# THE MIDDLE EAST

# THE MIDDLE EAST

## EIGHTH EDITION

CONGRESSIONAL QUARTERLY INC.

WASHINGTON, D.C.

Copyright © 1994 Congressional Quarterly Inc.
1414 22nd Street, N.W., Washington, D.C. 20037

Printed in the United States of America

Editor: Daniel C. Diller
Associate Editor: John L. Moore
Production Editor: Kerry V. Kern
Contributors: Joseph A. Davis, Rose Esber, Talia Greenberg, Max Gross, Joel Levin, Kristen Petrino, Ian L. Todreas

Front cover painting by Hossein Zenderoudi, *Del Miravad Ze Dastam*. From the book *Hafez: Dance of Life,* copyright © 1987 Mage Publishers, Inc.

Maps: William J. Clipson
Cover: Anne Masters Design

Photo credits: 58, Reuters; 99, R. Michael Jenkins; 123, U.S. Navy; 128, UN photo, J. Isaac; 222, Golestan/Reflex/Picture Group.

Library of Congress Cataloging-in-Publication Data

The Middle East / Daniel C. Diller, John L. Moore, editors. -- 8th ed.
    p.    cm.
   Includes bibliographical references (p.  ) and index.
   ISBN 0-87187-999-9 (pbk)
   1. Middle East--Politics and government--1979-   I. Diller, Daniel
C., 1959-  . II. Moore, John Leo, 1927-  . III. Congressional Quarterly, inc.
DS63.1.M484  1994
956.94--dc20                               94-17492
                                             CIP

# CONTENTS

# MAPS, BOXES, AND TABLES

PART I

# OVERVIEW OF
# THE MIDDLE EAST

# CHAPTER 1

# INTRODUCTION

Throughout history the Middle East has been a rich and diverse region of enormous cultural significance. It has spawned three of the world's great religions—Christianity, Islam, and Judaism—and has provided many other contributions to civilization. In the twentieth century the discovery of the largest petroleum deposits in the world made the Middle East vital to the international economy.

The region is also strategically important because of its oil assets and its location at the crossroads of three continents. What happens there affects not only local peoples and nations but also the entire world.

Perhaps more than any other region, the Middle East has been afflicted with conflicts that seem to defy solution. Disputes between Arabs and Israelis, Iranians and Iraqis, and other antagonists have gone beyond disagreements over territory or fears concerning a rival's geopolitical and economic goals. Middle East combatants have often hated each other because of decades of mutual hostilities and ethnic, religious, and cultural prejudices. Constructing long-term settlements requires not only carefully drawn compromises backed by international guarantees, but also fundamental changes in the attitudes of people toward their enemies.

## Movement Toward Peace

Since the end of World War II the Arab-Israeli conflict has been the central political issue in the Middle East. Through the 1980s the Arabs and Israelis fought five major wars and numerous smaller battles that demonstrated the intractability of the conflict and threatened to involve outside powers. In addition, the Arab-Israeli conflict caused or exacerbated other upheavals, such as the Jordanian civil war in 1970, the Lebanese civil war in 1975, and innumerable episodes of terrorism.

Israel's occupation of adjacent Arab lands during the 1967 Six-Day War has been the focal point of the conflict since that time. Arabs have demanded that Israel withdraw from the occupied territories and recognize a Palestinian state. Israel has countered that these lands are essential to its security. Any consideration of relinquishing all or part of them would require the Arabs to recognize Israel's right to exist and cooperate in establishing a secure peace.

Although Egypt and Israel concluded a separate peace in 1979, Israel's relations with other Arab states and the Palestine Liberation Organization (PLO) remained hostile. Events in the early 1990s, however, changed the region's political landscape and made serious negotiations possible between Israel and its Arab neighbors, including the PLO.

Ironically, the development that may have had the most to do with creating an overall climate favorable to the advancement of peace in the Middle East did not happen in the Middle East. This event was the breakup of the Soviet Union and the fall of Moscow's Communist government.

Although the Soviet Union had been less deeply involved in Middle Eastern affairs than the United States since the 1940s, it regarded the region as important. Soviet Middle East policy focused on extending Moscow's influence at the expense of the United States, while avoiding a superpower military confrontation in the region. Arabs in many countries, although suspicious of the Soviet Union's military power and Communist ideology, regarded Israel as a far greater threat to their security. To counter the United States' unflinching support for Israel, some Arab states, such as Syria, Egypt, and Iraq, developed close arms-supply relationships with the Soviet Union. Egypt's expulsion of Soviet advisers in 1972 dealt a heavy blow to Moscow's influence in the Middle East, but the Soviets adjusted to the setback by strengthening ties with Syria and the PLO.

Moscow's importance to Middle East politics rested less with its active military and diplomatic involvement than with its willingness to sell weapons to Arab states opposed to Israel and its ability to act as a counterweight that usually prevented, or at least limited, direct U.S. military intervention. So long as the Soviet Union continued to engage the United States in a nuclear arms race and global Cold War, neither power could intervene on the side of its client states without fear that such intervention could lead to a nuclear confrontation with the other power.

The decline of the Soviet economy in the late 1980s and the eventual dissolution of the Soviet Union in 1991 virtually removed Moscow's influence from the Middle East. The Arab entities that had depended on Moscow, especially Syria and the PLO, were left without a patron. They were pitted against Israel, the region's foremost military power, which retained the backing of the United States, the sole remaining superpower.

In 1990 the Iraqi invasion and occupation of Kuwait led to hopes among many Palestinians that Iraq would function as a rallying point for anti-Western and anti-Israeli sentiment. But the overwhelming defeat of Iraqi forces in 1991 by an American-led international coalition that included Arab nations compounded the Palestinians' isolation. The goal of establishing a Palestinian homeland did not appear to be achievable through confrontation.

Even as Israel's position had grown stronger because of the collapse of the Soviet Union and the defeat of Iraq, its internal situation dictated a move toward peace. In the occupied territories a Palestinian uprising (known as the *intifada),* which had been ongoing since late 1987, was taking an economic and morale toll on Israelis. In addition, the transformation of the Soviet Union had opened the way for hundreds of thousands of Soviet Jews to emigrate to Israel. The accompanying financial costs and social upheaval of this immigration made peace more urgent for many Israelis. In June 1992, Israeli voters returned the Labor party to power. Led by Yitzhak Rabin, the Labor party sought negotiations with the Palestinians, even as the intifada, terrorism, and Israeli military counter strikes remained a part of daily life.

After years of fruitless negotiations and intermittent warfare, diplomatic successes in 1993 and 1994 transformed the Arab-Israeli conflict. On September 13, 1993, PLO chairman Yasir Arafat shook hands with Israeli prime minister Yitzhak Rabin at a dramatic White House ceremony. That day the Declaration of Principles was signed, establishing a framework for Israeli transfer of the Gaza Strip and the city of Jericho to the control of a new Palestinian National Authority. In human history seldom have two such intractable enemies made peace.

The agreement was followed in May 1994 by the withdrawal of Israeli troops from the Gaza Strip and Jericho. In June, Arafat returned to the occupied territories for the first time in twenty-seven years. As extraordinary as the conclusion of the agreement was, establishing a successful Palestinian government that delivers services to its citizens and maintains order may be the greater challenge for Arafat.

The PLO-Israeli agreement was followed by successful negotiations between Jordan and Israel. On July 25, 1994, King Hussein of Jordan and Prime Minister Rabin of Israel signed the Washington Declaration, which formally ended the forty-six-year state of belligerence between their nations. Then, on October 26, a Jordanian-Israeli peace treaty was signed on the border between the two nations with President Bill Clinton in attendance.

Syrian-Israeli negotiations were not so fruitful through October 1994, but expectations were high among diplomats and the Syrian people that a peace agreement could be concluded within a year or two that would return the Israeli-occupied Golan Heights to Syria. During 1994 the government-controlled Syrian press toned down its criticism of Israel and the remaining several hundred Syrian Jews were granted exit visas. The Jordanian-Israeli agreement may put pressure on Syrian president Hafez al-Assad to compromise with Israel so that it can compete for foreign investment and trade.

## Crises in the Persian Gulf

Since 1979 the international attention received by the Arab-Israeli conflict has been rivaled by the world's attention to crises in the Persian Gulf region. In that year the Iranian revolution, the U.S. embassy hostage crisis in Tehran, a second round of oil price increases, and the Soviet invasion of Afghanistan converged to focus the world's attention on the Persian Gulf. During the 1980s the Iran-Iraq War underscored the Gulf's volatility as well as its strategic and economic importance. Touched off in September 1980 by Iraq's invasion of Iran, the eight-year war threatened the flow of oil throughout the Gulf and ultimately involved the United States and other countries outside the region.

In 1988 a tense peace was concluded between Iran and Iraq. But two years later the region was again engulfed in war when Iraq invaded and occupied oil-rich Kuwait in August 1990. A long-feared international economic nightmare threatened to come true: a belligerent military power was in a position to dominate the oil reserves of the Persian Gulf.

Although Iraqi president Saddam Hussein employed pan-Arabist rhetoric to justify the invasion of Kuwait, most Arab countries, including Saudi Arabia, Egypt, and Syria, rejected the invasion as naked aggression against a fellow Arab state. The Gulf oil-producing states in particular feared that

## Defining the Middle East

The Middle East is not a precisely defined area of the world. It is sometimes referred to as the "Near East" or "Southwest Asia," but not everyone agrees on what countries should be included within these geographic designations. If the Middle East is defined solely as the Arab states and Israel, Iran would be excluded. If it is thought to comprise Israel and the predominantly Muslim states, then all the North African states—Algeria, Tunisia, Morocco, and Libya, plus the Sudan, Afghanistan, Pakistan, and Turkey—would have to be included.

This book focuses on those countries that American readers most often associate with the Middle East and that have had a continuing and central role in two issues of critical importance to U.S. foreign policy: the Arab-Israeli conflict and the security of the Persian Gulf and its oil resources. These nations are Bahrain, Egypt, Iran, Iraq, Israel, Jordan, Kuwait, Lebanon, Libya, Oman, Qatar, Saudi Arabia, Syria, the United Arab Emirates, and Yemen.

if Saddam were left unchecked, he would eventually move against them. In early 1991 a powerful American-led international coalition operating out of Saudi Arabia drove Iraq from Kuwait.

The coalition destroyed much of Iraq's military might while humbling Saddam's army—reputed to be the fourth largest in the world. The totality of the Iraqi defeat largely undercut Saddam's appeal to Palestinians as an Arab champion willing to defy the West. But Saddam himself clung tenaciously to power in Baghdad despite rebellions by the Kurds in northern Iraq and the substantial Iraqi Shi'ite population in the south. The United Nations continued to enforce sanctions against Iraq that precluded it from selling oil or importing anything but food and medical supplies.

In October 1994 Saddam Hussein demonstrated that he could still cause his neighbors and the international community anxiety. He ordered the redeployment of two divisions of his best troops to southern Iraq near the Kuwaiti border. President Clinton responded by quickly sending American air and naval power, along with approximately thirty-six thousand U.S. troops, to Saudi Arabia and the Persian Gulf. Saddam backed down from his aggressive posture, but the episode showed that the Iraq problem required active containment and perhaps a beefed-up American military presence in the Gulf area.

Saddam's gambit likely was intended to draw new attention to Iraq and pressure the international community to lift the sanctions that were impoverishing the country. He may have calculated that the coalition would not have the will to reassemble a military force in Kuwait and would therefore have to appease Iraq's calls for a lifting of sanctions. Ironically, the Iraqi strategy brought about the opposite of its intended effect: the troop movements reawakened fears that Saddam still possessed sufficient military force to take aggressive action against Kuwait. As a result, the UN Security Council, which had been divided on the question of sanctions, voted unanimously to condemn the Iraqi deployment and appeared unlikely to consider a near-term lifting of the embargo.

## Continuing Arms Race

Even though the potential for war in the Middle East has been reduced by the defeat of Iraq and by the Arab-Israeli agreements, the consequences of a future war have been multiplied by the Middle East's regional arms race. The Middle East has led all regions of the world in arms imports since the end of the Vietnam War.

No controls exist on sales of conventional weapons to Middle East nations, and producers have been willing to sell increasingly sophisticated weapons systems, including surface-to-surface missiles, to countries there. When one supplier refuses to sell weapons to a nation for political or security reasons, the buyer can turn to numerous other suppliers for comparable weapons. Even nations not directly involved in hostilities have felt compelled to arm themselves in response to regional instability. The result has been an unrestrained arms race that not only could increase the devastation of a Middle East war but also could trigger a war by upsetting power balances and inducing nations to launch preemptive strikes.

The Iran-Iraq War, which began in 1980, saw the use of chemical weapons and ballistic missiles. Baghdad and Tehran both were hit with missile attacks, and chemical weapons were used extensively on the battlefield. During the Persian Gulf War in 1991, Iraq launched missile attacks against Israeli cities. Despite a significant chemical warfare capability, however, Iraq refrained from using such weapons against advancing coalition troops.

By far the most dangerous potential development in the Middle East arms race would be the acquisition of nuclear weapons by several states. As of 1994, Israel was the only country known to have a nuclear arsenal, although the Israeli government does not acknowledge its existence. Other states—such as Iraq, Syria, Libya, and Iran—have nuclear weapons programs or have tried to buy a nuclear weapon.

In contrast to the nuclear arsenals of the United States and the Soviet Union, which contributed to an atmosphere of stability during much of the Cold War, nuclear proliferation in the Middle East would likely have an opposite effect. Nuclear arsenals there would be small and vulnerable and the relatively short distances between countries would make adequate warning of an attack difficult. In addition, nuclear weapons could be transferred to regional terrorist groups for use in political blackmail.

Although international constraints on technology transfer have been somewhat successful in slowing the development of nuclear weapons, given enough time, concerted nuclear weapons programs will succeed. United Nations inspectors examining Iraq's nuclear program after the Gulf War, for example, have concluded that its nuclear program was far more extensive than previously believed. When additional Middle East states acquire nuclear weapons capabilities, many current assumptions about Middle East security will become obsolete.

## Optimism Amid Violence

Events during the first half of the 1990s have created great optimism that relative peace may be established in the Middle East, where warfare and political instability have been central features of life since the end of World War II. The Arab-Israeli conflict no longer appears to be capable of producing a major war at a moment's notice or of sparking a global confrontation. Israel now has formal peace treaties with Egypt and Jordan and constructive talks are going on with Syria and the PLO. Other Arab states, including Morocco, Tunisia, Oman, and Qatar, have established contacts with Israel. Iraq remains belligerent, but it no longer exercises much influence over other Arabs. Palestinians in Jordan, among Saddam's most enthusiastic backers in 1990, have responded with indifference to his saber rattling in 1994.

Yet peace between Israelis and Arabs is far from complete. The Israeli-Palestinian peace has strident opponents among both peoples. Many Israelis, as well as the Likud party leadership, continue to regard Yasir Arafat as a terrorist. Even those who embraced compromise generally see the initial agreement establishing Palestinian self-rule in Gaza and Jericho as a hopeful experiment, not the first step of an inevitable process culminating in a fully independent Palestinian state throughout the West Bank. If Arafat fails to abide by his promises, in particular if he cannot stop Palestinian violence, Israelis may lose patience with the Palestinian National Authority.

Meanwhile, terrorism and violence remain a prominent part of the lives of Israelis and Palestinians. In October 1994, Hamas, the Islamic Resistance Movement, launched a series of terrorist acts that shook Israel. On October 9 Hamas carried out a shooting spree in West Jerusalem that killed two and wounded thirteen. Two days later Hamas members kidnapped an Israeli soldier and demanded the release of 190 Arab prisoners held by Israeli. Then, on October 19, a suicide bomber blew up an Israeli bus in downtown Tel Aviv, killing twenty-one people.

The kidnapping in particular framed the dilemma faced by Israel and the Palestine National Authority in preserving peace amidst ongoing terrorist activities. Suspecting that the soldier was being held in Gaza or Jericho, the Israeli government demanded that Yasir Arafat's government secure his release and threatened to suspend peace negotiations if it did not. Arafat's police conducted a house-to-house search, arresting and temporarily holding two hundred militants in the process. The episode ended on October 14 when Israel discovered that the soldier was actually being held in the Israeli-controlled West Bank. A rescue attempt resulted in the death of the hostage, an Israeli commando, and three Hamas members.

After the October 19 bombing, Yitzhak Rabin immediately announced that attacks by Hamas would not prompt Israel to break off the peace process, because doing so would be a victory for Hamas. But the attacks placed Yasir Arafat in a precarious position. Failure to curb the violence carried out by Palestinians opposed to peace with Israel could cause the peace process to stall or collapse. The Israeli right wing pointed to each terrorist act as a reason to reconsider the peace process. But if Arafat moved too harshly against Hamas or cooperated too closely with Israeli security forces trying to root out Hamas, he risked undermining his own political support among large segments of the Palestinian population. In addition, Hamas could make Arafat and his administration a target. Arafat had attempted to co-opt the leadership of Hamas, without much success. A strong rejectionist element was likely to remain that would be capable of carrying out occasional, if not frequent, terrorist attacks. The scope of Hamas's October 1994 terrorist campaign demonstrated a growing expertise at carrying out terrorist acts designed to have the maximum psychological impact.

The future of Middle East peace depends on developing solid constituencies in Israel and its Arab neighbors who recognize that peace and normality will not be achieved overnight or without further bloodshed. Clear perceptual links between peace and prosperity must also be established. The rapidly expanding economic cooperation between

Jordan and Israel may provide tangible examples of the benefits of peace to Palestinians and Syrians who are tired of violence.

Middle East economies have been buffeted by falling oil prices, disruptions in commerce caused by warfare, and high foreign debt. A growing number of Arabs and Jews have recognized that they have a huge economic stake in making peace. A secure peace would allow nations in the region to expand trade and tourism, divert resources from defense spending, improve communication and transportation links, and construct a more efficient sharing of scarce water resources. For Jordan, Syria, and the new Palestinian entity, all of which lack huge oil resources, the economic rewards of making peace with Israel are a key to the ongoing peace process. If they can be realized, the march toward peace is unlikely to be reversed.

CHAPTER **2**

# ARAB-ISRAELI CONFLICT

For more than forty years, the conflict between Israel and its Arab neighbors remained one of the most dangerous and seemingly unresolvable conflicts in the world. Two events—the initiation of negotiations between Israel and its Arab neighbors at Madrid, Spain, in October 1991, and the breakthrough agreement between Israel and the Palestine Liberation Organization (PLO) signed in Washington on September 13, 1993—shattered many long-held assumptions about the Arab-Israeli conflict. Like the surprise decision of Egyptian president Anwar Sadat to visit Jerusalem in November 1977 and the resulting Camp David process, these events revised the rules used by diplomats, scholars, and journalists to interpret Middle Eastern politics.

Almost continuously since the 1967 Six-Day War, some type of negotiations or peace initiative aimed at an Arab-Israeli settlement has existed. But outbreaks of full-scale war, acts of terrorism, preemptive and retaliatory raids, civil strife, hostile propaganda, and unceasing mutual recriminations made the Arab-Israeli conflict seem intractable. One such war, in 1973, appeared to bring the United States and the Soviet Union close to a nuclear confrontation, when President Richard Nixon, worried about possible Soviet intervention, put American forces on worldwide alert. In 1991 Israel stood ready to retaliate with missiles and perhaps weapons of mass destruction if Iraq carried out a threat to attack Israel with chemical weapons.

Undoubtedly, now that long-maintained barriers to negotiations have been broken, an active peace process will continue to be a prominent feature of Middle East politics. Setbacks to this process are inevitable, as parties on both sides can be expected to resist compromises. The peace process continues to be punctuated by acts of violence in the Israeli-occupied West Bank and elsewhere. Moreover, relations between Arab states and Israel will not soon be governed by mutual trust. Yet the peace process will not easily be undermined. Palestinian recognition of Israeli legitimacy in 1988 has been balanced by official Israeli recognition of an as-yet-undefined Palestinian legitimacy in September 1993. These two breakthroughs denote a significant advance along the road toward mutual realism and perhaps even eventual settlement of the conflict.

## Origins of the Conflict

The Middle East is the inheritor of five thousand years of history. The ancient connection of the people of Israel with the land of Palestine is an integral part of the region's history. The Roman destruction of the Second Temple in Jerusalem in A.D. 70 and the forced dispersal of the Jews from Palestine left the Jewish people scattered around the world. Although many Jews assimilated into the many countries of their diaspora, for nearly two thousand years a significant number retained their Jewish identity and each year concluded Passover ceremonies with the determined prayer, "Next year in Jerusalem." The prophetic concept of an eventual ingathering of the Jewish exiles into the land of their origin influenced the beliefs and expectations of many Jews and Christians in the West.

Zionism, the political movement among European Jewry that led, beginning in the late nineteenth century, to increased Jewish migration to Palestine and ultimately to the successful establishment of an independent Israeli state in 1948, had its roots in specific conditions in nineteenth-century Europe. The growth across Europe and ultimately throughout the world of the idea of nationalism as an ideological basis for political organization caused many to ponder the ultimate meaning of Jewish identity in an age of emerging nation-states. Continuing anti-Semitism throughout most of Europe, culminating in the Nazi Holocaust of European Jewry during World War II, finally led most Jews and a great many others in the West to view with favor the idea of an independent Jewish state in Palestine, where more than half a million Jews had established themselves by the end of the war.

Establishing a Jewish state in Palestine, however, was not a simple matter. Much had happened there during the nearly two thousand years of Jewish diaspora. Since the rise of Islam in the seventh century, the Middle East had become largely an Islamic region, and the inhabitants of Palestine, Syria, Iraq, Egypt, and the Arabian Peninsula were now nearly all Arabs. Islam, a religion closely akin to both Judaism and Christianity, also had laid claim to Jerusalem as one of its holy cities. Most Arabs believed that, as "People of the Book," Jews, like Christians, were free to live peaceably in Arab areas so long as they recognized Arab-Islamic sovereignty. The Arabs, however, did not believe that Jews had a right to an independent state of their own on land that was now part of the Arab-Islamic world. From its inception, therefore, the Zionist movement faced general opposition in the Middle East, not only from the Arab inhabitants of Palestine but also from the larger Arab world of which Palestine was considered a part.

The Arabs of Palestine were ill equipped to meet the challenge posed by the determined Zionist movement. For four centuries, since 1516, the Ottoman Empire had ruled Palestine. Ottoman rule, although Islamic in character, was fundamentally oppressive and aimed at extracting as much wealth as possible from an increasingly impoverished Arab peasantry. As the twentieth century began, Palestine, like most Arab societies, was seriously underdeveloped. Moreover, long centuries of relatively oppressive foreign rule had fragmented the Palestinian Arabs politically and trained them effectively in the virtues of political accommodation. As a result, the Palestinian Arabs had no tradition of independent political organization, and although they were disturbed by the Zionist movement, they lacked effective political institutions to secure their own rights and interests.

The European powers, meanwhile, were competing for influence and domination in local regions throughout the rapidly declining Ottoman Empire. The European Zionists recognized that they could advance their cause by backing the imperial aims of the European power most likely to prevail in the contest for influence in Palestine. This ambition was achieved in the last days of World War I, when Great Britain concluded that support for the Zionist movement would significantly serve its imperial interests in the Middle East. On November 2, 1917, the British government issued what has come to be known as the Balfour Declaration, named after Lord Arthur James Balfour, the British foreign minister who enunciated it:

His Majesty's Government views with favor the establishment in Palestine of a national home for the Jewish people, and will use their best endeavors to facilitate the achievement of this object, it being clearly understood that nothing shall be done which may prejudice the civil and religious rights of existing non-Jewish communities in Palestine, or the rights and political status enjoyed by Jews in any other country.

Many observers regard this declaration as the beginning of what has come to be known as the Arab-Israeli conflict.

## The British Mandate

The Balfour Declaration committed Britain to support the establishment of an independent Jewish state, a goal the fledgling Zionist movement had been seeking since its first meeting in Basel, Switzerland, in 1897. Other powers, including France and the United States, soon issued resolutions of support for the principles enunciated in the Balfour Declaration. In July 1922 the League of Nations adopted the British mandate for Palestine, which incorporated the principles of the Balfour Declaration within its text. Article Two of the mandate document states:

The Mandatory shall be responsible for placing the country under such political, administrative and economic conditions as will secure the establishment of the Jewish national home, as laid down in the preamble, and the development of self-governing institutions, and also for safeguarding the civil and religious rights of all the inhabitants of Palestine, irrespective of race and religion.

With the official implementation of the British mandate in September 1923, the road was opened for unrestricted Jewish migration to Palestine and the establishment of legally sanctioned institutions that were to culminate in the state of Israel twenty-five years later.

### Barriers to a Jewish State

Even with such international support, however, the large-scale Jewish settlement of Palestine and eventual establishment of an independent Jewish state was not inevitable. Although the Zionist movement at this time received considerable support, this backing was more idealistic than practical. After an initial surge of migration in 1924 and 1925, the yearly number of Jewish settlers arriving in Palestine fell to an average of between twenty-five hundred and five thousand—hardly a sufficient number to repopulate a land and transform its basic national character. Only after the 1933 German elections that brought Hitler and the Nazi party to power was there a significant increase in Jewish migration, brought on by a growing belief among Jews that a Jewish national home was needed.

The considerable ideological conflict and politi-

cal factionalism within the early *Yishuv* (the Jewish settlement in Palestine) also threatened the Zionist movement. Socialist-labor Zionists, mainly from Eastern Europe and Russia, sought to collectivize all economic activity of the Yishuv while totally Judaizing it to the detriment of Arab labor. The labor Zionists often clashed with private Jewish capitalists and investors who hired Arab labor and criticized the labor Zionists for placing socialism above the effort to create a Jewish state. Both these Jewish groups were opposed by an even larger body of Orthodox Jews who denounced the whole Zionist vision of a Jewish state as being inconsistent with their spiritualist view of religion. In addition, conflicts between the leadership of the Yishuv and the Zionist leadership abroad also threatened the unity of the Zionist enterprise.

Another factor inhibiting the progress of the Zionist movement in Palestine was the coincidental growth of nationalist sentiment among the Arabs. The emergence of such sentiment predated World War I and gave rise first to movements opposed to continued Ottoman Turkish rule, and after the war to the imposition of European rule through the League of Nations mandate system. During the war the British had capitalized on the existence of Arab nationalist sentiment by striking an agreement with Hussein ibn Ali (Sherif Hussein) of Mecca, who had led an Arab revolt against the Turks in support of British military operations in Palestine and Syria. In return for this support Henry McMahon, the British high commissioner in Egypt, had promised Hussein British support for an Arab kingdom under his rule after the war. Such a kingdom with its capital at Damascus did come into being briefly in 1919, but it was suppressed in July 1920 by French forces acting to assert France's control over Lebanon and Syria in accordance with its own League of Nations mandate over these areas.

This division of the Arab Middle East into French and British spheres of influence resulted from wartime negotiations. While the British were negotiating with Hussein in 1915 and 1916 and making promises of support for an Arab kingdom after the war, the British and French in 1916

# Who Is a Palestinian?

The word *Palestine* is of Roman origin, referring to the biblical land of the Philistines. The term fell into disuse for centuries, but the British revived it as an official designation for the area that the League of Nations mandated to their supervision in 1920, following the World War I breakup of the Turkish-Ottoman Empire. The League approved the terms of the mandate—including the pledges made by Britain in the 1917 Balfour Declaration—on July 24, 1922.

The British mandate also applied to Transjordan (now Jordan). Transjordan lay entirely to the east of the Jordan River; Palestine lay entirely to the west of it. Because the league's mandate applied to both regions, however, the argument was made that "Palestinian" applied to persons east as well as west of the Jordan River and that the designation applied not just to the Arab inhabitants—as is the common practice today—but also to Jews and Christians living in the former mandated area.

Palestine as a legal entity ceased to exist in 1948 when Britain, unable to control Arab-Jewish hostility and the influx of Jewish immigrants to Palestine, relinquished its mandate and Israel declared its independence on May 14. The United Nations had voted in 1947 to partition Palestine into Arab and Jewish sectors.

During 1948-49 Israel enlarged its territory in a war of independence with neighboring Arab nations. But it did not take control of all Palestine. One region, the West Bank, came under the control of Jordan, which later annexed the territory, and another, the Gaza Strip, came under Egyptian control. These territories, however, were subsequently occupied by Israel during the Six-Day War of 1967.

made in the Hussein-McMahon correspondence, the Sykes-Picot agreement, and the Balfour Declaration came in the Paris peace talks after the war. During these talks Hussein's son, Faisal, who had been proclaimed king of the new Arab state in Damascus, expressed his willingness to collaborate with the Zionists and to accept the principle of a Jewish national home in Palestine. This brief possibility of Arab-Zionist cooperation quickly faded, however, with the overthrow of Faisal's kingdom by France in 1920.

With the demise of the Arab kingdom, Arab nationalist hopes that had been nurtured during the war turned to bitterness. Although some Arabs collaborated with the French and British during the 1920s and 1930s, an increasingly strong nationalist movement promoted strikes, demonstrations, occasional acts of terrorism, and other forms of resistance against European rule. To the nationalists, the European division of the Middle East into several countries was perceived as part of a larger Western strategy to divide and rule the Arab world and to prevent nationalist aspirations from being realized. Many Arabs also perceived Western support for Zionist aspirations in Palestine as an aspect of this strategy, aimed at creating a Western-sponsored base in the Arab world that would legitimize a permanent Western presence in the region to sustain and defend the Jewish national home. The between-wars struggle against European colonial domination, therefore, included opposition to Jewish migration to Palestine as well as to the perpetuation of the mandate system. Arab opposition to Zionist aspirations, consequently, had a pan-Arab character and influenced Arab opinion far beyond the boundaries of Palestine, which, then as now, constituted the central theater of the Arab-Israeli conflict.

A final factor that threatened the Zionist movement was British policy itself. Although Britain remained committed to the promises of the Balfour Declaration, successive British governments amended it in response to Arab nationalist challenges, both within Palestine and beyond. The first major compromise came at the Cairo Conference in March 1921, which was convened by Winston

signed the Sykes-Picot agreement that set aside Lebanon and Syria as areas of French interest, while giving Britain a free hand in the Arab region to the south.

The final sorting out of the conflicting promises

Churchill, then England's colonial secretary, to seek ways to consolidate British authority in both Palestine and Iraq in the face of growing Arab nationalist opposition and the need to cut costs of colonial administration. The conference decided to install Faisal, the recently deposed Arab king in Damascus, as king of Iraq. In addition, to further appease the embittered supporters of Faisal, the original Palestine mandate was divided at the Jordan River and Faisal's brother, Abdullah, was installed as king in eastern Palestine, which now took the name Transjordan. After this decision Transjordan was no longer open to Jewish migration and settlement, a circumstance that some Zionists saw as a betrayal of the British promise in the Balfour Declaration and a contravention of its responsibilities under the terms of its League of Nations mandate.

### British Reassessment

A major outbreak of Arab-Jewish violence around the Wailing Wall in Jerusalem in August 1929 spread to other parts of Palestine and led the British government to take still another look at its policy in Palestine. Two consecutive investigative reports (the Shaw Report of March 1930 and the Hope-Simpson Report of May 1930) concluded that insufficient attention was being paid to the second half of the British obligations under its mandate charter, namely "ensuring the rights and positions" of the non-Jewish inhabitants of Palestine. Both reports recommended restrictions on Jewish migration and limitations on future land transfers to "non-Arabs." The British government accepted these recommendations in the subsequent Passfield White Paper of October 1930. This new policy position provoked a political furor in England and appeared to threaten the survival of the government of Prime Minister Ramsay MacDonald. The prime minister subsequently issued a letter repudiating the white paper, and the perceived threat to Zionist aspirations in Palestine passed. The events, however, indicated to both Arabs and Jews that the British commitment to a Jewish national home in Palestine was not without limits.

# Who Is an Arab?

It is not easy to define accurately the term *Arab*. The British geographer W. B. Fisher, in his book *The Middle East: A Physical, Social and Regional Geography,* states: "From the point of view of the anthropologist, it is impossible to speak with accuracy either of an Arab or of a Semitic people. Both terms connote a mixed population varying widely in physical character and in racial origin, and are best used purely as cultural and linguistic terms, respectively." Thus the so-called Arab countries are those that share a common culture and speak Arabic as the primary language.

As Islam spread from the Arabian Peninsula there took place Arabization and Islamization— processes that are closely linked but not identical. Peter Mansfield writes in *The Arabs: A Comprehensive History* that "Arabization began some two centuries before the Prophet Muhammad, with the overflow of Arabian tribes into Syria and Iraq, and reached its greatest impulse during the first decades of the Arab Empire. Islamization lasted much longer and still continues today, especially in Africa."

The Arab countries are Egypt, Syria, Jordan, Lebanon, Iraq, Saudi Arabia, the Republic of Yemen, Kuwait, Bahrain, Oman, Qatar, a loose group of tiny sheikdoms on the Persian Gulf that form the United Arab Emirates, and the North African countries collectively known as the Maghreb—Morocco, Algeria, Tunisia, and Libya.

Islam is the predominant religion today in all of these countries. That in itself, however, does not define an Arab nation. Turkey, Iran, Afghanistan, Pakistan, Indonesia, the Sudan, and Somalia are Islamic, but not Arab. Similarly, not all Arabs are Muslims. Lebanon's population includes close to a million Arab Christians. In several other Middle Eastern countries there are significant Arab Christian minorities—some with ancestral roots antedating the Muslim conquests and others converted by missionaries. There are also several non-Arab Muslim minorities in the Middle East, including the Kurds in parts of Iraq, Iran, and Turkey.

Finally, following the upsurge in Jewish migration that accompanied the rise to power of the Nazi party in Germany in the mid-1930s, new violence erupted in 1936 that again led the British government to review its position in Palestine. The "Arab Revolt" of 1936-39, which in some respects was analogous to the Palestinian *intifada* of the late 1980s, was the first major outbreak of Arab-Israeli hostilities, although British authorities were present as a dominant third party to deal with it. The apparent irreconcilability of Zionist aspirations with Arab nationalist claims finally led the Peel Commission in July 1937 to recommend the partition of Palestine into Jewish and Arab states. This was the first time partition had been officially advocated as a potential solution to the emerging conflict in Palestine. The Arabs rejected the Peel Commission's recommendation of partition, however, and Zionist leaders, although accepting the principle of partition, objected to the limited territory that had been allotted to the Jewish state. The British government again reviewed its position and in May 1939 issued a final white paper, which effectively ended Britain's open-ended commitment to the establishment of the Jewish national home in Palestine.

Historians generally agree that, with the clouds of World War II looming over Europe, Britain's perceptions of its strategic interests in the Middle East now favored positions that would not alienate Arab nationalist sentiment. The British wanted to prevent the Arabs from looking to the Nazis as potential liberators from British control. Consequently, the 1939 white paper, which remained the basis of British policy in Palestine until the end of the British mandate in 1948, emphasized meeting Arab demands more than satisfying Zionist aspirations. It rejected the concept of partition and foresaw the establishment of an independent Palestine state within ten years.

During this period the British government in Palestine proposed to develop self-governing institutions that would include Arabs and Jews, even if both sides refused to collaborate. More importantly, however, the white paper enunciated the principle that the Jewish national home could be established only with Arab consent, and it proposed that the Jewish national home be established within the independent Palestine state. Regarding Jewish immigration, twenty-five thousand immigrants would be admitted immediately; over the next five years it would be restricted to fifteen thousand a year; and after the five-year period future Jewish immigration would occur only with Arab consent. Jewish land purchases and settlements also were restricted to the coastal and lowland areas of Palestine and were not permitted in the hilly and mountainous areas of the country. Finally, if after the ten-year period Palestine still did not seem ready for independence, Britain would undertake another review to determine what course of action it would take.

Despite its effort to satisfy Arab demands without totally abandoning its prior commitments to the Zionist movement, the 1939 white paper was rejected both by the Arabs and the Zionists. The Arabs opposed it because it did not halt Jewish migration and failed to grant immediate political independence to Palestine. The Zionists rejected it on the grounds that it constituted a violation of international law, namely the League of Nations mandate, which they believed obligated Britain to use its authority in behalf of Zionist goals. The Zionists believed that the British government had abandoned its commitment to the Jewish national home, and they vowed to resist the new British policy in Palestine, even while lending support to the British war effort in Europe and North Africa.

## Jewish Self-Reliance

The challenges faced by the Zionist movement led its Yishuv component toward increasing self-reliance, even though the Jewish settlement in Palestine remained dependent on diaspora Jewry for financial assistance, migration, and political activism in support of the Zionist cause outside Palestine. During the early 1920s institutions for organizing the Jewish presence in Palestine had been established. The most significant of these were the Jewish National Fund, which purchased land for Zionist settlement; the Keren Hayesod, a second fund that financed development projects in behalf of the Yishuv; the Histadrut, a countrywide labor organization that gradually became the dominant force in Yishuv and later Israeli affairs; and finally the Haganah, the forerunner of the Israel Defense Force. Overseeing all these activities after 1929 was the Jewish Agency, whose headquarters were in Jerusalem rather than in London, where the World Zionist Organization previously had exerted primary executive authority over affairs of the Yishuv. Increasingly through the 1930s and 1940s, Yishuv figures, notably David Ben-Gurion, Israel's first prime minister, strengthened their influence over the Jewish Agency and the Zionist movement.

Against this developing organization of the Jewish community in Palestine, the Arabs had no counterpart. Divided among various factions that reflected the rivalries among Palestine's traditional notable families, the Arabs generally reacted negatively to British rule and Jewish enterprise instead of constructing a positive political program of their own. Although some Arabs favored collaboration with the British as a means of co-opting British favor, they were usually intimidated into silence by more radical leaders who favored boycotts and general strikes to demand immediate political independence for Palestine. Many militant Arab nationalists were arrested by the British, or they fled abroad before World War II, just as British policy was becoming more supportive of Arab concerns.

Because Arab attacks during the revolt were directed against British authority as well as the Jewish presence, the British began to rely on Jews to perform police duties on their behalf. A Jewish settlement police was raised, trained, armed, and paid by the British to guard isolated Jewish settlements. Most of the Jews organized for this purpose turned out to be members of the Haganah, the secret and illegal paramilitary force being raised by the Yishuv. Police duties gave the Haganah a legal cover for conducting military training and carrying weapons.

The Haganah had since its origins in the early 1920s amounted to little more than a paper organization formally grouping local village defense committees. In 1936 as a consequence of the Arab revolt, however, one thousand men were selected for a standing force available for service anywhere in Palestine. Infiltrated into the British police, they gained useful training, acquired arms, and undertook special operations of their own against Arab groups involved in the revolt. At the same time, a rival Jewish militia, the Irgun Zvai Leumi, was formed under the leadership of Ze'ev Jabotinsky, a political opponent of the socialist-labor Zionists who dominated the politics of the Yishuv and controlled the Haganah. Less restrained than the Haganah, the Irgun favored more forceful tactics, including terrorism, against the Arabs.

The issuance of the British 1939 white paper put Palestinian Jewry on a collision course with the British and strengthened the resolve of the Yishuv to maintain and strengthen the still-secret and illegal Haganah. The restrictions on Jewish immigration into Palestine at a time of extreme anti-Semitism in Nazi-dominated Europe led the Haganah to facilitate illegal immigration in opposition to British policy. At the same time, however, the Haganah collaborated with the British by providing about twenty-seven thousand Jews to serve with British forces against Nazi Germany during World War II. This service provided further training and experience to the armed forces of the Yishuv.

A second result of the 1939 white paper was a decision of the World Zionist Organization to broaden its base of international support. No longer confident of British guarantees, the Zionist movement increasingly looked to the United States as a source of funds and political support. At the Biltmore Conference in New York City in May 1942, organized to mobilize the large American Jewish community, resolutions were adopted that called for the United States to support the opening of Palestine to Jewish migration, to recognize the Jewish Agency in Jerusalem as the sole authority in control of immigration and the economic development of Palestine, and to recognize all of Palestine after the war as "a Jewish Commonwealth integrated in the structure of the new democratic world." This appeal had great success, and Britain soon found itself increasingly on the defensive in matters pertaining to Palestine, especially as the Nazi holocaust of European Jewry grew more apparent during the second half of 1942.

## End of the British Mandate

The quest for a Jewish homeland in Palestine reached a climax during the three years following the end of World War II. With thousands of displaced Jews from the war living in refugee camps, Britain came under great international pressure, encouraged by the Zionists, to admit them to Palestine. At the same time, the Haganah, the Irgun, and a third breakaway Jewish militia known as the Stern Gang inaugurated a guerrilla campaign against the British in Palestine that included the use of terrorism. Britain was unable to maintain central authority in Palestine and unwilling to reverse the policy enunciated in its 1939 white paper because of perceived British interests among the newly independent Arab states of the region. The British government saw no resolution to its predicament and decided to get out of Palestine. In February 1947 it announced that it would end its responsibilities under the mandate and refer the problem to the newly formed United Nations.

Thus ended the British mandate for Palestine, a colonial enterprise that had been undertaken to serve British interests in the Middle East by fostering the establishment of a Jewish national home in Palestine. As Arab nationalists, including those of Palestine, strove with increasing success to achieve political independence and an end of European colonial rule in the Middle East, Britain perceived its interests to be associated with the maintenance of satisfactory relations with the newly independent Arab states. These, like the Palestinian Arabs, opposed Jewish migration and resisted any thought that Palestine might be partitioned into two states.

Unable to satisfy either Zionist aspirations as promised in the Balfour Declaration three decades earlier or the demands of the Palestinian Arabs, who had the support of their Arab neighbors, Brit-

ain turned the matter over to the international community. The United Nations would have to devise a resolution of the problem if violence in Palestine were to be avoided.

# Partition of Palestine, 1948 War

At the United Nations a special commission was appointed in May 1947 to investigate the situation in Palestine and to recommend action to the General Assembly. Known as the United Nations Special Committee on Palestine (UNSCOP), the commission was composed of representatives of eleven countries: Australia, Canada, Czechoslovakia, Guatemala, India, Iran, Mexico, the Netherlands, Peru, Sweden, and Yugoslavia. Feted and warmly received by the Zionists and boycotted completely by the Arab leadership in Palestine, the committee concluded that the British mandate should be terminated and that Palestine should be granted independence.

The implacable attitudes expressed by Arabs and Jews, however, led the commission to recommend partition as the basis for granting Palestinian independence. Members differed on how partition should be implemented. The minority report (India, Iran, Yugoslavia) recommended "an independent federal state" with its capital at Jerusalem, composed of two autonomous political entities (Arab and Jewish) but united by a central government that would include both Arab and Jewish representatives. The majority report recommended the establishment of two sovereign states, joined in an economic federation, but with Jerusalem having a separate status as an international city under UN administration.

The commission presented its report in August 1947, and after nearly three months the UN General Assembly voted on it. The newly independent Arab states that were now members of the assembly, while favoring Palestinian independence, opposed partition in any form. In the end, however, they supported the UNSCOP minority report in an effort to head off the majority recommendation. Zionist forces and their supporters favored the full partition plan and exerted extreme diplomatic pressure to obtain the votes even of countries whose delegates had gone on record against partition.

Following numerous postponements and delays until the requisite two-thirds vote could be obtained, UN General Assembly Resolution 181, adopting the majority recommendation of the UNSCOP report, was passed on November 29, 1947, by a vote of 33-13, with 10 abstentions.

The United Nations decision on the partition of Palestine was greeted with joy and celebration among Jews around the world, since it provided international sanction for the establishment of a Jewish state. The UN vote, however, caused Arab-Jewish hostilities to erupt throughout Palestine, as Arabs struggled to prevent implementation of the partition plan, and the forces of the Yishuv fought to ensure its implementation. On December 3, 1947, Great Britain, which had abstained from voting on the UN resolution, announced it was unwilling to implement a policy that it had not supported and that lacked support from both sides of the conflict. Britain declared that it would evacuate Palestine on May 15, 1948. On the same day, the two-year-old League of Arab States (Arab League) declared its united opposition to the partition of Palestine and encouraged league members to intervene in support of the Arab cause in Palestine.

With Arabs far outnumbering Jews in Palestine, especially with the support of the armies of neighboring Arab states behind them, it seemed unlikely that the Yishuv could prevail on its determination to establish a Jewish state. In early 1948 the Jewish population of Palestine, which lived mainly in that portion of the country assigned to the Jewish state by the UN resolution, numbered slightly over six hundred thousand, while the Arabs numbered about 1.3 million. At least half a million Arabs lived alongside Jews in the sector allotted to the Jewish state.

The Arabs, however, lacked institutions of self-government that the Yishuv had been creating since the early 1920s. The Jewish Haganah in late 1947 numbered about forty-three thousand. Consisting mainly of "home guards" who, although not well trained, were well organized to defend established Jewish settlements, the Haganah also possessed a rudimentary mobile field force of about eleven thousand, many of whose members had served with the British army during World War II. In addition the Irgun, now led by future Israeli prime minister Menachem Begin, fielded a militia numbering about five thousand, while the terrorist organization LEHI (the Stern Gang) included several hundred fighters.

Against these elements of the Yishuv, the Arabs had forces that could be construed as "village militias," but these lacked central direction. Closely monitored by the British since the Arab revolt in the 1930s, the Arabs found it impossible to develop coordinated military activity until after the November 1947 partition resolution. At that time, two different Arab forces gradually were established. The first, sponsored by Hajj Amin al-Husseini, the leader of the 1936 Arab revolt, who remained in Cairo and was prohibited by the British from returning to Palestine, was the Holy War Army. Never larger than five thousand loosely coordinated fighters in various parts of the country, Husseini's forces lacked the support of the Arab League, which sponsored a second force, the Arab Liberation Army (ALA). Composed of about thirty-eight hundred volunteers from the various Arab countries, including about a thousand from Palestine, its units entered northern Palestine during January-May 1948. Still a third force in Palestine were elements of Jordan's Arab Legion that remained under British authority, and therefore officially neutral. After Britain's departure on May 15, 1948, the Arab Legion came under Jordanian control.

Fighting during December 1947 and early 1948 consisted mainly of low-level guerrilla operations—sniping, ambushes, and acts of terrorism—as Jewish forces sought to hold the main roads linking Jewish settlements in Palestine. In February 1948 the leadership of the Yishuv announced a general mobilization, and in April the Haganah, which heretofore had conducted mainly defensive operations, went on the offensive. Operating in accordance with what was known as "Plan D,"

Haganah strategy was to secure control of all territory allotted to the Jewish state by the UN resolution prior to the departure of the British. This involved seizing all Arab towns and villages in the Jewish sector and expelling as many of the Arab inhabitants as possible. The Haganah also attempted to secure the road connecting the Jewish sector with West Jerusalem, where nearly one-fifth of the Jewish inhabitants of Palestine lived.

Jewish forces quickly proved victorious, seizing control of Tiberias on April 18, Haifa on April 22, Safed on May 10, and Jaffa on May 13. In the process, whether voluntarily or not (the issue has always been controversial), some three hundred thousand of the half million Arabs living in the Jewish sector became refugees by May 15, fleeing to other parts of Palestine or neighboring Arab countries. Historians generally agree that a systematic massacre on April 9 of some two hundred fifty Arab inhabitants of Dayr Yassin, a village overlooking the road to Jerusalem, conducted by the Irgun and Stern Gang, helped to create the psychological climate that encouraged the refugees to flee.

## Israel Proclaimed

As the British mandate came to a formal end and the last British forces evacuated Jerusalem on May 15, the armed forces of the Yishuv had laid effective claim to virtually all the territory allocated to it under the terms of the partition resolution. On May 14 David Ben-Gurion, head of the Jewish Agency, formally proclaimed the establishment of Israel as an independent state. Both the United States and the Soviet Union quickly recognized the new state of Israel, as did most other members of the United Nations. Of the Western states, only Britain delayed, waiting until January 30, 1949, to recognize the Jewish state.

At this point, if the recently independent Arab states surrounding Israel had acquiesced to the Jewish state's existence, the Arab-Jewish conflict in Palestine might have been effectively ended. The Arabs of Palestine were not in a position to continue the conflict, and an independent Palestin-

ian Arab state prescribed by the UN partition could have emerged. Although Israel had gained control of territory assigned to it in the UN resolution, it had failed to secure control of the road to Jerusalem, and it was possible that Jerusalem could have emerged as the neutral, UN-administered city envisioned by the partition resolution. Earlier hostilities between Jews and Arabs and the Arab states' commitment to their Palestinian brethren, however, made compromise impossible. As they had vowed and had been preparing to do since December 1947, the contiguous Arab states—Egypt, Jordan, Syria, and Lebanon, as well as Iraq—sent contingents of their armies into Palestine on May 15, as the last British forces were departing.

## The 1948 War

The entrance of the Arab armies transformed what had been fundamentally a religious-ethnic conflict in Palestine into a wider war among all the newly established states of the region. Conflicting Arab objectives resulted in uncoordinated military strategies that the new Israeli state was able to exploit to its advantage. In the process, the cause of the Palestine Arabs was submerged in the wider conflict. When the fighting subsided, the Palestine Arabs found themselves living under Israeli, Jordanian, or Egyptian rule, or as displaced refugees in hastily constructed camps around the margins of Israel's newly established, somewhat expanded frontiers. The Arab Palestinians not only failed to keep Israel from being established as a state, they also lost what had been assigned to them in the UN partition resolution.

Despite the attack on Israel by five Arab armies, the armed forces of Israel, now formally reincorporated as the Israel Defense Force on May 26, 1948, continued to hold a distinct manpower advantage. By this time Israel fielded a mobile army of nine brigades with twenty-five thousand front-line troops that would grow to nearly eighty thousand by the end of the year. Historians generally agree that initially the Arabs held the edge in terms of aircraft, armored vehicles, and artillery, but Israel quickly overcame these deficiencies. With the British departure, restrictions on Jewish immigration also were lifted, and Israel significantly increased its pool of available manpower.

The Arab-Israeli War of 1948 developed in three phases. During the first phase (May 15-June 11), Israel conducted primarily defensive operations that succeeded in halting Arab offensive thrusts into Israeli territory. Unable to break through Jordanian defenses defending the road to Jerusalem, Israel also managed to construct a secondary road, the so-called Burma Road, that enabled Jerusalem to be resupplied, thus securing West Jerusalem for Israel. A UN-brokered ceasefire gave time to all sides, especially Israel, to rearm, reorganize, train, and plan for the second phase of the war. When the truce ended on July 6, primarily because of Syrian and Egyptian unwillingness to extend it, Israel had greatly improved its military position in terms of weapons, manpower, and organization.

During this second phase (July 6-19), Israel took the offensive and delivered several crushing defeats to the various Arab armies. It took Lod and Ramle in central Palestine and Nazareth in the north, all areas designated for the Arab state in the UN partition plan. A determined Israeli effort to capture East (Arab) Jerusalem had failed by the time a second United Nations cease-fire was imposed on July 19.

This second cease-fire was meant to be permanent until final armistices were signed, but it left Egyptian and Jordanian forces in control of the Negev, which the UN partition resolution had assigned to Israel. Determined not to lose the Negev, Israel on October 15 seized the pretext of Egyptian sniping at an Israeli convoy to resume offensive operations that eventually isolated Egyptian forces. The withdrawal of Egyptian forces from the Negev following a new cease-fire on January 7, 1949, opened the way for complete Israeli occupation of the Negev, which it accomplished on March 6-10, 1949. Meanwhile, on October 29-31, 1948, Israel also resumed offensive operations in the north and quickly defeated Syrian, Lebanese, and ALA forces located there, bringing

all of Galilee under Israeli control. This further usurpation of territory assigned to the proposed Arab state by the UN partition resolution was soon complemented by the de facto annexation in December of the remaining portion of Arab Palestine (the West Bank) by King Abdullah of Jordan. As the war ended, Egyptian forces remained in occupation of the Gaza Strip, but unlike Jordan they never annexed it.

Effectively defeated by Israel and unable to continue the war, the Arab states finally signed United Nations-sponsored armistice agreements: Egypt on February 25, 1949; Lebanon on March 23; Jordan on April 3; and Syria on July 20. Israel had emerged as an independent state in the region, successfully defended its borders, expanded its assigned territory, and gained general international recognition. With Israel's acquisition of areas allotted to the proposed Arab state and Jordan's annexation of most of the rest of it, the Arab state envisioned in the resolution was left without territory. Moreover, out of Palestine's prewar Arab population of 1.3 million, approximately half had become refugees, either in the West Bank or Gaza or neighboring Arab countries. Jerusalem, moreover, emerged as a divided city, partitioned into Israeli and Jordanian sectors, rather than the united city under international administration proposed by the UN resolution.

Israel refused to negotiate away any of the gains it had made during the war to achieve a durable peace. The Arab states were similarly unwilling to conclude durable peace agreements with Israel. Despite the decisiveness of Israel's victory, therefore, the Arab-Israeli conflict continued.

## Early Arab-Israeli Relations

The nearly two decades between the establishment of Israel and the Arab-Israeli war of June 1967 was a time of momentous change in the Middle East. The newly established Jewish state, inhabited by many European emigrés who were highly motivated to build the new state and defend it, was better equipped and more effectively organized to take advantage of post-World War II

# Jewish Heritage Unites a Diverse Israel

Like the United States, Israel is a country founded and developed by immigrants from many different ethnic and cultural backgrounds. Israel has encouraged this "ingathering" of Jews from all parts of the world, counting on their common Jewish heritage to help cement their union with other Israelis—a task that has presented many difficulties. This drawing-together is the essence of *Zionism,* which might be called "the founding religion" of Israel.

Zionism emerged from a ferment of nationalist, socialist, populist, and utopian ideas that were inflaming the youth of that time. As nationalists, the Jews were not unlike other minority groups chafing under foreign rule within the Russian and Austro-Hungarian empires. The Jews had a special impetus, however, because of anti-Semitic persecutions.

## Earliest Settlements

The first Jewish settlements in Palestine arose through the efforts of Jews who in 1882 formed an organization called "Lovers of Zion." (Zion is the hill in Jerusalem on which King David's palace is said to have stood.) These young Jews conceived the idea of sending groups of colonists to Palestine, then a neglected backwater of the Ottoman Empire, to establish Jewish communities in the land of their forebears. The movement got its start when Theodor Herzl, a Viennese journalist, wrote *Der Judenstaat,* the rationale for creation of a Jewish state. He later founded the Zionist movement as it exists today.

"I imagine that the Jews will always have sufficient enemies, just as every other nation," Herzl wrote. "But once settled in their own land, they can never again be scattered all over the world."

Palestine at that time had a Jewish population of about twenty-five thousand, mostly descendants of refugees from the Spanish Inquisition and pious pilgrims to the Holy Land. They were poor, religious, and lived separatist lives among the largely Arab Muslim population. The resident Jews looked with hostility on the new arrivals, whom they considered dangerous radicals and religious renegades. The newcomers were confronted with a life style that seemed to contain the worst aspects of the ghetto life from which they had fled. Despite the unpromising conditions and the difficult climate, a succession of immigrants succeeded over the next few decades in founding several dozen communities.

The Jewish settlement of Palestine was marked by numerous waves of immigration, known by the Hebrew word *aliyah,* meaning ascension (to Zion). The first aliyah, 1882-1903, brought in some twenty thousand to thirty thousand Jews. The second aliyah, 1905-14, which brought thirty-five thousand to forty thousand, was the formative one that set the tone for the future nation. Immigrants of this period produced the first leaders of independent Israel, among them David Ben-Gurion and Isaac Ben-Zvi, later prime minister and president, respectively.

The first twentieth-century immigrants were young Jews in their late teens or early twenties, burning with zeal to create a utopia. They believed that only through socialism could a society be created free of the evils of materialism, exploitation, and the aberrations that produced anti-Semitism. The immigrants were driven by an intense, near-mystical devotion to their cause. Working the soil for them was not merely a pioneering necessity, but also a sacred mission.

## Founding of Kibbutzim

"The immigrants of the second aliyah brought with them to Palestine not only their powerful ties to Jewish history and traditions as well as to contemporary political and social movements ... in their countries of origin, but also ideologies and principles concerning the nature and institutions of the Jewish community and society they intended to create," wrote Judah Matras in a 1970 study in *Integration and Development in Israel.* This wave of immigrants became "the political, social, economic, and ideological backbone of the Jewish community in Palestine, and large sectors of life in Israel today are organized around institutions created by immigrants arriving in the second aliyah."

These were the founders of the *kibbutzim,* collective farms that gripped the Jewish consciousness. The first kibbutz, Degania, was founded in 1910 on swampland near Lake Tiberias; it was the cheapest land available. Soon many agricultural collectives were established. Although the kibbutzim never held more than 10 to 12 percent of the Jewish population of Palestine, they created the national ideal of the tough, vital, selflessly dedicated farmer-soldier and patriot. The kibbutz provided the nation with some of its governing elite and many of its best soldiers. Although only 4 percent of today's Israeli population has ever lived on a kibbutz, kibbutz members accounted for one-fourth of the Israeli fatalities in the 1967 Arab-Israeli War.

## World War I Immigration

World War I brought Jewish immigration to a halt. Furthermore, the Turkish regime, which was on the side of the Central Powers, expelled many Jews who had come from the Allied nations. Other Jews left voluntarily because of deteriorating economic conditions. During World War I the Jewish population of Palestine dropped from eighty-five thousand to fifty-six thousand. After the war, however, a third aliyah began, encouraged by the Balfour Declaration of November 2, 1917, in which the British government expressed sympathy for the Jewish dream of a homeland. Britain in 1917 was the occupying power in Palestine and from 1920 ruled the region under a League of Nations mandate.

Between 1919 and 1923, this third aliyah brought thirty-five thousand Jews to Palestine. This group was composed mainly of Russians, whose motives were similar to those of the prewar pioneers.

The fourth aliyah, 1924-31, brought some eighty-two thousand immigrants, mainly middle-class Jews from Poland. "An economic depression, combined evidently with anti-Semitism, touched off widespread economic, social and political sanctions and discrimination against the Jews in Poland," according to Matras. Another factor was new U.S. legislation restricting immigration from Eastern Europe.

## Impact of Nazi Persecution

The fifth aliyah, 1932-38, brought two hundred seventeen thousand Jews to Palestine. The rise of nazism in Germany and its expansionist moves in Central Europe occasioned the first sizable influx of immigrants from Germany and Austria, as well as from Czechoslovakia, Hungary, and Greece. The Nazi threat also accounted in large part for a renewed flow, totaling ninety-one thousand, from Poland. Unlike the pioneers, who were young, unattached, and eager to work the soil, the aliyah of the 1930s included large numbers of settled middle-class families, headed by men who had made their mark in business and in the professions.

Throughout the entire period of Jewish settlement, large numbers of immigrants decided not to stay in Palestine. Nevertheless, by the end of 1938 the Jewish population had risen to four hundred thirteen thousand.

Arabs protested the influx of Jews, and the British government responded by reducing immigration quotas and restricting Jewish land purchases. This policy, set forth in a British government white paper on May 17, 1939, remained in force throughout World War II. Nevertheless, seventy-five thousand Jews entered Palestine during the war years, twenty-nine thousand of them illegally. By the end of the war in 1945, the Jewish population of Palestine stood at five hundred sixty-four thousand.

## Post-World War II Immigrants

The next wave of immigration drew mainly from the two hundred thousand homeless Jews—Russian, Polish, and German—who were living in so-called displaced persons camps after World War II. In the years 1946-48 about sixty-one thousand came to Palestine, nearly half of them slipping through a blockade the British had imposed to halt further immigration. The ban drew protests from a world haunted by the revelations of Hitler's death camps, and it provided an additional ingredient fueling a three-sided civil war that developed among the Jews, the British, and the Arabs.

A hard-pressed Britain notified the United Nations in 1947 that it could no longer continue its role in Palestine and planned to withdraw its forces. With the ending of the British mandate, Jews in Palestine declared the existence of the state of Israel. Within three years Israel's population doubled to 1.4 million, 75 percent of it foreign born.

developments in technology and communications than the more traditional societies of its Arab neighbors. Liberated from the constraints of British rule, Israel embarked on a period of nation building that gradually transformed it into the most technologically advanced state in the region. Unrestricted immigration also led to rapid population growth during the early years of Israeli independence—from a Jewish population of 717,000 in November 1948 to nearly 2 million by 1961. Many of these immigrants were Jews from the Arab countries. From 1950 onward the Israeli government maintained that the influx of Jews from Arab countries amounted to a population exchange that freed Israel from responsibility toward the Palestine Arabs who became refugees during the 1948 Israeli war of independence.

For the Arab states surrounding Israel, however, the defeat of their armies by the new Jewish state was perceived as a disaster. So overwhelming did the defeat appear that the legitimacy of every Arab regime was seriously undermined, an era of general Arab political instability was inaugurated, and a popular desire to obtain revenge for the insult of 1948 fueled Arab political rhetoric for the next two decades. Under such circumstances the transformation of the various Arab-Israeli armistice agreements into a permanent peace settlement proved impossible.

Unable to force compliance with the UN partition resolution of November 1947, the UN General Assembly in December 1948 established the Conciliation Commission for Palestine to mediate the Arab-Israeli conflict. Consisting of France, Turkey, and the United States and headed by UN acting mediator Ralph Bunche, the commission presided over negotiations on the island of Rhodes. Its efforts led to the various Arab-Israeli armistice agreements. The commission was unable, however, to transform these agreements into a broader peace settlement. The Arab states insisted on negotiating as a unified bloc, while Israel would only negotiate with each individual Arab state. In addition, Israel rebuffed Arab demands for repatriation of Palestinian refugees. Finally, while some Arab leaders privately indicated their willingness to resolve the conflict in return for some territorial concession by Israel, the beleaguered Israeli government adamantly refused to give up any territory, especially after its formal admission into the United Nations on May 11, 1949.

Israel's refusal to permit even a partial repatriation of Arab refugees and the Arab states' refusal to grant them citizenship created an enormous refugee problem. In response, the United Nations in 1950 established the UN Relief and Works Agency (UNRWA) to fund and administer refugee camps in Lebanon, Syria, Jordan, the West Bank, and Gaza. The camps, which soon became permanent, demonstrated the impotence of the international community in leading the conflicting parties toward an overall settlement.

### Regional Arms Race

Aware of the unstable political situation that had emerged after the unresolved 1948 Arab-Israeli War, Great Britain, France, and the United States in May 1950 announced a Tripartite Declaration in which they agreed to limit arms supplies to the various parties of the Arab-Israeli conflict and to insist on a political rather than a military solution to the problem. This early effort to contain a potential arms race soon broke down, however, when Israel in 1954 concluded a major arms agreement with France. On February 28, 1955, Israel made use of its newly strengthened armed forces to launch a successful raid against an Egyptian position in the Gaza Strip. Ostensibly undertaken in retaliation for continuing border incidents by unknown Arab refugees, the raid was carried out primarily to demonstrate Israeli military strength and the futility of continued Arab nonrecognition of Israel.

Instead of intimidating Egypt into recognizing the permanence of Israel, however, the Gaza raid, along with other similar Israeli retaliatory raids into Arab territory, provoked the new military leadership in Egypt, headed by Col. Gamal Abdel Nasser, to seek a reliable source of arms for itself. Nasser preferred to obtain arms from the West, especially from the United States, which was seeking to draw Egypt into a Western-sponsored Middle East alliance system. When President Dwight D. Eisenhower refused to provide arms on terms that Egypt would accept, however, Nasser turned to the Soviets. The subsequent Soviet-Egyptian arms agreement, announced on September 27, 1955, marked the final collapse of the Tripartite Declaration arms limitation policy, gave impetus to the developing French-Israeli arms relationship, undercut U.S. efforts to contain Soviet influence in the Middle East, and provoked tensions that led to renewed war between Israel and Egypt in November 1956.

## Barriers to Peace

Despite continuing diplomatic efforts by the United Nations, the United States, and Great Britain to diminish tensions and suggest plans for an overall Arab-Israeli settlement, a variety of factors combined to thwart peace efforts. Foremost among them was the pattern of border clashes and incidents that developed almost from the moment the 1949 armistice agreements were signed. At first these clashes were often begun by Arab villagers on one side of the armistice line whose lands and crops had ended up on the Israeli side of the unofficially established Israeli border. The border incidents, however, gradually evolved into more organized attempts at sabotage and violence by refugee elements who, even in the early 1950s, began to coalesce into various resistance groups. Arab governments sometimes supported these groups, but more often governments sought to control them.

Israel tended to hold the appropriate Arab government responsible for patrolling the Arab side of the border, but Arab governments generally were unable or unwilling to perform this task. Israel's adoption in 1952 of a more aggressive reprisal policy led the Arab states to enhance their defensive preparations.

Israel's sense of isolation and vulnerability during the early 1950s was fueled by Arab rhetoric calling for its destruction, an Arab League boycott on trade with Israel, and frequent Egyptian blockades of sea traffic to or from Israel through the Strait of Tiran or the Suez Canal. The Soviet-Egyptian arms agreement of September 1955 dramatically increased Israeli fears of the Arabs' potential military capabilities. Pressure in Israel grew for a large preemptive strike against Egypt, mainly to secure Sharm al-Sheikh, the western flank of the Strait of Tiran, before Egypt could integrate its new weapons into its armed forces. Israel also signed a major new arms agreement with France.

## Western Hostility Toward Egypt

Israel's growing desire to attack Egypt was made increasingly feasible because of developing Western hostility toward Egypt's new military government, increasingly dominated from 1954 by Nasser. France viewed Nasser as an enemy because of the moral and material support he offered to the Algerian resistance fighters who opposed French rule in North Africa. Britain was alarmed by the nationalist policies of Nasser, who sought to end the British presence in Egypt and the Suez Canal Zone. Nasser also resisted British efforts to organize the Baghdad Pact, a Western-supported alliance (Turkey, Iraq, Iran, Pakistan) intended to check the expansion of Soviet influence in the Middle East.

Finally, the United States, whose policy was to encourage Egypt's inclusion in any Western alliance formed in the region, gradually became disenchanted with Nasser's policies as well. His official acceptance of Soviet arms assistance in September 1955, his refusal to lift a blockade against Israeli shipping through the Strait of Tiran and the Suez Canal, and his recognition of Communist China in May 1956 were all considered blows to U.S. interests. Nasser's recognition of China, however, was the act that led U.S. secretary of state John Foster Dulles, on July 20, 1955, to withdraw promised financing for the proposed Aswan High Dam, the principal symbol of Nasser's ambitious plans for Egypt's agricultural and economic development. Although Dulles's move was probably a bargaining maneuver aimed at

forcing Nasser to take more seriously U.S. interests in the region, Nasser reacted on July 26 by
nationalizing the French- and British-owned Suez
Canal Company. This action led Britain and
France to begin preparations for a joint military
operation to take back the canal.

Unable to secure support for an Anglo-French
military intervention from the United States,
which preferred a negotiated settlement of the
Suez crisis, the two Western allies and Israel
adopted a strategy of deception. Israel would
launch an attack on Egyptian forces in the Sinai
and appear to threaten the canal. At this point
Britain and France would intervene to separate the
warring parties, reoccupying the Suez Canal in the
process. The operation was timed for late October
1956, when the Soviet Union was preoccupied
with the uprising in Hungary and the United
States was faced with presidential elections. The
British and French believed the elections would
prevent the Eisenhower administration from taking any action.

### 1956 Suez Crisis

In accordance with the prearranged secret plan,
Israel launched its offensive against Egyptian positions in the Sinai on October 29. The attack included an Israeli paratroop drop near the Mitla
Pass to give the appearance of a threat to the Suez
Canal. The transparency of the allied strategy was
evident on the following day, however, when
France and Britain jointly issued an ultimatum
demanding an immediate cease-fire, a withdrawal
of Egyptian and Israeli forces from opposite sides
of the Suez Canal, and Egyptian acceptance of a
temporary occupation by French and British
forces of the Suez Canal Zone to separate the
belligerents and to ensure freedom of shipping
through the canal. At this point, Israeli-Egyptian
hostilities had barely begun near the Israeli frontier, far from the Suez Canal, and Egypt would
have had to evacuate its thirty-thousand-man force
from the Sinai to observe the terms of the cease-
fire.

Israel quickly indicated its acceptance of the

ultimatum, while Nasser rejected it but issued
orders that, in the event of an Anglo-French attack
on Egypt, all forces in the Sinai were to be withdrawn to defend the canal. These orders were
implemented on the nights of October 31 and
November 1, following French and British air attacks against Egyptian airfields on October 31.
The withdrawal of Egyptian forces from the Sinai,
coupled with the decimation of the Egyptian air
force by the allied air attacks, opened the way for
Israel's complete occupation of the Sinai Peninsula, almost without a fight, which it achieved by
the morning of November 5.

Meanwhile, on November 1 the United Nations
General Assembly adopted a United States-sponsored resolution calling for an immediate cease-
fire, a withdrawal of Israeli forces behind the 1949
armistice lines, the reopening of the Suez Canal
(which Egypt had closed), and all other United
Nations members (that is, Britain and France) "to
refrain from introducing military goods into the
area." Egypt immediately accepted this call for a
cease-fire, but Israel, Britain, and France would
not, the latter two because they had not yet introduced ground forces in the Suez Canal area, which
they were able to do only by November 5. Finally
caving in to both international and domestic pressure, Britain accepted the United Nations cease-
fire effective at midnight on November 6-7, long
before it had been able to achieve its military
objectives in the Suez Canal Zone, but well after
Israeli objectives had been achieved. Israel and
France also accepted the cease-fire.

Of the three attackers, Israel alone had
achieved its military objectives in the 1956 Suez
crisis. Nevertheless, as in 1949, it was unable to
translate military victory into a lasting political
settlement. Under strong pressure from the United
Nations, and especially from the United States
and the Soviet Union, to withdraw unconditionally
from all territories it had occupied during the
conflict, Israel ultimately did so. The last Israeli
troops left Gaza on March 9, 1957. The last
French and British troops had left Egypt on December 22, 1956.

In return for Israel's evacuation of the Sinai,

Israel and Egypt accepted the presence on the Egyptian side of the Israeli-Egyptian armistice line of a United Nations Emergency Force (UNEF), which began arriving in mid-November 1956. The force's mission was to help protect Israel's southern frontier from further Arab attacks as well as to ensure freedom of Israeli navigation through the Strait of Tiran. These being two primary goals of its 1956 war against Egypt, Israel in fact profited from its military campaign. It failed, however, to secure a general peace treaty as a result of the war or explicit Arab recognition of its legitimacy as an existing state. Therefore, it remained technically at war with Egypt, as with the rest of the Arab world.

## Arab Rivalries

The years immediately following the Suez crisis witnessed a significant downturn in Arab-Israeli tensions. This was primarily due to Arab preoccupation with inter-Arab politics and rivalries. Although anti-Israeli sentiment remained the staple of Arab political rhetoric, Israel took a back seat to instability and other problems that afflicted Arab regimes.

Despite the military defeat Egypt had suffered during the Suez crisis, Nasser emerged afterward as a popular hero for many Arabs. Whatever the military outcome of the war, the political result was that Britain and France, the traditional colonial powers in the Arab world, had been humiliated. Moreover, the Egyptian nationalization of the Suez Canal received permanent international recognition, Israel had been denied any territorial expansion, and Nasser was seen as the leader capable of restoring Arab unity and pride. Pro-Nasser parties and groups, perhaps encouraged by Egyptian funds, sprang up throughout the Arab world. Nasser enjoyed an era of leadership in the Arab world that lasted until Egypt's humiliating defeat in the Arab-Israeli War of 1967.

The popularity of Nasser and what came to be known as "Nasserism" provoked crises in several Arab countries during the late 1950s and early 1960s. Pro-Nasser groups and other opponents raised challenges to King Hussein's rule in Jordan that led to British intervention in support of the king in both 1957 and 1958. In February 1958 Syrian politicians, inspired by Nasser, went to Cairo offering their country as part of a Nasser-led United Arab Republic (UAR). This political union of Egypt and Syria lasted three years until disgruntled Syrian officers reclaimed Syrian sovereignty through a successful military coup in September 1961.

Inspired by the union of Egypt and Syria, large numbers of Lebanese in 1958 demonstrated in favor of union with the UAR. The subsequent destabilization of the existing Lebanese government led to United States' intervention during the summer in support of continued Lebanese sovereignty. Almost simultaneously, military officers in Iraq, again influenced by the example set by Nasser's Egypt, overthrew their pro-Western monarchy and withdrew Iraq from the Baghdad Pact. Rather than join the new United Arab Republic, however, the new military regime emphasized Iraqi independence and began to vie with Nasser for moral leadership in the Arab world.

Finally, in September 1962 pro-Nasser elements in the North Yemen military overthrew their traditional monarchy, leading ultimately to Egyptian military intervention against the Saudi-financed royalist opposition, which the new Yemeni military regime could not subdue. The heavy Egyptian commitment in soldiers, money, and materiel in North Yemen seriously drained Egyptian resources and decreased Nasser's capability to conduct a successful war against Israel in 1967.

Despite continuing popular support in the Arab world, by the mid-1960s Nasser experienced strained relations with other Arab regimes. Relations with Saudi Arabia were the most hostile because of the conflict in Yemen, but Jordan and Iraq also had disputes with Egypt.

In the midst of these Arab disputes, any Arab threat to Israel seemed remote. It was true that with Soviet support and assistance, Egypt and Syria were arming themselves for a potential third round of hostilities against Israel. The Jewish state, however, continued its reliable arms relationship with France and was developing its own arms manufacturing industry. In addition it was gradually building its highly trained citizen army to meet future Arab military challenges. Israeli victories in 1948 and 1956 also provided a measure of deterrence against an Arab attack. Even as late as the spring of 1967, the possibility of an Arab-Israeli war did not appear likely. Yet out of the conflicts spawned by developing inter-Arab rivalries lay the seeds of the war that broke out on June 5, 1967.

## The Six-Day War of 1967

Two developments in 1964 led to the gradual revival of Arab-Israeli border tensions that culminated in the Six-Day War of 1967. An Israeli project to divert water from the Sea of Galilee along an aqueduct to the Negev Desert led Syria to call for joint Arab action against the Israeli effort. Seeking to reassert his credentials as leader of the Arab world, Nasser called for a meeting of Arab heads of state under the auspices of the Arab League in Cairo. This first Arab summit convened in January 1964 and announced two significant decisions. The first was general Arab support for Syria to divert sections of the Jordan River lying in its territories, a step that would diminish the amount of water flowing into Israel. As Syrian construction crews began to undertake this project in late 1964, however, Israeli air strikes forced them to halt work.

The second decision taken at the Arab summit was the formal establishment of the Palestine Liberation Organization (PLO). Since the 1956 Suez crisis, many stateless Palestinian refugees from the 1948 war had been organizing political groups and attempting to mobilize public sentiment for their return to what was now Israel. In general, they still looked to the Arab regimes to help them achieve this mission, but many became increasingly skeptical about the capability and the will of the Arab governments to keep the issue alive.

Some Palestinians, such as George Habash, a leader of the Arab National Movement (ANM), which he had helped to establish in Beirut in the early 1950s, believed that general revolutionary upheaval and the achievement of Arab unity was a precondition for overcoming Israeli intransigence. Soon after the formation of the PLO in 1964, Habash established a Palestinian wing of the ANM known as the National Front for the Liberation of Palestine (NFLP—later to be called the Popular Front for the Liberation of Palestine, or PFLP). Still others, such as Yasir Arafat's Fatah (Conquest) organization, established about 1959, took the view that the Arabs of Palestinian origin had to develop their own independent political capacity, distinct from the Arab states, to foster an eventual return of the lands lost in 1948.

The proliferation and appeal of such groups led Nasser to favor the establishment of a formal Palestinian organization within the Arab League structure. In this way he sought to channel Palestinian irredentist energies into another base of support for himself and his leadership in the Arab world. At the same time he sought to exert control over the Palestinian movement. The language of the summit communiqué establishing the PLO was significant. Where previous gatherings of Arab officials since 1949 had called for the "application of the United Nations resolutions" on the issue, that is, that Israel should accept border rectifications and the return of Arab refugees, the new formulation called for "the liberation of Palestine," thus implying a resolution of the Arab-Israeli conflict through military force.

### Mounting Tensions

Nasser wanted to avoid direct confrontation with Israel in 1964 and refrained from mobilizing general Arab support against Israel's effort to stop Syria's water diversion project. Unable to count on Nasser's backing, Syria responded by providing arms and training to Yasir Arafat's Fatah organization, which began undertaking sabotage operations against Israel. The Fatah operations, which caused little damage but resulted in some Israeli casualties, continued through 1965 and escalated in 1966 and 1967. Complicating the problem for Israel was the fact that although the attacks originated in Syria, the missions were conducted over Jordan's West Bank armistice line with Israel. In accordance with its traditional policy, therefore, Israel held Jordan responsible for failing to control its border. In November 1966, after a particularly serious incident in which several Israelis were killed, Israel retaliated against the village of Samu near Hebron in the West Bank.

During this period tensions also had risen along the Syrian-Israeli frontier because of Syrian shelling of Israeli settlements from elevated positions in the Golan Heights. Although UN observers often held Israeli settlers responsible for these incidents because of their efforts to farm disputed territories whose status had not been resolved in the 1949 armistice agreement, the Syrian shells nevertheless often hit areas outside the disputed zones, including established Israeli settlements. Finally, a particularly intensive Syrian shelling on April 7, 1967, escalated into an air battle in which Israeli pilots shot down six Syrian aircraft.

Syrian and Jordanian reaction to these mounting tensions focused on criticism of Nasser. They accused him of hiding behind the UNEF troops along his armistice line with Israel and of being more interested in his empire in Yemen than in helping confront the common Israeli enemy. The regimes in Jordan and Syria, despite their own rivalry, in effect dared Nasser to assert his self-proclaimed leadership of the Arab world.

The terrorist attacks against Israel were not deterred by Israeli counterstrikes, and in early May 1967 the Israeli government announced that it was considering more decisive action, especially against Syria. Rumors of Israeli preparations for war along the Syrian border, apparently spread by Moscow, raised a challenge that Nasser could not avoid. On May 16 he demanded the withdrawal of the UNEF from the Sinai and began reinforcing Egyptian troops near the frontier with Israel. On May 22 Nasser announced his intention to reestablish the blockade of the Strait of Tiran. This last action, which violated the terms of the 1956 agreement that ended the Suez crisis, was considered an act of war by Israel.

War fever began to grip the Arab world, fueled by Jordan's decision on May 30 to join a mutual defense pact with Syria and Egypt. The latter two had entered into such an agreement the previous November. Meanwhile, paralyzed by indecision, the Israeli government fell, and on June 1 a new national unity government was formed that included Moshe Dayan, the architect of Israel's 1956 military campaign, as minister of defense.

With historical hindsight, it now seems possible that if Israel had not launched hostilities on June 5, no war would have occurred in 1967. Nevertheless, any diplomatic settlement of the crisis, which U.S. officials were trying to arrange, would likely have been reached at Israel's expense. Although Nasser insisted that any outbreak of war would be initiated by Israel, other Arab leaders spoke of destroying Israel. Egyptian movements in the Sinai also appeared to indicate a plan to break through the Negev to create a land corridor linking Egypt and Jordan, a goal of Egyptian diplomacy since 1949. Terrorist operations against Israel also would not likely have ended with a diplomatic settlement. Finally, Israeli military strategy, grounded in a perception of the country's geographic vulnerability, placed an emphasis on capturing the initiative by launching a preemptive first strike. These factors combined to lead the new Israeli government to decide to go to war.

### Israel Attacks

During the Six-Day War Israel executed a brilliant military strategy that resulted in its reconquest of the Sinai peninsula and the conquest of Jordan's West Bank and Syria's Golan Heights. Achieving total surprise, Israel launched its military campaign on June 5 at 8:45 a.m. (Egyptian time), after dawn alerts had ended at Egyptian airfields and the Cairo rush hour was in full swing. In three hours of precise wave attacks, Israeli aircraft struck Egyptian airfields, destroying 300 of the 431 aircraft in the Egyptian inventory. Then during the noon hour and early afternoon, similar attacks destroyed the air forces of Jordan and Syria and Iraqi aircraft deployed at a major airfield in western Iraq. The achievement of immediate Israeli air superiority enabled the outmanned Israeli ground forces to have the decisive advantage in the land battles that followed.

Meanwhile Israeli ground forces launched a multipronged attack into the Sinai. Unlike the campaign of 1956, which was designed to confront static Egyptian defensive positions, the 1967 attack aimed at breaking through Egyptian lines, severing lines of communication, and finally destroying the Egyptian army as it tried to retreat. With complete air superiority, the Israeli strategy proved highly effective. Egypt unconditionally accepted a UN Security Council request for a cease-fire on June 9. By this time, however, Israel had achieved full control of the Sinai Peninsula and the Jordanian West Bank.

The circumstances and motivations of Israel's attack on Jordan are less clear. Forty-five minutes after launching its air strikes against Egypt, Israel sent a message through UN mediators to the Jordanian king informing him that Israel would not attack the West Bank unless Jordan attacked first. Nevertheless, deceived by Nasser that Egypt was destroying the Israeli air force rather than being destroyed by it, Hussein ordered his artillery to open fire on various targets in Israel, apparently before receiving the Israeli message. Although this firing did not constitute a prelude to Jordanian offensive operations, it did supply a pretext for Israel to attack the West Bank.

Israeli military action against the West Bank began at 11:15 a.m. on June 5, shortly before its destruction of the Jordanian air force. The capture of East Jerusalem was the first Israeli priority. Fierce fighting around the city occurred June 5 and 6. Realizing the weakness of his position, the Jordanian commander in Jerusalem withdrew his forces during the night of June 6, and unopposed Israeli forces took control of the city the next morning. Meanwhile, Israeli columns moved in from the north, west, and south against Jordanian forces concentrated at Nablus. Aided by air superiority, they gradually overcame Jordanian resistance and converged on Nablus on June 7. Virtually surrounded by approaching Israeli forces, and with their morale broken, the defenders of Nablus fled in a disorga-

nized fashion across the Jordan River, leaving Israel in effective control of the West Bank. At 8:00 that evening, both Jordan and Israel accepted the UN appeal for a cease-fire, fully a day and a half before the cease-fire concluded in the Sinai. Israel now took up the problem of Syria.

Syria, whose actions and policies had done so much to provoke the war, did little once hostilities had started. After the destruction of its air force on June 5, Syria was vulnerable to Israeli interdiction of its military movements. As the magnitude of Israel's victories in the Sinai and West Bank became apparent, the Syrian government planned at the appropriate moment to accept the UN call for a cease-fire, which it did at 5:20 p.m. on June 8. Since the outbreak of the war four days earlier, however, Syrian artillery from the Golan Heights had kept Israeli forces and settlements under constant bombardment. The Israeli government faced strong public pressure from its population in the north and from army units in its northern territorial command to do something to silence the Syrian guns. Accordingly, without informing the rest of his government, Israeli defense minister Moshe Dayan ordered the army to attack Syria as soon as its units were ready on June 9. Syria may have accepted the cease-fire on June 8, but as Dayan later remarked wryly in his memoirs, it "went into effect a day and a half later."

Despite the formidable obstacle posed by the Golan Heights, Israeli columns advanced up the Heights without faltering, although they faced withering fire from dug-in Syrian positions along their routes. The Syrian government in Damascus sent an immediate protest concerning Israel's violation of the cease-fire to the United Nations and issued orders for its front-line units to withdraw from the Golan Heights to defensive positions near the capital. This withdrawal began even before the Israelis reached the crest of the Heights on the afternoon of June 9. Consequently, when Israel resumed operations the following morning, its units swept to their designated military objectives without opposition. Having achieved its military objectives, Israel accepted the UN cease-fire at 6:30 p.m. on June 10, the sixth day of the war.

## Aftermath of the War

The results of the Six-Day War greatly complicated the Arab-Israeli conflict. Before the war the key issues were quite simple: the final settlement of Israel's borders and the ultimate disposition of the Arab refugees. After the war several new issues emerged. Among these were the terms by which the Sinai Peninsula would be returned to Egypt and the Golan Heights to Syria; the status of the West Bank and Gaza Strip; the status of Jerusalem, which Israel now proclaimed to be the reunited capital of Israel and not subject to negotiation. Two other results of the war also would affect profoundly the Arab-Israeli conflict in the coming years. The war increased international involvement in the Middle East, especially that of the United States and the Soviet Union, and stimulated a sense of national identity among the Palestinian refugees of 1948 as well as among the Arabs living under Israeli occupation. This national identity eventually led to calls for Palestinian national self-determination.

Except for East Jerusalem, which it immediately annexed, Israel initially expressed its official willingness to return the territories it had occupied during the war. The Israeli government, however, stated that it would permit no return to the prewar status quo that had provided the conditions for the war to erupt in the first place. Israel insisted on negotiated peace agreements with its Arab neighbors in exchange for the occupied territories. In this view, Israel received the support of the United States, which in 1956 had insisted on Israel's unconditional withdrawal from the Sinai.

The Arab states convened an Arab summit in Khartoum in August 1967 and adopted the position that Israel should withdraw from the occupied territories without further conditions. Because the principle of the "inadmissibility of the acquisition of territory by war" was enshrined in the United Nations Charter, they expected the international community to support the Arab position. Unlike the United States, the Soviet Union, which had broken diplomatic relations with Israel during the war, did so. Moscow also agreed to rearm Egypt

*West Bank and Gaza*

and Syria, a gesture that strengthened their resolve to hold fast to the principles enunciated at the Khartoum summit: "no peace with Israel, no recognition of Israel, no negotiations with it, and insistence on the rights of the Palestinian people in their own country."

## UN Resolution 242

In an effort to reconcile these positions, the United States and the Soviet Union, now deeply immersed in the Arab-Israeli imbroglio, sought to reach agreement on a framework for encouraging a settlement of the conflict. The result of their effort was United Nations Security Council Resolution 242 adopted on November 22, 1967. *(Text, Appendix, p. 395)*

Emphasizing the "inadmissibility of the acquisition of territory by war and the need to work for a just and lasting peace in which every state in the area can live in security," the resolution also stressed that a "just and lasting peace" should include the application of both the following principles: "(i) Withdrawal of Israeli armed forces from territories occupied in the recent conflict; (ii) Termination of all claims or states of belligerency and respect for and acknowledgment of the sovereignty, territorial integrity and political independence of every State in the area and their right to live in peace within secure and recognized boundaries free from threats or acts of force." Other principles enunciated in the resolution included freedom of navigation through international waterways in the area; a just settlement of the refugee problem; and establishment of demilitarized zones, if necessary, to guarantee the territorial inviolability and the political independence of every state in the area.

Although the resolution clearly linked the establishment of peace with Israeli withdrawal, any insistence on direct negotiations among the hostile parties was notably missing from the text. The resolution concluded, however, by requesting the appointment of a special UN representative to conduct negotiations with the various parties in accordance with its provisions.

Gunnar Jarring, Sweden's ambassador to the Soviet Union, was appointed to mediate between the Arabs and Israel, but his efforts to secure movement in the peace process soon failed. Egypt, although it grudgingly accepted the UN resolution, mainly at Soviet insistence, held fast to the view that Jarring should focus solely on Israeli withdrawal. Syria, on the other hand, refused to accept the resolution at this time and continued to support Palestinian resistance groups willing to make raids into Israel. These hard-line attitudes, meanwhile, strengthened the hands of a rapidly growing body of Israelis who called for retention of the territories, or most of them. They claimed that the territories were needed for Israeli security because the Arabs would never agree to peace. Some Israelis also claimed that because the territories were part of historic Israel, they should not be returned in any case.

In the face of continued Israeli occupation of the territories, King Hussein tolerated the growth of Palestinian resistance organizations in Jordan. He had accepted Resolution 242, but he saw the organizations as a means of deterring any Israeli effort to annex the West Bank, which technically remained part of his kingdom.

The emergence of an increasingly significant Palestinian-based guerrilla movement against Israel proved to be one of the most salient new features of the Arab-Israeli conflict in the years after the 1967 war. The rapidly growing community of Palestinian Arab refugees was increasingly drawn to the idea, most effectively articulated by Yasir Arafat's Fatah organization, that the Palestinians needed to forge their own independent political identity in order to secure their liberation. The growth of such attitudes, however, was to bring them into conflict not only with Israel but also with their host states, especially those where their movement was able to take root.

### War of Attrition

As it became clear that the Jarring mission was not going to be successful and that Israel was consolidating its hold on the occupied territories, Nasser decided to renew military confrontation with Israel as a means of retaining superpower interest in the conflict. His determination to secure Israel's withdrawal from the Sinai on his own terms rather than Israel's was strengthened by continuing Soviet military assistance. By the summer of 1968 the Egyptian inventory of military hardware was superior in quality and quantity to what it had been on the eve of the 1967 war. Accordingly, in September 1968, Egypt began intensive artillery barrages of Israeli positions along the entire length of the Suez Canal. The tactic failed to raise an international response, however, and Israeli retaliation by air attacks against civilian targets and helicopter raids deep in Egyptian territory indicated the need for better defensive preparations. In addition, the Israelis built stronger fortified positions, the so-called Bar-Lev Line, along the east bank of the canal.

To meet these challenges, Nasser evacuated civilians from the Egyptian cities along the canal and began building, with Soviet assistance, an elaborate air defense network to counter Israeli air superiority. When these preparations were in place, he formally announced and launched on March 8, 1969, a "War of Attrition" against Israeli forces on the canal. Nasser now hoped to weaken Israeli resolve by resorting to an extended conflict that would inflict unacceptable Israeli casualties and destroy the Bar-Lev Line, making it possible for Egyptian forces to cross the canal and establish a beachhead in the Sinai.

Heavy Egyptian bombardment and Israeli counterfire continued for about eighty days. When in July an Egyptian commando unit succeeded in crossing the canal and inflicting heavy Israeli casualties, Israel decided to commit its air force. The Israeli air force sent a commando unit to destroy a key radar installation that controlled parts of Egypt's extensive air defense system. Then Israeli jets followed up with ten days of intensive air attacks causing great damage to Egyptian artillery and surface-to-air missile systems. This action made it possible for Israeli warplanes to strike virtually at will against Egyptian positions.

The War of Attrition continued, however, with no end in sight. Israel in early 1970 decided to expand the war with deep-penetration bombing of targets in the Egyptian interior. These actions led Nasser to seek increased Soviet support, which in due course was provided. Moscow sent Soviet personnel to help Egypt operate certain portions of its air defense system and to fly newly supplied Soviet aircraft. The influx of Soviet personnel soon improved Egyptian air defenses but provoked at least one instance of aerial combat between Israeli and Soviet pilots in which the Israelis were victorious. Most importantly for Nasser, however, the Soviet role prompted a new U.S. initiative aimed at implementing a cease-fire in the conflict.

This was the Rogers Plan, named after U.S. secretary of state William Rogers, who enunciated it. Firmly grounded in UN Resolution 242, it called for a cease-fire that included a memorandum of understanding that both Egypt and Israel agreed with the resolution as a basis for further negotiations.

Both Egypt and Jordan accepted the Rogers Plan, but Israel refused to make any commitment to withdrawal before negotiations and rejected it. Only after the United States applied strong pressure, promised continuing military assistance, and guaranteed that it would not insist on a full withdrawal to the 1967 borders did Israel finally agree to accept the Rogers proposal. Even then the Israeli decision provoked a minor government crisis when several cabinet members, including Menachem Begin, resigned from the government rather than be associated with it. Nevertheless, a cease-fire was implemented on August 8, 1970, but not before Nasser had been able to obtain from Israel a commitment in principle, guaranteed by the United States, to withdraw its forces from the Sinai.

## 1973 War

A few weeks after the cease-fire agreement with Israel, Nasser died in September 1970, and Anwar Sadat was chosen to replace him as president of Egypt. Although Sadat had been among the Free Officer cadre that had overthrown King Farouk in 1952 and had been part of Nasser's leadership council from the beginning, he was different from Nasser in many ways. He was less ideological and had a more relaxed style of leadership. He also proved to be less wedded to the concept of pan-Arabism and more oriented toward purely Egyptian interests. Many observers at the time thought of him as a transitional leader, partly because he seemed to lack Nasser's dynamic personality.

Following the achievement of an Egyptian-Israeli cease-fire, the United States focused on reviving UN ambassador Gunnar Jarring's efforts to secure a full implementation of UN Resolution 242. In February 1971 Jarring asked Sadat to enter into a peace agreement with Israel on the basis of the UN resolution. Sadat readily agreed, accepting even the principle of settling the refugee question on the basis of existing UN resolutions, a stance that was at variance with the policy of the PLO.

Israel, however, rejected Sadat's terms, indicating that it did not accept full withdrawal to prewar lines. It also refused to accept a negotiation process mediated by a third party, insisting on direct negotiations without preconditions. In rejecting Sadat's offer at this time, however, the Israelis gravely underestimated the new Egyptian president. He would in time achieve precisely what he now offered, but at a considerable cost to Israel. Soon after the breakdown of this mediation effort, Jarring abandoned his effort to achieve a settlement on the basis of UN Resolution 242.

## Preparations for War

As time passed, Sadat concluded that the new geopolitical situation produced by the 1967 war would not be reversed by diplomacy. As early as 1971 he began to prepare for war. Even as he did so he continued to privately communicate to the United States his desire to achieve a negotiated settlement. Sadat also made contacts with Hafez al-Assad, the new president of Syria, who eagerly supported the concept of a two-front war. They and their staffs held many planning meetings concerning the war under the cover of talks concerning a Libyan-proposed Federation of Arab Republics embracing Egypt, Syria, Libya, and the Sudan.

Receiving sufficient arms from the Soviet Union was the key condition needed by both leaders for a decision on war. Although the youthful Libyan leader Col. Muammar Qaddafi was excluded from the plans of Assad and Sadat, his generous infusions of Libyan oil wealth contributed significantly to the rearming of both countries. Sadat became frustrated by the slowness of Soviet arms deliveries, due, he believed, to U.S.-Soviet efforts to achieve détente, even while U.S. arms continued to flow to Israel. In July 1972 he took the surprising step of expelling all twenty-one thousand Soviet military advisers and operations personnel serving in Egypt. Ironically this step caused the Soviets to speed up weapons deliveries to both Egypt and Syria—to Egypt in an attempt to win back Sadat's favor, and to Syria in order not

to lose Assad's favor. The expulsion also made a favorable impression in Washington and seemed to diminish chances that Egypt could soon launch a war against Israel. By November 30, 1972, however, according to his memoirs, Sadat felt confident enough in his military preparedness to make his "firm decision" to go to war.

## Arabs Attack

At precisely 2:05 p.m. on Saturday, October 6, 1973, the high Jewish Holy Day of Yom Kippur, Egypt and Syria jointly launched their war on Israel. The Israeli high command, despite sufficient intelligence, was caught by surprise, having misinterpreted the evidence of an impending attack until just hours before it occurred. In accordance with a meticulously planned and methodically executed operation, nearly ninety thousand Egyptian troops, supported by intense artillery barrages and aerial bombardments, crossed the Suez Canal, overran existing Israeli defenses, and established defensive beachheads along the length of the canal's east bank. By the time Israeli mobilization could produce sufficient forces to counterattack on October 8, the Egyptian defensive positions had been made virtually impregnable. An elaborate air defense system behind the canal effectively neutralized Israeli air strike capability over the Egyptian positions. Meanwhile, effective deployment of antitank weapons neutralized the second principal element of Israel's military superiority, its capability in mobile armored warfare.

## Golan Heights Fighting

As it became clear that Sadat's intention was to consolidate his newly won defensive position and not strike off across the Sinai, Israel turned its attention to the Syrian front. Simultaneously with the Egyptian offensive, Syria had thrown thirty-five thousand troops and eight hundred tanks against Israeli defenses on the Golan Heights. Unlike the Egyptian strategy—which was to establish a strong position on the east bank of the Suez Canal, defend it, and use the crisis to consolidate its gains in subsequent negotiations—the Syrian objective was to drive the Israelis off the Golan Heights and to recapture the territory that had been lost in 1967. From October 6 to October 13, the Golan front remained the principal theater of the war as Israel devoted the bulk of its resources to holding its position there. In close and bitter fighting, the Syrians almost achieved their objective before breaking off offensive operations on October 9, after Israeli reinforcements had reestablished a firm defensive line at the crest of the Heights.

Israeli ground forces played the key role in defending Israeli positions in the Golan Heights. During the first days of the war, the Israeli air force faced a network of surface-to-air missiles and antiaircraft artillery similar to the one that had successfully challenged its control of the air over the Sinai front. By October 8, however, as the Sinai front began to stabilize, the Israelis, at great cost to their aircraft and pilots, undertook a systematic effort to destroy the Syrian air defense system. By October 11 Israel once again had achieved general control of the air. That day Israeli ground forces went on the offensive to recapture territories lost so far in the war and to carry the battle beyond the cease-fire line of 1967 toward the Syrian capital.

Despite a brave defense, Syria was unable to contain the advance of an Israeli salient along the eastern base of Mount Hermon toward Damascus. Syrian forces withdrew under fire to an established defensive line at Sasa and prepared to defend the approaches to Damascus with the support of newly arrived Iraqi and Jordanian units. Having reestablished its control of the battlefield and created a pressure point within Syria to absorb future Arab counterattacks, Israel after October 13 broke off offensive operations and turned its attention to the Sinai front.

## Israeli Counterattack in the Sinai

Even before turning back the Syrian offensive on the Golan, the Israelis had been planning their counteroffensive at the Suez Canal. It called for a breakthrough and crossing of the canal at Deversoir, just north of the Great Bitter Lake. The Israeli high command had hoped that their own attack would be preceded by an Egyptian thrust from the bridgehead into the Sinai. Israel hoped to blunt the Egyptian offensive and take advantage of the confusion to drive through Egyptian lines to the designated crossing point at the canal. When Egyptian forces failed to cooperate and remained secure in their well-defended position, Israel prepared for its breakthrough anyway for the night of October 14.

Meanwhile, as Syrian forces had begun to come under extreme Israeli pressure on October 11, President Assad had appealed to Sadat to attack in the Sinai. In their prewar planning, Assad had understood that Sadat contemplated a deeper drive into the Sinai. When this did not come, he began to feel betrayed. Egypt had indeed planned such an expanded offensive across the Suez, but not until its elaborate air defense system had been transported across the canal. Finally, against the advice of his generals, and after it was too late to relieve the Syrian front, Sadat ordered an October 14 Egyptian offensive to capture the Giddi and Mitla passes, thus providing Israeli generals with precisely the opportunity for which they had hoped.

The Egyptian forces advanced beyond their air defense cover and under an ill-conceived plan toward an increasingly strong and well-prepared Israeli army. In the Sinai nearly one thousand Egyptian tanks and eight hundred Israeli tanks, the latter now supported by air cover, fought the largest armored battle since World War II. Israeli tactics and superior mobility blunted the Egyptian advance, inflicting heavy casualties and causing confusion in the Egyptian ranks that allowed the Israelis to implement their own plan to cross to the west bank of the canal.

On the night of October 15 a small Israeli force commanded by Gen. Ariel Sharon broke through a gap in the Egyptian defenses, bridged the canal, and reached the west side by the morning of October 16. For two more days intense fighting continued as Egyptian forces attempted to close the gap.

Finally, by the afternoon of October 17, after nearly forty-eight hours of continuous battle, a much larger Israeli force succeeded in clearing the gap, opening the way for a major crossing of the canal and the establishment of an effective Israeli beachhead on its western side. For two more days the Israelis struggled to consolidate the beachhead and bring in more forces to strengthen the position while Egyptian forces encircling the beachhead attempted desperately to destroy it.

On October 19 Israeli forces on the western bank of the canal drove south along the canal toward Suez. Their goal was to trap the Egyptian Third Army on the east bank of the canal. When the UN-sponsored cease-fire came into effect in the evening of October 22, however, Israeli forces had been able to push only half way toward their goal against determined Egyptian resistance. Despite Israeli acceptance of the cease-fire, fighting continued in this sector until October 25 when Israeli units had effectively cut all supply lines serving the Third Army. Continued shelling and several other last-ditch efforts to secure final positions also occurred on the Golan front after the October 22 cease-fire.

## Cease-Fire

As the war ended, none of the participants had achieved the kind of military victory it would have preferred. Yet all had fought tenaciously and had achieved partial successes. There was no clear winner as had been the case in previous Arab-Israeli wars.

Syrian president Assad was furious with Sadat for agreeing to the cease-fire. In his view, the Syrian army was about to recapture the initiative from the Israelis. Beginning on October 8 a massive Soviet airlift of resupplies to both Egypt and Syria had begun, and Syrian units on the Golan front had been reequipped and had a tight ring around the Israeli salient pointing toward Damascus. Units from Morocco, Iraq, Jordan, and Saudi Arabia also had taken places along the front, and Israeli forces had been substantially weakened because of redeployment in the Sinai. Without con-

tinued pressure on the Egyptian front, however, Assad also finally agreed to the cease-fire.

Israel was not satisfied with its gains on the Egyptian front, and it continued to fight on for three days after its official acceptance of the cease-fire.

It was primarily Egypt that took the lead in responding to international appeals for a cease-fire, but only after it had become clear that the tide was turning against the Arabs. On October 16, after the disastrous Egyptian defeat in the Sinai, but before he had information about the Israeli breakthrough across the canal, Sadat in a major television and radio broadcast expressed his willingness to accept a cease-fire if Israel withdrew from all the territories occupied in 1967. In addition, however, he expressed willingness to attend a postwar peace conference with Israel and to endeavor to convince the other Arab states to participate also.

As the war had continued, it increasingly became the focus of great power concern, facilitating communication between Washington and Moscow, even as U.S.-Soviet tensions mounted. On October 21, in response to a U.S. congressional decision to appropriate $2.2 billion for a major military arms package for Israel, the states comprising the Organization of Arab Petroleum Exporting Countries (OAPEC), led by Saudi Arabia, announced a general boycott of oil sales to the United States.

After Sadat issued a strong appeal on October 19 to the Soviet Union to help him in arranging a cease-fire, the Soviets urgently requested that U.S. secretary of state Henry Kissinger visit Moscow. There, after two days of negotiations, procedures were agreed upon for a cease-fire and future negotiations. Presented to the United Nations Security Council, it was passed by unanimous vote on October 22 as Resolution 338. *(Text, Appendix, p. 395)*

Nevertheless, when Israel continued its effort, despite the cease-fire, to consolidate its position on the west bank of the canal, Moscow protested to Washington, suggesting the urgent dispatch of Soviet and U.S. troops to police the cease-fire and to implement the provisions of Resolution 338. If the

United States disagreed, the Kremlin continued, the Soviet Union was prepared to act alone. U.S. president Nixon, at the advice of Kissinger, interpreted the Soviet communication as an ultimatum and placed U.S. forces on worldwide alert to face down the Soviet challenge. Although the Arab-Israeli war was effectively over, the conflict still seemed to have the potential to threaten global nuclear war. The nuclear crisis probably was more artificial than real, and it passed quickly, as tensions diminished after the halting of Israeli offensive operations on October 25.

## Disengagement Agreements

Despite the joint U.S.-Soviet role in bringing an end to the 1973 war, Secretary of State Kissinger emerged as the central mediator in postwar negotiations. This was due in part to a growing perception among the Arabs, especially Sadat, that only the United States was in a position to extract compromises from Israel that the Arabs, even with Soviet support, could not obtain by themselves. As long as support for UN Security Council Resolution 242, which called for Israeli withdrawal from occupied territories, remained an element of U.S. policy, a basis for achieving this objective through diplomatic means continued.

In addition to demanding an immediate cease-fire in the 1973 war, UN Security Council Resolution 338 did reiterate the objective of the consenting parties to implement Resolution 242 in all its parts. Moreover, unlike Resolution 242, 338 also called for negotiations "between the parties concerned under appropriate auspices aimed at establishing a just and durable peace in the Middle East." Sadat was prepared to participate in such negotiations, and under the rubric of "appropriate auspices" a role was provided for Henry Kissinger.

Repeatedly traveling between the Arab capitals and Israel, Kissinger engaged in what came to be called "shuttle diplomacy." Kissinger's efforts gradually produced a series of "disengagement agreements." A first agreement on October 28, 1973, secured Israel's assent to relief for Egypt's encircled Third Army. A subsequent agreement on

November 11 committed both Egypt and Israel to implement Security Council resolutions 242 and 338 and to stabilize the cease-fire.

Finally on January 18, 1974, Kissinger's diplomacy resulted in the "Disengagement of Forces Agreement," which significantly reduced the chances of a surprise attack by either side. In it, Israel consented to withdraw its forces from the west bank of the Suez Canal. In return, Egypt accepted a stringent limitation on the number of its forces permitted on the east bank of the canal and a withdrawal of its surface-to-air missiles (a key component of its success in the war) and long-range artillery to a line thirty kilometers behind the demilitarized zone now established between the Egyptian and Israeli forces. A similar limitation was also placed on Israeli forces near the canal. United Nations Disengagement Observer Forces (UNDOF) were to be stationed in the demilitarized zone to monitor compliance with the agreement.

Following the Egyptian-Israeli agreements, Kissinger focused on negotiations between Syria and Israel. Sadat's decision to agree to provisions that reduced the chances for a renewed two-front war weakened Assad's negotiating position. So also did Sadat's promise to Kissinger to encourage the Arab oil-producing states to lift their boycott on sales of petroleum to the United States, which they did on March 18, 1974. As with Sadat, Kissinger's assurances that the United States would work for implementation of resolutions 242 and 338 enabled him to secure Assad's acceptance of a Syrian-Israeli "Separation of Forces" agreement on May 31.

In accordance with this agreement, Israel withdrew from the salient it had occupied during the war and gave up a narrow band of land it had captured in 1967, including the town of Qunaitra. This zone, however, became a demilitarized buffer zone controlled by UNDOF units established to monitor the agreement. On each side of the buffer zone Syrian and Israeli zones with restricted numbers of personnel and weapons also were established. Finally, in a separate agreement with Kissinger, Assad promised not to permit Palestinian

# The Rise of Arab Nationalism and the Arab League

The faint beginnings of Arab nationalism can be traced back to the nineteenth century, when it was strongest among Christian Arabs, who did not identify fully with the larger Islamic community and who were more susceptible to Western ideas. The British occupation of Egypt in 1882 sparked development of nationalism there, but until World War I it was the Muslim faith that supplied the predominant bulwark against the encroaching West.

As a popular movement, Arab nationalism first developed from 1908 to 1914 with the Young Turks' rise to power in the Ottoman Empire. The Young Turks advocated a constitution providing for the fusion of the different races of the empire into a single, Ottoman democracy. Once in control, however, the Young Turks used their power to promote Turkish interests and to rule the empire on the tenet of Turkish racial supremacy. In response, Arab leaders formed secret societies in Beirut, Cairo, and Paris and called for Arab political autonomy within the empire. Arab efforts culminated in the convening of the 1913 Paris Congress, at which the Young Turks agreed to the Arabs' request on the basis of further negotiation. The defeat of the Ottomans in World War I and the occupation of the Arab Middle East by the victorious European powers, however, provided the Arabs with an even stronger desire to pursue autonomy.

At the beginning of the war, most Muslim Arabs favored the Turks against the Allies. But in 1916 the British organized an Arab revolt, immortalized by the writings of T. E. Lawrence. Bedouin troops supported the British forces advancing through Palestine and Syria. Their leaders had been promised Arab independence, but once the war ended the Arabs found themselves divided into a series of states governed under British or French mandates. The mandates, as formalized by the League of Nations between 1922 and 1924, provided that the British and French would administer and develop the territories until they were ready for independence.

The British were given control of Palestine, Jordan, and Iraq. Both Transjordan (the area to the east of the Jordan River) and Iraq were ruled by Arab kings—under the supervision of British advisers and troops. Palestine was run by a British commissioner who, under the League of Nations mandate, was allowed to begin developing a national home for the Jews. Syria, which then included what later became Lebanon, was administered by the French. In 1923 the British agreed to independence for Egypt, but it retained advisers and the right to station troops to oversee the Suez Canal. Iraq's independence came with the end of the British mandate in 1932.

The situation in the Arabian Peninsula was different. The strength of the Ottoman Turks had never penetrated deeply there. There was a major rivalry for power between King Hussein, ruler of the Hijaz, and Ibn Saud, ruler of Najd. The French and British were content to let them fight it out, and in 1927 Ibn Saud became sovereign over both Najd and the Hijaz.

Between the world wars Saudi Arabia, while independent, was too inward-looking to lead the move for Arab unity that had begun during World War I. The other states, under their tutelary rulers, were concerned with achieving a greater degree of independence from occupying powers rather than with working for pan-Arab nationalism.

The pan-Arab movement was reawakened by World War II. The Arabs in 1939 had progressed beyond the complete servitude of 1914 to a semiautonomous existence based on treaties with Britain and France. The war removed the French from Syria and Lebanon and the Italians from Libya, leaving Britain the only colonial power in the Middle East. Arab nationalism intensified, and the eventual end of the British role appeared inescapable.

Near the end of the war the Hashemite Arab leaders of Iraq and Syria proposed to unite several Arab countries under their leadership. Non-Hashemite Arabs and the British opposed the plans. They supported instead the formation of a loose federation of the Arab states that would safeguard national sovereignties but enable them to work for the common interest. The federation concept grew out of two conferences among Egypt, Saudi Arabia, Yemen, Transjordan, Syria, Lebanon, and Iraq and became known as the Arab League.

The birth of the first pan-Arab organization in 1944 stirred high hopes among many Arabs, but its capacity for action was limited. The seven original states were unequal in wealth and prestige and had differing political goals. None wanted to sacrifice its own sovereignty to a federal ideal, and there were destructive personal rivalries among the rulers of Egypt, Saudi Arabia, Jordan, and Iraq.

The one area in which members of the league were in agreement in the early years was opposition to growing Jewish claims to Palestine. After the United Nations voted to partition Palestine in 1947, the Arab League declared war against the new state of Israel. But instead of acting in a truly coordinated fashion, each Arab state tried to help a particular client group in an effort to emerge as the champion of the Palestinian Arab cause. This uncoordinated and conflicting effort led to the Arabs' defeat in the first Arab-Israeli War, bitter feuds among the Arab governments, and the influx of unwanted Arab refugees into other Arab countries.

The 1948 war and subsequent emergence of Egypt as the leader in the Arab League wiped out British designs of a British-Hashemite plan for Arab unity and, consequently, British influence in the league. The formation in Gaza of the All-Palestinian government under Egyptian aegis, Jordan's annexation of eastern Palestine (which the league condemned and only two countries recognized), and a breakdown in the Syrian government in 1949 threatened to bring down the Arab League completely. It was resuscitated, however, by the signing of a mutual security pact aimed at protecting Syria from the ambitions of the Hashemite kings.

The factionalism of the Arab League and its failure to meet primary goals have been reflected in the history of the Arab world since World War II. As the British systematically gave up their remaining control, the newly independent nations endured dictatorships, coups, assassinations, and abdications. Moreover, the Arab countries were continually interfering in each others' affairs. Egypt, for example, attempted to instigate or support revolutions in Syria, Lebanon, Iraq, Jordan, Saudi Arabia, and Yemen. Egypt became involved in a full-scale war in Yemen during the 1960s and at one point had as many as seventy thousand troops there. Almost all of the Arab countries at some time were involved in machinations intended to bolster one state against another. Until 1973 attempts to achieve fruitful pan-Arab cooperation ended in failure.

For much of the postwar period Egypt, the most populous state, sought to lead the Arab world. In 1952 the monarchy was overthrown and supplanted by a military dictatorship headed by Gamal Abdel Nasser, a vigorous and charismatic figure. Nasser emerged as the champion of Arab nationalism, but his feuds with other leaders often made him a divisive force in the region. President Anwar Sadat, his successor, broke with the pan-Arab ideologues and advocated an Egyptian nationalist philosophy. This approach was dramatically exemplified by his trip to Jerusalem and the signing of the Egyptian-Israeli peace treaty in 1979. Egypt was expelled from the Arab League in 1979 after Sadat signed the peace treaty, but it was welcomed back into the organization in May 1989.

During the Persian Gulf War the Arab League was split when Iraq invaded fellow member Kuwait. Twelve of the twenty-one league members voted to commit troops to oppose Iraq. Three voted for the resolution with reservations, three abstained or were absent, and three—Iraq, Libya, and the Palestine Liberation Organization—voted against the measure.

Arab governments made their decision according to their own perceived self-interests, not according to their feelings toward Kuwait or their desire to preserve Arab unity. The wealthy Gulf states, which had the most to fear from Iraq, followed Saudi Arabia's leadership and joined with the West in opposing Iraq. Egypt, which received $2.3 billion a year in aid from the United States and which has traditionally been an Iraqi rival for Arab leadership, also sided with Saudi Arabia and the West. President Hafez al-Assad of Syria joined the coalition based on his personal enmity toward Saddam Hussein and his ambitions for Damascus to eclipse Baghdad as an Arab power center. He also was anxious to improve relations with the wealthy Gulf states. The Iraqi invasion of Kuwait and Arab reaction to it demonstrated that pan-Arab impulses were weak when they conflicted with the interests of individual Arab states.

guerrilla attacks on Israel along the Golan front, something he had never permitted in any case, despite general support for the guerrillas in neighboring Lebanon and Jordan.

Continuing efforts by Kissinger during the summer of 1974 to further the Arab-Israeli peace process were overshadowed by U.S.-Soviet summit talks, a Turkish invasion of Cyprus, and President Nixon's resignation because of the Watergate scandal. Issues were further complicated by the Arab League's decision made in October 1974 at a summit in Rabat, Morocco, endorsing the PLO as the sole legitimate representative of the Palestinian people. *(Text, Appendix, p. 396)*

The implication of this position from the Arab perspective was that, although Egypt and Syria were free to pursue recovery of territories lost to Israel in 1967, collective Arab policy toward a general resolution of the Arab-Israeli conflict was to focus on arrangements reached between the PLO and Israel. The Arabs' support of the PLO's claims to be the legitimate representative of all those Palestine Arabs living either as refugees outside of Israel or under Israeli occupation directly contradicted Israel's policy, buttressed by Resolution 338, of seeking peace through direct negotiations with its neighboring Arab states. In addition, Israel positively opposed negotiations with the PLO because of the latter's denial of Israel's right to exist and its opposition to resolutions 242 and 338.

## Sinai II

Kissinger's shuttle diplomacy resulted in a second Israeli-Egyptian disengagement agreement (Sinai II) on September 4, 1975. In this document Israel agreed to a further withdrawal of its forces from the Mitla and Giddi passes and the Abu Rudais oil fields to a new cease-fire line. Egyptian forces were permitted to move up to the line Israel had previously occupied. In between, a new UNDOF-monitored buffer zone was established, and early warning electronic monitoring systems operated by American technicians were put in place to warn both governments of any violations of the agreement.

The agreement also imposed limitations on forces in zones adjoining the neutral buffer zone, and both Israel and Egypt promised to observe their continuing cease-fire and to abjure the use of force or military blockade against one another. Egypt also agreed to allow Israel to use the Suez Canal for the passage of nonmilitary cargoes, and both countries pledged to continue negotiations toward a final peace settlement. Despite the guarantees embodied in the Sinai II accord, however, Israel's acceptance of them was conditional on two side memorandums signed by Kissinger. The first provided guarantees of continued U.S. economic and military assistance to Israel. In the second, the United States promised not to "recognize or negotiate with the PLO so long as the PLO does not recognize Israel's right to exist and does not accept Security Council Resolutions 242 and 338."

With the signing of the Sinai II accord, Kissinger's ability to advance the Arab-Israeli peace process came to an end. The position of the United States and Israel not to negotiate with the PLO was at odds with what now had become a collective Arab stand.

President Assad was especially disturbed by the implications of Sinai II for Syria. He feared that Egypt's agreement with Israel undermined his own effort to secure a return of the Golan Heights. As a result, he refused to cooperate with U.S. peacemaking and joined with Iraq, Algeria, Libya, South Yemen, and the PLO in a new alliance called the Rejectionist Front, which condemned Sadat's increasing accommodation with Israel and sought to undermine it.

# Role of the PLO

The growing importance of the PLO as a factor in the Arab-Israeli conflict in the years after 1967 was a function of the emerging sense of Palestinian identity. The PLO formed by the Arab summit of 1964 had been intended to be merely a bureaucratic arm of the Arab League, then effectively controlled by President Nasser of Egypt. Despite this effort to establish control of the Palestinian movement, however, the various independent resistance groups springing up in the 1950s and 1960s had avoided being dominated by the Arab League. When Arafat's Fatah began operations in Israel in the mid-1960s, contributing to the 1967 war, it had done so for itself, as well as on behalf of Syria, and not as an element of the PLO.

Only after the war, in February 1969, did the various commando groups seek and receive admission into the organization. By this time, however, they had become strong enough to take over the organization. Yasir Arafat, head of the largest Palestinian organization, became PLO chairman. Under his chairmanship the PLO, in accordance with Fatah policy, strove to be an independent political actor in inter-Arab relations. At the same time, Arafat's independence was constrained by the perceived need to maintain unity within the Palestinian movement and consensus among the different commando organizations belonging to the PLO.

The various commando groups were able to assert their influence over the PLO because of the moral support, funds, and recruits that began to flow toward them, especially Fatah, in the period following the 1967 war. As the Arab regimes slowly recovered from their military debacle and sought to regain their losses, the commando groups kept the Arab-Israeli conflict alive by launching raids and acts of terrorism in Israel or the occupied territories.

## PLO in Jordan and Lebanon

Jordan and Lebanon, where the largest numbers of refugees were located, were the two countries where the Palestinian movement and the resistance groups thrived. An incident in Jordan soon after the 1967 war greatly contributed to the fortunes of Arafat's Fatah. A major Israeli reprisal against the Jordanian town of Karameh in March 1968 encountered stiff resistance from Fatah fighters supported by Jordanian artillery. Although the Israeli unit accomplished its mission, it sustained many casualties. Arafat was able to claim that his fighters had fought more bravely than any of the Arab armies a few months earlier.

The Karameh incident brought great attention to Fatah and drew many new recruits into the organization. Further Israeli reprisals in Jordan and Lebanon now began to have the same effect, strengthening the resistance groups that gradually began to take control of the Palestinian refugee camps in those countries.

A major rival of Arafat at this time was George Habash, the leader of the PFLP. His organization was imbued with a far more revolutionary philosophy than Arafat's. It called for the overthrow of discredited Arab regimes and the unification of the Arab world under revolutionary leadership as a means to achieve the liberation of Palestine. In July 1968 the PFLP began hijacking Israeli El Al passenger aircraft and then aircraft of other Western airlines that serviced Israel. The purpose was to highlight the seriousness of the Arab-Israeli conflict and the intensity of its Palestinian dimension. Although these and subsequent acts of international terrorism did draw international attention to the Palestinian problem and the hapless condition of the Arab refugees, they also provoked international outrage and tended to discredit the Palestinian movement.

A government crisis in Lebanon in 1969 led to a new status for the PLO in that country. A developing pattern of PLO-Israeli violence over Lebanon's southern boundary with Israel provoked the crisis. Many Lebanese wanted their government to deal forcibly with the Palestinian fighters and disarm them. Still others lent support to the Palestinian cause and demanded that the government demonstrate solidarity with the PLO by mobilizing a stronger army to resist Israeli incursions. The result was political paralysis and a government crisis that was resolved only by the intervention of President Nasser of Egypt. Through his mediation, the "Cairo Agreement" was reached in October 1969. It spelled out specified areas of operation for the PLO in southern Lebanon and placed the Palestinian refugee camps under PLO control. Even though the Cairo Agreement resolved the immediate crisis, it amounted to a significant infringement on Lebanese sovereignty by giving the PLO virtual state-within-a-state status in Lebanon. It also strengthened Arafat's effort to be treated as an independent actor in inter-Arab politics.

A similar crisis developed in Jordan in 1970. Tensions between the army and the PLO that had increased throughout the year finally erupted into civil war in September, following the PFLP hijacking of four international airliners. The Palestinian hijackers had forced the planes to land at a remote airfield outside the Jordanian capital. When the crisis had passed and all hostages on the airliners had been released, King Hussein unleashed his army against the Palestinian guerrillas in his country. They were defeated after ten days of fighting. This setback for the PLO, which was remembered as "Black September," made Lebanon the sole remaining center of PLO organizational activity in its struggle against Israel.

Between 1949 and 1967 Lebanon had remained aloof from the Arab-Israeli conflict. Its emergence as the principal arena of the Israeli-PLO conflict placed strains on the Lebanese political system, which eventually led to civil war in 1975. Meanwhile, Lebanon increasingly became the center of PLO operations against Israel, both across Israel's borders and abroad, and the various PLO groups operating in Lebanon became targets of Israeli reprisals.

## Growing International Stature

During the early 1970s the PLO's support among Palestinian Arabs both outside and within Israel continued to grow. Arab and other governments increasingly accepted the PLO as the legitimate political representative of the unabsorbed refugees of the 1948 war with Israel. The strength and appeal of the PLO among the refugees and in the Arab world stemmed less from its proclivity toward violence, which tended to be counterproductive in most cases, than from its political symbolism. Since 1948 the Arab states had justified their continuing hostility toward Israel on the grounds of defending the rights of the Palestinian Arabs to return to the land whence they came. With the emergence of a grass-roots Palestinian political movement whose aim was increasingly to

shoulder the burden of their own liberation, the Arab states were progressively relieved of this perceived responsibility. To the degree that the PLO demonstrated its viability and capability to mobilize the Palestinians, it was in the interest of most Arab states to support it with funds and diplomatic backing.

By 1974, only five years after assuming the chairmanship of the PLO, Yasir Arafat achieved the first stage of his quest to formulate an independent Palestinian policy. At an Arab summit conference in Rabat, Morocco, in October, the assembled Arab heads of state recognized "the right of the Palestinian people to establish an independent national authority under the command of the Palestine Liberation Organization, the sole legitimate representative of the Palestinian people, in any Palestinian territory that is liberated." One month later, on November 13, Arafat and the PLO received international recognition when he spoke before the United Nations General Assembly, which granted the PLO observer status. The vote to admit the PLO was 105-4, with 20 abstentions. Only Israel, the United States, Bolivia, and the Dominican Republic voted against the PLO. In 1976 the PLO became the twenty-first full member of the Arab League, and by 1977 more than a hundred nations had granted the PLO some form of diplomatic recognition.

The PLO's new international stature and recognition carried several implications. First, it brought into question Jordan's 1950 annexation of the West Bank, which no Arab state had ever formally recognized. Accordingly, King Hussein's efforts to negotiate a return of the territory from Israel were undercut, although the concept of a joint Jordanian-PLO negotiating posture remained a possibility. Despite his bitterness toward the PLO, with which he had engaged in a bloody war in 1970, Hussein publicly accepted the decision of the Rabat summit "without any reservations." But he did not abjure Jordanian claims to the West Bank until 1988.

Second, the new recognition produced fissures in the PLO itself. Essentially an umbrella organization of various Palestinian commando groups, each with a different political outlook, the PLO maintained its unity by incorporating the views of even its most radical members. The growing acceptance of the PLO in international affairs, however, carried with it the burden of being responsive to the basic guidelines laid down by the international community for a settlement of the Arab-Israeli conflict, namely accepting Israel, aligning with existing UN resolutions, and abandoning the struggle for the total liberation of Palestine.

Some elements of the PLO, such as George Habash's PFLP, withdrew from the PLO rather than be a party to any compromise program. Arafat, ever anxious to maintain the unity of the Palestinian movement, tried to produce a compromise approach to Israel that would be acceptable to all factions and the international community, but he was unsuccessful. He insisted that any compromise settlement should be seen only as a prelude to the total liberation of Palestine. Such a formula was obviously rejected by Israeli leaders whose experience with the PLO disposed them to perceive it primarily as a terrorist organization bent on destroying Israel. Similarly unimpressed were potential U.S. interlocutors, such as Henry Kissinger, who sought to facilitate an Arab-Israeli peace process, but only with parties willing to accept and make peace with Israel.

## Israel's Position Hardens

A third implication of the enhanced international status of the PLO was a hardening of attitudes in Israel itself. Since the origins of the Zionist movement in the late nineteenth century, Zionism had been characterized by two prominent trends. The first was the socialist-labor tendency embodied in Israel's ruling Labor party. Ideological about the economic and social life of Israel, it nevertheless remained pragmatic and flexible in international relations and diplomacy. The second tendency, known as revisionist Zionism, cared little for the ideological formulations of the Labor party. Instead, it focused on the historic destiny of the Zionist movement to gain control of all Eretz Israel, composed of southern Lebanon, southern Syria, Jordan, and the territories occupied in the 1967 war. Revisionist Zionists dominated the Herut party, which had been led by Menachem Begin since 1948. They had opposed the 1947 UN partition of Palestine on the grounds that Jews could never agree to the partition of historic Israel. In the post-1967 period, the Herut party maintained that the occupied territories were parts of historic Israel that had been "redeemed." It called, therefore, for Israeli settlement of the territories and opposed any suggestion that Israel should withdraw from them.

The revisionists were supported by the Greater Land of Israel Movement, which emerged immediately following the 1967 war. The movement included many Labor party members, including then minister of defense Moshe Dayan, who favored the creation of Jewish settlements in the new territories. The intent was not necessarily to avoid returning some of the territories, but to "create facts" that would enhance Israeli security and strengthen Israel's bargaining position. Even in the summer of 1967 a number of unauthorized settlements were established in the occupied territories by various Israeli citizen groups. Menachem Begin and his supporters in the Israeli Knesset used their positions of influence to demand full government approval of the new Jewish settlements.

As time passed without movement toward an Arab-Israeli settlement, the view that Israel should retain most or all of the territories as the best guarantee of its security gained increasing support in Israel, especially in the military. In 1974, following the first disengagement agreements with Egypt and Syria, a new organization, Gush Emunim, made its appearance. The group was committed to creating illegal Israeli settlements near the main Arab population centers and forcing the government to accept them. Gush Emunim's efforts received behind-the-scenes support from many in the military, making it virtually impossible for the government to stop the settlements begun by the organization.

In the context of this increasingly contentious political environment, it proved impossible for Israel to consider even minor concessions to Jordan.

Israel's concern about the implications of the PLO's growing role was apparent in the September 1975 guarantee it sought from the United States that the latter country would not "recognize or negotiate with the PLO so long as the PLO does not recognize Israel's right to exist and does not accept Security Council Resolutions 242 and 338."

### Lebanese Civil War

A final implication of the international legitimization of the PLO was the impact it was to have in Lebanon. It being apparent that such legitimization would evoke no positive response in Israel, the field of PLO activity would remain Lebanon for the foreseeable future. This was a challenge to Lebanese sovereignty to which the Lebanese government, paralyzed over the issue of how to deal with the PLO, could not respond. As a result various militias, representing the different sectarian and political groups in the country, began to acquire arms, and in April 1975 the Lebanese civil war broke out.

At first the PLO avoided involvement in the conflict, but in the winter attacks on some of the vulnerable Palestinian refugee camps in Maronite Christian territory led it to enter the conflict on the side of its National Movement allies. As fighting continued during the spring, PLO involvement helped to tip the balance toward National Movement forces, which appeared to be achieving victory. In response Lebanese president Suleiman Franjieh requested Syrian intervention in behalf of his government. President Assad, apparently worried about the possibility of an Israeli intervention if he did not intervene himself, sent Syrian units into Lebanon in June 1976. The Syrian intervention in behalf of the Maronite forces was not meant to assist them in achieving victory, but rather to restore the balance. Among the forces engaged by the Syrians was the PLO, whose military units were forced back into southern and coastal Lebanon. The PLO, however, survived and suffered no loss of international stature.

## Camp David Agreements

On March 26, 1979, President Sadat completed the process of normalizing relations between Egypt and Israel by signing a treaty of peace in Washington. In return for peace and the establishment of diplomatic relations, Israel agreed to withdraw completely from the Sinai within a period of three years. Most of the Sinai was defined as a demilitarized zone with UN and multinational forces posted to ensure compliance with the treaty. Egypt accepted a fixed limitation on the size of the military force it was permitted to keep in a fifty-mile-wide area east of the Suez Canal. Finally, the treaty guaranteed freedom of navigation for Israeli shipping through the Strait of Tiran and the Suez Canal. *(Text, Appendix, p. 396)*

Sadat had been frustrated by the lack of progress in achieving a final agreement on Israeli withdrawal from the Sinai after the signing of the Sinai II accord in September 1975. He had concluded that only a dramatic gesture could break the psychological barrier which, in his view, made the Arab-Israeli conflict so intractable.

Such a gesture seemed especially necessary following Menachem Begin's assumption of the office of Israeli prime minister in June 1977. Begin and his Likud bloc (of which the Herut party was a member) had campaigned on a promise never to return any portion of Samaria and Judea, as he referred to the lands of the West Bank. Rather, he was a proponent of accelerated Jewish settlement of all the occupied territories. Begin referred to the PLO as a Nazi organization with whom he would never deal, even if it accepted UN Resolution 242. Moreover, he had adamantly opposed the concessions Israel already had made to Egypt in the two disengagement agreements.

### Sadat Goes to Israel

On November 9, 1977, Sadat announced his willingness to go to Israel to discuss, directly and in person, the issue of Arab-Israeli peace with the Israeli government. Given the history of the Arab-

Israeli conflict up to this time, Sadat's announcement astounded the world, although careful groundwork had been made through preparatory contacts in Morocco. Such an initiative coming from the leader of the most powerful and populous Arab state required a positive response, even by the recalcitrant and suspicious Menachem Begin.

In his address to the Israeli Knesset, after expressing his desire that Egypt and Israel live together in "permanent peace based on justice," Sadat listed the conditions he thought necessary to achieve Arab-Israeli peace. In addition to the usual references to permanent borders, mutual recognition, nonbelligerency, and settling disputes through peaceful means, he specifically called for an Israeli withdrawal from the occupied territories and the achievement of the fundamental rights of the Palestinian people, including their right to self-determination and their right to establish their own state.

In response to Sadat's initiative, Begin on December 25, 1977, visited Ismailia, Egypt, where he presented Israel's response to the Egyptian proposal. He focused primarily on points related to a settlement of issues in the Sinai but also presented his proposal for a settlement of the West Bank and Gaza issue. He proposed abolishing the military administration in these territories and replacing it with "administrative autonomy of the residents, by and for them." Security and public order were to remain the responsibility of Israel, however. Begin asserted that "Israel stands by its right and its claim of sovereignty of Judea, Samaria and the Gaza district." But he added, "In the knowledge that other claims exist, [Israel] proposes for the sake of agreement and peace, that the question of sovereignty be left open." He proposed that the status of the Holy Places and Jerusalem be considered separately in other negotiations. Begin did not address ending the Israeli occupation and granting the Palestinians the right to establish their own state.

## Framework Agreements

Despite the disparity between the two positions, negotiating committees were formed to continue the dialogue. Discussion continued sporadically but unsuccessfully throughout the first half of 1978. As negotiations broke down, however, President Jimmy Carter intervened in an effort to keep the talks alive. He invited Sadat and Begin to Camp David, his presidential retreat in Maryland, for face-to-face talks, hoping to resolve their differences.

The Camp David talks, as they came to be called, convened with President Carter in attendance on September 5, 1978, and continued for thirteen days. After difficult negotiations, which apparently would have failed without the mediation of the U.S. president and his advisers, agreement was reached on September 17. *(Camp David summit, Chapter 3, p. 70)*

The Camp David talks actually produced two agreements. Neither was a treaty, but rather an agreement to agree. Called "frameworks for peace," the first dealt with issues relating to Egypt and Israel and provided the basis for the treaty signed between the two countries in March of the following year.

The second, a "framework" for settling the future of the West Bank and Gaza, represented an agreement among Israel, Egypt, and the United States, also a signatory to the accords, on an approach for resolving this contentious aspect of the Arab-Israeli conflict. Sadat was under extreme pressure from other Arab states not to sign a separate peace treaty with Israel. He therefore was anxious to arrive at a formula that would take into account the larger Arab perspective toward Israel. Begin was annoyed by Sadat's insistence on including issues that in his view rightfully belonged to negotiations with Israel's other Arab neighbors. Nevertheless he continued pursuing a treaty that would bring peace with Egypt. The result was an agreement which, depending on how it was interpreted and negotiated, satisfied either Sadat's or Begin's objectives in the negotiations.

In summary, the main points of the West Bank and Gaza framework were as follows:

- Egypt, Israel, and Jordan were to agree on modalities for establishing an elected self-governing authority in the West Bank and Gaza.

- Egypt, Israel, and Jordan were to negotiate an agreement establishing the powers and responsibilities of the self-governing authority in the West Bank and Gaza.
- After agreement, Israeli armed forces were to withdraw from the West Bank and Gaza except in specified security locations.
- During a five-year transition period, Egypt, Israel, Jordan, and the West Bank-Gaza authority were to negotiate the final status of the Israeli-occupied territories.
- Israel and Jordan were to negotiate a peace agreement taking into account the agreement reached on the final status of the West Bank and Gaza.
- All negotiations were to be based on UN Security Council Resolution 242.

A remarkable document, the West Bank and Gaza framework left every issue open, subject to negotiation, but it confined the debate within the boundaries of the original Palestine mandate (which included Jordan). It made no mention of Syria or the Golan Heights. It provided for the principle of Israeli withdrawal from occupied territory, but without specifying the extent of this withdrawal.

The framework left open the possibility of a variety of options on achieving a final settlement of the conflict. Among them:

- Jordanian option—a West Bank-Gaza self-governing authority under Jordanian sovereignty, or in confederation with Jordan.
- Israeli option—a West Bank-Gaza self-governing authority under Israeli sovereignty, or in confederation with Israel.
- Independent state option—possible achievement of an independent state by Arab inhabitants of the West Bank-Gaza, expressing their right of self-determination.

Other potential options also were conceivable, depending on the outcome of negotiations. Most importantly, the framework placed an emphasis on political negotiation rather than military force as the means to reach a final settlement.

## Arab Response

The key to proceeding on the West Bank-Gaza framework was to secure the participation of Jordan. Although King Hussein appeared to consider seriously the possibility of joining the negotiations, he resented not having been invited to Camp David. He also had not been consulted during the talks, and he was offended at the presumption that he would follow along meekly. By agreeing to participate, he also would have implicitly accepted the premise that Jordanian sovereignty over the West Bank was negotiable. Moreover, Hussein had to take into account the attitude of his powerful neighbors—Syria, Iraq, and Saudi Arabia—and his own large population of Palestinian citizens.

Although Hussein did not condemn Sadat's initiative, most of the Arab world did and put intense pressure on Sadat not to sign the peace treaty with Israel and subsequently on Hussein not to collaborate with it. Syria and the PLO, which perceived Egypt's withdrawal from the Arab-Israeli conflict as weakening their own positions, were especially critical of it. When Sadat did sign the treaty on March 26, 1979, nineteen members of the twenty-two-member Arab League, including Jordan, convened in Baghdad the following day and agreed to a package of political and economic sanctions against Egypt. Egypt had not been invited to attend; Oman and Sudan chose not to attend. Egypt was also expelled from the Arab League, and the league's headquarters was moved from Cairo to Tunis. All Arab League members broke diplomatic relations with Egypt, except Oman, Sudan, and notably the PLO. Egypt also was expelled from most regional political and economic institutions, such as the Organization of Arab Petroleum Exporting Countries, the Islamic Conference Organization, and the Organization of African Unity. Arab nations also endorsed a general economic boycott on trade with Egypt.

## West Bank-Gaza Talks

Under these circumstances, King Hussein did not attend the first meetings in Beersheba between

Sadat and Begin on May 25, 1979, concerning the West Bank-Gaza framework. The nonparticipation of Jordan in this and subsequent meetings held through May 1980 played into the hands of those Israelis who, like Prime Minister Begin, opposed Israeli withdrawal from the West Bank and Gaza. Begin used his position of leadership to encourage accelerated Jewish settlement in the territories and to develop administrative mechanisms that would strengthen the degree of Israeli authority and Jewish ownership of land in the territories. In 1977 only seventeen Jewish settlements existed on the West Bank with a combined population of about five thousand. By 1982 there were about one hundred Jewish settlements with a combined population of more than twenty thousand.

As the Begin government pursued these policies, the "autonomy talks" between Egypt and Israel stalled for a number of reasons. Israel sought to limit autonomy to the inhabitants of the territories; Egypt believed it should extend to the territory itself. Each promoted its own version of a "self-governing authority." Egypt sought total Israeli withdrawal from the territories (including East Jerusalem), the dismantling of Israeli settlements, and the right to self-determination for the Palestinians. Israel opposed these concepts because they "would set in motion an irreversible process which would lead to the establishment of an independent Arab-Palestinian state."

Thirteen months after the talks broke down, Begin was narrowly reelected prime minister in June 1981, an election he interpreted as a mandate for his policies. After Sadat's assassination on October 6, 1981, the new Egyptian government of Hosni Mubarak proved no more amenable than Sadat to Israel's autonomy proposals. The Begin cabinet responded by moving to implement unilaterally its concept of autonomy, claiming that it fulfilled the intent of the Camp David agreement.

On November 8, 1981, the Israeli government established a new civilian administration to replace the military administration that had governed the occupied territories since 1967. This civilian administration, which nevertheless was a department of the military, began the process of constituting a "self-governing authority" in the territories. It sought to structure a system of administrative councils of the type Israel had been advocating in the Camp David talks. The civilian administration's efforts, however, were based on a reorganization of the so-called village leagues, groups of armed Palestinian informants and enforcers upon whom the military administration had relied to intimidate uncooperative Arabs.

These policies provoked strong resistance from Arabs across the territories, followed by the use of an "iron fist" policy by the army. Violence in the West Bank and Gaza escalated throughout the first six months of 1982. The Begin government believed the source of the violence was the continuing influence of the PLO among Arabs in the territories. Therefore, Israel moved in June 1982 to attack the problem at its source by invading Lebanon.

## The Israeli Invasion of Lebanon

After Egypt signed a peace treaty with Israel in March 1979, the focus of the conflict turned to Israel's northern frontiers. Despite the continuing harsh anti-Israeli rhetoric emanating from Syria, the Golan front, monitored by United Nations observer forces, had been quiet since the Syrian-Israeli separation of forces agreement of 1974. The Egyptian-Israeli peace treaty diminished chances that Syria would launch an attack on Israel to regain the Golan Heights, because the Syrians could not count on Egypt to open a second front. Egypt's involvement in the Camp David process had prompted Syria to pursue parity with Israel in military capability. But Syrian leaders did not contemplate a major military action against Israel until they had substantially built up their forces. The only area where the Arab-Israeli conflict was likely to erupt, therefore, was Lebanon.

### Israel's 1978 Intervention

With the entry of Syrian forces into Lebanon in June 1976 and the return of PLO units to southern

Lebanon, Israel designated a "red line" in that country, which it warned Syria not to cross. At the same time it began arming a southern Lebanese militia commanded by a renegade Greek Catholic Lebanese officer, Maj. Saad Haddad. Israel hoped that this force would help it control infiltration of PLO commandos into Israel from Lebanon. Shortly after a terrorist attack by eight Fatah commandos on an Israeli beach between Haifa and Tel Aviv, however, Israel on March 14, 1978, launched a major invasion into Lebanon involving twenty thousand troops. Ostensibly undertaken as a retaliatory raid in response to the terrorist attack, the real purpose of the military operation, which had been months in the planning, was to clear an area about ten kilometers wide along Israel's northern frontier that would serve as a security zone controlled and patrolled by Haddad's Free Lebanon Militia (FLM).

Soon after the Israeli invasion, the United Nations dispatched a six-thousand-troop peacekeeping force, the United Nations Interim Force in Lebanon (UNIFIL), to patrol an area in southern Lebanon separating PLO forces from the northern Israeli border. Israel and Haddad would not permit the deployment of UNIFIL into the Free Lebanon security zone, and numerous violent acts between UNIFIL and FLM units occurred during the first weeks of the United Nations mission. Despite the UNIFIL-FLM buffer, PLO units continued to find their way into Israel. More important, they made increasing use of rockets and long-range artillery to launch attacks on northern Israeli towns over the heads of the FLM and UNIFIL troops. PLO and Israeli attacks against one another became particularly violent during the last months before the signing of the Egypt-Israel peace treaty in March 1979.

In addition to sponsoring Haddad's militia, Israel in mid-1976 had begun to provide arms and training to the Maronite Lebanese Forces militia as another means of countering the PLO and its allies in Lebanon. As this relation deepened following the Lebanese civil war, Syria's President Assad feared an Israeli challenge to Syrian preeminence in Lebanon. Assad responded with policies aimed at securing regional hegemony to promote his new concept of "strategic parity" with Israel.

Such a policy involved combating the Lebanese Forces militia and asserting Syrian control over the PLO in Lebanon. Arguing that the Arab-Israeli conflict was an Arab problem and not simply a Palestinian one, Assad operated through Syrian-supported Palestinian groups to weaken Arafat's leadership of the PLO. In addition, he sponsored new Lebanese militia groups such as the Shi'ite organization Amal as a counterweight to the PLO and the Israeli-supported Lebanese Forces. Amal had an inherently anti-PLO bias, as its Shi'ite members had suffered greatly from the PLO-Israeli violence in southern Lebanon.

Confronted by a variety of opponents in Lebanon in the early 1980s, the PLO became increasingly isolated. It was in this context that it agreed to a cease-fire with Israel in July 1981. The cease-fire resulted from a series of negotiations mediated by U.S. special envoy Philip Habib.

## Precursors to Invasion

In April 1981 an eruption of hostilities between the Syrians and Lebanese Forces militia in the Bekaa Valley led the Maronites to appeal for Israeli support. When Israel responded by shooting down two Syrian helicopters, Assad installed surface-to-air missiles within Lebanon near the city of Zahle. Israel's Prime Minister Begin vigorously protested the missile installations and threatened to destroy them if Syria did not remove them. The "missile crisis" prompted the United States to send Special Envoy Habib to the Middle East to negotiate a solution.

As if to demonstrate its force following Syria's installation of these missiles, Israel conducted a series of air raids on PLO targets, while the PLO retaliated with rocket barrages into northern Israel. An escalation of this violence over a three-week period in July prompted complex negotiations among Arafat, the UNIFIL commander, Saudi Arabia, Habib, and Israel that finally culminated in a PLO-Israeli cease-fire on July 24.

Despite Israeli assertions that the PLO could

not adhere to a cease-fire, it did so. And the longer the cease-fire endured, the more it seemed to alarm the government of Menachem Begin in Israel. The cease-fire implied an indirect Israeli recognition of the PLO, gave time to the PLO to build up its forces in Lebanon, and enhanced Arafat's stature as a responsible political figure who could impose discipline throughout his organization. The possibility that international pressure could build to resolve the problem of Lebanon at the expense of Israeli aspirations on the West Bank and Gaza could not be discounted. As resistance to Israeli rule in the territories increased during the spring of 1982, Israel made preparations for a major military operation against the PLO.

### Expulsion of PLO from Beirut

On June 6, 1982, Israel launched its invasion of Lebanon. The publicly stated purpose of "Operation Peace for Galilee" was to clear all PLO forces from a forty-kilometer area north of Israel's border with Lebanon, thus putting northern Israel out of range of PLO artillery. As the operation developed, however, it became clear that Israel had larger objectives, including:

- The full destruction of the PLO leadership and infrastructure, thus eliminating the main perceived obstacle to Israel's consolidation of its rule over the West Bank and Gaza.
- Arrangement for the election of Bashir Gemayel as president of Lebanon. Israel hoped he could restore law and order and bring remaining Palestinians there under Lebanese government authority.
- Conclusion of a peace treaty with Lebanon.

In a rapid three-prong advance complemented by extensive naval landing operations along Lebanon's coast, Israeli units drove PLO forces back into Beirut. Israel effectively surrounded the city by June 14. In the Bekaa Valley, Israeli warplanes completely destroyed Syrian surface-to-air missile installations in a June 9 air battle. Israeli and Syrian army units on the ground engaged in heavy

fighting until the two governments agreed to a cease-fire on June 11.

Israel decided to lay siege to Beirut and demand the surrender of the PLO instead of entering the city and engaging in costly urban fighting. The siege, marked by sporadic bombing and shelling of PLO centers in the city, continued through the summer until August 12, when negotiations again mediated by Special Envoy Habib finally achieved a cease-fire and an agreement allowing the PLO to evacuate southern and coastal Lebanon.

The departure of the PLO from Beirut, which was completed by September 2, deprived it of its last base in the Arab world from which to make direct attacks on Israeli territory. The organization was now scattered throughout a variety of Arab countries, none of which bordered Israel except Syria, whose policy was to not allow them autonomy of decision. It appeared that the PLO's significance to the Arab-Israeli conflict had greatly diminished. This was an illusion, however, because the strength of the PLO, although forged on the concept of armed struggle against Israel, had never rested with its military capability. The broad range of international diplomatic support the PLO had garnered over the years as the institutional symbol of Palestinian nationalism had become the principal basis of its legitimacy. In the years after the PLO's departure from Lebanon, it was this aspect of the PLO's strength that Arafat sought to husband and enhance.

Israel had achieved the key objective of its invasion of Lebanon, the expulsion of the PLO, but it found itself mired in a war it was unable to end. It opened up a second front of the Arab-Israeli conflict that was only indirectly related to the PLO or the Palestinian problem. The new conflict pitted Israel against Muslim militia groups in Lebanon that now mobilized themselves—with Syrian, Iranian, and other sources of external support—to resist the continuing Israeli occupation of southern Lebanon.

Israel's second objective of fostering a strengthened central government with which it would sign a peace treaty was shattered by the assassination of president-elect Bashir Gemayel on September

14, 1982. The Israelis succeeded in negotiating a treaty signed May 17, 1983, with the less amenable successor government of President Amin Gemayel. This treaty, however, foundered because of widespread Lebanese resistance to it and the refusal of the Syrian government to withdraw its troops from Lebanon. As it became clear that even U.S. support could not strengthen the Lebanese government sufficiently to enable it to overcome the resistance engendered by the Israel-Lebanon agreement, Israel began undertaking a series of unilateral withdrawals. By July 1985 Israel had extricated itself from Lebanon.

### Israeli-Shi'ite Conflict

Israel's withdrawal from Lebanon did not end its conflict with forces in the country. As it departed, Israel left an expanded security zone in southern Lebanon controlled by its surrogate force, now called the Army of South Lebanon (ASL), commanded by Antoine Lahad, a retired Lebanese general. Israel justified the zone by pointing to the continued presence of Syrian forces in the northern parts of Lebanon and the probability of PLO reinfiltration into southern Lebanon in the absence of strong central government authority.

For the Shi'ite inhabitants of southern Lebanon, who at first welcomed the Israeli invasion but turned against it as the Israeli occupation became prolonged, the security zone was perceived as a joint effort of Israel and Lebanon's Maronite Christians to perpetuate the second-rate status Shi'ite Muslims had long held in Lebanese society. Armed and funded by Syria and Iran, two major Shi'ite militias, Amal and Hizballah (the latter inspired by the religious appeals of revolutionary Iran), continued to attack ASL and Israeli troops in the security zone throughout the 1980s. Israel often responded by arresting Shi'ites who had reputations as especially strong militants.

The presence of Shi'ites in Israeli prisons provoked others to engage in acts of international terrorism to secure their release. An example was

in June 1985 when three Lebanese Shi'ites hijacked a TWA airliner out of Athens, Greece. After landing in Beirut, they killed one American and held thirty-nine Americans hostage in an effort to make Israel release some seven hundred Lebanese Shi'ites imprisoned in Israel. The American hostages were freed, and Israel eventually released the Shi'ites, whom it said were previously scheduled to be released.

## 1982-87 Diplomacy

Following the evacuation of the PLO from Beirut, the focus of the Palestinian component of the Arab-Israeli conflict tended to be on diplomacy rather than military confrontation. In September 1982 a flurry of international diplomacy provided momentum in the Arab-Israeli peace process.

### The Reagan Peace Initiative

The diplomatic activity began with an American initiative proposed by President Ronald Reagan on September 1, 1982. In a nationwide telecast, Reagan outlined a new initiative to give a "fresh start" to the Camp David process.

Taking advantage of the diminished stature of the PLO, and clearly trying to appeal to King Hussein of Jordan, whose participation in the Camp David process was vital for it to achieve any meaningful success, Reagan committed U.S. policy to a "Jordanian Option." He reiterated U.S. opposition to further Israeli settlement in the West Bank or Gaza and to annexation or permanent control of the territories by Israel, while asserting that the United States would exclude the PLO from negotiations and oppose creation of an independent Palestinian state. Reagan then proposed some type of self-government by the Palestinians in the territories in association with Jordan. He further called for negotiations to decide the disposition of Jerusalem.

The Begin government immediately rejected the proposal, saying it "deviated" from Camp David in that it tended to predetermine the outcome of negotiations. On the other hand, opposition Labor leader Shimon Peres called it "a basis for dialogue with the U.S."

Hussein, who had been consulted on the substance of the Reagan initiative prior to its announcement, initially indicated interest, but he noted his need to secure general Arab support and PLO approval before entering the negotiation process. Indeed the Reagan announcement was deliberately timed to precede a forthcoming Arab summit. His administration hoped that the summit would empower Hussein to respond positively to the Reagan initiative.

### The Fez Summit Peace Proposal

The Arab summit, which met in Fez, Morocco, September 5-8, 1982, did not respond to the U.S. initiative as the Reagan administration had hoped. At the same time, the summit did endorse a set of principles that was the first collective Arab expression of an intent to reach a settlement of the Arab-Israeli conflict. Passed unanimously by all members present, including the PLO and Jordan (Libya had not attended because of the agenda; Egypt, no longer a member of the Arab League, also did not attend), the Fez proposal adopted a hard-line approach.

The proposals' provisions included an Israeli withdrawal from all territories occupied in 1967;the administration of the territories by the UN Security Council for a short transition period, which would not to exceed several months; the establishment of a Palestinian state with Jerusalem as its capital; and UN Security Council guarantees to protect the peace and security of states in the region.

By continuing to designate the PLO as the sole legitimate representative of the Palestinian people and calling for the creation of an independent Palestinian state, the summit reinvigorated the PLO, so recently battered in Beirut. At the same time, it undercut any effort by King Hussein to participate in the Camp David process or indeed even to consider Jordanian sovereignty over the West Bank as legitimate.

### The Hussein-Arafat Initiative

Because the Reagan initiative failed to draw Jordan into the Camp David process, that process lost its momentum. The position of Israel's government remained firm. Although Shimon Peres, the head of the more accommodating Labor party, took over as prime minister in 1984 under a coalition agreement with the rival Likud bloc, Israel was preoccupied with economic problems and the effort to withdraw Israeli forces from Lebanon. In addition Labor's Likud coalition partners did not give Peres a free hand to make any decision relating to the West Bank and Gaza that contradicted their own position.

King Hussein and Yasir Arafat held talks during late 1982 and early 1983 in an effort to find a formula that would enable Jordan to negotiate on behalf of the PLO. Two concepts dominated the dialogue: establishing a Jordanian-West Bank Palestinian confederation or creating a joint Jordanian-Palestinian delegation to participate in the Camp David process.

Arafat's efforts to reach agreement with Hussein, however, faced opposition from two sources. The first of these were PLO factions that were wedded to the concepts of armed struggle and the total liberation of Palestine. These had taken refuge mainly in Syria following the evacuation from Beirut and opposed Arafat's temptation to follow the path of diplomacy. The second source of opposition was President Assad of Syria, whose determination to dominate regional affairs, including the Palestine issue, clashed sharply with any Jordanian or PLO effort to pursue an independent policy.

The PLO-Syrian feud reached a crisis point in May 1983, when Assad supported a mutiny against Arafat's leadership of Fatah and the PLO. Intra-PLO fighting continued in eastern and northern Lebanon throughout the summer and fall until December, when Arafat and four thousand followers once again were evacuated from Lebanon, this time from the port city of Tripoli.

To the surprise of the world, Arafat's first stop after his departure from Lebanon was Egypt, where he was received by President Mubarak. This symbolic visit marked a formal split in the PLO over management of the Arab-Israeli conflict. While Arafat moved toward reconciliation with the Camp David process (and to mold the process according to Palestinian terms), a rejectionist element of the PLO, controlled by and subordinated to Syria, held fast to an uncompromising collective Arab position. Despite sharp Israeli opposition, Mubarak lent support to the idea of developing a "new approach" that would bring Jordan and the PLO into the negotiations with Israel. So also did King Hussein, who resumed efforts with Arafat in early 1984 to seek a joint Jordanian-Palestinian policy for negotiations with Israel.

Although the two leaders shared interests in finding a common position that would secure Israeli withdrawal from the occupied territories, they did so for different reasons. For his part, Hussein was obliged to obtain a PLO mandate in order to negotiate on behalf of the Palestinian people; a 1974 Rabat summit resolution, reaffirmed at the Fez summit, had specified these terms. Meanwhile, Arafat sought to use his leverage to gain the approval of Jordan, Egypt, and ultimately the United States for the concept of an independent Palestinian state, to be achieved through the venue of an international conference, as stipulated by the Fez resolution. During 1984 Hussein reconvened the Jordanian parliament (half of whose members were West Bank Palestinians), restored diplomatic relations with Egypt in September, and sought the support of the more moderate Arab states and the United States for an enhanced Jordanian role in the peace process. Meanwhile, Arafat sought to build world support for an international peace conference and recognition of Palestinians' self-determination rights.

Because of the opposition of Syria and Syrian-based elements of the PLO that opposed his leadership, however, Arafat required reaffirmation of his role as PLO chairman before he could conclude any agreement with Hussein. Accordingly, despite Syrian threats and a boycott of Arafat's opposition, the king permitted a convocation of the Palestine National Council (PNC—equivalent to a Palestinian parliament in exile) in Jordan in November 1984. Arafat dominated its deliberations and was reelected as PLO chairman. He obtained authorization to continue his diplomatic strategy, but not to conclude any peace settlement on the basis of UN Resolution 242. Although this resolution called for Israeli withdrawal from occupied territories, it treated the Palestinian issue as a refugee problem and did not recognize the right of the Palestinian people to self-determination.

With his role as PLO chairman reconfirmed, Arafat was able to reach an agreement with Hussein on a joint diplomatic initiative, which the two signed on February 11, 1985. Its provisions included:

- An exchange of land for peace as provided for in resolutions of the United Nations, including those of the Security Council.
- The right of self-determination of the Palestinian people in the context of a Jordanian-Palestinian Arab confederation.
- The settlement of the Palestinian refugee issue in accordance with UN resolutions.
- An international peace conference in which the five permanent members of the Security Council and all parties to the conflict would participate, including the PLO.

*Peace Efforts Founder*

Announcement of this agreement was followed by visits to the United States by King Fahd of Saudi Arabia, President Mubarak, and King Hussein in May 1985 to solicit U.S. support for the initiative. Hussein proposed that a preliminary meeting between U.S. representatives and the joint Jordanian-Palestinian delegation, excluding PLO representatives, be held before an international conference. In addition, Hussein delivered a list of Palestinians suggested by the PLO for U.S. consideration as members of the joint Jordanian-Palestinian delegation.

The United States responded cautiously because of suspicions that hidden within the term *self-determination* lay the seeds of an independent Palestinian state. The Reagan administration reiterated its requirement for a "publicly and unequivocally" clear PLO statement that it accepted UN resolutions 242 and 338 and Israel's right to exist before the United States would meet with PLO representatives. The PNC had just as unequivocally denied Arafat the authority to make such a statement during its November meeting in Jordan. In addition, the bitter opposition of the Syrian-based PLO rejectionists constrained Arafat politically from meeting the U.S. condition unless the United States first declared its acceptance of the right of the Palestinian people to self-determination.

Deadlocked, the Hussein-Arafat initiative finally collapsed. Two terrorist actions contributed to the demise of the diplomatic process. The first was the killing of three Israeli tourists on a yacht at Larnaca, Cyprus, on September 25, 1985, by assassins alleged to be members of Force 17, a PLO unit personally loyal to Arafat. Although Arab commentary insisted that the three Israelis were members of Mossad, the Israeli intelligence organization, and not just innocent tourists, Israel responded by bombing Arafat's PLO headquarters in Tunis on October 1.

The second terrorist action was the October 8 hijacking of the *Achille Lauro,* an Italian cruise ship, by members of the Palestine Liberation Front, a pro-Arafat group within the PLO. The hijackers' killing of Leon Klinghoffer, an American tourist confined to a wheelchair, made it impossible for moderate Arab leaders supporting Arafat to depict the PLO as a similarly moderate element suitable for inclusion in the peace process. Although the action was almost certainly sponsored by Syrian-based radical Palestinian elements opposed to Arafat and his diplomatic strategy, the continuing association of the Palestinian movement with brutal acts of terrorism against innocent civilians was gravely damaging to the Hussein-Arafat initiative.

Faced with Arafat's inability to escape his own ambiguous political situation, the Reagan administration's caution, and the lack of responsiveness

from a politically paralyzed Israel, King Hussein finally repudiated the agreement with Arafat in February 1986. Jordanian-PLO relations rapidly deteriorated, and in July 1986 all PLO offices in Jordan were ordered closed. In April 1987 Arafat also repudiated the accord as a first step in an attempt to effect a reconciliation with his PLO opposition.

Hussein managed to convene an Arab summit conference in Amman in November 1987. The outcome was a personal triumph for the king. The conference endorsed his request to convene an international peace conference, and it placed him rather than Arafat squarely in the position of Arab leadership. It also gave leave for individual Arab countries to restore relations with Egypt, broken since the signing of the Camp David treaty, although Syrian opposition still precluded Egyptian readmission into the Arab League. Finally, the summit, with Syrian approval, endorsed Iraq's position in the Iran-Iraq War, and Hussein was able to arrange a personal meeting between the two feuding leaders, Saddam Hussein of Iraq and Hafez Assad of Syria.

## The Intifada

Hussein's mandate to enter the peace process was to be short-lived, however. Within a few weeks of the summit, the outbreak of a sustained general uprising among the Arab population of the West Bank and Gaza, known as the *intifada,* was to transform the Arab-Israeli conflict. The intifada shifted the focus of the conflict away from the disputes between Israel and its Arab neighbors to Israel's relations with the Arabs who lived under its occupation.

The Israeli army was unable to put down the uprising, which quickly became an established fact of life throughout the West Bank and Gaza. The sight of Palestinian children armed with rocks facing Israeli soldiers increased international sympathy for the cause of Arabs in the occupied territories. The critical problem for Israel was that the young rock throwers, and local Palestinian leaders who emerged to explain the intifada, regarded the

PLO—in particular the part led by Yasir Arafat—as the only legitimate representative of the Palestinian people. The uprising, although not directly inspired by the PLO, returned international attention to Arafat.

The intifada was a reaction to determined Israeli efforts for nearly a decade to control life in the occupied territories. The Israeli government had expropriated available land in the territories, built Jewish settlements, controlled the territories' water and electricity, destroyed houses of the families who resisted, arrested and detained Arabs arbitrarily, and in extreme cases deported Arabs engaged in anti-Israeli activity. In general the government tried to create conditions that would induce the Arabs to absolutely respect Israeli authority. The intifada represented a massive and popular upheaval against the continuing Israeli occupation. Violence and resistance to the occupation, however, were not new. What distinguished the intifada from previous violence was its universal presence throughout the territories and the inability of Israeli authorities to contain it, despite the Israeli army's use of beatings, massive arrests, curfews, and violent confrontations with the demonstrators.

Possibly inspired by the perceived success of resistance to Israel's occupation of southern Lebanon between 1982 and 1985, the intifada was also an expression of Palestinian frustration at the failure of Arab diplomacy to reach any accommodation with Israel in the years since the Camp David treaty.

In an effort to revive momentum toward a diplomatic settlement, U.S. secretary of state George Shultz embarked on a diplomatic mission in the spring of 1988—the first official American peace initiative since the Reagan plan of 1982. The initiative laid down a tight timetable for completion of the negotiation process by the end of the year, but it was otherwise similar to the agreement reached between Foreign Minister Peres and King Hussein the previous April, and for which King Hussein now had an Arab summit mandate to pursue. Where United States mediation of that agreement had been low key due to the delicacies

of negotiating an agreement with a foreign minister operating without the approval of his prime minister, the urgency of the situation now led Shultz to lend it the prestige of his personal involvement.

His mission encountered two primary obstacles, however, the opposition of Prime Minister Shamir and the noncooperation of West Bank Palestinians because of the lack of a place in his plan for the PLO. Despite initial cautious support in both Syria and Jordan, Syria eventually demanded a conference with a unified Arab delegation, and King Hussein noted that he no longer could represent either the PLO or the Palestinian people. By May it was clear that the concept of an international conference as originally conceived by Peres was no longer possible.

The changed nature of the situation was revealed at a three-day emergency Arab summit convened by Algerian president Chadli Bendjedid in Algiers June 7-9. The summit decided to withdraw from Syria, Jordan, and the PLO annual funding that previously had been allotted to confrontation countries bordering Israel. Instead, the summit endorsed general Arab support for the intifada and urged all Arab funds to be distributed to the territories through the PLO. These funds were to be allocated state by state, however, not by the Arab League as a whole. Rather than condemn the Shultz initiative, moreover, the Arab leaders reiterated their support for an international conference under UN auspices and urged the PLO to declare the establishment of an independent Palestinian state, which the Arab states proposed to designate as the principal Arab interlocutor in such a conference.

In July 1988 King Hussein—so recently authorized by the November Arab summit to seek a peace settlement with Israel—relinquished Jordan's claims to the West Bank and Gaza, which it had maintained since 1949. Hussein's action appeared designed to free Jordan, with its large Palestinian population, from the disruptive effects of the intifada and force the PLO into a more conciliatory position by making it solely responsible for representing the Arabs in the occupied territories.

Although Hussein's announcement did not completely remove him from Middle East diplomacy, it was a blow to U.S. and Israeli leaders who had anticipated a prominent role for Jordan in any settlement. *(Text of Hussein statement, Appendix, p. 399)*

As the intifada continued and the Israeli government sought to contain it with force, Arafat convened a meeting of the Palestine National Council in Algiers. On November 15, 1988, the council took the historic step of proclaiming the establishment of an independent Palestinian state and announced its recognition of UN Resolution 242, implicitly recognizing Israel. A declaration rejecting terrorism also was adopted. The council called for the convening of an international conference under sponsorship of the UN, the purpose of which would be to negotiate a resolution of the Arab-Israeli conflict.

Although the Reagan administration maintained that these initial pronouncements did not satisfy its conditions for beginning a dialogue with the PLO, Arafat on December 14 explicitly accepted resolutions 242 and 338, recognized Israel's right to exist, and renounced terrorism. The United States responded by opening talks with the PLO in Tunis despite Israeli objections. *(Text of Arafat statement, Appendix, p. 401)*

## U.S.-PLO Dialogue

The U.S. decision to open talks with the PLO occurred in the last days of the Reagan administration. The incoming Bush administration sought to build on the legacy by giving priority to achieving a settlement of the Arab-Israeli conflict. Bush's election in late 1988, however, had followed soon after the reelection of the Likud party and its leader Yitzhak Shamir as prime minister of Israel in June. Shamir made clear his total opposition to conducting direct negotiations with PLO chairman Arafat or to accepting the principle of an independent Palestinian state. These ideas were taboos for Israel under his leadership. Instead Shamir in May 1989 put forth his own plan calling for elections in the occupied territories that would produce a local Palestinian delegation to conduct negotiations with Israel on some type of Arab autonomy formula in accordance with the Israeli interpretation of the Camp David accords. A halt to the intifada was a precondition for the holding of these elections, however.

Difficult to resist in principle, the electoral proposal was not rejected outright by the PLO. The organization insisted, however, that before elections could take place, Israel had to agree in principle to give up the occupied territories and to allow the Arab residents of East Jerusalem to participate in the election. Both conditions were at odds with the Israeli position, and the impasse continued.

In an effort to break the impasse, the new U.S. secretary of state, James A. Baker III, sought to find ways to implement the Shamir plan while reassuring Palestinians that U.S. policy was sensitive to their concerns. These assurances included public statements by Baker suggesting that Israel ultimately would have to negotiate with "representatives of the PLO" and urging Israel to "lay aside once and for all the unrealistic vision of greater Israel" and to "reach out to Palestinians as neighbors who deserve political rights."

American efforts were abetted by an Egyptian ten-point plan put forth in September 1989 that, among other things, called for international observers to monitor the election and agreement by Israel to accept any and all results of the election. This initiative was followed by a Baker five-point plan that called for Egypt, Israel, and the United States to begin a round of negotiations aimed at finding a compromise between the Israeli and Palestinian positions. Interpreting these initiatives as amounting to virtually direct Israeli-PLO negotiations, even if through third parties, the Shamir government finally rejected them, but at a considerable cost to U.S.-Israeli relations.

The Egyptian and U.S. initiatives, however, put considerable pressure on the Israeli political system. Israel's Labor party, which remained part of the ruling coalition, favored responding to both initiatives and criticized Shamir vehemently for rejecting his own plan and disrupting relations with the United States. More hard-line figures in his own Likud party also leveled criticism at him, probably to preempt any possibility of his reaching a compromise with Labor. Pressure mounted until mid-March 1990, when the government fell. The inability of Labor leader Shimon Peres to form a new government, however, gave Shamir a second chance, and he succeeded by June in forming a new government without calling new elections. His new government, which included most of Israel's religious parties, excluded Labor and was considerably more hard-line than the previous one.

The PLO, meanwhile, seeing the prospects slipping away for compromise and increased PLO involvement in the peace process, began altering its position accordingly. Following Israel's rejection of the Mubarak and Baker initiatives, the PLO adopted the position that any Palestinian delegation engaged in talks with Israel should represent the PLO, a stance it previously had not insisted on, despite strong opposition from many Palestinians.

At the same time, a complex set of changes in the overall international environment led Arafat to develop closer relations with Iraq's president Saddam Hussein, both as a source of funds and of firmer diplomatic support for the PLO. These changes included: the end of the Iran-Iraq War and the return of Iraq as an Arab actor with interest in the Arab-Israeli conflict; the collapse of Communist regimes in Eastern Europe that previously had been reliable supporters of the PLO; the changing nature of the Communist regime in the Soviet Union, which, beginning in late 1989, was permitting the emigration of tens of thousands of Russian Jews to Israel; diminishing financial support from the Arab Gulf states; and finally a late 1989 Syrian-Egyptian rapprochement that raised hopes of broadening the peace process, possibly at the PLO's expense.

The linkage between Arafat's changing situation and the new role of Saddam Hussein was made clear at an emergency Arab summit held in Baghdad on May 28-30, 1990. Convened at Iraq's initiative to discuss the status of the intifada, the stagnation of the peace process, and perceived American-instigated "campaigns" against Iraq and Libya, the summit aimed, an Iraqi spokesman stated, at forging a "new Arab order" to meet these challenges. Limitation of America's role in the Middle East was a central theme of the summit's official communiqué. The conference also endorsed "the PLO's desire" to shift away from the current U.S.-Israel-Egypt venue for negotiations and called for the convening of an international conference regarding the Arab-Israeli conflict as an "urgent necessity."

As if to herald the change in Arab and PLO approaches to the Arab-Israeli conflict, a failed attack by dissident members of the PLO on Israel's beaches near Tel Aviv on May 30, the last day of the Arab summit, revived tensions and undercut the peace initiative that had been inaugurated by the PLO's recognition of Israel in November 1988. The United States soon broke off its dialogue with the PLO, after Arafat refused to condemn the event or its perpetrator—the same group that had been responsible for the notorious *Achille Lauro* hijacking in October 1985.

It was in this psychological environment of heightened tension and increasingly hard-line politics that the Persian Gulf crisis of 1990 erupted on the entire international community.

## Toward a Peace Agreement

The Arab summit and changed directions for the Arab world reflected in the summit's communiqué clearly resulted from efforts by Iraqi president Saddam Hussein to assume a position of decisive leadership in the Arab world. The "blood and iron" nature of this leadership was revealed in early August 1990 by Iraq's blitzkrieg invasion and subsequent annexation of Kuwait.

Immediately challenged by outraged international opinion, Saddam publicly rationalized his action by pointing to the Israeli occupation of the West Bank, Gaza, and south Lebanon. He offered to withdraw from Kuwait only in an exchange for an Israeli withdrawal from these territories. This argument, which gained the Iraqi leader considerable support among the Arabs of the occupied territories and refugee camps, was rejected by the United States, which assembled an anti-Iraq coalition to resist Saddam's pretensions. Despite U.S. resistance to any effort by Saddam to link his personal aggression to unresolved issues of the Arab-Israeli conflict, he persisted. On the eve of the opening of allied military operations he referred to the coming war as the "great battle for Palestine."

American efforts to put together a successful anti-Iraq coalition were at least in part dependent on the maintenance of a broad international consensus. Not all members of the international community, however, were so adamant as the United States in rejecting the linkage between the occupied territories and Kuwait. The Arab members of the anti-Iraq coalition in particular were at least as concerned about the prospects for regional instability provoked by the unresolved Arab-Israeli conflict as they were about Iraq's occupation of Kuwait. The Soviet Union too made it known that it was prepared to cooperate fully with the United States in working toward the resolution of both the Persian Gulf crisis and the Arab-Israeli conflict. To maintain a sufficient allied consensus and the solidarity of the Anti-Iraq coalition, therefore, American leaders found it both necessary and useful to coordinate U.S. activities on both fronts with a broad array of international leaders whose views had to be taken into account. Accordingly, on January 29, 1991, two weeks into the Gulf war, the United States and the Soviet Union issued a joint communiqué that not only called for Iraq to withdraw unequivocally from Kuwait, but also committed the two powers to work together after the Gulf War to promote both Arab-Israeli peace and regional stability.

## Madrid Talks

The U.S.-led coalition victory over Iraq produced a situation quite different from that called for by the Iraqi-dominated Arab summit of the previous summer. Instead of limiting America's role in the Middle East, the successful outcome of the Gulf crisis made the United States the decisive external arbiter of Middle Eastern affairs, at least in the short term. The Bush administration sought to exert this leadership role, as it had in the Gulf crisis, through international consensus and dialogue. Thus, continuing sanctions against Iraq and efforts to contain future Iraqi military reconstruction were undertaken as United Nations actions. Efforts to promote regional stability necessarily meant focusing quickly on the Arab-Israeli conflict as well.

Almost immediately after the end of the Gulf War on February 28, 1991, Secretary of State Baker returned to the region on March 7 with a principal aim, among others, of reviving the Arab-Israeli peace process. Baker made eight trips to the Middle East during the summer of 1991, successfully concluding his mission by achieving agreement among all the major parties to the Arab-Israeli dispute to convene for preliminary talks in Madrid, Spain, on October 30. Given the long history of the conflict, Baker's achievement was remarkable, as the Madrid summit represented the first direct, diplomatic encounter between Israel and all its neighboring Arab states since the aborted United Nations-sponsored peace talks on Rhodes in 1951. Several factors, in addition to his own indefatigable sense of mission, accounted for Baker's success.

First, and perhaps most important, was the changed structure of the international order that had followed the collapse of communism in Eastern Europe in 1989, including the reformed nature of the ruling party in the Soviet Union and the end of the Cold War. As had been illustrated in the Gulf crisis, it was now possible for the United States and the Soviet Union to work cooperatively in international affairs, despite lingering disagreements over matters of substance. A key reason for Baker's success was that the invitation to Madrid was issued jointly by both the United States and the Soviet Union, and the two presidents of each country were present at Madrid to preside over the summit. Such great-power cooperation would have been virtually unthinkable just a year or two earlier. In addition, both the United Nations and the European Community had been mobilized as supporters of the process and had representatives present at the Madrid summit as observers. The weight of international opinion, therefore, clearly favored a transformation of the Arab-Israeli conflict from a struggle conducted on the battlefield to one conducted in the corridors of diplomacy. The risk of resisting such strong international pressure by any one of the principal parties to the conflict was too great.

Second, the overwhelming defeat of Iraq in the Gulf War represented a decisive defeat for more radical forces in the Arab world who favored a military solution to the Arab-Israeli conflict. The huge role played by the United States in the war in behalf of its Arab allies meant that it, together with its allies, would play the decisive role in formulating the shape of the peace that followed. If U.S. policy favored a diplomatic settlement of the Arab-Israeli conflict as one outcome of the Gulf crisis, few were in a position to resist diplomatically the power that the United States had just demonstrated militarily.

Certainly those Arab states that had fought with the United States in the anti-Iraq coalition—Saudi Arabia and the lesser Gulf states in whose defense the Gulf War had been fought; Egypt, which already had a peace treaty with Israel; and Syria, which by joining the coalition sought to escape its previous regional isolation by cultivating better relations with the United States and its key Arab allies in the region—had done so for benefits they hoped to gain and were not about to sacrifice by noncooperation with U.S. postwar policy.

Baker's success also was probably abetted by certain anomalies of the Gulf War. The loyalty PLO leader Yasir Arafat had demonstrated for Iraqi president Saddam Hussein ironically facilitated the peace process. As a loser in the war, the PLO had lost the support of those same key Arab states who were to be represented at Madrid, a necessary condition for Israel to accept the invitation. At the same time, the marginal role played by Israel in the Gulf crisis, and indeed even the protective role the United States had played in deploying Patriot antimissile batteries to Israel to help defend against Iraqi Scud missile attacks,

had the effect of weakening Israel's bargaining position with the United States, possibly a necessary condition for some of the Arab states to go to Madrid.

Finally, undoubtedly a function of the international consensus politics conducted by Baker, and also to ensure the cooperation of the key Arab states, Baker insisted that Palestinians be included at Madrid. Israeli insistence on a veto over who among the Palestinians might be included in such a delegation was not in the end sustained, nor were the delegates chosen by the electoral process requested by Prime Minister Shamir a year earlier. In line with U.S. policy since the Reagan years, they were present as part of the Jordanian delegation and they consisted solely of Arab inhabitants of the occupied territories who had no affiliation with the PLO. Inclusion of non-PLO Palestinians unquestionably reflected the impact of the intifada, the continuation of which implied that no resolution of the Arab-Israeli conflict would be possible without some voice for the Palestinians.

Syrian acceptance on July 18 of the joint U.S.-Soviet invitation to Madrid proved the key to unlocking the door of the diplomatic process. Within days, Lebanon and Jordan had announced acceptance of their invitations, and Saudi Arabia, attending only as an observer, had announced its support of the process. Egypt had worked with the United States to facilitate the diplomatic process and also accepted its invitation to attend in observer status.

In the end, ironically, it was the hard-line Israeli government of Yitzhak Shamir that proved the most hesitant party, withholding a decision to attend until October 20. Concerned mainly with the composition of the Palestinian delegation and fears that the delegation would prove, de facto, to be representative of the PLO, the Israeli government sought assurances that could not be delivered.

## Eleven Rounds of Negotiations

Between the Madrid summit of October 30-November 1, 1991, and the Israel-PLO Declaration of Principles of September 13, 1993, eleven meetings of the so-called bilateral negotiations between Israel and its immediate Arab neighbors took place in Washington. A series of multilateral negotiations involving many other countries to discuss wider-ranging issues, such as arms control, water sharing, and refugees also occurred in a variety of world capitals. Although no great diplomatic progress occurred in any of these meetings, their very occurrence marked an important stage in the evolution of the Arab-Israeli conflict. Gradually it became clear that the bilateral talks involved four sets of negotiations rather than three as originally conceived. In addition to Syria, Jordan, and Lebanon, Israel increasingly found itself negotiating separately with the Palestinian members of the joint Jordanian-Palestinian delegation. Moreover, despite efforts by Israel to avoid direct negotiations with the PLO, it gradually became clear that the Palestinian members of the Jordanian-Palestinian delegation did not feel empowered to make decisions without consulting PLO headquarters in Tunis.

The growing indirect role of the PLO in the negotiating process provided a serious challenge to Shamir's hard-line government in Israel. In June 1992 elections, Shamir's Likud party was ousted in favor of the Labor party, now led by Yitzhak Rabin. The election, among other things, was a mandate for continuing the peace process begun at Madrid.

Perhaps the most important issue in the Israeli election, however, had been the status of the country's relations with the United States. On September 6, 1991, just as the U.S. government had been seeking Israel's agreement to attend the Madrid summit, the Shamir government had formally submitted a request for $10 billion in loan guarantees to be used to fund the construction of housing for the many Jewish immigrants arriving in Israel from the Soviet Union.

Coming when it did, the loan guarantees request had the appearance of pressuring President Bush to respond favorably to ensure Israel's acceptance of the invitation to Madrid. Bush reacted negatively, however, asking the U.S. Congress to defer action on the request until after the summit.

Shortly thereafter he reacted even more strongly, insisting that Israel freeze all settlement construction activities in the occupied territories as a condition for receiving the loan guarantees. Shamir retaliated by criticizing the Bush administration for trying to pressure Israel. The impasse continued, poisoning U.S.-Israeli relations and becoming yet another issue used by Labor to weaken Likud's hold on the Israeli electorate.

The election of the Labor party and its leader Yitzhak Rabin as the new prime minister marked a significant departure from the hard-line policies followed by Israel under successive Likud-led governments since 1977. Although having a reputation as one of the most hard-line politicians within the Labor party, Rabin nevertheless was eager to restore frayed U.S.-Israeli relations. In one of his first acts, he froze all new settlements in the occupied territories but did not stop work on settlements already under construction. This step proved sufficient for the Bush administration to conclude that U.S. conditions had been met, and during Rabin's first state visit to the United States in August 1992 the Bush administration announced its decision to authorize the $10 billion in loan guarantees. (*Loan guarantees, box, Chapter 3, p. 96*)

During his first weeks in office, moreover, Rabin announced his willingness to meet personally with Arab heads of state and, perhaps anticipating the inevitable, indicated his government's preparedness to negotiate with Palestinians directly affiliated with the PLO.

## The Oslo Breakthrough

In late August 1993, while Arab and Israeli delegates returned to Washington to meet for the eleventh round of the increasingly stalemated peace talks, they and the rest of the world were startled by the surprise announcement that a secretly negotiated agreement had been reached between representatives of the Israeli government and the PLO. The roots of the agreement lay in informal, indirect contacts between moderate Israelis and PLO figures concerned about the lack of

*President Bill Clinton looks on as Israeli prime minister Yitzhak Rabin (left) and PLO leader Yasir Arafat shake hands September 13, 1993, after signing the Declaration of Principles, which laid the foundation for Palestinian self-rule in lands occupied by Israel since 1967.*

progress in the bilateral talks in Washington. Working on the basis of establishing a "statement of principles" that might be acceptable to both Israel and the PLO, the two parties, working largely through the government of Norway, discovered merging areas of agreement sufficient to interest both the PLO leadership and the new Israeli government of Yitzhak Rabin in pursuing further dialogue. Following the January 1993 lifting of the ban in Israel against any contact with representatives of the PLO, the contacts became direct in a long series of increasingly formal meetings by ever-higher echelons of negotiators from both sides. Meeting in the strictest secrecy at various locations outside Oslo, Norway, the negotiations continued, unknown to the rest of the world, until the breakthrough agreement in August.

In fact, there were two agreements. In the first,

signed by Arafat in Tunis on September 10 and by Rabin a few hours later, the PLO formally recognized Israel's right to exist in peace and security, renounced the use of terror and violence, and pledged to remove the clauses in the PLO charter that called for the elimination of Israel as a state. In return Rabin, by affixing his signature, formally extended Israeli recognition to the PLO as the legitimate representative of the Palestinian people.

This first historic agreement paved the way for a second, the "Declaration of Principles on Interim Self-Government and Arrangements," signed in Washington on September 13, 1993. Known also as the "Gaza-Jericho first" plan, this agreement, following closely the formula first developed at Camp David fifteen years earlier, envisioned a five-year plan in which Israel gradually would lift its military occupation of the occupied territories, and Palestinian self-rule gradually would be estab-lished in the same territories. As a first-stage, mutual confidence-building measure, both sides agreed to an initial implementation of the agree-ment first in Gaza and Jericho by December 13, 1993, three months after the signing of the agree-ment. Then a Palestinian Council, elected by July 1994, was to begin assuming responsibility for a variety of government services throughout the ter-ritories, as the Israeli armed forces simultaneously began withdrawing from the major Arab towns and cities of the territories. The exact organization and powers of the council were not spelled out but were to be worked out in further negotiations be-fore the end of the five-year period. Finally, in December 1995, final negotiations were to begin on reaching a final settlement of the Israel-Pal-estinian conflict in the occupied territories. The results of these negotiations were to take effect in December 1998, five years after the withdrawal of Israel from Gaza and Jericho.

## After the Declaration of Principles

Israeli forces did not withdraw from Gaza and Jericho on December 13, 1993, as called for in the Israel-PLO agreement. Difficulties with regard to two issues—whether the term *Jericho* referred to the town or the district of that name, and which security forces, Israeli or PLO, would remain posted on the borders of Egypt and Gaza and of Jordan and Jericho—kept the agreement from be-ing implemented on time. The delay demonstrated how difficult the process of further negotiating and implementing the full agreement would be. Nevertheless on May 11, 1994, the Israelis did withdraw, opening the way for Palestinian admin-istration of Gaza and Jericho.

The agreement faced difficulties from other directions as well. On both sides of the conflict, rejectionist forces strongly opposed it. Hard-line groups in Israel denounced Rabin as a traitor who had sold out to the enemy by signing the agree-ment. Many Israelis continue to see Arafat as the primary enemy of the Jewish state and a man responsible for the killing of hundreds of Jews.

Among the Palestinians, some members of the militant Islamist Hamas movement also opposed Arafat's compromise and threatened to undermine it by continuing terrorism and violence. Nor did all member groups of the PLO support the agree-ment. Both these categories of rejectionists re-ceived moral and financial support from Islamist groups external to the Arab-Israeli conflict, such as Iran. The strong dissent of these groups raised the possibility that changed political circum-stances might one day reverse the fragile progress made toward an Arab-Israeli settlement. At the very least, their existence indicated that even a comprehensive settlement might not entirely still the violence historically associated with the Arab-Israeli conflict.

### Establishing Palestinian Autonomy

Beyond threats from Jewish and Arab extrem-ists, the success of the autonomy scheme estab-lished by the Israeli-Palestinian agreement rested on the ability of Yasir Arafat and his PLO to bring effective government to the territory relinquished by the Israelis. Many observers questioned whether Arafat, known for his disorganized and dictatorial leadership style, could satisfy Israeli demands for order and local Palestinian demands for democracy, an effective judicial system, and an improvement of living conditions. Arafat appeared more inclined to continue his role as the interna-tional spokesman of the Palestinians than to move to Jericho and submerge himself in the bureau-cratic details of running a government.

On July 1, 1994, Arafat returned in triumph to the Gaza Strip after twenty-seven years in exile. Although the occasion was jubilant, some Pal-estinians complained that Arafat had not stated an intention to stay in Gaza permanently with his people. Arafat's large entourage, his extensive security precautions, and his visits to Europe project an imperial approach that could weaken his popularity among Palestinians. Inevitably, Palestinians, most of whom already live in squa-lor, would have to make further sacrifices. If they perceived Arafat as refusing to share in those sacrifices, Palestinians may reject his leadership.

Arafat was likely to have a grace period, given the euphoria of many Palestinians in Gaza and Jericho over the Israeli withdrawal. But a significant delay in bringing noticeable improvements to the economy could open the door for Hamas and other militant forces that oppose the peace accord. Under a pact signed with Israel on April 19, 1994, the new Palestinian authority will have the power to collect its own taxes and customs duties and oversee most economic matters. Nevertheless, the economy of the Palestinian-administered areas will be closely linked through trade and currency to the Israeli economy.

International aid will be critical to the development of Palestinian-controlled areas and the operation of a Palestinian government. Although the United States and other Western countries pledged aid, the Palestinians had not received the windfall that Egypt received when Anwar Sadat signed a peace treaty with Israel. About $2.2 billion over five years was pledged, but delivery of the money has been slow and uncertain. Many donors expressed concern that their funds could be used by Arafat and the PLO as patronage money rather than effective development aid. Arafat has denounced conditions for aid that donor countries have sought to impose.

## Looking to the Future

The Arab-Israeli peace process received a significant boost on July 25, 1994, when Jordan's King Hussein and Israel's Prime Minister Rabin signed a document in Washington ending the forty-six-year state of war between the two countries. The "Washington Declaration" was followed by a formal peace treaty between Jordan and Israel signed October 26, 1994, at a ceremony on the Israeli-Jordanian border. The treaty resolved border and water disputes and established cooperation in many areas,

including trade, tourism, communications, and transportation links. In addition, both sides pledged not to allow their territory to be used as a base for third-country attacks against the other.

The Israeli-Jordanian peace treaty left Syria as the one major front-line Arab state that had not ended hostilities with Israel. Yet the prospects were good that an agreement between these two states could be reached. Both nations have an interest in making peace, and the issues involved are much simpler than those that exist between the Israelis and Palestinians. A peace treaty would likely involve a gradual Israeli withdrawal from the Golan Heights in exchange for Syrian normalization of relations with Israel. The Golan Heights would be demilitarized and the area would be monitored by international peacekeepers.

Many major issues remained that could derail a final and complete peace between Israel and the Palestinians, including the status of Jerusalem, Palestinian refugees, and Jewish settlements on the West Bank. Although a consensus in Israel to give up Gaza existed, many Israelis will vigorously oppose giving up more territory in the West Bank. Israeli leaders have emphasized that negotiations on the many remaining issues could take years. "You cannot solve a conflict of one hundred years in one month, two months, or even six months," Prime Minister Rabin warned.

Nevertheless it was clear that the Arab-Israeli conflict had entered a new phase. The maximalist, idealistic politics of the past seemed to be giving way to a more pragmatic, realistic political approach on both sides that took into account the existence and rights of the other. Political leaders appeared to be striving to achieve the possible rather than struggling indefatigably for the impossible. The future of Arab-Israeli relations undoubtedly will remain rocky, but the gradual opening of new channels of negotiation raises hopes that future crises in relations will have mechanisms for conflict resolution available other than warfare.

CHAPTER 3

# U.S. POLICY IN
# THE MIDDLE EAST

Minutes after Israel declared its independence on May 14, 1948, the United States became the first country to recognize the Jewish state. The establishment of Israel marked the beginning of extensive U.S. political, economic, and military involvement in the Middle East. Since the time of the 1967 Six-Day War, achieving peace and stability in the Middle East has been one of the most important U.S. foreign policy concerns.

American policy in the Middle East has traditionally focused on four major objectives: ensuring the security of Israel, achieving an Arab-Israeli peace settlement, maintaining U.S. and Western access to Middle Eastern oil, and—until 1989—blocking Soviet expansionism in the region. The United States also has pursued several lesser policy goals that are related to its four main objectives, including combating terrorism, preventing the spread of nuclear and chemical arms, and improving economic and security ties with moderate Arab states.

These policy objectives have often conflicted with one another. In particular the special relationship between the United States and Israel has made other U.S. policy goals more difficult to achieve. American support for Israel during the 1973 Arab-Israeli War led to an Arab oil boycott against the United States. The U.S.-Israeli relationship also caused many of the Arab states to be skittish about joining the U.S.-led coalition against Iraq in the Persian Gulf War. Had Saddam Hussein succeeded in his efforts to bring Israel into the

war, it might well have caused many of the Arab states to drop out of the coalition. Nevertheless, successive U.S. administrations have agreed that these major objectives must all be pursued, and they have retained wide public and congressional support.

One stable factor in the search for Middle East peace has been the ability of the United States to fill the role of mediator. In spite of its close ties with Israel, the United States maintains relations with nearly all Arab countries, and even in times of crisis U.S. diplomats gain access throughout the region.

## Palestine Partition

President Woodrow Wilson set the framework for U.S. policy in the Middle East when he endorsed a 1917 letter from British foreign secretary Arthur Balfour to Lord Lionel Rothschild, leader of the British Zionists, pledging that Britain would support the establishment in Palestine of a "national home" for the Jewish people, on the understanding "that nothing shall be done which may prejudice the civil and religious rights of existing non-Jewish communities in Palestine." The U.S. Congress adopted a resolution approving the declaration in September 1922.

Wilson also strongly influenced the post-World War I peace settlement that established national boundaries for the Middle East. He conceived the interim League of Nations mandates, which led to

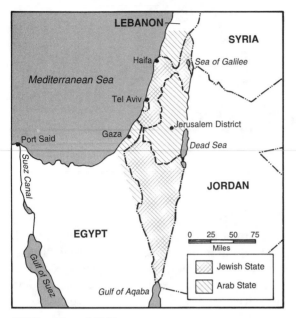

*UN Partition of 1947*

the formation of most of the countries that exist in the Middle East today. In July 1922 the League of Nations approved an arrangement giving Great Britain a mandate over Palestine. The mandate, which went into force September 22, 1923, contained a preamble incorporating the Balfour Declaration and stressing the Jews' historical connection with Palestine. Britain was made responsible for placing the country under such "political, administrative, and economic conditions as will secure the establishment of a Jewish National Home."

Between 1923 and 1939 more than four hundred thousand Jews immigrated to Palestine, causing growing resentment against the British among the Arabs. In 1939, however, Arab unrest and German and Italian attempts to improve relations with the Arabs led the British to issue a white paper that reduced the flow of Jewish immigrants to Palestine—primarily European Jews suffering from Nazi persecution—to fifteen thousand a year for five years. After that, no more Jewish immigration was to be allowed unless agreed upon by the local Arab population. Jews denounced the restrictions and tried to circumvent them.

The United States led the effort after World War II to lift the immigration restrictions. In August 1945 President Harry S. Truman called for the free settlement of Palestine by Jews to a point consistent with the maintenance of civil peace.

Later that month he suggested in a letter to British prime minister Clement R. Attlee that an additional hundred thousand Jews be allowed to enter Palestine. In December both houses of Congress adopted a resolution urging U.S. aid in opening Palestine to Jewish immigrants and in building a "democratic commowealth."

Meanwhile in November, Great Britain, eager to have the United States share responsibility for its Jewish immigration policy, joined with the United States in establishing a commission to examine the problem of admitting European Jews to Palestine. Great Britain also agreed to permit an additional fifteen hundred Jews to enter Palestine each month.

In April 1946 an Anglo-American Committee of Inquiry recommended the immediate admission of a hundred thousand Jews into Palestine and continuation of the British mandate until a United Nations trusteeship was established. Truman immediately endorsed the proposal, but Britain stipulated that, before it would agree to continue its mandate, underground Jewish forces in Palestine would have to be disbanded.

On October 4 Truman released a communication sent to the British government in which he appealed for "substantial immigration" into Palestine "at once" and expressed support for the Zionist plan for creation of a "viable Jewish state" in part of Palestine. In response, the British government said it regretted that Truman's statement had been made public before a settlement was realized. The British feared that such an unqualified expression of American support for a Jewish state would reduce the chances of reaching a compromise between the Arabs and Israelis.

When a London conference of Arab and Zionist representatives failed to resolve the Palestine question, Britain turned to the United Nations in early

1947. The United Nations set up a committee of inquiry, which ultimately recommended that Palestine be divided into separate Arab and Jewish states, with Jerusalem becoming an international zone under permanent UN trusteeship. On November 29, 1947, the UN General Assembly ratified that decision. Britain set May 15, 1948, as the date its mandate would end.

Sporadic violence by Arab and Jewish guerrillas that had become a part of life in Palestine escalated to open civil war after the UN decision. In March 1948 the United States voiced its opposition to the forcible partitioning of Palestine and called for suspension of the plan. The Truman administration requested a special session of the UN General Assembly to reconsider the issue.

In April the Security Council adopted a U.S. resolution calling for a truce in the civil war in Palestine and a special session of the General Assembly. This effort, however, was too late to stop the division of Palestine. On May 14 the British high commissioner left Palestine and the state of Israel was proclaimed. The United States immediately granted Israel de facto recognition.

## Arab-Israeli Struggle and the United States

From the moment the United States recognized Israel, U.S. commitment to the Jewish nation became a fundamental element of American Middle East policy. That commitment initially stemmed from concern for the terrible plight of Jewish refugees from Hitler's Germany. It was sustained by considerable public support for a special friendship with Israel and by the politically active and influential Jewish population in the United States. Support for Israel, however, created strong anti-American feelings in the Arab countries, subsequently opening many of them to the influence of the Soviet Union.

The United States assumed the role of Israel's chief arms supplier with some reluctance. Throughout the 1950s and early 1960s, Washington had shunned Israeli arms requests so as not to jeopardize its friendships with moderate Arab

*Israel After 1948-49 War*

countries or its Middle East oil interests. But with the French decision in 1967 to cut off arms to Israel, U.S. policy makers felt they had no alternative but to step into the arms supplier role to counter Soviet assistance to Israel's enemies.

The United States, however, did not conclude a formal security pact with Israel for fear that such an agreement would provide a rallying point for Arab hostility. Moreover, U.S. leaders were concerned that a treaty would encourage intransigence by Israel in any future negotiations with the Arabs. Although the United States clearly had become Israel's arms lifeline and its most important ally, it avoided defining exactly what that commitment entailed in an attempt to maintain the appearance of impartiality. The commitment to Israel, however, while not in the form of a treaty, has been reaffirmed by all U.S. administrations since Truman.

### First Arab-Israeli War (1948-49)

The day after Israel declared its independence, contingents from five Arab countries—Egypt,

Transjordan, Iraq, Syria, and Lebanon—invaded Palestine. Although the population of the Arab states involved in the fighting was forty times larger than that of the infant Jewish state, the Arabs were torn by various rivalries and were unable to agree on common objectives. They never succeeded in placing their armies under effective joint command. Meanwhile, the outnumbered Jews profited from their greater cohesion and their paramilitary experience fighting the Palestinian Arabs during the British mandate period. Their war effort was augmented by an influx of men and aid from abroad.

The shooting war stopped January 7, 1949, and by February 24 Egypt had signed a separate armistice agreement with Israel. Lebanon signed the armistice in March, Transjordan in April, and Syria in July. Iraq refused to sign an armistice agreement and simply withdrew from Palestine. When the fighting was over, Israel held over 30 percent more territory than had been assigned to the Jewish state under the UN partition plan. The Palestinian state envisaged by the UN plan never materialized. Israel gained about twenty-five hundred square miles. Transjordan, which annexed territory on the West Bank of the Jordan River and transformed itself into the state of Jordan, gained twenty-two hundred square miles. Egypt took the Gaza Strip, about one hundred thirty-five square miles. Jerusalem was divided between Israel and Jordan. UN armistice commissions were established to police the frontiers, and several demilitarized zones were established between Israel and the bordering Arab states of Egypt, Jordan, and Syria.

The United Nations also set up the United Nations Relief Works Agency (UNRWA) to assist Palestinian Arabs who had fled or been driven from their homes. Although the number is disputed, it has been estimated that more than seven hundred thousand Palestinian Arabs who had lived in the area taken over by Israel became refugees.

## Suez Crisis

In an attempt to bring stability to the Middle East and reassure both Israel and the Arab states, the United States joined with Britain and France in issuing the Tripartite Declaration of May 1950. The three powers pledged to limit arms shipments and to oppose any attempt to alter the existing armistice lines by force. Yet the armistice lines were repeatedly violated by Arab commando raids into Israeli territory and retaliatory raids into Arab territory by Israel. The level of hostilities escalated, culminating in a second Arab-Israeli war in 1956.

In the fall of 1955, President Gamal Abdel Nasser of Egypt asked the Soviet Union for military equipment. Moscow began funneling arms to Egypt through Czechoslovakia and quickly became Egypt's major arms supplier. Soviet arms shipments to Egypt in 1955 and 1956 persuaded Israel that it must prepare for a preventive war against Egypt before the military balance shifted in Cairo's favor. Israel's request for U.S. arms was rejected by President Dwight D. Eisenhower who, on March 7, 1956, warned that it could provoke an "Arab-Israeli arms race."

On July 26 Nasser, emboldened by Soviet arms shipments and the withdrawal of eighty thousand British troops from the Suez Canal zone, nationalized the British-run canal and refused to guarantee the safety of Israeli shipping. Nationalization of the canal followed a U.S. refusal on July 20, 1956, to provide Egypt financing for the Aswan Dam, a mammoth project on the Upper Nile intended to furnish Egypt with cheap electricity and irrigation. The United States had been interested in the project, but it withheld assistance when Nasser moved Egypt closer to the Soviet Union.

Nationalization of the canal directly threatened British and French interests. The British government held 44 percent of all shares in the Suez Canal Company; private French investors held more than three-quarters of the remaining shares. In addition, both nations were heavy users of the canal, which provided the shortest waterway to their oil supplies in the Persian Gulf. To them, nationalization was intolerable because Nasser could bar their vessels and British and French investors would suffer financial losses. The two governments froze Egyptian assets and began planning for joint military action, secretly enlisting Israel's participation in the plan.

Israeli armed forces attacked Egypt October 29 and by October 31 had occupied the Sinai Peninsula to within ten miles of the Suez Canal. Britain and France began air strikes against Egyptian targets October 31, and British and French troops joined the battle November 5. By November 7 British and French forces had secured control of the canal.

Despite the close U.S. relationship with Britain and France, President Eisenhower vigorously protested the Suez invasion. He opposed in principle the use of arms to settle the dispute and hoped to improve relations with Egypt and Arab nationalists throughout the Middle East by forcing the allies to withdraw. After intense international pressure from the United States, Britain and France withdrew their forces from Egypt in December 1956. The last Israeli units were not withdrawn from the Sinai until March 1957, and then only when the United States threatened to impose economic sanctions on Israel if it failed to do so.

The U.S. condemnation of the invasion mitigated Nasser's defeat on the battlefield, and the outcome was a severe political and moral setback for Britain and France in the Middle East. In the end, Nasser's stature in the Arab world was bolstered. Despite the U.S. efforts in behalf of Egypt, there was no significant improvement in U.S.-Egyptian relations. The Soviet Union, however, succeeded in portraying itself as a defender of the Arab cause by issuing ultimatums to the British, French, and Israelis to end the invasion after U.S. opposition had already made the allies' withdrawal inevitable.

The 1956 war did not solve the Arab-Israeli territorial conflict and only temporarily altered the military balance in the area. The Soviet Union immediately began replacing the military equipment lost by Egypt during the war. The war increased Arab hostility toward Israel, and Nasser began to successfully promote the concept of Arab unity.

## The Six-Day War (1967)

Middle East tensions exploded again on June 5, 1967, with the start of the Six-Day War. Diplomatic efforts immediately preceding the war had failed to lift a blockade of the Gulf of Aqaba that Egypt's Nasser imposed on May 23. The blockade halted most Israeli shipping and threatened to strangle the Israeli economy. Nasser imposed the blockade following his demand that the UN Emergency Force be removed from the Gaza Strip and the Gulf of Aqaba outpost at Sharm el-Sheikh. The United Nations relented and withdrew the Emergency Force. At the same time, Nasser moved a substantial Egyptian force into the Sinai Peninsula, and Syria, Iraq, and Jordan signed a treaty of mutual defense and began to mobilize their forces.

Fearing an imminent attack, Israel decided to strike first. Its warplanes surprised Egyptian airfields, destroying the bulk of the Egyptian air force on the ground. Then, in a lightning move across the Sinai Peninsula, the Israeli army broke the Egyptian blockade of the Gulf of Aqaba and once again put Israeli soldiers on the banks of the Suez Canal. Hundreds of Egyptian tanks and artillery pieces were destroyed in the Sinai. In the east, Israel's forces ousted Jordanian troops from the old section of Jerusalem and seized control of all Jordanian territory west of the Jordan River. In the north, Israel captured the Golan Heights. For two decades Syria had used these heavily fortified borderland hills to harass Israel's northeastern settlements. (Six-Day War, Chapter 2, p. 26)

The 1967 war substantially altered the political balance in the Middle East. Israel's smashing victory stunned the Arabs and their Soviet backers and left Israel in a position of strength. In contrast to 1956, when Israeli forces were withdrawn in response to strong Washington pressure, Tel Aviv at once announced that Israel would remain in the occupied territories until decisive progress toward a permanent settlement had been made.

A few hours after Israel's initial attack on June 5, Robert J. McCloskey, deputy assistant secretary of state for public affairs, declared that the

*Middle East After 1967 War*

U.S. position was "neutral in thought, word, and deed." The McCloskey statement was criticized by many members of Congress and other supporters of Israel, who pointed to the longstanding ties between the two countries. Later the same day, George Christian, President Lyndon B. Johnson's press secretary, said the McCloskey statement was "not a formal declaration of neutrality." And at a news conference Secretary of State Dean Rusk said the term "neutral" in international law meant that the United States was not a belligerent. He said it was not "an expression of indifference." Nasser, charging that U.S.-made aircraft had contributed to Egypt's defeat, severed diplomatic relations with Washington, as did six other Arab states.

On June 19 President Johnson, in his first major statement on U.S. Middle East policy since the outbreak of the war, outlined a five-point formula for peace in the Middle East. "Our country is committed—and we here reiterate that commitment today—to a peace [in the Middle East] that is based on five principles: first, the recognized right of national life; second, justice for the refu-

gees; third, innocent maritime passage; fourth, limits on the wasteful and destructive arms race; and fifth, political independence and territorial integrity for all." Johnson also said the victorious Israeli troops "must be withdrawn" from the lands occupied during the Six-Day War. But he made it clear he would not press for a withdrawal to prewar lines in every respect.

The Soviets lost significant prestige in the region by not providing the Arabs with much assistance during the Six-Day War. In fact, the Soviet decision to back a cease-fire while Israel was in Arab territories angered the Arabs. The only significant measure that Moscow and its Communist allies took was severance of diplomatic ties with Israel. Partially to make up for its inaction during the war, Moscow rebuilt the armed forces of Egypt, Syria, and Jordan.

On November 22, 1967, the United States voted with the rest of the UN Security Council members in unanimously approving a resolution (Security Council Resolution 242) aimed at bringing peace to the Middle East. The document called for (1) withdrawal of Israeli forces from the occupied Arab areas; (2) an end to the state of belligerency between the Arab nations and Israel; (3) acknowledgment of and respect for the sovereignty, territorial integrity, and political independence of every nation in the area; (4) the establishment of "secure and recognized boundaries"; (5) a guarantee of freedom of navigation through international waterways in the area; and (6) a just settlement of the refugee problem. *(Text of UN Resolution 242, Appendix, p. 395)*

Although UN efforts to end the Arab-Israeli conflict once again foundered, the resolution remained the basis for subsequent UN peace initiatives. Before the 1967 war, the Arabs had insisted that Israel return all lands in excess of the territory assigned to the Jewish state by the 1947 UN partition plan. After the 1967 war, however, the Arabs gradually modified their demands and came to insist only that Israel adhere to the principles of the 1967 Security Council resolution, which they interpreted as calling for Israel to return to its pre-1967 borders.

## No War, No Peace

Sporadic fighting was renewed in 1969 along the Suez Canal front after Egypt repudiated the 1967 cease-fire. During this "war of attrition" period Egypt tried to wear down the Israelis and bring about territorial withdrawals. Although frequently violated, the cease-fire technically continued on the other fronts.

In a departure from previous U.S. policy, the administration of President Richard Nixon agreed early in 1969 to a series of bilateral talks on the Middle East with the Soviet Union as well as to four-power talks including Britain and France. The talks were held throughout the year, but little progress was made.

At the same time, the United States continued to support the efforts of UN envoy Gunnar V. Jarring to mediate a peace settlement. On January 25, 1970, Nixon reaffirmed U.S. support for Israel's insistence on direct peace negotiations with the Arabs. A few days later he asserted that the United States was "neither pro-Arab nor pro-Israeli. We are pro-peace."

With the situation highly volatile, and scattered border clashes continuing, Secretary of State William P. Rogers in June 1970 submitted another proposal for a cease-fire and called for a resumption of UN mediation efforts aimed at implementing the 1967 Security Council resolution. Egypt and Jordan and then Israel agreed to a ninety-day cease-fire, beginning August 8, in conditionally accepting the U.S. formula for peace negotiations.

Once the agreement to seek a peace settlement was announced, however, protests arose in many parts of the Middle East. Arab guerrilla groups and the governments of Syria and Iraq rejected the peace initiative and denounced Nasser for accepting it. In Israel, six members of the Gahal minority party resigned from the cabinet of Premier Golda Meir when she announced the government's acceptance of the Nixon administration's peace formula. Palestinian commandos dramatized their opposition by carrying out a series of spectacular commercial aircraft hijackings.

Hopes for a peace settlement were dashed September 7, 1970, when Israel announced it was withdrawing from the peace talks. Israel's decision followed charges it had made on several occasions (later validated) that Soviet missile batteries had been placed in the Suez Canal cease-fire zone in direct violation of the cease-fire agreement.

Militarily defeated and politically humiliated after the 1967 war, Nasser tried to improve Egyptian prestige and get Israel to pull back from the cease-fire lines. Sporadic fighting with Israel, however, yielded little and exposed Egyptian territory to Israeli air attacks. Nasser, seeking help from the Soviet Union to halt the Israeli raids, persuaded Moscow to provide an air defense system. This commitment was a departure from those of the past because it allowed the introduction of Soviet pilots and troops into Egypt to oversee the installations.

President Nasser died in September 1970. He was succeeded by Anwar Sadat, a relatively obscure and inexperienced man whose view of Egypt's future was not widely known. Unlike Nasser, Sadat was not saddled by guilt over defeat in the 1967 war, but he believed that a no-war and no-peace situation was not in Egypt's long-range interests.

Sadat had his own agenda for Egypt, which did not correspond perfectly with the Soviet Union's regional interests. He wanted and needed to rebuild Egyptian prestige and Arab pride. The Soviet Union was more interested in limiting Western influence in the region, while avoiding a confrontation with Washington. Sadat asked repeatedly and unsuccessfully for increased Soviet military aid to prepare for a war with Israel. The Soviets continued to press for a peaceful solution of the conflict, repeatedly stating their support for UN Security Council Resolution 242.

As Sadat's differences with the Soviet Union became more acute, he concluded that Egyptian and Soviet goals were incompatible. On July 18, 1972, Sadat ordered all twenty thousand Soviet Union military advisers out of Egypt. Sadat's action severely damaged the Soviet position in the Middle East. The Soviet Union responded by expanding ties to Syria, Iraq, and the Palestine Liberation Organization (PLO).

## October War (1973)

The "no-war, no-peace" stalemate held until October 1973, when Arab frustrations over the deadlock triggered the fourth Arab-Israeli War on October 6. Egypt and Syria launched an attack on Yom Kippur, the holiest day of the Jewish calendar. Egyptian and Syrian troops broke through Israel's forward fortifications and advanced into the Sinai Peninsula and the Golan Heights.

The war that began on October 6, 1973, has different names. In Israel it is known as the Yom Kippur War. The Arabs sometimes call it the War of Ramadan, since it began during their month-long period of daytime fasting. As in 1967, Israel had good intelligence that troops were being mobilized for a possible strike. However, Israeli leaders were sternly warned by President Nixon that if Israel dealt the first blow, it could not rely on U.S. assistance during the war.

Despite the success of the initial Egyptian and Syrian strikes into Israeli-occupied territory, Israeli forces recovered. They broke through the Egyptian lines and drove to the western bank of the Suez Canal. On the other front, they advanced to within twenty miles of the Syrian capital of Damascus. Nixon carried out a massive airlift of war materiel, the prolonged fighting having stretched Israeli resources to their limits.

To avoid further defeat and humiliation of the Arabs, the United States and the Soviet Union joined in pressing for an end to the fighting. Following a visit by Secretary of State Henry A. Kissinger to Moscow, a joint U.S.-Soviet resolution calling for an immediate cease-fire and implementation of the 1967 UN Security Council Resolution 242 was presented to the Security Council October 21. Egypt and Israel agreed, and the cease-fire was expected to go into effect the next day.

But the fighting continued, and Egyptian president Sadat, concerned for the fate of his army, called on both the United States and the Soviet Union to send in troops to enforce the cease-fire. On the evening of October 24 Soviet general secretary Leonid Brezhnev sent a message to Nixon proposing joint U.S.-Soviet supervision of the truce. Brehznev warned, "If you find it impossible to act together with us in this matter, we should be faced with the necessity urgently to consider the question of taking appropriate steps unilaterally." The proposal was rejected by the United States, which preferred a plan setting up a UN observer force without big-power participation.

In the early morning hours of October 25, U.S. armed forces were placed on worldwide alert in response to the possibility of a unilateral move by the Soviet Union to send troops to the Middle East. The crisis was defused later that day when Moscow agreed to a Security Council resolution establishing an international peacekeeping force without the participation of the five permanent members of the Security Council.

## Kissinger "Shuttle Diplomacy"

American diplomacy was instrumental in bringing about a cease-fire between Egypt and Israel and then, under the Ford and Carter administrations, a series of agreements that led finally to a peace treaty between the former belligerents. Secretary Kissinger negotiated a six-point cease-fire agreement on November 11, 1973, that was signed by Egyptian and Israeli military representatives at kilometer 101 on the Cairo-to-Suez road.

On December 21, 1973, largely through Kissinger's efforts, the Geneva Conference on an Arab-Israel peace was convened in accordance with UN Security Council Resolution 338 establishing the cease-fire. The talks were attended by the Soviet Union, the United States, Israel, Egypt, and Jordan. Syria boycotted the conference.

The first round of the conference ended the following day with an agreement to begin talks on separating Israeli and Egyptian forces along the Suez Canal. Egypt and Israel signed a troop disengagement accord January 18, 1974, and the troop withdrawal was completed March 4. Meanwhile, efforts to negotiate a similar agreement between Israel and Syria were concluded May 31. In early 1975 Kissinger sought a second-stage disengagement in the Sinai Desert, but after fifteen days of shuttling between Egypt and Israel he declared in March that his efforts had failed.

The Soviet Union's position as cosponsor of the Geneva negotiations would mark Moscow's last involvement with the Middle East negotiations until the opening of the Madrid Conference in 1991. The United States proved itself to be an honest broker even with its close ties to Israel, and it was able to improve its position in many parts of the Arab world as a result.

When Kissinger returned from his shuttle talks, he and President Gerald R. Ford let it be known they were upset with Israel's negotiating position and that the United States would begin a "reassessment" of its policy in the Middle East. Consideration of Israel's request for $2.5 billion in U.S. aid was suspended until completion of the reassessment, a thinly veiled form of pressure on the Israeli government to be more forthcoming in talks with Egypt.

### Second Sinai Accord

Negotiations began again in June 1975. President Ford met first with Sadat in Salzburg, Austria, and then with Israeli ambassador to the United States Yitzhak Rabin in Washington. This time the talks proved to be more successful. As the culmination of Kissinger's shuttle diplomacy, a second Sinai disengagement pact was signed by Israeli and Egyptian representatives on September 1. Israel agreed to withdraw from the Sinai mountain passes and to return the Abu Rudeis oil fields to Egypt in return for Egyptian political concessions. The United States agreed to station an observation force in the Sinai.

Compared with the basic issues of recognition of Israel, the future of the Palestinians, permanent boundaries, the status of Jerusalem, and peace guarantees, the issues settled in the Sinai troop disengagement accords were minor. In two respects, however, the accords accomplished a major breakthrough. First, they introduced Americans into the midst of the Arab-Israeli conflict. Somewhat hesitantly, Congress approved the stationing of U.S. technicians between the Israeli and Arab

armies to monitor military activities. Second, they established a modest basis of trust necessary to pursue more basic issues.

The second disengagement agreement also resulted in considerable tension among the Arab parties to the conflict. President Assad and the PLO vigorously denounced Sadat for agreeing to what amounted, in their view, to a separate, though partial, peace with Israel.

When Arab unity was restored at the end of 1976, a new Arab strategy began to emerge. By presenting a moderate image to the world, Sadat and most of the Arab leaders hoped to affect U.S. policy and create the conditions for resumption of the Geneva negotiations. Even the Palestine Liberation Organization began to make gestures, however ambiguous, indicating a willingness to accept the existence of Israel if the occupied territories were returned to the Palestinians.

## Egyptian-Israeli Peace

By 1977 it was widely recognized that the United States had become the key outside participant in the Middle East conflict. "The U.S. holds 99 percent of the cards," Sadat said repeatedly. Accordingly, the Arabs launched a major diplomatic effort in 1977 to persuade the United States that the Arabs no longer challenged Israel's existence but did oppose its 1967 occupation of Arab lands and its refusal to recognize "Palestinian rights." In February 1977 Sadat said in an interview, "I want the American people to know that never before have the prospects for peace been better. Not in the last twenty-eight years—since Israel was created—have we had a better chance for a permanent settlement in the Middle East. We must not lose the chance."

It was in this atmosphere of renewed hope for achieving a comprehensive peace settlement that newly elected Israeli prime minister Menachem Begin came to the United States on July 19, 1977, for two days of talks with President Jimmy Carter. Although the atmosphere was cordial, it was clear that the new American administration and the new Israeli government were far apart on many important issues. Not only did Begin refuse to even consider agreeing to a Palestinian homeland, he also was elected on a platform of never returning the West Bank and Gaza to Arab sovereignty.

The initial Carter strategy for achieving a comprehensive peace settlement focused on reconvening the Geneva Conference, which had met in December 1973. The Soviet Union responded favorably, and the result was a joint statement on the Middle East, issued October 1, 1977, calling for a conference "not later than December 1977" to work out a full resolution of the Arab-Israeli conflict "incorporating all parties concerned and all questions."

The Israeli reaction to the prospect of bringing the Soviet Union into the forefront of the peace negotiations was negative. In addition, the radical Arab governments in Algeria, Iraq, and Libya still rejected any direct negotiations with Israel. Israeli officials opposed the idea because, among other factors, they feared the Soviets might succeed in drawing the PLO into the negotiations.

The Egyptian reaction to the joint statement was equally cool. Since 1972, when Sadat had expelled Soviet military advisers from Egypt, relations between Cairo and Moscow had turned increasingly sour. A Geneva Conference cochaired by the Soviet Union was no more appealing to Sadat than it was to Israel. The unpleasant prospect of another conference was seen by some observers as one reason behind Sadat's momentous decision to visit Jerusalem and proffer his terms for peace.

## Initial Peace Efforts

In addition to Sadat's desire to preempt Soviet involvement in the Middle East peace process, other reasons have been cited for his dramatic visit to Jerusalem on November 19, 1977. Analysts speculate that Sadat was motivated by his belief that if the Middle East conflict degenerated again into war the Arabs would suffer a 1967-type defeat, his fear of a radical upheaval in economically depressed Egypt, and his desire to get U.S. economic aid.

The Carter administration was taken by surprise by Sadat's initiative and only later gave its full support to the peace effort, in effect abandoning the comprehensive approach and supporting direct Egyptian-Israeli discussions for a separate agreement between those two nations. Sadat's Jerusalem visit was followed by meetings between Israeli and Egyptian officials in Cairo. Then the leaders of the two nations met on December 25 in Ismailia, Egypt, where Begin presented his West Bank proposal. It offered only local "autonomy" for the Palestinians over a five-year period. Israeli troops and settlements were to remain. The plan contained no mention of eventual sovereignty for the West Bank, a critical point with Sadat.

## Camp David Summit

The talks ended in a stalemate, and lower-level discussions over the next few months were unproductive. As negotiations broke down, the United States undertook a series of emergency attempts to rescue the situation, among them sponsoring a foreign ministers' conference at Leeds Castle outside London on July 18, 1978. The meeting was attended by American secretary of state Cyrus R. Vance, Israeli foreign minister Moshe Dayan, and Egyptian foreign minister Muhammad Ibrahim Kamel. Although Vance saw some flexibility in the discussions, the conference failed to produce concrete results. In August, with Egypt and Israel renewing strong criticism of one another, President Carter became concerned that the impasse could jeopardize the fragile relations between the two nations and wreck any chance for peace in the Middle East. He then invited the two leaders to Camp David, the presidential retreat in Maryland, for informal face-to-face talks aimed at breaking the stalemate. Both accepted immediately.

Carter's decision to call the Camp David summit was widely seen as a brash gamble that paid off beyond all expectations. The announcement of the summit came in August, when the president's popularity was at a low point. In thirteen days of arduous negotiations, Carter persuaded Sadat and Begin to make compromises that led to an agreement. Both Sadat and Begin later said Carter's firmness was the key to the breakthrough. The accords reached at Camp David essentially represented agreements to agree, rather than an actual settlement of the difficult issues dividing the two nations or the even broader disputes between Israel and other Arab nations. "This is one of those rare, bright moments of history," Carter declared as the historic accords drafted at Camp David were signed September 17 by Prime Minister Begin and President Sadat. There were two agreements at Camp David, one dealing with Israeli withdrawal from the Sinai Peninsula and peace arrangements between Israel and Egypt; the other a "framework" for settling the future of the West Bank and Gaza.

By the end of 1978, however, that success was threatened by a renewal of the discord. As negotiations continued and the euphoria of the Camp David summit dissipated, both Israeli and Egyptian leaders found that agreeing to the specifics of a treaty while under pressure from domestic groups who opposed a settlement was more difficult than agreeing to a "framework" in the seclusion of the presidential retreat in the Maryland mountains. Carter repeatedly expressed frustration that Israel and Egypt would quibble over what he viewed as minor issues. But to both sides, none of the issues were minor. Israeli and Egyptian leaders were being asked to resolve disputes that had been perpetuated by years of hostility and to give up positions they considered essential to their national interests. In return for a peace treaty, Israel was asked to give up territory that for more than eleven years had served as a buffer against one of its major enemies. Egypt was pressured by other Middle East nations not to sign a separate peace treaty with what they considered to be the Arab world's common enemy.

## Egyptian-Israeli Peace Treaty

Shortly after the Camp David accords were signed, Secretary of State Vance optimistically predicted that a treaty establishing peace between Egypt and Israel could be concluded by November 19—the anniversary of Sadat's 1977 visit to Jerusalem. It soon became obvious, however, that negotiating the treaty would be a slow process. Predictions of a treaty signing were pushed back to December 10, the date Sadat and Begin were to receive the Nobel Peace Prize, and then to December 17, the date specified in the Camp David agreement. As the end of the year approached, officials stopped predicting when the treaty would be concluded.

Even before the treaty negotiations began, disagreements developed over what actually had been said and agreed on at Camp David. Before Begin had left the United States after the Camp David summit, he and Carter locked horns over the terms of an agreement on Israeli settlements on the West Bank and Gaza. Begin said Israel could establish new settlements after a three-month moratorium, but Carter said Begin had agreed at Camp David not to establish any new settlements during the five-year transition period. While they were being pressured by the United States to reach a final agreement, both Sadat and Begin also came under intense pressure at home not to make concessions. Other Arab nations, including Jordan and Saudi Arabia, warned Sadat not to renounce Palestinian rights in the rush toward a peace treaty. In Israel, Begin was sharply criticized for his apparent willingness to abandon Israeli claims to some of the territories occupied in the 1967 war.

As negotiations proceeded, the main question became whether, and to what extent, the peace treaty between Egypt and Israel would be linked to the West Bank and Gaza issues. The United States and Egypt insisted that the treaty be linked to the resolution of the occupied territories issue. Israel wanted the treaty but did not want to include provisions dealing with the occupied territories. Begin fueled the Palestinian controversy early in the negotiations by announcing plans to expand Israeli settlements on the West Bank. Those plans were bitterly protested by Carter and Sadat and then put aside, where they simmered throughout the peace talks.

At a summit meeting in Baghdad November 2-5, 1978, the hard-line Arab countries charged Sadat with treason, then offered Egypt $5 billion if Sadat would cut off negotiations with Israel. Sadat refused the offer, making it clear he expected assistance from the United States instead. American officials were distressed that Saudi Arabia and Jordan, two moderate Arab nations, joined in the hard-line attacks on Egypt.

The Israeli cabinet on November 21 finally accepted a vaguely worded link between the peace treaty and the West Bank-Gaza issues, but it flatly rejected any timetable for elections. With the disagreement over a timetable unresolved, the United States early in December offered a compromise that would have put the issues in a "side letter" rather than in the treaty itself. Under that compromise, the two sides would have agreed to begin negotiations on the West Bank and Gaza within a month of ratification of the peace treaty. A target date of December 31, 1979, was proposed for elections in the territories.

Throughout the negotiations, the PLO rejected all the timetables and self-rule proposals. PLO leader Yasir Arafat said his group was the only true representative of the more than one million Palestinians on the West Bank and Gaza. He rejected Sadat's claim that the Egyptian leader was negotiating on behalf of the Palestinians.

Just as important as the PLO objection was the refusal of Jordan's King Hussein to participate in the negotiations. Jordan had administered the West Bank before the 1967 war, and the Camp David accords were based on the assumption that Hussein would participate in the peace settlement.

Implicit in the negotiations was the assumption that the United States would provide substantial aid to both Egypt and Israel once a peace treaty was signed. Although peace in the Middle East generally was accepted as being in the long-term interest of all parties, the short-term costs were heavy for both Israel and Egypt. Israeli officials estimated that moving its military forces from the Sinai Peninsula to the Negev Desert in southern Israel would cost approximately $3 billion over three years, a huge sum for that nation. To help pay for that move, and for other costs of peace, the Israelis asked the United States for an additional

$3.3 billion over three years. At Camp David, Carter committed the United States to building two replacement military bases for Israel in the Negev.

For his part, Sadat quietly spread the word that he expected the United States to pay a major share of the cost of economic development in Egypt, possibly as much as $10 billion to $15 billion over five years. The United States had been providing Egypt $1 billion a year.

After preliminary discussions among Vance, Israeli foreign minister Moshe Dayan, and Egyptian premier Mustafa Khalil in February 1979, Carter suggested that Begin and Sadat meet with him in a second round of summit talks at Camp David. The two leaders declined. Faced with the possible collapse of the treaty talks, Carter then invited Begin to meet with him alone in Washington. Begin accepted, and the talks opened March 1. Before leaving for the United States, Begin said Israel and Egypt remained far apart and accused the Carter administration of supporting Egyptian proposals that were "totally unacceptable to us." Among the points at issue were Sadat's insistence on Israeli acceptance of Palestinian autonomy for the West Bank and Gaza within a year; deletion of a clause in the Camp David accords giving an Israeli-Egyptian peace treaty priority over Egyptian treaties with other nations; and a delay, until all other treaty issues were resolved, in discussing Israel's request that Egypt supply Israel with oil from the Sinai oil fields. On February 17 Sadat said Egypt would make no further concessions in the peace treaty negotiations and that it was "now up to the Israelis."

On March 5 Carter announced that he would press his personal mediation efforts by visiting Cairo and Jerusalem. A White House statement said: "There is certainly no guarantee of success, but ... without a major effort such as this the prospects for failure are almost overwhelming." Carter's Middle East trip bore fruit. After agreeing to most aspects of the compromise proposals put forward by the American president, the Israeli cabinet March 14 approved 15-0 the two remaining points that had blocked an agreement. The

Egyptian cabinet approved them the next day. Under the terms of the agreement, Israel accepted an arrangement whereby Egypt would sell it 2.5 million tons of oil a year for an "extended period." For its part, Israel agreed to submit a detailed timetable for withdrawing its forces from the Sinai.

The Israeli Knesset gave its overwhelming approval of the treaty on March 22. The vote was 95-18. Both Carter and Sadat hailed the Knesset's action. On March 26, 1979, Israel and Egypt formally ended the state of war that had existed between them ever since Israel declared its independence in 1948. *(Egyptian-Israeli Treaty of Peace, text, Appendix, p. 396)*

The treaty provided for the normalization of relations between Egypt and Israel. It implemented the "framework" for a treaty agreed on at Camp David. Annexes to the treaty spelled out the details of further negotiations on trade, cultural, transportation, and other agreements and of a phased Israeli withdrawal from the Sinai Peninsula. Egypt and Israel were to undertake negotiations on the future of the West Bank and Gaza. The negotiations on Palestinian self-rule, to be supervised by the United States, were to begin one month after the formal exchange of treaty ratification documents and were to be completed within one year. The treaty did not mention East Jerusalem, occupied by Israel since 1967 and claimed by both Israel and Jordan. Egypt insisted that East Jerusalem was part of the West Bank and thus subject to negotiation. Israel rejected that view.

## Security, Oil Agreements

Two hours after the peace treaty was signed, Secretary Vance and Foreign Minister Dayan signed a "memorandum of agreement" providing specific American assurances to Israel if the treaty fell apart. The memorandum reaffirmed, and broadened, U.S. assurances given Israel at the time of the 1975 Sinai disengagement agreement.

If the treaty were violated, the memorandum stated, the United States "will consult with the parties with regard to measures to halt or prevent the violation. . . ." And the United States "will take such remedial measures as it deems appropriate, which may include diplomatic, economic and military measures. . . ."

The agreement brought a sharp protest from Egypt. In a letter to Vance, Egyptian prime minister Khalil said Egypt was "deeply disappointed to find the United States accepting to enter into an agreement we consider directed against Egypt." The agreement "assumes that Egypt is the side liable to violate the treaty," Khalil said. In a March 28 statement, Sadat said the memorandum violated the Israeli-Egyptian accord and that it "could be construed as an eventual alliance against Egypt." The State Department issued a response saying Khalil's complaints were "based on a misreading of the document." The agreement "does not assume that Egypt is likely to violate the pact," the response said. Carter administration officials emphasized that the specific pledges would be carried out only in response to a violation of the treaty by either Israel or Egypt, and it insisted the agreement did not constitute an alliance or a mutual defense treaty with Israel.

Potentially one of the most controversial assurances given by Carter to Israel was the guarantee to supply oil. At the time of the September 1975 Sinai agreement, President Ford agreed to guarantee Israel an adequate oil supply for a five-year period if that nation's normal supplies were cut off. As an incentive to sign the peace treaty, Carter agreed to extend the guarantee to fifteen years. Under the agreement, the United States was to supply Israel with enough oil "to meet all its normal requirements for domestic consumption." The promise was contingent on the United States' being able to obtain enough oil "to meet its normal requirements." Israel was to pay the United States "world market prices" for any oil supplied under the emergency agreement.

## Aftermath of the Treaty

On May 25, 1979, in keeping with the agreed timetable, Sadat and Begin met in Beersheba to begin the Palestinian autonomy negotiations. The goal of the first stage was full autonomy for the West Bank and Gaza under a freely elected self-governing authority that would serve for a five-year transition period. Agreement on the region's final status was reserved for a second stage to begin not later than three years after the self-governing authority was inaugurated.

Several meetings were held in 1980 but little progress was made. Sadat suspended Egyptian participation in mid-August after the Knesset passed a law confirming Jerusalem's status as Israel's "eternal and undivided capital." Early in 1981 Israel requested a resumption of the talks, but the new U.S. administration reacted cautiously. President Ronald Reagan's position contrasted sharply with the policies of the Carter administration, which had placed great emphasis on the negotiations and, through its special envoy, had been instrumental in keeping the negotiations alive.

The Israeli Sinai withdrawal was more successful. Under the terms of the treaty, once withdrawal was completed in April 1982, the United States was obligated to organize a peacekeeping force if the United Nations did not do so. Subsequently, the United Nations declined, largely because of opposition from the Soviet Union. "Normal relations" between Egypt and Israel officially began January 26, 1980, by which time Israel had withdrawn from two-thirds of the Sinai. Borders were opened between the two countries, travel was permitted, and embassies were established.

When the peace treaty was signed in March 1979, there was little doubt that the so-called hard-line Arab states—Algeria, Iraq, Libya, South Yemen, Syria, and the Palestine Liberation Organization—would indulge in virulent condemnation of the treaty. Both Egypt and the United States anticipated some criticism from traditionally pro-Western, pro-Sadat Arab nations such as Saudi Arabia, Jordan, Morocco, and the Persian Gulf states. The so-called moderates might not like the treaty, but, it was thought, they would seek to minimize any anti-Sadat or anti-American measures demanded by the hard-liners.

However, a day after the Washington signing, nineteen members of the Arab League—Algeria, Bahrain, Djibouti, Iraq, Jordan, Kuwait, Lebanon, Libya, Mauritania, Morocco, the Palestine Liberation Organization, Qatar, Saudi Arabia, Somalia, Syria, Tunisia, the United Arab Emirates, the Yemen Arab Republic (North Yemen), and the Yemen People's Democratic Republic (South Yemen)—met in Baghdad and adopted a package of tough political and economic sanctions against Egypt. Of the twenty-two Arab League members, only Oman and the Sudan, close allies of Sadat, boycotted the meeting. Egypt was not invited. Within weeks, all of the Baghdad participants had severed diplomatic ties with Egypt. Egypt was also expelled from the Arab League, the Islamic Conference, and many other Arab international organizations.

## Gulf Security

During the 1970s, while the United States was pursuing a negotiated peace between Israel and its Arab enemies, it also was strengthening its strategic relationship with Iran and Saudi Arabia. These two nations, which successive U.S. presidents saw as bulwarks against potential Soviet expansion southward, were allowed to buy billions of dollars of sophisticated U.S. arms.

The United States began an arms supply relationship with Saudi Arabia in the 1950s, but it was the Nixon administration in the early 1970s that made the oil-rich kingdom one of the "two pillars" of U.S. policy in the Persian Gulf region. Between 1950 and 1987, Saudi Arabia purchased more than $30 billion of U.S. defense articles. Much of this was spent on sophisticated aircraft and ultramodern air, naval, and army bases.

The Shah Muhammad Reza Pahlavi, the leader of Iran, was considered to be one of Washington's most important allies because of the close proximity of Iran to the Soviet Union, the growing U.S.-Iranian trade relationship, and close military and intelligence cooperation. Moreover, the U.S.-Israeli friendship was not an impediment to the United States' relationship with the shah, as it sometimes was with Saudi Arabia and other Arab nations.

## Hostage Crisis

The Middle East had been the setting for President Carter's most celebrated foreign policy achievement. But late in 1979, less than eight months after the signing of the Egyptian-Israeli peace treaty, the Iran hostage crisis paralyzed the Carter administration and created its biggest foreign policy embarrassment.

Although U.S. arms sales had strengthened the shah militarily, by the late 1970s his repressive regime faced enormous domestic opposition. On January 16, 1979, the shah left Iran for what turned out to be a permanent exile. The Iranian revolution was capped by the return to Iran of the exiled charismatic religious leader Ayatollah Ruhollah Khomeini on February 1. On April 1 of that year, Iranian voters approved the establishment of an Islamic republic. *(Iranian revolution, Iran profile, p. 216)*

On November 4, 1979, Iranian students seized the U.S. embassy in Tehran, taking sixty-six hostages. Thirteen of the hostages were released later in the month and one hostage was released in July 1980. But fifty-two Americans were held for 444 days. The students demanded that the shah, who was receiving medical treatment in the United States, be returned to Iran to stand trial. The students were backed by Khomeini and his Revolutionary Council.

Carter took several steps to pressure Iran to free the hostages. On November 14, 1979, he froze all Iranian assets in domestic and overseas branches of U.S. banks. In April 1980 he severed relations with Iran and instituted trade sanctions. On April 25 a U.S. rescue mission ended in disaster after it was aborted because of equipment failure. Two of the departing aircraft collided on the ground and eight U.S. servicemen were killed. The shah died of cancer in Egypt on July 27, but the hostage crisis continued, fueled by the virulent anti-American sentiments of the Iranians and the exploitation of those sentiments by Iran's leaders for domestic political purposes.

The frustration of the American people at Carter's inability to free the hostages contributed to his defeat in the 1980 election by Ronald Reagan. The hostages were not released until January 20, 1981, a few minutes after Reagan took the presidential oath of office. Following release of the hostages, Reagan largely ignored Iran during his first term, aside from ritual denunciations of terrorism and calls for an end to the Iran-Iraq War.

## Soviets in Afghanistan

On December 24, 1979, less than two months after the U.S. embassy in Tehran had been seized, the Soviets invaded Afghanistan in force to prop up a pro-Soviet government in that country. The invasion took the United States by surprise. Carter said in a December 31 television interview that the invasion changed his opinion of the Soviets more than any other event. On January 20, 1980, he called the invasion the "most serious threat to peace since the Second World War."

Although the Soviet invasion of Afghanistan did not constitute a strike into the heart of the Persian Gulf oil producing region, it was seen by many analysts as a serious threat to the security of the Persian Gulf and its oil supplies. With the Soviets in Afghanistan and the Iranian hostage crisis ongoing, the Carter administration elevated the importance of Persian Gulf security.

On January 23 Carter announced what would become known as the Carter Doctrine. In his State of the Union Address, he warned that "An attempt by any outside force to gain control of the Persian Gulf region will be regarded as an assault on the vital interests of the United States of America, and such an assault will be repelled by any means necessary, including military force." The statement was a direct challenge to the Soviet Union.

Ironically, Moscow's Afghanistan adventure did not advance Soviet interests in the Middle East, but rather it set them back. Islamic nations, including Iran and Saudi Arabia, regarded the Soviet invasion as proof of Soviet aggressiveness and lack of respect for Islam. The Soviet Union retained influence with some Arab states through its arm sales and its ability to act as a counterweight to the United States, but Soviet credibility was severely damaged. Saudi Arabia and the small Gulf states, in particular, moved toward a closer relationship with the United States in response to the Soviet invasion.

## Reagan Policies

During President Reagan's first term, his administration continued efforts toward mediating a Middle East peace. It concentrated on getting Jordan and "moderate" Palestinians into the peace process with two goals in mind: a second peace treaty between Israel and an Arab country, and an agreement giving Palestinian residents of the West Bank some form of political autonomy.

Almost from its first days in office, the Reagan administration was forced by events to focus on Lebanon, a country that had suffered nearly ten years of civil war and occupation by Syrian and Israeli troops and the forces of the Palestine Liberation Organization. American prestige and power in the region suffered badly in the early 1980s when the Reagan administration's diplomatic and military efforts failed to bring peace to war-torn Lebanon. Moreover, continued hostility toward Israel by the Arab states wiped out the optimism engendered by the 1979 peace treaty between Israel and Egypt. The 1981 assassination of Egyptian president Sadat removed from the scene America's most loyal and important ally in the Arab world. Meanwhile, the political consensus at home on the policies the United States should pursue in the region disintegrated. As the administration shifted from diplomacy and mediation to an increased reliance on the use of American troops and large arms sales to moderate Arab states, the administration and Congress clashed repeatedly.

President Reagan brought to office a vigorous anti-Communist view of the world. In his campaign he had charged that earlier administrations were too accommodating to the Soviet Union and had allowed America's strength and reputation to decline. He identified Moscow as the source of most major international political problems, including those in the Middle East. Reagan, in con-

trast to Carter, placed relatively little importance on the role of Third World nations in U.S. foreign policy. The focus of Reagan policy, rather, was on countering communism.

Reagan viewed Israel as the most reliable friend in the region, and he believed Israel's democratic system made it a natural ally for the United States. Few of Reagan's senior advisers had Middle East experience. During the first months of the administration, important Middle East policy-making posts remained vacant. An overall U.S. approach to the Middle East would not emerge until after Israel's invasion of Lebanon in June 1982. The Arab-Israeli conflict was placed on a back burner, partly because the administration wanted to wait for the upcoming Israeli elections and partly because there was no pressing need to do otherwise.

### Strained Relations with Israel

Despite President Reagan's inclinations toward a close relationship with Israel, Israeli air strikes in mid-1981 against Iraq and Lebanon precipitated a temporary U.S. suspension of F-16 aircraft deliveries to Israel. The use of American-made jets in the raids raised the touchy question of whether Israel had violated a U.S. law limiting U.S. arms to defensive purposes. But beyond that, the air strikes had political repercussions in the United States, raising doubts about Israel's normally unquestioned support in Congress and in the country.

Using American F-16 fighter bombers escorted by F-15 fighters, Israel on June 7, 1981, attacked and quickly destroyed the Osirak nuclear reactor under construction near Baghdad, Iraq. Israeli prime minister Begin called the raid "an act of supreme, legitimate self-defense," claiming Iraq planned to use the facility to produce nuclear weapons that would threaten Israel. Critics, including many members of Congress, labeled the strike as aggression and accused Begin of launching the raid to bolster his chances in Israel's June 30 general election. The Reagan administration June 10 suspended delivery of four F-16s scheduled to be shipped to Israel June 12. Not since

Eisenhower in the 1950s had an American president postponed aid in response to an Israeli action.

Nevertheless, this demonstration of U.S. displeasure did not alter the fundamental relationship between the United States and Israel. On June 16 President Reagan said Israel appeared to have violated the defense-only legal requirements but added, "I do think one has to recognize that Israel had reason for concern in view of the past history of Iraq."

In July 1981 Reagan broadened the suspension of F-16 aircraft deliveries to Israel amid intense clashes between Israel and the PLO in southern Lebanon, where Israel had implemented air and commando raids to quell PLO artillery and rocket fire against Israeli border settlements. Although the attacks and counterattacks spanned nearly two weeks, the catalyst for Reagan's action was Israel's July 17 bombing of a PLO headquarters in downtown Beirut—an air strike that reportedly killed more than three hundred persons and wounded eight hundred.

The most direct U.S. criticism of Israel came July 23 from Deputy Secretary of State William P. Clark, who said Begin "is making it difficult for us to help Israel. Our commitments are not to Mr. Begin, but to the nation he represents." Defense Secretary Caspar W. Weinberger said Begin's actions "cannot really be described as moderate at this point." The Beirut attack also damaged (at least temporarily) Israel's support in Congress.

On August 24 U.S.-Israeli relations were strained further when Reagan formally notified Congress of his intention to sell Saudi Arabia five Airborne Warning and Control System (AWACS) planes. He had first signaled the possibility of such a sale on April 21.

Nevertheless, within several months, propelled by the desire of Secretary of State Alexander M. Haig, Jr., to form a "strategic consensus" to counter Soviet expansion in the region, Israeli prime minister Begin met with Reagan in September 1981 to discuss improved ties.

At the end of November, Israeli defense minister Ariel Sharon met with American defense secretary Weinberger to make final a "strategic memorandum of understanding." The memorandum was designed to counter Soviet-inspired political instability and pledged the signatories to meet threats in the Middle East "caused by the Soviet Union or Soviet-controlled forces from outside the region." It provided for military cooperation and coordination between Israel and the United States, but it did not obligate the United States to aid Israel if the Jewish state were attacked by the Arab states.

Although the agreement was hailed by the Likud party in Israel, the opposition Labor party was critical, claiming that it did nothing to ensure Israel's security and only committed Israel to defending U.S. interests in the region.

Debate over the merits of the agreement would soon become irrelevant. On December 14, 1981, the Israeli Knesset voted 63-21 to extend Israeli law to the Golan Heights, thereby annexing the territory it had occupied since 1967. Reagan strongly criticized the action and, in response, ordered that the memorandum of understanding with Israel not be implemented.

## Israel Invades Lebanon

On June 6, 1982, Israeli armed forces invaded Lebanon with the stated purpose of creating a twenty-five-mile-wide buffer zone in southern Lebanon free of Palestinian guerrillas. In the initial stages of the war the United States appeared ambivalent toward the Israeli moves. However, after Israel went beyond its self-declared twenty-five-mile limit the administration begin to voice opposition to Israeli actions.

The administration's immediate concerns were to prevent the war from expanding to include Syria. Philip Habib—President Reagan's special envoy who had already conducted a number of the negotiations between the Arabs and Israelis—was sent back in an effort to prevent hostilities from expanding. On June 9 Israel and Syria fought a massive air battle over Lebanon's Bekaa Valley, in which Israel destroyed Syrian surface-to-air missiles and decimated the Syrian air force. After this crippling blow, Moscow through Syria and Washington through Israel were able to prevent Syria

# Reagan Policy Foundered in Lebanon Morass

In 1982 President Ronald Reagan sought to assist peace efforts in Lebanon by sending a contingent of American marines to Beirut. This led to a near constitutional confrontation at home, the deaths of several hundred marines, and the evaporation of U.S. public support for an American role in the Lebanese morass. The president was left with little choice but to pull out the marines and concede political influence in Lebanon to Syria.

By August 1983 the U.S. Marine contingent in Lebanon had grown to eighteen hundred. On August 29 two marines were killed by artillery fire from Druze Muslim forces fighting the U.S.-backed Christian government. This sparked a movement in Congress to force the president to invoke the War Powers Resolution. That law, passed over President Richard Nixon's veto in 1973, set a ninety-day limit on any presidential commitment of U.S. troops abroad without congressional authorization. Reagan, however, argued that the U.S. forces were "essential to the objective of helping to restore the territorial integrity, sovereignty, and political independence of Lebanon." It was not possible to predict how long the marines would have to stay in that country, he said.

Congressional leaders of both parties insisted the president invoke the War Powers Resolution and acknowledge the right of Congress to share in setting the terms of the marine deployment. The president opposed any invocation of the War Powers Resolution and, like other presidents before him, questioned the law's constitutionality. A compromise was reached in which Reagan signed a joint resolution invoking the War Powers Resolution and imposing an eighteen-month limit on the deployment. In turn, the president declared in writing that he did not recognize the validity of the War Powers Resolution and that he retained his constitutional authority as commander in chief to deploy U.S. forces. The joint resolution was approved by Congress September 29 and signed by Reagan October 12, 1983. Events in Lebanon quickly diminished the relevance of the compromise.

On October 23 a suicide truck bomb attack on the marine headquarters killed 241 Americans. The deaths of the servicemen erased what support had existed for a long-term commitment of U.S. troops in Lebanon. A group calling itself the Islamic Revolutionary Movement claimed responsibility for the barracks bombing. The president, however, laid much of the responsibility for the attack and Lebanon's troubles on Soviet-backed Syria. Reagan suggested that U.S. abandonment of Lebanon might lead to a Middle East "incorporated into the Soviet bloc."

Some members of Congress argued that the president appeared to be shifting his reasons for U.S. involvement in Lebanon. Sen. Patrick J. Leahy, D-Vt., said the U.S. role originally "was a peacekeeping mission" but, as explained by Reagan, had become an effort "to stop the spread of communism."

The administration position was undercut by the December 1983 report of a blue-ribbon Pentagon panel that concluded that the marines could not perform their avowed role of neutral peacekeepers, partly because warring Lebanese factions no longer saw them as "even-handed and neutral" because of the gradual involvement of U.S. military units in direct combat assistance of the Lebanese armed forces controlled by President Amin Gemayel, a Maronite Christian. The government's force was seen by rival religious factions as an arm of the right-wing Maronite Christian "Phalange" faction in the struggle for power, the commission said.

By year's end, after other American soldiers had been killed in the first direct military clash between U.S. and Syrian forces in Lebanon, Congress was rapidly backing away from its September agreement to keep the marines in Lebanon through mid-1985. House Democrats reached general agreement February 1, 1984, on a nonbinding resolution calling on Reagan to order the "prompt and orderly withdrawal" of the marines, a move Senate Democrats endorsed the next day.

On February 7 Reagan announced that the sixteen hundred U.S. Marines in Lebanon would be moved in stages to ships offshore. In a March 30 letter to Congress, the president said he was ending U.S. participation in the peacekeeping force in Lebanon. With the departure of the marines and the near collapse of the Gemayel government, Syria emerged once again as the dominant force in Lebanon.

and Israel from engaging in an all-out ground war. On June 11 Israel and Syria signed a cease-fire, thus ending the brief encounter between the two. Even though the administration opposed Israel's invasion it seemed to support some of its goals. U.S. officials said they would seek the withdrawal of all foreign forces from Lebanon. This expansion of the original U.S. request that Israel pull out of the country reflected Israel's goal of ending the PLO and Syrian presence in Lebanon.

In spite of Israel's original claim only to a twenty-five-mile buffer zone, its armed forces continued their advance until they reached the outskirts of Beirut and surrounded thousands of PLO guerrillas in West Beirut. Quiet opposition to Israeli actions ended when the Israelis reached Beirut. Reagan made clear that the United States did not want Israel to enter Beirut, an Arab capital.

Divisions within the Reagan administration over Middle East policy widened during the war. Although opposed to the invasion, Haig saw benefits in the Israelis' eliminating the PLO presence in Lebanon and in their pressuring the Syrians to leave. This, he thought, would change the political conditions in Lebanon, enabling the Lebanese government to regain control of the country. Then, on June 24, 1982, Haig abruptly resigned. Most analysts suggest that internal administration conflict over Lebanon war policy was only the final in a long list of reasons for Haig's resignation.

The nomination of George P. Shultz as Haig's replacement was widely seen as portending changes in the administration's view of the Middle East. During Reagan's presidential bid in 1980, Shultz, who had been advising Reagan on other issues, was critical of the candidate's views toward Israel. Shultz stated often that the United States should have a "balanced approach" to the Arab-Israeli conflict.

With the Israelis on the outskirts of Beirut, the administration tried to reassure friendly Arab states that Israel would not enter Beirut. In attempting to negotiate an end to the crisis, Philip Habib managed to conclude a number of cease-fire agreements, all of which were broken almost immediately. Habib eventually secured agreement

for PLO forces to leave Beirut, but the evacuation did not occur until after the Israelis engaged in a day-long bombardment of the city on August 12.

Although the PLO had agreed in principle to leave Beirut, the final agreement was delayed while negotiators hammered out details of the evacuation and searched for a destination. President Hafez al-Assad of Syria refused to allow the PLO to come to his country. Jordan also refused to take the PLO because of tensions dating back to the Jordanian civil war in 1970 when factions of the PLO attempted to overthrow King Hussein.

Finally, Habib was able to get all the parties to agree to a PLO evacuation of West Beirut to various Arab countries, including Syria, that would be monitored by a multinational peacekeeping force of American, French, and Italian troops. In addition, the United States guaranteed the safety of the Palestinians living in the refugee camps in and around Beirut.

The U.S. Marines in the multinational force left Lebanon September 10 after the PLO evacuation was completed. On September 14 Lebanon's president-elect, Bashir Gemayel, was assassinated. In apparent retaliation during the following days, Phalange militiamen massacred hundreds of Palestinian civilians in the Shatila and Sabra refugee camps near Beirut. The violence prompted Reagan to send a contingent of twelve hundred marines back into Lebanon September 29 as part of a multinational peacekeeping force. The president's action was criticized by members of Congress who thought Reagan was evading the requirements of the 1973 War Powers Resolution by refusing to seek congressional approval for the deployment of troops in Lebanon. The War Powers Resolution proscribed the use of U.S. forces in hostile situations for more than ninety days without congressional authorization.

## Reagan's Peace Initiative

In 1982 President Reagan tried to revitalize the Arab-Israeli peace process that began at Camp David in 1978. However, Reagan's Middle

East peace initiative, launched in a televised speech September 1, made little headway. Reagan said the United States would support self-government for Palestinians on the West Bank of the Jordan River and in the Gaza Strip in association with Jordan, but not in an independent state or under Israeli sovereignty. He also called upon Israel to "freeze" further Jewish settlement in the West Bank and Gaza as a prelude to resuming negotiations under the 1978 Camp David accords. He added, however, that Israel could not be expected to pull back totally from the occupied territories.

The president pledged U.S. support for the Camp David plan for an interim agreement to provide self-government for the Palestinians in the West Bank and Gaza for five years while the ultimate status of the territories was negotiated by Israel, Egypt, the United States, and Jordan. "The final status of these lands must, of course, be reached through the give and take of negotiations," Reagan said. "But it is the firm view of the United States that self-government by the Palestinians of the West Bank and Gaza in association with Jordan offers the best chance for a durable, just and lasting peace."

Reagan said the U.S. position was based on the principle "that the Arab-Israeli conflict should be resolved through negotiations involving an exchange of territory for peace," as set out in United Nations Security Council Resolution 242 in 1967. Reagan ruled out the possibility of PLO participation in the negotiations. This continued the long-standing U.S. policy of refusing to recognize or deal with the PLO until that organization repudiated violence and terrorism, accepted Israel's right to exist, and declared its support for UN resolutions 242 and 338. Israel promptly rejected the Reagan plan. Jordan's King Hussein initially gave it cautious support and opened talks with PLO chairman Arafat. But Hussein failed to secure permission from the PLO to negotiate on behalf of West Bank Palestinians, and by April 1983 when the Palestine National Council meeting in Algiers rejected the plan, Hussein backed away from further involvement.

## Lebanon Linkage

The Reagan administration linked its initiative to a resolution of the Lebanese crisis. It viewed the possible resolution of the Lebanese situation as a first step in a broader Middle East peace. Fears grew in Congress, however, that the United States was getting too deeply involved in Lebanon and the lives of marines stationed in that country were in danger. That concern was confirmed when the U.S. embassy in Beirut was the target on April 18, 1983, of a bomb attack that killed sixty-three persons, including seventeen Americans.

The Reagan administration was intent on reducing Syrian influence in Lebanon and moving peace negotiations forward. To achieve these goals, U.S. officials sought an agreement between Lebanon and Israel. A long and difficult series of negotiations, involving top Israeli, Lebanese, and American officials, produced an agreement that in the end came to naught. The agreement, signed in Lebanon and Israel on May 17, 1983, was not called a treaty because the Lebanese were concerned about Arab reaction. Moreover, formal diplomatic relations were not to be established immediately. The agreement did, however, provide for an end to the state of war that had formally existed since 1948, a buffer security zone in south Lebanon to protect Israel, and absorption into the regular Lebanese army of the pro-Israeli militia, led by Saad Haddad, that operated in southern Lebanon. It also ensured Israeli air superiority and established in both countries semi-diplomatic missions that would have immunity privileges. Lastly, the agreement provided for negotiations to reestablish normal relations between the nations.

The United States, in a separate letter to Israel, promised to guarantee the agreement, acknowledged Israel's right to retaliate against attacks from Lebanese territory, and assured the Israelis that they did not have to withdraw until Syria and the PLO pulled out. The pact had a very short life. Even though it was signed by both parties and the Israeli Knesset ratified it, the Lebanese parliament delayed action. The Syrians, who were never part of the negotiations and who saw their influence in

Lebanon being undercut, refused to accept the agreement, which rendered it meaningless. Without a withdrawal by Syria and the PLO, the Israelis would not withdraw. Under increasing Syrian pressure, Gemayel's government abrogated the accord.

American policy in Lebanon continued to focus on preserving Gemayel's government, which was being opposed with increasing hostility from opposition forces within Lebanon. Reagan's limited use of U.S. air and naval power to support Gemayel in late 1983 and early 1984, however, drew increasing criticism from Congress. American air strikes and naval bombardments against Syrian and Lebanese Shi'ite forces appeared only to increase Lebanon's chaos, further endanger U.S. peacekeepers, and undermine the status of the United States as a mediator in the Middle East. On October 23, 1983, 241 U.S. Marine and Navy personnel were killed in Beirut when a suicide truck-bomb crashed into their barracks. Lawmakers, and by extension the public, pressured the administration to withdraw the marines from Beirut and end U.S. military involvement in Lebanon. That withdrawal, announced on February 7, 1984, concluded the American policy of trying to support Gemayel's teetering government. Syrian domination of Lebanese affairs became nearly complete.

## Bouts with Terrorism

Ronald Reagan entered office in 1981 just as the American hostages were being released by Iran. Reagan had vowed that his administration would give no quarter to terrorists. During 1985 and 1986 a wave of Middle East terrorism against the United States and other Western nations dominated headlines, pressuring the Reagan administration to back up with action its hard-line rhetoric toward terrorism. On June 14, 1985, Arab gunmen hijacked Trans World Airways Flight 847 from Athens to Rome with 153 people aboard. The hijackers forced the pilot to fly to Beirut where one American was killed and thirty-nine Americans were held hostage. The hijackers and their Shi'ite supporters demanded, among other things, that Israel release

some seven hundred Shi'ite prisoners it was holding. Over the following two weeks of the crisis U.S. officials avoided both negotiating with the terrorists and publicly pressuring Israel to release the prisoners. Nevertheless, it appeared at one point as though American officials were privately pushing Israel to release its prisoners. The American hostages were released at the end of the month, and Israel began releasing its prisoners. Israeli officials, however, pointedly noted they had intended to release the Shi'ites prior to the hijacking.

A second hijacking in 1985 caused even wider international ripples. On October 14 gunmen identified as being members of the Palestine Liberation Front (PLF), a faction of the PLO, seized the Italian passenger liner *Achille Lauro.* The gunmen surrendered to Egyptian authorities a few days later and released the hostages, but not before they killed an elderly, wheelchair-bound American passenger.

In accordance with its stern antiterrorist campaign, the United States sought to capture the hijackers. American intelligence sources soon learned that the terrorists were on an Egyptian airliner heading first toward Tunisia, where it was denied permission to land, and then to Athens. Under orders from President Reagan U.S. F-14 fighters intercepted the Egyptian airliner and forced it to land in Sicily. There Italian authorities took the hijackers into custody to await trial. Then, much to the United States' astonishment and anger, the Italians released Muhammad Abu'l Abbas, the leader of the PLF, whom the Egyptians said acted as a mediator but the United States claimed was the mastermind of the hijacking.

Although Syria and Iran had been implicated in supporting terrorist activities, the Reagan administration focused its antiterrorism efforts on Libya. That nation was of less importance to American strategic interests than Iran and did not have a major role in the Arab-Israeli peace process like Syria. Moreover, the fanatical and unpredictable ideas of Libyan leader Col. Muammar Qaddafi and Libya's aggression in Africa had alienated many Arab governments and caused the Soviets to keep their Libyan allies at arm's length.

Military action against Libya, therefore, was likely to involve fewer risks than action against Iran or Syria.

In 1985 Abu Nidal, a terrorist leader who had defected from the mainstream of the PLO, moved his base of operations from Syria to Libya. In December 1985 members of his group attacked the check-in counters of El Al airlines at the Rome and Vienna airports with automatic weapons and hand grenades. They killed eighteen persons and wounded more than one hundred. On January 7, 1986, Reagan announced that there was "irrefutable evidence" that Libya had supported the Palestinian terrorists who carried out the attack. He ended all economic activity between the United States and Libya and ordered all American citizens to leave Libya. The next day he froze Libyan assets in the United States. The United States had little success, however, in persuading its European allies to enact similarly tough sanctions against Tripoli.

In March, Reagan ordered the U.S. Navy to conduct maneuvers in the Gulf of Sidra off the coast of Libya in defiance of Qaddafi's declaration that the gulf was Libyan territorial waters. During the maneuvers Libya fired antiaircraft missiles at U.S. planes. In response, U.S. planes bombed several Libyan ships and a Libyan missile installation.

The U.S. show of strength in the Mediterranean, however, did not deter further terrorist violence. On April 2 a bomb blew a hole in the side of a TWA jet over Greece, killing four people. On April 5 a bomb exploded in a Berlin discotheque frequented by American military personnel. The blast killed two persons, including an American soldier, and wounded more than two hundred.

After intelligence indicated that Qaddafi played a role in the Berlin attack, Reagan ordered an air strike against Libya. On the night of April 14 U.S. F-111 bombers based in Britain and carrier planes in the Mediterranean staged a large-scale raid on Libya. The warplanes' targets included a naval academy, air bases, and Qaddafi's home and headquarters. The raid killed at least fifteen people, including Qaddafi's infant daughter, and injured sixty.

One U.S. F-111 bomber was shot down, and its two crewmen were killed. The attack was overwhelmingly supported by the American public and Congress. A *Washington Post*-ABC News poll showed 76 percent of Americans surveyed approved of the strike. The U.S. attack, however, did not receive the same approval overseas. The British government was the only European government to support the bombing, which was widely condemned in the Arab world. France had refused to allow U.S. bombers based in Britain to fly over its territory. Moscow canceled a scheduled visit to Washington by Foreign Minister Eduard Shevardnadze to protest the strike.

The raid did not end terrorist attacks against the United States. Indeed, on April 17 one American and two British hostages in Lebanon were found executed in retaliation for the attack, and the same day an Arab tried unsuccessfully to smuggle a bomb on board an Israeli airliner in London. Nevertheless, Libyan involvement in terrorism appeared to decline after the raid.

### Iran-Contra Scandal

In addition to bombings and hijackings, the Reagan administration had to contend with the kidnappings of Americans by pro-Iranian Shi'ite groups in Lebanon. During 1984 and 1985 nine Americans had been kidnapped there. Although a few had been released, the Shi'ite groups continuously held several Americans captive.

The administration was particularly concerned with the fate of William Buckley, the CIA station chief in Beirut, who was kidnapped in March 1984. Intelligence reports indicated that Buckley was being tortured to extract his knowledge of U.S. antiterrorist operations. While not of the magnitude of the 1979 Iranian hostage crisis, the plight of Buckley and the other American hostages in Lebanon frustrated the Reagan administration and led it to seek their release through methods that conflicted with the administration's policy of not dealing with terrorists.

In 1985 the Reagan administration began considering secret arms sales to Iran through Israel as a way to win the release of U.S. hostages and open a dialogue with "moderate Iranians." Reagan authorized three shipments of U.S. antitank and antiaircraft missiles from Israel to Iran in the late summer and fall. The shipments coincided with the release of one U.S. hostage in September 1985.

On January 17, 1986, President Reagan signed a secret finding authorizing a covert U.S. diplomatic initiative to Iran. The document identified three goals of the plan: "(1) establishing a more moderate government in Iran, (2) obtaining from them significant intelligence not otherwise obtainable, to determine the current Iranian Government's intentions with respect to its neighbors and with respect to terrorist acts, and (3) furthering the release of the American hostages held in Beirut and preventing additional terrorist acts by these groups." During 1986 U.S. representatives communicated with Iran through intermediaries and on one occasion traveled to Iran to seek the release of hostages in Lebanon. During these dealings the United States transferred (with Israel's assistance) additional arms and spare parts for military equipment to Iran. Although two American hostages were released during 1986, three more were kidnapped to take their place.

On November 3 a pro-Syrian Beirut magazine reported on the secret trip by U.S. representatives to Iran earlier in the year. This disclosure led to investigations in the United States that uncovered the Iranian initiative and forced Reagan to admit on November 13 that the United States had shipped arms to Iran. Although Reagan insisted that he had not traded arms for hostages, the initiative appeared to undercut his administration's policy of not negotiating with terrorists. Moreover, critics charged that Reagan had undermined U.S. standing in the Persian Gulf region, where moderate Arab nations such as Saudi Arabia had been opposing Iran in its war with Iraq. The revelation that the world's leading antiterrorist had sent arms to a nation that had been implicated in terrorist activities weakened U.S. credibility and international determination to fight terrorism.

On November 25 the Iranian initiative was further complicated by the disclosure that National Security Council officials had used some of the proceeds from the arms sales to aid the Nicaraguan contra rebels, despite a U.S. law prohibiting such assistance. This revelation transformed what had been an embarrassing and contradictory policy into a full-fledged scandal. Although a number of his top-level aides were implicated, no conclusive evidence was found that Reagan himself had known of the diversion of funds to the contras.

In 1987 U.S. ships began escorting reflagged Kuwaiti vessels through the Persian Gulf. The Reagan administration hoped the naval escorts of ships threatened by the continuing Iran-Iraq War would restore confidence in the United States among the Gulf states, put pressure on Iran to end the fighting, and ensure the flow of oil from the Gulf. The escorts brought U.S. ships and planes into direct conflict with Iranian forces on a number of occasions. American naval forces destroyed several Iranian ships and oil platforms in retaliation for Iranian attacks and minings in the Gulf.

The U.S. presence, however, did lead to tragedy on July 3, 1988, when the USS *Vincennes* mistook an Iranian airliner for an attacking Iranian warplane and shot it down after the airliner failed to respond to several warnings. All 290 passengers and crew were killed.

Later in July, Reagan's high-risk policy in the Gulf was partially vindicated when Iran accepted a cease-fire in the eight-year war with Iraq. Although the U.S. naval presence in the Gulf had not been the dominant factor in pushing Iran to end the war, the escorts had helped to check Iranian aggression in the Gulf and reestablish some measure of U.S. credibility with the Gulf states. The cease-fire officially began on August 20, allowing the United States to reduce its naval presence in the Gulf.

## Intifada and the Shultz Plan

Middle East peacemaking efforts were given a new impetus in December 1987 by the Arab uprising in the West Bank and Gaza. This uprising, known as the *intifada,* differed from previous violence in the occupied territories in that it pervaded all areas of the West Bank and Gaza and became a permanent feature of life there. Palestinian youths armed with stones daily confronted Israeli soldiers. *(Intifada in the Arab-Israeli conflict, Chapter 2, p. 51)*

In response to the intifada, Secretary of State Shultz took up Middle East peacemaking with a new urgency in early 1988. He made several trips to the Middle East, where he shuttled between capitals promoting his plan to start Arab-Israeli negotiations. His plan called for talks between Israel and a joint Palestinian-Jordanian delegation. By the fall the two sides were to agree on arrangements for local elections that would give Palestinians in the occupied territories some autonomy over their affairs for a period of three years. By December the parties were to begin talking about what and how much occupied territory Israel would eventually relinquish. The plan also called for an international peace conference attended by all five permanent members of the UN Security Council, including the Soviet Union. Shultz's plan was not greeted enthusiastically by the Likud government, which opposed the idea of giving up occupied territory.

In July, King Hussein surprised the international community and dealt a blow to Shultz's peace proposal by renouncing Jordan's claims to the West Bank and relinquishing administrative responsibility for it to the PLO. Hussein's action virtually foreclosed Jordan's participation in the peace process, which many Israeli and U.S. leaders had regarded as essential for progress toward a settlement. With Hussein out of the picture and U.S. and Israeli elections approaching in the fall, Shultz's peacemaking efforts made no progress.

## U.S.-PLO Dialogue

In a 1975 memo to Israeli leaders, Secretary of State Henry Kissinger had reaffirmed the policy of three U.S. administrations that the United States would not negotiate with the PLO until it renounced terrorism, acknowledged Israel's right to exist, and accepted UN resolutions 242 and

338. Successive administrations abided by this approach to the PLO. Yasir Arafat and his organization refused to meet U.S. conditions, and the United States along with Israel rejected any participation by the PLO in Middle East negotiations.

In late 1988, however, Arafat was being pushed to adopt a more moderate stance toward Israel and peace negotiations by the Soviet Union, Egypt, Jordan, and other moderate Arab states. The intifada had not only raised questions about the viability of the Israeli occupation of the West Bank and Gaza but also had increased international sympathy for the Palestinian cause. The PLO determined that it could best take advantage of the intifada by being less confrontational and searching for recognition of a new Palestinian state. Meanwhile, the renunciation of Jordan's ties to the West Bank by King Hussein in July 1988 had caused the United States to take a more careful look at the prospect of negotiating with the PLO. *(Hussein's Renunciation of Claims to West Bank, text, Appendix, p. 399)*

On November 15, 1988, in Algiers, the Palestine National Council (PNC) declared the existence of an independent Palestinian state. The PNC accepted UN Security Council resolutions 242 and 338 but issued ambiguous statements about its willingness to recognize Israel and renounce terrorism. The U.S. State Department rejected contentions by the PLO that it had satisfied U.S. conditions for a U.S.-PLO dialogue. Nevertheless, the PNC's statements led to a month of diplomatic activity in which the PLO inched its way toward meeting the U.S. conditions.

On November 26 progress toward a U.S.-PLO dialogue appeared to be scuttled when Shultz announced that he would deny Arafat a visa to enter the United States to address the United Nations. The General Assembly, however, voted overwhelmingly to hold a session in Geneva, Switzerland, so Arafat could address the body. In Arafat's UN speech on December 13 he came closer than ever before to uttering the precise words that Shultz wanted to hear, but Shultz again rejected Arafat's statement as insufficient.

Then on December 14 Arafat held a hastily

arranged press conference in which he "renounced" rather than just "condemned" terrorism,
accepted UN resolutions 242 and 338 without
qualification, and affirmed "the right of all parties
concerned in the Middle East conflict to exist in
peace and security, including the states of Palestine, Israel and their neighbors." Four hours later
Shultz announced that Arafat's words had finally
satisfied U.S. conditions and that "the U.S. is
prepared for a substantive dialogue with the
PLO." Shultz instructed the U.S. ambassador in
Tunisia to begin negotiations with representatives
of the PLO. *(Arafat Statement on Israel, Terrorism, text, Appendix, p. 401)*

Although little progress was made in the negotiations between the PLO and the United States
during their first eight months, the talks significantly changed the Middle East peace process.
They reaffirmed the position of the United States
as the dominant outside peacemaker in the Middle
East and made Palestinian nationalism more sensitive to American opinion. The meetings between
Israel's closest ally and its most bitter enemy also
put pressure on Israeli leaders to construct peace
proposals of their own. In addition, the talks gave
Yasir Arafat's Fatah branch of the PLO something to lose if it engaged in terrorist acts, since
the dialogue was conditioned on a PLO renunciation of terrorism.

## Bush Administration

Even with its early protests over Israel's use of
American weapons and the opening of a dialogue
with the PLO, a move the Israeli government
vigorously protested, the Reagan administration's
Middle East policy was characterized by its strong
support of Israel. The election of George Bush,
Reagan's two-term vice president, seemed to promise continuity in U.S.-Israeli relations and Washington's approach to achieving Middle East peace.
But it became evident early on that Bush and his
foreign policy team would be less patient with
Israel than Reagan had been.

At two congressional appearances in March
1989, Secretary of State James A. Baker III said
that Israel some day might have to negotiate with
the PLO about the status of the occupied territories, an approach that the Israeli government had
consistently rejected. Then in a May speech to the
American-Israeli Public Affairs Committee, a
powerful pro-Israel lobbying group, Baker said:
"For Israel, now is the time to lay aside, once and
for all, the unrealistic vision of a greater Israel.
Israeli interests in the West Bank and Gaza—
security and otherwise—can be accommodated in
a [peace] settlement. Forswear annexation; stop
settlement activity; allow [Arab] schools to reopen;
reach out to the Palestinians as neighbors who
deserve political rights."

Although Baker's comments came within a
speech that was pro-Israeli and he was reiterating
longstanding U.S. positions, his blunt tone angered
Israeli leaders and caused staunch American supporters of Israel to worry that the Bush administration was trying to put more distance between itself
and the Jewish state.

While increasing the pressure on Israel to nego-
tiate, the Bush administration nevertheless maintained the traditional strong U.S. support of Israel
at the United Nations. On June 9 Bush vetoed a
UN Security Council resolution that denounced
Israel for violating the human rights of Palestinians in the occupied territories. In addition, the
Bush administration opposed efforts to grant the
PLO the status of a state in UN organizations.
When the PLO petitioned for membership in the
World Health Organization (WHO), an affiliated
agency of the United Nations, the United States
threatened to withhold its contribution to the
WHO as well as to any other international orga-
nization that admitted the PLO.

### Shamir Election Plan

After a summit in April, Israeli prime minister
Yitzhak Shamir feared that Bush might accept the
longstanding Arab demand for an international
peace conference—where Israel perceived itself at
a disadvantage. As an alternative, Shamir advanced a plan to hold elections in the occupied
territories to select local Palestinians who would

represent their people in peace negotiations with Israel. Many Palestinian leaders as well as conservative Israelis had rejected the idea, but Bush immediately backed it as the best option for advancing the peace process. Jordan's King Hussein gave a qualified endorsement to the proposal in April 1989.

On June 8 Ambassador Robert H. Pelletreau, Jr., the U.S. envoy to Tunisia who was holding regular talks with the PLO in Tunis, urged the PLO to accept Shamir's election plan. The PLO refused to endorse the plan but indicated some interest in it. Administration officials had hinted that if the PLO accepted the Israeli election proposal, the United States would upgrade its dialogue with the PLO to higher-ranking officials.

Ariel Sharon, the leader of the right wing of Shamir's own Likud party, however, opposed the plan and maneuvered to force Shamir to accept conditions that most observers believed would make it unacceptable to any Palestinian leader. On July 5, before a Likud party convention, Shamir accepted the hard-line conditions of party conservatives, which stated that Arab residents of East Jerusalem could not vote in the elections or run for office; no elections would be held until the Palestinian uprising ended; Israel would not give up any territory and no Palestinian state would ever be established; and Jewish settlements would continue to be built in the occupied territories. Because the riders were backed by a large faction of his party, Shamir could not reject them without risking a no-confidence vote from his party. The Labor party, the junior member of Israel's unity government, threatened to resign over the riders, but it did not do so, partly because the United States urged it to remain in the government.

The Bush administration responded to the Likud's move by warning that if the vote plan were crippled by unreasonable conditions it might have to consider organizing an international conference to reinvigorate the Middle East peace process. Secretary of State Baker told reporters July 8, "Our calculus all along has been that if things totally bog down, if you can't make progress with this election proposal, then we would have to look

a little bit more closely at the prospects for an international conference. There is an awful lot of support for that out there from other countries. We have always said that an international conference, properly structured, at the right time, might be useful."

In response to the new conditions, PLO leader Arafat announced his organization would no longer consider supporting the plan.

In early September, nearly six months after Shamir's plan was initially floated, Egyptian president Hosni Mubarak offered a ten-point proposal to bring together Israeli and Palestinian negotiators in Cairo. Movement on Shamir's plan had halted and Mubarak hoped to restart the process on a new track. After struggling with Mubarak's proposal for several weeks, the divided Israeli government finally rejected it on October 6 over the proposed rules for the composition of the Palestinian delegation.

## Bush Struggles with Lebanese Hostages

By 1989 eight Americans were being held hostage by pro-Iranian groups in Lebanon. With a civil war between Christians and Muslims raging, authority in the country had effectively fallen into the hands of the many private militias. Despite extensive efforts, no American hostages had been released since 1986, when it was disclosed that the Reagan administration had sent arms to Iran in the hope that Tehran would use its influence to have hostages freed in Lebanon.

For some time, Iran had been indicating its desire to improve relations with the United States. Bush repeatedly made clear, however, that no improvements could be made until the hostages were released. Beginning in late April, several of the American hostages were released, with Bush making a point of publicly thanking Iran and Syria for their efforts.

On July 28, 1989, Israeli commandos abducted Sheik Abdul Karim Obeid, a spiritual leader of the pro-Iranian Shi'ite Hizballah group that was holding several Americans and Israelis hostage in Lebanon. In response, a Shi'ite organization released a videotape that purported to show the hanging of Lt. Col. William R. Higgins, a U.S. Marine being held hostage in Lebanon.

American investigators determined that the man in the video was Higgins, although they could not verify when he had been hanged. The Shi'ite group threatened to kill another hostage unless the Israelis released Obeid. The Israelis offered to trade Obeid and other Shi'ite prisoners for all Israeli and Western hostages being held by the Shi'ites. The Bush administration, while saying it would not make concessions to terrorists, explored ways to release the remaining U.S. hostages in Lebanon and welcomed an offer in August from the Iranian government to help secure their freedom.

## Soviet Immigrants

For decades, the United States had pressed the Soviets to allow Jews and other oppressed groups to freely emigrate. The trickle that was permitted to leave was automatically offered refugee status in the United States on the presumption that they had a "well-founded fear of persecution." Beginning in 1989, the trickle became a flood as Soviet emigration restrictions were relaxed.

In response to the wave of immigrants and because of the internal changes in that country, refugees from the Soviet Union were no longer admitted without specific proof of persecution. On October 1 President Bush capped Soviet immigration at fifty thousand a year, redirecting much of the flood to Israel, where the immigrants were welcomed with open arms. The same day, Israel announced that it did not have the resources to handle the huge influx and formally asked the United States for $400 million in loan guarantees so that it could borrow money cheaply to build housing for the new arrivals.

By January 1990 immigration had accelerated to more than one thousand a week. Noting that a "big Israel" would be needed to handle the flood of immigrants, Shamir indicated that the refugees could be a factor in Israel's decisions regarding the status of the occupied territories. "This is

the best thing that could happen to Israel," he declared.

In response to fears that Likud would use the influx to further settle the occupied territories, Shamir said, "The Government has no specific policy of directing immigrants to Judea, Samaria [the biblical names for the West Bank] and the Gaza Strip, just as it is incapable of preventing immigrants from opting for living in those places. . . . Every immigrant is free to choose his place of residence as he pleases." Nevertheless, huge new settlements began to appear in the territories. Arab countries, the United States, and the Soviet Union became alarmed that the growth of the settlements might lock in the West Bank as a permanent part of Israel. King Hassan II of Morocco declared that "the nightmare of Soviet Jews' emigration to the occupied territories, haunting the Arab nation, is considered a catastrophe." Soviet leader Mikhail Gorbachev began to hint that the flow of refugees would be cut if they were being settled on the West Bank.

In February 1990 Moscow bowed to Arab pressure and—despite U.S. appeals—refused to allow direct flights from Moscow to Tel Aviv, which would have accelerated the flow even further. American Jewish groups feared that in the unstable Soviet Union political forces might quickly turn against the refugees and the flow could be stopped at any time. Thus they sought every means to move the immigrants out of the USSR as fast as possible.

## Stalled Diplomacy

On March 13, 1990, Israel's National Unity Government fell when Prime Minister Yitzhak Shamir dismissed Finance Minister Shimon Peres, head of the Labor party, and the rest of the Labor party ministers followed him out of the government. This left Shamir as head of a caretaker government until new elections could be held. The immediate cause of the collapse was American efforts to restart the peace process.

Baker had proposed that Israel allow one Palestinian with a second address in East Jerusalem to be on the negotiating team. Likud and Labor's disagreement over accepting this proposal led to the collapse. Earlier in the month, Bush had stated that "the foreign policy of the United States says that we do not believe there should be new settlements in the West Bank or in East Jerusalem." Likud officials later said that accepting the Baker proposal in light of President Bush's statement could be seen as backing down from their stance that the status of Jerusalem is not negotiable.

On June 8, after elections in which Likud came out ahead of Labor by a razor-thin margin, Shamir announced the formation of a new government coalition of Likud and several small rightist parties, the most conservative government ever in Israel. Sharon, an outspoken advocate of expanded settlement in the occupied territories, was appointed housing minister, in charge of a massive program of building new housing for the refugees still pouring in. With Shamir one of the most moderate members of the government, few observers expected a serious return to the peace process.

On June 13 Shamir laid down new and more rigorous preconditions for Palestinian negotiators, prompting a furious rebuke from Baker. If that is going to be the Israeli approach, Baker stated, "there won't be any dialogue and there won't be any peace, and the United States of America can't make it happen." If the Israelis did not make a good-faith effort to restart the process, Baker said, then the United States would simply "disengage" from Middle East diplomacy and Shamir could "call us when you are serious about peace."

On June 20 President Bush announced the suspension of the eighteen-month-old U.S. dialogue with the PLO as a result of an attempted May 30 terrorist attack against Israel. Six speedboats carrying Palestinian guerrillas tried to attack a beach in Tel Aviv but were thwarted by Israeli forces. Although he distanced himself from the attack—responsibility for which was taken by the Lebanon-based Palestine Liberation Front—PLO chairman Arafat refused to condemn the attack, despite repeated U.S. prodding.

Robert Pelletreau, the American ambassador to Tunisia, who was conducting the talks, stated that the United States was operating under the assumption that Arafat spoke in the name of the PLO and its eight constituent groups and that it was the PLO's responsibility to exercise control over those groups. In the event of a terrorist action by one of its members, Washington expected the PLO to publicly condemn the action and discipline those responsible. Despite the setback for the peace process, Bush felt that he had no choice but to break off the talks, given Arafat's weak response to the attack. Combined with the hard line taken by the new Israeli government, most observers felt that the peace process was essentially stopped. Neither side seemed able or willing to make the necessary gestures to break the deadlock. For emphasis, at the same time that Bush announced the end of talks with the PLO, he repeated Baker's statement that the Israelis should "call us" when they get serious about peace.

During 1990 the flow of immigrants increased to more than ten thousand a month, holding close to this level through 1991—even during the Gulf War. On June 24, as a result of further U.S. and Soviet pressure, the Israeli government stated that as a matter of policy it would not settle immigrants on the West Bank or Gaza Strip. Nevertheless, the settlements in the territories continued to grow.

On October 2, after a full year of hesitation, Baker announced that the United States had agreed to provide Israel with the requested $400 million in housing loan guarantees as a result of private assurances that none of the aid would be used in the territories. Relations between the United States and Israel, which had steadily worsened since Bush's inauguration, warmed noticeably.

## Persian Gulf War

The invasion and occupation of oil-rich Kuwait by Iraq in August 1990 set in motion a crisis that would remain at the forefront of the international agenda for seven months. President Bush responded to the invasion by pulling together an international coalition authorized by the United Nations Security Council to oppose Iraq. Nearly forty nations contributed combat forces, transport assistance, medical teams, or financial aid to the joint effort to force Iraq from Kuwait. The Persian Gulf crisis was the first major test of the effectiveness of the UN Security Council to confront international aggression in the post-Cold War era. *(Persian Gulf War, Chapter 4, p. 120)*

In his August 8 speech announcing the first deployment of U.S. forces in Saudi Arabia, President Bush declared:

Four simple principles guide our policy.

First, we seek the immediate, unconditional, and complete withdrawal of all Iraqi forces from Kuwait.

Second, Kuwait's legitimate government must be restored to replace the puppet regime.

And third, my administration, as has been the case with every president from President [Franklin D.] Roosevelt to President [Ronald] Reagan, is committed to the security and stability of the Persian Gulf.

And fourth, I am determined to protect the lives of American citizens abroad.

Bush and Secretary of State Baker directed a major diplomatic initiative aimed at Security Council adoption of a resolution to authorize the use of force against Iraq if it did not withdraw from Kuwait. The campaign culminated in the Security Council's adoption on November 29 of Resolution 678, which set January 15 as the deadline for Iraq to pull out of Kuwait. After that, the resolution authorized member states to use "all necessary means" to enforce previous UN resolutions demanding the withdrawal.

Congress supported the president's actions from the start of the crisis, but at times the support was wary. Lawmakers generally endorsed Bush's economic embargo against Iraq and his deployment of hundreds of thousands of troops to Saudi Arabia to ward off a possible Iraqi invasion of that country. But many members opposed an early resort to force, hoping instead that the pain of severe economic sanctions would force Iraq to abandon Kuwait.

Most Americans backed Bush's initial deployments of troops to Saudi Arabia. As the crisis continued, however, public support for Bush's strategy weakened as fears of a recession and a long stalemate in the desert increased. A *New York Times*/CBS News public opinion poll taken October 8-10 showed that 57 percent of Americans supported the president's Gulf policies, as compared with 75 percent in early August.

## War Decision

Many journalists, politicians, and scholars who followed the administration's policy explanations commented that Bush had failed to make a coherent case for the need to use force if Iraq refused to withdraw from Kuwait. The difficulty the Bush administration was having in explaining its actions stemmed partly from the nature of the Iraqi threat and partly from the administration's haphazard presentation of the motivations behind its policy.

Saddam Hussein's invasion of Kuwait certainly did not threaten American shores. Instead, it threatened U.S. interests overseas, the international economy, and principles of international law. No single reason for going to war against Iraq was entirely compelling by itself. The Iraqi invasion required citizens to weigh a complex balance sheet of variables for and against the use of force, instead of responding to a ringing cry to arms in the interest of national defense. Moreover, for Americans who saw Iraq as a threat but had doubts about the wisdom of war, continuing a policy of enforcing severe economic sanctions against Iraq offered a compromise option through which a person could oppose both Saddam's barbarous acts and the launching of what might be a very bloody war in the desert.

During the crisis the Bush administration expanded on the reasons the president cited in his August 8 speech for his strong response to Iraq's invasion of Kuwait. Often the justifications were moral. Bush announced that the United States would not stand for Iraq's brutal aggression against Kuwait. The administration cited Iraq's duplicity before the invasion; Kuwait's peaceful history; reports of atrocities by Iraqi troops; and Iraqi efforts to depopulate Kuwait, strip it of its valuables, and annex it to Iraq. Bush stressed that the Iraqi invasion was an opportunity to establish a "new world order" in which collective action would deter and combat aggression and uphold international law. In mid-November growing concerns among Americans about the economy led the Bush administration to emphasize the importance of liberating Kuwait to the economic health of the nation. Secretary of State Baker said November 13 that the administration policy in the Gulf was motivated by economic concerns: "If you want to sum it up in one word, it's jobs. Because an economic recession worldwide, caused by the control of one nation—one dictator, if you will—of the West's economic lifeline [oil], will result in the loss of jobs for American citizens."

Similarly, when public opinion polls in late November showed that Americans were more concerned about Iraq's potential for developing nuclear weapons than any other aspect of the Gulf crisis, administration officials focused on the Iraqi nuclear threat. Bush aides noted that Iraq's aggressive nuclear research program could succeed in developing rudimentary nuclear weapons within several years. Some experts disputed that Iraq could build nuclear weapons that quickly, but the prospect of a nuclear-armed Iraq some time in the future was a potent argument for going to war against Iraq.

The deployment of large numbers of American forces in Saudi Arabia also triggered a constitutional debate on the division of war powers between the executive and legislative branches in the United States. Most lawmakers asserted that because the responsibility to declare war rested with Congress, the president did not have the power to launch a military offensive against Iraq without prior congressional approval—unless Iraq attacked U.S. forces. The administration disputed this assertion, claiming that the president's role as commander in chief empowered him to order offensive actions against Iraq.

The president, however, promised to consult closely with Congress with regard to his Gulf policy. In January 1991, when war became likely and Bush appeared to have enough votes in Congress to win approval for the war option, he sought to unite the government and the country behind his policies by asking Congress to authorize an attack against Iraq if one became necessary in his judgment. The request satisfied most members of Congress that the president had not usurped their war-making role.

In early January last-ditch diplomatic efforts to persuade Iraq to withdraw failed. As the U.S.-led coalition prepared for war, Congress debated resolutions authorizing the president to use force to expel Iraq from Kuwait. The debate concluded January 12 with the adoption of identical resolutions (S J Res 2, H J Res 77) authorizing Bush "to use United States armed forces" to end Iraq's "illegal occupation of, and brutal aggression against, Kuwait." The Senate voted 52-47 for approval; the House vote was 250-183.

Once the UN deadline had passed, Bush acted swiftly. On January 16 he ordered coalition forces to begin a sustained bombing campaign against Iraq. On February 24, after thirty-eight straight days of bombing, the allies launched a ground offensive into Kuwait and Iraq that overwhelmed Iraqi defenders with surprising ease. On February 27 Bush announced a cease-fire and declared Kuwait liberated.

## Aftermath of the War

By most measures the U.S.-led coalition's war against Iraq was enormously successful. Kuwait was liberated and the legitimate Kuwaiti government was restored to power; coalition forces sustained fewer casualties than almost anyone predicted; Iraq's offensive military potential and nuclear weapons research facilities suffered a serious setback; the wave of terrorism that Saddam had threatened to loose upon his enemies had not appeared; and the international community had demonstrated that it could collectively respond to aggression.

The victory was less complete than it might otherwise have been, however, because Saddam Hussein managed to retain power despite the ravages his leadership had brought to his country. His repression of dissent, frequent purges of the military and his Ba'ath party, and efforts to prevent anyone from accumulating too much authority had blocked the emergence of rival centers of power in Baghdad that could lead a coup against him. Though toppling Saddam had never been a stated purpose of the coalition military effort, his continued belligerence toward his own people and the international community created perceptions that President Bush had stopped the war too soon.

The Bush administration and the United Nations settled into the task of containing a weakened, but still dangerous Iraq. As of the fall of 1994 the United Nations continued to maintain stringent, U.S.-backed economic sanctions against Iraq, and its inspectors engaged in a long-running struggle to force Saddam to reveal and relinquish the elements of his massive effort to develop nuclear, chemical, and biological weapons.

With Saddam still in power, the president's decision to end the war continued to be questioned by the press and rival politicians. Bush's opponents coupled his decision to end the war early with his administration's failure to oppose Saddam before the Iraqi invasion of Kuwait to take some of the luster off his performance as commander in chief.

Even in defeat, Saddam managed to create headaches for the United States and the international community by refusing to cooperate fully with nuclear weapons inspectors sent to Iraq under the terms of the cease-fire agreement. Iraq's conventional military strength had been sharply reduced by the war, but policy makers worried that if it acquired a nuclear weapon it could again menace the region. Inspectors determined that Iraq's program to develop nuclear bombs was far more extensive and advanced than the Bush administration or independent experts had predicted.

## Iraqi Rebellions

Soon after the cease-fire with the U.S.-led coalition forces was declared, Iraq was torn by civil violence. Realizing that much of the Iraqi military's best equipment and some of its best units had been destroyed, Kurdish resistance fighters in northern Iraq and Shi'ite Muslim rebels in southern Iraq began waging open warfare against Iraqi

troops loyal to Saddam. With the war for Kuwait over, Saddam Hussein ordered what was left of his military to put down the rebellions.

During the Persian Gulf War, Bush had repeatedly said he would welcome the overthrow of Saddam. Many commentators noted that his statements may have contributed to the confidence of Iraqi rebels that the United States would come to their aid. But during the postwar insurrections Bush emphasized that he had never promised to intervene in Iraq's "internal affairs."

"We're not going to get sucked into this by sending precious American lives into this battle," Bush said April 4. "We have fulfilled our obligations."

But when the Iraqi army brutally turned back the Kurdish and Shi'ite rebellions, large numbers of Kurd and Shi'ite refugees were placed in peril. The Bush administration took limited measures designed to prevent disaster.

On April 5 Bush announced that U.S. cargo planes would drop food and other relief supplies to Kurdish refugees thronging the mountains along Iraq's border with Turkey. He also earmarked $11 million in relief funds for victims of the Persian Gulf War and for refugees from the failed uprisings against Saddam. The Bush administration announced April 10 that it had warned Iraq the previous weekend to keep its military forces away from a large section of northern Iraq where relief agencies were trying to aid hundreds of thousands of Kurdish refugees.

Democratic critics in Congress, some of whom had originally opposed going to war, urged Bush to take more effective steps to protect the Kurds, including banning Iraqi armed helicopter flights. The anti-Iraq coalition had prohibited any use of Iraqi combat airplanes since the end of the Gulf War, but flights by armed helicopters had not been banned.

Bowing to the necessities of a human tragedy, Bush announced on April 16 that U.S., British, and French forces would go back into Iraq to aid the Kurdish refugees. The administration said that U.S. troops, running supply operations out of Turkey, would construct tent cities in dry, relatively low terrain and then would encourage and assist the movement to those sites of hundreds of thousands of Kurds huddled in cold, inaccessible mountain encampments near the Turkish border.

The deployment of an estimated sixteen thousand U.S., British, and French troops in the resettlement operation risked Bush's commitment to avoid interference in Iraq's internal affairs. But Bush justified the deployment saying, "I think the humanitarian concern . . . is so overwhelming that there will be a lot of understanding about this."

Iraq denounced the U.S. plan April 18 as an interference in its affairs. But the same day it agreed under pressure to a UN plan to conduct relief efforts inside Iraq.

On April 25, the administration sent Congress a letter formally requesting a $150.5 million supplemental appropriation to underwrite "Operation Provide Comfort," as the administration's refugee relief effort was called.

In late April the United States broadened the scope of its relief efforts, providing direct aid for the first time to an estimated 1 million people who had fled from southern Iraq into neighboring Iran. Allied forces also greatly expanded the size of a security zone established for hundreds of thousands of Kurdish refugees. The allies, encountering no resistance from Iraqi forces, created a safe haven for the refugees that encompassed more than eighteen hundred square miles in northern Iraq.

During the week of April 29, Kurds began to leave their squalid encampments in the mountains, some returning to their villages and others staying in a camp constructed by allied troops. But the slow process was complicated by the Kurds' lingering fear that Saddam still threatened their survival.

On May 22 Congress sent the president a $572 million supplemental appropriations bill for fiscal 1991 (HR 2251) that included $556 million in disaster and refugee relief aid, much of it for the Kurdish aid effort. The conference report on the bill (H Rept 102-71) passed the House 387-33. The Senate cleared it by voice vote. President Bush signed the bill (PL 102-55) on June 13.

## Toward a Peace Agreement

The U.S.-led coalition victory over Iraq produced a situation quite different from that called for by the Iraqi-dominated Arab summit of the previous summer. Instead of having its role in the Middle East limited, as the summit wished, the United States emerged from the Gulf crisis with its prestige and influence greatly strengthened, improving the climate for diplomatic achievement. The Bush administration recognized that it now had an opportunity to advance the Arab-Israeli peace process and other U.S. goals.

The American position also had improved because of the continuing disintegration of the Soviet Union. Moscow was increasingly turning inward to address its domestic political and economic crises. Since its withdrawal from Afghanistan, completed in 1989, it had shown much less interest in an assertive role abroad. Soviet allies in the Middle East, especially Syria, could no longer expect financial or diplomatic backing from their patron. The United States was the only remaining superpower. By the end of 1991 the Soviet Union had completely dissolved. Its main successor state was not in a position to project military or financial influence into the Middle East.

Within weeks after the war, Baker began the first of numerous shuttle trips to Middle East capitals. After Baker's meeting with Prime Minister Shamir on March 12—his first official visit to Israel—many observers were surprised that he had not laid down an ultimatum for Israeli attendance at an international conference. In Damascus and elsewhere in the Middle East, Baker's performance was the same. He listened to Assad's and other Arab leaders' requirements for attending a conference and made suggestions of steps they could take to help create the proper atmosphere for negotiations. Yet, as Thomas Friedman of the *New York Times* observed, Baker found doors open but minds sealed.

On April 7 Baker began a second swing through the Middle East during which he began to discuss the specifics of his proposed peace conference. Yet, in a concluding press conference on April 24, he admitted that he still found little support for the conference among Middle East nations, particularly in Israel and Syria. Outside of the region, however, support had begun to develop. Soviet foreign minister Alexander Bessmertnykh announced that the Soviet Union was willing to co-sponsor a conference. The European Community also expressed its interest in attending.

Baker's first breakthrough came with the announcement on May 10 that the Gulf Cooperation Council—which represents Saudi Arabia, Kuwait, Bahrain, Qatar, the United Arab Emirates, and Oman—was willing to send an observer to a peace conference between Israel and its neighbors. This about-face came after a personal appeal from President Bush to the Saudi monarch and represented tangible evidence of the new diplomatic clout the United States wielded in the Middle East.

The real turning point for the conference, however, came with the announcement by Hafez al-Assad on July 18 that Syria would participate, although a number of issues remained regarding the conference format. In the words of Baker, the commitment of Assad, who had long led the Arab rejectionist front opposing direct talks with Israel, "gives us something to work with." Within days, Lebanon and Jordan followed suit—Palestinian willingness to participate had never been in question since they had few other options—and Baker found himself with a full deck of Arab participants. Only Israel's Yitzhak Shamir still refused to commit.

For Shamir, Syria's acceptance created a serious dilemma. Rejecting the conference could well cause irreparable damage to Israel's already sagging relationship with the United States, putting at risk the $3 billion in annual aid Israel received. But attending the conference might cause his fragile right-wing coalition government to collapse.

## The Conference Format

While setting up the conference Baker became bogged down, not in the substance of what the participants would discuss but in the procedural issues and the format. Syria had insisted that any talks be held in the framework of an international conference, with the participation of the United Nations, the United States, and the Soviet Union. This would blur the fact that Syria was doing what it had always refused to do in the past—sitting down at a table with Israel.

Israel rejected such a format, instead calling for the conference to be no more than a one-day ceremonial affair with no UN participation, before proceeding to direct bilateral talks with each of its neighbors. It also rejected Soviet participation until the Soviet Union consented to reestablish the diplomatic ties it had cut off in 1967. From the Israeli view, Palestinians could participate only as part of the Jordanian delegation. Allowing a separate Palestinian delegation might imply that Israel was amendable to the formation of a Palestinian state—something the Shamir government absolutely opposed.

The Syrians ultimately accepted a procedural compromise which was largely on the Israeli terms. The full conference would break up after a day of ceremonial speeches into three bilateral negotiations: Israel-Lebanon, Israel-Syria, and Israel-Jordan/Palestinians. On the question of reconvening, Syrian foreign minister Farouk al-Sharaa blurred this concession by noting that "our interpretation is that a conference in practice does not finish its plenary session until it fulfills its objective. That is peace. It can adjourn, but it does not finish until it fulfills its objective." The UN would be represented at the full conference by a single observer who would not be permitted to speak.

## Shamir Agrees

On July 23, still suspicious that the Syrian concessions were not genuine, Shamir gave Baker a tentative yes to attending the talks, with the condition that he be allowed a veto over the list of Palestinians with whom Israel would negotiate. One of the small parties in his coalition immediately announced its departure from the government, leaving him on shaky political footing. Discussions now turned on Shamir's insistence that no

Palestinians from East Jerusalem could attend, nor anyone with ties to the PLO, which Israel still viewed as a terrorist organization. Shamir was adamant that, since the annexation of East Jerusalem, its status was not a point for discussion and its residents lived in Israel proper, not in the territories. This was especially problematic because much of the Palestinian leadership within the territories lived in East Jerusalem. Nevertheless, with some fine-tuning of the Palestinian delegation still to be worked out, the Israeli cabinet voted on August 4 to attend the proposed conference.

On October 18 the United States and the Soviet Union (severely weakened since the Moscow coup two months earlier) issued formal invitations to a conference to be held October 30 in Madrid. The opening session would last three days and include only ceremonies and speeches. Then, in mid-November, multilateral talks would open for all governments in the region to discuss topics such as arms control, water rights, and the environment.

The same day invitations were issued, Israel and the Soviet Union announced the resumption of full diplomatic relations. Consular ties had been established in 1987 and relations had slowly crept forward from that time. Nevertheless, Israel had long refused to allow the Soviets a role in Middle East peace-making until diplomatic formalities were fully restored. The Palestinian team ultimately was composed according to Israeli specifications, mostly of medical men, writers, and academics from the territories with no real links to the PLO. They would formally be part of the Jordanian delegation. To Israel's frustration, however, a second team of Palestinian "advisers" with close PLO ties also showed up in Madrid to coordinate with the primary delegation.

## Peace Negotiations

On October 30, 1991, the Madrid conference opened as scheduled with speeches by the two sponsors, Presidents Bush and Gorbachev. The following day, representatives of each delegation spoke. The rhetoric, on the whole, was inflammatory, with little to indicate that the sides were in a mood to compromise. For many, it was evident that little more than U.S. pressure was keeping them at the conference. In the words of Lotfy al-Khouli, a well-known Arab columnist, "Everyone is inside the peace cage and the door has been closed. It's an American cage from which Syrians, just like Israelis and Palestinians, cannot really get out. Anyone who thinks otherwise is engaged in wishful thinking."

Shamir opened the second day of the conference by bluntly warning that if the Arabs insisted on proceeding immediately to a discussion of returning the occupied territories, then there was nothing for them to discuss. At a news conference later the exasperated Jordanian foreign minister, Kamal Abu Jaber, responded, "If we can't talk about Jerusalem, if we can't talk about withdrawal, what on earth are we doing here?"

The chief Palestinian negotiator, Haidar Abdel-Shafi, all but dared the Israelis to walk out, invoking the name of Yasir Arafat and referring to "our acknowledged leadership, clearly and unequivocally recognized by the community of nations, with a few exceptions." Nevertheless, no one walked out of the conference.

Invectives peaked in the closing statements. Shamir denounced Syria as having "the dubious honor of being one of the most oppressive tyrannical regimes in the world." Then the Syrian foreign minister accused the Israeli prime minister of being a terrorist and pulled out a British wanted poster from 1947 for a thirty-two-year-old terrorist named Yitzhak Shamir. The opening session was formally completed on November 1. The delegates went home on November 4 with no agreement on where—or if—the talks would resume.

Despite the harsh tone of the conference, most observers were upbeat in their views. One commentator used the metaphor of the talking dog to explain the significance of the conference: It's not what he says that counts, the amazing thing is that the dog speaks at all. The fact that such implacable enemies had even sat down and listened to speeches together was what mattered. On November 22 the United States issued invitations to the participants to continue the peace talks in Washington as a compromise location on December 4. However, because the invitations were issued on the eve of a meeting between Bush and Shamir, the Israelis perceived the timing as a as a snub. They bitterly complained that they had been effectively ordered to show up in Washington on the prescribed day. In response, they proposed that the direct talks be delayed five days, then be moved quickly to a site in or near the Middle East.

When December 4 arrived, all of the Arab delegates were in Washington, but the Israeli delegates did not arrive until five days later, as promised. Opposition parties in Israel heaped scorn on Likud for this "infantile" behavior.

Finally, on December 10, the negotiators were ready to sit down and begin one-on-one talks. The Palestinians insisted, however, on breaking away from the Jordanian delegation and meeting separately with the Israelis. While this issue was unresolved neither delegation would enter the meeting room. After a week spent in a State Department corridor discussing the ground rules, the talks adjourned December 18.

In mid-January 1992 the talks resumed. Although the participants finally had reached the meeting rooms, much of their time was spent talking past each other with little result. In the three months since Madrid, what little initial enthusiasm there had been for the talks seemed to have dissipated. By prior agreement, no American official was present in the room for any of the talks. Baker had insisted from the start that he had no intention of forcing an American solution on the parties; they would have to hammer one out on their own. But his strategy seemed to be producing few results.

Partly this was the result of the shaky political ground under the Shamir government. When the topic of interim Palestinian self-rule came up in the talks, it caused two small right-wing parties to announce their departure from the government on January 19, leaving Shamir without a majority in the parliament. Bowing to the inevitable, Shamir scheduled early elections for June 23, staying on until then as the head of a caretaker government. This had the advantage for Shamir of relieving the American pressure for concessions until after the elections. Any chances for a breakthrough in the talks were effectively put on hold until June.

On January 28-29 the first session of regional multilateral talks took place in Moscow. Although separate from the bilateral talks, they originally had been intended to take place in mid-November. Most observers expected little from the Moscow talks, but at least they threw no new snares into the peace process. Other Arab states from the Persian Gulf and the Magreb also took part in the talks on economic cooperation, water sharing, refugees, the environment, arms control, and other regional concerns. Syria and Lebanon declined to attend, arguing that such matters should not be discussed with Israel until after diplomatic normalization had taken place.

In late February and April, two more rounds of bilateral talks took place in Washington. These rounds achieved little, but the United States had insisted on them, fearing a gap of too many months would stall the "momentum" of the talks. In May the five sets of multilateral talks that had opened in Moscow in January (refugees, environment, water, arms control, and economic development) met in five different capitals with more than twenty participants. Israel boycotted the refugee talks, complaining that the participation of Palestinians from outside the territories violated the agreement worked out in Madrid.

## Israeli Elections and U.S. Ties

With Baker's frustration at Likud intransigence, and Shamir's complaints that U.S. pressure to stop building settlements was interference in Israeli affairs, U.S.-Israeli ties had sunk to nearly historic lows. Once Israeli elections were announced, Bush and Baker made little secret of their anger at Shamir and their hopes for a Labor victory. They were confident that, with Labor's more flexible approach to territorial compromise, more could be achieved at the peace negotiations.

Bush's sharpest weapon against Shamir was the long-delayed loan guarantees. On March 17 Bush effectively buried them and placed the blame on the Shamir government, declaring, "We're simply

# Israeli Settlements and the Loan Guarantees

During 1990 and 1991 the pace of Russian immigration to Israel continued to accelerate. By June 1991 more than three hundred thousand immigrants had arrived since the wave began in 1989. Their most immediate need invariably was housing. The Likud government—and more specifically rightwing housing minister Ariel Sharon—made political use of this need by starting massive new settlements in the occupied territories, creating built-in constituencies for Likud's argument that "not one inch" was to be returned.

As U.S. secretary of state James A. Baker III worked to set up a peace conference, he found that no issue angered Arabs more than Likud's policy of settling the territories, making any future territorial compromise less likely. "Nothing has made my job of trying to find Arab and Palestinian partners for Israel more difficult than being greeted by a new settlement every time I arrive," an exasperated Baker declared in testimony before Congress. "The Arabs ... argue that this proves that the Israeli government is not interested in negotiating outcomes, but it's really interested in creating facts on the ground."

Absorbing the immigrants was placing a huge strain on the Israeli economy. Thus, in June 1991 the Israeli government indicated that in September it would formally request $10 billion in U.S. housing loan guarantees over five years. These would allow Israel to borrow from private banks at a lower rate than it otherwise would receive. Similar guarantees had been offered to Israel in the past, but never on such a scale or at a time of such tension with the United States.

The loan guarantees became the focal point for U.S. critics of the Israeli settlements. A common question was, "Why should U.S. taxpayers provide the financing for an Israeli policy that flies in the face of U.S. policy?" President George Bush began to hint that it would be best if Prime Minister Yitzhak Shamir delayed his request so that it would not interfere with the proposed peace conference. Supporters argued that the loan guarantees were a humanitarian gesture supporting the end results of the decades-old U.S. policy of pushing for greater Soviet immigration, and that they should not be tied to political conditions.

With the support of strong majorities in Congress, however, Israeli ambassador Zalman Shoval made a formal request on September 6, ignoring White House requests for a 120-day delay so as not to interfere with the conference. Supporters of Israel in Congress declared their confidence that they could muster a two-thirds majority in both chambers to override a White House veto, despite Bush's warning that "a contentious debate ... would raise a host of issues that could destroy our ability to bring one or more of the parties to the peace table." In a statement that angered the American Jewish community, Bush declared that he was "one lonely little guy" battling "powerful political forces."

Congressional leaders conceded that overriding a veto would be too bruising even if it succeeded. Ultimately, Bush and Congress approved the loan guarantees after Shamir's party was defeated in Israel. Nevertheless, the anger raised in the debate permanently damaged Bush's standing among American Jews and left U.S.-Israeli relations at their lowest level ever. Bush's perceived hostility toward Israel was cited by large numbers of Jews who had supported Bush in 1988, but who chose to support Bill Clinton in 1992.

---

not going to shift and change the foreign policy of this country."

The loss of the loan guarantees was a blow to the Israeli economy, but it alarmed Israelis more as an indication that Shamir had allowed something to go seriously wrong in Israel's strategic relationship with the United States, which had rarely denied Israel anything it asked for.

This was certainly a factor in the sweeping electoral victory of Yitzhak Rabin and the Labor party on June 23. Also, Israelis had grown tired of the Likud vision of a "Greater Israel" and were no longer willing to pay the price in blood and re-sources. Another significant factor in Likud's defeat, besides blame for the loss of the loan guarantees, was an awareness that longstanding ties with the United States were not to be taken for granted.

With the new government in place, U.S.-Israeli tensions eased immediately. Within days of his election, Prime Minister Rabin began to dramatically scale back settlement activity in the occupied territories and moderate the harsh statements of the Likud government. Even Hanan Ashrawi, one of the Palestinian negotiators, admitted that there had been a "shift of tone" from Israel. However, Rabin refused to tie his hands by categorically stopping new building, declaring that he would continue to build "security" settlements but not "political" settlements—although the difference has never been made clear. Nevertheless, Baker quickly reciprocated by hinting that the loan guarantees might now be possible and telling Israel's Arab negotiating partners that with this new compromise by Israel, it was time for them to show some flexibility.

On August 10 at Bush's family retreat at Kennebunkport, Maine, President Bush and Prime Minister Rabin announced that they had reached agreement on terms for the U.S. loan guarantees, and that another round of the peace negotiations would open in Washington on August 24. Rabin indicated his hopes that the new round would continue for a full month and begin to include discussions of the terms for Palestinian autonomy, leading to some future "territorial compromises."

As was hoped, the August 24 round did last a full month, with nearly all of the talk on substantive issues. Procedural questions, which had tied previous rounds in knots, were quickly resolved by the new Israeli negotiating team, which had shown up with a concrete thirty-three-page proposal for establishing Palestinian autonomy. Nevertheless, despite substantial progress, no breakthrough was achieved. Another short round of negotiations was squeezed into late October, but with U.S. elections and the looming defeat of George Bush overshadowing everything else, little was accomplished.

## Clinton Administration

With the election of Bill Clinton to the presidency, many observers feared for the future of the peace process. Clinton was far more sympathetic to Israel than Bush had been, and it was unclear whether the Arabs would find him to be a credible mediator. Baker's Middle East team would be leaving the State Department and, at the very least, it was assumed that the talks would be delayed while the new administration filled vacancies and got up to speed, despite Clinton's early insistence that there would be no delay.

Shortly after the 1992 election the outgoing administration was host to another negotiating session in Washington. The talks quickly stalled against a tide of rising violence and reprisals in the territories. After weeks of attacks and counterattacks between Palestinians and Israeli settlers, the Israeli government rounded up and deported to Lebanon more than four hundred Palestinians connected with the radical Hamas movement. This led to a Palestinian declaration that they would boycott the talks until the deportees were returned. Clinton called on Israel to relax the deportation order, but he used the threat of an American veto to block efforts in the UN in January 1993 to establish sanctions against Israel.

On February 2 Rabin relented somewhat, accepting one hundred of the deported back to Israel and promising to allow the others to return after a year. The Palestinians insisted that this was inadequate to bring them back to the table. However, after a number of other concessions by the Israelis and promises against further deportations, the talks resumed on April 27.

Recognizing that almost nothing had been achieved in more than a year of talks, Secretary of State Warren M. Christopher sought to change the U.S. role from mediator to active participant. He tried unsuccessfully to get the two sides to adopt a U.S.-proposed statement of principles. Meeting again in late June, the two sides still showed little interest in Christopher's proposals.

## Secret Negotiations

In mid-August reports began to appear in the Arab press that PLO and Israeli officials were meeting secretly, bypassing the stalled official negotiations in Washington. On August 29 the reports were confirmed by announcements that Israeli foreign minister Shimon Peres and Mahmoud Abbas of the PLO had been meeting secretly in Oslo, with the assistance of Norwegian foreign minister Johan Jorgen Holst, and had reached rough agreement on mutual recognition and establishment of Palestinian autonomy in Gaza and Jericho within six months, with other areas to be added later. After an interim period of five years, the final status of the territories would be determined.

The sudden turnaround caught almost everyone by surprise. Hard-liners on both sides quickly began to complain. Israeli settlers declared that they would shoot Palestinian policemen. Radical Hamas supporters called Arafat a traitor for agreeing to start with such a tiny piece of land and without clear guarantees for the withdrawal of Israeli forces. Although also caught off guard, Clinton and Christopher quickly promised their support and invited the sides to Washington for a formal signing ceremony.

The official talks resumed in Washington on August 31, although they were effectively superseded by negotiations continuing in Norway. Members of the Palestinian team even complained that Arafat had not discussed the Norwegian negotiations with them.

On September 1 Jordanian officials hinted that they would be ready to sign a peace agreement with Israel once a final deal was signed with the Palestinians. Although technically at war with Israel since 1967, Jordan had long since given up its claims to the West Bank. Its remaining disputes with Israel were minimal, involving only a few small slivers of borderland.

While most Arab leaders quickly moved to support the plan, Syria continued to voice its suspicions. Hafez al-Assad did not personally condemn the agreement, but he allowed the radical Palestinian movements based in Damascus free reign to attack it, making it clear where his feelings lay.

## Peace Treaty

On September 13, 1993, at a sun-drenched ceremony on the White House lawn, Yitzhak Rabin and Yasir Arafat, veterans of numerous Arab-Israeli wars, shook hands and their foreign ministers signed a historic document, the first ever between Israel and the PLO, recognizing each other and agreeing on the outlines of a plan to end their long conflict. Although the agreement specified that the Israeli withdrawal would begin on December 17, many of the details remained to be worked out.

Cognizant of the drama of lifelong enemies shaking hands, President Clinton observed that "the children of Abraham . . . have embarked together on a bold journey." While Rabin declared, "we the soldiers who have fought against you, the Palestinians—we say to you today, in a loud and clear voice: Enough of blood and tears. Enough." *(Peace accord documents, Appendix, p. 404)*

Many analysts have speculated on the reasons that, after so many years of conflict, Israel and the PLO were finally able to come together. Although American pressure for negotiations had brought the parties together, it did not bring about the movement toward a settlement. On the Palestinian side, it is evident that Arafat feared being forced out. Since the Gulf War, the PLO had few cards left to play. It had alienated its wealthy Arab backers with its support of Saddam Hussein, and the rise of the more radical Hamas movement in the territories had left it with weakened popularity among Palestinians. Without such a dramatic move, Arafat might soon have found himself marginalized. The secret talks allowed Arafat to negotiate without the pressures from radical elements in the PLO. For his part, Rabin had come to power promising peace and yet had presided over worsening violence and stalled talks in Washington. Failure to deliver an agreement with at least one of Israel's enemies would have sooner or later threatened his government's mandate.

*Jordan's King Hussein (left) and Israel's Prime Minister Yitzhak Rabin addressed a joint session of Congress July 26, 1994, following the signing of a peace agreement July 25 that ended a forty-six-year state of war between the two countries.*

## Broadening Peace

The Clinton administration remained committed to expanding the Arab-Israeli peace, though it generally stayed out of issues related to implementation of the Israeli-Palestinian agreement. With the president's foreign policy in several parts of the globe being sharply criticized by Republicans and many commentators, the Middle East was perceived as an area of success for Clinton. Secretary of State Christopher sought to build on this success by conducting shuttle diplomacy between Syria and Israel. Clinton lent the prestige of his office to this enterprise by meeting with President Assad on January 16, 1994, in Geneva. By the fall of 1994 an agreement had not been reached.

Should the Syrians and Israelis reach an accord on a staged Israeli withdrawal from the Golan Heights, it was expected that Clinton would approve the stationing of U.S. troops in that area as part of an international peacekeeping mission.

The Clinton administration also pledged financial aid to the new Palestinian entity. In 1993 it promised $500 million over five years for the development of Gaza, Jericho, and any additional areas coming under Palestinian autonomy. Congress, however, would have to appropriate the money. Half of the amount was to be in the form of loans, the other half in grants. The United States also continued its own talks with the PLO. Like other donors, the United States has considered placing conditions on its aid to help ensure democratization and the efficient use of funds for development purposes.

The conclusion of an agreement between Jordan and Israel in July 1994 gave a further boost to the momentum for peace in the Middle East. Once again, though the accord had been reached without American involvement in negotiations, Washington played host to the formal signing ceremony. On July 25 King Hussein and Prime Minister Rabin signed the "Washington Declaration" at the White House. The document ended the state of war between the two countries. It was followed on October 26 by the signing of a formal peace treaty between Jordan and Israel. President Clinton attended the signing at a ceremony on the Jordanian-Israeli border. *(Israeli-Jordanian declaration text, Appendix, p. 410)*

## U.S. Goals in the Middle East

During the early 1990s the United States saw all four of its traditional goals in the Middle East significantly advanced. The security of Israel was improved by the weakening of Iraq during the Persian Gulf War and the conclusion of peace agreements between Israel and the PLO and Jordan. Those same agreements brought tangible hope that a second objective might be achieved—a permanent Arab-Israeli peace. Although the United States remained dependent on Persian Gulf oil for a growing share of its energy needs, the victory over Iraq preserved U.S. access to that oil. The war's success also strengthened U.S. strategic relationships with Saudi Arabia and the smaller Gulf oil-producing states. Finally, the collapse of the Soviet Union had eliminated Moscow from the Middle East picture, ending fears that conflict in the Middle East could touch off a superpower confrontation.

While these developments and accomplishments were cause for great optimism in Washington, the Middle East was still a potential area of crisis because oil and the U.S. commitment to Israel made the stakes high. Instability in the Arab producing nations could threaten the U.S. oil lifeline, while a breakdown of the Arab-Israeli peace process could enlarge the prospects for anti-American terrorism.

In particular, the threats from Iran and Iraq continued to pose a challenge to the United States. Although Iraq was badly weakened by the war and was still besieged by the UN embargo, Saddam Hussein remained in power. In early October 1994 Saddam demonstrated that he still could command the world's attention. He deployed many of his best Republican Guard troops to positions close to the Kuwaiti border. President Clinton responded to the provocation by deploying thirty-six thousand U.S. troops to the Gulf region. The U.S. show of force caused Saddam to pull back his troops from the border. Iraq's aggressive move, an apparent attempt to pressure the United Nations to lift sanctions, actually weakened support in the international community for an early lifting of sanctions. Eventually, however, international sanctions may be lifted, giving Saddam some breathing space. His hatred of the United States and propensity to use Iraqi military power could eventually re-create a threat to U.S. interests in the region.

Under the Clinton administration's policy of "dual containment," Iran was regarded as a threat as least as great as Iraq, and probably greater. The United States sought to slow the development of Iranian military technology and weapons of mass destruction by lobbying other nations to tighten controls on technology and weapons going to Iran. The United States also opposed World Bank loans for Iran and other nations' bilateral rescheduling of Iranian debt. Nevertheless, the United States had not precluded exploratory talks with Tehran, even as it used diplomacy to weaken Iran.

Of prime importance during the second half of the decade will be U.S. efforts to keep weapons of mass destruction out of the hands of terrorists. That prospect could make nuclear nonproliferation the most critical U.S. goal in the Middle East.

CHAPTER **4**

# THE PERSIAN GULF

The Persian Gulf is a strategic body of water that is home to more than half the world's oil deposits. It is fed by the two great rivers of antiquity—the Euphrates and the Tigris—and empties into the Arabian Sea through the Strait of Hormuz. Eight countries with a combined population of more than 111 million ring the Gulf: Iran, Iraq, Saudi Arabia, Kuwait, Bahrain, Qatar, the United Arab Emirates, and Oman. Iran, the only non-Arab country on the Gulf, has more than 65 million people—more than all of its Gulf neighbors combined.

Collectively these nations are the primary source of oil for much of the world, producing millions of barrels each day. Much of the petroleum is loaded on supertankers at vast but vulnerable terminals in the Gulf, and it flows in these carriers to the Indian Ocean through the narrow Strait of Hormuz. Although recent efforts throughout the region to build pipelines have reduced the Gulf nations' dependence on tanker shipments through the strait, the threat of disruption to the region's oil flow remains an international and local concern.

The effect of a disruption of Persian Gulf oil on the world's economy was demonstrated by the Saudi Arabian-led 1973 Arab oil embargo. This action was a response to the Arab-Israeli War of that year and resulted in a temporary cutoff of oil from most Gulf states to the United States and a slowing of the flow to most of the rest of the world. The action contributed to a worldwide recession as the price of oil skyrocketed from less than $3 a barrel in early 1973 to about $11 a barrel in 1974. *(Oil embargo, Chapter 5, p. 142)*

Another round of oil price increases that began in 1979 again rocked the world's economy. That year three events occurred that raised fears in Washington and the capitals of other major industrialized nations that the Persian Gulf oil supply was vulnerable to disruption. In February the Iranian revolution resulted in the overthrow of the shah and the establishment of a fundamentalist Islamic republic under the leadership of the Ayatollah Ruhollah Khomeini. In November the seizure of the U.S. embassy in Tehran and the holding of American diplomats hostage confirmed the implacable hostility of the new government toward the West and the United States in particular. Finally, in December 1979 the Soviet Union launched a massive invasion into nearby Afghanistan to prop up the pro-Soviet government there.

Although most analysts discounted the possibility of a Soviet military move beyond Afghanistan, the Soviet invasion and the upheaval in Iran prompted President Jimmy Carter to declare in his State of the Union address on January 23, 1980, that "an attempt by any outside force to gain control of the Persian Gulf region will be regarded as an assault on the vital interests of the United States of America, and such an assault will be repelled by any means necessary, including military force." The statement came to be known as the Carter Doctrine, and it reinforced perceptions that what happened in the Persian Gulf region was of vital importance to the United States and the rest of the world.

While the 1970s demonstrated the significance

of the Gulf region, the 1980s and 1990s underscored its vulnerability. In September 1980 Iraq launched an offensive into Iran that turned into a bloody eight-year war of attrition. The Iran-Iraq War left hundreds of thousands dead, disrupted vital oil tanker traffic in the Gulf, and led to U.S. intervention in the form of naval escorts for Kuwaiti oil tankers. Meanwhile the economies of the Gulf states, all of which depend to some degree on oil, were rocked by the crash of oil prices in the mid-1980s. Plummeting oil revenues forced Gulf states to cut back severely on domestic development projects and services.

Despite these shocks the Gulf states and their governments survived. The Iran-Iraq War ended in a stalemate. Radical Islamic fundamentalism inspired by Iran did not lead to the overthrow of any Gulf government, the Soviets began withdrawing from Afghanistan in 1988, and oil prices recovered somewhat in the late 1980s as world oil consumption began to increase.

But peace in the region was fleeting. On August 2, 1990, Iraq invaded and occupied Kuwait, setting in motion an international crisis that ended with Iraq's suffering a humbling military defeat at the hands of a U.S.-led international coalition.

In the mid-1990s, Iran and Iraq remain the focus of Persian Gulf security concerns. Both nations have demonstrated aggressive international ambitions, both have a nuclear weapons development program, both have significant oil reserves, and both have grievances against their Arab neighbors.

Iraq's defeat did not remove Saddam Hussein from power, and his regime remains hostile to the West. Potential points of conflict include Iraq's continued pursuit of weapons of mass destruction and the government's struggle with its own Kurdish population in the north and its Shi'ite population in the south. Nevertheless, the war greatly diminished Iraq's military strength and the continued enforcement of an oil embargo and other stringent economic sanctions have crippled Iraq's economy. The Iraqi threat to its neighbors is unlikely to be resolved soon, but meanwhile it is well contained.

In part because Iraq has been weakened, many U.S. analysts since the end of the Gulf War have considered Iran to be the greater threat to Persian Gulf security. Iran's large population, its backing of subversive activities abroad, and its proximity to the Strait of Hormuz choke point combine to make it a serious threat. Yet Iran is experiencing internal political and economic problems that have limited its international ambitions and its military resources.

Few observers expect that the Persian Gulf region will achieve a stable peace any time soon. Ethnic conflicts, volatile personalities, territorial disputes, the enmities developed during two bloody wars, and the high financial stakes associated with oil wealth will ensure that the Persian Gulf remains an international hot spot.

Yet some positive developments have emerged from the war-torn years of the 1980s and early 1990s. The wealthy Gulf oil states are far more aware of their vulnerability and are more open to constructive security cooperation with outside powers, including the United States. Attention has been focused on the nuclear weapons programs in the region, and nations are less likely to be able to quietly build a nuclear weapon capacity. With the collapse of the Soviet Union, there no longer is a significant Russian threat to the security of the Persian Gulf. And the movement in the Arab-Israeli peace process has begun to diminish the usefulness of anti-Israeli sentiment as a rallying point for aggressive or radical ideologies.

## The Iran-Iraq Rivalry

The Iran-Iraq disputes that led to their war in 1980 are rooted in historic, territorial, and ideological differences. Some analysts say the enmity goes back to the sixteenth century when the Ottoman Sunni-Persian Shi'ite struggles began. Others trace it all the way back to the Arab invasion of Persia in the seventh century and the Persians' subsequent defeat at Qadissiya. In fact, the Iraqis at times described the Iran-Iraq War as the "Second Qadissiya" or "Saddam's Qadissiya."

## Origins of Conflict

Despite the longstanding rivalry between Iran and Iraq, their relations during the late 1970s were cordial. Then the Ayatollah Khomeini's Islamic Revolution succeeded in overthrowing the shah of Iran in 1979. This development reopened two historically contentious issues that eventually led to war: which country would control the Shatt al-Arab waterway (the 120-mile confluence of the Tigris and Euphrates rivers that discharges into the Gulf) and how much influence would the two countries exercise over the Persian Gulf region in general and the minorities in each other's country in particular.

Relations between the two countries were complicated in the early 1970s by Iran's support of the Kurds' fight for independence from the Iraqi government. The Kurds make up 20 percent of Iraq's population and predominate in the isolated mountains of the north. Iran had supplied the Kurds with arms and given them asylum in Iran when necessary. Iraq, in turn, backed religious and secular opponents of the shah and gave financial and military assistance to Baluchi, Kurdish, and Arab secessionist movements in Iran. Iran-Iraq relations reached a low point in 1974 when Iran, with U.S. and Israeli encouragement, began to increase aid to Iraq's Kurds. The combination of border clashes and support for rebel and dissident groups in each other's country brought Iran and Iraq close to open warfare.

By March 1975, however, the tensions began to decrease. Iraq believed it was imperative to avoid a full-scale war with Iran and to attempt to consolidate domestic power by putting an end to Iranian subversive activities. To accomplish these objectives, the shah of Iran and Saddam Hussein (then vice president of the Revolutionary Command Council) met at a session of the Organization of Petroleum Exporting Countries (OPEC) in Algiers. Assisted by the mediation efforts of the president of Algeria, the Iran-Iraq leaders issued a joint communiqué on March 6, 1975, announcing the reaffirmation of the 1913 Constantinople Protocol land boundaries but defining the thalweg line

in the river as the new frontier on the Shatt al-Arab. Iran and Iraq signed a treaty on June 13, 1975, with three additional protocols concerning international borders and good neighborly relations. Each party also agreed to refrain from assisting insurgents in the other's country.

The Algiers treaty ushered in a period of friendly relations welcomed by Iran, Iraq, and neighboring Saudi Arabia. Iraq was scorned by some of the more radical Arab states—Syria and South Yemen—for "selling out" Arab territory. Despite the apparent rapprochement, the treaty conflicted with the Arab nationalist ideology of the Ba'ath party in Iraq. In retrospect, it is clear that the Iraqi leaders had no intention of accepting the agreement indefinitely; when Iraq was strong enough, it planned to reassert its authority over the Shatt al-Arab.

Relations between Iraq and the shah's regime in Iran remained stable throughout the late 1970s. In July 1977 the two states signed six bilateral agreements covering trade, cultural relations, agriculture and fishing, railway linkages, freedom of movement for Iranians visiting the Shi'ite Muslim holy places in Iraq, and coordination of activities concerning the movement of "subversive elements." In October 1978 the Iraqi government complied with the nervous shah's request to evict Khomeini from Najaf, Iraq, where he had been in exile since 1964 when he was forced to leave Iran.

## Changes After the Iranian Revolution

The Iraqi government initially welcomed the Iranian revolution in February 1979. Iran broke off unofficial relations with Israel, left the Western-dominated Central Treaty Organization (CENTO), and announced that it would no longer police the Gulf. Iraq welcomed these changes. It hoped that the new government in Iran would turn inward and address domestic concerns, leaving the Gulf open to Iraqi influence.

By mid-1979 Iraqi-Iranian relations had changed dramatically. Iranian clerics had renewed Iran's claims to Bahrain and had urged Shi'ite communities in the Gulf to rebel against their

*The Persian Gulf Region*

ruling regimes. Shi'ites demonstrated in Saudi Arabia, Kuwait, and Bahrain. In Iraq dozens of Shi'ites were reportedly arrested in Najaf for planning demonstrations; several were executed. In response, Saddam warned Iran: "Iraq's capabilities can be used against any side which tries to violate the sovereignty of Kuwait or Bahrain or harm their

people or land." In October Iraq broke diplomatic relations with Iran, branding the revolution as "non-Islamic."

In April 1980 several incidents further harmed Iraqi-Iranian relations. On April 1 Iraqi deputy premier Tariq Aziz was wounded by a hand grenade thrown by an Iranian. On April 6 Iraq cabled the United Nations to demand that Iran withdraw from from the disputed islands Abu Musa and the Greater and Lesser Tunbs. Iran placed its border troops on alert in response. Harsh verbal attacks then followed. Khomeini called on the people of Iraq to bring down their government: "Wake up and topple this corrupt regime in your Islamic country before it is too late." Saddam responded: "Anyone who tries to put his hand on Iraq will have his hand cut off." An attack on the Iranian embassy in London by Arabs from the Iranian province of Khuzistan was widely believed to have been instigated by Iraq.

Clearly, the confrontation between Iran and Iraq had gone far beyond the dispute over the river boundary of the Shatt al-Arab. The pan-Islamic ideology of the Khomeini revolution to unite all Muslims, despite ethnic or cultural divisions, directly opposed the pan-Arab ideology of the Ba'athist government in Baghdad. Khomeini and Iran's other religious leaders viewed their revolution not only as an Iranian event, but also as the beginning of a worldwide Islamic revolution. Because of Iraq's religious composition and close proximity to Iran, it felt threatened by Iran's intentions.

Despite the absence of a significant upheaval among Iraq's Shi'ites, the presence of a hostile Iranian government preaching Islamic fundamentalism and aggressively challenging Iraqi interests in the Persian Gulf was disconcerting to Saddam Hussein's regime. Even if Iran did not pose an immediate danger, its large population (almost three times the size of Iraq's) made it a significant long-term military threat, and its subversive activities and intransigence on territorial issues ran counter to Iraq's regional ambitions. Given these considerations, Iraq began preparing for war in the summer of 1980.

## The Iran-Iraq War

For eight years the Iran-Iraq War threatened the stability and security of the Persian Gulf region. The war, which appeared to be lopsided in favor of Iraq when it began in 1980, turned into

the longest war in recent Middle East history. Analysts have estimated that 1 million people were killed in the war, which cost the combatants hundreds of billions of dollars.

Each side possessed distinct advantages that led analysts at various points during the war to predict that it would prevail. Iraq had a more advanced arsenal of weapons and about five times as many combat aircraft as Iran. In addition, Iran's international isolation made it difficult for that country to purchase advanced weaponry and spare parts for its prewar arsenal. Iraq also enjoyed the support of most of the Arab world, including Saudi Arabia and Kuwait, which provided billions of dollars to the Iraqi war effort. In contrast, support for Iran in the Middle East was limited to Syria, Libya, and Algeria. Iran, however, had more people and greater territorial depth to aid defense efforts. In addition, Iranian leaders successfully portrayed the war as a religious crusade to many of the country's young fighters, who were generally more motivated than Iraqi troops through much of the war.

Neither side, however, was able to translate its advantages into victory. In the end Iran accepted a UN cease-fire after Iraqi battlefield gains in 1988. The war came to an end with both combatants in possession of about the same territory with which they started. Both societies, however, had been devastated by the war, which produced some of the most brutal tactics of the twentieth century, including rocket attacks on city centers, "human wave" assaults against fortified positions, and the use of chemical weapons.

### Iraq Attacks

By mid-1980 the situation in Iran seemed to present Iraq with an ideal opportunity to end Iranian interference in the Gulf and to turn the clock back to the favorable border situation it had enjoyed until 1975. Iran's central authority appeared to be disintegrating, and there was a purge in July of the remnants of the regular armed forces in Khuzistan.

On September 17, 1980, amid escalating border clashes, Iraq terminated the 1975 treaty and claimed exclusive sovereignty over the entire Shatt al-Arab. The government announced that all vessels using the estuary and waterway should fly the Iraqi flag and take on only Iraqi pilots. Iraq accused Iran of violating the 1975 agreement by supporting Kurdish rebels. In a statement published in 1979 the Iranian government said it would no longer abide by the shah's promise to stop aid to Iraqi insurgents: "The Iranian government blocked any Kurdish moves against Iraq, but the situation is different now. The Iranian government does not uphold this agreement."

On September 22 massed Iraqi forces pushed across the Iranian border east of Baghdad. In a second move the Iraqis crossed the Shatt and attacked key cities and oil installations in Khuzistan (called *Arabistan* and claimed by Iraq because most of its people are Arab and Sunni). Iraq's strategy was to destroy Iran's oil sources, refineries, and transportation routes and thus debilitate the Iranian regime. Within a month Iraq had occupied an area within Khuzistan of close to thirty-five hundred square miles. Meanwhile, Iranian jets knocked out the principal Iraqi oil installations at Kirkuk and Baghdad.

All mediation efforts by the United Nations, the Islamic Conference Organization, the Palestine Liberation Organization (PLO), Pakistan, Algeria, Turkey, and others failed. The UN Security Council unanimously adopted Resolution 479 on September 28 calling upon Iran and Iraq "to refrain immediately from any further use of force and to settle their dispute by peaceful means." The resolution urged other states to refrain from "any act which may lead to a further escalation and widening of the conflict."

## The Tide Turns

Despite initial success on the battlefield, Iraq failed to achieve its ultimate objective: the fall of Khomeini's regime. In fact, the invasion seemed to create a surge of Iranian patriotism. The war gave the Khomeini government an excuse to suppress dissent—an issue around which it could rally nationalist and religious fervor.

By November the Iranians had stopped the enemy offensive and were engaging the Iraqis in a war of attrition inside Iran. In the face of high casualties, the Iraqi government had expressed its willingness to negotiate, provided Iran acknowledged Iraq's sovereignty over the Shatt al-Arab and pledged nonintervention in Iraq's affairs. Iran, however, rejected international appeals for mediation.

In October 1980 the Iraqi National Assembly had appealed to parliaments around the world to urge Iran to accept peaceful means to end the war. Iraq also had sent cabinet ministers to meet leaders of Turkey, India, Saudi Arabia, Kuwait, and some European states to express "Iraq's peaceful attitude before and during the war."

The Ayatollah Khomeini, in response to all mediation attempts, repeatedly stated that Iran would fight the war until it was won. He called Saddam "more criminal than the shah." Khomeini said his goal was "to establish an Islamic government in Iraq and to destroy the Iraqi regime in the same way as we destroyed the shah." In the late summer of 1981 Iranian forces launched heavy counterattacks designed to drive the Iraqis from Iranian territory. By April 1982 Iranian forces had recaptured the Khuzistan cities of Abadan, Dezful, and Khorramshahr. The Iraqi government decided to withdraw from the remaining Iranian territories under its control.

Iran planned next to cut off southern Iraq from Baghdad, thus splitting Iraqi forces and creating conditions under which the large Iraqi Shi'ite population in the south could be induced to unite with Iran. In July 1982 Iranian troops entered Iraqi territory near Basra just across the Shatt al-Arab. Iraqi resistance stiffened, however, and the Iranian offensive was blunted.

In the fall Iran continued attacks in the territory east of Baghdad and penetrated three miles into Iraqi territory. A large-scale Iranian offensive continued into the winter and spring of 1983. The apparent goal was to cut off Basra, Iraq's second-largest city and its main port on the Gulf. An Iranian offensive in February 1983, described as the "decisive and last," failed. It involved about a hundred thousand Iranian soldiers—many of whom attacked Iraqi lines in human waves. Thousands were left dead and wounded. Another major offensive, in April, netted Iran about twelve miles of Iraqi territory after bloody hand-to-hand fighting. Throughout the fighting Iraq's Shi'ite population generally remained loyal to the regime of President Saddam Hussein.

During the summer of 1983 Iraq embarked on a deliberate plan to internationalize the war, and to a degree it succeeded. The French sold Iraq Exocet missiles, and the Soviets increased arms sales to Baghdad. Member states of the Gulf Cooperation Council (GCC), especially Saudi Arabia and Kuwait, increased their financial support of Iraq. The United Nations, meanwhile, passed resolutions that were tougher on the Iranians than on the Iraqis. This success was primarily due to a worldwide fear of an Iranian victory in the war.

Fierce fighting continued in the spring of 1984. Iraq claimed it crushed the Iranian offensives involving as many as four hundred thousand troops. Iraq, however, was accused by Iran and the United States of using chemical weapons in violation of the 1925 Geneva agreement outlawing these weapons. The United States also accused Iran of throwing untrained units of teenagers against Iraqi lines to wear down the enemy before attacking with regular army units.

## Attacks on Tankers and Cities

In May 1984 the war entered a new and more dangerous stage. Iraq delineated a zone with a fifty-mile radius around the Iranian port of Kharg Island and began striking at tankers sailing within the zone. Baghdad justified escalating the conflict by asserting that its Gulf ports had been unusable since the beginning of the war because of shelling, while Iranian ports remained open to export oil that provided revenue to finance Iran's war effort.

Iraq hoped that the Iranian government would choose to negotiate an end to the war rather than risk having its oil exports cut off. Iran responded, however, by attacking ships calling on ports of Arab states in the Gulf that supported the Iraqi

war effort. In fact, throughout 1983 Iran had declared that if its own ports were attacked, it would make the entire Gulf unsafe.

The Arab Gulf states vehemently protested Iranian strikes against Gulf tankers. The Arab League also condemned Iran, and the UN Security Council adopted a similar resolution of disapproval. Despite protests, the tanker attacks continued through September 1985; by then seventy-seven ships—mostly commercial vessels not involved in the war—had been attacked in the Gulf by either Iran or Iraq.

Although both Iran and Iraq had occasionally bombed the other's cities during the first four and a half years of the war, neither had launched intensive bombing campaigns against civilians until March 1985. At that time Iraq began systematically attacking Iranian population centers in an attempt to force Iran to accept a negotiated settlement. The Iraqi attacks continued sporadically until the end of the war. The campaign against Iranian cities created many refugees and hurt Iranian morale. The Iraqis believed this campaign was the best chance they had of ending the conflict on their terms. Iran countered with surface-to-surface missile attacks on Iraqi cities. The Iranians had a limited supply of missiles, however, and their attacks inflicted much less devastation on Iraqi cities than Iraqi missiles and planes were inflicting on Tehran and other Iranian cities.

## Iranian Offensives

During 1985 neither side could claim much progress in the ground war. Iran's superior numbers had not enabled it to breach the more sophisticated Iraqi defenses, but Iraq was unable to launch a counteroffensive to drive Iran from southern Iraq. Then in February 1986 Iranian forces launched a daring attack across the Shatt al-Arab that resulted in their capture of the Iraqi port city of Fao. The attack contrasted with previous Iranian offensives in that it was a well-planned military assault that relied on deception and mobility rather than on frontal assaults by poorly trained and ill-equipped Revolutionary Guards (volunteers known for their loyalty to Khomeini and their religious fervor).

The attack led many observers in the Arab world and the West in mid-1986 to predict an Iranian victory. Iraq appeared to be in a tenuous position with the key city of Basra vulnerable to a successful Iranian offensive. All subsequent Iranian offensives failed, however. Iraqi resistance again stiffened, feuds within the Iranian government led to the dismissal of key military officers, Arab states increased their financial support of Iraq, and in the summer of 1987 the U.S. Navy began escorting Kuwaiti oil tankers in the Persian Gulf and challenging Iranian forces there. *(Tanker reflagging, Chapter 3, p. 83)*

In December 1986 Iran launched a major offensive against Basra that had been planned for a year and publicized as the final blow that would topple Saddam Hussein's regime. After two months of human wave assaults, Iran had failed to take any significant territory and had suffered huge losses of men and equipment. The failed offensive seriously damaged Iranian capabilities and morale. A UN-appointed team of observers also disclosed that Iraq had used chemical weapons on a large scale against the Iranian attackers, while Iran had employed such weapons on a smaller scale.

In the late spring of 1988 the Iraqi army, supported by heavy air cover, began dislodging the weakened Iranian forces from their positions. For several months the Iraqis won major victories on the battlefield as Iranian forces retreated. Finally, in July, Iranian leaders accepted UN Security Council Resolution 598, which had called for a cease-fire in the war. The Ayatollah Khomeini, who had vowed to continue the fight until Saddam was ousted from power, called the acceptance of the cease-fire "more deadly than taking poison." The Iranian decision appeared motivated by the deteriorating situation on the battlefield, continued Iraqi air and missile attacks on Iranian cities, Iran's extreme international isolation, and a bleak economic situation caused by the war and diminished oil revenues. The cease-fire called for in UN Resolution 598 was implemented August 20, 1988, a month after Iran accepted it. *(Texts of UN resolution and Iran's acceptance, Appendix, p. 399)*

## The Persian Gulf Crisis

During 1989 and early 1990 the Persian Gulf region was commanding less of the world's attention than it had in recent years. Compared with the monumental changes taking place in Germany, the Soviet Union, and Eastern Europe, events in the Persian Gulf seemed less central to world affairs than they had in the past. The region also appeared less turbulent. The Iran-Iraq War had ended in 1988 with an inconclusive but stable cease-fire. After the death of the Ayatollah Ruhollah Khomeini in 1989, Iran's leaders moderated their efforts to export their brand of Islamic fundamentalism and focused greater energies on domestic reconstruction.

This apparent lull in the turbulence of the Middle East was misleading. On August 2, 1990, any illusions that the Persian Gulf region had become more stable or predictable were shattered when Iraqi troops stormed into neighboring Kuwait. The invasion and subsequent annexation of Kuwait by Iraqi president Saddam Hussein set in motion a crisis that would remain at the forefront of the international agenda for more than seven months. By early March 1991 a U.S.-led coalition force had driven the Iraqi army from Kuwait and occupied much of southern Iraq. Virtually every target of military significance in Iraq had been bombed, and Saddam's regime was fighting for its life against an array of domestic rebel forces emboldened by the coalition's defeat of the Iraqi military.

The most widely felt consequence of the crisis, however, was the dramatic rise in the price of oil. After the invasion of Kuwait and the subsequent imposition of an international economic embargo against Iraq, oil prices skyrocketed in response to the marketplace's loss of Iraqi and Kuwaiti oil and fears that war would damage Saudi oil facilities. The price increases affected peoples and economies throughout the world, but developing economies dependent on oil were especially hard hit.

Three factors distinguished the Iraqi invasion of

Kuwait as a situation that demanded an international response. First, Kuwait's importance to the international economy is far beyond its size. It sits atop the fourth largest oil reserve in the world. If Saddam could have added Kuwait's oil resources to Iraq's and used his superior military might to bully Saudi Arabia and the smaller Gulf oil states into supporting Iraq's positions in OPEC, he could have dominated oil production and pricing policies. Oil prices still would have been tied to supply and demand, but Saddam would have been in a position to push prices up, thereby straining the world economy. Second, Iraq's efforts to acquire nuclear weapons and its existing stocks of conventional, chemical, and biological weapons made that country a long-term military threat to the entire Middle East and perhaps beyond. Third, Iraq's government had demonstrated an appetite for military conquest and a capacity for brutality. Since 1980 Iraq had invaded Iran, resorted to the use of chemical weapons against Iranian soldiers and ballistic missiles against Iranian citizens, and used poison gas against its own Kurdish population during a campaign to snuff out the Kurdish resistance movement.

Because much of the Arab world and the international community during the 1980s considered Iraq to be a counterweight to a more threatening Iran, world reaction to Iraqi behavior had been restrained. But the invasion of Kuwait revealed an unmistakable pattern of Iraqi aggression.

The multinational coalition destroyed Iraq's offensive military capacity. The war left unanswered, however, many political and economic questions concerning the Persian Gulf region. By forcing Middle East countries to choose sides in an expanding conflict, Iraq's act of aggression inflamed regional problems seemingly unrelated to the invasion. The crisis demonstrated that peace and stability in the Middle East would remain elusive until such time as the nations of that area and the entire international community dealt with the Arab-Israeli conflict, the regional arms race, the disparities in wealth among Middle Eastern countries, and other contentious issues.

## Road to Aggression

Iraq's aggression against Kuwait grew out of Iraqi economic problems produced by the Iran-Iraq War. The war had left Iraq $80 billion in debt. Almost half of this was owed to Saudi Arabia, Kuwait, and the Gulf states. Iraqi leaders believed that debts to Arab nations related to the war with Iran should be forgiven. They reasoned that Iraq had served as a shield against Iran, which threatened all Arabs, especially those on the Persian Gulf. During the eight years of war, Iraq had paid a steep price—hundreds of thousands of Iraqis had been killed or maimed and the country was left with few funds for reconstruction, despite its huge oil reserves. Given these circumstances, Saddam Hussein regarded as an injustice the refusal of his Arab brothers to forgive Iraq's debts. Moreover, he maintained that forgiving Iraqi debts was in his creditors' self-interest because Iraq's economic health remained crucial to the security of the Arab world. Arguments that Iraq had started the war against Iran in pursuit of its own objectives, not as a defensive action to block Iranian aggression toward the Arab world, had little persuasive power in Baghdad.

During the spring and summer of 1990, Kuwait became the focus of Iraqi resentment against its Arab creditors. Besides refusing to write off Iraqi war debts, Kuwait was exceeding its oil-production quota set by OPEC, thereby contributing to low international oil prices. Iraqi reconstruction from its war with Iran could only be based upon revenues from its oil resources. But the low price limited the cash Iraq could earn through oil sales. Iraq blamed quota violators—specifically, Kuwait and the United Arab Emirates—for the depressed prices. According to Saddam Hussein, the overproduction by his Arab brothers amounted to economic warfare that threatened his country's security and prosperity. That Iraq, like most other OPEC members, also had engaged in overproduction made little difference to Saddam. He had problems, and he believed he could profit by blaming Kuwait and the United Arab Emirates.

Iraq also charged that Kuwait had pumped

# UN Security Council Resolutions on Iraq

*August 2—Resolution 660.* Condemns Iraq's invasion of Kuwait. Demands an unconditional and immediate withdrawal. *Vote:* 14 for, 0 against, 1 abstention (Yemen).

*August 6—Resolution 661.* Imposes mandatory economic sanctions against Iraq that include a complete trade embargo. Only food and medicine "in humanitarian circumstances" are exempted. *Vote:* 13 for, 2 abstentions (Yemen and Cuba).

*August 9—Resolution 662.* Declares Iraq's annexation of Kuwait null and void. *Vote:* Unanimous (15-0).

*August 18—Resolution 664.* Condemns Iraq for holding foreign nationals hostage and demands their immediate release. Demands that Iraq refrain from closing diplomatic and consular missions in Kuwait. *Vote:* Unanimous (15-0).

*August 25—Resolution 665.* Authorizes coalition warships to use force if necessary to prevent circumvention of the trade embargo against Iraq. *Vote:* 13 for, 2 abstentions (Yemen and Cuba).

*September 13—Resolution 666.* Establishes guidelines for humanitarian food aid to Iraq and occupied Kuwait. Reaffirms that medical supplies are exempt from the embargo. *Vote:* 13 for, 2 against (Yemen and Cuba).

*September 16—Resolution 667.* Condemns Iraq for violence against foreign embassies and diplomats in Kuwait. Demands protection for diplomatic and consular personnel. *Vote:* Unanimous (15-0).

*September 24—Resolution 669.* Agrees to consider exceptions to Resolution 661 for shipment of humanitarian supplies to Iraq and authorizes the examination of requests by states for economic assistance under Article 50. *Vote:* Unanimous (15-0).

*September 25—Resolution 670.* Tightens the embargo on air traffic to and from Iraq and authorizes the detention of Iraq's merchant fleet. *Vote:* Unanimous (15-0).

*October 29—Resolution 674.* Holds Iraq responsible for all financial losses resulting from its invasion of Kuwait and calls on UN members to gather evidence of human rights abuses by Iraqi troops in Kuwait. Demands that Iraq release third-country nationals and provide food to those being held against their will. Reiterates demand that diplomatic missions in Kuwait be protected. *Vote:* 13 for, 2 abstentions (Yemen and Cuba).

*November 28—Resolution 677.* Condemns Iraqi attempts to alter the demographic composition of Kuwait and to destroy the civil records maintained by the legitimate government of Kuwait. Mandates the UN secretary general to take custody of a copy of the Kuwaiti population register. *Vote:* Unanimous (15-0).

*November 29—Resolution 678.* Authorizes "member states cooperating with the government of Kuwait" to use "all necessary means" to uphold the above resolutions if Iraq has not complied with them by January 15, 1991. *Vote:* 12 for, 2 against (Yemen and Cuba), 1 abstention (China).

---

$2.4 billion worth of oil that rightfully belonged to Iraq from the Rumaila oil field, only a small part of which lies under Kuwaiti territory. These communications alarmed other Arab leaders who feared that Iraq was not bluffing about its intention to force changes in the oil-production policies of Kuwait and the United Arab Emirates.

On July 25 tensions eased somewhat. Egyptian president Hosni Mubarak, who had been the focus of Arab efforts to mediate the dispute, announced that Iraq and Kuwait had agreed to hold talks in Jiddah, Saudi Arabia, on August 1 to discuss their differences. Mubarak also said that Saddam Hussein had assured him that Iraq did not plan to attack Kuwait.

The talks in Jiddah on August 1 lasted only two hours before they broke down. The following day Iraqi army units invaded Kuwait. The quick Iraqi resort to military force following a token attempt at direct negotiations with Kuwait appeared premeditated. It is almost certain that Iraq planned before the Jiddah talks to invade Kuwait.

Although Kuwait's oil-production policies contributed to the Iraqi regime's aggressive posture toward Kuwait, it is possible that even if Kuwait had appeased Iraq fully by agreeing to cut oil production, write off Iraq's debts, and compensate Iraq for oil taken from the Rumaila oil field, Saddam Hussein would still have found a pretext to invade the country. Iraq's invasion was more than a response to its neighbor's oil production policies. It was an attempt to provide a quick fix to Iraq's severe economic problems and to obtain funding for continued expansion of Iraqi military capabilities by seizing Kuwait's immense wealth. The invasion also was intended to improve Iraq's access to the Persian Gulf and to redraw colonial borders to which Iraq had long objected.

## Invasion and Occupation of Kuwait

Before dawn on August 2, 1990, Iraqi armored divisions drove into Kuwait. The well-equipped, battle-hardened Iraqi army, led by elite Republican Guard troops, quickly seized control of the country. Saddam claimed that his forces were responding to a call for help from Kuwaiti revolutionaries who had overthrown the al-Sabah regime. Iraq's government indicated the day after the invasion that it planned to withdraw from Kuwait by August 5. In actuality there was no revolution, and Iraq had no intention of withdrawing. On August 8 Baghdad ended the pretense by announcing that it was annexing Kuwait, which would become Iraq's "nineteenth province."

International outrage at Iraq's aggression and duplicity was compounded by stories of Iraqi atrocities told by people who had fled Kuwait. The behavior of Iraqi troops and commanders revealed a deep-seated resentment among many Iraqis of Kuwait's wealth and superciliousness. The occupation was deliberately bloody, destructive, and vindictive; much of the damage done had no strategic or military purpose or benefit. Refugees described torture and summary executions of Kuwaiti citizens and widespread looting by Iraqi troops. The invasion force appeared to be systematically stripping Kuwait of everything of value. Throughout its occupation, Baghdad refused to allow journalists or Red Cross observers to visit Kuwait to investigate human rights abuses.

While robbing Kuwait of its wealth, Iraq initiated a campaign to depopulate it and replace its citizens with Iraqis. Iraqis were being moved into Kuwait, and Kuwaitis who were allowed to leave the country had their identity papers and passports confiscated. Kuwaitis who were out of the country at the time of the invasion were barred from returning. Some Kuwaitis were forcibly deported to Iraq. By October intelligence reports estimated that only two hundred forty thousand of Kuwait's six hundred thousand citizens remained in the country.

## American and Saudi Response

Like much of the world, the administration of President George Bush and the U.S. intelligence community were caught off guard by the Iraqi invasion. Although the massing of Iraqi forces on the Kuwait border had caused U.S. leaders concern, few officials or analysts believed that Saddam was audacious enough to invade Kuwait.

President Bush's primary concern in the days after the invasion was deterring an Iraqi attack on Saudi Arabia. The Saudis' massive oil reserves were vital to the world's economy. An Iraqi move against them or the Saudi government would force the United States to take military action, almost regardless of the circumstances or the relative strength of American and Iraqi troops in the region at the time.

Bush pressed the Saudi Arabian government to allow American soldiers to be stationed in that country. Although the Saudis maintained a close relationship with and bought most of their military equipment from the United States, they had never sought or consented to an American military presence in Saudi Arabia. Because of U.S. support for Israel, most Arab countries were wary of accommodating American troops. The Saudi government, as the guardian of the Islamic holy places in Mecca and Medina, also could expose itself to criticism that it was allowing the holy places to be defiled by the presence of a large non-Islamic army.

In the early days of August, however, Saudi officials considered the threat from Iraq to be much greater than the damage an American military presence might do to Saudi Arabia's domestic stability and standing within the Muslim community. After U.S. defense secretary Dick Cheney on August 6 showed King Fahd ibn Abdul Aziz satellite intelligence of Iraqi missiles pointed at Saudi Arabia and Iraqi forces massing near the Saudi border, the king threw his lot in with the United States. American forces began arriving in Saudi Arabia the next day.

During the initial stages of the deployment, American forces and their Saudi allies were outnumbered greatly by Iraqi forces in Kuwait and southern Iraq. By the end of the third week in August, however, the threat of an Iraqi offensive had diminished as the United States, Great Britain, and several other nations assembled formidable air and naval forces in the Gulf region. Meanwhile the United States continued its deployments of ground forces. They were joined in August by troops from Great Britain, France, Egypt, Syria, Morocco, Pakistan, and a number of other countries.

### Anti-Iraq Coalition

The United States encouraged broad international participation in the military effort to defend Saudi Arabia and enforce UN sanctions. The Bush administration succeeded in building a broad multinational coalition that proved to be enduring and resilient. More than two dozen nations contributed combat forces to the defense of Saudi Arabia and the eventual liberation of Kuwait. Other nations provided medical teams, transport assistance, or financial aid to the coalition. *(Contributors to the Multinational Coalition, table, p. 113)*

Aside from Saudi Arabia, Egypt and Syria were the most important Arab members of the coalition. Egypt's President Mubarak led Arab opposition to the Iraqi invasion. By January 1991 Egypt had deployed thirty thousand troops in the region. Syria long had denounced U.S. patronage of Israel, and the United States had declared Syria to be a supporter of international terrorists, but both temporarily set aside their differences to pursue their common interest of forcing Iraq out of Kuwait. President Hafez al-Assad sent nineteen thousand troops to Saudi Arabia. Combat forces from the Arab states of Morocco, Bahrain, Oman, Qatar, the United Arab Emirates, and Kuwait also participated in the coalition under Saudi command. The Bush administration placed a high value on the continuing participation of the Arab members of the coalition. The presence in Saudi Arabia of troops from a variety of Arab countries weakened Iraqi claims that the United States and its Western allies were waging a war of aggression against Arab nations and peoples.

Throughout the Gulf crisis, Great Britain was the staunchest Western ally of the United States. It contributed thirty-five thousand troops—the largest Western contingent to the multinational force next to the United States—and it provided unswerving support for American initiatives. The British also felt some responsibility for Kuwait, which had been under British protection until it received its full independence in 1961.

With seventeen thousand troops committed to the coalition, France also made a sizable contribution. Italy and Canada provided warplanes and many other Western nations sent combat ships to the region. Pakistan and Bangladesh each sent several thousand troops to Saudi Arabia, and Turkey maintained an imposing military presence on Iraq's northern border that both guarded against an Iraqi attack and forced Iraq to keep several divisions near its northern border.

Although the Soviet Union declined to send significant forces (it did have ships in the Gulf) and sometimes pursued its own agenda during the crisis, Moscow backed the United States in every important vote in the United Nations Security Council, including the votes imposing a total economic embargo against Iraq and authorizing coalition forces to go to war.

Despite wide participation, the coalition arrayed against Iraq was clearly an American-led operation.

# Contributions to the Multinational Coalition

*Argentina*—100 troops, 2 transport planes, and 2 warships.

*Australia*—2 warships and 1 supply ship.

*Bangladesh*—6,000 troops.

*Belgium*—2 minesweepers, 1 supply ship, 3 other ships, and 6 transport planes.

*Bulgaria*—Medical personnel.

*Canada*—2 warships, 1 supply ship, 18 combat aircraft, and 12 other planes.

*Czechoslovakia*—200 chemical defense troops and 150 medical personnel.

*Denmark*—1 ship.

*Egypt*—30,000 troops and 400 tanks.

*France*—17,000 troops, 350 tanks, 38 combat aircraft, and 14 ships.

*Germany*—5 minesweepers and 3 other ships in the eastern Mediterranean and 18 warplanes in Turkey as part of a defensive NATO deployment.

*Great Britain*—35,000 troops, 120 tanks, 60 combat aircraft, and 18 ships.

*Greece*—1 ship.

*Gulf Cooperation Council (Saudi Arabia, Bahrain, Oman, United Arab Emirates, Qatar, and Kuwait)*—Combined force of 10,000 frontline troops. Each country also made individual contributions of planes and ships.

*Kuwait*—7,000 frontline troops, 34 combat aircraft.

*Italy*—4 minesweepers, 6 other ships, and 8 combat aircraft.

*Morocco*—2,000 troops.

*Netherlands*—3 warships and 18 combat aircraft.

*New Zealand*—2 transport planes and medical personnel.

*Niger*—480 troops.

*Norway*—1 support ship.

*Pakistan*—2,000 troops in Saudi Arabia and 3,000 troops in the United Arab Emirates.

*Poland*—Medical personnel and 1 hospital ship.

*Portugal*—1 transport ship.

*Saudi Arabia*—66,000 troops (20,000 serving at the front lines), 550 tanks, 300 planes (about 135 of which were modern combat aircraft), and 8 ships.

*Senegal*—500 troops.

*Soviet Union*—4 ships on patrol in the region but not involved in coalition operations.

*Spain*—3 warships.

*Sweden*—Medical personnel.

*Syria*—19,000 troops deployed in Saudi Arabia, 50,000 deployed along the Iraqi-Syrian border, and 270 tanks.

*Turkey*—100,000 troops deployed along the Iraqi-Turkish border, 2 warships in the Persian Gulf, 7 ships in the eastern Mediterranean.

*United States*—430,000 troops, approximately 2,000 tanks, 1,800 combat aircraft, and more than 100 ships (including 6 aircraft carriers).

*Note:* Figures were as of January 15, 1991, and included ships stationed in the Red Sea and eastern Mediterranean.

*Sources:* Associated Press; Center for Defense Information; *The Economist; New York Times; Time; Washington Post.*

No other Western nation possessed military forces large enough to form the core of an anti-Iraq coalition. Had the United States sat on the sidelines, an international military force would not have been deployed in Saudi Arabia and economic sanctions might not have been strictly enforced.

The Japanese did not want to be seen as taking advantage of the crisis by sitting on the sidelines while their major industrial competitors and trade partners committed huge resources to defending Saudi Arabia and liberating Kuwait. Consequently, the Japanese government pledged financial aid instead of troop deployments. By early 1991 Japan had pledged a total of almost $11 billion to the United States and $3 billion to Middle East nations.

Like Japan, Germany chose to make a financial contribution instead of sending military forces. It pledged $2 billion to the Gulf effort on September 15 and later increased its total contribution to almost $8 billion, $6.5 billion of which would go to the United States. The biggest financial contributors to the military effort against Iraq, however, were Saudi Arabia and Kuwait, both of which pledged more than $16 billion. All the major donors delivered on their pledges, which totaled $54 billion.

## UN Sanctions

In tandem with the U.S. military effort to defend Saudi Arabia, the Bush administration launched a diplomatic campaign to create an anti-Iraq consensus within the international community. The United Nations Security Council became the focus of this campaign.

On August 2, the same day as Iraq's invasion, the UN Security Council met in emergency session and unanimously passed Resolution 660, which condemned the invasion and called for an immediate Iraqi withdrawal. Four days later the Security Council passed Resolution 661, which established an almost total embargo on Iraqi commerce. The embargo was to include all imports going to and exports coming from Iraq, except for humanitarian shipments of medicine and some food. Iraq was particularly vulnerable to a complete economic embargo because it depended almost completely on oil exports for foreign earnings and it imported about 75 percent of its food. Iraqi oil could be exported only through the Persian Gulf sea route and through pipelines running across Saudi Arabia to the Red Sea and across Turkey to the Mediterranean. All three avenues of export were quickly cut off by the embargo, depriving Iraq of hard currency earnings.

Resolution 661 only called on UN member states to observe the embargo. It provided no explicit authorization of a military blockade to enforce the sanctions. The United States insisted that it had the right to use military force to prevent circumvention of the embargo. On August 16

U.S. naval forces in the Persian Gulf began interdicting ships carrying cargoes to or from Iraq. The British concurred in this judgment, but the other three permanent members of the council, the French, Chinese, and Soviets, claimed that a new resolution was necessary if military force were to be used to prevent leakage through the embargo.

On August 25, after much lobbying by the United States, the Security Council passed Resolution 665, specifically authorizing the use of force necessary to ensure compliance with the embargo against Iraq. Any commerce between Iraq and the rest of the world would have to occur over land. While circumvention of the embargo by traders operating out of Jordan (and to a lesser extent, Turkey and Iran) would help keep Iraq supplied with foods and certain other goods, its economy would be crippled by the embargo. The UN blockade quickly succeeded in cutting off virtually all of Iraq's exports and, by some estimates, 90 percent of its imports.

## Hostages

When it became obvious that the United States and other Western nations were going to oppose the invasion of Kuwait with military deployments and severe economic sanctions, the Iraqi regime moved to play one of the cards in its hand—Westerners stranded in Iraq and Kuwait. On August 9 Iraq announced that it was sealing its borders and allowing only diplomatic personnel to leave. Four days later Iraqi officials confirmed that foreigners would not be allowed to leave Iraq (or Kuwait) until the crisis was over. Iraq avoided calling the foreigners hostages, referring to them instead as "guests." In late August the Iraqi government began rounding up Westerners in Iraq and Kuwait, many of whom had gone into hiding, for the purpose of holding them at strategic military sites throughout Iraq. The Iraqis primarily used American and British citizens as "human shields," but citizens of a number of European nations and Japan were detained at military sites as well.

Iraq's detention of Westerners was intended to

deter a coalition air attack against military targets inside Iraq and Kuwait, stimulate peace movements in Western countries, and paralyze governments that might otherwise vigorously oppose Iraq. But by holding hostages, Iraq was taking a big propaganda risk. Only hard-core Iraqi supporters in a few Arab countries would condone the use of innocent civilians as hostages and human shields. Western leaders repeatedly pointed to the hostage taking as another example of Saddam Hussein's brutality.

Saddam's incomplete understanding of how his holding of hostages would be perceived was demonstrated by a bizarre meeting between Saddam and a group of British hostages August 23. Iraqi television broadcast a forty-minute videotape of the meeting, which was intended to portray Saddam as a benign, patriarchal leader concerned for the welfare of his "guests." Images of the Iraqi leader smiling as he spoke with tense Britons through an interpreter, posing with the hostages for a group photograph, and patting the head of a distrusting young boy reinforced Saddam's reputation in the West as manipulative and maniacal.

Sensing that holding the hostages could backfire, the Iraqis announced August 28 that they would release foreign women and children. By September 22 all Western and Japanese women and children who wanted to leave Iraq and Kuwait had been flown out on chartered Iraqi flights, for which their governments had to pay Iraq hard currency. The Iraqis, however, held on to most male adult hostages, continuing to house many of them at strategic locations. On December 6, a week after the UN Security Council passed a resolution authorizing the coalition to use military force against Iraq after January 15, Saddam Hussein informed the Iraqi National Assembly that all foreign hostages would be released.

## Arab Politics

The Iraqi invasion of Kuwait forced Arab governments to choose sides in a conflict that was fraught with dangers for the individual countries of the Middle East and the region as a whole.

Saudi Arabia was directly and immediately threatened by Iraqi forces, and was therefore willing to join the United States in opposing Baghdad.

Almost every Arab state regarded Saddam Hussein's annexation of Kuwait as unlawful. Fourteen of twenty-one Arab League nations condemned the Iraqi invasion the day after it happened. Like Kuwait, the boundaries of most Middle East countries had been created arbitrarily during colonial times. Saddam's argument that his invasion of Kuwait merely was an effort to redress past colonial injustices threatened to set the precedent that all Middle East boundaries could be subject to reinterpretation.

Arab leaders also understood that Saddam's ambitions, which stretched far beyond Kuwait, could place their own regimes in jeopardy. However, they were hesitant to abandon the myth of Arab unity or take a position that could place them on the side of a Western military intervention against a fraternal Arab state, especially one with menacing military strength.

After a week of indecision in the Arab world, President Mubarak of Egypt called an emergency meeting of the Arab League that was held in Cairo August 10. Mubarak announced that the meeting would attempt to find an "Arab solution" to the crisis in an effort to avert outside intervention. Iraq, however, refused to make any concessions on Kuwait. Its delegation to the Cairo summit even asserted that Baghdad's August 8 annexation of Kuwait gave it the right to control Kuwait's seat at the meeting. The summit ended with twelve of the twenty-one Arab League members voting to send troops to Saudi Arabia to defend it against Iraq. Arab troops were to operate under Saudi command, distinct from Western contingents that might also be deployed in Saudi Arabia. The twelve Arab nations opposing Iraq were Bahrain, Djibouti, Egypt, Kuwait, Lebanon, Morocco, Oman, Qatar, Saudi Arabia, Somalia, Syria, and the United Arab Emirates. Iraq, Libya, and the Palestine Liberation Organization (PLO) voted against the measure. Jordan, Mauritania, and Sudan voted for it "with reservations." Algeria and

Yemen abstained, and Tunisia did not attend the meeting.

Arab governments made their decision according to their own perceived self-interests, not according to their feelings toward Kuwait or their desire to preserve Arab unity. The wealthy Gulf states, which had the most to fear from Iraq, followed Saudi Arabia's leadership and joined with the West in opposing Iraq. Egypt, which received $2.3 billion a year in aid from the United States and which has traditionally been an Iraqi rival for Arab leadership, also sided with Saudi Arabia and the West. President Assad of Syria joined the coalition despite longstanding differences with the United States. His personal enmity toward Saddam Hussein and his ambitions for Damascus to eclipse Baghdad as a power center in the Arab world made an Iraqi defeat a tantalizing prospect. He also was eager to improve relations with the wealthy Gulf states who could replace dwindling Soviet financial support.

In contrast, poorer Arab nations tended to side with Saddam or declare their neutrality. As the leader of a militarily powerful Arab nation confronting the oil-rich Gulf Arabs, Israel, and the West, Saddam had a strong appeal among poorer segments of the Arab population. Jordanians and Palestinians in particular rallied to support Saddam, but pro-Iraq demonstrations also were common in Yemen, Lebanon, Algeria, Libya, Tunisia, and the Sudan. Demonstrations of support for Iraq also were reported in some nations whose governments joined the coalition, including Egypt, Syria, and Morocco.

## Limits of Pan-Arabism

The Iraqi invasion of Kuwait and the willingness of Arab governments to pursue their own interests, even if it meant allying themselves with foreign troops, demonstrated that the notion of pan-Arabism did not reflect the realities of the Arab world. Pan-Arabism was the concept that all Arabs in the Middle East could unite to form a single Arab nation. That Iraq could invade its Arab neighbor and subject Kuwaiti citizens to torture was powerful evidence that pan-Arabism could not be taken seriously.

Although Arab states share common linguistic, religious, historical, and cultural roots, and have sought to limit outside influence in the Middle East, they have evolved into independent nations with widely different needs and objectives since the Ottoman Empire was fragmented after World War I. The twenty-one members of the Arab League, an organization founded in 1945 on pan-Arabist principles, were divided by their ties to foreign powers, sectarian and ethnic compositions, levels of wealth, and other factors. Yet despite the obvious limits of Pan-Arabism in the modern Middle East, the concept has a strong appeal among poorer Arabs who have seen their individual countries dominated by Western powers and militarily threatened by Israel and Persian Iran. Pan-Arabism has held out the hope of achieving Arab military strength, economic independence from the West, and a more equal distribution of oil wealth among the Arab people. Saddam Hussein sought to take advantage of the pan-Arabist romanticism of many poor Arabs. Ironically, he portrayed his invasion of Kuwait as a first step toward a broader Arab union that would restore the Arab world's glorious past. Saddam attempted to create an image of himself as a strong Arab nationalist who would defend the rights of poor Arabs against Israel and the wealthy Gulf rulers.

Saddam's march into Kuwait and his lonely stand against the West appealed to longstanding Arab resentments and frustrations. To Arabs who hated their colonial past, his confronting a coalition that included the United States, Great Britain, France, and other Western nations signaled the beginning of a new era of Arab independence. To Arabs frustrated by several military defeats at the hands of Israel, the apparent might of Iraq's army proved that Arab states were not necessarily doomed to military inferiority. To poverty-stricken Arabs the sight of Kuwait's elite being transformed from wealthy oil barons with extravagant lifestyles into refugees was satisfying. When Saddam Hussein promised an equal distribution of oil wealth among the Arab people, he was seen as a modern-day Robin Hood, whose brutal means could be justified by his goals. He also was compared with Saladin, the twelfth-century Muslim military leader who defeated European crusaders and liberated Jerusalem.

Although Saddam was hailed in the streets of Amman, the villages of the West Bank, and in many other parts of the Arab world, the fact remained that most Arab governments opposed him. Moreover, the three most powerful and influential Arab nations besides Iraq—Egypt, Saudi Arabia, and Syria—all were deploying sizable military forces on the Saudi-Kuwaiti border. Eight Arab nations had refused to sanction military deployments against Iraq, but the twelve that did contained 60 percent of the people living in Arab countries and a much larger percentage of Arab wealth. With this level of Arab participation in the multinational coalition, Saddam would find it difficult to persuade Arabs not already inclined to support him that he was fighting a holy war against invaders.

## Toward War in the Gulf

Once U.S. and allied military deployments in Saudi Arabia had removed the possibility that Iraq could launch an offensive that could threaten Saudi Arabia and its oil fields, the Bush administration had to decide on a strategy for dealing with Saddam's occupation of Kuwait. There was broad consensus among Americans and members of Congress that Saddam should be opposed and Saudi Arabia should be protected. The public's support for a possible U.S.-led military action against Iraq was less certain.

On November 8, two days after midterm congressional elections in the United States, President Bush announced that he was reinforcing the two hundred thirty thousand U.S. troops already in the Gulf participating in what was known as "Operation Desert Shield." He provided no specific total of how many troops would be sent, but Pentagon sources said that approximately two hundred thousand more troops would be deployed in the region.

The new deployments to Saudi Arabia and the end of troop rotation plans alarmed critics in Congress, who complained that the administration's policies shortened the time economic sanctions would have to take effect and force Iraq out of Kuwait. Military experts agreed that the United States could not sustain such a large force in an inhospitable desert environment indefinitely, and the new deployments would force the administration to choose between withdrawing part of the force, which would be perceived as a moral victory for Saddam Hussein, or going to war.

The massive military buildup in Saudi Arabia reflected a change in President Bush's strategy. He appeared to be rejecting the long-term approach of relying on economic sanctions to force Iraq out of Kuwait. In announcing the deployments on November 8 Bush said that the additional forces being sent to Saudi Arabia were intended to "insure that the coalition has an adequate offensive military option should that be necessary to achieve our common goals." Bush believed that his best chance to force Iraq out of Kuwait peacefully was to present Baghdad with a coalition force capable of inflicting terrible damage on Iraqi forces. Until such a coalition force was in place, Bush did not believe that the threat of attack would be credible. The new buildup, therefore, was a high-stakes gamble. It increased the pressure on Saddam to withdraw, but greatly heightened the likelihood of war if he did not.

Saddam Hussein was believed to be a ruthless tyrant willing to sacrifice many lives for his purposes, but he also was seen as a leader who could be counted on to act in his self-interest. Sanctions might not force Saddam out of Kuwait, even if he were faced with a complete embargo imposed over a number of years. But if he could be made to see that his armies, upon which he depended for his personal power and prestige, would be destroyed in a war with the United States and its coalition partners, Bush and his advisers believed that Saddam would find a face-saving way to withdraw from Kuwait.

The Bush administration also took this approach because the perceived fragility of the anti-Iraq coalition created a sense of urgency. It was feared that unrest motivated by support for Iraq within Arab countries supporting the coalition could topple friendly governments or weaken the resolve of these governments to remain in the coalition. In addition, the October 8 killings of as many as twenty-one Palestinians in Jerusalem by Israeli security policy demonstrated that events in the occupied territories or any provocative Israeli military strike could cause Arabs to reconsider their opposition to a fraternal Arab nation that was militarily strong enough to be a counterweight to Israel.

The timing of an offensive, if one became necessary, was an additional consideration. After the middle of March, extreme desert heat would return to the Gulf region, and this would favor the defenders. Also, the Muslim holy month of Ramadan would begin in March, complicating Arab participation in the coalition. These factors weighed heavily on the side of employing the military option sooner instead of later.

Perhaps the most important factor in the Bush administration's decision, however, was that many officials at the Pentagon and the White House and their Arab counterparts feared an Iraqi withdrawal from Kuwait almost as much as a war. A pullout would have left the formidable Iraqi military (as well as its nuclear research facilities and its chemical and biological weapons industries) intact and capable of threatening its neighbors, including Saudi Arabia and Kuwait. Even if the international community agreed to impose indefinite restrictions on sales of arms and technologies with military uses to Iraq, Baghdad would already be in possession of military power that none of its neighbors could match. Consequently, President Bush stated that if Iraq withdrew an international peacekeeping force would be needed on the ground and U.S. naval forces in the Persian Gulf would need to be strengthened.

Meanwhile, seeking to prove that his withdrawal from Kuwait was not an act of cowardice or betrayal of the cause of poor Arabs, Saddam Hussein would be tempted to pursue other aggressive policies, particularly against Israel. Such conditions would heighten Arab-Israeli tensions and dramatically increase the possibility of another Arab-Israeli war. Israel already had hinted that it could not allow Iraq to make further progress toward developing accurate missiles and atomic weapons. Its air attack against the Iraqi Osirak nuclear reactor in 1981 had demonstrated that Israel was quite willing to use military force against Iraq without a direct Iraqi military provocation. If Iraq threw its military weight behind an Arab attack against Israel, the conflagration would far exceed previous Arab-Israeli wars. The military threat posed by Iraq, especially its chemical and biological weapons, might even induce Israel to use nuclear weapons against Iraq. Consequently, the Bush administration regarded peace based on an Iraqi withdrawal as an outcome nearly as dangerous as a war. The official U.S. policy objectives continued to be the ouster of Iraq from Kuwait through economic sanctions and the threat of military force, but implicit in Bush's willingness to make the military threat was an underlying belief that war might be the wise option.

## UN Deadline

After announcing the new military deployments to Saudi Arabia, the Bush administration began pursuing the possibility of a UN Security Council sanction for the use of force against Iraq. On November 29 the UN Security Council voted 12-2 (with Yemen and Cuba dissenting) to implicitly authorize coalition nations to use force to expel Iraq from Kuwait. Security Council Resolution 678, however, allowed for a month and a half of diplomacy by authorizing force only after January 15. Diplomats would have forty-seven days to persuade Iraq to withdraw from Kuwait peacefully or to construct a compromise.

Diplomatic efforts came to a climax on January 9, 1991, when U.S. secretary of state Baker met Iraqi foreign minister Tariq Aziz in Geneva. The negotiations began amidst general pessimism that neither the Americans nor the Iraqis would make compromises necessary to avoid war. After six and a half hours Baker and Aziz emerged from their meeting and reported that neither side had budged

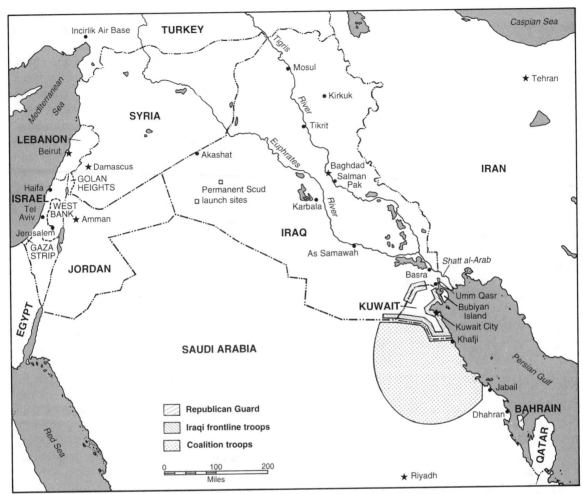

*Before the Gulf War began on January 17, 1991, coalition ground forces were concentrated opposite Iraqi fortifications along the Saudi-Kuwaiti border. Iraqi commanders hoped to bloody the attackers as they tried to breach frontline minefields and obstacles. Republican Guard units were stationed behind Iraqi lines with the mission of responding to coalition breakthroughs. The Iraqis intended to draw Israel into the conflict by firing Scud surface-to-surface missiles at the Jewish state from fixed launch sites and mobile missile launchers positioned in Western Iraq. After the bombing campaign began, the coalition secretly moved much of its attacking ground forces west to positions along the Saudi-Iraqi border, which Iraq had left almost undefended.*

from its original position. Aziz had refused even to accept a letter written by Bush to Saddam Hussein, saying the letter's language was "not compatible with the language that should be used in correspondence between heads of state." American officials said the letter called on Saddam to

withdraw from Kuwait and described the military capability of the international force arrayed against him. Bush later called Aziz's performance at the meeting "a total stiff-arm, a total rebuff."

Both houses of Congress voted January 12 to empower the president to use force to drive Iraq from Kuwait. The vote was 250-183 in the House and 52-47 in the Senate. Bush had claimed the authority as commander in chief to order an attack against Iraq regardless of congressional action, but the vote strengthened his domestic position. Most members of Congress who had voted against authorizing war accepted the decision of the body and closed ranks behind the president. The coalition would go to war unless Iraq took steps to withdraw from Kuwait by January 15.

## Persian Gulf War

On the morning of Tuesday, January 15, 1991, President Bush signed an executive order in Washington, D.C., authorizing an aerial offensive against Iraq that would begin the following night unless a diplomatic breakthrough occurred before the deadline passed at midnight EST January 15. Wednesday afternoon Secretary of Defense Cheney ordered the U.S. commander in Saudi Arabia, Gen. H. Norman Schwarzkopf, to launch the attack. The coalition's strategy was to wage an extended air campaign against strategic targets in Iraq and Kuwait. Coalition military leaders were confident that they could quickly establish air supremacy over the badly outmatched Iraqi air force. Coalition warplanes could then methodically destroy Saddam Hussein's military machine and soften Iraqi defenses, so that when a ground offensive was launched, fewer coalition casualties would be suffered.

### Initial Bombing Raids

The first coalition airplanes left Saudi airfields at 12:50 a.m. Saudi time January 17 (4:50 p.m. EST January 16). The world learned that the air campaign had begun at 2:35 a.m. Saudi time when journalists in Baghdad reported thunderous bomb explosions amidst a torrent of antiaircraft fire.

American, British, Saudi, and Kuwaiti warplanes participated in the first wave of bombing. They were soon joined by French and Italian aircraft. The coalition had assembled more than two thousand planes in the Persian Gulf theater. Coali-

tion air forces would average about two thousand sorties (one round trip mission by one plane) per day during Operation Desert Storm.

Much of the world greeted news of the attack with resigned support. But, within a first few hours after the bombardment began, positive reports on the bombing created a euphoria in the United States and elsewhere in the international community, raising hopes that the chore of driving Iraq from Kuwait might be less costly in lives and wealth than previously imagined. This confidence resulted from the seeming inability of the Iraqi military to defend itself against air attacks or to take any significant offensive action against coalition forces.

### Scud Attacks

Early on January 18 the Iraqis struck back amid the unrelenting allied bombing campaign by launching a salvo of Scud missiles armed with conventional high explosive warheads at Israel. Eight Scuds struck the Jewish state in and around the cities of Tel Aviv and Haifa. The Scuds injured more than a dozen people, but no one was killed. Later in the day the Iraqis launched a Scud missile at Saudi Arabia. A U.S. Patriot antimissile missile intercepted and destroyed the Scud before it reached the ground. During the coming weeks, Iraq would fire dozens of Scuds at Israel and Saudi Arabia.

The Scud missile was a Soviet-made surface-to-surface weapon designed to deliver nuclear weapons over a short distance. The Soviets had sold hundreds of them to Iraq during the 1980s and Iraq had used them during the Iran-Iraq War to terrorize the population of Tehran with conventional warheads. Iran had fired its own Scuds at Baghdad in a dual that became known as "the war of the cities."

Because of their small payloads and inaccuracy, the Scuds had negligible strategic value. Iraq could not use them to destroy coalition military targets. They did, however, demonstrate to the Iraqi people and Saddam Hussein's supporters outside Iraq that the Iraqi military could strike back in some fashion against the coalition. More important, Saddam Hussein hoped that these missile attacks against Israel would draw the Jewish state into the war.

### Keeping Israel Out of the War

Israel's military reputation in the Middle East is based on its consistent retaliation for attacks against the Jewish state and its citizens and on its use of superior technology to defeat its opponents. Saddam was counting on Israel's behaving as it had in the past. If Israel retaliated against Iraq in response to Scud attacks, Arab members of the coalition would be placed in the uncomfortable position of fighting on the same side as Israel. Even if the Arabs did not back out of the coalition in response to an Israeli counterattack, Israeli participation in the war would increase sympathy for Iraq in the Arab world and thereby intensify the domestic political problems of Arab leaders supporting the anti-Iraq effort.

After the initial Scud attacks against Israel, the Israeli leadership came under extreme pressure from some cabinet members and citizens to strike back. The domestic pressure to retaliate was largely emotional, however. Most Israelis understood that if their government could resist the temptation to attack Iraq, the coalition would be stronger and better able to destroy Iraq's military quickly. They also knew that restraint on the part of their government could yield substantial political benefits and financial aid when the war was over.

The primary worry of Israeli officials was that Iraq would place chemical weapons on their Scuds. Although Iraq had substantial experience delivering chemical weapons with artillery and warplanes, delivering chemical weapons effectively on missiles traveling hundreds of miles was a technically difficult task. The Iraqis had never placed chemical weapons on missiles during the Iran-Iraq War. A chemical weapons attack against Israel may have been only marginally more dangerous to Israeli citizens than a conventional weapons attack, but poison gas used against Israelis would call up memories of the Holocaust, during which millions of Jews died in Nazi gas chambers. The Israeli government promised retaliation if Iraq used its Scuds to deliver chemical weapons against Israel.

An Israeli entry into the war against Iraq could conceivably have unraveled President Bush's careful diplomacy and splintered the anti-Iraq coalition. Regardless of their attitude toward Iraq, Arab states were united in their opposition to and distrust of Israel. No Arab leader would want to be perceived by his people as fighting alongside Israel against an Arab country. Nevertheless, Kuwait and Saudi Arabia appeared committed to the coalition regardless of whether the Israelis chose to retaliate. President Mubarak of Egypt said before the attack on Iraq that he would not withdraw his support for the coalition in response to Israeli retaliation for missile attacks. The Syrian government indicated after the first few Scud attacks on Israel that it also might not withdraw its forces from Saudi Arabia if Israel launched a limited retaliatory attack. Consequently, a proportional Israeli retalition would not have necessarily caused the coalition to fall apart as some analysts worried. Nevertheless, an Israeli attack against Iraq could have placed leaders of Arab nations participating in the coalition, especially Hosni Mubarak, in a difficult position domestically.

The Bush administration vigorously pressed the Israeli government to stay out of the war. Bush promised Israeli leaders that mobile Scud missile batteries in Western Iraq would be a top priority target of U.S. pilots. He also dispatched Patriot antimissile missile batteries and their U.S. crews to Israel. This deployment represented the first time that U.S. combat forces had ever been stationed in Israel. The Israeli government declared that the U.S. troops would remain only until Israeli units could be trained to operate the Patriot batteries.

Israeli leaders understood that, because Saddam's purpose in attacking Israel was to draw Israel into the war, an Israeli retaliation would be playing into his hands. The Israeli government abandoned its usual policy of retaliation. Because the circumstances of the Iraqi attacks were unique, by declining to retaliate Israel was not likely to weaken the effect of its long-term deterrence strategy. Israeli officials continually hinted that they might retaliate, but despite frequent Scud attacks, Israel stayed out of the war.

## Success of the Air Campaign

The air campaign was an unqualified success, given the minimal number of aircraft lost by the coalition and the destruction inflicted upon the Iraqi military, defense industries, and weapons research facilities. In a January 23 briefing, Gen. Colin Powell, chairman of the Joint Chiefs of Staff, declared that the coalition had achieved air superiority.

Iraqi warplanes had been so ineffective that during late January the Iraqi leadership had sent more than a hundred of its best planes to the safety of airfields in Iran. The few Iraqi warplanes that had challenged coalition aircraft or attempted to penetrate air defenses in Saudi Arabia and the Persian Gulf had been shot down. Meanwhile, allied air attacks were destroying many of Iraq's hardened aircraft shelters, presumably concealing warplanes inside them. Little would be left of the Iraqi air force if it tried to wait out the bombing in Iraq. Therefore, planes were sent to Iran in the hope they could be recovered after the war, or perhaps later in the present conflict. Iran, however, declared that it would return the planes to Iraq only after the war was over. Thus, dozens of Iraqi warplanes, many of which only two and a half years before had been bombing Iranian targets, sat out the fighting on Iranian airfields. After the war, Iran announced that it would keep the Iraqi planes.

Despite the destruction experienced by Iraq, the coalition air war had not forced an Iraqi capitulation as some military analysts had speculated might be possible. Nor had it triggered an internal Iraqi uprising against Saddam Hussein's regime. If coalition forces were going to reclaim Kuwait, they would have to do it on the ground.

## Ground War

The international community feared the beginning of the ground campaign almost as much as it had feared the opening of hostilities. The Iraqi army appeared to be much more formidable than the Iraqi air force, and Saddam had pinned his hopes of bloodying the attackers on the ground phase of the battle.

The Iraqi force in the Kuwait theater was estimated at approximately five hundred forty thousand troops (after the war, U.S. military officers with access to revised intelligence reports of Iraqi troop strength said that the number of Iraqis in the Kuwait theater might actually have been as few as three hundred fifty thousand). Any force this large had the potential to inflict thousands of coalition casualties, even if it had been bombed for five and half weeks. The coalition had assembled nearly seven hundred thousand troops in and around Saudi Arabia, but fewer than four hundred thousand would be directly involved in the attack against the Iraqis. Commentators pointed out that many Iraqi soldiers had gained extensive experience during the eight-year Iran-Iraq War, while most coalition forces would be seeing combat for the first time. The Iraqis also had the advantage of defending heavily fortified positions. Finally, the Iraqis were almost certain to use their stocks of chemical weapons against the attackers as they had done effectively during the Iran-Iraq War. Coalition forces were equipped with high-quality protective gear and were very mobile, but chemical attacks were dangerous and would slow the pace of any battle.

## Battle Plan

The official goal of the coalition offensive against Iraq had been the liberation of Kuwait. But President Bush and other coalition leaders hoped to destroy Saddam's army in the process, so he would be unable to threaten his neighbors in the near future. The coalition battle plan, therefore, sought not only to drive Iraqi forces from Kuwait, but also to cut off and destroy retreating Iraqi units. In his January 23 briefing, General Powell had declared bluntly, "Our strategy to go after this army is very, very simple. First, we're going to cut it off, and then we're going to kill it."

The battle plan included two major deceptions. First, naval and amphibious maneuvers were held before the ground offensive to make the Iraqis think that the coalition was preparing to attack the Kuwaiti coastline. Coalition commanders deployed eighteen thousand marines on ships off the Kuwaiti coast to reinforce this impression, and once the ground campaign had begun U.S. Marines faked a helicopter assault against Iraqi coastline defenses. As a result, Iraq committed one hundred twenty-five thousand troops to defend against a coastal attack that would never happen. Second, before the air campaign began, coalition forces had concentrated along the Saudi-Kuwaiti border to give the Iraqis the impression that the attack would be confined to that area. After American warplanes achieved air superiority, preventing Iraqi aircraft from flying surveillance missions, approximately two hundred seventy thousand American, British, and French troops, along with their heavy equipment and sixty days of supplies, were moved far to the west along the Saudi-Iraqi border. These forces were in a position to launch an attack around the Western flank of the Iraqi army in Kuwait. Even if Iraqi military leaders had known about the massive coalition force in the West, they could have done little about it because any column of troops or tanks sent west to reinforce the few Iraqi units facing the coalition army would have been vulnerable to air attacks.

The battle plan called for the coalition forces in the west to encircle the Iraqi army by sweeping around the Iraqis' right flank all the way to the Euphrates River. Republican Guard armored units would be forced to come out of their dug-in positions, making them vulnerable to attack from the air. Other coalition units would punch holes in the Iraqi defensive positions in Kuwait and drive on to Kuwait City. Meanwhile, the bombardment of Iraq and Kuwait by coalition warplanes would be intensified to give ground units as much air support as possible.

*American soldiers made up the largest contingent of the 270,000-member multinational force that drove Iraqi invaders from Kuwait in a remarkably brief ground war in early 1991. Superior weaponry and heavy aerial bombardment helped to end the war quickly, with few coalition casualties.*

## Soviet Peace Initiative

As the ground war approached, and Iraqi losses from the coalition air campaign mounted, Baghdad showed interest in a negotiated settlement. The Iraqi regime announced February 15 that it was willing to withdraw from Kuwait, but it attached numerous conditions to the withdrawal offer. President Bush and other coalition leaders immediately rejected the proposal.

Iraqi officials then turned for mediation assistance to the Soviet Union, their longtime patron, which had been urging them since August to withdraw peacefully from Kuwait. President Mikhail

Gorbachev presented a Soviet withdrawal plan to Foreign Minister Aziz on February 18. Bush, who had been informed of the proposal, told Gorbachev the following day that it was inadequate. On February 21 the Soviets announced that Iraq had accepted a modified Soviet plan that called for a "full and unconditional Iraqi withdrawal" from Kuwait. The six-point proposal, however, neglected to meet a growing list of U.S. conditions for an end to the war, including Iraqi willingness to pay reparations to Kuwait, disclose the location of all mines, and abide by all UN Security Council resolutions related to the Gulf War. The Bush administration also insisted that Iraqi forces withdraw from Kuwait within one week so that they would be unable to take all of their equipment with them. The Soviet plan allowed the Iraqis three weeks to leave.

Increasingly confident that a coalition ground campaign (which was ready to be launched) would be successful, Bush moved to head off further Iraqi peace proposals that he feared could divide the coalition by offering terms that came close to, but fell short of meeting, all coalition demands. On February 22 he announced that Saddam Hussein had until noon EST February 23 to begin a withdrawal and accept "publicly and authoritatively" all coalition requirements for a cease-fire. The U.S. conditions appeared designed to allow Saddam no room to save face if he accepted them. They mandated a swift and humiliating retreat that the Bush administration hoped would disgrace Saddam in the eyes of his supporters in Iraq and the Arab world. Reports that Iraqi troops had begun committing systematic atrocities in Kuwait and setting Kuwaiti oil wells ablaze stiffened coalition resolve to go to war immediately if Saddam did not agree to Bush's terms. The February 23 deadline passed without signs of an Iraqi withdrawal, and Bush ordered the offensive to proceed.

## One Hundred Hours

At 4:00 a.m. Saudi time February 24 the coalition launched its coordinated ground offensive. The assault would last exactly one hundred hours.

The huge American, British, and French force to the west penetrated deep into Iraq at a blitzkrieg pace. With French forces guarding their left flank, American troops reached the Euphrates River during the evening of February 25. Because allied bombers had destroyed bridges over the Euphrates, Iraqi units could not escape the coalition envelopment. Meanwhile American, Saudi, Egyptian, Syrian, Kuwaiti, and other Arab forces quickly breached Iraq's supposedly formidable frontline fortifications, consisting of barbed wire, sand berms, bunkers, minefields, and trenches filled with oil that could be ignited. These forces pushed toward Kuwait City, taking tens of thousands of Iraqi prisoners along the way.

With his army collapsing, Saddam Hussein delivered a radio speech on February 26 announcing an Iraqi withdrawal from Kuwait. He maintained a defiant tone, suggesting that the Iraqi retreat was a strategic withdrawal and telling Iraqis that "Kuwait is part of your country and was carved from it in the past." Most Iraqi forces were already engaged in a disorganized retreat by the time the speech was broadcast. With most Iraqi troops giving up without a fight, coalition troops suffering unbelievably light casualties, and domestic public opinion strongly in favor of pressing the advantage to ensure that Saddam would not soon be able to threaten his neighbors, Bush was not inclined to call off the attack unless Iraq agreed to severe terms. He responded to Saddam's speech later on February 26 by saying that the withdrawal did not meet his terms for a cease-fire and that the coalition would continue its offensive.

The American and British forces that had penetrated deep into Iraq in the west drove eastward February 26 toward Republican Guard divisions and other Iraqi forces trapped below the Euphrates. In the ensuing battles, large numbers of Iraqi tanks, artillery pieces, and military vehicles in the Kuwaiti theater that had escaped the air campaign were destroyed. The most intense fighting occurred February 27 when coalition armored units destroyed several Republican Guard divisions that were trying to shield other Iraqi troops retreating from Kuwait. More than two hundred Iraqi tanks

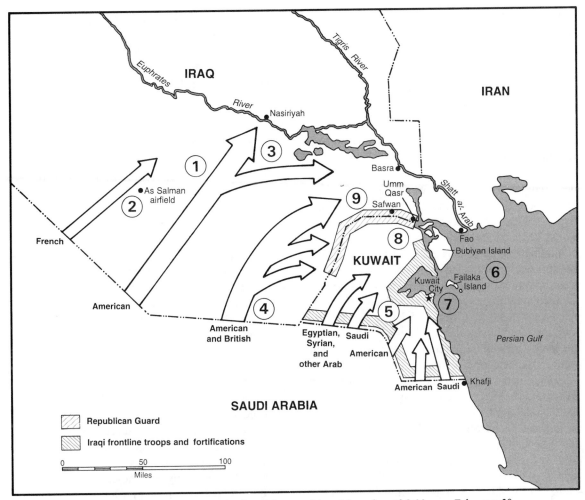

The ground attack began at 4:00 a.m. Saudi time February 24 and lasted until 8:00 a.m. February 28.

1. American special forces landed deep behind Iraqi lines before the attack to provide strategic reconnaissance.

2. A French division supported by an American brigade destroyed an Iraqi division and established defensive positions to guard the western flank of coalition forces.

3. The U.S. Army's Eighteenth Airborne Corps launched an attack toward the Euphrates River city of Nasiriyah. American forces reached the river and severed the main highway leading north to Baghdad.

4. The U.S. Army's Seventh Corps and the First British Armored Division drove into Iraq and toward Kuwait.

5. Saudi, Egyptian, Syrian, Kuwaiti, and other Arab forces, along with two U.S. Marine divisions and an Army brigade, breached Iraqi frontline defenses and converged on Kuwait City.

6. An 18,000-troop U.S. Marine force in naval vessels positioned off Kuwait feigned a helicopter-borne assault on the Kuwaiti coast to persuade 125,000 Iraqi defenders that an amphibious landing was imminent.

7. Saudi and Kuwaiti troops supported by U.S. Marines entered Kuwait City on February 27. Coalition forces found Kuwaiti resistance fighters in control of much of the capital.

8. Iraqi troops attempting to flee Kuwait were attacked on February 26 by coalition pilots who jammed roads by bombing vehicles at the front and rear of Iraqi convoys headed north.

9. American and British forces engaged Iraqi Republican Guard units in a massive tank battle February 27-28.

were destroyed without the loss of a single coalition tank.

American marines and Arab coalition troops marched into Kuwait City February 27 after fighting several pitched battles on the outskirts of the city. They found that all but a few stranded Iraqis had fled the capital the previous day. Kuwaiti resistance fighters and citizens welcomed home Kuwaiti troops who led the coalition march into the city.

At 9:00 p.m. EST February 27, President Bush declared in a televised address, "Kuwait is liberated. Iraq's army is defeated. Our military objectives are met." He announced that coalition forces would cease offensive operations three hours later at midnight EST (8:00 a.m. February 28 in the battle zone). Bush said a permanent cease-fire would require the Iraqis to accept all UN Security Council resolutions pertaining to the Gulf crisis, release all prisoners of war and Kuwaiti hostages, and disclose the locations of mines. Iraqi commanders also were required to meet with coalition military leaders within forty-eight hours to work out the military details of the cease-fire. Earlier on February 27, a letter from Foreign Minister Aziz to the UN Security Council had declared Iraq's willingness to observe all UN Security Council resolutions. On March 3 General Schwarzkopf met with Iraqi military representatives, who agreed to abide by all coalition conditions for the military cease-fire. By March 5 Iraq had released all coalition prisoners of war.

Throughout the ground campaign, many Iraqi soldiers surrendered as soon as they encountered coalition troops or after giving only token resistance. Thirty-eight days of coalition bombing had destroyed many units' equipment and supplies and cut their communications with their military commanders. Some Iraqi soldiers did not even have water.

The war weariness of Iraqi troops, the technological superiority of coalition weapons, the lack of Iraqi air cover, and an efficient U.S. battle plan led to coalition casualty levels that Lt. Gen. Sir Peter de la Billiere, the commander of British forces in Saudi Arabia, called "the smallest number for the size of the campaign in the history of warfare." On March 22 the United States reported that 125 Americans had been killed in combat during the entire six-week war. Of these, 28 were killed by a single Iraqi Scud missile that struck a barracks in Dhahran, Saudi Arabia, on February 25. The total number of American soldiers killed in action was less than the 202 American soldiers who had been killed in accidents related to operations in the Middle East since August 2.

The coalition attack left the Iraqi army in disarray. Approximately sixty-three thousand Iraqis were taken prisoner and between twenty-five thousand and one hundred thousand were killed or wounded, according to widely varying unofficial coalition estimates. Tens of thousands of others were reported to have deserted before or shortly after the coalition ground campaign. Schwarzkopf estimated that as many as 30 percent of Iraqi troops in the Kuwait theater had deserted before the ground battle began. More important to the weakening of Iraq's offensive military potential was the destruction of most of its heavy equipment. British military officials estimated February 28 that Iraq lost about thirty-five hundred of its forty-two hundred tanks in Kuwait and southern Iraq, two thousand of its three thousand artillery pieces, and two thousand of its twenty-seven hundred troop carriers. American estimates of Iraqi equipment losses were slightly higher. These losses, along with the destruction of more than a hundred Iraqi warplanes and seventy Iraqi naval vessels, weakened Iraq's ability to wage war against its neighbors in the short run. Iraq retained a large army—more than three hundred thousand troops and about one thousand tanks stationed near the Turkish and Iranian borders and around Baghdad were not involved in the ground war. But the loss of such a high percentage of its best troops and equipment would limit the Iraqi military's offensive capability.

## Continuing Security Concerns

The Persian Gulf region after the war has remained one of the most volatile in the world. In stopping the threat at hand—Iraq's military might and aggressiveness—the coalition created or exacerbated other problems. The defeat of Iraq's military opened the way for Iran to reexert its regional ambitions. The destruction of a large portion of Iraq's conventional arsenal did nothing to stem the impulse of Iran, Iraq, and other Middle Eastern nations to acquire more sophisticated and destructive weapons. The shock of the war also did not bring on a renaissance of political reform in the Gulf region, causing disillusionment among some inhabitants.

Although Iraq was humiliated and its offensive military capacity weakened by the war, the government of Saddam Hussein remained in power. The Iraqi leader has continued to denounce the West and its Persian Gulf allies and to resist full implementation of the cease-fire agreements. The result has been a continuation of the international embargo against Iraq that was put in place after the Iraqi invasion of Kuwait.

Even as the international community continued a policy of containment of Iraq, many analysts argued that in the long run Iran was the greater threat to Persian Gulf security. The concern that a dismembered Iraq would encourage Iran to be more assertive was one reason why the Bush administration did not move more aggressively in support of Iraqi Kurdish and Shi'ite rebels after the Persian Gulf War. Commentators warned that Iraq could go the way of Lebanon—a splintered nation where regions were controlled by warring factions based on nationalist and religious loyalties. The Gulf Arabs, in particular, were concerned that a fractured Iraq would open the way for Iran to dominate the Persian Gulf region—a scenario that had led the Gulf states to cooperate closely with Iraq during the eight-year Iran-Iraq War.

Although the Gulf War strengthened Iran's position, the country continued to be plagued by poor economic performance and internal political problems. In addition, the United States under President Bill Clinton was continuing a policy of "dual containment" of Iran and Iraq. Nevertheless, Iran was clearly the giant of the Persian Gulf area.

The failure of most wealthy Gulf states, including Saudi Arabia, to achieve meaningful political and social reforms compounded the risk of Islamic upheaval in the Gulf. Saudi Arabia has depended on its huge oil wealth to keep its population contented and on its pro-Western stance to maintain the backing of the United States. But financial problems, severe human rights violations, and the refusal of the Saud family to share power could eventually lead to instability in Saudi Arabia.

The invasion of Kuwait by Iraq proved how unprepared the Gulf Cooperation Council countries were to meet security threats. That experience has led Kuwait, Saudi Arabia, and the smaller Gulf states to upgrade their defenses. But military analysts agree that only the United States can provide for the security of the Persian Gulf and its oil supplies.

### Containing Iraq

Since its defeat in 1991 Iraq has resisted full implementation of the cease-fire agreements. As a result the United Nations has continued to enforce an embargo against Iraq. The key component of this embargo has been a ban on Iraqi oil sales. Iraq's economy is heavily dependent on oil exports, but since August 6, 1990, the embargo has prevented it from selling oil.

The UN Special Commission on Iraq (UNSCOM) was created after the Persian Gulf War to identify and destroy Iraq's weapons of mass destruction, its scientific development programs related to these weapons, and its ballistic missiles. At the completion of this task, UNSCOM was to establish a comprehensive monitoring system to prevent programs related to weapons of mass destruction from going forward again.

Until late 1993 Iraq provided minimal cooperation to UNSCOM inspectors, grudgingly complying with their requests only when it appeared that failing to do so would lead to military confrontation. Baghdad denied inspectors access to many key sites, hid nuclear equipment, and refused to destroy weapons facilities that were found. On January 13, 1993, U.S.-led coalition forces conducted a coordinated air strike against Iraq in

*Kurdish men haul water on the streets of Erbil, Iraq, to cope with a shortage of drinking water. In the aftermath of the war, the general population faced a scarcity of consumer goods, as Iraq's refusal to fully implement the cease-fire agreements forced the UN to continue its economic embargo.*

response to repeated Iraqi incursions into Kuwait and Iraq's refusal to allow entry of seventy UNSCOM inspectors returning to Iraq from the Christmas holidays. The air strike included more than one hundred planes.

On June 26, 1993, President Clinton ordered an attack by twenty-three cruise missiles against the Iraqi Intelligence Service headquarters in Baghdad. The attack was a response to evidence that Iraq was behind a plot to assassinate former president George Bush during a visit to Kuwait earlier in the year. The attack also followed a UNSCOM report issued five days earlier citing Iraq's lack of cooperation.

Despite Iraqi defiance on several fronts, the international embargo was taking a toll. Even though the embargo provided for humanitarian exceptions of food and medicine, disease rates and the price of food were rising dramatically. Basic consumer goods were scarce for the general population. The June missile attack generated despair among many Iraqis who had hoped that the embargo was close to being lifted and that the Clinton administration would be inclined to take a softer line than had the Bush administration.

On November 26, 1993, responding to deteriorating conditions, Iraq formally agreed to abide by UN Security Council Resolution 715 requiring Iraq to provide a full inventory of its assets related to weapons of mass destruction. This decision opened the way for UNSCOM inspectors to begin a more unobstructed campaign to establish positive verification over the elements of Iraq's weapons infrastructure.

In July 1994 UNSCOM announced that all known banned weapons had been destroyed, although the commission had not been able to verify that certain parts of Iraq's weapons programs were eliminated. The long-term monitoring program was nearly in place. It would include the monitoring of more than one hundred fifty research, industrial, and military sites within Iraq through the use of remote cameras, unannounced inspections, and overflights.

It was anticipated that the oil embargo could be lifted if Iraq fully cooperated with the monitoring system and repudiated its claim to Kuwaiti territory. Saudi Arabia and the Gulf states, in particular, were insisting that this condition be met. Through the summer of 1994, Baghdad had refused to accept the UN-established Iraqi-Kuwaiti border, though this was a condition that Iraq was likely to accept in the end to break the embargo.

Even if the inspection system were proven to be effective, the United States and Great Britain had expressed deep reservations about allowing the embargo to end. Washington has cited the implacable hostility of Saddam's regime, its repression of minorities, and its failure to account for missing Kuwaitis as reasons to continue the embargo. Underlying these concerns is the fear that allowing Iraq to resume earning oil revenue will give Saddam the resources he needs to rebuild Iraq's military capacity and jump-start a covert nuclear weapons program.

Even if the Iraqis cooperated with the UNSCOM inspection regime, inspectors have admitted that it would not be foolproof. Moreover, if inspectors did uncover violations, the United States and its coalition partners would likely have difficulty reaching a consensus on reinstating effective sanctions or taking military action against Iraq.

American arguments against lifting the embargo were strengthened in October 1994, when Iraqi Republican Guard divisions were deployed in a threatening posture near Kuwait. The Iraqi's withdrew after President Clinton dispatched thirty-six thousand U.S. troops to the region.

But there is also a recognition in the West that the embargo cannot be continued indefinitely and that Saddam, barring an unforeseen military coup, is well entrenched in power. In the UN Security Council Russia and China have supported a lifting of the embargo. Iraqi neighbors Turkey and Jordan, which have been shouldering financial burdens because of the embargo, want it ended. The humanitarian costs of the embargo on the Iraqi people have also been cited as a compelling reason for lifting it.

In anticipation of an ending of the embargo, European businesses have been jostling for favorable trading positions with Iraq. Iraq still possesses the second-largest oil reserves in the world, however, and when the embargo is removed Saddam's government will have substantial resources with which to rebuild itself.

## The Iranian Threat

After its revolution, Iran's new government declared that spreading Iranian-style revolutions to other states was a primary precept of its foreign policy. Ayatollah Khomeini, Iran's spiritual leader for ten years until his death in June 1989, said it plainly: "Islam is a sacred trust from God to ourselves, and the Iranian nation must grow in power and resolution until it has vouchsafed Islam to the entire world."

According to Iran's leaders an ideal Islamic state would establish a "true Islamic government," which means that it must be ruled by antimonarchal, pro-Iranian religious leaders. It also would attain "true independence," through an anti-Western and anti-Soviet Islamic foreign policy. Finally, it would be a government of the common people, that would champion the interests of oppressed groups around the world.

Arab governments have continuing reasons to fear uprisings in their Shi'ite communities. Iran has the most people in the region, an overwhelming majority of them Shi'ites. Nearly two hundred thousand Iranians are dispersed throughout the Gulf Arab countries. Shi'ites are believed to constitute almost 70 percent of Bahrain's population and a substantial Shi'ite population inhabits the Eastern Province of Saudi Arabia.

Fears of the Iranian expansionist threat led Gulf sheiks to align themselves with Iraq during the Iran-Iraq War. Saudi Arabia provided the Iraqi war effort with more than $40 billion during the course of the conflict.

In pursuit of its revolutionary goals, Iran has supported subversion and terrorism in neighboring Gulf states, as well as in nations outside the region such as Lebanon. In 1979 Iranian cleric Ayatollah Ruhani threatened to lead a revolutionary movement to Bahrain unless Bahrain's rulers adopted "an Islamic form of government similar to the one established in Iran." Iran later denied any responsibility for the statement after strong reactions from Arab governments. Then in December 1981 Iran was accused of fomenting coups in Bahrain and other Gulf states. Although Iran again denied responsibility, Bahrain deported the Iranian chargé d'affaires for his alleged involvement in the plot.

Iran also was accused of instigating multiple bombings in Kuwait in December 1983. Armed terrorists allegedly entered Kuwait from Iran by boat. Western sources reported that final approval of the plot "came directly from a message carried to Kuwait by courier from Iran." The Tehran government again denied any involvement. As a result of the bombings, Kuwait expelled more than a thousand Iranians, and other Gulf states tightened security measures.

Kuwait, however, could not insulate itself from further terrorism. In May 1985 the emir of Kuwait narrowly escaped harm when an Iraqi Shi'ite drove a car bomb into a royal procession. The Kuwait regime blamed Iran for bombings in 1986 and 1987. In April 1988 a Kuwaiti airliner was hijacked by individuals believed to belong to a pro-Iranian Shi'ite organization in Lebanon. The hijackers forced the plane to land in Iran and demanded the release of seventeen terrorists convicted in the 1983 embassy bombings in Kuwait. After the plane was refueled, the hijackers ordered the pilot to fly to Cyprus, then to Algiers, where Algerian officials negotiated the release of the hostages in return for safe passage out of the country for the hijackers.

In addition to its subversive activities, Iran has attempted to export Islamic fundamentalism by proselytizing. Iran organizes and hosts international congresses for foreign religious leaders and uses the season of al-hajj, the Islamic pilgrimage to Mecca, to spread Khomeini-styled Islam to other Muslims.

In July 1987 political demonstrations by Iranian pilgrims and their attempts to take over holy shrines in Mecca during al-hajj sparked riots that resulted in the deaths of more than four hundred people, two hundred seventy-five of whom were Iranian. The demonstrations did not appear to have been ordered by the Iranian government, which had been trying to improve relations with the Saudis. Nevertheless, in the days that followed, the Tehran government accused Saudi security forces of brutality in dealing with the riots and vowed to oust the Saudi ruling family. Huge anti-Saudi riots in Tehran led to the sacking of the Saudi embassy, and two explosions at Saudi oil facilities in Saudi Arabia's eastern province were attributed to Shi'ite saboteurs.

During the first ten years after the establishment of the Islamic Republic in Iran, that government was largely unsuccessful in its attempts to export its revolution. Except for groups of Shi'ites in Lebanon, Arabs generally rejected Iranian influence, viewing Khomeini as the spokesman not for a broad-based Islamic revival but for an Iranian, Shi'ite brand of Islam foreign to most Arab cultures. In addition, Iran's goal of destroying Iraq's government caused most Arabs to rally around their Iraqi brethren against the Iranians. The repressive aspects of the Iranian regime and its support of terrorism also cost it the support of many Arabs.

The death of Ayatollah Khomeini on June 3, 1989, reduced, but did not end, Iran's efforts to export its Islamic revolution. Iran's new leaders were inclined to spend a greater share of their attention and resources on economic reconstruction after the long Iran-Iraq War.

Although Iran continued to back terrorism and subversion against neighboring governments, it has been much more selective in choosing what operations it would support. Iran's president, Ali Akbar

Hashemi Rafsanjani, and its spiritual leader, Hojatolislam Ali Khamenei, have both called for a concentrated effort to rebuild Iran's economy that would include selected foreign investment. Such an effort would benefit greatly from economic links to nearby Arab neighbors.

Iran has reason to seek accommodation with its neighbors because its oil industry is deeply affected by their production and pricing policies. In December 1991 Saudi Arabia and Iran restored diplomatic ties, but relations remain strained over disputes on oil-pricing policies and Saudi restrictions on the number of Iranian pilgrims allowed into Saudi Arabia.

Exporting revolution remained a stated goal of the Tehran regime. Iranian leaders who rejected such action risked undermining their revolutionary credentials. The United States continued to cite Iran as a prime "state sponsor of terrorism." Iran is the main patron of the Hizballah Shi'ite militia in Lebanon. Iran also has been one of the most vocal opponents of the Arab-Israeli peace process, and it has provided funding to Palestinian groups that have opposed an agreement.

Iran's economic difficulties have hampered the growth of its military arsenal. Yet Iran has continued its efforts to acquire more sophisticated weapons. In 1992 and 1993 it purchased two Kilo-class diesel submarines from Russia, presenting a new challenge to American warships in the Persian Gulf. A third was expected to be delivered in late 1994. Tehran also has bought several hundred Scud missiles from North Korea, and it concluded an agreement with China to build a nuclear power plant outside the capital. Although Iran is a party to the Nuclear Non-Proliferation Treaty, it may have nuclear weapons ambitions. R. James Woolsey, U.S. director of central intelligence, estimated in testimony before the Senate Intelligence Committee on January 25, 1994, that Iran was eight to ten years away from a nuclear weapons capability.

## Gulf Cooperation Council

To strengthen regional security and improve economic, political, and military cooperation,

Saudi Arabia, Kuwait, Bahrain, Qatar, the United Arab Emirates, and Oman founded the Gulf Cooperation Council (GCC) in February 1981. Biannual meetings of heads of state are held, and a conference of ministers meets four times a year. The council set up a permanent secretariat in the Saudi capital of Riyadh.

Since its creation, the GCC has tried to foster economic cooperation that would reduce tariffs and other barriers to trade between members. The GCC's primary purpose, however, was to enhance its members' security. The GCC established a joint military command to oversee GCC defense activities and conducted a series of joint military maneuvers—the first maneuvers ever held among Arab states—to test coordination of the six member states' Western equipment and command systems. These exercises were a visible symbol in the region that the GCC was working toward diminishing needs and pretexts for outside intervention.

Long before the Iraqi invasion of Kuwait, however, analysts predicted that the GCC joint defense system could not stop an attack by a major regional power. The Gulf states' small populations, diversity of weapons systems, and divergent domestic interests have impeded mutual defense efforts. Even Saudi Arabia's large purchases of expensive arms did not relieve the vulnerability of the alliance.

After the Gulf War, the Damascus Agreement between the Gulf states and Egypt and Syria provided for Egyptian and Syrian ground forces that would be stationed in the Gulf states to deter further regional aggression. This arrangement has not come about, however, in part because of Saudi Arabia's reluctance to allow large numbers of secular Arab forces to be stationed in the country on a permanent basis.

As a result, U.S. naval forces in the Gulf have been granted greater access to port facilities in Gulf states. Bahrain hosts the permanent U.S. naval headquarters in the Gulf and the United Arab Emirates is a frequent port of call. American ships in the Gulf enforce the ongoing embargo against Iraq, boarding and inspecting ships headed for Iraq every day.

The willingness of the GCC countries to host

an American military presence contrasts to the 1970s and 1980s when Gulf states desired the American military to be available, but "over the horizon." The aggressive deployment of Iraqi forces near the Kuwait border in October 1994 likely will make Gulf regimes even more accommodating to a permanent U.S. military presence. Yet Gulf Arabs continue to be suspicious that the United States will some day move to dominate them, perhaps in response to a global energy crisis. The regimes of the Gulf also fear that accommodating Americans could open them to attacks from fundamentalists. But for the foreseeable future the GCC countries have no alternative but to accept a strong American military presence.

CHAPTER **5**

# MIDEAST OIL

In 1971 oil-importing nations paid about $2 a barrel for petroleum produced by the Organization of Petroleum Exporting Countries (OPEC). By 1981 the price of OPEC oil had jumped to about $35 a barrel. This 1,700 percent increase fundamentally changed the rules that had governed international economic and political relationships. The effects of that change were still being felt worldwide in the mid-1990s.

Of all known world reserves, two-thirds of the oil and one-half of the natural gas were in the Middle East, home to half the OPEC member nations. The concentration of these vast supplies meant that whatever happened in the Middle East affected the economies of countries everywhere. This was true not just of industrialized nations, whose lifeblood was petroleum, but also of poorer developing nations. Those countries were plunged deeply into debt to meet their much simpler energy needs and then were pushed, in some cases, to the brink of economic disaster as world recession decimated the export earnings they needed to handle the debt.

The impact of a seventeen-fold increase in oil prices stunned nations dependent on foreign oil, but it had even more dramatic consequences for the oil-rich exporting countries themselves. The most obvious and immediate effect of the two rounds of oil price increases was a redistribution of wealth. While many non-Communist industrialized nations sank into economic recession, several of the oil-producing states in OPEC (then a total of thirteen) suddenly were gorged with money. With the transfer of wealth came a dra-matic shift in political and economic power. Not only did the major oil-producing states control a vital resource, but they also had accumulated by the end of 1983 some $400 billion in foreign assets.

At the start of the 1970s, the Western oil companies largely controlled the spigot to the oil. By the end of the decade, after two major surges in prices and a wrenching oil embargo that traumatized industrial countries, the members of OPEC had gained firm control over oil production and prices.

During the 1980s, however, OPEC's control over oil production and supply receded. When the industrial economies went into recession between 1980 and 1982, following the 1978-79 round of oil price increases, world oil usage began to change. Conservation, fuel switching, and reduced economic activity caused the demand for oil to fall.

Meanwhile, the oil-exporting nations that were not members of OPEC continued to increase production. Mexico brought ever-greater amounts of oil to market from new fields in the Yucatan Peninsula, and the British and Norwegians expanded production from the North Sea. During the early 1990s OPEC lost even more control. The organization could not prevent the fall of international oil demand, a world oil glut, and downward pressure on petroleum prices. Religious, economic, and military conflict among OPEC's member nations hampered the organization's ability to act with the unity required to make the cartel effective.

Nobody expected pre-1970 oil prices to return, but by 1994 prices in real, inflation-adjusted dollars were almost that low again. The 1980s and early 1990s demonstrated that market forces would have as much influence as cartel decisions on oil prices in the longer run. Nevertheless, the enormous Middle East petroleum reserves and the significant cost advantages in extracting oil and gas enjoyed by nations there left little doubt that OPEC nations would continue to have influence over the world's oil supply.

## Vast Reserves, Low Cost

While petroleum has been discovered in dozens of countries, by far the largest concentrations of oil and natural gas reserves in the non-Communist world are found in the countries adjacent to the Persian Gulf.

Smaller but still important reserves are found in the Arab countries of North Africa. At the end of 1991, just before the collapse of the Soviet Union, Middle East reserves were estimated at 597-662 billion barrels of oil and 1,319-1,345 trillion cubic feet of natural gas, representing about two-thirds of the non-Soviet world's oil reserves and three-fifths of its natural gas. The countries of Abu Dhabi, Iran, Iraq, Kuwait, and Saudi Arabia each contain greater oil reserves than the still-considerable reserves found in the United States. Saudi Arabia alone has known oil reserves ten times greater than the United States possesses, while Iranian gas reserves are more than triple the size of those in the United States. *("Estimated Crude Oil and Natural Gas Proved Reserves," table, p. 138)*

The largest and most important oil fields in the Middle East, such as the giant Ghawar field in Saudi Arabia, which stretches for a hundred miles, contain easily extracted oil. It is found in formations that are well understood geologically, close to the surface, and permeable enough to permit easy flow of oil to the wells. Most new oil fields being developed in other regions, such as Alaska, the North Sea, or the Gulf of Guinea, all present difficult and expensive technical challenges. Offshore drilling platforms or other unusual logistical support facilities, such as the trans-Alaska pipeline, add to oil-production costs.

### Persian Gulf Oil Advantages

The cost of producing a barrel of oil in the Persian Gulf (before royalties or taxes) has been estimated at about two dollars. Oil from most other regions is considerably more expensive to extract because of higher production and exploration costs. For the expensive frontier production areas such as Alaska the cost of each barrel of oil is as high as $15 to $18. Consequently, major declines in world oil prices are more harmful to oil producers outside the Middle East. A price drop of $5 a barrel can make large offshore and remote projects unprofitable and force some production to be shut down.

A second advantage enjoyed by Middle East producers is that there has been relatively little exploratory and development drilling in the Middle East, compared with nations such as the United States. By the 1980s the United States had already found and pumped most of the low-cost oil on its own territory, while Middle East nations were still finding large new reserves practically every time they drilled.

The magnitude of Middle East oil reserves may also be seen by comparing the Middle East's potential production rates per barrel of known oil reserves with the production rates of other producers. If the countries of the Persian Gulf tapped their oil reserves at the same rate as the United States they would produce 44 billion barrels each year, instead of the 4.2 billion actually produced.

### Location and Defense Problems

Although the Arab members of OPEC enjoy distinct advantages in oil production, they also must deal with important disadvantages.

The bulk of Middle Eastern oil reserves are far from where the petroleum will be refined and consumed. The two principal markets for Persian Gulf oil are Western Europe and Japan. Oil destined for either region must cross thousands of miles of ocean in slow, difficult-to-defend supertankers. This lifeline is vulnerable to interruption at a number of points, but perhaps none so danger-

## World Crude Oil Production and Petroleum Consumption, 1992

| CRUDE OIL PRODUCTION | | | PETROLEUM CONSUMPTION | | |
|---|---|---|---|---|---|
| Country/region | Thousands of Barrels Per Day | Percentage of Total | Country/region | Thousands of Barrels Per Day | Percentage of Total |
| Saudi Arabia[a] | 8,438 | 14.0 | United States[b] | 17,033 | 25.5 |
| Russia | 7,386 | 12.3 | Japan[b] | 5,454 | 8.2 |
| United States | 7,171 | 11.9 | Russia | 4,301 | 6.4 |
| Iran[a] | 3,429 | 5.7 | Germany[b] | 2,843 | 4.3 |
| China | 2,838 | 4.7 | China | 2,632 | 3.9 |
| Mexico | 2,668 | 4.4 | Italy[b] | 1,936 | 2.9 |
| Venezuela[a] | 2,334 | 3.9 | France[b] | 1,929 | 2.9 |
| United Arab Emirates[a] | 2,325 | 3.9 | Mexico | 1,845 | 2.8 |
| Norway | 2,122 | 3.5 | United Kingdom[b] | 1,803 | 2.7 |
| Nigeria[a] | 1,982 | 3.3 | Canada[b] | 1,644 | 2.5 |
| United Kingdom | 1,825 | 3.0 | South Korea | 1,508 | 2.3 |
| Canada | 1,598 | 2.7 | Brazil | 1,410 | 2.1 |
| Indonesia[a] | 1,566 | 2.6 | India | 1,252 | 1.9 |
| Libya[a] | 1,483 | 2.5 | Spain[b] | 1,108 | 1.7 |
| Algeria[a] | 1,217 | 2.0 | Other OECD nations[b] | 5,014 | 7.5 |
| Other Eastern Europe and former USSR | 1,204 | 2.0 | Middle East nations | 3,705 | 5.6 |
| Kuwait[a] | 1,029 | 1.7 | Other Eastern Europe and former USSR | 3,330 | 5.0 |
| Iraq[a] | 450 | 0.7 | Other nations | 7,997 | 12.0 |
| Qatar[a] | 396 | 0.7 | | | |
| Gabon[a] | 298 | 0.5 | | | |
| Other nations | 8,495 | 14.1 | | | |
| World Total | 60,255 | | World Total | 66,744 | |

[a] Organization of Arab Petroleum Exporting Countries (OPEC).
[b] Organization for Economic Cooperation and Development (OECD) nations. OECD members not listed separately are Australia, Austria, Belgium, Denmark, Finland, Greece, Guam, Iceland, Ireland, Luxembourg, Netherlands, New Zealand, Norway, Portugal, Puerto Rico, Sweden, Switzerland, Turkey, and U.S. Virgin Islands.

*Notes:* Figures are preliminary totals for 1992. Total production figures are smaller than consumption, indicating that some nations were drawing down reserves; in addition, some by-products from crude oil result in more for consumption than the amount of oil that was used to create the product. Consumption includes internal consumption, refinery fuel and loss, and bunkering; also included, where available, are liquefied petroleum gases sold directly from natural gas processing plants for fuel or chemical uses.

*Source:* Department of Energy, Energy Information Administration, *International Energy Annual 1992.*

ous as the narrow Strait of Hormuz where the Gulf enters the Arabian Sea, and through which much of the world's oil passes daily. *(Persian Gulf, map, p. 104)*

The damage caused to hundreds of ships in the Persian Gulf during the 1980-88 Iran-Iraq War demonstrated the vulnerability of oil that must pass through the Strait of Hormuz. Early in the war, the Iraqis lost the capability to load oil for passage through the Gulf. After several unsuccessful attempts, Iraq inflicted heavy damage on the principal Iranian terminal facilities at Kharg Island. Iran threatened to close the strait if its own loading facilities were ever totally knocked out. The war's effects caused some Gulf states, particularly Iraq, to emphasize oil transportation by pipeline.

Pipelines connect Saudi oil fields to the Red Sea. Before the Iraqi invasion of Kuwait in 1990, the Iraqis had shipped oil through this Saudi pipeline as well. But passage of goods through the Red Sea, while safer than Gulf passage, is not without

World Oil Consumption, Selected Years, 1960-91 (Millions of Barrels Per Day)

| Year | United States | Germany[a] | Japan | China | USSR | Mexico | France | Italy | United Kingdom | World Total |
|------|------|------|------|------|------|------|------|------|------|------|
| 1960 | 9.80 | 0.63 | 0.66 | 0.17 | 2.38 | 0.30 | 0.56 | 0.44 | 0.94 | 21.34 |
| 1965 | 11.51 | 1.61 | 1.74 | 0.23 | 3.61 | 0.34 | 1.09 | 0.98 | 1.49 | 31.14 |
| 1970 | 14.70 | 2.61 | 3.82 | 0.62 | 5.31 | 0.50 | 1.94 | 1.71 | 2.10 | 46.81 |
| 1975 | 16.32 | 2.65 | 4.62 | 1.36 | 7.52 | 0.75 | 2.25 | 1.86 | 1.91 | 56.20 |
| 1980 | 17.06 | 2.71 | 4.96 | 1.77 | 9.00 | 1.27 | 2.26 | 1.93 | 1.73 | 63.07 |
| 1985 | 15.73 | 2.34 | 4.38 | 1.89 | 8.95 | 1.47 | 1.78 | 1.72 | 1.63 | 60.10 |
| 1986 | 16.28 | 2.50 | 4.44 | 2.00 | 8.98 | 1.49 | 1.77 | 1.74 | 1.65 | 61.76 |
| 1987 | 16.67 | 2.42 | 4.48 | 2.12 | 9.00 | 1.52 | 1.79 | 1.86 | 1.60 | 63.01 |
| 1988 | 17.28 | 2.42 | 4.75 | 2.28 | 8.89 | 1.55 | 1.80 | 1.84 | 1.70 | 64.83 |
| 1989 | 17.33 | 2.28 | 4.98 | 2.38 | 8.74 | 1.66 | 1.86 | 1.93 | 1.74 | 66.03 |
| 1990 | 16.99 | 2.38 | 5.14 | 2.30 | 8.39 | 1.73 | 1.82 | 1.87 | 1.75 | 66.16 |
| 1991 | 16.71 | 2.83 | 5.27 | 2.46 | 8.20 | 1.80 | 1.90 | 1.92 | 1.76 | 66.56 |

*Note:* Entries are for selected countries and do not add to world total.

[a] Through 1990 the data for Germany are for the former West Germany only.

*Source:* Department of Energy, Energy Information Agency, *Annual Energy Review 1992.*

risks. In late 1984 mines laid by an unknown country caused damage to many ships. Western nations and Egypt cooperated in a successful mine-sweeping operation that cleared the Red Sea. *(Pipelines and oil fields, map, p. 161)*

Natural gas transportation can be even more problematic. While oil from Algeria, on the North African coast, can be transported easily to European markets, Algeria's natural gas must be liquefied before it can be shipped across the Mediterranean to Europe and across the Atlantic to the United States. Algeria has the third-largest reserves of natural gas in the Middle East, but its liquefaction plants have been expensive.

Most natural gas associated with Middle Eastern oil production is still flared (burned off), but Arab countries are beginning to use the gas in domestic development projects, either by reinjecting it into oil fields to sustain production pressure or by using it as the principal fuel for domestic industries. Some countries, notably Saudi Arabia, Kuwait, and Iran, also are trying to overcome the difficulty of transporting natural gas to distant markets by using it as the raw material for new petrochemical and fertilizer complexes. Once converted to other products, the chemicals can be transported to European markets in smaller ships able to pass through the Red Sea and Suez Canal.

Another disadvantage that Middle Eastern producers face is the difficulty of defending their production operations. For the most part, the region's oil is located in sparsely populated countries that have neither the manpower nor the topography needed to defend against a military attack by a determined aggressor.

Despite the vast spending on military weaponry by the Persian Gulf states, most of them would be overwhelmed by a military attack by a major industrial power. Yet direct attack by outside countries has not occurred. Any unilateral hostile action in the region by an outside power would likely be opposed by other nations with an interest in the same oil supplies. Many countries, including the United States, consider continued access to Middle East oil vital to their national interests.

During the Cold War, the United States was concerned about a Soviet military move to control Middle East oil-producing regions. Both the Carter and Reagan administrations sought access to military bases close to the Persian Gulf as support facilities for any military action that might be required to prevent Soviet intrusion into the oil fields. The key oil-producing countries of the Gulf, however, were unwilling to permit a permanent military presence by a superpower and seemed determined to avoid creating a pretext for having one forced upon them. Before the Iraqi invasion of Kuwait, only Oman granted the United States military-base rights on its territory and even that nation was under pressure from other Arab states to deny the United States access.

The Iraqi invasion, however, finally broke this taboo. The United States and allies staged operations from Saudi territory involving hundreds of thousands of troops. The Iraqi aggression demonstrated that the greatest and most consistent danger to Middle East oil supplies would be from regional powers that gained military superiority over their neighbors.

## Recycling Oil Dollars

When oil prices soared in the 1970s, corresponding upheavals occurred in the world banking system. A vast transfer of wealth took place in less than a decade, producing unprecedented surpluses of money for oil-exporting countries, large but manageable trade deficits for industrial countries, and dangerously large trade deficits and accumulations for some developing countries.

After each round of price hikes, surplus petrodollars (as international oil revenues came to be called) flooded into OPEC bank accounts at a faster rate than they could be spent. Oil-exporting nations rapidly pushed national development programs to take advantage of the new riches, which increased spending on goods and services from nations abroad.

As oil prices and sales volumes declined by the middle of the 1980s, OPEC countries reduced their imports of goods and services, but not fast enough to prevent a trade deficit. A $15 billion deficit was incurred in both 1982 and 1983. This was still a relatively minor offset against the cumulative surplus of nearly $400 billion earned over the previous decade, but it was growing.

The flow and use of surplus petrodollars became extremely important to the world financial system. In 1983 about 37 percent of OPEC's $400 billion cumulative surplus was held as bank deposits in large industrialized countries, with 70 percent of bank deposits in dollars. About 13 percent of the surplus went into short-term government securities. Six percent of the surplus went into foreign exchange reserves such as gold and Special Drawing Rights at the International Monetary Fund. OPEC countries also made increasing investments (29 percent of the surplus by 1983) in corporate securities and agricultural and commercial real estate in industrial countries. About 15 percent was loaned to or invested in developing countries.

Until oil revenues began to decline during the 1980s the oil-producing countries of the Middle East all undertook extensive development programs. These programs later were cut back, but the weak oil market pushed producing nations to diversify their economies.

OPEC countries have always favored investment in industries related to their petroleum production, and they increasingly sought to develop refining, fertilizer, petrochemical, and oil-transportation industries. One of the most ambitious efforts was Saudi Arabia's construction of two new industrial cities at the Red Sea ports of Yanbu and Jubail. Other big projects included the $3.5 billion Iranian petrochemical complex at Bandar Khomeini, which was damaged in the war with Iraq. Kuwait also was active, purchasing refineries in Denmark and Holland, and acquiring gasoline marketing networks throughout Europe.

## Early Oil Cartels, OPEC

The world's first multinational oil empire was John Rockefeller's Standard Oil Trust (predecessor of Exxon, Mobil, Amoco, Sohio, and Chevron), which by 1880 controlled more than 70 percent of the then-known supply. By 1885 at least 70 percent of Standard's business was overseas. The second worldwide oil empire was built by Marcus Samuel and his syndicate after they gained control over the Russian fields at Baku

## Estimated Crude Oil and Natural Gas Proved Reserves

| Region/Country | Crude Oil[a] | | Natural Gas[b] | |
|---|---|---|---|---|
| | Reserves | Percentage of Total | Reserves | Percentage of Total |
| North America | 81.6 | 8.2 | 335.3 | 7.7 |
| Canada | 5.6 | | 96.7 | |
| Mexico | 51.3 | | 71.5 | |
| United States | 24.7 | | 167.1 | |
| Central and South America | 68.5 | 6.9 | 167.0 | 3.8 |
| Argentina | 1.6 | | 20.4 | |
| Brazil | 2.8 | | 4.0 | |
| Venezuela | 59.1 | | 110.0 | |
| Other | 5.0 | | 32.6 | |
| Western Europe | 14.7 | 1.5 | 181.4 | 4.1 |
| Italy | 0.7 | | 11.4 | |
| Netherlands | 0.1 | | 69.6 | |
| Norway | 7.6 | | 60.7 | |
| United Kingdom | 4.0 | | 19.2 | |
| Other | 2.3 | | 20.5 | |
| Eastern Europe and USSR | 58.5 | 5.9 | 1,763.5 | 40.3 |
| USSR | 57.0 | | 1,750.0 | |
| Other[c] | 1.5 | | 13.5 | |
| Middle East | 661.6 | 66.7 | 1,319.1 | 30.1 |
| Iran | 92.9 | | 600.4 | |
| Iraq | 100.0 | | 95.0 | |
| Kuwait | 96.5 | | 48.5 | |
| Oman | 4.3 | | 9.9 | |
| Qatar | 3.7 | | 162.0 | |
| Saudi Arabia | 260.3 | | 184.5 | |
| United Arab Emirates | 98.1 | | 199.3 | |
| Other | 5.8 | | 19.5 | |
| Africa | 60.5 | 6.1 | 310.2 | 7.1 |
| Algeria | 9.2 | | 116.5 | |
| Egypt | 4.5 | | 12.4 | |
| Libya | 22.8 | | 43.0 | |
| Nigeria | 17.9 | | 104.7 | |
| Other | 6.1 | | 33.6 | |
| Far East and Oceania | 44.1 | 4.5 | 299.3 | 6.8 |
| Australia | 1.5 | | 15.1 | |
| China | 24.0 | | 35.4 | |
| India | 6.1 | | 25.8 | |
| Indonesia | 6.6 | | 64.8 | |
| Malaysia | 3.0 | | 59.1 | |
| Other | 2.9 | | 99.1 | |
| World Total | 989.4 | | 4,375.8 | |

*Note:* Estimates as of January 1, 1992. Percentages may not total 100 due to rounding.

[a] Billions of barrels.

[b] Trillion cubic feet.

[c] Albania, Bulgaria, Czechoslovakia, Hungary, Poland, and Romania.

*Source:* Department of Energy, Energy Information Agency, *Annual Energy Review 1992.*

and exported oil to Western Europe and the Far East in competition with Standard. Samuel, after refusing a Rockefeller buyout offer, formed Shell Transport and Trading Company. In 1907 this company merged with Royal Dutch, which controlled Indonesian production, to form Royal Dutch Shell.

In 1906 William D'Arcy began the search for oil in the Middle East, hoping to form his own empire. However, he did not obtain the funds necessary for exploration until the eve of World War I. At that time the British government funded D'Arcy's company, Anglo Persian (predecessor of British Petroleum), in the hope of securing oil supplies for its navy. The British government took a controlling interest in the company.

Anglo Persian had earlier entered into a deal with Shell Oil and German interests to divide up the oil rights to the former Ottoman Empire. Since few of the participants in the deal knew exactly what parts of the Middle East were included, one who did, Armenian financier Calouste Gulbenkian, mapped a red line around the affected areas of what is now Turkey, Jordan, Syria, Iraq, and Saudi Arabia. The "red-line" agreement ultimately became the basis of British domination of Middle East oil. The parties were prohibited from competing with each other within the confines of the red line. Gulbenkian was awarded a 5 percent share, for which he thereafter became known as Mr. Five Percent for his part in arranging the deal. He died one of the world's wealthiest men.

In the late 1920s oil was flooding into the markets and the three rival empires engaged in intensive price competition. This competition proved short-lived, however, because representatives of the three met at Achnacarry Castle in Scotland in 1928 to form the "as-is" agreement. The agreement established principles to correct overproduction, reduce competition, and freeze individual market shares at their 1928 levels.

Even though the cartel controlled production of most oil outside the United States and the Soviet Union, and it had established a system for pricing oil anywhere in the world at the prevailing U.S.

Gulf Coast price, it could not prevent competition from producers outside the cartel.

One of the most important challenges came from U.S. companies such as Socal (Standard Oil of California, now Chevron), Gulf, and Texaco, which were not parties to either the red-line or as-is agreements. They had taken an active role in the search for Saudi Arabian and Kuwaiti oil but had been hindered from developing their interests by the British government. After World War II the American government insisted its companies be allowed to develop Middle East concessions. So in 1948 the red-line agreement was scrapped and the Arabian American Oil Company (ARAMCO) was formed by Esso (now Exxon), Texaco, Socal, and Mobil to develop the Saudi concession. Huge deposits of oil were soon discovered and the American companies reaped profits by supplying low-cost oil to Europe and Japan, and later to the United States. Other American companies gained access to concessions in Kuwait, Iran, and other important Middle East oil producers.

## Oil Company Control

The Middle East oil-producing nations during the first half of the twentieth century played a subservient role to the major international oil companies that had developed their oil fields. Foreign oil companies were given a free hand to exploit the oil reserves under concessions granted by the local ruler. Those agreements required the companies to pay only a nominal royalty, an average of twenty-one cents a barrel, to the oil-producing countries. In return, the oil companies were exempted from taxes and were given a blank check to determine production and pricing policy.

The oil-producing countries remained satisfied with these arrangements during times when demand was slow, prices were fluctuating or dropping, and prospects for discovering oil were uncertain. During and after World War II, however, inflation reduced the purchasing power of the fixed royalty payments given the producing countries. In other words, their share of the value of the oil being produced declined.

One of the first challenges to these arrangements came in Venezuela, where in 1945 the government demanded and received an even split in oil profits with the companies. The new rules and tax system were formulated by the Venezuelan oil minister, Juan Pablo Perez Alfonzo, later a founder of OPEC.

In subsequent years the oil-producing countries of the Middle East, which had been getting royalties of 12.5 percent of oil profits, adopted the Venezuelan sharing plan. By the early 1950s all the producing countries had negotiated agreements providing for oil profits to be divided on a 50-50 basis with the oil company or consortium producing the oil. These agreements increased the revenues of the Middle East governments almost tenfold between 1948 and 1960, to nearly $1.4 billion from about $150 million.

Another important development was the entry into the oil-production business in the 1950s of many new, independent companies. The original seven major corporations that had controlled the world oil market discovered that smaller, aggressive companies were eager to produce at high levels. Gulf, Texaco, Socal, Mobil, and Esso were the five major American corporations, with the Royal Dutch Shell Group and the British Petroleum Company rounding out the so-called "Seven Sisters." In the past they had reduced overseas production when the world oil market was saturated, thus preventing a drop in price.

The independents, among them Occidental, Amoco, and Getty, made it more difficult for the major companies to control prices. The smaller businesses set lower prices for gasoline and other oil products, upsetting the ordered market structure. By the end of 1957 prices were dropping. As a result, in February 1959 the major companies cut posted oil prices to reflect the lower market prices. The posted price, also known as the tax reference price, was used to establish the taxable, per-barrel profits a company was deemed to have earned on the oil produced from a particular country. The tax on this amount and a royalty payment were the producing countries' source of oil revenue. Therefore, by cutting the posted price, the oil companies reduced the royalty and tax income received by the producing nations.

The turmoil in the producing structure was felt in the United States, where producers found sales of oil from domestic wells being undercut by cheaper foreign oil. The federal government studied the situation and publicly expressed concern about dependence on foreign oil while privately considering measures to protect U.S. oil companies. The Eisenhower administration asked the suppliers of foreign oil to limit their imports voluntarily to about 12 percent. The effort failed, however, and President Dwight D. Eisenhower decided in 1959 to impose mandatory oil import quotas. Venezuela and the Arab producers suddenly found themselves unable to expand their share of the world's biggest oil market.

Producing countries were also angered by a second price cut in August 1960 by Esso, a move soon copied by the other companies. In September 1960 Iraq called a meeting of oil-producing governments to discuss the situation. Saudi Arabia, Iran, Kuwait, and Venezuela responded quickly and favorably. Leaders of the group were Perez Alfonzo of Venezuela, whose country was then the top world producer, and Sheik Abdullah Tariki, the oil minister of Saudi Arabia. The result of their session was a decision to establish OPEC. The initial goal of OPEC was to return oil prices to their earlier levels and to gain the right to consult with oil companies on future pricing decisions.

No further cuts in posted prices were made by the oil companies. Instead the United States government helped to ensure that producer-nation revenues could increase without forcing the companies to raise the price. This was accomplished by an expansive interpretation of the foreign tax credit that lowered the taxes oil companies paid to the U.S. government, thereby offsetting the extra taxes they paid to producer governments. The policy proved controversial, because it appeared to permit part of the price of a barrel of oil to be considered eligible for the special tax treatment afforded payment of true foreign income taxes. Critics charged that this tax treatment amounted to a subsidy for foreign oil production.

## Unified OPEC Action

During the 1960s several new nations joined OPEC. Qatar, Libya, and Indonesia were the first to join, followed by Algeria, Nigeria, Ecuador, Gabon, and the United Arab Emirates (UAE—Abu Dhabi, Dubai, and Sharjah), bringing OPEC membership to thirteen.

OPEC had been successful in preventing further cuts in posted prices for oil, but it failed during the early 1960s to restore prices to their earlier levels or to agree on a formula to limit output among its members. Although individual countries continued to make progress through negotiations with particular oil companies that during this period tried to ignore OPEC, the 50-50 split on oil profits was increasingly criticized by the producing states. Consequently, in the late 1960s OPEC began to agitate for higher revenues.

In June 1968 OPEC held a conference at its Vienna headquarters that produced a declaration of principles asserting the right of member nations to control world oil production and prices—a goal that at that time seemed unlikely to be realized. OPEC also agreed on a minimum taxation rate of 55 percent of profits, more uniform pricing practices, a general increase in the posted prices in all member countries, and elimination of allowances granted to oil companies. That same year, the Organization of Arab Petroleum Exporting Countries (OAPEC) was established.

It was the 1969 revolution in Libya that tilted the balance of power toward the producing countries, making it possible for OPEC to press for further authority. In September 1969 a group of officers headed by Muammar Qaddafi seized control of the Libyan government. He moved to force oil-production cuts and to demand, and eventually get, higher oil prices and a greater percentage of profits in the form of taxes.

It did not hurt Qaddafi's cause when in May 1970 a bulldozer accident severed the Trans-Arabian Pipeline, known as the Tapline. The Tapline carried Saudi oil to the Mediterranean Sea, where it was transported to Europe. With the pipeline out of operation, Libya's oil suddenly was in even greater demand, particularly by the Occidental Petroleum Company, the focus of Qaddafi's efforts. After Armand Hammer, owner of Occidental, gave in to higher prices and taxes, Qaddafi moved on to the major companies, which eventually agreed to raise their posted price by 30 cents a barrel.

The lesson was not lost on the rest of OPEC. In February 1971 the Persian Gulf states of Abu Dhabi, Iran, Iraq, Kuwait, Qatar, and Saudi Arabia met in Tehran with oil company officials. Following the precedent set by Libya, they demanded and won what was considered at the time a major price increase of thirty cents to fifty cents a barrel. The Tehran agreement also raised the minimum tax rate on oil profits from 50 to 55 percent. Two similar agreements benefiting Iraq and the Mediterranean producers followed later in the year.

The price agreements reached in 1971 were short-lived. In December 1971 the United States devalued the dollar. By January 1972 the OPEC countries were demanding adjustments to reflect their loss of buying power. The companies gave in to OPEC's demands in 1972, and they did so again in June 1973 to adjust for a second devaluation in February 1973. The companies agreed to raise the posted price of crude oil immediately by 6.1 percent, making a total increase of 11.9 percent since the 1973 devaluation. The agreement, scheduled to be in effect through 1975, also set a new formula under which posted prices would reflect more fully and rapidly any changes in the dollar's value.

The OPEC countries also were increasing their power at the expense of the oil companies on another front. Algeria, long frustrated with the leftover colonial presence of the French oil company, in 1971 nationalized the French holdings. Libya took over British Petroleum's interests in its country in the same year, and it later nationalized other foreign companies. Iraq joined in 1972, nationalizing the consortium operating there. Iran, which had taken over its fields in 1951, assumed full control of the companies in 1973.

Other, less radical, countries such as Saudi Arabia wanted to have a more orderly transfer of control. In December 1972 a participation agreement was reached between various oil companies and Saudi Arabia, Kuwait, the United Arab Emirates, and Qatar. These countries agreed to accept an immediate 25 percent interest in the oil companies, increasing to 51 percent by 1982. As it turned out, the countries gained a controlling share of the companies by the mid-1970s, although management for the most part remained in the hands of Westerners. The change in control meant that the share of Middle East oil owned by the international oil companies declined sharply. In 1972 the companies had an equity interest in 92 percent of the oil leaving the Middle East. By 1982 the proportion was less than 7 percent.

## OPEC's Market Domination

Representatives of the major oil-exporting countries had been scheduled to meet in Vienna with officials from the world's major oil companies on October 8, 1973. The OPEC negotiators apparently were going to the October 1973 session with the aim of winning a substantial price increase. In mid-1973 they had seen the market price of oil for the first time exceed the posted price. To take advantage of this opportunity for higher oil revenues, the producing countries wanted the posted price to be higher than the market price, not just equal to it.

Many of those gathering in Vienna already were on their way to the meeting on October 6 when news came from the Middle East. An Egyptian attack on the Israeli army in the Sinai had started what became the fourth major Arab-Israeli war since 1948. For the OPEC representatives, the war served to strengthen their resolve for higher prices. They asked for $6 a barrel, up from the existing $3. The companies countered with $3.50. When OPEC officials finally offered $5.12 as their minimum acceptable price, oil company officials tried to stall, asking for a two-week recess. OPEC representatives, led by Sheik Ahmed Zaki Yamani of Saudi Arabia, rejected any delay and stood by their demand. The oil companies refused, and the meeting broke up.

OPEC then met October 16 in Kuwait. At this historic meeting the OPEC representatives agreed to set the posted oil price at $5.12 a barrel. They informed the oil companies this decision was not subject to negotiation. For the first time, the OPEC countries themselves had unilaterally set the price. In doing so they were acting in accordance with the philosophy adopted in 1968 in Vienna.

The success of OPEC's pricing decision was ensured October 17, when the Organization of Arab Petroleum Exporting Countries agreed to cut production by 5 percent each month until Israel withdrew from Arab territories occupied since the 1967 war and agreed to respect the rights of Palestinian refugees. Saudi Arabia the next day stiffened the sanction, announcing it would cut oil production by 10 percent and end all shipments to the United States if America continued to supply Israel with arms and did not modify its pro-Israel policy.

On October 19 President Richard Nixon asked Congress for $2.2 billion in emergency military aid for Israel. Libya announced an embargo the same day. On October 20 Saudi Arabia reduced production by 25 percent and completely cut off supplies to the United States. By October 22 most other Arab producers had joined in the additional production cutback and the embargo against the United States.

The world oil market reacted frantically to these developments. Fears of inadequate supplies pushed prices upward, making even the once-shocking OPEC price of $5.12 a barrel seem reasonable. Premium oil was sold at auction for $20 a barrel. With renewed confidence, OPEC met again in Tehran on December 22. On December 23 the oil ministers announced a new posted price of $11.65 a barrel.

Suddenly and painfully aware of its dependence on a dozen once-obscure countries, the Western world paid the price that OPEC asked. The result of the quadrupling of world oil prices was a worldwide recession in 1974-75 that most economists at the time labeled the worst since the Great Depression of the 1930s.

## Effects of Arab Oil Embargo

Although the Arab world had tried to impose oil embargoes during previous Arab-Israeli conflicts, success did not come until 1973. In 1956 the Egyptian-Israeli war resulted in the closing of the Suez Canal, blocking the shipment of Middle East oil to Europe. But the United States was able to draw on its excess production capacity and send extra oil to Europe, thus alleviating the crisis.

In 1967, during the Six-Day War between Israel and the Arab states, the Arab oil-producing countries shut down their wells to protest support of Israel by consuming countries. But the consumers turned to the United States again and to Venezuela and Indonesia, which raised production levels to maintain the balance between supply and demand. Eventually, the Arab countries broke ranks, as shipments leaked out and eroded the effectiveness of the shutdown. The production halt had been undermined by Saudi Arabia's lack of enthusiasm for the boycott.

By 1973, however, the Arab nations were asserting a new role in the world market. They had become a significant power in the international economy, producing 37 percent of the oil consumed by the non-Communist world. In contrast, U.S. production had been falling since about 1970. The excess American oil capacity that had been called on before was gone. In addition, Saudi Arabia was a leader in the decision by OAPEC to reduce production and to place an embargo on the United States and other countries. That leadership was extremely important because the Saudis then were producing 7.6 million barrels of oil a day, or 42 percent of the Arab countries' production.

The Arabs were systematic in their embargo, with countries divided into categories. On the boycott list were nations considered to be friends of Israel. The United States was at the top. The Netherlands was included in the total boycott because the Arabs were angered by what they saw as a pro-Israel stance and reports that the Dutch had offered to aid in the transit of Soviet Jewish immigrants to Israel. In late November, Portugal, Rhodesia, and South Africa were officially placed on the embargo list. Shipments of oil to Canada were cut off because the Arabs feared the oil might be reshipped to the United States.

Exempted nations included France, Spain, other Arab and Muslim states, and on a conditional basis Britain. These nations were permitted to purchase the same volume of oil as they had purchased in the first nine months of 1973, but, since the fourth quarter of a year normally was a heavy buying period, these nations felt the pinch. All the remaining countries fell into the nonexempt category, which meant that they would have to divide what was left after the needs of the exempted nations had been met.

In addition to the embargo, the Arab states made monthly reductions in production. The effect of the oil squeeze was quickly felt in the consuming nations. Measures taken to cope with the oil shortage included gas rationing, bans on Sunday driving, lowered speed limits, greater use of temperature controls in public buildings, switching to alternative fuels, and the restriction of gasoline purchases to odd or even days. Most major oil-importing industrial countries joined in the formation of the International Energy Agency, which helped coordinate the allocation of supplies between nations and oversee appropriate conservation measures.

Although estimates varied, the embargo was said to have cost the United States about 2 million barrels of oil a day. A 1974 Federal Energy Administration report estimated that the five-month embargo cost half a million American jobs and a gross national product loss of between $10 billion and $20 billion. However, Arab oil did leak through the embargo, reportedly from Iraq and Libya. In October 1974 the United States began withholding data on its oil imports to prevent these leaks from being plugged.

Hardest hit were Japan and Western Europe, areas most dependent on foreign oil. Most of Northern Europe suffered from the embargo against the Netherlands because the Dutch port of Rotterdam was Europe's largest oil-refining and transshipment center.

Share of U.S. Oil Consumption Supplied by Imports, 1960-92 (Millions of Barrels Per Day)

| Year | Total Consumption | Total Imports | Percentage Imported | Imports from OPEC Countries | Percentage Imported from OPEC |
|------|------|------|------|------|------|
| 1960 | 9.80 | 1.82 | 18.6% | 1.31 | 13.4% |
| 1961 | 9.98 | 1.92 | 19.2 | 1.29 | 12.9 |
| 1962 | 10.40 | 2.08 | 20.0 | 1.27 | 12.2 |
| 1963 | 10.74 | 2.12 | 19.7 | 1.28 | 11.9 |
| 1964 | 11.02 | 2.26 | 20.5 | 1.36 | 12.3 |
| 1965 | 11.51 | 2.47 | 21.5 | 1.48 | 12.9 |
| 1966 | 12.08 | 2.57 | 21.3 | 1.47 | 12.2 |
| 1967 | 12.56 | 2.54 | 20.2 | 1.26 | 10.0 |
| 1968 | 13.39 | 2.84 | 21.2 | 1.30 | 9.1 |
| 1969 | 14.14 | 3.17 | 22.4 | 1.34 | 9.5 |
| 1970 | 14.70 | 3.42 | 23.3 | 1.34 | 9.1 |
| 1971 | 15.21 | 3.93 | 25.8 | 1.67 | 11.0 |
| 1972 | 16.37 | 4.74 | 29.0 | 2.06 | 12.6 |
| 1973 | 17.31 | 6.26 | 36.2 | 2.99 | 17.3 |
| 1974 | 16.65 | 6.11 | 36.7 | 3.28 | 19.7 |
| 1975 | 16.32 | 6.06 | 37.1 | 3.60 | 22.1 |
| 1976 | 17.46 | 7.31 | 41.9 | 5.07 | 29.0 |
| 1977 | 18.43 | 8.81 | 47.8 | 6.19 | 33.6 |
| 1978 | 18.85 | 8.36 | 44.4 | 5.75 | 30.5 |
| 1979 | 18.51 | 8.46 | 45.7 | 5.64 | 30.5 |
| 1980 | 17.06 | 6.91 | 40.5 | 4.30 | 25.2 |
| 1981 | 16.06 | 6.00 | 37.4 | 3.32 | 20.7 |
| 1982 | 15.30 | 5.11 | 33.4 | 2.15 | 14.1 |
| 1983 | 15.23 | 5.05 | 33.2 | 1.86 | 12.2 |
| 1984 | 15.73 | 5.44 | 34.6 | 2.05 | 13.0 |
| 1985 | 15.73 | 5.07 | 32.2 | 1.83 | 11.6 |
| 1986 | 16.28 | 6.22 | 38.2 | 2.84 | 17.4 |
| 1987 | 16.67 | 6.68 | 40.1 | 3.06 | 18.4 |
| 1988 | 17.28 | 7.40 | 42.8 | 3.52 | 20.4 |
| 1989 | 17.33 | 8.06 | 46.5 | 4.14 | 23.9 |
| 1990 | 16.99 | 8.02 | 47.2 | 4.29 | 25.3 |
| 1991 | 16.71 | 7.63 | 45.7 | 4.09 | 24.5 |

*Source:* Department of Energy, Energy Information Agency, *Annual Energy Review* 1992.

## Embargo as a Political Weapon

The embargo was immensely effective for the Arabs from an economic standpoint but it had a powerful political effect as well. On November 6, 1973, representatives of the European Economic Community (Common Market), meeting in Brussels, adopted a statement urging Israel and Egypt to return to the October 22 cease-fire lines that had been drawn before Israeli troops completed the encirclement of Egypt's Third Army. They called on Israel to "end the territorial occupation which it has maintained since the conflict of 1967" and declared that peace in the Middle East was incompatible with "the acquisition of territory by force." Moreover, they declared that any settlement had to take into account "the legitimate rights" of the Palestinian refugees.

Later in the month Japan followed suit. On November 22 the Japanese cabinet announced that it might reconsider its policy toward Israel. The Arabs rewarded Western Europe and Japan by exempting them from the 5 percent cut in oil production for December. On December 13 Japan appealed to Israel to withdraw to the October 22 cease-fire lines as a first step toward total withdrawal from occupied Arab territories. OAPEC made further concessions to Western Europe and Japan on December 25 by canceling the January cutback and announcing a 10 percent oil production increase.

The United States, too, was influenced by the embargo. Although Washington officials repeatedly denounced the Arab tactics and declared that the country would not submit to such coercion, the oil squeeze undoubtedly contributed to the desire of the U.S. government and people to push for a Middle East peace.

Secretary of State Henry A. Kissinger shuttled relentlessly throughout the Middle East attempting to mediate a settlement. A series of peace missions produced the November 11, 1973, cease-fire agreement between Israel and Egypt, resumption of diplomatic relations between the United States and Egypt, the first round of Geneva peace talks, the Egyptian-Israeli disengagement accord, and a disengagement agreement between Israel and Syria.

President Anwar Sadat of Egypt led the way toward ending the boycott. On January 22, 1974, he said Arab oil states should note the "evolution" in U.S. policy toward the Middle East and later predicted that the United States would be more evenhanded in its approach to the Arab-Israeli conflict.

OAPEC's formal announcement of an end to the embargo against the United States came at a Vienna meeting on March 18, 1974. Libya and Syria, however, refused to formally end the boycott until later in the year.

## Postembargo Oil Prices

After the embargo there was hope, and some expectation, among the consuming countries that OPEC would fall apart. But the OPEC nations showed their acumen by moving cautiously in 1975 when a worldwide recession depressed de-

mand for oil. Saudi Arabia cut production sharply, from 8.5 million barrels a day in 1974 to 7.1 million barrels in 1975. Iran, Venezuela, and Kuwait also reduced production. The average OPEC price actually dropped somewhat in 1975 to $11.02 a barrel. While these cuts were undoubtedly in response to weaker oil demand during the recession, the fact that OPEC nations were willing to respond flexibly to demand rather than continue production at former levels helped keep the price from falling even further.

In October 1976, at an OPEC meeting in Bali, Indonesia, the Saudis argued that the world economy was still too fragile to risk further price increases in 1977. Although other countries were eager to add to their earnings, Saudi Arabia's rank as OPEC's leading producer gave it great influence, and it prevailed. This influence was also due to Saudi Arabia's willingness to unilaterally use its huge productive capacity to shape the world oil market.

The Saudis were less successful, however, at preserving the appearance of unity at a December 1976 OPEC session in Qatar. Unable to agree on a single price, OPEC ended up with a two-tier pricing system. Iran and ten other countries agreed to raise prices by 10 percent in January 1977 and another 5 percent that July. Saudi Arabia and the UAE limited their total increase to 5 percent. Nevertheless, the countries that pushed for the larger increase were unable to implement it during 1977.

## Price Lull Ends

During this time OPEC members were arguing among themselves about the need for more revenues, with the loudest complaints coming from Algeria, Libya, and Iraq. Inflation was shrinking their revenues, they contended, and prices had to be increased to reflect the reduced value of the dollar, the currency in which oil payments are generally made. In fact, rising inflation had caused the price of oil to decline in real terms between 1974 and 1978.

The position of those OPEC members pushing

for higher prices was enhanced in late 1978 when oil-field work stoppages and other political disruptions in Iran began to cause declines in that country's production, while Western economies were still growing vigorously. The price lull was over.

### Market Takes Over in 1979

In December 1978 OPEC members met in Abu Dhabi and agreed to end the eighteen-month freeze on prices. The oil ministers decided to make the 1979 increase effective in four stages, beginning January 1, 1979. By the last stage, on October 1, the price was to go up to $14.54 a barrel, for a total increase of 14.5 percent. The market, however, quickly superseded the schedule the organization had set.

Iran's output dropped in early 1979 to less than 1 million barrels a day, down from the 1978 average of 5.5 million barrels. Even though Saudi Arabia and others increased production, there still was not enough oil to meet the strong world demand. The pressure prompted OPEC to decide in March to move at once to a price of $14.54 a barrel, the level originally scheduled for October. The organization also agreed to allow countries to add surcharges to the official price, the first time it had authorized members to set prices individually.

Importers bid hungrily for oil. Spot prices, the price of oil sold in shipload lots among the web of oil traders based primarily in Rotterdam and Paris, were the first to reflect the competition for oil. Reports of oil being sold at spot prices of $25 and $30 a barrel spurred the scramble.

Evidence of the tight world oil market, and the vulnerability of importers, was particularly visible in the United States. For the first time since the winter of 1973-74, Americans were lining up for gasoline. The lines began in California in the spring and by May had spread to the East Coast. Stations closed at midday, purchases were limited, and daily routines were thrown into disarray by the apparent lack of fuel.

When he took office in 1977 President Jimmy Carter proposed a comprehensive program de-

signed to force energy users to switch fuels. It banned new oil- or gas-fired electricity generation and encouraged the development of synthetic and alternative fuels. Carter also attempted to promote conservation programs through tax benefits and phased-in price increases, while denying the oil companies the benefit of the higher prices through a windfall profits tax. It retained price controls on natural gas but proposed to decontrol the price of oil and gas production from newly discovered domestic resources. A "strategic petroleum reserve," originally of 500 million barrels, was to provide protection from embargoes and other supply disruptions.

Carter's plan met with congressional opposition, although some provisions were passed, including the strategic reserve, new tax credits for homeowners installing solar heating, and federal grants to schools and hospitals for energy conservation.

Fears of instability in the Persian Gulf region contributed to rising oil prices. Iran's Shah Muhammad Reza Pahlavi had left that country on January 16, 1979. On February 1 the Ayatollah Khomeini returned triumphantly to Iran after a fifteen-year exile. He quickly moved ahead with his plans to establish an Islamic republic. The Iranian revolution had turned on the long-simmering conflict between ancient, conservative religious mores and a modern society created with oil money and protected by Western arms. The situation was not unique to Iran. Other Muslim oil-producing states facing the strains of modernization brought on by their enormous oil revenues were Saudi Arabia, Iraq, Libya, Kuwait, Qatar, and the UAE.

Although Iran's production was back up to about 3.6 million barrels a day by the summer months, the market was still extremely tight. Nothing had happened to alleviate the fears of importers that political unrest might lead to further disruption in world supplies.

When OPEC oil ministers met again in June 1979, they ratified the market price. Saudi Arabia, along with the UAE and Qatar, increased prices to $18 a barrel. But the others raised prices to $20 a barrel and surcharges were authorized by

OPEC so long as the contract price did not exceed $23.50.

Leaders of the United States, Japan, Canada, Italy, Britain, West Germany, and France met in Tokyo in June, and for the first time agreed to cut imports by specific amounts and to work together to increase coal use and develop alternative energy supplies.

In the past, the consuming nations had spent most of their time competing with one another for oil instead of working together. President Carter said the United States would limit future oil imports to less than 8.5 million barrels a day. The Europeans agreed to a ceiling of 10 million barrels a day.

The new cooperation came in part because Carter in April 1979 had agreed to lift price controls on domestic oil by October 1981. The Europeans had complained since the embargo that the U.S. controls were encouraging, even subsidizing, imports, thus taking oil from the rest of the world. When Ronald Reagan took office in 1981, one of his first acts was to speed up oil decontrol by abolishing price controls on January 28.

The move demonstrated Reagan's strong free-market orientation and set the tone for his energy policies. Favoring the elimination of the U.S. Department of Energy and opposing an activist government role, the Reagan administration throughout its first term was largely content to encourage market forces to bring down demand, while dismantling most of the Carter programs on conservation, mandatory fuel substitution, and alternative and synthetic fuels.

Although Reagan campaigned on the theory that this approach would stimulate increased domestic oil production, no significant increases occurred. Price decontrol instead was followed by a reduction in petroleum industry capital spending to locate new oil supplies. Indeed, much of the search for oil took place on Wall Street as companies found it cheaper to purchase other companies, and their reserves, than to discover new oil through exploration.

By the early 1980s efforts in industrial nations to reduce their dependence on OPEC oil were showing significant results. The amount of electricity generated worldwide by atomic power increased by 33 percent between 1982 and 1984. Nations such as Japan also tried to diversify sources of supply by importing liquefied natural gas. Japan increased natural gas usage by 31 percent between 1983 and 1984. Most nations, other than the United States, also increased gasoline taxes to cut petroleum consumption. At the same time, support continued for already-extensive mass transportation networks.

A number of nations began to exploit newly discovered oil-production areas. Britain and Norway, for example, began to reap the benefits of oil discovered in the North Sea before the embargo.

## Uncertainties and Disunity

Any confidence the new accord provided consuming nations was dashed by two other events in 1979: Iran's taking of American hostages on November 4 and the Soviet invasion of Afghanistan on December 27. These events were stark reminders of the dangers of instability in the Middle East. Oil buyers assumed they were purchasing from a supply of oil that probably would get tighter in the future.

In this mood of uncertainty, OPEC was set to meet again in Caracas in December 1979. Aware of upcoming demands for major price increases by the Africans and others, Saudi Arabia and three other countries tried to head off the "price hawks" by raising prices in advance of the scheduled session. The Saudis raised their price from $18 to $24 a barrel, a one-third increase. Nevertheless, this "moderate" hike was still lower than the $26-a-barrel price that Nigeria, Algeria, and Libya already were asking, and getting, for their premium oil. So the Saudis and others raised their prices again, as did the price hard-liners. On some markets the price of oil reached $30 a barrel. The Caracas meeting ended without agreement on either a price ceiling or a price floor. For the first time OPEC had been unable to achieve even a semblance of accord.

By the time OPEC met again in Algiers in June

1980, the Saudis had raised their price to $28 a barrel. This time the countries were more successful in reaching general agreement. Although Saudi Arabia continued to refuse to increase its price, the other countries did. The base price, they announced, would be $32 a barrel, and the ceiling would be $37 a barrel for top-quality crude oil. OPEC was still split, and Saudi Arabia had not regained control, but some order had been restored.

In December 1980 the range of allowable prices was increased again, with the base price going to $36 a barrel and the ceiling on premium oil reaching $41 a barrel. Saudi Arabia continued to lag behind, charging $32 a barrel.

Divisions within OPEC continued in the fall of 1980 and into 1981. Despite the decline in the demand for oil accompanied by some reductions in prices, OPEC members were unable to agree on a unified pricing and production policy. Tensions within the organization were exacerbated when war broke out between Iran and Iraq in September 1980.

Eight months later, with the worldwide demand for oil still lagging, the thirteen OPEC nations convened in Geneva. A majority called for price increases as well as production cutbacks to end the world oil glut and the price downturn. (Since November 1980 the spot market price of Arabian light crude oil had dropped from about $40 a barrel to about $34-$35 a barrel.) But Saudi Arabia refused to bow to the majority demand to raise prices, arguing that they already were too high and that it was unrealistic to raise them in a situation of slackening demand. The Saudis found themselves alone; the other members voted unanimously to cut oil production a minimum of 10 percent. Iran and Iraq were exempted from the cut to allow them to return to their prewar production levels.

The Saudis announced they would maintain their oil production at a record level of 10.3 million barrels per day until the others agreed to reform the price structure. Except for the Saudis, who continued to charge $32 a barrel, OPEC members agreed on a benchmark price that ranged from $36 a barrel to the $41 charged by Algeria, Nigeria, and Libya. The two-day meeting broke up in bitterness.

After another OPEC meeting in August 1981 ended in disunity, the oil ministers called on the heads of government to resolve the deadlock. Iraq offered a "compromise" that would have set the price at $35 a barrel and frozen it there through 1982. Again the Saudis, joined this time by the UAE, rejected the proposal and said they would not support any rise beyond $34 a barrel. Iran also opposed the proposal because it would have meant lowering its price. Venezuela, Libya, and Algeria insisted on $36 a barrel.

However, the Saudis this time did agree to a million-barrel-per-day decrease in their oil production. It proved to be just one of many decreases that would be required to prop up the price of oil.

OPEC had been forced to reduce output before as the world recovered from the 1974-1975 recession. The necessary reductions then had not been that great, however, as United States demand for imported oil soon recovered. But the drop-off in world oil demand, while slow in coming, was surprisingly sharp and deep. Oil demand was relatively inelastic to changes in price in the short term, but with oil prices remaining high for several years, demand fell.

World oil production continued to decline. From a peak of 62.5 million barrels per day (bpd) in 1979 it dropped in each of the following four years to 59.5 million bpd in 1980, 55.9 million in 1981, 53.5 million in 1982, and 53 million in 1983. By 1984, with the world beginning to recover from the effects of recession, it increased to an average of 54.1 million bpd. Further recovery was slow in coming, with production reaching only about 56.1 million bpd by 1987.

### Production Ceilings

A cartel must be able to control the price impact of a general drop in consumption by reducing supply. Oil producers who were not members of OPEC were not, in the early 1980s, interested in reducing their output. Production from the Western Hemisphere, notably Mexico, and from the British and Norwegian sectors of the North Sea, continued to increase as world consumption declined. So OPEC was forced to implement the bulk of the necessary cutbacks in oil production itself.

OPEC was compelled for the first time ever to agree on production quotas. In March 1983 OPEC introduced a collective production ceiling of 17.5 million barrels per day and sharply reduced prices. The key grade of OPEC crude, Saudi light, fell in price from $34 a barrel to $29 a barrel.

For about fifteen months these arrangements helped maintain a rough balance in the world market. As economic activity picked up in the oil-importing countries, energy consumption increased in the first half of 1984. But economic growth slipped in the second half, and oil consumption again fell, aided by warm winter weather. Further pressure on prices developed because some OPEC members exceeded their quotas and engaged in secret price discounting.

The previous quotas eventually turned out to be too loose, so on October 23, 1984, the oil ministers of six OPEC countries, together with Mexico and Egypt, agreed in principle to a further cutback. Following emergency meetings in Geneva beginning October 29, OPEC members agreed to restrict production by a further 1.5 million bpd to defend the $29 a barrel price of Saudi light. The official price of Saudi light remained $29 a barrel until the beginning of 1985 when it was dropped to $28.

OPEC also agreed on December 20, 1984, to establish a committee to police pricing and production policies. Official responsibility for this function was assigned to OPEC's Ministerial Executive Council, chaired by Ahmed Zaki Yamani, the Saudi oil minister. The oil ministers of Venezuela, Nigeria, Indonesia, and the United Arab Emirates also sat on the council, which audited individual nations' production.

By early 1985 OPEC production had fallen 57 percent from preembargo levels. OPEC was producing only about 46 percent of its maximum sustainable capacity, and of this amount the great-

est declines had been absorbed by OPEC's Middle East members. They had been willing to produce only 41 percent of the amount they otherwise could, while allowing the non-Arab OPEC members to produce at 65 percent of capacity.

## Iran-Iraq War

In September 1980 OPEC was jolted politically when two member states went to war against each other. For almost eight years Iran and Iraq remained locked in a bloody war of attrition. Other OPEC members, while refraining from active military involvement, gave financial assistance and other logistical support to the combatants. Iran's allies included Syria and Libya, while Iraq was helped by Kuwait, Saudi Arabia, and the UAE. Although oil was neither the cause nor sole focus of the dispute, both sides tried to destroy the other's production and loading facilities to reduce the revenues available for military purposes. Ironically, the war at first helped keep oil prices higher than they would otherwise have been: damage caused by the combat kept at least 4 million barrels of oil per day from the world market. This reduced the oversupply in a time of glut and meant that other OPEC members were able to produce more than they otherwise could.

The tensions within OPEC extended beyond the war. The Middle East members of OPEC tended to have small populations and disproportionately large oil revenues in relation to their size. When times became difficult, they were able to draw upon the credits amassed in Western banks during the years when oil prices were rocketing upward. Countries such as Nigeria and Indonesia were quite different. Nigeria's 1983 gross national product per capita was $771; Indonesia's was $502. Oil revenues were crucial to each country's financial health, and even a moderate dip in revenues could mean hardship for the millions of impoverished people who depended directly or indirectly upon a high oil price. Falling oil prices caused rising political pressures against the governments of those nations. In the summer of 1985 the Nigerian government was replaced after a coup, at least in part because of dissatisfaction with falling oil revenues.

Even OPEC's richest members were having a relatively difficult time coping with the oil glut. By May 1985 Saudi Arabia's production had fallen to a twenty-year low of 2.5 million barrels per day, and it declined even further during the summer. Meanwhile, the Saudi government was running a budget deficit of at least 46 billion rials, or more than 27 percent of revenues. The ambitious Saudi domestic development program depended on the use of gas produced with oil. With oil production so low, gas production was inadequate to meet the development program's requirements. Tired of bearing the burden of holding down production while other OPEC members cheated on their quotas, Saudi Arabia in late 1985 announced that it would no longer take up all the slack between supply and demand by producing well below its own quota. It began to sell the additional quantities up to its quota limit at market rather than official prices.

## The 1986 Crash

Saudi Arabia had watched its oil revenues shrink from about $110 billion in 1980 to about $26 billion in 1985, eroded less by the falling price of oil than by the kingdom's own declining production. Having cut its production repeatedly in those years in an effort to prop up prices, the Saudis in 1985 were producing as little as 1.3 million barrels a day, less than half of their OPEC quota. From 1983 to 1985 the Saudis' oil revenues dropped by nearly two thirds, forcing them to cut back development projects and imports each year and to finance budget deficits by spending cash reserves. Saudi dissatisfaction with this trend was intensified by awareness that the deficit was subsidizing non-OPEC as well as OPEC producers.

King Fahd decreed a major shift in Saudi oil policy, aimed at restoring some of the lost oil revenue by producing more and competing aggressively for a larger share of the market. The policy, first threatened at the fall 1985 OPEC meeting, went into effect that winter. Its chief tool was the

"netback agreement," whereby the actual price a buyer paid for Saudi crude oil depended on the price for which the buyer could resell the refined product. With the buyer's risk limited by the built-in profit margin, Saudi Arabia's sales began booming.

The new Saudi policy was partly intended to jolt cheating OPEC members into a new respect for cartel price and production discipline. Fahd determined that his kingdom would no longer bear the burden alone and would no longer play the role of "swing producer," cutting output to support the OPEC price.

The policy was also aimed beyond OPEC. As articulated by Oil Minister Ahmed Zaki Yamani and others, its stated goal was to induce non-OPEC producers such as Britain, Norway, Mexico, and the Soviet Union to reduce their production to support the world price.

As higher oil prices had spurred energy efficiency and brought new producers into the world market, OPEC's share of the total oil production in the non-Communist world had shrunk from about 67 percent in 1973 to 42 percent in 1985. As it tried to maintain prices, OPEC tightened its belt and ratcheted production down from a high of about 31 million barrels a day in 1981 to 16 million barrels a day in 1985.

### Oil Prices Plummet

The results of the Saudi initiative were dramatic. The world's largest oil producer increased sales by underpricing oil in an already glutted market. Demand was flat. Since world crude prices had peaked in the $35-per-barrel range during 1981, they had eased down toward $28 during the next five years. The decline from $28, still the official OPEC price, began in earnest around Thanksgiving 1985. By January 20, 1986, prices had sunk below the crucial psychological threshold of $20 a barrel. That was a ten-year low, and the lowest price even the most pessimistic forecasters had imagined. Analysts used terms like "free fall" and "price war" to describe the oil market.

In the face of all this, the government of British

prime minister Margaret Thatcher maintained a firm and unflappable demeanor. Britain, which had developed its North Sea oil fields over a decade, had become the fifth-largest producer and the third-largest exporter, after Saudi Arabia and the Soviet Union. Britain's position would have made it a special target of the Saudi effort to gain production cuts outside OPEC. Thatcher was stoutly committed to a free-market philosophy, and she presided over a nation that was not only a major oil producer, but was also a major oil consumer. As the market plunged, her government declared its determination not to tamper with North Sea production.

Sheik Yamani responded to the British hands-off declaration by warning on January 23, 1986, that without non-OPEC nations' cooperation in production cuts, "there will be no limitation to the downward price spiral, which may bring crude prices to less than $15 a barrel, with adverse consequences for the whole world economy." His words triggered more selling and further price plunges in oil commodity markets, with futures for Britain's North Sea Brent crude losing more than $1.50 per barrel the same day, a billion-dollar hemorrhage in revenues.

Although Saudi Arabia's policy was meant to gain a larger market share for OPEC as well as for itself, it was not exactly an OPEC policy. Some OPEC nations such as Kuwait and the UAE, still holding cash reserves and feeling the same pressures as Saudi Arabia, seemed to support the market-share strategy. But some of the poorer OPEC nations, starved for cash or burdened with debt, such as Venezuela, Nigeria, Indonesia, Iran, Algeria, and Libya, resisted it. When a five-member OPEC committee met February 3 to assess the situation, they were unable to agree on specific production goals.

News that the OPEC meeting had ended inconclusively February 4 sent oil contracts skidding down toward $15 a barrel on the New York Mercantile Exchange. "It's just about every man for himself with OPEC," observed Daniel Yergin, a Cambridge, Massachusetts, energy consultant, after the meeting.

Oil markets continued looking for a floor through the spring and summer of 1986, and they finally found one in the $10-$12 range, although some prices dipped as low as $8. Oil prices, once adjusted for inflation, were almost comparable to those that had prevailed before the 1973 shock.

Action by OPEC itself finally halted the long price slide. At a meeting in early August 1986, members reached an agreement to cut combined output to 16.8 million barrels a day, about 4 million barrels less than they had been pumping earlier in the summer. Even though the agreement covered only a two-month trial period, rumors that it was coming started prices back upward. The fever, it seemed, had broken.

Whether a world "free market" in oil had developed was still questionable. But the editorial page of the *Wall Street Journal,* a bastion of free-market philosophy, declared: "Oil is becoming once more what it should always have been, just another commodity."

The dramatic crash had both good and bad results for the OPEC nations. Falling prices had produced circumstances that stopped the erosion of OPEC's market share. Discovery and production in many non-OPEC countries was far more costly than in most OPEC countries. As prices fell, drilling for new oil in unproven locations ceased to be profitable. In the United States there was a significant decrease in exploration drilling, and production began to fall. At the same time, in response to lower prices, consumption started to inch up again for the first time since 1979.

Nonetheless, the price drop brought serious revenue losses in the near term for most OPEC producers. OPEC Secretary General Fahdil al-Chalabi told a group of economists that reasserting its market influence had cost its members $50 billion in lost revenues during 1986. It was the inability to endure these revenue losses any longer that forced OPEC to stop its market-share offensive.

The ouster in October 1986 of Sheik Yamani, who had been Saudi Arabia's oil minister since 1962, was perhaps indicative of the changing times. He had dominated OPEC during its heyday and had become a symbol of its continuity. His departure signaled a break with past policies and a recognition that new strategies were needed to address new conditions. He was replaced by Hisham M. Nazer.

### Recovery and Adjustment

After prices hit their bottom in August 1986, they gradually recovered during the fall of that year. OPEC members renewed their production control agreement in December. Shortly after the beginning of 1987, the world price leveled off near $18 a barrel.

That $18 figure also happened to be the official OPEC benchmark price. The price stability of 1987 suggested that OPEC could still function effectively as a cartel. Its members agreed to abandon netback arrangements and return to the "fixed" benchmark price during most of 1987. An alternative explanation for the stability was that a relatively "free" market had found a new equilibrium point. In fact, analysts estimated that only about 20 percent of OPEC's production was being sold at the official price.

After a meeting in mid-December 1987 OPEC members virtually abandoned the benchmark price and relied on production controls instead. Despite the protests of Saudi Arabia, the main backer of the benchmark price, the postmeeting communiqué did not even mention it. To defend a fixed price, one or more members would have to stand ready to adjust their output, and Saudi Arabia was still insisting, as it had back in 1985, that it would no longer play the role of the single swing producer.

There were still serious problems with any production-based system. Cheating on production quotas, which had been a chronic problem undercutting OPEC's effectiveness during much of the 1980s, remained rampant. In August of 1987 OPEC was producing 20 percent more oil than the quotas to its individual members allowed.

One sign that the problem was not getting better was the establishment in the fall of 1987 of the "Committee of Three," a new mechanism to police production cheating. This committee, made up of OPEC's chairman (Rilwanu Lukman of Nigeria) and two member oil ministers (from Venezuela and Indonesia), was to visit the heads of state in each of the organization's thirteen countries in an effort to persuade them to stick to their quotas. The group had no actual enforcement powers beyond verbal persuasion.

The apparent stability of prices in 1987 was also offset by a drop of about 15 percent during the year in the value of the dollar, the currency used for most oil transactions.

As the year ended, 1987 seemed to offer some vindication for the Saudi market-share strategy. For the first time since oil prices had begun dropping in 1982, OPEC's annual revenues exceeded those of the year before. For 1987 revenues were an estimated $93 billion or one-fifth higher than those for 1986.

### Oil Politics and the Iran-Iraq War

Oddly, prices stayed stable during 1987 despite the flare-up that year of naval warfare in the Persian Gulf related to the Iran-Iraq War. Ordinarily, an increased threat to Gulf tanker traffic would raise fears of shortages and push prices higher. In actuality, the 1987 fighting seemed to exert only the most transient upward pressure on prices.

The two nations had pounded each other's oil production and shipping facilities from the war's start in 1980, removing millions of barrels per day from the export market. The oil markets, long before the 1987 attacks on Gulf shipping, had adjusted prices and taken that supply reduction into account. The grinding war itself and the sporadic attacks on tankers in 1987 became just another hazard of doing business. War jitters caused refiners to build further inventory cushions during 1987, and their tanks were full by September. This inventory surplus exerted a downward push on prices.

Oil was a critical strategic variable in the grueling war of attrition between Iran and Iraq. The war pitted not only two armies against each other but also two economies, and both depended on oil for revenue to buy weapons. Iran's economy, devastated by the 1978 revolution, was especially dependent on oil.

By 1987 Saudi Arabia had provided about $40 billion in grants and loans to support Iraq's war effort, and it was oil revenues that made that aid possible. Furthermore, Saudi Arabia and Kuwait had through most of the war given Iraq three hundred thousand barrels of oil a day for "war relief," which Iraq could then sell for cash. The war showed that Mideast nations could use the "oil weapon" not only against Western consuming nations, but also against one another.

The Iran-Iraq War had profound effects on OPEC's internal politics. Surprisingly, the cartel continued to operate by "consensus," its standard operating procedure, despite the difficult circumstance of having two of its most important members engaged in a bloody war. Both continued to participate in order to pursue vital economic interests, and OPEC's internal politics increasingly became a continuation of the war by other means.

Perhaps the most important way the Saudis and other Gulf sheikdoms supported and subsidized Iraq was to wink at its cheating, first by tacitly allowing it to ignore and exceed production quotas and eventually by exempting Iraq from quotas altogether. As a result, Iraq could maximize its revenues with unrestrained production.

Iraq had long taken the position that it would not recognize any OPEC production limits until it was given a quota equal to Iran's. Finally, at a December 14, 1987, meeting when OPEC refused again to grant Iraq that parity, Iraq simply dropped out of the production agreement, and OPEC subtracted Iraq's nominal quota from its overall production limits. Iraq's demand that it be allowed greater production was opposed by Iran and non-Gulf OPEC members such as Venezuela, Nigeria, Indonesia, Ecuador, and Gabon.

Unlike Iraq, Iran sought not a sanction to produce more oil, but an increase in its price. Since Iraqi attacks had damaged Iran's shipment facilities, making it impossible for Iran to export more oil, higher prices were the only way that country

could increase its revenues. Algeria and Libya were, to some degree, sympathetic to Iran's call for higher prices. Although Iran called for production cuts and higher prices in OPEC meetings, in the oil markets it cut prices to sell as much oil as possible, and it was rarely able to exceed its quota.

At the beginning of December 1987, for example, Iran's quota was 2.7 million barrels per day. Yet Iraqi attacks left Iran able to export less than 1 million bpd. Iraq, on the other hand, with an official quota of 1.6 million bpd, was producing at a rate estimated by some analysts to be as high as 2.6-2.8 million bpd and claimed production capacity of 4 million bpd.

Iraq had acquired by 1986 the Exocet missile, deadly when used by fighter planes against tankers at sea. Once it perfected in-the-air refueling, Iraq showed it could strike Iranian oil industry targets such as Sirri Island and Larrak Island, 900 miles from its own airfields. Iran's refineries, pumping stations, shuttle tankers, and terminals all suffered damage.

To export its oil, Iran had to rely on tanker shipments from Kharg Island, which were vulnerable to Iraqi attack. Because Iran could not get credit, it had to pay for needed war supplies and food imports in cash. Since Iran was almost totally dependent on its oil exports as a source of cash, Iraqi attacks on Iranian oil targets seriously hindered Iran's war effort. Moreover, Iraqi damage to Iran's refineries forced Iran to import kerosene and heating oil for its own domestic use.

Iraq's situation was quite different from Iran's. Early in the war Iranian attacks had curtailed oil shipments from the main Iraqi terminal on the Faw Peninsula, cutting Iraqi exports from 2.5 million bpd in 1980 to 1 million bpd in 1981. The Iraqis responded over the next few years by building a network of land pipelines to transport their oil to the Red Sea through Saudi Arabia and to the Mediterranean through Turkey. Thus, Iraq reconfigured its oil transportation system so that it was largely invulnerable to Iranian attack and raised its exports above 1980 levels.

Unable to inflict further damage to Iraq's oil economy, Iran had widened its attacks to interdict the tankers of the Gulf allies, such as Kuwait, that were supporting Iraq's war effort. Iran's expanded mining of shipping lanes and positioning of new Silkworm antiship missiles along its coast in 1987 were part of this effort.

### Saudi Arabia Versus Iran

Another key ingredient in OPEC and Persian Gulf politics was the relationship between Saudi Arabia and Iran, historically the two largest producers among OPEC nations.

A suspension of old antagonisms between Saudi Arabia and Iran in 1986 helped staunch overproduction and restore prices after the crash. Then, in late July 1987, 400 people died in Mecca during riots in which Iranian pilgrims fought Saudi police. Iran's Ayatollah Khomeini responded by calling for the overthrow of the Saudi royal family. The Saudis accused Iran of provoking the riots and called for Khomeini's removal. This hostile atmosphere spilled over to proceedings at an OPEC meeting in September.

The Saudis and Iranians, despite frequent political disagreements, had always managed to separate politics from their own economic interests. By September 1987, however, analysts were saying that the Saudi-Iranian feud and the Iran-Iraq War were beginning to overshadow economic self-interest for Persian Gulf OPEC nations.

Indeed, some analysts said that hurting Iran had been a motive for the Saudi market share offensive of 1985. Saudi policy in 1985 and 1986 had caused enormous economic damage to Iran. At the end of 1987 the prices the Saudis had helped hold up for most of the year were beginning to slip, again hurting Iran's oil revenues, and Saudi Arabia showed no signs of trying to stop the decline.

### OPEC Courts NOPEC Nations

OPEC's "committee of five" oil ministers (the pricing committee) invited representatives of at least seven non-OPEC oil-producing nations (nicknamed "NOPEC") to a meeting at OPEC headquarters in Vienna on April 23, 1988. Cartel president Rilwanu Lukman of Nigeria said the meeting's purpose was to discuss "methods of cooperation," which was presumed to mean possible production cuts. The OPEC overture was seen as acknowledgment that the thirteen cartel members were finding it difficult to exert enough control on production to keep prices from falling.

What was significant about the April meeting was how close OPEC and non-OPEC powers came to an agreement on cutting back production. The meeting ended April 27 with an offer by six non-OPEC nations to cut their oil output by 5 percent if OPEC also cut output 5 percent. Those six were Angola, China, Egypt, Mexico, Oman, and Malaysia. Colombia attended the talks but did not endorse the proposal. Brunei was invited but did not attend. Norway sent an observer. The United Kingdom did not take part.

During the six weeks before the meeting the news that the meeting was to take place had set off a rally in the spot market that raised the price of one representative crude, North Sea Brent, from $14 to $17 a barrel.

The principal advocates of production cuts, as well as the opening to non-OPEC countries, were Iran, Algeria, and Libya. The leader on the other side of this debate was Saudi Arabia, joined by the UAE, Kuwait, and Qatar.

When a full meeting of OPEC convened the next day (April 28) to consider the non-OPEC offer, it was clear that Saudi Arabia intended to block any deal. In a statement just hours before the meeting, King Fahd himself came out against it.

### OPEC's Petroleum Industry Investments

OPEC nations adapted to the emergence of an ever-more-open and volatile oil market in the 1980s in a number of ways beyond competing for sales. Multibillion-dollar barter deals, usually involving oil-for-arms swaps, became common. There was also a growing effort by OPEC producers to acquire new positions "downstream" from the wellhead, in the refining and distribution sectors of the petroleum industry. While low prices for crude hurt the producers who pumped it from the ground, they helped refiners by widening their profit margins. It was a lesson not lost on OPEC that, during and after the price crash of 1986, earnings stayed healthy and even grew for the major oil companies. The majors were "vertically integrated"; that is, they were involved in every step of the supply process from exploration and production to petrochemicals and gasoline stations.

OPEC members wanted to hedge against price uncertainty by moving downstream as well. The most prominent example of such "downstream re-integration" was the June 1988 $1.2 billion acquisition by Saudi Arabia of 50 percent ownership of three Texaco Inc. refineries in the United States, as well as marketing access to 11,420 gasoline stations in twenty-three states. Kuwait had already expanded marketing of its product in Europe under the "Q-8" brand. Some Americans and Europeans were uneasy about such foreign investment by Middle East oil powers, but the deals seemed to promise greater security for consuming nations. After all, Middle East nations would only be hurting their own business if they implemented another large-scale embargo.

## Iran-Iraq Peace and Parity

Iran and Iraq began moving toward a cease-fire in July of 1988 and formally agreed to one in August. Some analysts, counting on the end of the war to heal the divisions within OPEC, predicted the peace would bring oil price increases. Other analysts and traders, however, correctly predicted a downtrend. Production capacity in Iran and Iraq that had been put out of commission by the war, such as Iraq's export terminals at Mina al-Bakr and Khor al-Amaya on the Persian Gulf, gradually would come back on line. Both countries would have strong need for revenues to rebuild their economies and pay war debts and could be expected to produce near their capacity.

Moreover, major market fundamentals remained unchanged: inventories were high, production capacity far exceeded demand, and demand

was scarcely growing at all. OPEC still controlled a minority share of the market in the non-Communist world. OPEC discipline on production quotas was getting worse as the summer of 1988 wore on, and top officials were acknowledging that it was in shambles as the world price slumped toward $13 a barrel.

By September the Saudis were increasing production further, reaching an output rate of about 5.5 million barrels a day, unabashedly violating their OPEC quota of 4.3 million barrels a day. That pushed prices for some grades of Persian Gulf crude below $10 a barrel, or about as low as they had gone during the 1986 crash. It was, in fact, a renewal of the earlier market share offensive aimed this time more at competitors inside OPEC (namely Iran and Iraq) than those outside. Iraq's overproduction would no longer be indulged by the Saudis.

The Saudis and their close allies (Kuwait, the United Arab Emirates, and Qatar) proposed that collective OPEC production (including Iraq's) be limited to 18.5 million bpd. Iraq's quota would be raised to 2.3 million bpd, the same as Iran's. Historically, Iraq's quota had been 1.6 million bpd, but Iraq had never followed it. Instead, Iraq had produced as much as possible, which in the fall of 1988 was about 2.7 million bpd. New pipeline capacity expected to come on line in 1989 was expected to increase Iraq's capacity to 4 million bpd. Iran argued that it deserved a higher quota because its population was three times larger than Iraq's.

At an October meeting in Madrid, Iran angrily rejected the proposal, saying it would never accept "parity" with Iraq on principle. But after intense pressure at another OPEC meeting in Vienna in late November, Iran finally gave in. Although Iran accepted parity, OPEC members allowed Iran to save face by keeping its former proportional share of overall OPEC production.

That agreement seemed to help restore some order to OPEC. Oil prices rose immediately upon news of the agreement. During the first six months of 1989, the term the agreement covered, prices stayed in the $18-$22 range.

OPEC Crude Oil Production, 1979-92 (Millions of Barrels Per Day)

| | 1979 | 1980 | 1981 | 1982 | 1983 | 1984 | 1985 | 1986 | 1987 | 1988 | 1989 | 1990 | 1991 | 1992 |
|---|---|---|---|---|---|---|---|---|---|---|---|---|---|---|
| **Middle East OPEC** | | | | | | | | | | | | | | |
| Algeria | 1.22 | 1.11 | 1.00 | 0.99 | 0.97 | 1.01 | 1.04 | 0.95 | 1.05 | 1.04 | 1.10 | 1.18 | 1.23 | 1.22 |
| Iran | 3.17 | 1.66 | 1.38 | 2.21 | 2.44 | 2.17 | 2.25 | 2.04 | 2.30 | 2.24 | 2.81 | 3.09 | 3.31 | 3.43 |
| Iraq | 3.48 | 2.51 | 1.00 | 1.01 | 1.01 | 1.21 | 1.43 | 1.70 | 2.08 | 2.69 | 2.90 | 2.04 | 0.31 | 0.45 |
| Kuwait | 2.50 | 1.66 | 1.13 | 0.82 | 1.06 | 1.16 | 1.02 | 1.42 | 1.59 | 1.49 | 1.78 | 1.18 | 0.19 | 1.03 |
| Libya | 2.09 | 1.79 | 1.14 | 1.15 | 1.11 | 1.09 | 1.06 | 1.03 | 0.97 | 1.18 | 1.15 | 1.38 | 1.48 | 1.48 |
| Qatar | 0.51 | 0.47 | 0.41 | 0.33 | 0.30 | 0.39 | 0.30 | 0.31 | 0.29 | 0.35 | 0.38 | 0.41 | 0.40 | 0.40 |
| Saudi Arabia | 9.53 | 9.90 | 9.82 | 6.48 | 5.09 | 4.66 | 3.39 | 4.87 | 4.27 | 5.09 | 5.06 | 6.41 | 8.12 | 8.44 |
| United Arab Emirates | 1.83 | 1.71 | 1.47 | 1.25 | 1.15 | 1.15 | 1.19 | 1.33 | 1.54 | 1.57 | 1.86 | 2.12 | 2.39 | 2.33 |
| Subtotal | 24.33 | 20.81 | 17.34 | 14.25 | 13.11 | 12.84 | 11.68 | 13.63 | 14.08 | 15.63 | 17.04 | 17.79 | 17.42 | 18.77 |
| **Other OPEC** | | | | | | | | | | | | | | |
| Ecuador[a] | 0.21 | 0.20 | 0.21 | 0.21 | 0.24 | 0.26 | 0.28 | 0.29 | 0.17 | 0.30 | 0.28 | 0.29 | 0.30 | 0.32 |
| Gabon | 0.20 | 0.18 | 0.15 | 0.16 | 0.16 | 0.16 | 0.17 | 0.17 | 0.16 | 0.16 | 0.21 | 0.27 | 0.29 | 0.30 |
| Indonesia | 1.59 | 1.58 | 1.61 | 1.34 | 1.34 | 1.41 | 1.33 | 1.39 | 1.34 | 1.34 | 1.41 | 1.46 | 1.59 | 1.57 |
| Nigeria | 2.30 | 2.06 | 1.43 | 1.30 | 1.24 | 1.39 | 1.50 | 1.47 | 1.34 | 1.45 | 1.72 | 1.81 | 1.89 | 1.98 |
| Venezuela | 2.36 | 2.17 | 2.10 | 1.90 | 1.80 | 1.80 | 1.68 | 1.79 | 1.75 | 1.90 | 1.91 | 2.14 | 2.38 | 2.33 |
| Subtotal | 6.67 | 6.18 | 5.50 | 4.90 | 4.78 | 5.01 | 4.95 | 5.10 | 4.77 | 5.16 | 5.52 | 5.96 | 6.45 | 6.50 |
| Total | 31.00 | 26.99 | 22.84 | 19.15 | 17.89 | 17.85 | 16.63 | 18.73 | 18.85 | 20.79 | 22.56 | 23.75 | 23.87 | 25.27 |

[a] Ecuador left OPEC in September 1992.

*Source:* Department of Energy, Energy Information Administration, *International Energy Annual 1992.*

## OPEC Roller Coaster

In late 1989 several factors combined to increase oil prices. Unexpectedly cold weather in the winter of 1989 had driven up oil demand. Falling oil output from the troubled former Soviet fields created an Eastern European market for OPEC oil. As 1990 began, the market price of oil was $2 to $5 above the $18 OPEC reference price. Prices had jumped so fast in late 1989 that OPEC raised its production quota by about 3 million barrels to 22 million barrels a day.

Prices stayed high. It seemed, for a moment, that OPEC producers were back on top of the world: able to sustain both high prices and high production. While OPEC production was at its highest level since 1981, United States production took its biggest single-year drop ever in 1989.

As the March 16, 1990, meeting of OPEC approached, Iraq, Saudi Arabia, and Kuwait met in Kuwait the weekend of March 3. In a departure from past policy, Saudi Arabia sided not with its traditional oil ally Kuwait, but with Iraq. Kuwait wanted to raise or scrap OPEC production quotas (which it was already exceeding) regardless of price. But Iraq and the Saudis wanted to push prices up by moderating production.

The issue before OPEC at its March meeting was whether to defend the $18/barrel reference price with some kind of controls on production. On one side was Kuwait. Kuwait's oil minister in February had acknowledged that nation was producing above its OPEC quota of 1.5 million barrels (an estimated 1.9 million barrels). Kuwait argued that production should be increased to keep the price from going above $18.

On the other side was Iraq, together with traditional price hawks such as Libya and Algeria. They wanted to keep the price from going below $18 by restricting production. Iraq announced pointedly before the meeting that it would stick to its own quota, and that OPEC's quota system would not be abandoned at this meeting. Iraq's quota was 3.14 million barrels a day, and it

OPEC Oil Revenues, Selected Years, 1974-91 (Billions of U.S. Dollars)

| Country | 1974 | 1979 | 1980 | 1981 | 1983 | 1985 | 1986 | 1987 | 1988 | 1989 | 1990 | 1991 |
|---|---|---|---|---|---|---|---|---|---|---|---|---|
| Saudi Arabia | $22.6 | $57.5 | $102.0 | $113.2 | $46.1 | $25.9 | $19.3 | $22.2 | $20.9 | $25.3 | $43.8 | $47.6 |
| Iraq | 5.7 | 21.3 | 26.0 | 10.4 | 8.4 | 12.1 | 6.8 | 11.7 | 11.8 | 15.2 | 8.7 | 0.4 |
| Iran | 17.5 | 19.1 | 13.5 | 8.6 | 21.7 | 15.9 | 7.4 | 10.7 | 8.9 | 12.2 | 18.4 | 15.0 |
| Libya | 6.0 | 15.2 | 22.6 | 15.6 | 11.2 | 10.4 | 4.7 | 5.6 | 4.8 | 6.4 | 10.8 | 10.3 |
| Nigeria | 8.9 | 16.6 | 25.6 | 18.3 | 10.1 | 13.2 | 7.0 | 7.4 | 6.7 | 9.4 | 14.0 | 12.5 |
| Kuwait | 7.0 | 16.7 | 17.9 | 14.9 | 9.9 | 9.5 | 6.3 | 6.8 | 6.5 | 8.3 | 5.8 | 0.08 |
| United Arab Emirates | 5.5 | 12.9 | 19.5 | 18.7 | 12.8 | 12.2 | 6.6 | 8.9 | 7.4 | 10.6 | 15.5 | 15.0 |
| Venezuela | 8.7 | 13.5 | 17.6 | 19.9 | 15.0 | 13.1 | 6.8 | 8.3 | 7.3 | 7.3 | 11.0 | 11.7 |
| Algeria | 3.7 | 7.5 | 12.5 | 10.8 | 9.7 | 5.7 | 2.7 | 3.4 | 2.8 | 6.6 | 8.2 | 7.8 |
| Indonesia | 3.3 | 8.9 | 12.9 | 14.1 | 9.9 | 18.5 | 4.3 | 5.7 | 4.8 | 6.4 | 8.9 | 8.2 |
| Qatar | 1.6 | 3.6 | 5.4 | 5.3 | 3.0 | 3.1 | 1.6 | 1.9 | 1.5 | 2.1 | 3.0 | 2.5 |
| Ecuador | — | 1.0 | 1.4 | 1.5 | 1.1 | 2.0 | 0.9 | 0.7 | 1.2 | 1.3 | 1.5 | 1.3 |
| Gabon | — | 1.4 | 1.8 | 1.6 | 1.5 | 1.7 | 0.7 | 1.0 | 0.9 | 1.2 | 2.0 | 1.8 |
| Total | $90.5 | $195.2 | $278.8 | $252.9 | $160.4 | $143.3 | $75.1 | $94.3 | $85.5 | $112.3 | $151.6 | $134.2 |

Sources: *Petroleum Economist;* Petroleum Finance Company; American Petroleum Institute, *Guide to Petroleum Statistical Information, 1993-1994.*

claimed capacity to produce as much as 5 million barrels for export.

At the full OPEC meeting in March, oil ministers seemed to settle the issue temporarily by agreeing to do nothing: changing neither the quota system nor the $18 reference price.

## Prices Tumble

In April crude prices went into a nose dive in response to reports that OPEC's production had continued to climb, reaching the highest level since 1981. They fell about $3 by late March, and were now threatening to sink below the $18 price. OPEC output exceeded 24 million barrels a day in March (well above the 22.1-million-barrel ceiling OPEC had set for itself in November 1989).

OPEC president Sadek Boussena, Algeria's oil minister, suggested an emergency meeting was needed to deal with the price drop. Saudi oil minister Hisham Nazer announced that he would meet with Kuwait's oil minister, Sheik Ali Khalifa al-Sabah, and his United Arab Emirates counterpart, Sheik Mani Said al-Otaiba, in Jidda in hopes of convincing them to stick to their quotas. The UAE was the other major over-producer at the time, pumping almost double its quota of 1 million barrels a day.

At the meeting, those two nations agreed they would cut back production, but they committed themselves to no specific numbers. Oil traders were unimpressed, and prices continued downward toward $17.

The picture of a revived OPEC, once more in the driver's seat with cartel-like powers, had been replaced by an image of an organization in disarray. Some OPEC members argued against an emergency meeting of the full organization, fearing it would degenerate into an unseemly blame session.

An emergency meeting was convened May 1 in Geneva, and discussions were indeed rocky. Ministers finally announced commitments from major producers to cut production a further 1.445 million barrels (to the old target of 22 million for OPEC as a whole). The bulk of this cut was to be borne by Kuwait, Saudi Arabia, and the UAE. The Saudi cabinet pronounced itself "deeply satisfied with the successful results." This was not enough to persuade the market that supply and demand would be brought back into balance, and prices continued to slip.

## Iraqi Assertiveness

By the end of June, the price of oil was in the $14 range. On June 26 Iraq served a chilling warning on Kuwait to curtail its overproduction. It was in the form of a personal message from President Saddam Hussein to Sheik Jaber al-Ahmed al-Sabah, emir of Kuwait, hand-delivered by Iraq's deputy prime minister, Saadun Hamadi. The move was seen by some as a bid by Iraq for leadership within OPEC, now that "jawboning" by Saudi Arabia, hitherto the dominant force in OPEC, had proved ineffective. Events would reveal that there was considerably more to this Iraqi ultimatum than met the eye.

Kuwait was particularly vulnerable. Not only had the Saudis seemingly gone over to the Iraqi side on the oil price vs. production debate, but in 1989 the Saudis also had signed a nonaggression treaty with Iraq. This came at the same time as the Iraqis were seeming to reconcile with Iran over both oil policy and diplomatic issues.

On July 12 the Saudis boosted the sagging oil markets by announcing that they were temporarily and unilaterally cutting production. As the regular midyear OPEC meeting, scheduled for July 26, approached, the market reflected returning confidence.

Then on July 17 Iraqi president Saddam Hussein publicly threatened to use force against other Arab OPEC nations (whom he meant was no mystery) if they did not curb overproduction. Saddam charged that the policies of the overproducing nations were "inspired by America to undermine Arab interests and security." During that same week, Iraq made several other accusations against Kuwait that had nothing to do with oil pricing. Iraq said Kuwait had been drilling for oil and deploying troops on Iraqi territory. By July 23, Western intelligence sources began reporting that Iraq was massing tens of thousands of troops near its border with Kuwait.

It was an inauspicious backdrop for the opening of the July 26 OPEC meeting in Geneva. Few observers believed the threats would be carried out; many, however, believed that OPEC had fi-nally found a stick big enough to enforce quotas. Since Saddam's first public threat, oil prices had jumped by some $4 a barrel.

Iraq got virtually everything it wanted at the July 26 OPEC meeting. The thirteen oil ministers signed an agreement raising their target price from $18 to $21 a barrel. (The price OPEC used to measure against the target was actually a "market basket" of seven crudes. Thus the OPEC price was actually somewhat lower than the top-grade indicator crudes commonly used in market reports.) To achieve that price, they agreed to a new production ceiling of 22.5 million barrels a day—higher than the previous ceiling but below the amount members were actually pumping. The tacit understanding seemed to be that this quota, unlike previous ones, would be followed, because Iraq, the new "policeman of OPEC," would enforce it. The market reacted to this news with almost no change in price.

# Persian Gulf War

On August 2, 1990, Iraq invaded Kuwait. The geopolitics of Mideast oil played a major part in motivating that invasion. At the same time, it is possible to overemphasize the role of oil—which is important primarily because of the economic, political, and military power it represents. Saddam may have seen oil as simply another means to achieve power.

The price versus production dispute of 1990 was, if not merely a pretext for the invasion, a surface manifestation of much deeper tensions. It was an issue that had galled and rankled various OPEC nations throughout most of OPEC's three-decade history.

Even in 1990 the price vs. production issue was a legitimate question of strategic philosophy. The positions of various OPEC nations on the question tended to reflect, as always, their particular circumstances as well as market conditions. During much of the 1980s nations such as Saudi Arabia had been arguing against pushing the price of oil up too far. Too high a price only encouraged conservation by consuming nations, brought more non-OPEC production on line, reduced OPEC's market share and economic leverage, raised supply, and eventually drove prices down again. Many hard lessons of the previous two decades had suggested that price stability (at the "right" price, of course) was in the best interests of both producers and consumers. Kuwait and Saudi Arabia had shared this view during much of the 1980s. The $18 reference price of 1990 was the "right" price, not because all OPEC nations favored it but because there were almost as many OPEC members trying to push the price higher as there were trying to push it lower.

Kuwait's "cheating," then, could hardly be seen as the moral outrage that Saddam claimed it was—even if it was a nuisance to some members. Cheating had been a way of life for many nations during OPEC's history. During much of the Iran-Iraq War, Iraq had openly and unabashedly ignored its own quota as the Saudis and Kuwait encouraged it to do so.

Iraq's treasury was affected by far more than the price of oil. Iraq owed Kuwait and other Gulf states some $30 billion to repay loans they had given to support Iraq in its war against Iran. Saddam was, at the time the Gulf War began, demanding that Kuwait forgive these debts. Kuwait charged in July that Iraq's belligerence was designed to force Kuwait to write the debt off. But Iraq needed the money for more than just repayment of debts; it wanted to finance the expensive arms buildup it had been conducting since 1988.

The Rumaila oil field also was a point of contention between Iraq and Kuwait. This crescent-shaped reservoir, nearly two miles deep and fifty miles long, was thought to be one of the world's biggest, perhaps several times larger than that at Prudhoe Bay, Alaska. It lay beneath both sides of the Iraq-Kuwait border, although more was thought to be under Iraq. When Iraq refused to negotiate a deal for sharing the oil, Kuwait began pumping without an agreement. Before the Iran-Iraq War, Iraq had pumped intensively from its side of the reservoir. But during the war Iraq mined it to keep it out of Iranian hands and was not able to keep up with the rate at which Kuwait

was draining the pool. Iraq considered Kuwait to be "stealing" its oil.

The price of oil was important to Iraq in a much broader geopolitical context. Saddam was trying to use it as a key issue in his bid for leadership and power in the Arab world. The fundamentalist revolution that had swept Iran, like the socialist revolutions that had swept countries such as Libya and Algeria years before, were, in part, reactions of the impoverished masses against wealthy property-owning elites. No one symbolized those rich elites better than the ruling families of Kuwait and Saudi Arabia. By blaming them for perpetuating low oil prices and rhetorically linking them with the United States, Saddam was boosting his own particular form of populist pan-Arabism.

## Gulf War Effects

Iraq's invasion brought a jump in the price of oil, as commodity markets reacted to expected decreases in production and heightened levels of uncertainty. The August 6 decision by the United Nations Security Council to impose a trade embargo on Iraq effectively removed from the market Iraq's production of almost 3 million barrels a day. Kuwait's production, almost 2 million barrels, also was lost. By mid-August, the price had reached the $27 range and was still rising.

Saudi Arabia partially offset that effect by agreeing to raise its own production by 2 million barrels a day. The United States' declaration that it would protect Saudi Arabia militarily gave markets confidence that the Saudis actually could produce more. Venezuela, the UAE, and other OPEC nations seemed ready to follow suit. They had the capacity to make up the rest of the lost production. Venezuela alone could have contributed five hundred thousand extra barrels a day, but it wanted authorization from OPEC to raise its quota before doing so. The Saudis signaled they were ready to raise production even without OPEC endorsement. Meanwhile, Iraq was threatening any nation that did raise production.

By August 22 it was clear that a faction of price

hawks sympathetic to Iraq would block the effort by Saudi Arabia and Venezuela to call an official OPEC meeting. That group consisted of Iran, Algeria, and Libya. The war had divided OPEC along the old fracture lines. OPEC, as an organization, was showing itself unable to respond to an event of profound importance to oil markets. Whether production decisions by the thirteen OPEC nations could be made within the organizational framework of OPEC was of vital importance to the organization's future credibility.

On August 29, however, OPEC members meeting in Vienna approved the production increase. The UAE would add another six hundred thousand barrels a day to the amount committed by Venezuela and Saudi Arabia. Nigeria, Ecuador, and Gabon were expected to add smaller amounts. This, together with news of peace possibilities in the Iraq-Kuwait situation, pushed oil prices down further.

The relief in oil prices was only temporary. Despite the belief of many analysts that supplies were adequate for the immediate future, war speculation pushed the price up to $31 by mid-September. This pattern continued through the fall, with prices extremely volatile, shooting as high as $40 on rumors of war and dropping giddily on rumors of peace. By the end of October, the price of oil future contracts for December delivery was up to $34.25. Ironically, the price increase helped Saudi Arabia, boosting the income yield from its higher production, and helping it fund military and diplomatic measures against Iraq.

OPEC oil ministers met again in Vienna on December 12 and agreed that they would return to the July agreement on output quotas once the Gulf crisis was over. The accord seemed to represent OPEC's acknowledgment that it had starkly diminished power to set oil prices at all, at least in the near term. Oil traders, not OPEC, were now setting the price. By the end of 1990 OPEC had made up the entire shortfall caused by the removal of Iraqi and Kuwaiti oil; production by OPEC as a whole was at a ten-year peak. Yet fear of the consequences of war kept prices high.

Representatives from Iraq and Kuwait sat at the same table during the December 12 meeting. It was a sign of a new sobriety within OPEC. As their control over the market diminished, OPEC members could no longer afford to use oil as a political weapon; they had to treat it simply as an economic commodity if the organization was to survive at all. "OPEC is not involved in the political aspect of the present crisis," said Sadek Boussena before the meeting.

The artificially high prices of 1990 did produce more revenue for OPEC members. Once the production decision had been made, even nations sympathetic to Iraq took care of their own treasuries first. OPEC nations exported about $160 billion worth of oil, bringing in some 42 percent more revenue than in 1989.

### War and Its Aftermath

After the allied bombing campaign began on January 16, 1991, at 4:50 p.m. EST, the oil market generally stabilized. News that the war had begun brought a sharp but brief rise in oil prices on markets that were open. A few hours later, however, as highly optimistic reports of the bombing reached traders, oil prices went into a steep decline. The quick neutralization of the Iraqi air force removed most danger to Saudi oil facilities, traders believed. This result belied the predictions of some veteran oil traders that war could cause oil prices to jump above $50 a barrel. Although the embargo closed some pipelines, few outside Kuwait had war damage. The success of the initial raids resulted on January 17 in the biggest-ever one-day drop (almost $11) in oil prices on the New York Mercantile Exchange. At the end of trading, oil prices closed at $21.44, ten cents lower than the price on August 1, 1990, the day before Iraq invaded Kuwait.

With the start of the allies' shooting war, President George Bush kept a promise to release a million barrels a day from the U.S. Strategic Petroleum Reserve—a commitment originally intended to dampen the upward volatility of oil prices. But with the price having already tumbled, the move added to the downward pressure on

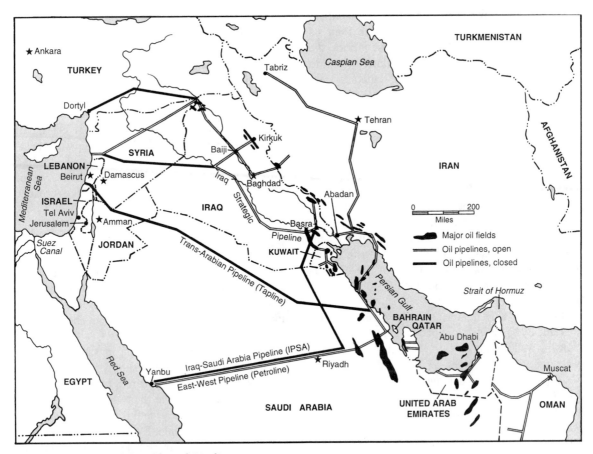

*Major Middle East Oil Fields and Pipelines*

prices. The International Energy Agency, often called the "consumers' club," on January 28 followed suit, releasing almost another million barrels a day. After the February 28 cease-fire, even with the Kuwaiti oil fields set ablaze by the departing Iraqis, prices remained well below $20 until March 11, when OPEC ministers held their first postwar meeting in Geneva.

OPEC's problem at that meeting was to bolster the price or at least keep it from sagging further, and this could only be done by reining in production. Indeed, the prewar price spike had been caused partly by hoarding, and now inventories were high. The higher price had actually brought new supplies on line and encouraged demand re-duction (perhaps as much through economic recession as through energy conservation). Worldwide, oil production in 1990 reached the highest level in eleven years, while consumption actually dropped for the first time in thirteen years.

At the March 11-12 meeting, OPEC decided to cut production by about 1 million barrels a day, or about 5 percent. Algeria and Iran had wanted a bigger cut, saying one was needed to support a $21 target price. But Saudi Arabia disagreed. Saudi financial reserves had been drained by some $50 billion of costs incurred from the Gulf War, and Riyadh wanted to recoup some of that through greater oil production. The March 12 "voluntary" agreement allowed the Saudis to produce 8 million barrels a day—down from its claimed 8.45-million-barrel wartime peak, but much higher than its previous quota of 5.4 million. For most nations, the decision was an easy one, since it allowed them to produce more than their previous quotas. Iraq, whose oil was still under international embargo because of its aggression in Kuwait, did not attend. With Kuwaiti wells still ablaze, that country could produce little in the short term.

Because the Saudis got what they wanted from other OPEC members, the March meeting was taken as a sign that their dominance in OPEC had been restored. By contrast, the influence Iraq had asserted before its invasion of Kuwait was completely lost. At a June 4, 1991, meeting in Vienna, the Iraqi oil minister asked OPEC to write to the United Nations asking for an end to the international embargo on Iraqi oil. OPEC rejected the request.

Oil from Kuwait was slow to return to the market. By early May, only 10 percent of Kuwait's burning wells had been extinguished. Allied navies were still clearing mines set by Iraq around Kuwaiti ports. Iraq had damaged or destroyed much of Kuwait's oil production infrastructure—pipelines, refineries, and ports. Not only was Kuwait's considerable output of refined product off the market, but the nation actually had to import gasoline and other fuels for domestic use. In July Kuwait finally announced that it would begin exporting crude oil again. At this point, Kuwait could export only about one hundred forty thousand barrels a day, but that increased steadily to almost six hundred thousand barrels by the end of the year.

During the summer, the United Nations discussed whether to allow a partial lifting of the embargo on Iraq's oil exports so that Baghdad could use the revenue to buy food and compensate the many individuals and businesses that had claims against Iraq stemming from its invasion of Kuwait. The prospects for a broader lifting of the embargo were dim so long as Saddam Hussein continued to be belligerent and Iraq resisted compliance with cease-fire requirements. Finally, on September 19, the United Nations proposed that

Iraq be allowed to export under strict conditions some $1.6 billion worth of oil over six months. Within the next week, however, Iraq was detaining UN inspectors assigned to monitor Iraq's capacity to produce weapons of mass destruction. At the end of October 1991, Iraq's oil minister denounced the UN's $1.6 billion plan as too burdensome on Iraq and urged his government to reject it. In November, reports surfaced that Iraq was cheating on the embargo through small-scale trading with its immediate neighbors. Nonetheless, as of 1994, Iraq remained cut off from the broader world market.

## Return to Oversupply

After the war ended, any worries about a shortage of oil on the world market receded into the indefinite future. Even with the absence of Iraqi and Kuwaiti oil, there was more than enough oil to meet world demand.

The June 4 OPEC meeting in Vienna took no significant action to adjust supply and price. The price issue had not disappeared, but with some six hundred of Kuwait's one thousand wells still burning, members felt they could afford to avoid the divisive issue for a while. By the end of the month, OPEC members combined had blithely pumped more than their official production ceiling of 22.6 million barrels a day. This high production continued through the year, making 1991 production OPEC's highest in more than a decade.

The unraveling of the Soviet Union made the situation easier for OPEC. Although the proven oil reserves in Soviet bloc nations were smaller and more difficult to reach than those of Saudi Arabia, the Soviets had always pumped from them as if there were no tomorrow. Oil and gas not only were essential to fuel the Soviet military-industrial complex in its heyday, but they also helped to bind various satellite nations to the bloc through their dependence on subsidized Soviet oil. The Soviet Union had during the 1970s and 1980s been rated the largest producer in the world. The Soviets did export some oil to get hard currency, but those amounts were limited. For a long time, Soviet production made little real impact on the "world" market, because it was consumed almost entirely within the closed system of the Eastern bloc.

Soviet output was about 11.5 million barrels a day in 1990, of which about 3 million barrels a day were net exports. But the turmoil of political dissolution and economic collapse caused Soviet oil production to slide. Production fell in 1989, 1990, and 1991.

For OPEC this meant a new market in Eastern Europe had opened up to their exports. Farther ahead, there seemed to be potential for exporting oil to the former Soviet republics themselves.

## Saudi Dominance

By September 1991 it was clear that Saudi Arabia was dramatically increasing its stored inventories of crude oil above the ground. Markets usually respond to such assurance of adequate supply by pushing down prices. The Saudis seemed to be sending just such a signal, and sending it deliberately. It was also a signal to the price hawks in OPEC that the price of oil, below $19 in September, was satisfactory to the Saudis.

When OPEC met in Geneva on September 24, Saudi Arabia called for a 10 percent increase in the total OPEC production ceiling. The Saudis argued that this would keep shortfalls in Soviet production from driving the price up over the winter. Not only were the Saudis acknowledging publicly that they sought a price several dollars lower than OPEC's $21 target—they also were signaling their intention to impose this price on OPEC through its own production increases. "Nobody has to approve what Saudi Arabia produces," Saudi oil minister, Hisham M. Nazer, told reporters at the meeting.

The market price edged lower in reaction to the news. OPEC gave in to Saudi pressure and raised its production ceiling to 23.6 million barrels a day, an increase of at least a million barrels. The price hawks—Iran, Libya, Algeria, and Indonesia—left the meeting grumbling. But encouraging consumption of oil in the longer term by keeping the price low was a reasonable strategy with the world econ-

omy still struggling through a recession. The European Community was proposing a pollution tax on oil that could eventually amount to $10 a barrel.

The September 1991 OPEC meeting marked a reassertion of the old Saudi dominance over OPEC. Just as importantly, perhaps, it marked a reascendance of the old Saudi "market share" policy. Of course, the Saudis had achieved a larger "market share" within OPEC itself—now producing around a third of OPEC's total output (up from one-quarter before the invasion of Kuwait).

The Saudis followed the same line at the November 26, 1991, OPEC meeting in Vienna. They announced plans to raise their production capacity to 10 million barrels a day by 1994, bidding to replace the former Soviet republics as the world's largest producer. Soviet production was steadily sinking toward the 10-million-barrel level. The Saudis presented this policy to OPEC on what seemed to be a take-it-or-leave-it basis, causing resentment among other members. The best that other members could win at the meeting was a Saudi promise not to raise production significantly in the coming quarter.

The meeting helped to produce a marked sag in oil prices during December, to an unseasonable low of about $17.40 a barrel. This prompted some OPEC members to call for an emergency meeting to trim production, an idea the Saudis resisted.

As the February 12, 1992, OPEC meeting in Geneva approached, five member nations announced production cutbacks. They were Venezuela, Libya, Nigeria, Iran, and Algeria. The production cuts were hardly enough to have much effect on the market; their importance was as internal OPEC political maneuvering. It was enough, however, to cause the Saudis to blink. On January 21 Saudi Arabia announced it was cutting its own production by one hundred thousand barrels a day—again a token, but a signal that it was willing to discuss production curtailment. The UAE, Indonesia, and Gabon followed suit with cuts of their own.

After three days of behind-the-scenes negotiations, OPEC February 15 announced agreement on a production cut of 1.2 million barrels a day.

But in a rare show of disunity OPEC's two largest producers, Iran and Saudi Arabia, both publicly dissented. Iran said further cuts were needed. The Saudis said they would not abide by the quota the other OPEC members had given them. No longer the patient "swing producer," the Saudis had insisted on keeping the larger share of OPEC production they had gained during the Gulf War. The market sagged in response.

OPEC held another meeting on April 24 in Vienna. By this time Kuwait, whose production had recovered steadily since the war, was exporting enough oil to play a significant role in the world market again. The problem was that other nations would have to give up some production to make room for Kuwait, if OPEC hoped to hold down its total output. OPEC avoided this problem by deciding to keep the total ceiling unchanged. But Kuwait was already producing well above its nominal 850,000 barrel-per-day quota.

OPEC was for a while spared from the consequences of its indecision by favorable market conditions. Forecasts suggested that demand for oil was moving toward a twelve-year high. Despite concern about low prices, oil stayed in the $18-$20 range during the first quarter of 1992. When OPEC met again in late May, the Saudis hinted strongly that they might be willing to curtail production and let prices rise. The market price shot up a dollar on the mere rumor. In the end, this was revealed as a tactical move aimed at quashing an EC proposal for a clean energy tax, which the Saudis feared would gain momentum from the Rio de Janeiro "Earth Summit" in mid-June. The Saudis seemed almost to be saying that if anyone was going to collect a surcharge on oil, it would be the producers. The incident seemed to prove that OPEC's $21 "target price" might, after all, be achievable. But all through May, OPEC's production continued to rise.

OPEC got further advantage from the continuing slide in production from the former Soviet republics. When the end-of-year statistics for 1992 were posted, Saudi Arabia had replaced the former Soviet Union as the world's largest producer of oil, at a level of 8.5 million barrels a day.

## Troubles for OPEC

At the September 16, 1992, OPEC meeting in Geneva, Iran declared that it would not limit its production, despite quotas. The most ominous blow to OPEC, however, was the announcement by Ecuador that it was leaving the organization, dropping the membership to twelve. Although Ecuador's production was small, this was the first time any member had quit the organization. Newly elected Ecuadoran president Sixto Duran Bellen, a free market advocate, complained that membership held Ecuador below its desired level of oil production without providing enough benefits in return.

That month actual OPEC production rose again, to a new eleven-year high. It rose further in October, to the highest volume since 1980. Prices again started to slide. When OPEC met again on November 25 in Vienna, more squabbling sent prices tumbling again. Only after intense haggling was a deal struck: a cut in the production ceiling of about four hundred thousand barrels a day, or 2 percent. This "cut" was scarcely more than the 290,000 barrel-a-day production of Ecuador, which was leaving the cartel. (And it seemed insignificant since OPEC at the time was producing 1.8 million bpd over its ceiling.) The agreement was to be temporary, effective only during the first quarter of 1993. Market prices, nudged up initially by the perception that OPEC was finally finding some self-discipline, soon headed downward on the belief the cartel had not found enough of it.

January 1993 brought new military tensions between Iraq and the U.S. allies over Iraq's anti-aircraft missiles and failure to comply fully with UN Security Council resolutions. Oil prices remained almost unchanged even though war jitters normally raise prices. It was a sign that the fundamental forces affecting the market were tending to push prices downward.

On January 24 Saudi Arabia surprised the world petroleum market with a call for OPEC production cuts of at least a million barrels a day. It seemed to be a reversal in basic Saudi policy, and the oil price rose strongly on the strength of this news. When OPEC met February 13 in Vienna, there was already a clear consensus among members that a cut of at least one million barrels was in order. But the three-day session was rancorous and difficult. Some nations wanted deeper cuts. Kuwait, the only dissenter against cuts of some type, was now producing some 1.7 million barrels a day, and was aiming for 2 million barrels by summer.

Finally, on February 16, OPEC announced a cut of 1.5 million barrels a day. Kuwait, Iraq, and Algeria, however, publicly dissented from the agreement. Kuwait had settled for a 1.6-million-barrel temporary quota. The Saudis agreed to cut production from 8.5 million barrels to 8.0 million barrels a day. Iraq denounced the agreement as a hostile action against it. The disunity sent prices downward, as traders doubted OPEC's ability to enforce a common discipline. By May OPEC nations were pumping six hundred thousand barrels a day more than the new ceiling of 23.6 million barrels.

Oil traders, in fact, were settling into a deep and longer-term skepticism about OPEC's ability to restrain members from producing. When OPEC met again in Geneva on June 8, the price of oil was still about $3 below the OPEC target of $21. But many believed that lowering the all-OPEC production ceiling would just encourage further cheating. The issue before this weakened twelve-member OPEC was whether to raise the quota to curtail cheating, in hopes of restoring market confidence in OPEC discipline.

Kuwait came to the meeting demanding to increase its own production. Kuwait took the view that other OPEC members had in February promised it a quota increase at this June meeting. Published accounts of the February agreement had mentioned only a "review" of Kuwait's quota. Kuwait now insisted on at least 2 million barrels a day. Iran opposed this bitterly, saying if Kuwait's share increased, Iran would pump more to keep its proportional share of the total.

After two days of haggling, OPEC decided to keep the production ceiling unchanged. But Ku-

wait rejected the agreement and publicly announced that it would go its own way and produce as much as 2.16 million barrels a day. Oil prices headed downward to a three-year low.

By September 1993 the world price for indicator crudes was running in the range of $14-$16 a barrel. Most of the big OPEC producers other than Saudi Arabia—for example Iran, Kuwait, and Nigeria—were cheating on quotas. OPEC as a whole was estimated to be producing 25 million barrels a day, well above its 23.6 million barrel ceiling. Oil prices had fallen some 20 percent since early summer. Adjusted for inflation, the real price of oil was no higher than it had been in 1963. Former Algerian energy minister Nordine Ait-Laoussine told the New York Times: "OPEC is dying. . . . The organization will not survive if it stays on its present course."

OPEC met September 24-27 in Geneva to struggle with the crisis, but the results were insubstantial and unconvincing. The final communiqué announced agreement by OPEC nations to "reduce" production to 24.5 million barrels a day. It would have been a "reduction" only in comparison with actual production. Measured against the 23.6 million barrel OPEC ceiling, it was an increase. Built into the logic of this communiqué was the premise that any production limits OPEC tried to impose on itself were meaningless.

The old antagonism between OPEC's two largest producers, Saudi Arabia and Iran, so acute during the years of Iran's fundamentalist revolution, was still alive. One of Iran's motives for producing more was to push down the Saudi share of total OPEC production, thus reducing Saudi influence within OPEC. Kuwait, unchastened by the Gulf War, now used the war as a justification for full-bore production. Kuwait's oil minister Ali Ahmad al-Baghli put it bluntly: "We are a special case."

Economic and political factors outside the control of OPEC also worked against OPEC's interests. Britain and Norway were producing record amounts of oil from the North Sea. Because Iraq, in September 1993, had still not come to terms with the United Nations, the possible resumption

Energy Consumption in the United States, by Source, Selected Years, 1950-92 (in percentages)

| Year | Coal | Natural Gas | Petroleum | Nuclear Electric Power | Hydroelectric Power | Geothermal | Total Consumption[a] |
|------|------|------|------|------|------|------|------|
| 1950 | 37.3% | 18.0% | 40.2% | — | 4.4% | — | 33.08 |
| 1955 | 28.8 | 23.1 | 44.4 | — | 3.6 | — | 38.82 |
| 1960 | 22.4 | 28.3 | 45.5 | — | 3.8 | — | 43.80 |
| 1965 | 21.9 | 29.9 | 44.3 | 0.1% | 3.9 | — | 52.68 |
| 1970 | 18.4 | 32.8 | 44.4 | 0.4 | 3.9 | — | 66.43 |
| 1975 | 17.9 | 28.2 | 46.3 | 2.7 | 4.6 | 0.1% | 70.55 |
| 1980 | 20.3 | 26.8 | 45.0 | 3.6 | 4.1 | 0.1 | 75.96 |
| 1985 | 23.6 | 24.1 | 41.8 | 5.6 | 4.6 | 0.3 | 73.98 |
| 1986 | 23.2 | 22.5 | 43.3 | 6.0 | 4.6 | 0.3 | 74.30 |
| 1987 | 23.4 | 23.1 | 42.7 | 6.4 | 4.1 | 0.3 | 76.89 |
| 1988 | 23.5 | 23.1 | 42.7 | 7.1 | 7.1 | 0.3 | 80.22 |
| 1989 | 23.3 | 23.8 | 42.1 | 7.0 | 3.5 | 0.2 | 81.33 |
| 1990 | 23.5 | 23.8 | 41.2 | 7.6 | 3.6 | 0.2 | 81.26 |
| 1991 | 23.1 | 24.2 | 40.5 | 8.1 | 3.8 | 0.2 | 81.14 |
| 1992 | 22.9 | 24.7 | 40.6 | 8.1 | 3.4 | 0.2 | 82.36 |

[a] Quadrillion Btu.

*Source:* Energy Information Agency, *Annual Energy Review 1992.*

of Iraqi oil sales hung over the market like the sword of Damocles, ready to fall at any time.

Throughout the fall of 1993, the world price of oil slid lower. OPEC met again in Vienna November 23-24 but ended the meeting with an announcement that there would be no cut in production levels. Various explanations were offered by analysts for this action—such as OPEC's expectation that demand would increase over the winter. But many analysts, observing OPEC's behavior, concluded that it had simply stopped trying to be a cartel. The market made its own analysis in December 1993, by sending the price of oil to new record lows.

## A Cloudy Future

The Gulf War and the events of the 1980s reinforced the geopolitical importance of the Middle Eastern oil reserves. Yet, the future of OPEC as a cartel remained uncertain in 1994.

By their military action in the Gulf War, the United States and its allies demonstrated what had long been understood: that they considered Middle Eastern oil vital to their national security and economic interests. Yet those interests, and the threats to them, were not what they had appeared during the Cold War, when the West's worst nightmare was seizure of the oil fields by the Soviet Union or a Soviet-backed client government. Not only had the former Soviet Union evaporated as a military presence in the Middle East by 1993, but it was also in the process of turning from the world's biggest producer into another energy-hungry mouth for the Middle East to feed.

What was clear, as both U.S. production and former Soviet production continued to decline, was that the United States and many other nations of the world sorely needed access to Middle Eastern oil. Over the long term, U.S. reliance on foreign oil imports had been increasing and seemed likely to keep increasing. The threats to energy security now seemed to come less from external forces like the Soviets than from internal strife among the Middle Eastern nations themselves. Both the Iran-Iraq War and the Gulf War emphasized this lesson.

After the Gulf War, the strategic alliance between the United States and Saudi Arabia had become stronger and more openly acknowledged. Even with the Soviets out of the picture, some Middle Eastern states felt they needed U.S. strength to protect their oil fields. Saudi Arabia and other Gulf states had for the first time openly allowed U.S. troops to operate on their territory. Public alliance with the United States still brought perils, for hostility to the U.S. persisted in many quarters of the Middle East. That hostility had many sources: nationalism, Muslim fundamentalism, Pan-Arab populism, the Arab-Israeli conflict, and the quest by some Middle East states for regional economic and military power.

Saudi Arabia's market share offensives and the apparent eagerness of many OPEC members to increase their individual market shares at the expense of other members illustrated the fundamental, persistent debate that had spanned all three decades of the organization's history. OPEC had long been divided into two competing camps: the price moderates, typified by Saudi Arabia, and the price hawks such as Libya, who hoped to push the price higher despite market conditions. This division had often made it difficult for OPEC to operate as an effective cartel.

Yet the decline of OPEC's power and resolve can be exaggerated. Although it was telling that OPEC began exceeding its own production ceiling by increasing amounts in the mid-1980s, it was perhaps even more significant that OPEC was able and willing to eventually agree on substantial production cuts to restore oil prices. OPEC lost some control over oil prices as market forces continued to realign supply and demand, but it demonstrated market leverage when its members summoned the self-discipline and collective resolve to do so.

Cheating was chronic. OPEC, well into its third decade, still lacked any formal, institutionalized mechanism for enforcing its policies on its members. It relied on its members' perceptions of their own economic interests, and during the 1980s and 1990s those interests seemed ever more divergent. One nation, Saudi Arabia, with the world's largest reserves, served as OPEC's primary enforcer. Saudi Arabia proved repeatedly in the 1980s that

it alone, or perhaps joined by a small circle of Gulf allies, was big enough to dominate OPEC. Less certain, however, was whether OPEC was strong enough to control world oil prices.

The Saudis had learned, however, that there was such a thing as too much success. OPEC's ability to drive up the price of oil in the 1970s was the source of most of its problems during the 1980s. Demand slackened as conservation, fuel switching, inflation, and economic recession followed the price increases. New oil fields in non-OPEC countries were waiting to come on line as soon as rising prices made them profitable. This increase in world production robbed OPEC of the market power it needed to keep prices high.

While Saudi domination of OPEC, and indeed the world market, was as strong in 1994 as it had ever been, there were no guarantees it would continue. It seemed possible that other nations, such as Iran, or even Russia, could regain lost status as major producers. And Iraq's capacity could be brought back into the market if political changes occurred in that country that would cause the international community to lift the embargo.

The 1980s produced further economic and foreign policy liberalization in China and Russia, two sleeping energy giants that had been virtually walled off from the rest of the oil market. A more complete integration of these countries into the international economy as oil exporters or importers promised to change the world oil market significantly.

Another global uncertainty that arose during the 1980s was the so-called greenhouse effect—climate warming caused partly by the burning of fossil fuels. Some scientists predicted that the dangers of climate change would force cutbacks in petroleum consumption within the next few decades, long before underground reserves of petroleum are exhausted. To date, however, the amount of energy conservation inspired by global warming has been only a slim fraction of total consumption.

Despite such uncertainties, the importance of the Middle Eastern oil states remains unquestioned. By the mid-1990s the three biggest Gulf countries, Saudi Arabia, Iran, and Iraq, could supply 50 percent of the oil in world trade. If they cooperated with each other, as they had in the past, they could dominate the world oil market.

Prospects for such cooperation were not good in late 1994, suggesting that the world oil market could continue to be subject to chaotic fluctuations in price and supply.

# CHAPTER 6

# FOURTEEN CENTURIES OF ISLAM

From Morocco on the Atlantic through North and East Africa and into sub-Saharan Africa, across the broad expanse of central and southwest Asia to the headwaters of the Indus in the lofty tableland of Tibet, and swinging southward to the far reaches of the Java Sea, the call of Islam goes forth to the world five times a day: "God is most great! I testify that there is no god but Allah. I testify that Muhammad is the messenger of Allah." This is Islam's credo and it is intoned in Arabic, the language of Islam's holy book, the Koran.

For fourteen centuries, the faith of Islam has been shaping the lives of nations and peoples that form a mosaic of nationalities, races, languages, regions, and cultures. Today, about 800 million people living in Asia, Africa, Europe, and, to a much lesser extent, the Americas profess faith in Islam.

## Islam Divided

The catchall term *Islam* fails to convey the substantial differences among the many Islamic sects, races, nations, and cultures. The Islamic world is no more monolithic and homogeneous than the world of Christianity. From an anthropological point of view, there are vast differences between an Uzbek Muslim of Central Asia and a Berber from North Africa, or between a Muslim from Sumatra and a Fulani Muslim from Mali.

Political differences within the Muslim world are extensive, as evidenced by the varying ideological commitments of Muslim governments: the conservative monarchy of Saudi Arabia, the revolutionary Islamic fundamentalism of Iran, the secular socialism of the Ba'athist regimes of Syria and Iraq, and the disestablishment of Islam by the westernizing government of Turkey. This ideological diversity has promoted interstate conflict and tension. Moreover, divergent ideologies within Islamic nations have threatened to destabilize many Muslim governments.

The geographic spread of the forty or so Islamic countries (and of the approximately thirty other countries with sizable Muslim populations) has, of course, produced different societies. The cultural and historical development of Indonesia, for example, is quite distinct from that of Morocco. In the Middle East, Iran, Turkey, and Egypt are all Islamic countries, but they have little else in common.

On the theological level, Muslims also differ over interpretation of the Koran and the teachings of Muhammad. Some seventy sects and offshoots of Islam have arisen because of these doctrinal differences, which in some cases have remained irreconcilable. As in other religions, some sects of the Muslim faith are intolerant of others.

## Islam as Unifier

This said, one should not overemphasize the differences and ignore the factors that unite Muslims all over the world. Islamic ideals and precepts have provided the most important element of cultural continuity and tradition in most of the Islamic countries. Although it remains largely an ideal, the notion of "the nation or community of Islam" still holds the majority of Muslims together in an informal allegiance. With the formation of the Organization of the Islamic Conference in 1972, this bond took on a more formal meaning.

A way of life as well as a religion, Islam has provided Muslims with a powerful frame of reference. Both on the conscious and subconscious levels, Muslims draw their identity, habits, and attitudes largely from Islam. This common heritage and tradition has been reinforced by most Muslim nations' shared experience of having been dominated and exploited by European colonial powers.

In spite of the ascendance of nationalism as the principal focus of political identity in modern times, in many Muslim countries the lines between national and religious identities are blurred. The two identities often overlap, so that to Arabs, Pakistanis, and Iranians, for example, national identity is largely synonymous with affiliation to Islam. Many Muslim nations expressly state in their constitutions that Islam is the official faith. In these countries Islam is more than a religion. It is a centuries-old system of values, norms, and beliefs that permeates all aspects of social, political, and cultural life.

## Western Hostility

In the past the image of Islam in the West tended to be totally foreign, almost sinister. Many Muslims feel that this stereotypic image of Islam prevails in the West even today.

The negative image of Islam is due in part to ignorance about that "exotic" and "strange" religion, but it also has deep roots in history. Of all the world's religions, Islam is the closest to Christianity. Yet Christian Europe had denigrated it and ridiculed its founder, the Prophet Muhammad, throughout the medieval age and even into the modern era. Works by Dante, Voltaire, Carlyle, and other European writers, thinkers, theologians, and Orientalists attacked the Koran or Muhammad and thus influenced the attitudes of generations of Westerners.

This hostility to Islam was the result not so much of theological differences as of history and geography: it was Islam that had conquered parts of Europe and threatened much of the rest of it for several centuries. Islam's early empire expanded through conquests in the West, starting with Byzantium. The Arab armies that carried the faith to new horizons and frontiers overran Spain, Sicily, and parts of Eastern Europe and ruled them for centuries. They crossed the Pyrenees and raided France as far as Nimes. The armies of the last Islamic empire, the Ottoman, which was Turkish, not Arab, twice stood at the gates of Vienna and almost occupied the city.

Triggered by Islamic conquests in the West, the Crusades to the Holy Land by Western nations between the eleventh and thirteenth centuries deepened the hostility between the followers of the two religions and reinforced mutual suspicions and insecurities.

The legacy of alienation germinated by the Islamic conquests and counter-conquests by the West was perpetuated in literature and folk culture. Later, during the nineteenth and twentieth centuries, Western industrialization and military strength spearheaded Western hegemony in much of the Islamic Middle East. Muslims felt victimized and dehumanized, their national identities suppressed and their cultural heritage and contributions to civilization denigrated.

More recent years have witnessed a significant revival of Islamic sentiment—a product of the continuing effort of nearly all Muslim countries to shake free of the legacy of Western colonialism. For example, the overthrow of the shah of Iran and the rise to power of the Ayatollah Ruhollah Khomeini were motivated in part by the impulse of the Iranian people to establish independence from the West. The revival of Islamic sentiment, in turn, has renewed historically rooted fears in the West of the specter of "Islam on the march." Events such as the Iranian revolution of 1978-79 and the U.S. embassy hostage crisis of 1979-81 contributed to these fears that never had fully disappeared in Western culture. Mutual suspicions and misperceptions on both sides created hostility that shows few signs of subsiding.

## The Historical and Cultural Setting

Alexander the Great was barely twenty-two when his Macedonian forces swept through the Middle East and India as far east as the Indus River. His goal as leader of a powerful Greek empire was to unify the Middle East into a lasting empire, which he hoped would rekindle the spirit and brilliance of "the glory that was Greece."

Alexander's imperial dream was dashed by his death in 323 B.C. His empire soon broke up into several successor states ruled by his generals. Divided and poorly led, these states warred and feuded with each other until the Romans arrived a century later and, with the exception of Mesopotamia and Iran, brought the Middle East under their tutelage.

Some eight centuries later the Roman Empire itself was ravaged by the northern Teutonic barbarians, who severed its western half in the fifth century A.D. His empire decimated, the Emperor Constantine transferred his seat of power eastward from Rome to Constantinople, giving birth to the Byzantine Empire.

The eastern Roman emperors of Byzantium controlled the Roman provinces of the Middle East, while farther east the Sasanids of Persia established a rival empire in Mesopotamia and areas of present-day Iran. The Byzantines found themselves ruling diverse peoples and cultures, including Greeks, Syrians, Phoenicians, Egyptians, Jews, several Palestinian tribes, and Arabs.

The Arabs, Semitic people who originally came from the hinterlands and shores of Arabia (present-day Saudi Arabia), had fanned out into the Middle East and established several communities and states. They were mostly pagan, but as Christianity began to spread through the Middle East in the second century A.D. many of them embraced the new religion. For example, the Arab states of Ghassanid and Lakhmid, which allied themselves

## Facts About Islam

● With about 800 million followers, Islam is the world's second-largest religion after Christianity. About forty nations have overwhelming Muslim majorities and roughly thirty other countries have sizable Muslim populations.

● Although Islam has been associated with the Middle East and the Arabs, the largest Islamic country is non-Arab—Indonesia. India, which does not have an Islamic majority, nevertheless has the second-largest Muslim population.

● Jerusalem is the third holiest place in Islam after Mecca and Medina—both in Saudi Arabia. Tradition has it that the Prophet Muhammad journeyed at night from Mecca to Jerusalem and from there ascended to heaven on a winged horse, Al-Buraq, and returned the same night.

● Most Muslim countries follow the Western (Gregorian) calendar, but a few use the lunar calendar adopted over thirteen centuries ago by Umar, second of the Rashidun caliphs. Muslim dates are referred to by the notation A. H. (Anno Hegira).

● The Muslim year has three hundred fifty-four days and twelve months. Each month begins with the new moon. Months vary between twenty-nine and thirty days and have no fixed relation to the seasons. Therefore, the months—as well as Muslim holidays—come at different times each year and may fall in different seasons. In the countries that have retained the Muslim calendar—especially Saudi Arabia—the day goes from sundown to sundown rather than from midnight to midnight. A rule of thumb is that the date of any Islamic holiday will advance eleven days from one year to the next.

with the Byzantines and the Sasanids, respectively, were Christian. Their kinsmen in Arabia, however, remained largely pagan and immune to the control of the two rival empires to the north.

## Arabia: Islam's Birthplace

Arabia at the time was by no means an isolated desert removed from the civilized world or populated merely by nomads who roamed the desert. There were sedentary populations living in towns and oases scattered across Arabia and having a modicum of social order and links to the outside world. The camel had revolutionized life there by bringing city and desert together into a well-integrated system and by linking Arabia—primarily through trade—with the outside world, particularly with the prosperous and cultivated states of the Mediterranean.

The demands and prosperity of the Byzantine and Roman worlds, especially their growing appetite for spices, incense, and silk, gave a powerful impetus to trade between India and Africa, on the one hand, and the Mediterranean world, on the other. Trade had been established between them over two major routes—the Persian Gulf and the Fertile Crescent (Syria, Lebanon, Iraq, Jordan, and Palestine). But the wars between the Byzantines and the Sasanids and their Ghassanid and Lakhmid satellites made these routes increasingly risky. In time, traders shifted to new routes along the Red Sea through the rugged western part of Arabia known as the Hijaz. Soon, caravans were carrying goods from Yemen by way of the Hijaz to Syria and the Mediterranean.

The booming caravan trade worked especially to the advantage of one city in Arabia, Mecca, which was to become the largest city and most important and powerful trading center on the peninsula. Located in a long, rocky valley among bare, mountainous hills, some forty miles inland from the Red Sea, and fed by a permanent spring, Mecca first became a settlement located around a shrine called the Ka'bah (literally, cube).

The Ka'bah housed a black stone, believed by some non-Muslims to be a meteorite, which was held sacred by the Bedouins in the desert and the townsfolk of Mecca and nearby settlements. Tradition has it that the black stone was brought to earth by the archangel Gabriel and delivered to the Prophet Abraham and his son Ishmael, who encased it in the Ka'bah. The Ka'bah thus became a pilgrimage site, but pagan practices distorted its significance.

The Meccans revered Abraham as a patriarch and prophet and claimed descent from Ishmael. Later, Muslims claimed Abraham as the first Muslim, while Arabs in general claimed Ishmael as the progenitor of all Arabs.

By the sixth century A.D., when Muhammad was born, the enterprising Meccan merchants had developed into a powerful mercantile oligarchy not unlike the Italian mercantile republics of the Middle Ages. Lying in a strategic position at the crossroads of overland trade routes linking Asia and the Mediterranean by way of the Hijaz, Mecca thrived even when Constantinople and other northern centers in the eastern Mediterranean were importing more and more luxury goods from the East by way of the Black Sea and central Asia.

The prosperity of Mecca gave added prominence and power to the Quraysh, the major tribe and part of the aristocracy inhabiting the city. The Quraysh consisted of several clans and families, one of which was the family of Banu Hashim, from whom Jordan's Hashemite dynasty claims descent. It was into this family that Muhammad was born.

## The Prophet Muhammad

Very little is known about the early life of Muhammad. No biography of him was written until a century after his death, and its authenticity is marred by extravagant embellishments and idealization. His date of birth generally is given as A.D. 570.

It is known that his father, Abdullah, probably died before Muhammad was born, and that his mother died when he was about six. His grandfather became his guardian and protector, and when his grandfather died the boy was left in the custody of an uncle. Without inheritance from his father, the young Muhammad had to fend for himself, and he did so by working as a caravan trader. His efficiency and honesty eventually caught the eye of a wealthy and influential widow many years his senior, who made him her business agent. Eventually, he married her and they had many children, but only four girls lived to maturity.

The Mecca in which Muhammad grew to manhood was the center of Arabia's polytheistic animism, attracting tribal pilgrims from all over the Arabian Peninsula. The Meccans at that time generally were pagan, although, as a center of trade, Mecca had come into contact with certain influences outside Arabia. These included Christianity, Judaism, and some Christian heretical and gnostic sects, some of whose adherents lived in Mecca and other Arabian towns. Zoroastrianism, a monotheistic religion practiced by Persians, also was known to some Meccans.

Through their contacts with Jews and Christians the Meccans acquired a certain awareness of monotheism and developed vague notions of a Supreme Being. They believed, however, that they could gain access to the Supreme Being only through intercessors—gods and goddesses in the form of idols. So they installed 360 such idols in the Ka'bah, which remained there until the Prophet Muhammad destroyed them and reconsecrated the Ka'bah, which subsequently became the holiest shrine of the Islamic religion.

The sect thought to have had the deepest influence on Muhammad's thinking was the Hanifis—a pious group with monotheistic leanings who were very critical of the rampant paganism and the growing commercialism and materialism of Mecca. In time Muhammad, too, became deeply troubled by the low moral fiber of Meccan society. Following ancient Middle East custom, he is said to have retreated on occasion to lonely places to think and contemplate. According to some unsubstantiated accounts, he was influenced by Christian heretics and hermits he met during his caravan trips to Syria.

Tradition has it that Muhammad chose a cave in a hillside near Mecca to meditate. His marriage had brought him material comfort, thus enabling him to stay away from work for long periods of time.

*Muhammad's Revelations.*    It was in a cave that Muhammad, according to his seventh-century biography, experienced his first revelation. The year probably was A.D. 610, when Muhammad was about forty. He was supposed to have had a vision in which the archangel Gabriel commanded him to read a message sent from God saying that man was a creature of God and subservient to him.

Muhammad, who was believed to have been illiterate, is said to have memorized the message and repeated it to his wife and his friends, who called it a divine revelation. This first revelation was followed by others, on and off, for some twenty years, both in Mecca and Medina, another city in Arabia. These revelations became the basis of the Koran. Muslims refer to the Koran as "glorious," not holy.

Muhammad's revelations established his role as the "Prophet" and "Messenger of God" and marked the birth of Islam. The adherents of the new religion became known as Muslims.

Slowly, Muhammad began to attract believers. Most Meccans, however, spurned his teachings and ridiculed his claims of prophethood. They were outraged particularly by his audacious denunciation of Mecca's paganism and his condemnation of the Ka'bah, which gave Mecca its position of prestige and eminence in Arabia and which enjoyed the protection and sponsorship of the Meccan aristocracy.

*Islam Finds a Home.*    The disdain of Meccan leaders eventually turned into hostility when the ruling class became aware of Muhammad's growing appeal to some segments of the population and the serious implications of his teachings. His message clearly threatened the established order and jeopardized the city's income from trade and pilgrimages. To avoid persecution Muhammad secretly fled with about seventy of his followers for Yathrib, a city to the north of Mecca, in A.D. 622. The flight from Mecca—termed the *Hegira* by Muslims—marks the beginning of the Islamic calendar.

Yathrib, later named Medina al-Manura ("City of Enlightenment") and subsequently shortened to Medina, welcomed Muhammad in the hope he would help alleviate the serious divisions and civil disorders caused by the large influx of outsiders—mostly Yemenis and Bedouins—and internal feuds among rival groups and clans. The success that Muhammad achieved in Medina was the first test for the nascent religion.

With Medina as his base, Muhammad set out to subjugate Mecca. He succeeded in A.D. 630 after years of intermittent wars. Entering Mecca in triumph, Muhammad proceeded to the Ka'bah, where he destroyed the idols of paganism.

The Islamic commonwealth now began to emerge and take shape through raids and conquests in which the Bedouin's free spirit and love for movement and booty were channeled to the call of *jihad,* meaning "striving" or "struggle"—a term often associated with the concept of religious or holy war. In fact, however, jihad has a broader meaning of striving for the common well-being of Islam and Muslims, and not necessarily by military means.

Islamized Arabs in Muhammad's lifetime carried their religion to many parts of Arabia, but the Prophet Muhammad did not live long enough to see the spectacular expansion of Islam. When he died in A.D. 632, only two years after seizing Mecca and making it the center of Islam, he had bequeathed to his followers not only a religion but also a sociopolitical system and even an ideology. It became the task of his followers to propagate that ideology and carry it beyond the confines of Arabia.

## Islam After Muhammad

To the extent that Muhammad was God's prophet on earth, no one could succeed him. Some provision had to be adopted, however, for filling Muhammad's other roles as the spiritual and secular head of Islam. The succession question produced a major schism in Islam that has endured to this day. Some of Muhammad's followers claimed that the mantle of leadership should pass within the Prophet's family to his cousin and son-in-law, Ali, and argued that Muhammad had made this designation. Upholders of this view evolved into the Shi'ite sect of Islam. *("Schisms and Sects of Islam," box, p. 175)*

Most Muslims, however, opposed this claim and relied instead on tribal tradition, where inheritance or legal claim always had been superseded by a process of selection in which tribal elders chose a leader according to the prestige and power of his family or position in the tribal system. This view prevailed, laying the basis for the Sunni (orthodox) tradition in Islam.

*Muhammad's Early Successors.* Muhammad's trusted lieutenants were able to agree on one of their own, Abu Bakr, who was perhaps the first convert to Islam outside Muhammad's immediate family. He was the father of Ayshah, Muhammad's last wife. Abu Bakr thus became the first of four early *caliphs*—a term derived from Abu Bakr's title as successor of God's messenger—who promoted the expansion of Islam. Abu Bakr's first goal was to Islamize and exert control over the rest of the Arabian Peninsula. This was accomplished by his brilliant military commander, Khalid ibn al-Walid, who conquered eastern and southern Arabia and even subdued tribes that had revoked their allegiance to Islam after Muhammad's death. With Islam secure in Arabia, Khalid and other generals conquered the Sasanids in what is now Iraq, wrested Syria from the Byzantines, and opened all of Palestine to the Muslims.

Abu Bakr was followed as caliph by Umar ibn al-Khattab, whom Muslims sometimes call the second founder of Islam. During his ten-year reign the theocratic foundations of Islam were consolidated and Islamic conquests were pushed into new lands. Persia, central Asia, western India, and Egypt—bastions of great empires and earlier civilizations—were overrun by his Islamic forces. This expansion was driven as much by economic considerations as by religious zeal. Under Umar, the Middle East was reunified into a single, great empire, which it had not been since the age of Alexander the Great.

Umar was succeeded by the Uthman ibn 'Affan, the third of the Rashidun (rightly guided) caliphs. Like his two predecessors, Uthman had

# Schisms and Sects of Islam

About 90 percent of all Muslims are *Sunnis*—considered the orthodox sect. Of the dissident sects of Islam, the largest and most important is the *Shi'ite* sect. *Shi'ah,* or *Shi'ism,* refers to the "partisans of Ali."

When the Prophet Muhammad died without making any provisions for succession, his cousin and son-in-law, Ali ibn Abi Talib, claimed to be the Prophet's successor. But most of Muhammad's followers rallied around Abu Bakr, reputed to be the first person outside the Prophet's immediate family who converted to Islam.

Appointed to succeed the Prophet as the leader of the Muslim community, Abu Bakr became the first of the four *caliphs,* meaning "successors," of Muhammad.

Muhammad's son-in-law was rebuffed two more times when Muslims elected Umar ibn al-Khattab and Uthman ibn'Affan as the second and third caliphs. Eventually, twenty-three years after Muhammad's death, the caliphate passed to Ali, but the governor of Syria at the time, Mu'awiyah, and other members of a powerful tribe, the Umayyads, refused to recognize his authority. Ali ruled from Kufah, in Iraq, but his reign was marked by strife and dissension.

The first war between Muslims was waged during his reign when Ali's army defeated the rebellious forces of Mu'awiyah. Among other things, Ali was accused by his adversaries of having condoned the murder of his predecessor, Uthman, a member of the powerful Umayyad family.

In A.D. 661 Ali was assassinated by a Muslim dissident and his eldest son, Hasan, succeeded him as caliph. Challenged by the powerful Umayyad governor of Syria, Mu'awiyah, the easygoing and irresolute Hasan abdicated in favor of his rival, who was proclaimed the caliph of all Muslims, with his capital in Damascus.

Before his death, Mu'awiyah designated his son, Yazid, as his successor to the caliphate. Hasan's younger brother, Husayn, rose in rebellion against Yazid but was routed and slain in Karlbala, in Iraq, in A.D. 680. The dreadful manner in which Husayn was tortured and killed by the Sunni followers of Yazid led to the creation of Shi'ism—the first schism in Islam.

Each year Shi'ites mark the anniversary of Husayn's martyrdom with an astounding display of emotional intensity and religious frenzy marked by breast beating and self-flagellation. The martyrdom of Husayn became the major symbol of Shi'ism.

The political dispute that gave rise to Shi'ism was reinforced later by doctrinal differences. The Shi'ites replaced the Sunni term *caliphate* with that of *imamate* and focused their belief on a hereditary line from Muhammad through twelve imams, beginning with Ali. The major Shi'ite sect draws its name of *Twelvers* from the twelve imams. The twelfth imam reportedly disappeared in mysterious circumstances in A.D. 878. Shi'ites disagree on how and when he died, but they agree his name was Muhammad al-Muntazar, "the expected one," and that he must reappear to complete the mission of God on earth.

Twelver Shi'ism is the state religion of Iran, the only Muslim country with an overwhelming Shi'ite majority. Among the large Arab countries of the Middle East (Iran is non-Arab), only Iraq, where the sect originated, is predominantly Shi'ite. The other Arab nations are mostly Sunni, although Lebanon has a sizable Christian population.

Shi'ism itself has its own dissidents, those who became *Isma'ilis, Alawites,* and *Druzes.*

In the eighth century a mystical movement called *Sufism* developed in protest against the formalism and legalism of conventional Islam. The name is derived from the Arabic word for wool, *suf,* since the first Sufis wore coarse woolen garments, probably in imitation of the Christian hermits of Syria. The Sufis practiced a form of hermitic mysticism by withdrawing from the world and seeking a personal relationship and direct communion with God.

Sufism has had great influence, both within the Islamic world and beyond it. Many Sufi orders exist, each centered around different rites. Although both Sunni and Shi'ite fundamentalists reject it, Sufism retains wide appeal among those who view Islam fundamentally as a religious experience rather than as a basis for political action.

been one of Muhammad's companions, but unlike them he belonged to a powerful family, the Umayyad. It was from this family that Uthman appointed some of his senior aides as governors and generals. His most significant and historically important appointment was that of his dynamic and able cousin, Mu'awiyah ibn Abi Sufyan, as governor of Damascus. Mu'awiyah soon became the ruler of all Syria.

Uthman's weak leadership, and his policy of appointing many members of the Umayyad family to high office, angered other Muslims, including those who considered themselves keepers and protectors of Muhammad's legacy. Uthman eventually was murdered by rebels outraged by what they saw as his favoritism and deviation from the path set by Muhammad.

Under pressure from those rebels, Muhammad's cousin and son-in-law, Ali ibn Abi Talib, was chosen as successor to Uthman. His selection, however, was opposed by some of the powerful and influential Muslims, who accused Ali of condoning the murder of Uthman.

*The Umayyad Islamic Empire.* There followed an unstable period in which first Muhammad's widow and then the ruler of Syria, Mu'awiyah, challenged Ali for control of the Islamic movement. Eventually, Mu'awiyah, a member of the Umayyad family, prevailed over all his challengers, and he was proclaimed the caliph of all the Muslims in A.D. 661. Damascus then became the center of the Umayyads and their Arab empire.

The Umayyad dynasty lasted from A.D. 661 to 750 and initiated a new wave of conquests that complemented the breathtaking expansion by the first four Rashidun caliphs. The Muslim empire extended its hegemony to the fringes of India and China, overran North Africa, and, in A.D. 717, pushed across the Strait of Gibraltar. The occupation of Spain by the Muslims—given the name "Moors"—lasted until A.D. 1492. During the Umayyad dynasty Muhammad's followers gained control of an empire that surpassed in size the empire of Alexander the Great.

This was a period in which the newly conquered peoples, including the Syrians, Egyptians, and Berbers, became Arabized, adopting the faith, culture, and language of the Arabs. The Berbers retained certain local attributes, such as a native dialect, and the Persians, Turks, and some Indian groups adopted the Arabic alphabet and script but retained their own language. The Arabs themselves were exposed to a process of acculturation as the new faith acquired millions of converts among the non-Arab peoples. As a result, the Arab character of Islam became diluted.

A combination of powerful trends finally brought about the demise of the Umayyad empire that Mu'awiyah had established. The most decisive were the growing decadence of the Umayyad court in Damascus; the persistent opposition to the Umayyad dynasty by Shi'ite Muslims; the emergence of rebellious and alienated forces in Iraq and in a region of Iran known as Khurasan, once centers of great power that resented their subordinate status under the Umayyads; and the constant feuding among the Sunni tribes of Arabia.

*The Abbasid Islamic Empire.* About the year 740, the Abbasids, led by Abu al-Abbas, a descendant of an uncle of Muhammad, emerged as the major opposition group to Umayyad rule. They became the main rallying point of all the anti-Umayyad forces, especially the non-Arab Muslims of Khurasan. In 747 the Abbasids, led by Abu al-Abbas, openly revolted. Within three years they had defeated the Umayyads.

The Abbasids ruthlessly hunted down the Umayyad rulers. Only a few managed to escape, among them Abd al-Rahman, who fled to Spain, where he established the Umayyad caliphate of Cordoba. The Umayyads at Cordoba were threatened by internal factionalism, Berber invasions from North Africa, and resistance by Spanish Christians in the north of Spain. The regime survived these challenges, however, and then prospered under subsequent Berber/Arab dynasties that arose in North Africa. Moorish power in Spain finally came to an end in 1492 with the capture of the last Islamic stronghold at Granada by the Christian forces of King Ferdinand and Queen Isabella.

The emergence of the Abbasid Empire, with its capital in Baghdad, ushered in great changes. Non-Arab Muslims achieved greater prominence and influence than ever before. The Abbasids extended the Islamic empire to some of the Mediterranean ports in southern France and Italy and took control of Sicily and Sardinia and, in the east, part of present-day Turkey and India.

The imperial munificence and wealth of the court in Baghdad far outstripped its Umayyad predecessor in Damascus and was immortalized in the tales of *The Arabian Nights*. The arts flourished, and a great cultural movement flowered along the banks of the Tigris and Euphrates rivers. The works of the ancient Greeks, Romans, Iranians, and Hindus in philosophy, medicine, astronomy, mathematics, and science were translated into Arabic and became part of Islamic culture. A whole generation of Arab and Arabized Muslim scholars left their imprint on Western civilization.

The Abbasids leaned heavily on Persian administrators and Turkish soldiers in running their burgeoning empire, which extended almost from the borders of China to the Pyrenees. The influence of the Persians and Turks grew until the caliphs themselves became little more than figureheads of the new administrative elite.

As the power of the caliphs diminished, they became easy prey for their governors and generals, who proceeded to carve out their own principalities. Ultimately, many little dynasties and states sprouted within the Abbasid Empire, rendering it an empty shell ruled by caliphs appointed or deposed at will by the Turkish soldiers or Persian administrators. In Spain, Morocco, Tunisia, Egypt, Syria, Persia, and other areas, new self-styled caliphates and sultanates arose, maintaining a semblance of allegiance to the caliph in Baghdad. By the year 1000, the Abbasid caliph in Baghdad was rivaled by self-proclaimed independent caliphs in both Cairo and Cordoba.

The fiction of the Abbasid dynasty continued through the eleventh century, when a group of Turks, called Seljuks, captured Baghdad and won recognition from the Arab caliph there. The Seljuk rulers captured most of Anatolia (Turkey) from the Byzantines and triggered the chain of events that culminated in the Crusades.

*The Ottoman Empire.*  The final blow to the Abbasid Empire came in 1258 when Mongols overran Baghdad. As the Middle Ages drew to a close, Muslim power shifted decisively to Anatolia, where a small Turkish tribe led by Osman began to accumulate power and territory at the expense of the Byzantine Empire. By 1453 the Ottomans, as they are called in English, had captured Byzantium. Constantinople was renamed Istanbul and became the capital of the Ottoman Turks.

The greatest of the Ottoman sultans, Suleiman the Magnificent (1520-1566), extended the frontiers of the empire to include the Middle East and North Africa as well as most of present-day Hungary and southeastern Europe. In India, another Turkish dynasty, the Moguls, established an Islamic empire that reached its height in the period between 1556 and 1658. It was during that era that the Taj Mahal was built at Agra.

The Ottoman Empire began to break up even before the European powers emerged in the nineteenth century as the new masters of the international order. The "sick man of Europe," as the tottering Ottoman rule was labeled at the turn of the century, was finally defeated in World War I, and its territories were partitioned. The remnants of the empire were centered in Turkish-populated Anatolia, which became the Turkish Republic in 1923 under the leadership of Mustafa Kemal (Ataturk).

# The Doctrine of Islamic Faith

Of all the major religions, Muslims proudly point out, only Islam is named neither for its founder, as in Christianity or Buddhism, nor after the community in which it emerged, as in Judaism. They see this as proof of the uniqueness of Islam as a universal religion—neither the product of a human mind nor of a religion that is identified with a particular community.

Islam incorporates both the spiritual and temporal aspects of life into a social as well as a religious system that seeks to regulate a believer's relationship to God and relations with other persons. Its precepts and tenets, though clearly the product of a particular society and historical period, were considered to be good for all people and all times and, therefore, unalterable.

In Islam there is no separation between the religious and the secular. Almost all Islamic nations ostensibly declare their adherence to this concept. Although these nations are guided by modern, practical norms, Muslims find it necessary to seek an Islamic explanation for world events. Turkey is the only Islamic country that has made a formal separation between the religious and secular spheres. At the other extreme, Saudi Arabia and now Iran are the only countries that claim the Koran as their constitution. That, however, does not bar the Saudis from following secular practices and policies.

*Islam* in Arabic means "submission"—in this case, submission to the will of God. The one who submits is a Muslim. That submission is total and irrevocable. Indeed, the central theme of the Islamic faith is an uncompromising assertion of the unity, uniqueness, and sovereignty of *Allah,* the Arabic equivalent of God. Accordingly, Muslims vehemently reject the Christian doctrine of the Trinity as sinful and blasphemous.

The affirmation of the oneness of God is linked symbolically to another fundamental tenet, namely that Muhammad is the messenger, or apostle, of God and that he is the last prophet. These two affirmations constitute the *Shahadah*—the Muslim's confession of faith.

## Doctrine's Sources

The Islamic doctrine has four sources: the *Koran,* the *Hadith-Sunnah,* consensus, and inference by analogy.

*The Koran.*   The Koran (literally, "reading or recitation") is the primary source of Islamic teachings and doctrine. Considered the word of God, it is therefore divine, eternal and immutable. Muslims believe that the Koran is a replica of an archetype in heaven. Because the Koran was revealed to Muhammad in Arabic, Muslims are prohibited from using it liturgically in any other language.

The Koran consists of 114 chapters of varying lengths which, Muslims believe, were revealed to Muhammad piecemeal over a period of about twenty years by the archangel Gabriel. Each chapter bears the name of a person, animal, or object prominently cited in the text.

The various utterances in the Koran initially were memorized or written on parchment, leather, palm leaves, stone tablets, and other objects. They remained scattered and were not finally pieced together and collected into a standard text until well after Muhammad's death in A.D. 632. The first canonized version was set down under the caliph Uthman in the seventh century.

Islam has no priestly or clerical caste and no central body, and Muhammad has no divine attributes, but simply is considered God's messenger. Thus the Koran has an overwhelming spiritual importance in the lives of Muslims. It is the purveyor and preserver of the faith, and it exercises a powerful hold as much for its spiritual content as for the sheer majesty of its prose.

The Koran is a work of such beauty that Muslims, particularly Arabs, are sometimes transformed into a state of emotional and spiritual elation when they listen to the verses of the Koran. The verses are always chanted or intoned, perhaps to accentuate the rhythmic cadence and elegance of the text. The mutually reinforcing link between the linguistic and the spiritual importance of the Koran underlies the Muslims' deep belief in the inimitability of the holy book.

The Koran also provided a religiously sanctioned linguistic model, which protected the Arabic language from the ravages of local fragmentation and from Ottoman domination. During the Ottoman rule, Arab culture and the Arab component of Islam were diluted and nearly pushed to extinction.

Westerners, including some Orientalists, in the

past applied the association of Christianity and Christ to Islam, calling it "Mohammedanism." But, unlike Christ, Muhammad ("Mohammed" still is a common Western spelling of his name) never was deified in the Koran. His attributes remained those of a prophet and messenger of God. Muslims venerate him as such and always follow his name with the phrase, "May God bless him and grant him salvation," but they do not worship him. Nevertheless, that veneration often approximates worship. It is, therefore, the Koran, not Muhammad, that is the cornerstone of Islam.

*The Hadith-Sunnah.*   The Koran contains a wide variety of devotional regulations as well as specific rules for everyday living—rules on matters such as marriage, divorce, inheritance, and contracts. Like the testaments of other religions, however, it did not address many problems, especially those caused by the growth of the community of Islam after Muhammad's death and the twentieth-century establishment of modern secular states. The lack of comprehensive guidance in the Koran led Muslims to seek guidance elsewhere, primarily in the so-called *Hadith-Sunnah,* meaning "tradition" and "prophetic practice." *Hadith* specifically refers to Muhammad's sayings, while *Sunnah* refers to his actions or his attitude toward the actions of others. In modern usage, the two words generally are used interchangeably.

The codification of the Hadith-Sunnah did not begin until the second half of the second Islamic century (767-795), and it was not completed until the third (869-896), during the reign of the Abbasid dynasty. Since the sources of what Muhammad said and did were oral testimonies and reports handed down from one generation to another, a great deal of distortion and even spurious attributions to Muhammad slipped into the record. Sifting through the mass of oral history that had accumulated after Muhammad's death, Islamic scholars in the Abbasid era faced the formidable task of verification and compilation. Finally, the process was boiled down to six collections or compilations—the so-called Six Books.

*Consensus.*   The third source of Islamic doctrine is consensus, which is practiced by leading Muslim scholars recognized as interpreters of Islamic doctrine. When the Muslim community is faced with an issue for which the Koran or the Hadith-Sunnah has no provision, scholars may study the matter to determine how to deal with it. At least three scholars are required to reach a consensus on any issue.

*Inference by Analogy.*   Inference by analogy is the fourth source of Islamic doctrine. Basically, this is the process by which judges and scholars devise a solution to a new problem or case based on solutions or principles inferred from the previous three sources. Inference by analogy corresponds to the use of precedents in the Anglo-Saxon legal tradition.

### The Five Pillars of Islam

The four sources provide the system of Islamic doctrine. That doctrine entails certain obligations that are as important as faith in determining and defining the complete identity of a Muslim. The most significant obligations are the so-called Five Pillars of Islam:

*I. The Confession of Faith.*   This is the oral declaration, "I testify that there is no God but Allah; I testify that Muhammad is God's messenger." Implicit in this testimony is commitment to belief in one true God (monotheism) and affirmation that God's revelation through the Prophet Muhammad (the Koran) is true. Islamic scholars concur that confession of the faith before witnesses is the distinction between a Muslim and a non-Muslim.

*II. Prayer.*   Several conditions have to be met before prayers can be performed. The person must be a Muslim, decently attired, physically clean, and should turn his face toward Mecca.

Prayers should be performed five times daily: at daybreak, noon, afternoon, sunset, and evening. Kneeling and touching their foreheads to the ground, Muslims repeat ritual prayers always beginning with the declaration, "God is most great."

Muslims can perform daily prayers anywhere, and many carry a prayer rug with them. On Friday, the Sabbath, Muslims flock to mosques for what is equivalent to the Sunday mass in the Catholic church.

*III. Alms.*  The giving of alms, like the tithe in Christianity, is obligatory for Muslims. Alms can be given to the poor or to an institution that supports the Muslim community.

*IV. Fasting During Ramadan.*  Ramadan, the ninth month in the lunar Islamic calendar, is the month in which the Prophet Muhammad customarily retreated to fast and pray and in which the Koran was first revealed to him. In memory of the Prophet's practice and in honor of Allah's revelation, Muslims are required to fast and pray during the entire month.

Because Ramadan follows the phases of the moon, it may occur during any of the four seasons. Nothing is to be consumed between sunrise and sunset, not even water. Sexual activity and smoking are forbidden during fasting.

When the traditional cannon is fired to signal the breaking of the fast at sunset, Ramadan usually takes on a festive character in which families gather around tables laden with traditional dishes and gifts are exchanged. The month of fasting culminates in the colorful three-day holiday of *'Id al-Fitr,* one of the most important Muslim holidays.

Traditionally, the sick, the elderly, travelers, pregnant women, and nursing mothers are exempted from the rites of fasting during the month of Ramadan.

*V. Pilgrimage.*  The twelfth and last month of the Islamic calendar is the season of *al-hajj,* the ritual pilgrimage to Mecca. Muslim males and females of sound body and mind are required to journey to Mecca at least once in a lifetime. *("The Pilgrimage to Mecca," box, page 182)*

### Articles of Faith

Muslims also adhere to a set of beliefs that can be summed up as follows:

*Belief in God.*  Muslims are believers in one God. They pride themselves on being the only true monotheists.

*Belief in God's Angels.*  Angels, Muslims believe, are spiritual beings created by God to carry out His orders. Angels have no independent will of their own.

*Belief in God's Messengers or Prophets.* These are men inspired by God to communicate His orders to mankind. The Koran speaks of a line of prophets beginning with Adam and ending with Muhammad. Both Jesus and Moses are part of this line.

*Belief in God's Books.*  Only four books revealed to the prophets are specifically mentioned in the Koran and, therefore, recognized by Muslims: the Torah (the first five books of the Old Testament); the Psalms; the Gospel or New Testament; and the Koran. Muslims believe in the first three books to the degree that they were preserved as originally written. They contend, however, that only the Koran was so preserved, the implication being that it remains the only true book. Christians and Jews are called "People of the Book" and Muslims respect their places of worship, law codes, schools, and property.

*Belief in the Day of Judgment.*  Both in the Koran and in the Hadith-Sunnah, man is constantly enjoined to conduct his life with awareness that he will ultimately confront the day of God's judgment. For this reason, he must be attentive to Allah's commands, submit himself to them, and act with compassion and justice toward others.

According to Islamic doctrine, at the end of the world there will be a day of resurrection. All humans will be revived and come before God for judgment. The deeds of people will be assessed, and those found guilty of evil acts will be punished in hell. The righteous believer will live eternally in paradise, a green, well-watered place of ease and comfort. Believers guilty of evil will serve a certain time in hell before being restored to paradise. Eternity in hell is reserved for nonbelievers. Martyrs in the cause of Islam are believed to pass directly to paradise.

*Belief in Predestination.*    Muslims believe that Allah is both creator and sustainer of the world, upholding its existence moment by moment. Reality is but an expression of Allah's will, and man cannot change what Allah has willed. Man nevertheless is free to accept or reject Islam, which is an expression of Allah's will. Submission to Islam implies living in harmony with God's will, which is designed to produce peace and accord among men as the natural order of things. Rejection of Islam implies rebellion against the natural order created and sustained by Allah and is responsible for the chaos and confusion that exists in the world.

## Islamic Canon Law

The concept of Islamic Law *(shari'a)* embraces all aspects of human life and endeavor, both private and public, devotional and secular, civil and criminal. It deals with rituals as well as with matters such as commercial activities, property, marriage, divorce, inheritance, personal conduct, personal hygiene, and diet. It sets forth penalties for crimes and offenses, but in most Muslim states secular legal and penal codes are based on Western models. A few Muslim countries, notably Saudi Arabia, still apply penalties provided for in the canon law. For example, adultery can be punishable by stoning or beheading; theft by the amputation of a hand. The canon law also covers political concerns such as war and peace, relations among states, and treaties. In sum, the canon law is the most important and comprehensive representation of Islam at the practical level.

The canon law was compiled by Islamic theologians, scholars, and jurists during the first three centuries of Islam (the seventh, eighth, and ninth centuries of the Christian era), on the basis of the Koran, the Hadith-Sunnah, inference by analogy, and, significantly, *ijtihad,* individual interpretations of Islamic law.

*Sunni Schools of Thought.*    The free exercise of analogical reasoning among Islamic scholars lent itself to several variations and systematized formulations of the canon law. These differing formulations developed into schools of thought. Four of these legalistic schools have survived within the orthodox Sunni sect of Islam to this day. They are the Hanifi, the Maliki, the Shafi'i, and the Hanbali.

The *Hanifi* is the official school in most of the Middle East, except in the Arabian Peninsula and Iran. It also is predominant in Turkey, Pakistan, Afghanistan, and among Muslims in India. Developed in Iraq and named after a prominent Islamic scholar, Abu Hanifa, a Persian by origin, the Hanifi school placed considerable emphasis on the role of reason and independent legal opinion in the development of Islamic doctrine and law. It is considered the most liberal and adaptable of the four schools and has the most followers.

The oldest school, the *Maliki,* developed in Medina, emphasized the Hadith-Sunnah and the opinions of the Islamic scholars of Medina, who were thought to retain the best memory of the state and society that had existed during the lifetime of Muhammad. Today, it is followed pervasively in North and West Africa, but it has little attraction elsewhere in the Islamic world.

Considered the most legally rigorous of the four schools, the *Shafi'i* originated from an attempt to reconcile the Maliki and Hanifi schools, but instead became a third school of legal doctrine. It remains influential in Egypt, the Republic of Yemen, East Africa, and Indonesia and other parts of Southeast Asia.

The *Hanbali,* the most conservative of the four schools, rejects all other sources of Islamic law except the Koran and the Hadith-Sunnah and emphasizes imitation of Arabian society during the lifetime of Muhammad. Today, it is the official school of law in Saudi Arabia and Qatar.

# The Pilgrimage to Mecca

Once a year, Mecca—Islam's holiest city—becomes a teeming, sweltering microcosm of the Islamic world. Muslims of every race and color converge on it from all corners of the earth to perform the rites of *al-hajj* (pilgrimage). There, in Mecca's Sacred Mosque, the world of Islam comes together around the Ka'bah, the shrine rising majestically in the middle of the mosque's large open court.

The ritual of al-hajj, a Muslim ceremony known as the Fifth Pillar of Islam, is rooted in the pre-Islamic era of paganism when Arab tribesmen trekked to the Ka'bah at least once a year to worship the idols it housed. With the advent of Islam, Muhammad destroyed the idols and reconsecrated the Ka'bah as Islam's holiest shrine, thus restoring it, according to Muslims, to the temple of God built by the Prophet Abraham and his son Ishmael.

Today, the cube-like stone structure of the Ka'bah stands forty-nine feet high and is shrouded by the *kiswah,* a brocaded black cloth adorned with quotations from the Koran. The kiswah is made anew every year.

The Ka'bah's focal point is a piece of rock, twelve inches in diameter, called the Black Stone. Set in silver and mounted in the east corner of the holy shrine, this sacred rock is thought by Muslims to have been delivered to Ishmael by the archangel Gabriel. It is said to be the only remaining relic from the original structure built by Abraham and Ishmael.

## A Holy Ritual

Muslims of both sexes who are physically and financially able to do so are admonished by the Koran to perform the hajj at least once in their lifetime. To devout Muslims, the hajj is the crowning event of their lives. There, with thousands of other Muslims, they renew their communion with God and rededicate themselves to Islam.

The formal pilgrimage lasts only ten days, beginning on the first day of Dhul-Hijjah, the twelfth and last month of the Muslim lunar calendar. In another sense the pilgrimage begins when the Muslim leaves home for Mecca and does not end until the Muslim returns. During the whole period, the pilgrim is considered to be in a dedicated state and participating in a holy ritual.

Before entering the sacred territory around Mecca, Muslims have to be in a state of *ihram* (restriction). The men remove their clothes and don simple garments consisting of two large pieces of white fabric that cover their bodies. Nothing else is worn. The women wear their customary dress and can remain unveiled. But, unlike the men, they have to keep their heads covered. The state of ihram also

---

*Shi'ite School of Thought.* On the whole, the differences among the four majority schools of thought are slight, and each accepts the other three as orthodox expressions of Sunni Islamic doctrine. Muslims belonging to Islam's minority Shi'ite sect, however, do not recognize them and maintain their own school, sometimes called the *Ja'afari* school.

Liberal Sunni scholars sometimes refer to this school, which is representative of Twelver Shi'ism, as a fifth school of Islamic law. Centered around certain traditions that are not accepted by the other four schools, such as Muhammad's alleged appointment of his nephew Ali as his successor,

the Ja'afari school is clearly heterodox in certain of its interpretations of Islam.

Nevertheless, the similarities between Sunni and Shi'ite Muslims are far greater than their differences, and neither sect denies the Islamic character of the other.

Governed by the canon law, all Muslims are required to abide by certain rules. They are forbidden to drink alcoholic beverages or engage in gambling and usury. They also have to follow dietary laws that are reminiscent of Jewish laws. The eating of pork is prohibited, and beef or lamb can be eaten only if the animal is ritually slaughtered and drained of blood.

requires Muslims to refrain from cutting their nails or hair, hunting, wearing jewelry, or engaging in sexual relations.

At the Sacred Mosque, tradition requires that the pilgrims perform the *tawaf,* the rite of walking around the Ka'bah seven times counterclockwise, during which they kiss or touch the Black Stone. Then comes the ceremony of *sa'y,* in which pilgrims make seven trips between the hills of Safa and Marwah, which are within the walls of the great mosque.

The ceremony is a reenactment of the desperate search by Hagar, Abraham's wife, for water when she and her son Ishmael were left alone in a desolate valley. The ordeal of Hagar and her son ended when the Well of Zamzam was revealed to them. Pilgrims ritually drink from that well.

### The Final Days

On the eighth day of Dhul-Hijjah, the final days of the hajj begin. Pilgrims proceed to the village of Mina, four miles east of Mecca, where they rest, then advance the next day to the Plain of Arafat for the ritual prayers of "standing" from noon to sunset. More than a million and a half persons have been known to assemble on that sultry plain where Muhammad prayed and delivered his farewell sermon on the ninth day of Dhul-Hijjah.

On the return trip to Mina, the pilgrims stop for the night at Muzdalifah. There they collect pebbles for the ritual stoning of Satan's three pillars, which are located in Mina and symbolize evil and temptation.

On the tenth day pilgrims celebrate 'Id al-Adha (Festival of Sacrifice) by sacrificing an animal. That ritual, which marks the end of the pilgrimage season, recalls the time when Abraham offered up his son Ishmael as a sacrifice to God, but his son was delivered when the archangel Gabriel brought a ram that was used as a sacrifice instead.

(The biblical version of the same story has Abraham offering up his son Isaac, rather than Ishmael, as a sacrifice to God.)

While the 'Id al-Adha is being celebrated at Mina, Muslims throughout the world are conducting similar ceremonies in their homes and towns. 'Id al-Adha is the highest holy day in the Islamic calendar and commemorates the sacrifice of Abraham as well as the end of the pilgrimage.

With the completion of the sacrifice ceremonies, the pilgrimage is considered completed, although many pilgrims return to the Ka'bah for final prayers and often visit the Prophet's tomb in Medina before returning home.

Muslims can go to Mecca any time of the year, but the real pilgrimage is the one performed during Dhul-Hijjah.

## Islam Today: A New Assertiveness

In many parts of the Islamic world, recent years have seen a reawakened religious consciousness favoring a return to Muslim puritanism. This movement has encouraged an idealized vision of the past and an internal and global Islamic assertiveness.

In some Muslim countries, fundamentalists are challenging contemporary regimes and calling for an outright reincarnation of ancient Islamic society. In others, Muslims advocate the more moderate course of increasing the involvement of Islam in the political and social structures of the nation and re-emphasizing Islam as a principal factor in public life. Meanwhile, more mosques are being built and younger people, in particular, are going to them in larger numbers.

Islam has been a major factor behind many recent political developments in Muslim countries. It has contributed to political power struggles, xenophobia (particularly anti-Westernism), and calls for pan-Islamic solidarity. In Afghanistan, opposition to the Soviet occupation and the Soviet-supported Afghan regime took on the character of a jihad or "holy war." Opposition groups in countries where Muslims are in the minority, such as the Philippines, India, and some African nations, have invoked Islam in their drive for greater autonomy. In a number of Islamic countries, notably Egypt, Syria, and Turkey, Islamic militants and dissidents have been quite visible and active. Islam has been used as a pretext by Libya to aid one of the major factions in Chad. In Libya itself, Col. Muammar al-Qaddafi's commitment to Islamic ideals is a major part of his worldview.

Iran is the most dramatic example of Islam's impact on recent political developments. A regime led by Islamic scholars—the closest thing to a theocracy since the dawn of Islam—took power in 1979 after bringing down one of the strongest dynasties in the Middle East. The regime succeeded in whipping up a wave of religious fervor that helped to sustain its war effort against neighboring Iraq for nine years.

In January 1991, when elections in Algeria appeared on the verge of producing a parliamentary majority for the Front for Islamic Salvation (FIS), the Algerian military intervened to stop the elections. Rather than halting the momentum of the Islamist movement, the military intervention resulted in civil disorder and a revolutionary atmosphere in Algeria. On the other hand, the election of a substantial minority of Islamist deputies to the parliament in Jordan in 1989 and again in 1993 demonstrated that the movement could have impact through democratic as well as revolutionary means.

The cumulative effect of these developments has clearly jolted the West, reviving a latent antipathy toward and suspicion of Islam. The literature generated in the West by references to "Islamic resurgence," "militant Islam," "the dark side of Islam," and similar phrases tended to frighten many Westerners. Islamic scholars have criticized the West for failing to comprehend the regenerative dynamics of Islam or to understand the complex political, economic, and social forces that have moved non-Western developing societies. The result, these scholars maintained, has been an alarmist perspective in the West about the meaning and potential of the contemporary wave of Islamic fervor.

The West's negative attitudes toward Islam were reinforced in 1989 by the reaction in many parts of the Islamic world to the publication of Salman Rushdie's novel *The Satanic Verses*. The book was unquestionably blasphemous from a Muslim perspective because of the doubts it raised about the authenticity of some verses of the Koran. Despite the fictional manner in which the doubts were phrased, its appearance at a time of general revival of Islamic belief and commitment was certain to make it controversial. The call for Rushdie's death by Iran's late Ayatollah Khomeini and efforts by Muslims to prevent the book's publication and distribution in the other parts of the world clashed with liberal Western traditions of freedom of speech and press. Muslims and many Western observers pointed out, however, that efforts in 1988 by some Christians in the West to prevent the showing of the film "The Last Temptation of Christ" also trampled on freedom of expression.

## Impact of Modernization

Like other countries emerging from colonial rule or discarding the old order, the modern Islamic nation-states had to borrow heavily from the West to build political and social institutions and run increasingly complex societies.

Nationalism—itself a secular European innovation—was fervently adopted by peoples whose national identity and impulses had long been suppressed by foreign rule and control. Once these peoples achieved independence, their ruling elites, many of whom were educated in the West, turned to Western ideas as a model for nation building. To a large extent, their choice of models was predetermined by the legacy of their former rulers—that is, the actual presence in their societies of European-type administrative, legal, and educational systems. These systems were too deeply entrenched to dismantle; moreover, they worked.

Direct Western influence in Islamic societies had begun to accelerate the process of modernization well before the emergence of independent nations in the Middle East. From the West came industrialization, urbanization, technology, commercialization, constitutionalism, and other notions that were powerful forces of change. The economic and political benefits of these methods and ideas heightened expectations and aspirations in the Islamic world, motivating the political elites that stepped into power to continue the process of modernization.

The effect of this acculturation was a gradual dismantling of the old order. There were limits to this process, however, that were directly related to the role of Islam in society. Given the powerful mix of politics and religion in the Middle East, where religious doctrine, cultural and behavioral patterns, and political values intersect at various levels of daily life, borrowing from the West could not proceed without some degree of religious sanction.

The exception to this proposition was Turkey, the only Islamic country formally to institute a secular system. At the other end of the spectrum, Saudi Arabia based its government and social system on a fundamentalist model. In these two nations, the role of Islam in society and government was clear. But in those Muslim states that had little experience in a governing system that separated religion from secular matters, the political elites could not ignore Islam's central role. Thus, officials sought to justify their actions in Islamic terms and to relate modern political concepts to their countries' Islamic heritage.

Working primarily through official religious organizations long accustomed to accommodating the ruling groups and sanctioning the established order, the secular officials modified and reinterpreted legal and theological aspects of Islamic doctrine. In doing so, they were drawing on the historical precedent of Islamic scholars and jurists who had adapted Islamic doctrine to current conditions. They rationalized that the Islamic canon law should not be taken literally as a fixed repository of commandments and prohibitions but rather as a model to be emulated.

The process of modifying Islamic doctrine to accommodate modernization and new social and political realities has not been easy. Many traditionalists and fundamentalists have contended that Islamic doctrine—immutable and sacred—had all the answers and provided an ideal and coherent model for society that was superior to that found in the West, whose values they rejected as corrupt and debased. Consequently, they viewed departures from that ideal model as both religiously heretical and socially detrimental. Predictably, this approach was popular among the guardians of Islamic traditions, but it often was supported by other groups that felt alienated or threatened economically by modernization, including merchants and shopkeepers in the small cities and small landowners and peasants in the countryside.

Because they had to take into account these deep-seated Islamic impulses—and they themselves wished to preserve at least the essence of their traditions—the governing elites sought to reconcile traditional values and secularism. The result was a set of compromises that produced systems incorporating elements of traditionalism, modernism, secularism, socialism, and other political ideas. Not all regimes in the Islamic world subscribed to this amalgam, but most did.

This marriage of convenience worked well to a point. It began to crack under the accelerated pace of industrialization and the evolution of a new set of norms and practices brought about by materialism, individualism, a certain degree of moral laxity, a breakdown in some of the traditional Islamic codes of behavior, greater access to information and knowledge, universal education, and higher expectations of achievement.

The resulting strains in the traditional fabric of Islamic society were compounded by economic dislocations. On the one hand, the pressures of modernization widened the gap between the rich minority and the poor majority, further impoverished the peasantry, and created a class of urban poor leading squalid lives in congested cities. On the other hand, sudden and enormous increases in wealth from oil revenues in some hitherto backward societies created acute problems as the pressures of rapid development began to unravel the old order and clash head-on with the forces of traditionalism.

# Islam in the United States

An estimated 2-3 million Muslims live in the United States—about 1 percent of the U.S. population. But their number is growing, along with American interest in Islam.

The Islamic presence in the United States dates back to just before the turn of the century when Middle Eastern Muslims, mostly from Lebanon, began to emigrate to the United States. More Muslims came after World War II, this time from other Arab, as well as non-Arab, countries. Most of the immigrants settled in large cities.

Today there are a substantial number of Muslims living throughout the United States who have emigrated from Lebanon, Syria, Yemen, Palestine, Albania, Yugoslavia, India, Pakistan, Turkey, Egypt, Iraq, Iran, and most of the other Islamic countries.

Their Muslim identity notwithstanding, religious solidarity among Muslims in the United States is nominal. They still primarily associate with their own national and sectarian groups and rarely mix with each other.

As Christians and others always have done, Muslims perpetuate their sectarian and national differences and distinctions, even after immigrating to the same foreign country.

With the growth of their population in America, leaders of the Muslim community set out to organize and create organizations to aid fellow Muslims in practicing their faith. Today, mosques and Islamic centers have been established in many American cities, and they play an important role in transmitting the cultural and religious values and teachings of Islam.

Muslim students also have organized the Muslim Students Association of the United States and Canada, which has approximately two hundred chapters. Islamic bookstores serving local and mail-order customers have mushroomed in many metropolitan areas.

The February 1993 bombing of the World Trade Center in New York, apparently the work of a small group of recent Muslim immigrants, reflected a mood of militant Islamic radicalism found in some parts of the Muslim world. The deed was condemned by most American Muslims, who called it an un-Islamic act and emphasized that the terrorist incident was not indicative of the attitudes and contributions of the Muslim community in the United States. So far inexplicable in terms of motive, the bombing appeared to be related to U.S. policies in the Middle East.

While most Muslims living in the United States are first- or second-generation immigrants, black Americans who have accepted Islam constitute a visible minority of the American Muslim community. These are the Black Muslims, a movement founded in Detroit in 1930 by W. D. Fard, who was succeeded by Elijah Muhammad in Chicago. The movement was influenced by the Ahmadiyyah Movement, which was founded in India in 1879 to reinterpret Islam, but Elijah Muhammad, whose followers were drawn to Islam by its principles of social and racial equality, subverted those principles to "black supremacy." "God is black" became one of the movement's mottoes. As a result, other Muslims disassociated themselves from the Black Muslims.

With the death of Elijah Muhammad, the Black Muslim movement modified its extremist position vis-à-vis the white society and, under the leadership of Elijah's son, Wallace Muhammad, and strongly influenced by the example of Malcolm X, a former disciple of Elijah Muhammad who had broken with the movement, began to draw closer to the mainstream of Islam.

Despite the more mainstream character of the Black Muslim movement, today called the "Nation of Islam," some of its spokesmen retain radical views. One of its leaders, the controversial Louis Farakhan, has drawn negative publicity on several occasions through expression of anti-Jewish and anti-Christian views.

Many other members of the movement have drawn favorable publicity through their community activism in drug- and crime-infested neighborhoods in several American cities. In general, the Nation of Islam remains a separate organization from the larger community of Muslims in the United States and reflects an aspect of African-American politics, as well as acceptance of Islamic values and doctrines.

Many of the systems that eventually emerged in the Middle East lacked an essential ingredient of most successful Western societies: citizen participation. The governing groups usually failed or were unwilling to create the necessary mechanisms and institutions to allow their people to participate in decisions. Colonial domination simply dissolved into variations of native repression or authoritarianism, regardless of the socialist, progressive, and democratic labels attached to them. While these modern economic and governing systems were sanctioned by most religious establishments and used Islamic symbols of identification, they failed to gain grass-roots support and popular mandates. Popular responses to the modernizing experiences buffeting Middle East societies primarily took political forms, but with an Islamic hue.

## Fundamentalist Movements

The history of Islam, almost from its inception, is replete with fundamentalist attempts to reaffirm Islamic ideals or resurrect the past in the face of internal crises or external challenges. Such revivalist movements have been a common feature of Christian and Jewish histories as well. The nineteenth century, during which European power and hegemony reached its zenith in the Middle East, produced many Islamic fundamentalist movements: Mahdism in Sudan; Muhammad Abduh's *salafiyah* movement in Egypt; Jamal al-Din al-Afghani's pan-Islamism movement in Egypt; Wahhabism in Saudi Arabia, and Sanusism in Libya. Some of these fundamentalist movements were forward-looking, in that they advocated a rejuvenated and purified Islam while encouraging the assimilation of the political organization and technical advances brought by European colonial administrations.

The Islamic revolution in Iran and the Muslim Brotherhood in Egypt, Syria, Jordan, and other parts of the Arab world are the best-known fundamentalist movements in existence today. These contemporary Muslim fundamentalists actively seek a return to orthodoxy and puritanism as the path to salvation and emancipation from external threats and internal disarray. Their appeal has struck a chord among sectors of the population that normally have shunned fundamentalist approaches, such as the university students in Egypt and the middle class in Iran.

Iran is the only Islamic country to date in which the fundamentalist movement replaced a modernizing, though repressive, regime. The Iranian case, however, is unique and should not be seen as an example of what is likely to occur elsewhere in the region. In Iran the Shi'ite *mullas* (scholars) always had played a political role, unlike their counterparts in Sunni Muslim countries. When the shah outlawed political opposition, dissidents among the Western-educated middle class, the shopkeepers, and various leftist groups joined the only existing pocket of organized resistance in the country—the religious community, which had been a longstanding source of opposition to the government.

Unlike their counterparts in Iran, Sunni religious leaders are not self-supporting, have no priestly hierarchy, are not politically organized, and have no history of political activism. Their record generally is one of religious orientation and support of the established political order. In extreme cases, however, they may encourage dissidence. In recent years, some Sunni religious leaders in Algeria, Tunisia, Egypt, Jordan, and Yemen have been involved in opposition political movements. The leaders have sought increased political influence as a means of forcing existing governments to adopt policies more in line with their own rigid view of Islam.

One other country in which the religious establishment wields significant political clout is Saudi Arabia. By virtue of its descent from Shaykh Muhammad ibn 'Abd al-Wahhab, founder of the dominant Wahhabi movement in Saudi Arabia, the al-Shaykh family traditionally has assumed the religious leadership of the country.

The Saudi monarchy today has to pay close attention to what the religious establishment says, but this has not inhibited the kingdom's strides toward modernization. The religious establishment by itself does not represent a major threat to the Saudi regime. A combination of several other forces—disaffected elites in the military and among the technocrats, for example—would have to coalesce to jeopardize the existing government.

The modern experiences of Iran and Saudi Arabia demonstrate that although religious considerations can play a supportive or catalytic role in politics, turmoil is more likely to derive from unfulfilled political and social expectations, lack of participation in government, and the absence of social justice.

The so-called Islamic movement represents a resurgence by Arab, African, and west Asian peoples who are beset by political, economic, and social crises to which they are unable to respond because they remain outside the political system—unrepresented, dispossessed, and impotent. Their turn to Islam is only one expression of their disenchantment with political leadership and the ideological alternatives over the past few decades. Nevertheless, the movement is no less authentic because of these limitations. For most Muslims, regardless of region, Islam remains the most genuine expression of their inherited cultural tradition. Any search for social and political recovery among the peoples of a Muslim society must include an assertion of Islamic values and traditions.

## Islam as a Political Force

It is difficult to visualize the emergence of a large-scale united Islamic revolutionary movement that transcends national boundaries. Recent back-to-the-roots stirrings in some parts of the Islamic world were responses primarily to local circumstances and political crises rather than a spontaneous spiritual rebirth of a messianic nature.

*Leadership.*  As one scholar noted, an Islamic nation encompassing many present-day countries is bound to remain an ideal—a superficial goal blocked by political and economic realities. There are several reasons for this. Islam has no powerful, organized central body or hierarchy that can coordinate, mobilize, and regulate such a movement. Recently created organizations such as the Jiddah-based Islamic Conference Organization established in 1972 will probably remain *inter*national, as distinct from *trans*national, mechanisms, effective only when the interests of the individual member states coincide. Even then, their role will be exhortative, much like the United Nations.

Cairo's Al-Azhar University and Saudi Arabia's dual religious centers of Mecca and Medina have not functioned as springboards for universal Islamic action. Their role will continue to be that of supporting learning and worship. In addition, Shi-'ism's limitations as a minority sect within Islam severely restrict Khomeini's successors in Iran from leading a pan-Islamic movement. The Islamic Republic in Iran also has demonstrated that a religiously run regime can be as repressive as any secular regime. Given its antiquated worldview, it is not likely to be capable of managing a complex, decentralized, and quickly changing Middle East. It can and does, however, lend aid and support to other activist Islamist groups elsewhere in the Muslim world, such as Shia Hizballah of Lebanon, the Hamas movement among Palestinians, and the National Islamic Front (NIF) in Sudan.

Nevertheless, certain international events, such as the Serbian-Croatian strangulation of Muslim Bosnia, the perceived injustice imposed on the Muslims of Palestine by Israel, and the now-ended Soviet occupation of Afghanistan, can serve as catalysts for concerted Muslim action, at least at the diplomatic and popular levels.

*Secular Influences.*  Almost daily, events in Islamic countries indicate that the pull of modernization and progress is equal to or greater than the pull of traditionalism. In Kuwait, for example, a crisis developed in 1980 over the government's decision to ban Arab students from private Kuwaiti schools that followed non-Arab curriculums and to end the licensing of new private foreign schools. The Kuwaiti government's decision outraged the elite Arab community, Kuwaitis included, whose children attended, or were expected to attend, those schools.

In Saudi Arabia today, women are beginning to demand greater freedom and to reject their inferior role in traditional Saudi society. Many Saudi women want to join the labor force and live in a modern environment. They argue that this will lessen the country's need for foreign workers.

Iranian women have been even more forceful in pressing their views. After an initial embrace of traditional mores and customs, including the reversion to traditional garb and the veil, many modern Iranian women now are renouncing their inferior, restrictive status.

The connections between governments and religious establishments also have the potential to change. In Saudi Arabia, the government's close identification with the religious establishment poses a political threat to its power. Growing numbers of people, especially among the educated classes, resent the fact that the government has given religious leaders a large voice in the nation's affairs while denying political expression to others. This has led to talk, so far unfulfilled, of establishing a national assembly and provincial councils, and even of the need to adopt a civil, secular constitution to replace the Koran.

The obscurantism and superstition of the past have given way, in varying degrees, to the acceptance and practice of modern, pragmatic, and rational modes of thought. Fundamentalists concede that Western technology has to be acquired—but without Western culture and social norms. The dilemma for fundamentalists is whether Muslim nations can take the one without the other. Can women be educated, for example, and still be expected to accept their home-bound role? And if they are allowed to work, can they continue to be segregated from men?

Despite the arguments for economic, social, and technological modernization in Islamic countries, Islam will remain an important political force in Middle East societies. Even highly secular Muslim regimes will have to contend with the Islamic ethos of the masses and mold society and government so that they can be perceived as at least minimally compatible with Islam.

PART II

# COUNTRY PROFILES

EGYPT

IRAN

IRAQ

ISRAEL

JORDAN

KUWAIT

LEBANON

LIBYA

PERSIAN GULF STATES

SAUDI ARABIA

SYRIA

YEMEN

# EGYPT

As Egypt begins the second half of the 1990s, President Hosni Mubarak is facing the same economic problems that have plagued his government since he assumed power in 1981. Mubarak realizes that he must improve the economy's performance to prove his leadership. After years of relying on foreign aid and enacting minimal reforms, he was forced by grim prospects in 1991 to accept a comprehensive structural reform package monitored by the International Monetary Fund (IMF) and the World Bank.

Nevertheless, Mubarak refuses to compromise on opening up the political system because militant Islamist groups have waged a campaign of violence against his regime. At the same time, he has made no attempt to address the rampant bureaucratic corruption that is damaging Egypt's economy and eroding his own popularity.

The Islamic groups that have rejected the government and declared that an Islamic system is the answer to the country's problems find willing adherents among the poor, unemployed, and university students. Yet, the violent tactics of some groups threaten their popular appeal among ordinary Egyptians.

Despite its domestic woes, Egypt has reassumed its historical role on the international scene as a leader among Arab countries. Geography, history, and culture lie behind Egypt's traditional preeminence in the Arab world. Egypt is centrally situated in that world, which stretches westward through North Africa to the Atlantic Ocean and eastward through the Fertile Crescent and the Arabian Peninsula. Egypt is also by far the most populous Arab nation. But size alone does not account for the influence it has long exerted among its neighbors.

Egypt also has left a large imprint on the politics of individual Arab nations and on the region as a whole. The 1952 coup in Egypt, in which Col. Gamal Abdel Nasser and his colleagues seized power and broke with colonial rule, transformed Egyptian society and had a powerful effect on the Arab world. Nasser became the chief Arab spokesman, and he cast his spell on at least two generations of Arab political leaders. He was the model for military leaders who came to power by leading coups in North Yemen (1962), the Sudan (1969), and Libya (1969). During Nasser's years in power, his calls for pan-Arabism and socialism echoed all over the Arab world and influenced Third World nations around the globe.

Upon Nasser's death in 1970 his successor, Anwar al-Sadat, exercised Egypt's leadership in another way. After several years of military confrontation and a major war with Israel, Sadat courted capitalism, broke Egypt's alliance with the Soviet Union, sought American aid and friendship, and boldly made peace with Israel. For that audacious act, he made Egypt a pariah among Arab nations and incurred the wrath of Muslim fundamentalists. The Arab League promptly expelled Egypt from membership and adopted a package of political and economic sanctions against it.

Sadat's assassination in 1981 elevated Mubarak to the presidency. Unlike his two predecessors, the charismatic and radical Nasser and the flamboyant and impulsive Sadat, Mubarak is pragmatic

## Key Facts on Egypt

**Area:** 386,660 square miles, including 22,500 square miles of the Sinai Peninsula.
**Capital:** Cairo.
**Population:** 60,765,028 (1994).
**Religion:** 94 percent Muslim (mostly Sunni), 6 percent Coptic Christian and others.
**Official Language:** Arabic; English and French are widely spoken by upper and middle classes.
**GDP** $139 billion; $2,400 per capita (1993).

*Source:* Central Intelligence Agency, *CIA World Factbook 1994.*

and cautious—some have said plodding. He has managed, however, to return Egypt to the good graces of its Arab neighbors without reneging on the peace treaty with Israel or weakening ties to the United States. Beginning in 1988 he gradually assumed a leadership role among Arab nations—just as had Nasser and Sadat at their heights of power. After being shunned for nearly a decade for signing the 1979 peace treaty with Israel, Egypt is once again at the political center of the Arab world. Mubarak led the Arab nations opposed to Iraq's invasion of Kuwait in 1990. He brought Egypt into the international coalition arrayed against Iraq, and Egyptian troops helped to expel Iraq from Kuwait in early 1991. Egypt's diplomatic backing also contributed to the historic agreement between the Palestine Liberation Organization (PLO) and Israel in September 1993.

## Problems in a Crowded Land

Egypt's reassertion of leadership in the Arab world has done little to mitigate a host of intransigent internal problems. Overpopulation creates many of them and compounds others. Egypt's population rose to 60.8 million in 1994, with another 2.6 million estimated to be living abroad.

Although the rate of increase decreased to 2.3 percent a year in 1993, from a high of 3 percent in 1985, that still means more than 1 million more mouths to feed every ten months. The country, which once fed itself, now must import more than half of its food.

Although Egypt has a land area of 386,660 square miles, roughly equal to the combined size of Texas and New Mexico, most of it is barren desert. Less than 4 percent of the land is arable. In a country where rainfall is only an inch or two a year, nearly all of the food that Egypt grows comes from the acreage that is within reach of irrigation from the Nile River, the source of life in Egypt since earliest recorded times. The river, the world's longest, rises in the mountains of interior Africa and flows northward to the Mediterranean, running the length of Egypt.

The Nile Valley in Egypt is never more than nine miles wide until the river branches into tributaries north of Cairo and widens into the delta. As seen from the air, the valley is but a green ribbon bisecting the brown desert for 500 miles between Cairo and the High Dam at Aswan. Lake Nasser, formed by the dam and extending 185 miles southward, some 62 miles into the Sudan, is hemmed in by geologic formations that make irrigation extremely difficult along its edges.

The Western (or Libyan) Desert, running the length of the country west of the Nile, makes up about two-thirds of present-day Egypt. It is a low plateau punctuated by depressions and basins, some of which form oases, and the great Sand Sea. This desert in Egypt and Libya itself is probably best known to the world for the extensive tank warfare conducted there in World War II. British prime minister Winston Churchill considered the battle of El Alamein, some seventy miles west of Alexandria, the war's turning point. There, in 1942, British and Commonwealth forces turned back the hitherto victorious Afrika Korps and saved the vital Suez Canal from German capture.

Stretching eastward from the Nile to the Red Sea is a sloping plateau that develops into dry, barren hills and is known as the Eastern (or Arabian) Desert. There and in the plateau- and mountain-strewn Sinai Peninsula across the Suez Canal and Red Sea, the habitation is confined chiefly to a few seaside villages and resort communities and some nomadic Bedouin groups and their flocks.

In the Nile Valley and delta are concentrated 99 percent of the people, creating some of the highest population densities on Earth. About one-fourth of the Egyptian people live in and around Cairo, the capital, making it the biggest and possibly the fastest-growing metropolis in Africa or the Middle East. Their numbers have overwhelmed many of the basic municipal services, caused massive traffic congestion, and resulted in housing shortages so severe that makeshift quarters litter the urban landscape. Untold thousands live in the city's ancient cemeteries; others make do in shacks perched atop high-rise buildings in downtown Cairo. The city has spread outward into the desert as far as the famous pyramids at Giza, twenty miles west of the Nile, and up and down the river, removing thousands of valuable acres from cultivation.

Since 1971 when the High Dam at Aswan started controlling the release of irrigation water, Egypt has put 2 million additional acres in cultivation, increasing its total by a third. With an adequate year-round water supply, farmers can grow as many as three crops a year. In the past, the growing season was limited principally to the season after the river's annual flooding. (It was during the flood seasons, when the peasants had no crops to tend, that the ancient pyramids were built.) The post-1971 gains in farm production, however, have not kept pace with population growth. In addition, an unintended side effect of the dam has been to deprive the farm lands of soil-enriching silt that the flood waters left behind. Consequently, the fertility of the soil has been depleted, requiring the use of commercial fertilizers that Egypt can barely afford on export commodities that are highly sensitive to world trade prices.

The government advocates birth control, and Muslim authorities in Egypt have said that it does not violate Islamic doctrine. But birth control is said to be practiced almost exclusively in the cities where middle-class Egyptians find they cannot ad-

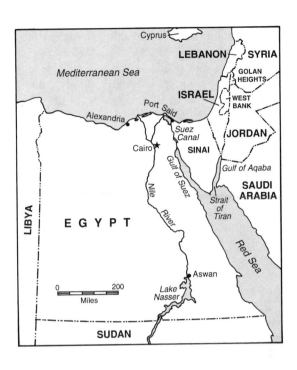

equately support large families. Egyptian officials say rural peasants (fellahin) believe each family needs five or six children to assure the parents security in old age. Migratory patterns in Egypt indicate that when the children come of age, many leave their family's small plots—a legacy of Nasser's breakup of great estates into small units for the peasants—and go to already-crowded cities seeking jobs.

Unemployment and underemployment are pervasive. The government's estimate of joblessness is about 20 percent of the national work force, but some observers believe it is probably twice as high. Per capita income is approximately $600, and half of the population is illiterate. For educated Egyptians, the government is the employer of last resort.

Since Nasser's time, the government has guaranteed all qualifying students a free education through college and then a job until retirement. Out of the large university system, thousands upon thousands of graduates have marched directly into low-paying jobs in already-bloated bureaucracies.

These days, however, graduates may wait eight years to obtain that $35-a-month government job, only to be assigned to an isolated village. The dominance of the public sector is widely recognized as hampering growth and certainly cannot provide the number of jobs necessary for the ever-increasing population.

## History

Unlike many Arab states that are the product of political unification in this century, Egypt has existed as a nation-state since ancient times. The Egyptian people share a nationality that predates even the Islamic conquest in the seventh century. They claim a civilization continuously recorded for more than five thousand years, which at various times reached great heights of cultural attainment.

Egypt's lack of natural barriers has always made it vulnerable to invasion. The Hyksos, Nubians, Ethiopians, Persians, Greeks, Romans, Arabs, French, Turks, and British were among the invaders of the lower Nile Valley. After the last pharaoh fell to Persian invaders in 525 B.C., Egypt continued under foreign rule or influence until the 1952 coup. The advent of Islam in the seventh century changed Egyptian life permanently. By the tenth century Cairo had become a center of Islamic scholarship. The mosque of Al Azhar, which became Al Azhar University, remains one of the preeminent centers of Islamic learning and exerts a strong influence on Egyptian political life.

Ottoman rule of Egypt was interrupted in 1798 by the invasion of the French emperor Napoleon, who dominated Egypt until 1801. Many scholars mark the beginning of modern Egyptian history with the Napoleonic invasion. The French brought in some liberal ideas, the printing press, and a lively interest in both modern science and Egypt's glorious but half-forgotten past.

The last dynasty to rule Egypt emerged following the French evacuation. Muhammad Ali, who was appointed by the Ottoman sultan in 1805, ruled Egypt until 1849. He brought Egypt into the modern world. Seizing complete control of the Egyptian state, Muhammad Ali imported European ideas and technology. During his autocratic reign, he transformed the country—building canals and other transport systems, introducing cotton cultivation, fostering education, and bringing scholars from Europe to Egypt. Through skill, daring, and intrigue, Muhammad Ali gained virtual independence in Egypt from his nominal overlord, the sultan in Constantinople.

Although the first survey for the Suez Canal was carried out by French engineers under the direction of Napoleon, it was one of Muhammad Ali's successors, Said, who granted a concession to the French entrepreneur Ferdinand de Lesseps for construction of the canal. In 1869 the Suez Canal was opened, reducing the length of the sea route from Europe to Asia.

In 1882 Britain sent troops into Egypt to protect its extensive financial holdings, including partial ownership (with France) of the Suez Canal. Six years later the Egyptian khedive Ismail (*khedive* is a ruler under sovereignty of the Ottoman Empire) faced bankruptcy and sold his shares in the canal to the British. They gained indirect political control of Egypt through the khedives, whom they kept in office. In 1914, at the outbreak of World War I, Britain declared Egypt a protectorate, ending the legal fiction that Ottoman sovereignty still prevailed. In 1922 it granted nominal independence, declaring Egypt a monarchy and placing Fuad, a compliant khedive, on the throne. The Ottoman Turks' subjugation had lasted four and a half centuries, except for the brief interruption of French rule.

By the end of World War I a new organization had emerged as the focus of Egyptian nationalist sentiment, the *Wafd al Misri* (Egyptian Delegation, known as the Wafd). Led by educated, upper-class Egyptians, the Wafd favored complete Egyptian independence as a republic.

A new agreement was reached with Great Britain in 1936, and the British military occupation was terminated. British troops remained along the Suez Canal, however, and London continued to exercise influence over internal Egyptian affairs. During World War II Egypt was a base of operations for Great Britain and its allies. Nevertheless, disputes between the British and the Egyptians continued, as did disagreements between the king and the Wafd. British actions in 1942 to compel the king to appoint a pro-Allied, Wafdist prime minister were repugnant to many Egyptians, who resented continued British domination of Egyptians politics.

Egypt joined other Arab states in establishing the Arab League in 1945. Three years later the king sent Egyptian troops to fight against the Israelis in the first Arab-Israeli War. The Arab armies were stunned by the victory of the Israelis, whom they imagined they would overcome within a few days. An armistice was signed between Egypt and the new state of Israel in February 1949, and the Gaza Strip—a small parcel of land along the Mediterranean coast—became a territory administered by Egypt. (*Arab-Israeli wars, Chapter 2, p. 16*)

Blame for the poor showing of the Egyptian army fell on the government, which was guilty of corrupt military procurement and incompetent leadership. The Muslim Brotherhood, intent upon achieving Islamic rule, became openly active and was banned in 1948. It engaged in violent attacks on the government and the British. Anti-Western rioting broke out in Cairo in January 1952, and the political situation became increasingly volatile.

## 1952 Coup and Nasser's Regime

On July 23, 1952, a group of young military men who called themselves the Free Officers took power in Egypt in a bloodless coup. Col. Gamal Abdel Nasser and his military colleagues brought about the abdication of King Farouk (the son of King Fuad) and ended decades of de facto British rule. Nasser defied the West, befriended the Soviet Union, introduced socialism, and appealed to the downtrodden masses.

The revolution was at first only a coup staged by a group of officers distressed by the Egyptian army's poor showing in the 1948 invasion of the newly declared state of Israel. Their initial goal was "cleaning up" the army and the state. The message they broadcast on the day of the coup—a day that became almost sacred to most Egyptians—did not go beyond their intention to "purify ourselves and to eliminate traitors and weaklings." Yet the coup developed into a genuine political, cultural, and economic revolution.

As viewed by Egyptian political scientist Nazih N.M. Ayubi, these young officers were basically an urban middle-class group who

must have had a certain feeling of alienation, a feeling that Egypt was not quite Egyptian. For in spite of formal independence, the British were still there. And if the civil service was already Egyptianized, the greater part of the wealth was owned by foreigners. The problem was not simply political, economic, or administrative. It was also a cultural one—that of the search for a national identity.

Nasser spoke often of "Islamic socialism" even as he pushed for Egypt's modernization essentially on a secular basis. In fact, the heterogeneous group of young officers who carried out the coup included Muslim fundamentalist sympathizers as well as leftists. Their first domestic policy initiative was land reform. In September 1952 the new regime began breaking up large landholdings in an attempt to destroy the economic and political grip of wealthy, absentee owners—both foreigners and Egyptians. Soon to follow were minimum-wage decrees and reduced working hours. Meanwhile, Nasser emerged as the regime's strongman, articulating the pent-up frustrations of poor Egyptians and winning their hearts as no other ruler had done.

## Foreign Policy Under Nasser

In foreign policy Nasser's regime at first declared that it favored neither East nor West, but by the mid-1950s his course of nonalignment and anti-imperialism brought him into direct conflict with the West. Nasser played a prominent role in the 1955 conference of nonaligned nations in Bandung, Indonesia, and he was granted equal international status with leaders such as Josip Broz Tito of Yugoslavia, Jawaharlal Nehru of India, and Chou En-lai (Zhou Enlai) of China. That year, in response to the reluctance of Western nations to sell Egypt arms without strings attached, Nasser agreed to purchase weapons from Czechoslovakia. This action, the first Soviet-bloc arms deal with an Arab nation, was welcomed by many Arabs as a step away from traditional Western domination, but U.S. president Dwight D. Eisenhower's secretary of state, John Foster Dulles, viewed it as a step toward the Communist world—despite Nasser's clear aversion to communism and his banning of the Egyptian Communist party.

Moreover, Nasser opposed Dulles's attempts to build an anti-Communist alliance in the Middle East. On July 19, 1956, Dulles played his trump card against Nasser. He announced that the United States was withdrawing financial support for the Aswan High Dam, the centerpiece of Nasser's economic planning. Seven days later, to the roaring approval of a Cairo crowd, Nasser spat out the words: "O, America, may you choke on your fury!" Then he seized the British- and French-owned Suez Canal Company and applied the canal's revenues to the dam project.

Egypt promised to pay off the stockholders, but Britain and France were in no mood to let Cairo control the waterway, Europe's petroleum lifeline to the Middle East. After months of secret negotiations among Britain, France, and Israel—whose ships were barred from the canal—Israeli forces launched an attack on Egypt across the Sinai Peninsula in October 1956. Britain and France, pretending to react to a surprise threat to the safety of the canal, seized it by force. Under pressure from the United States, the Soviet Union, and the United Nations, however, they were forced to withdraw, as was Israel. Eisenhower was infuriated that his two European allies had acted without consulting him, and he denied them much-needed U.S. support. By March 1957 a peacekeeping force, the United Nations Emergency Force (UNEF), was installed on the Egyptian side of the 1948 Egyptian-Israeli armistice line.

America's stand on the Suez crisis improved its relations with Nasser only slightly, and briefly. For Nasser it was a sweet victory. He had thumbed his nose at the West and gotten away with it. Egyptian

control of the Suez Canal was confirmed. When Nasser gained Soviet support for his Aswan Dam project, he made it clear that he did not need to depend on the West and that the Western nations could not take the Arab states for granted. The Soviets soon assumed an important position in Egyptian foreign policy and became Egypt's major weapons supplier.

In 1958 Nasser enjoyed another triumph. He was asked by Syrian leaders to lead a union of Egypt and Syria. Nasser, who had long espoused Arab unity, found it difficult to say no, even though he was wary of an instant union. He agreed, only on the condition that the union be complete. Syrian parties were abolished, Cairo became the capital of the new United Arab Republic (UAR), and a new political party (the National Union) was created. The union fared badly, however, and it was dissolved when Syrian anti-unionists seized control of the Damascus government in 1961. The party created to be a vehicle of unification, the National Union, was replaced in Egypt by a new Nasser creation, the Arab Socialist Union.

In contrast to the period from 1955 to 1961, which saw the rise of Nasser's influence in the Arab world and the achievement of personal successes, the years from 1961 to his death in 1970 were marked by a series of policy failures, notably Egyptian involvement in the Yemeni civil war and the Arab defeat in the June 1967 Arab-Israeli War.

Nasser responded to a call from pro-Nasser officers in the Yemen army who overthrew the Yemeni king in September 1962. He sent troops to bolster the new government against royalist forces that retreated to the Yemeni highlands and, with Saudi Arabian aid, threatened the survival of the republican government. With as many as eighty thousand Egyptian soldiers engaged in the fighting, the Yemeni war became a drain on the Egyptian treasury. The Egyptian image was tarnished by Nasser's arrogant efforts to control the Yemeni republicans and by the brutal measures Egyptian forces used against royalist villages in Yemen.

Perhaps the most damaging consequence of Egypt's involvement in the Yemeni civil war was its weakening effect on Egyptian defenses. When the 1967 war erupted, Nasser's best troops were tied down far from home. That war, a turning point in regional relations, was triggered by growing tensions between Israel and its Arab neighbors. In November 1966 Israel had destroyed a village in the West Bank (controlled by Jordan) in retaliation for Palestinian guerrilla raids across the border, and in April 1967 there were air clashes between Israel and Syria. Nasser engaged in a series of threatening steps short of war. He asked the United Nations to remove some of its peace-keeping troops from the Sinai, closed the Strait of Tiran to Israeli shipping, and signed a mutual defense treaty with Jordan.

Israel, fearing an invasion, launched a surprise attack on Egypt, Jordan, Syria, and Iraq on the morning of June 5. The air forces of the four Arab states were virtually destroyed on the ground within the first hours of the attack. Without air support the Arab armies were devastated, and by the time a cease-fire went into effect June 11, the Israelis had taken the eastern sector of Jerusalem and all of the West Bank from Jordan, seized the Golan Heights from Syria, and pushed the Egyptians out of the Gaza Strip and the whole of the Sinai Peninsula all the way to the Suez Canal.

The Egyptian army and people were again humiliated, as in 1948. Nasser publicly blamed himself for the defeat, implicitly agreeing with the verdict of history that the war resulted from his miscalculated brinksmanship. He provoked Israel in the belief that the United States would prevent the Jewish state from going to war and that the Soviet Union would come to his rescue if there were a war.

Nasser resigned as president, but a massive outpouring of support persuaded him to remain in office. The effects of the defeat were significant. Nasser withdrew Egyptian troops from Yemen, purged the top echelons of the army, and reorganized the government. Perhaps most important, Nasser's foreign policy objectives shifted. Regaining Egyptian territory held by Israel became a top priority. The quarrel with Israel was no longer only a matter of securing Palestinian rights. The return

of the Sinai—approximately one-seventh of Egypt's land area—was Nasser's chief aim.

Nasser's position became more moderate after the war. He accepted UN Security Council Resolution 242, recognizing the territorial rights of all states in the area (including Israel), despite opposition from many Arabs, including the Syrian government and the PLO. *(Text of resolution, Appendix, p. 395)*

The disagreement over the UN resolution foreshadowed a rift that would widen during Anwar Sadat's leadership. In September 1970 heavy fighting broke out in Jordan between the government of Jordan's King Hussein and the PLO. It was fitting that the chief proponent of Arab nationalism, Nasser of Egypt, should be chief mediator in the September 27, 1970, cease-fire between the two sides. The strain of the critical negotiations may have taken its toll: the following day Nasser died of a massive heart attack.

Tens of thousands of Egyptians took to the streets, passionately mourning the man who, more than any other single figure in modern Egyptian history, had confirmed Egypt's preeminent position in the Arab world. He had been an authoritarian leader, intolerant of dissent from any quarter. He had failed to provide any genuine institutions of political participation. He had presided over the most disastrous military defeat in modern regional history. His economic policies had not produced prosperity. Yet Nasser changed the life of the average Egyptian and he was loved by the masses of lower-class Egyptians in a way that was never understood by Western political leaders.

## Sadat's Leadership

As first vice president, Anwar Sadat succeeded Nasser. It was whispered that he had remained one of only two of the original Free Officers still in government because he was never a political threat to Nasser. Few would have guessed that he was destined to become a daring and powerful leader. It was widely presumed that stronger rivals would soon divest him of power. Sadat, however, proved to be shrewder. He outmaneuvered his rivals, emerged from Nasser's shadow, and transformed Middle East politics. His primary goals were to regain the territory lost to Israel and improve Egypt's Third World standard of living. He achieved the first goal but not the second.

Training his sights on Western capitalism, Sadat introduced his "open door" economic policy in 1971. At first disguising it as a mere widening of Nasser's socialism, he set out to lure foreign investment and build a job-creating entrepreneurial class. Disillusioned with Nasser's Soviet connection, Sadat became confident enough of his power by mid-1972 to expel thousands of Soviet military advisers and civilian technicians—though without breaking diplomatic relations with Moscow—and offer Washington an olive branch. According to Alfred Leroy Atherton, Jr., a former ambassador to Cairo (1979-83), the Nixon administration was preoccupied with a reelection campaign and the Vietnam War. President Richard Nixon did not respond promptly or fully to Sadat's overtures. So Sadat, unable to draw upon America's diplomatic clout to win back the Sinai, went to war.

Egyptian forces, better prepared than in 1967 and this time with surprise on their side, crossed the Suez Canal on October 6, 1973, and advanced deep into the Sinai. By the time a UN-arranged cease-fire took effect October 22, an Israeli counterattack had retaken most of the ground, and in one area held both sides of the canal. The final position of the armies, however, was less important to the Egyptian people than the enemy's initial rout.

The effect of the war on Sadat's public image in Egypt was enormous. Once viewed as a colorless, former Nasser "yes-man," Sadat achieved the title, "Hero of the Crossing" (of the canal), an epithet he treasured. The high level of Arab solidarity during the war, when an Arab oil embargo was successfully implemented against Western nations that supported Israel, was also a great boost to Sadat's standing in the Arab world.

Sadat now had Washington's attention. Secretary of State Henry Kissinger began a "shuttle diplomacy" between Jerusalem and Cairo to bring about a peace settlement. His efforts led to the first of two disengagement agreements between Egypt and Israel that went beyond the original cease-fire on January 18, 1974. That year, Egypt and the United States restored diplomatic relations, which Nasser had broken after the 1967 war. In addition, Nixon became the first president to visit Egypt since Franklin D. Roosevelt went there in November 1943, during World War II. American aid, cut off in the Nasser years, was resumed. The U.S. Navy helped to clear the canal of wartime wreckage, permitting its reopening in 1975.

Sadat, clearly cultivating a closer relationship with the United States, envisioned it as a "full partner" in Egypt's drive for peace and prosperity.

He came increasingly to view the United States as the key to resolving the Arab-Israeli conflict. Although he was often disappointed in the United States, his trust in successive administrations did not diminish publicly. When negotiations with the Israelis bore no fruit, he made his historic trip to Jerusalem in November 1977, carrying a message of peace to the heart of the enemy's country and capturing the attention of the world.

The trip set in motion a chain of events that led to the Camp David agreements. President Jimmy Carter prevailed upon Sadat and Israeli prime minister Menachem Begin to meet at Camp David, the presidential retreat in Maryland, for twelve days in September 1978. There they hammered out two documents, "A Framework for Peace in the Middle East" and a "Framework for the Conclusion of a Peace Treaty Between Israel and Egypt." On March 26, 1979 they returned to sign the peace treaty in a White House ceremony. *(Treaty text, Appendix, p. 396)*

The peace with Israel cost Sadat and Egypt their standing in the Arab world. Most Arab leaders and peoples saw Sadat's compromises with Israel as a betrayal. Five days after the peace treaty was signed, eighteen Arab nations and the PLO expelled Egypt from the Arab League and instituted an economic boycott against Egypt. Of the twenty-one remaining league members, all but Oman, Somalia, and the Sudan severed relations. In May

Egypt was expelled from the forty-three-member Organization of the Islamic Conference. Similarly, Egypt was cast out of the Organization of Arab Petroleum Exporting Countries (OAPEC).

By that time most Arab governments had severed diplomatic ties with Cairo.

Sadat was more successful in attaining peace with Israel than prosperity for Egypt. His new economic policies created a class of much-resented nouveau riche without invigorating the nation's sluggish economy. Few jobs or *piasters*—the small change of Egyptian currency—trickled down to the workers. Average income remained below $500 a year. Part of Nasser's "social contract" with the people was that prices of food, housing, public transportation, and electricity would be subsidized by the government. In January 1977, however, Sadat was under budget-cutting pressures from Egypt's foreign creditors, and he reduced food subsidies. His action touched off weeks of rioting that threatened to undermine his regime.

Sadat had already loosened some of the tight restrictions on political dissent that he inherited from Nasser. In 1975 he permitted three ideological groups *(platforms)* to organize within the confines of the Arab Socialist Union. The following year the three were permitted some freedom to perform as political parties. The centrist *party,* the Egyptian Arab Socialist Organization, became the government party, and in 1978 it was reorganized as the National Democratic party, continuing to serve as a vehicle of autocratic control and manipulation. The second *party* consisted of fundamentalists (for example, the Muslim Brotherhood, whose leaders had been freed along with other dissidents in 1973), and the third—perhaps a counterweight to the second—was made up of small leftist groups.

Sadat's political liberalization ended when the political groups outside his direct control, principally Nasserites on the left and Islamic fundamentalists on the right, began to criticize his peacemaking with Israel. Sadat cracked down repressively on dissidents—most dramatically in September 1981 when he abruptly jailed fifteen hundred foes. He was assassinated the following month by Muslim extremists who wanted not a takeover of the government but simply the death of the man they regarded as a traitor to Egypt, the Arab world, and Islam.

Death came October 6, 1981, on the anniversary of the canal crossing, as Sadat reviewed a military parade commemorating the event. He was slain by soldiers who belonged to a militant Muslim faction, al-Jihad. His murder surprised Egyptians less than it did Westerners. He was remembered in the West as the instigator of the peace treaty, a corecipient (with Begin) of the 1978 Nobel Peace Prize, and the man who moved Egypt out of the Soviet orbit of influence. To fellow Arabs, Sadat's difficulties with fundamentalist Muslims and other dissidents had become increasingly clear, erasing much of the popularity he enjoyed in the heady days following the October 1973 war. There was no outpouring of grief in Egypt for Sadat as there had been for Nasser. Three former American presidents—Richard Nixon, Gerald R. Ford, and Jimmy Carter—attended his funeral, but no Arab head of state publicly mourned the Egyptian president.

## Mubarak's "Cold Peace" with Israel

Hosni Mubarak, trying to steer a middle course in all matters, foreign and domestic, did not embrace the "partnership" with the United States with Sadat's fervor. He recognized, however, that U.S. assistance was crucial to Egypt both economically and militarily. American officials generally gave him high marks for trying to keep irritants in the relationship from being magnified.

Mubarak has promoted the central tenet of Sadat's notion of peace with Israel—that the treaty with Israel meant the end of military hostilities and the establishment of a proper relationship. But it often has been a "cold peace" beset by many problems. Mubarak criticized Israel's annexation of the Golan Heights in 1981 and protested Israel's invasion of Lebanon in June 1982. That invasion was seen by the treaty's foes as confirmation that Israel could act with impunity since it no longer had to consider a military attack from Egypt.

*Hosni Mubarak*

For Mubarak, the Israeli invasion came just when Egyptian-Israeli relations seemed to be smoothing out. Egypt was still savoring the sweetest fruit of the treaty. On April 25, 1982, Israel turned over the last remaining section of the Sinai territory it had held since the 1967 war—except for a tiny beach strip called Taba, where the Israelis built a resort hotel on the Gulf of Suez. After a seven-year dispute, Israel handed Taba over to Egypt, March 15, 1989.

In September 1982 Mubarak recalled his ambassador from Israel to protest a massacre of Palestinians by Lebanese Christians in refugee camps outside Beirut that were guarded by Israeli soldiers. The ambassador later returned to his post, but the relationship was further jolted by three shooting incidents in Cairo in 1984-86 that left five Israeli diplomats dead and one wounded. On another occasion, in 1985, an Egyptian military conscript killed seven Israeli tourists in the Sinai.

On the tenth anniversary of the signing of the peace treaty, Begin said in a radio interview from his home in Jerusalem that a "full normalization of relations [with Egypt] still hasn't arrived, and we're waiting for it."

From a "cold peace" the relationship has sometimes deteriorated into an "angry peace." The massive immigration of Jews from the Soviet Union, especially their settlement on the occupied West Bank, became a contentious issue. The October 1990 incident that left nineteen Palestinians dead and both Israelis and Palestinians wounded at the Temple Mount near the Al-Aqsa Mosque, the third holiest Islamic shrine, set off a fury of recriminations. Despite deep-rooted mistrust, the two countries continue to uphold the peace and maintain bilateral ties based on solid national interests.

## Reconciliation with Arab Nations

A pivotal event on Egypt's road to reconciliation with its Arab neighbors occurred in November 1987. At that time, sixteen Arab League heads of state met in the Jordanian capital of Amman and issued a surprisingly strong-worded resolution attacking Iran for its "procrastination in accepting" a United Nations cease-fire proposal in what was then its seven-year war with Iraq. Jordan's King Hussein, the conference host, used the occasion to ask the participants—in the interest of Arab unity—to drop the league's ban on formal relations between its member countries and Egypt. They answered his appeal by declaring that a renewal of relations with Egypt would be considered "a sovereign matter to be decided by each state in accordance with its constitution and laws; and is not within the jurisdiction of the Arab League." Most Arab nations felt compelled to close ranks against Iran and the potentially subversive Islamic radicalism that it was attempting to export. They needed Egypt, by far the biggest Arab country, as a counterweight to Iran.

Jordan had already renewed relations with Cairo, and subsequently all the members did so except the hard-line states of Syria, Syrian-dominated Lebanon, and Libya. The next step was readmission to the Arab League itself. On May 23, 1989, after a ten-year absence, Egypt took its seat at an Arab League summit meeting, in Casablanca, Morocco, where Mubarak was accorded the honor of making the opening address. In addition to newly readmitted Egypt, the 1989 membership consisted of Algeria, Bahrain, Djibouti, Iraq, Jordan, Kuwait, Lebanon, Libya, Mauritania, Morocco, Oman, the PLO, Qatar, Saudi Arabia, Somalia, Sudan, Syria, Tunisia, the United Arab Emirates, the Yemen Arab Republic, and the Yemen People's Republic (newly reunited as the Republic of Yemen). Only weeks before the Casablanca summit, OAPEC readmitted Egypt; in 1984 it had reentered the Organization of the Islamic Conference.

The 1987 Amman conference's focus on Iran had an unintended side effect. It reportedly added to the level of frustration among the 1.5 million Palestinians living under Israeli control in the West Bank and Gaza Strip. They felt their cause had been demoted, possibly deserted, by the Arab leaders. Less than a month after the conference, the Palestinian *intifada* (uprising) began in the occupied territories. Palestine again became the region's foremost concern, and the Iranian threat seemed to recede. In July 1988 Iran's exhaustion from years of fighting compelled the Ayatollah Ruhollah Khomeini to accept a cease-fire agreement with Iraq.

Mubarak, meanwhile, had become a leading supporter of the PLO and its leader, Yasir Arafat. "There is no war without Egypt, and there is no peace without Egypt," Arafat said in December 1988 on one of his frequent visits to Cairo. His very presence symbolized Egypt's new harmony with the PLO leadership, which in 1981 had applauded Sadat's assassination. In this new era of buried hatchets, Mubarak joined with Arafat and Arafat's old nemesis, King Hussein, in pushing for an international conference to negotiate the Palestinian demand for statehood.

In late 1988 Mubarak implored Arafat to satisfy the U.S. government's conditions for holding talks with the PLO. In November 1988 the Palestine National Council met in Algiers and formally declared Palestinian statehood—and implicitly recognized Israel's right to exist. But U.S. secretary of state George P. Shultz demanded that Arafat explicitly renounce terrorism, accept UN Security Council Resolution 242—the basis for a Middle East peace conference—and recognize Israel's sovereignty. The resolution, adopted in the aftermath of the June 1967 Six-Day War, called for Israel's withdrawal from the territories it seized in the war—the West Bank and eastern Jerusalem from Jordan, the Gaza Strip and the Sinai Peninsula from Egypt, and the Golan Heights from Syria—in return for the Arabs' acceptance of Israel's "right to live within secure and recognized boundaries free from threats or acts of force."

After much prodding by Mubarak and a few false starts, Arafat on December 14 uttered the precise words that Shultz demanded. Within hours, the secretary of state said talks with the PLO could begin. This announcement created euphoria in the Arab world, even though the United States pointedly restated its support for Israel and withheld any backing for an independent Palestinian state. According to diplomatic sources in Cairo, Mubarak was one of several Arab and Western European leaders who urged Shultz and President Ronald Reagan to accept Arafat's words as genuine.

Mubarak paid his first White House call on Reagan's successor, George Bush, in April 1989. At the conclusion of their talk President Bush told reporters: "Egypt and the United States share the goals of security for Israel, the end of the occupation, and achievement of Palestinian political rights." The statement was considered significant in that an American president was bluntly calling for something unacceptable to Israel: the end of the occupation of the West Bank and Gaza.

At the end of 1989 Syria restored ties to Egypt, and President Hafez al-Assad of Syria visited Egypt for first time in thirteen years. To further promote regional economic cooperation, Egypt, together with Iraq, Jordan, and Yemen, founded the Arab Cooperation Council (ACC) in 1989.

## Persian Gulf War

The Iraqi invasion and occupation of Kuwait in 1990 created a serious dilemma for Egypt and President Mubarak. Opposing Iraq would put Egypt on one side of an intra-Arab conflict, just as it was solidifying relations with most Arab states. Failing to oppose Iraq, however, would invite further aggression by Iraqi president Saddam Hussein, poison relations with the wealthy Gulf Arabs, and weaken Egypt's crucial ties to the United States. Under these circumstances, Mubarak chose to lead the Arab military and diplomatic effort against Iraq.

He hosted a meeting of the Arab League in Cairo on August 10, eight days after the Iraqi invasion. Out of that meeting came a decision by most Arab countries to oppose Saddam and send troops to help defend Saudi Arabia. The first Egyptian troops began to land in Saudi Arabia the next day.

The opposition of Egyptian Islamists to Egypt's participation in the anti-Iraq coalition was largely drowned out by a government campaign to win over popular support by reporting the brutality of the Iraqi occupation. Egyptian-Iraqi ties were already strained by widespread reports of violent discrimination against Egyptian workers in Iraq. Domestically, Mubarak also earned credit for his early call for the Arab League summit to discuss the crisis.

Mubarak's anti-Iraqi position during the 1991 Gulf War, and his success in persuading other Arab countries to participate in the multinational force, earned him the gratitude of the United States and the Gulf countries. Egypt persuaded other Arab countries to participate in the UN coalition and sent four hundred tanks and thirty thousand troops to Saudi Arabia, the most of any Arab nation. The participation of Egypt and other Arab nations undercut Saddam's claims that his invasion of Kuwait was a blow against American imperialism that advanced the Palestinian cause. Mubarak also held Egypt solidly in the coalition when it appeared that Israel might enter the war against Iraq. American leaders worried that if

Israel retaliated for Iraqi missile attacks, Arab nations would withdraw from the coalition rather than fight on the same side as their old enemy Israel. But Mubarak said he would not withdraw Egypt, even if Israel did retaliate. In the end, the United States prevailed on Israel not to attack Iraq.

Military cooperation between Egypt and the United States continued on an expanded basis after the Gulf War, and Egypt was promised preferential treatment in receiving sophisticated military equipment being withdrawn from bases in Europe.

Egypt expected to reap major economic benefits for its role in the coalition against Saddam Hussein. The United States rewarded Egypt by forgiving a $7 billion debt for arms purchased in the 1970s and by rescheduling its remaining debts. Saudi Arabia wrote off outstanding Egyptian debts of $4 billion. By early 1991, Egypt's debt had been reduced from more than $50 billion to $36 billion. Nevertheless, Egypt claimed to have lost as much as $20 billion in revenue during the war as the Gulf crisis weakened three of the four pillars of the Egyptian economy. Egyptian oil revenues went up temporarily, but these gains were more than offset by the depression in Egypt's tourist industry brought on by fears of traveling in the Middle East, the loss of remittances from the half million Egyptian expatriate workers who fled the Gulf region, and the dwindling of Suez Canal revenues as fewer commercial ships chose to sail in Middle Eastern waters.

Mubarak hoped Egypt's contributions to Gulf security would bring badly needed aid and investment from the Gulf states. In March 1991 the Damascus Declaration was signed. It provided that Egypt and Syria would join the Gulf Cooperation Council (GCC) countries in a new Gulf security arrangement—the GCC plus two. Saudi reluctance to station a permanent non-Gulf Arab force in the area and its preference to rely on Western forces resulted in Mubarak's withdrawing Egyptian troops from the Gulf. At the same time, the GCC countries, suffering from their own financial difficulties, cut back on their committed aid.

Egyptian expectations for increased contracts, assistance and cooperative ventures for its efforts have been largely unfulfilled.

Nevertheless, Egyptian prestige in the Arab world rose dramatically because of its leadership during the Gulf War. In March 1991 the Arab League transferred its headquarters back to its original location in Cairo.

## Government and Politics

With their characteristic touch of self-deprecatory humor, Egyptians are fond of recalling King Farouk's last words to the rebellious officers who sent him into exile: "Your task will be difficult. It is not easy to govern Egypt." Since the time of the pharaohs, successful rulers of Egypt have learned to play off one set of potential foes against another. The fact that Mubarak has never named a vice president has inspired observers to say that he exerts more political leverage by leaving the office open than choosing among leading contenders. The absence of a designated successor, however, has raised troubling questions about Egypt's political stability.

Mona Makram Ebeid, a professor of political science at American University in Cairo, speaks of "Egypt's continued experiment with democracy—we can't yet call it democracy." The press is free enough to be critical of the government and offer readers a wide range of opinion. But in December 1988, in the very month the Egyptian novelist Naguib Mahfouz was awarded the Nobel Prize in literature, religious authorities blocked a newspaper serialization of one of his books on grounds it was "destructive of Islamic values and defamatory to Islamic prophets." In 1980 Egypt amended its 1971 constitution to stipulate that Islamic law, the *shari'a,* is the "principal" source for legislation and the legal system. However, the governmental structure is essentially that of a Western democracy.

Executive power is vested in the president, who is nominated by the national parliament, the People's Assembly, and elected for six-year terms by popular referendum. The president may appoint vice presidents, in addition to government ministers and all other officials. He is also supreme commander of the armed forces and may rule by decree when granted emergency powers by the People's Assembly. That is of little relevance to Mubarak, who has held emergency powers since Sadat's assassination. In addition, Mubarak's own National Democratic party (NDP) holds 79.4 percent of the seats in the People's Assembly and commands the patronage system and the broadcast media.

While overshadowed by the Gulf crisis, the 1990 parliamentary elections were nonetheless an important milestone in Egypt's development of a multiparty system, the regime's safety valve for sociopolitical pressures. Faced with the second constitutional crisis in three years, Mubarak was forced to call new elections to preserve the democratic image he has been attempting to foster.

In the 1990 parliamentary elections, the NDP won 348 of the 444 directly elected seats (compared with 346 in the 1987 general election). It also had scored a landslide victory in the 1984 parliamentary election, the only previous one held after Mubarak became president.

The 1990 elections were characterized by low voter turnout. The official estimate of 44.9 percent turnout was regarded as inflated. Four of the NDP's main opposition groups—the New Wafd, Socialist Labor party, the Liberal party, and the banned but officially tolerated Muslim Brotherhood—boycotted the elections to protest the government's refusal to repeal the emergency regulations or allow election supervision by the judiciary rather than by the Ministry of Interior.

The final results of the 1990 elections left the NDP in control of the legislature. The National Progressive Unionist Grouping won six seats, making it the largest opposition bloc in the assembly. All the elected candidates were Muslim, although none were known to be active in the Muslim Brotherhood. Acting on his constitutional prerogative, Mubarak nominated ten additional members to the assembly including three Copts and three women.

"None of these parties, including the regime's

NDP, has a solid social base," according to Saad Eddin Ibrahim, an Egyptian sociologist. The main opposition party, New Wafd, is led by members or descendants of the upper and middle classes who opposed British rule. The New Wafd party may be the only opposition party with the prospect of wide popular support. It is made up of Copts, Nasserites, Muslim fundamentalists, former army officers and socialists, and liberal businessmen championing the advancement of the private sector. The original Wafd was the majority party between 1922, when Egypt was accorded nominal independence, and the 1952 revolution. When Nasser came to power, he abolished it. The successor party was formed in 1978 at Sadat's behest; at the same time he created the NDP to replace Nasser's Arab Socialist Union (ASU). The NDP has performed much like the ASU. It has followed the president's lead and mobilized political strength, especially at election time.

Among the other legalized political groups is the increasingly Islamist, Socialist Labor party (SLP). By forming a coalition with the Liberal Socialist party, and opening its ranks to the Muslim Brotherhood—which is forbidden its own party—they became the main parliamentary opposition in the 1987 elections. Socialist Labor was another old party, outlawed by Nasser, that was permitted to start up again in 1982 after it supported Mubarak for president. Sadat founded it as the "loyal opposition" to the NDP. At the far left is the splinter National Progressive Unionist Grouping (NPUG), composed mostly of well-known Marxists and Nasserites. The political influence of the party's intellectuals is disproportionate to the size of its following. The People's (Umma) party, a tiny organization with a strong religious orientation led by Ahmad Al-Sabbahi, has little popular support or political consequences.

Two sizable groups without legal status as political parties—Nasserites and the Muslim Brotherhood—are active in Egyptian politics. Nasserites, who dream of restoring Nasser's brand of nationalism, are reported to be well represented among military officers. But Mubarak, himself a general who once commanded the air force, has cultivated the officers' loyalty by providing them many special benefits. In what has been described as a test of that loyalty, the army in 1986 answered the government's call to quell a mutiny in suburban Cairo by twenty thousand conscripts of the Central Security Force who were angered by low pay and bad living conditions. However, in a seeming effort to prevent the establishment of an alternative power base in the military, Mubarak has frequently changed his minister of defense, once in 1989 and most recently in 1991.

Several members of the Muslim Brotherhood have sat in the People's Assembly as elected representatives of officially recognized parties. The group is the strongest voice of the diffuse Islamic movement in Egypt, but there is a pronounced disagreement as to whether it represents the movement's main thrust. Since the brotherhood's founding in 1928, it has been the embodiment of Egyptian opposition to a secular, Westernized society. Militant spinoffs from the brotherhood have attempted to achieve that objective by violence. Nasser, the target of an assassination attempt, suppressed the brotherhood. Partly rehabilitated by Sadat, it emerged under Mubarak as a political and economic force, attesting to the fact that Egypt shares in the religious resurgence that swept the Islamic world during the 1980s.

A presidential election was held in 1993, but the results were never in question. Mubarak was nominated by the ruling National Democratic party for a third six-year term which began October 14, 1993. He garnered 94.9 percent of the more than 15 million votes cast. The opposition parties refused to back the president's nomination, arguing that the people should directly elect the president from a choice of candidates, instead of approving the assembly's chosen candidate by referendum.

President Mubarak announced that his third-term priorities were security and stability, economic reform, social justice, educational reform, fighting unemployment, addressing the problem of high population growth and tackling the country's cumbersome bureaucracy.

## Religion and Society

Nasser and Sadat both tried to enlist Islamic backing for their governments, although without permitting Muslim factions to achieve any real degree of control. In speeches Nasser appealed to Islamic history and culture, even as he followed a secular model of modernization.

About 94 percent of Egyptians are Muslims, and almost all of them are of the majority Sunni branch. Coptic Christians account for most of the non-Muslims in Egypt and in actual numbers form the biggest non-Muslim minority in any Arab country. The country's estimated 3-4 million Copts make up 4-6 percent of the population, but they form a larger share of the middle and professional classes than their share of the overall population. However, many live in villages and are poor farming people. In addition to the Copts, the small remnant of Egypt's once-large Jewish population continues to attend several remaining synagogues.

Coptic Egyptians view themselves as the descendants of the ancient people of the Nile Valley. They embraced Christianity in the first century but broke with its orthodoxy in the fifth century over a theological question. The Copts accepted the divinity of Christ, but they rejected the doctrine then accepted by the rest of Christendom that Christ was also fully human. The Coptic Church survived not only its break with the mainstream of Christianity but also the Islamic conquest of Egypt in the seventh century. Nevertheless, over the centuries, it has suffered several persecutions at the hands of the country's Muslim majority.

Nasser attempted to improve Coptic-Muslim relations by integrating Egyptian society and by forcing members of the two faiths to live together in the same neighborhoods. The experiment seemed to increase hostility between the two groups. By the 1970s, as Islamic resurgence became more widespread, and demands grew for the government to implement Islamic law, several Coptic-Muslim clashes occurred. In Sadat's crackdown on dissidents shortly before his murder, he dismissed Muslim critics from their posts in the mosques and banished the Coptic pope, Shenuda, from Cairo for inciting Coptic-Muslim strife. Moreover, Sadat banned publications that had been issued by Coptic associations and by the Muslim Brotherhood. Only after Mubarak became president did the hostilities between the government and the Copts begin to subside. In 1985 he permitted Pope Shenuda to return.

Despite the relative tolerance of Egyptian Muslims, the Islamic revival has been troubling to the Coptic-Muslim relationship. Copts perceive demands for the complete implementation of Islamic law as a direct threat to their political, economic, and social status. Although Copts pose no direct threat to Mubarak's power, their often-strong reactions to Islamic resurgence sometimes fan the flames of religious hostility. By mid-March 1993 violence against Copts had claimed between one hundred fifty and two hundred lives. The attacks on Christians, concentrated primarily in southern Egypt, are manifestations of chronic sectarian tension but are also a part of radical Islamists' strategy to challenge Mubarak's government.

Although Egyptian authorities tried and executed Sadat's assassins, Mubarak has quietly attempted to co-opt some religious dissent by allowing greater incorporation of Islamic principles into the political system. In trying to steer a middle course between Islamic and secular demands, Mubarak allowed previously banned opposition and religious newspapers to circulate, but he refused to overturn court decisions such as a 1985 ruling that abolished the 1979 women's rights laws. In response to the furor resulting from the abrogation of progressive law on women's rights, enacted with persuasion from Sadat's wife, Jihan, Mubarak took no public position. He did ensure, however, the assembly's passage of a new law that was a compromise between the position espoused by the fundamentalists and the rights guaranteed by the old law.

By the mid-1980s clashes between security forces and Islamic militants were increasing. In December 1988 violent battles occurred between police and Muslim extremists in Cairo's Ein Shams slum district, resulting in five deaths and three hundred arrests. The following April, the government cracked down on what Interior Minister Zaki Badr called "extremist groups fueling religious strife in this country." After more Muslim clashes with police, this time in the town of Fayoum, southwest of Cairo, authorities attributed the violence to Islamic Jihad groups—the movement that brought about Anwar Sadat's assassination—and arrested fifteen hundred persons.

Determined to keep militants in prison or under close surveillance, the Egyptian government had an estimated ten thousand Islamists arrested during 1989, including the spiritual leader of Islamic Jihad, Sheikh Omar Abd Al-Rahman, who was later tied to the 1993 terrorist bombing of the World Trade Center in New York. The sheikh's followers are believed to have received military training from Afghan guerrillas in Afghanistan.

The *Gamaat Islamiya* (Islamic groups) are offshoots of the politically and spiritually influential Muslim Brotherhood. The number of Islamic groups in Egypt is estimated at between thirty and sixty, ranging from the large, officially tolerated mainstream Muslim Brotherhood to medium-size violent groups like Islamic Jihad, to small militant groups operating clandestinely. New groups seem to be forming continually. Although the more militant groups draw their support from the lower-middle classes, especially in the deprived areas of Upper Egypt and the slums of Cairo, membership in Gamaat Islamiya is composed of a cross-section of society, the common thread being the belief that a return to Islamic roots will solve Egypt's problems. Islamic Jihad has claimed responsibility for many recent assassination attempts on political figures, policemen, intellectuals, and tourists.

Critics claim that the Islamists lack the resources, unity of purpose, and leadership to be a serious threat to the government. Their strengths, however, seem to be their ability to channel widespread discontent into popular support, and their organizational skills, which they demonstrated during the devastating Cairo earthquake of 1992. Islamic-controlled professional societies quickly provided food, shelter, and emergency medical care to the victims, many of whom were killed or injured by the collapse of substandard housing. The government was criticized for its slow response to the disaster, and its corruption was vehemently blamed for the dangerously shoddy construction.

In the past Mubarak often attempted to meet some of the Islamic fundamentalists' demands. But in response to the wave of attacks on foreign tourists during the 1990s that seriously damaged Egypt's economy, he has overseen an unprecedented security crackdown. The People's Assembly passed antiterrorist legislation in July 1992 that introduced the death penalty for members of terrorist groups and three-day detention for suspects. Human rights organizations have condemned reported torture and beatings by government security police, but the government denies these charges.

## Economy

Most analysts see Egypt's exhausted economy as the greatest potential peril to Mubarak's government. The country has enormous foreign debts from loans secured in the early 1980s. At that time oil commanded high prices in the world market, and Egypt was cashing in on new fields along the Red Sea and the return of older ones from Israel in the Sinai. Additionally, the Middle East oil prosperity provided jobs for as many as 4 million Egyptians in other Arab countries. The Suez Canal's reopening, after peace with Israel, restored another important source of revenue.

Oil prices plummeted in 1986, however, affecting not only the government's royalties but also the amount of money Egyptians were sending home from abroad. Many Egyptians in the Gulf region lost their jobs. Moreover, sporadic terrorism in the Middle East crimped the tourist trade, another source of national income. Even in the "good years" early in the 1980s, the government was incurring annual budget deficits. Then, however, big international banks were eagerly extending credit. More and more of the debt incurred during that period came due in the late 1980s.

In return for the government's pledge to stimulate production and exports, the International Monetary Fund and Western creditor nations agreed in May 1987 to let Egypt reschedule $8 billion of its $44 billion in foreign debts at generous repayment terms. For its part, Egypt moved to satisfy the IMF demand by devaluing its currency 60 percent to make exports cheaper in foreign markets and thus increase demand, even though Egyptian officials complained that devaluation increased the price of consumer goods and fueled inflation.

Chronic budget deficits have perpetuated Egypt's dependence on foreign aid. Since the Camp David accords, Egypt has received $30 billion in aid from Washington; only Israel received more. That assistance, both military and economic in their various forms, has been totaling about $3 billion a year for Israel and $2.2 billion for Egypt—in line with an unwritten policy in Washington that Egypt will be given a somewhat smaller amount than Israel. Because Egypt's aid is pegged to Israel's, it has risen as Israel's has gone up. Although both countries received U.S. aid before the treaty, the amount of aid increased dramatically after the peace was concluded. Aid to Egypt (but not to Israel) is explicitly conditioned on its continued observance of the Camp David agreements and, a more recent stipulation, its pursuit of economic reforms. American aid accounts for about half of the economic assistance that Egypt receives from all foreign sources. The rest comes chiefly from international lending institutions, such as the IMF and the World Bank, and the governments of Western Europe and Japan.

Increasingly under pressure from the United States and the IMF to reform Egypt's economy, Mubarak has gradually continued Sadat's conversion from a centrally controlled economy to a market economy, more open to private enterprise and foreign investment. The IMF's demands include unifying the exchange rate (effectively raising prices), eliminating state subsidies on consumer goods, reforming tax collection and reducing imports. The dilemma for Mubarak's government is maintaining the delicate balance between the conflicting demands of foreign creditors and the masses of Egyptians living at or below the poverty line. Memories of food riots in 1977 and 1984 remain strong, and Mubarak wants no recurrence.

In 1991 Mubarak finally agreed to a comprehensive structural adjustment program under the aegis of the IMF and the World Bank. Mubarak signed an agreement whereby the IMF would provide $372 million in assistance over eighteen months to support Egypt's reforms. The IMF agreement paved the way for the Paris Club of Western creditors to reschedule a $10 billion debt and cancel the remaining $10 billion debt over a three-year period. According to economic indicators, the World Bank concluded in early 1992 that the Egyptian reform program was broadly on track.

## Outlook

With the support of 4 million bureaucrats and a half-million-strong army, Mubarak's government is not facing imminent collapse. However, the corrosive effects of an inefficient state-controlled economy, ossified political structures, endemic corruption, and Islamist violence have demonstrated the regime's vulnerability.

Egypt's economic dilemma created by debt, unemployment, inflation, and reliance on revenues from oil, Suez Canal tolls, tourism, and worker remittances forced it to accept a three-year IMF structural reform program. Fearing the repercussions of higher unemployment and austerity, Mubarak has been tentative in implementing economic reforms. Critics charge he is not moving ahead fast enough with reforms and see caution ultimately as immobility.

Egypt's involvement in the coalition forces of the Gulf War sealed its return not only to the Arab fold but also as the predominate leader of the Arab world. Nevertheless, controversy surrounded Egypt's participation with the West in the destruction of Iraqi military forces, fueling Islamists' criticism that Mubarak is more responsive to the demands of Western creditors than to Egyptian national interests.

The United States has been Egypt's most important ally since Sadat ousted the Soviets, and the United States is Egypt's chief supplier of arms and military equipment. At times, however, Egypt has asserted its independence from Washington. American unconditional support for Israel remains a controversial issue in Egyptian-American relations, one that Islamic fundamentalists exploit to political advantage against the regime. The United States has staked a great deal of strategic interest on the regime and the American government is concerned about a perceived lack of vision in addressing Egypt's persistent problems. Washington is urging the Egyptian government to improve its human rights record, curb corruption, and open up the political system.

President Mubarak has stated that his priority is the "preservation of the security and stability of the homeland." Clearly, security takes precedence over democratization and political reforms. Concessions will not be made to the opposition while the government is under attack by radical Islamist groups. At the same time, reform of the political system is seen as a prerequisite for economic reform. Ironically, instead of addressing the Islamists' criticism, with which most Egyptians agree, the government alienates the people by its harsh repression of the critics. And the instability wrought by the violent struggle between the Islamists and the government terrifies ordinary Egyptians who have a natural aversion to extremism.

A deepening malaise is gripping the country. Discontented Islamic groups strike out in fury at a corrupt, entrenched bureaucracy amidst the general apathy of the average Egyptian. Unless the deadlock is broken, and an improvement in the overwhelming domestic problems is felt, Mubarak's current six-year term will not be so stable as his first.

# IRAN

Fifteen years after the Ayatollah Ruhollah Khomeini led the 1979 revolution that drove Shah Muhammad Reza Pahlavi from the country, the Islamic Republic of Iran has survived, defying early predictions by many analysts that its government would collapse or be defeated by Iraq.

Iran is struggling through yet another major test of its durability: the restructuring of its crippled economy and the shaking off of its deep social malaise before a political crisis is precipitated. President Ali Akbar Hashemi Rafsanjani, elected for a second and final four-year term in June 1993, faces the enormous task of rebuilding Iran's broken economy and overcoming the country's international isolation against strong opposition from conservatives.

After a spending spree during the relative boom days following the eight-year Iran-Iraq War, the bills have come due. The economy is being squeezed to pay off Iran's external debt, and the austerity measures being employed are raising the specter of popular discontent. Demonstrations protesting food shortages and the lifting of subsidies already have shaken major cities during the early 1990s. Overreliance on oil revenues in a volatile international market remains a major structural weakness of the Iranian economy. The government is shifting its emphasis to the private sector and is moving slowly toward the privatization of most industries nationalized in 1979. Despite strong opposition from radicals, the consensus in the regime was that change could be delayed no longer.

To secure access to international financial capital, Iran began making overtures to Western countries and to its Gulf neighbors immediately after the Iran-Iraq War. Iran has not found shedding its hostile, subversive image to be easy. Consequently, Iran accuses Washington, Tel Aviv, and Cairo of attempting to prevent its political dominance abroad and economic development at home. Its neutral stance during the 1991 Gulf War presented Tehran with an opportunity to mend fences. Nevertheless, there is a reluctance to permit a reemergence of Iran as the preeminent power in the Gulf, a role it had played unquestioningly until the 1979 revolution.

For now, the economic hardships and widespread frustration have not seriously threatened the political stability of Iran. There is a widespread domestic perception that there is no viable political alternative to Rafsanjani's government. The Islamic regime has moderated its domestic and foreign policies since the revolution; nevertheless, hard-liners continue trying to turn the clock back.

## The Land and People

Iran lies on a four-thousand-foot-high plateau that is almost entirely surrounded by mountains. Where there are no mountains, vast deserts form equally impenetrable barriers. These conditions restrict internal movement by land and have contributed to the development of numerous ethnically and linguistically distinct groups.

Iran is bounded by the Caspian Sea, Azerbaijan, and Turkmenistan on the north, Turkey and Iraq to the west, the Persian Gulf and the Gulf of

# Key Facts on Iran

**Area:** 636,293 square miles.

**Capital:** Tehran.

**Population:** 65,615,474 (1994).

**Religion:** 95 percent Shi'ite Muslim, 4 percent Sunni Muslim, 1 percent Jews, Bahais, Zoroastrians, and Christians.

**Official Language:** Persian or Farsi; Kurdish, forms of Turkic, and Arabic are spoken by leading minorities.

**GNP:** $303 billion; $4,780 per capita (1993).

*Source:* Central Intelligence Agency, *CIA World Factbook 1994.*

Oman to the south, and Pakistan and Afghanistan to the east. The Zagros Mountains, which stretch southeastward from the junction of the borders of Turkey, Azerbaijan, Turkmenistan, and Iraq, cover much of western Iran, and then extend eastward fronting the Arabian Sea and into Baluchistan. With few primary roads, villages there have remained isolated. Transportation networks are only slightly better on the eastern edge of the Zagros range in central Iran. Annual rainfall averages about fifty inches in the western mountains and less than an inch in the central plateau. Iran's rural population and farms are found in its fertile mountain valleys.

Iran's rugged terrain conceals large deposits of oil, the country's most important natural resource. Most of Iran's fields are located in the southwest corner of the country in a 350-mile corridor beginning north of Dezful and running southeast almost to Bushehr. Iran also has the world's second-largest natural gas reserves.

Mountains and deserts also separate groups living in northern and eastern Iran. The Elburz Mountains, which run along the southern shores of the Caspian Sea, form a rugged barrier north of Tehran. Two uninhabited deserts, the Dasht-e-Lut and the Dasht-e-Kavir, cover much of eastern Iran,

isolating Iranian settlements along the Afghanistan and Pakistan borders. The salt swamps of the Kavir are very dangerous to travelers and therefore remain largely unexplored. Iran suffers from occasional, but severe earthquakes. In June 1990, more than forty thousand people were reported killed and more than sixty thousand injured in an earthquake that struck northwestern Iran. Severe flooding inflicted heavy damage in eleven southern and western provinces in February 1993, and near the Afghan border in April 1993. The climate is one of extremes, ranging from scorching hot summers with high humidity, to sub-freezing winters with heavy snowfall in the northwest.

## Strong Local Identification

Because of Iran's geographic barriers, many Iranians have a greater allegiance to their local ethnic group than to the nation. Kurds in the Zagros Mountains have maintained their separate ethnic traditions. The rugged terrain of the northwest corner of Iran has enabled the Azerbaijanis to maintain their distance from Tehran. Turkic-speaking tribes around Mashad are isolated from the capital by the Dasht-e-Kavir, and the Baluchis, the poorest and least integrated of all Iranians, remain separated from the rest of the nation by the deserts of the east.

Farsi, the language of Iran's dominant ethnic group, the Persians, is the first language of only about half of Iran's estimated 65.6 million people. Most Persians are urban dwellers, although they also occupy fertile mountain valleys in the central part of the country. Persians comprise the bulk of the upper class, occupy the most important bureaucratic positions, and dominate the ranks of the economic elite. Since 1502 all the rulers of Iran have been Persians.

The Kurds, numbering around 4 million, are the second-largest ethnic group. Most live in northwest Iran along the Iraqi and Turkish borders. Kurds are generally Sunni Muslims, but most of Iran's population are Shi'ite Muslims. The Kurds' social organization is tribal.

In northern Iran, Turkic-speaking ethnic groups

that entered the area around the eleventh century predominate. Like the Kurds, they are tribally organized, and some are seminomadic. The largest Turkic ethnic group is the Azerbaijanis, who live in northwest Iran between the Caspian Sea and the Turkish border. The Turkic tribes have resisted efforts by the Persians to control them.

The Bakhtiari and the Lurs, distant relatives of the Kurds, inhabit the remote mountain areas in the southeast. Sixty percent of these people are nomadic. Leadership alternates every two years between the families that head the various tribes. The leader, or khan, serves as a sort of ambassador to Tehran; he lives in the city and takes frequent trips to the tribal areas.

Other groups, such as the Baluchi and the Arabs, consider themselves as peoples distinct from the ruling Persians. They have great pride in their ancestry, and their tribal loyalties are far stronger than any national ties.

There are also 1 million to 2 million Afghan refugees living in Iran, and more than half a million Iraqi refugees, most of whom fled Iraq during the 1991 civil war.

*Shi'ite Muslims Predominate*

The Islamic religion is the most powerful unifying force in Iran. While Shi'ite Islam is closely identified with Iran, its origins are not Iranian but Arab. During the mid-seventh century, following the death of the Prophet Muhammad, the great schism of Islam occurred over leadership of the Islamic community. Muslims split into Sunni Muslims (the majority in the Middle East), and Shi'ite Muslims (95 percent of Iran's population). Sunni Muslims held that succession should follow to the most able leader of the Islamic community. The Shi'ites maintained that only a descendant of the Prophet Muhammad could be the rightful leader, and that Ali, a cousin who had married the Prophet's daughter, was the rightful successor.

In 661 Ali was assassinated. His supporters, calling themselves Shiat Ali, or the partisans of Ali, revolted against the Sunnis but were defeated in 680 at Karbala in Iraq. Their leader Husayn,

Ali's youngest son, was executed. Husayn's death is commemorated annually as a day of mourning for all Shi'ite Muslims. Large numbers of Shi'ites fled to Iran. Proselytizing increased their numbers until they became the majority in Iran under the Safavids during the sixteenth century.

Shi'ite Muslims believe there are seven pillars of faith. In addition to the first five pillars of Islam, which are shared by the Sunnis—confession of faith, ritualized prayer, alms giving, fasting during Ramadan, and the pilgrimage to Mecca and Medina—the Shi'ites also add *jihad,* the struggle to protect Islamic lands, beliefs, and institutions, and the requirement to do good works and avoid evil thoughts, words, and deeds. *(Schisms and Sects of Islam, box, p. 175)*

The Imamate is the distinctive dogma and institution of Shi'ism. Of the several Shi'ite sects, the Twelve Imam or Twelver is dominant in Iran. The principal belief of the Twelver is that spiritual and temporal leadership of the Muslim community passed from the Prophet Muhammad to Ali, the first imam, and continued the line of imams to eleven of Ali's direct male descendants.

In addition to a political leader, the imam must be a spiritual leader who can interpret the inner mysteries of the Holy Koran and the *shariat,* Islamic canon law. The twelfth and final imam is believed to have gone into hiding because of Sunni persecution, and will reappear as the *Mahdi,* or Messiah, on the day of divine judgment.

Since the emergence of Twelver Shi'ite Islam, the *ulama,* or religious authorities, have played a prominent role in the development of scholarly and legal tradition. The hierarchy in the ulama dates only to the early nineteenth century. Since then, the highest religious authority has been vested in the *mujtahids*—scholars who by their religious studies and virtuous lives act as leaders of the Shi'ite community and interpret the faith as it applies to daily life. Prominent mujtahids with near-total authority over the community are accorded the title of *ayatollah.*

The principle of the *velayat-e-faqih,* or guardianship of the religious jurist of the community of believers, was expounded by the Ayatollah Khomeini to justify political rule by the clergy. According to this principle, the clergy, with their superior knowledge of Islamic law, are the best qualified to rule the community of believers. A *faqih* is an expert in religious jurisprudence whose authority and piety permits him to render binding interpretations of religious laws and principles. The innovative concept of *velayat-e-faqih,* incorporated into the constitution, provided Ayatollah Khomeini with the doctrinal basis for theocratic government.

# A Turbulent History

Iran's history as a continuous civilization spans at least twenty-five centuries. According to the Old Testament, ancient Persia existed as a civilization even before that. In the sixth century B.C., however, Cyrus the Great established the Persian Empire, which, with his grandson Darius's subsequent conquest of Babylonia and Egypt, was extended to the Nile Valley and almost to Asia Minor.

The empire gradually shrank because of Greek and Roman conquests and its own internal decay. By the seventh century A.D. it was beset by Arab invaders who brought with them Islam and foreign rule. The Persians gradually overthrew Arab rule, but Islam remained.

Modern Iranian history begins with nationalist protests in 1905 that forced the ruler of Iran, Muhammad Ali Shah, to establish a parliament (the *Majlis*) and grant a constitution in 1906. He was forced to abdicate in 1908 after repudiating the constitution, and he was replaced by his son Ahmad.

## Importance of Oil

In 1901 the Iranians had granted William Knox D'Arcy, an Australian, a concession to search for oil. The discovery of oil in Iran in 1908 intensified the developing British-Russian rivalry over Iran. On the eve of World War I Britain purchased 51 percent of D'Arcy's company, the Anglo-Persian Oil Company (renamed the Anglo-Iranian Oil Company in 1935). Persian oil helped fuel the British fleet during World War I.

The war interrupted the sporadic growth of constitutionalism in Iran. Although Iran officially remained neutral during the war, the importance of oil to Britain and Russia's desire to secure its southern flank resulted in British and Russian soldiers invading and occupying Iran. In 1919 Iran concluded a trade agreement with Britain that formally affirmed Iranian independence but in fact established a British protectorate over the country. After Iran's recognition of the new Communist government in the Soviet Union, Moscow renounced the imperialistic policies of the czars toward Iran and withdrew the Soviet troops that remained there.

A second revolutionary movement, directed largely by foreigners, was initiated in 1921 by Reza Shah, an Iranian military leader and the founder of the Pahlavi dynasty. In 1925 he was placed on the throne and he proceeded to implement major domestic programs, including the establishment of a modern education system and the construction of roads and a trans-Iranian railroad. During World War II, however, his close relationship with the Germans led to another occupation in 1941 by the British and Soviets, who saw

Iran as a key supply route from the West to the Soviet Union. The two powers forced him to abdicate in favor of his son, Muhammad Reza. After the war the Soviet Union attempted to establish separatist Azerbaijani and Kurdish regimes in northern Iran. This effort failed, however, after strong protests from the United States led the Soviets to withdraw their forces.

## Postwar Period

The Anglo-Iranian Oil Company became a symbol of Western influence in Iran's postwar affairs and served to bolster Iranian nationalism. This consortium of British and American interests antagonized both the political right and the left in Iran. The domestic political climate was further aggravated by deteriorating economic conditions resulting from the Allied occupation in World War II. Dissatisfaction with the shah, who had tried to accommodate foreign oil interests, led in April 1951 to the election of Muhammad Mossadeq, the leader of the rightist National Front, as prime minister.

In May, with the support of the Iranian nationalist movement, Mossadeq nationalized Iran's oil industry. Iran, however, did not have the technical resources to operate its oil facilities without foreign help, and its production fell. Growing national discontent with Mossadeq led him to take repressive measures to protect his power. He dissolved the Majlis in the summer of 1953 and tried to take over the government. Muhammad Reza Shah was forced to flee the country in August. Within days, however, shah loyalists in the military, apparently with the backing of the U.S. Central Intelligence Agency (CIA), defeated military units controlled by Mossadeq, and the shah returned to power.

With Mossadeq imprisoned and his National Front allies in parliament reduced to marginal effectiveness, the shah moved to consolidate his power. He smashed the Communist Tudeh party, and hundreds of its members in the army's lower ranks were rooted out, as were its sympathizers in all significant interest groups and associations. The shah rewarded his supporters—chiefly in the officer corps—and made peace with the nationalist-minded clerical authorities.

Although Iran's oil industry remained nationalized, the shah negotiated a deal with foreign oil companies under which the companies managed Iran's oil operations for a substantial profit. In foreign affairs the shah developed close relations with the United States, which became Tehran's main arms supplier. In 1955 Iran joined the Baghdad Pact, an alliance with Britain, Iraq, Pakistan, and Turkey that was intended to deter Soviet aggression in the Middle East. Although the United States was not a member, it encouraged formation of the alliance.

In 1961, amidst growing internal criticism and the resurgence of the National Front, the shah announced the "White Revolution," an ambitious plan to stimulate economic growth and social development. The plan promoted women's suffrage, literacy, health, the nationalization of natural resources, the sale of state-owned factories, and profit sharing for workers. The cornerstone of the White Revolution, however, was land reform. The landed classes, with allies among the Shi'ite clergy, incited violent demonstrations in June 1963 to protest the threat to their holdings. Predictably, the shah crushed this dissent. After that, he instituted reforms to mollify those with moderate demands and used repression to silence the others.

The shah used his nation's oil riches to turn Iran into a regional power. He bought billions of dollars' worth of sophisticated military equipment from the United States, which considered him a bulwark against communism. Following the 1973 war in the Middle East and the ensuing Arab oil embargo imposed on Israel's supporters, Iran's oil revenues soared. Before October 1973, Iran's oil revenues were $2.5 billion a year. By 1979 annual oil revenues had grown to $19.1 billion.

As international oil consumption grew, so did the West's dependence on Iran and its fellow Organization of Oil Exporting Countries (OPEC) members. According to CIA figures, the United States depended on Iran for 9.1 percent of its crude oil imports in August 1978, compared with 5.9 percent in September 1973. American exports to Iran increased about sevenfold from 1973 to 1978. During this five-year period, Iran bought more than $19 billion worth of military equipment from the United States. At the time of the shah's fall in 1979, Iran had a foreign debt of $7.2 billion, including $2.2 billion to U.S. banks.

## The Revolution

In February 1979, after months of civil violence, a broad-based movement led by the Ayatollah Khomeini ended the thirty-seven-year reign of the shah of Iran. The Iranian revolution did not spring up with a wave of Khomeini's hand. Social, economic, and religious pressures had been building within the country for several decades. These pressures led to widespread opposition to the shah from highly diverse groups that combined their efforts to accomplish a genuine grass-roots revolution.

The coalition of forces against the shah consisted of an urban-based alliance of traditionalists and modernists formed into loosely organized groups usually working independently. National religious figures close to Khomeini, who was in exile, shaped the movement inside Iran. Lesser figures among the religious hierarchy, or ulama, who possessed enormous local influence, particularly among the urban poor and bazaar merchants, gave the movement its strength.

On the eve of the revolution, the shah imposed price controls to curb inflation. While enforcing them, the government closed nearly two hundred fifty thousand small shops. This move alienated the merchant class, many of whom were jailed or excessively fined for "profiteering." The urban poor opposed the shah mostly on moral grounds, seeing his attempts to Westernize Iranian society as attacks on revered Islamic institutions.

Modernists made up a much smaller faction within the opposition to the shah. Islamic modernists such as the Marxist Mujaheddin-e-Khalq opposed him for his capitalist economic policies. Progressive intellectuals both religious and secular wanted a modernized Iran but no monarch. Secular modernist groups such as the Fedayin-e-Khalq

and the Communist Tudeh party, both longtime opponents of the shah, were joined by the professional middle class, which viewed the shah's highly centralized control over the political and economic process as the greatest obstacle to their advancement. Estimated at between 10 and 15 percent of the population, the professionals shifted their commitment from a nationalist secular cause to an Islamic one because it was the only available means of mobilizing the masses.

Khomeini's followers mark the start of the revolution with the White Revolution riots in June 1963, when wealthy landowners and Islamic clergy joined to oppose the shah's land reform program. The ulama also opposed a new law allowing women to vote and education programs that substituted secular classes for religious instruction and permitted coeducation. The shah further alienated his people by bringing in foreigners, especially Americans, to support his programs and provide technical skills.

The shah's brutal suppression of dissent forced Khomeini and other opposition leaders into exile. During the 1960s and 1970s sentiment against the government was growing in nearly every segment of Iranian society. Middle-class Iranians who opposed the government found allies in the religious hierarchy.

The clerics were incensed not only by the secularization of the education system, which they viewed as a direct assault on their position within Iranian society, but also by the Family Protection Law that allowed women to disobey Islamic teaching and divorce their husbands. The monarchy increasingly became an anti-Islamic symbol. By relying on non-Muslim foreigners and by reducing the traditional role of the ulama in government, the shah disrupted the balance that had existed between religious and secular authority in Iran. The ulama called upon conservative elements of the Iranian population to rebel.

The opposition found its leader in the Ayatollah Khomeini. When he was exiled in 1964, Khomeini believed that the political role of the clerics was to provide moral guidance to secular forces who would manage the technical aspects of the state.

Statements made by Khomeini in Paris left modernists with the impression that they would run the government once the shah was defeated.

After mass demonstrations in 1976 protesting the shah's switch from the Islamic calendar to one based on the coronation of Cyrus the Great, Iran was relatively quiet for a time. Sporadic protests did occur, however in response to the repressive activities of SAVAK, the shah's hated intelligence service. These protests escalated into large-scale riots in 1978 after a government-inspired article in the Tehran newspaper *Etelaat* impugned Khomeini's character and accused him of conspiring with Communists against the shah's regime. In January Khomeini supporters protested the article in Qom, a religious center dominated by the nation's Shi'ite clergy. During the march, army troops fired into the crowd. The victims were the first of an estimated ten thousand people killed during riots in 1978. The level of violence increased as the protests became more widespread. Demonstrators rioted against the shootings, and the shah's forces put down the riots with increased fervor. The government closed Iran's universities in June, creating greater support for the demonstrators among students.

Khomeini took an active part in encouraging the increasingly frequent and intense demonstrations from Iraq. The Iraqi government, concerned with maintaining good relations with Iran, expelled Khomeini, who set up headquarters in France on October 6, 1978. In France he attracted even more worldwide attention than he had enjoyed in Iraq.

In November, Iranian workers staged strikes in sympathy with the anti-shah demonstrators. The most important strikes were those by oil workers, whose walkout soon produced a fuel shortage, causing serious damage to the economy of the beleaguered nation.

Once the breadth of the opposition to the shah had become apparent, he made several last-minute efforts to appease his opponents. He granted amnesty to Khomeini, but the demonstrations and strikes continued. Soon even civil servants refused to report to work.

The shah then offered to step down as head of the government, but not as the shah. He appointed Shahpur Bakhtiar as premier. Bakhtiar, a member of the National Front who had always opposed the shah, accepted the appointment and quickly moved to placate the opposition. He promised to disband the SAVAK, proclaimed that no more Iranian oil would be sold to Israel or South Africa, turned over the Israeli embassy to the Palestine Liberation Organization (PLO), and openly criticized U.S. policies supported by the shah.

These efforts, however, came too late. Bakhtiar was denounced by his own party for accepting the premiership from the shah, and rioting continued. As a last-ditch measure, the shah ordered members of his royal family to turn in their millions of dollars in Iranian holdings to the Pahlavi Foundation, a family trust and charitable organization under his absolute control, but the revolution had become irreversible.

With the end near, the shah announced, "I am going on vacation because I am feeling tired." He flew to Egypt on January 16, 1979, never to return to his country. Two weeks later on February 1 Khomeini returned triumphantly to Iran. His supporters overthrew Bakhtiar's government on February 11. Bakhtiar fled to France, and Mehdi Bazargan was installed to replace him as premier. After a referendum, in which the only form of government to appear on the ballot was an Islamic republic, the public overwhelmingly voted for the establishment of an Islamic republic. The Islamic Republic of Iran was declared on April 1, 1979.

## Role of the Intellectuals

Bazargan was part of a group of liberal intellectuals, both secular and religious, who had belonged at various times to organizations such as the underground Freedom Front and the National Front—the backbone of the nationalist coalition built by former prime minister Muhammad Mossadeq. In 1979, however, the intellectuals had no political base.

Their middle-class support collapsed in the face of worsening economic conditions, political persecution, and the rising power of the clerics. The clerics were able to neutralize and eventually prevail over other national figures, such as Ibrahim Yazdi and Sadegh Ghotbzadeh, who were among the Westernized exiles with Khomeini in France just before the overthrow of the shah. Although these men were devout Muslims, their Western education and ideas made them suspect in the eyes of the fundamentalists. Nevertheless, one of these exiles, Abolhassan Bani-Sadr, gained ascendancy in Iran's postrevolutionary power structure. Bani-Sadr was a Sorbonne-educated economist and intellectual who became Iran's first popularly elected president in January 1980 after winning 75 percent of the vote.

Bani-Sadr, as the son of a prominent religious leader, was perhaps more acceptable to the clerics than his peers. Yet when Bani-Sadr ran for president he was opposed by the clerical leadership of the Islamic Republican party (IRP).

## Consolidation of Power

After the fall of the shah's government, Iran's internal security apparatus collapsed, and bands of armed youths calling themselves Revolutionary Guards (or the *Pasdaran*) ran amok, attacking anyone associated with the former ruler. The IRP had overthrown the shah without establishing an initial domestic program of government. Civil authority was exercised by thousands of self-appointed committees *(komitehs)* that took it upon themselves to stamp passports, distribute food, set prices for goods, and police the streets—mostly without state supervision.

In this atmosphere, a struggle for power ensued between the Shi'ite clerics and secular nationalists. Although these two general groupings had cooperated with each other in overthrowing the shah, they had different goals that were likely to clash. The clerics and their Islamic Republican party sought the establishment of a conservative society based on fundamentalist Shi'ite tenets and dominated by religious leaders. The secular nationalist groups sought various forms of secular government depending on their orientation, envisioned an advisory role for religious leaders, and were generally more receptive to foreign ties and influence.

The clerics had several advantages over the secular nationalists. First, the secular nationalists were merely a broad group of many organizations, including the Tudeh party, the Fedayin-e-Khalq, and the National Front, without common goals or a united leadership like that of the IRP. Second, the clerics had the support of Khomeini, who commanded enormous respect among many segments of the Iranian population. Finally, when competing for support, the clerics were able to tap the deep religious convictions of many Iranian citizens.

From 1979 to 1983 the clerics, led by Khomeini, used political maneuvering, propaganda, and terror to sweep their secular rivals aside. The liberal intelligentsia represented by President Bani-Sadr were gradually removed from positions of power. Bani-Sadr's presidency was crippled by the Iran-Iraq War that began on September 22, 1980, when Iraqi forces invaded Iran. As commander in chief, Bani-Sadr received blame for the military's failings, while his efforts to reorganize and reinvigorate the military led to suspicions that he was plotting to use the military to increase his own power.

Bani-Sadr survived only so long as Khomeini protected him and maintained some balance between him and the IRP. When Khomeini withdrew his support, Bani-Sadr's downfall was swift. The Majlis declared him politically incompetent and Khomeini removed him from office on June 22, 1981. Bani-Sadr fled the country in an Iranian air force jet in July. With him was Massoud Rajavi, leader of the Mujaheddin-e-Khalq. The two men were granted asylum by France.

One week after Bani-Sadr and Rajavi were forced into exile, the Mujaheddin bombed IRP headquarters, killing seventy-four of the nation's political elites, including the founder of the IRP, Ayatollah Mohammed Beheshti. The Mujaheddin espoused Islamic Marxism, arguing for a divinely integrated classless society with nationalized major industries and banks. The Mujaheddin's views on the direction of the revolution were not irreconcilable with the clerics' views, but the IRP was unwilling to share power with anyone.

In reprisal for the bombing of IRP headquarters, Khomeini turned the full force of the Revolutionary Guards against the Mujaheddin, and by the end of 1982 it was forced underground. Amnesty International estimates that between forty-five hundred and six thousand of the Mujaheddin were killed by Revolutionary Guards and thousands were put in prison. In late 1989 the Mujaheddin was operating as an underground opposition group in Iran.

Khomeini's regime also suppressed the extreme left-wing groups such as the Iranian Communist Tudeh party and the Fedayin-e-Khalq. The Revolutionary Guards' treatment of the Fedayin-e-Khalq was so harsh that in December 1982 Khomeini publicly criticized the komitehs for their excesses. In 1983 the Khomeini faction banned the Tudeh party and jailed more than a thousand of its members.

Khomeini even attacked the merchants, *bazaaris,* who played an important role in his rise to power and remain a key element in Iran's economy. In December 1980 Khomeini, like the shah, accused them of profiteering, and in June 1981 he ordered the execution of two well-known merchants for alleged counterrevolutionary activities. When Bani-Sadr was dismissed, bazaaris distanced themselves from IRP policies.

Throughout the consolidation period the military remained loyal to the revolution. Many officers owed their positions to Khomeini's regime, and rank-and-file soldiers had demonstrated intense loyalty to Khomeini. The military also was probably reluctant to confront the disorganized but ubiquitous Revolutionary Guards, whose propensity for violence was demonstrated time and again in the streets.

## U.S. Embassy Hostage Crisis

An event of central importance to the Iranian power struggle was the occupation of the American embassy on November 4, 1979, by revolutionary students. The students, who soon received the support of Ayatollah Khomeini and most of the fundamentalist clerics in the government, took sixty-one Americans hostage. Nine were released within a few days, but fifty-two of the embassy staff members remained prisoners of the students.

The hostage crisis, which continued for 444 days until Iran released the diplomats on January 21, 1981, as Jimmy Carter left office and Ronald Reagan became president, was used by Iran's hard-line, anti-Western clerics to weaken the position of moderates in the Iranian government. The hard-liners pointed to the diplomatic, military, and economic measures taken by the Carter administration to obtain the release of the hostages and the admission of the shah into America for medical treatment as evidence of the malevolence of the United States. In addition, publication of documents captured by the students who took over the embassy revealed U.S. intelligence activities in Iran and confirmed the suspicions of many Iranians that the United States was interfering in their internal affairs. In this atmosphere, Iranian moderates who had had contacts with U.S. officials became suspect, while extremists in Tehran gained credibility. Moreover, the refusal of some moderate Iranian leaders to actively support the hostage taking hurt their standing and made them more vulnerable to the machinations of the hard-liners.

## Government Structure Under Khomeini

After the elimination of the secular nationalists and other opponents, Iran's fundamentalist clerics dominated the government. As faqih, Khomeini became the final authority in all matters of government and social policy. In 1979 he asserted that "there is not a single topic of human life for which Islam has not provided instruction and established norms." Nevertheless, he remained aloof from the everyday decision-making process, maintaining his offices in Qom rather than Tehran, the capital. Because of his eminent position, however, all important decisions had to receive his approval.

The government was presided over by a president and prime minister, who were responsible for running the ministries and executing government policy. The 270-seat Majlis, which wrote and passed new laws subject to Khomeini's approval, was led by a Speaker.

In addition to these familiar instruments of government, several councils unique to revolutionary Iran played an important role in Khomeini's government. The Council of Experts—an elected body of seventy to eighty eminent Islamic scholars—was responsible for such high matters of state as revising the 1979 constitution and selecting a successor to Khomeini. The twelve-member Council of Constitutional Guardians screened and modified all legislation from the Majlis before passing it on to Khomeini for his approval. Laws that did not meet the council's Islamic standards were sent back, often in modified form with the expectation that they would be passed and resubmitted as returned.

The Revolutionary Council was in charge of the Pasdaran, or Revolutionary Guards. In addition to the council's military section, which had been responsible for most of the regime's civil violence, there were economic and political sections linked to tens of thousands of mosques. The clerics connected with the mosques functioned as local administrators. They provided food, clothing, and ration cards; ran the courts; collected taxes; and rounded up volunteers for the war against Iraq. They maintained detailed records on their flock and served as the Pasdaran's grass-roots intelligence service.

## War with Iraq

The apparent weakness of Iran's political center encouraged Iraq to attack Iran in September 1980. Captured documents published by Iran indicated that Iraq's president, Saddam Hussein, expected that the chaos in Tehran would bring a quick victory. Instead of collapsing, however, the Iranian government responded with surprising speed, mobilizing what was left of the shah's army. Waves of untrained young zealots, some of them unarmed, threw themselves into the conflict and halted the Iraqis' advance.

The Iranian army's counterattacks in late 1981 and 1982 forced the Iraqi army to retreat. In June 1982 Iraq began to seek peace. Saddam withdrew his troops into Iraq and unilaterally called a cease-

fire. Khomeini ignored these moves and in July ordered a major attack across the border toward Basra. The Iranian force, however, had been weakened by purges of officers and shortages of equipment and was unable to sustain this offensive. The assault failed, and the war deteriorated to a brutal standoff with the two armies inside Iraqi territory.

During the war both countries attacked the oil facilities of the other, as well as neutral tankers in the Gulf. Iranian attacks succeeded in substantially reducing Iraqi exports early in the war, although the construction of pipelines restored Iraqi export capacity by 1987. Iraqi attacks in 1984 and 1985 on Iranian refineries, oil tankers doing business with Iran, and Kharg Island, Iran's principal Gulf oil terminal, sharply reduced Iran's oil revenues. In 1983 Iran had earned $21.7 billion from its petroleum exports, but by 1985 revenues were just $15.9 billion. In 1986 the worldwide collapse of oil prices limited Iran's oil export earnings to just $7.3 billion. The loss of oil revenue further weakened an economy already suffering from poor management by inexperienced clerics and the resource drain caused by the war.

In addition to economic strains, the war brought Iran increasing international isolation. Its stated goal of exporting its revolution to neighboring states and its attacks on ships in the Gulf pushed Arab nations to back Iraq financially and diplomatically. Saudi Arabia and Kuwait provided billions of dollars for the Iraqi war effort, and the Gulf states formed the Gulf Cooperation Council (GCC) to coordinate their defenses.

The war also led to military confrontations between Iran and the United States. A covert attempt by the Reagan administration to use arms sales to Iran to improve U.S. relations with Iranian moderates and obtain the release of American hostages held in Lebanon by pro-Iranian groups caused a scandal in the United States. Not only had the plan contradicted President Reagan's policies of not negotiating with terrorists and not selling arms to Iran, but investigations disclosed that administration officials had also used proceeds from the Iranian arms sales to illegally fund the contra resistance fighters in Nicaragua.

In an effort to repair its image among Gulf states and head off growing Soviet involvement in the region, the United States began escorting reflagged Kuwaiti oil tankers through the Persian Gulf. These American naval escorts fought Iranian forces on several occasions and increased the Iranians' sense of encirclement.

Iranian morale was reduced further by Iraqi air and missile attacks on Iran's largest cities, Iraq's use of chemical weapons on the battlefield, and the failure of major Iranian offensives in 1986 and 1987 to breach Iraqi defenses around Basra. In early 1988 Iraqi forces began pushing the Iranians back toward their border. By July the Iraqis had recaptured virtually all occupied Iraqi territory and appeared poised to achieve significant territorial gains in Iran.

Faced with this prospect, Khomeini agreed to United Nations Resolution 598 providing for a cease-fire, despite his earlier vow to fight until Iraqi leader Saddam Hussein had been driven from power. The war had resulted in the deaths of hundreds of thousands of Iranians and left the nation financially bankrupt. *(Details on the Iran-Iraq War, Chapter 4, p. 105)*

## Iran After Khomeini

On June 6, 1989, the Ayatollah Khomeini was buried amidst a chaotic display of national grief. Hundreds of thousands of mourners showed up at the War Martyrs' Cemetery in Tehran and thousands pressed through elaborate barriers at the burial site, trying to touch Khomeini's body. The crowd overwhelmed security personnel and mourners grabbed at the corpse, causing it to fall from its wooden litter. Soldiers fought to retrieve the body as helicopters scattered the crowd. The body was airlifted away and officials were forced to delay the burial for six hours.

It seemed impossible to many Iranians that their preeminent religious and political leader was gone. For years Khomeini had defied premature predictions of death, while Western observers speculated on the government that would emerge when he was gone. Many analysts forecast that in his absence there could be a lengthy power struggle among the religious elite for control of the government. Such a power struggle had the potential to cause domestic terrorism, internal chaos, or even civil war.

In March 1989 the eighty-nine-year-old Khomeini had forced Ayatollah Hussein Ali Montazeri to resign as his designated heir. The resignation of Montazeri, who was considered a moderate on social and economic issues, appeared to indicate that radical factions opposed to expansion of private enterprise and a greater opening to the West had gained ascendancy. Montazeri's ouster confused the succession issue, increasing the possibility of a power struggle after Khomeini's death.

While the crowds at Khomeini's burial reinforced Western perceptions that Iran was out of control, the country's leadership was defying Western speculation about a power struggle by effecting an apparently smooth and peaceful transition of power. Within twenty-four hours of Khomeini's death Iran's Council of Experts had chosen outgoing president Ali Khamenei, a compromise candidate, to succeed Khomeini as supreme religious leader. Ali Akbar Hashemi Rafsanjani, the Speaker of Iran's parliament and leading candidate to succeed Khamenei as president, remarked: "We astonished the world and right now all of those wrong interpretations of power struggles and radicals versus moderates are dismissed."

In August Rafsanjani was overwhelmingly elected president as expected. Rafsanjani had repeatedly stated his intention to give priority to reinvigorating the economy. Khamenei and Rafsanjani were roommates in their early revolutionary days, and Khamenei gave Rafsanjani's presidential candidacy an effusive endorsement. Few prominent hard-liners were given positions of power in the new regime, although they maintained a strong presence in the Majlis. Despite the smooth transition, Khomeini's death created a vacuum in Iranian politics. Neither Rafsanjani nor Khamenei commanded the reverence and respect of Khomeini, who served as the final arbiter of all leadership disputes.

*Ali Akbar Hashemi Rafsanjani*

During the 1989 presidential elections, voters also approved 45 amendments to the constitution, including the elevation of the president to the government's chief executive and the elimination of the post of prime minister. The new Council of Ministers was regarded as a balanced coalition of conservatives and liberals.

Rafsanjani emerged as Iran's single most powerful political leader, but he still required Khamenei's backing. In October 1990 Khamenei and Rafsanjani worked jointly to prevent the election of many powerful conservatives to the eighty-three-seat Council of Experts.

To the outside world, the government presented a solid and unyielding front. But internally, pragmatists and radicals were deeply divided over objectives and policy. Throughout 1990 the leadership concentrated its efforts on domestic issues and moved to consolidate its rule.

Rafsanjani understood that the population was tired of the privations of war and revolution. Without marked improvement in living standards, the possibility existed that large segments of Iranian society could turn against the government. While considered to have a pragmatic vision, Rafsanjani was caught between the urgent need to implement reforms to reinvigorate the economy, and the continuing struggle for political dominance with his domestic rivals. Measures likely to improve the economy, including economic openings to the West and selected privatization, could draw the fire of radicals.

Supporters of Khomeini's teaching agreed that conditions should be improved for ordinary people. They were against the involvement of foreign capital, however, and felt that it should be excluded at all cost. As a result, Rafsanjani adopted a policy of gradual change to avoid factionalism. To revive the economy, Rafsanjani put forth a five-year development plan that allocated a large share of national resources to economic reconstruction and allowed modest economic openings to the West. Iran sought renewed relations with Saudi Arabia and Great Britain and accepted foreign loans. Reestablishing ties with the United States, however, remained a political impossibility.

Iran appeared to be headed toward a reconciliation with Western Europe in early 1989, following several months of cultivating economic contacts with Western European governments and business leaders. On February 7 Ali Akbar Velayati made the first visit to Great Britain by an Iranian foreign minister since the 1979 revolution. Then on February 14 Khomeini derailed the initiative by calling on Muslims to assassinate author Salman Rushdie, whose book *The Satanic Verses* was considered by much of the Islamic world to be blasphemous. Khomeini's assassination order was immediately denounced in the West. Great Britain and the other eleven nations of the European Economic Community recalled diplomats from Tehran to protest Khomeini's action. The Rushdie incident left Western European nations wary of moving too quickly to expand economic contacts with Iran.

## 1991 Gulf War

The cease-fire achieved at the end of the Iran-Iraq War had kept the peace between the two nations, but no resolution of outstanding issues was forthcoming as the 1990s began. In early 1990, however, Iran and Iraq agreed to resume negotiations in the Soviet Union. Iraq was aggressively pressuring Kuwait to limit its oil production, forgive Iraqi debts, and resolve border and oil rights issues on terms favorable to Iraq. Saddam Hussein was anxious to resolve outstanding issues with Iran. These negotiations were overtaken by events, as Iraq invaded Kuwait on August 2, 1990, setting in motion the Gulf crisis. Iran condemned Iraq's invasion of Kuwait and offered to defend other Gulf States.

Saddam, seeking to prevent the possibility of having to fight a two-front war, capitulated to Iranian terms for a resolution to the Iran-Iraq War. On August 15, 1990, he offered to return Iranian territory still occupied by Iraq and recognize Iranian control of the eastern half of the Shatt al-Arab waterway. Iran accepted these favorable terms. On August 18, Iraqi troops began withdrawing from Iranian territory. The two countries also began the exchange of an estimated eighty thousand prisoners of war. On September 10, 1990, they agreed to reestablish diplomatic relations.

As the multinational forces began deploying, Iran called for the simultaneous withdrawal of all Western forces from the Gulf and all Iraqi forces from Kuwait. Iran's extreme conservatives demanded that Iran ally itself with Iraq in a jihad against Western forces, while Rafsanjani held the position that the multinational coalition was tolerable so long as it withdrew immediately after the conflict in Kuwait was resolved. The Iranian government recognized that Iran stood to gain from a war between the coalition and Iraq. Iraq would be weakened militarily while Iran could appeal to people throughout the Middle East who were uncomfortable with both Iraq's aggression and the Western presence.

On January 17, 1991, the coalition began an air bombardment campaign against Iraq. The fighting was an Iranian dream come true. It pitted Iran's two most recent and hated antagonists, Iraq and the United States, against one another in a war that promised to destroy much of Iraq's military might while increasing opposition to the United States in some parts of the Middle East.

Despite Iran's declaring neutrality in the conflict, Iranian interests were threatened by Iraq's annexation of Kuwait. Permanent Iraqi control of Kuwait would have substantially strengthened Iran's primary rival in the region. An Iraq bolstered by the oil reserves of Kuwait and possessing an excellent port and a wide outlet to the Persian Gulf would be in a position to launch another war against Iran, or at least to severely restrict Iranian influence in the Persian Gulf region.

It was certain that the Iranian leadership wanted Iraq out of Kuwait and the Iraqi military destroyed, both as retribution for the war Iraq unleashed upon Iran in 1980 and because Iraq has been the most important Arab counterweight to Iranian regional influence. Iran therefore pledged its cooperation with the UN embargo against Iraq. The strong coalition response to the invasion allowed Iran to sit out the conflict, as sanctions and then coalition military power weakened Iraq and forced it from Kuwait. Throughout the crisis, Iran presented itself as a responsible mediator that denounced all military aggression and foreign military deployments in the region.

Soon after the war began, Iran agreed to receive Iraqi aircraft that Baghdad wished to shelter from allied air attacks. A total of 137 Iraqi warplanes, many of them among Iraq's best, were sent to Iranian airfields. Iran assured the coalition that it would not return the aircraft until the fighting was over.

After the coalition drove the Iraqis from Kuwait and destroyed a large part of Saddam's military power, Iran adopted a harder line toward Baghdad. Tehran informed the Saddam regime that it would keep the Iraqi warplanes, thereby substantially boosting the strength of the Iranian air force. In addition, Iran began supporting the Shi'ite rebellion in southern Iraq. It gave rebels sanctuary in Iranian territory and supplied them with weapons and supplies. Iran also provided weapons to Kurdish groups in northern Iraq, who had close relations with Iran in the past.

Iran-Iraq relations deteriorated after the conflict in response to Saddam Hussein's suppression of the Shi'ite rebellion in southern and central Iraq. Iraq accused Iran of providing support to the rebels and countered by resuming support for the military activities of the largest Iranian dissident groups, the Muhahidin-e-Khalq and the Kurdish Democratic party.

## Current Issues

*Internal Affairs.* The most important domestic problem facing the government is rebuilding an economy that has not recovered from the uncertain aftermath of the revolutionary period and eight years of war with Iraq. Compounding problems are rapid population growth and urbanization, which are severely straining social services, particularly housing. Despite government advocacy of birth control, the population is growing by approximately 2 million people every year.

The direction of economic policy is tied to the broader question of rapprochement with the West. Adopting decisive economic policies has been nearly impossible because the regime is divided over how much private sector and foreign involvement to permit. Hard-liners have argued that any foreign involvement could undermine Iranian independence and that opening up the economy to domestic private enterprise could erode Islamic values and weaken the control of religious leaders who advocate a tightly controlled state economy.

While Rafsanjani regards Western investment and technology as vital to Iran's reconstruction, he needs to gain access to them without alienating the conservative faction within the leadership. Those voicing the strongest opposition to a more pragmatic economic approach are often the same relentless voices criticizing the government's economic failures.

Even if the government could formulate a cohesive economic reform policy, Iran's leadership suffers from a lack of governmental and technical experts who would be capable of implementing the policy. Many of its most experienced administrators and technocrats fled Iran in the wake of the revolution. Ministerial nominees and other officials have often been chosen according to their religious standing, rather than their governmental experience. Although Iran's religious leaders have shown that they possess the political skills to maintain themselves in power, they may lack the skills necessary to solve the nation's domestic problems.

For the leaders, who had pledged to ease the burden of the dispossessed, the situation is potentially dangerous. Financial pressure on the government caused by the estimated $30 billion external debt has forced it to impose harsh and unpopular measures, including the reduction of imports by 50 percent in 1993 and an increase in the prices of some basic commodities, including bread. Widespread rumors circulate that the price of fuel, which is deeply discounted, may be raised.

Meanwhile, the decline of oil prices and the flat demand for oil have frustrated Iran's attempts to augment its oil revenues. Inflation is estimated at 35 percent, and unemployment is officially recognized at 14 percent. Growing discontent and disillusionment among the lower classes were evident with increased incidents of protests against food shortages and high prices in early 1990. Mass riots protesting the removal of squatter settlements in 1992 and against the lifting of housing subsidies shook several cities in 1993.

While industrial output has plunged to 50 percent of capacity, there are some signs that the private sector is focusing on higher-quality goods with export potential. The March 1993 devaluation of the currency is forcing industrialists to upgrade quality to international standards in order to compete in the local market and abroad.

The quickest fix for Iran's economic crisis may be to secure the cooperation of the United States and other Western nations in rescheduling its external debt. Germany, Japan, and France, which have fostered economic links to Iran, are eager to bail out Tehran. The Clinton administration, however, has not shown an inclination to cooperate in an easing of Iran's credit troubles or its broader economic difficulties. The United States has, however, increased its exports to Iran, albeit through third countries in the Gulf. Despite U.S. pressures to prevent debt relief, Iran's leading creditors may break ranks and conclude bilateral refinancing agreements.

Growing discontent with Rafsanjani's rule was manifest in low voter turnout during the June 1993 presidential elections. Rafsanjani received 63.2 percent of the vote, down from 94.5 percent in the 1989 election. Rafsanjani is also faced with mounting opposition from the conservatives within the 270-member Majlis. The conservatives are strongly allied to the powerful merchant class, the bazaaris, who hold a near monopoly on the purchase and distribution of most goods. The bazaaris feel threatened by Rafsanjani's plan to build up the domestic manufacturing sector.

An assassination attempt against President Rafsanjani on February 1, 1994, was seen by many analysts as the latest signal that political disillusion and economic hardship could erupt into open unrest. The same day rioting took place in the southeastern Sunni-dominated town of Zahedan in protest of the destruction of a Sunni mosque in Mashad. Besides breathing life into the economy, Iran's leaders must try to pacify ethnic and political movements opposed to the regime. The Kurds continue to rebel, and Mujaheddin attacks continue to terrorize the cities. The government has often reacted violently to perceived threats. More than a thousand followers of the Bahai faith have been killed or imprisoned. The Revolutionary Guards commit acts of violence against the populace, and the regime holds thousands of political prisoners in its jails.

For the first time since the revolution, the human rights organization Amnesty International was allowed access to Iran in May 1991, despite its having issued a critical report in 1990 condemning the execution of thousands of dissidents. But the assassination in Paris in August 1991 of Shapour Bakhtiar, Iran's last prerevolutionary prime minister, indicates that the Islamic regime has not abandoned the practice of eliminating its exiled opponents.

To the consternation of the Gulf Cooperation Council (GCC) countries and Western allies, Iran has been quietly rebuilding its armed forces. Most disconcerting to its neighbors is Iran's purchase of combat aircraft from Russia and Ukraine. In 1990 and 1991 more than twenty-four MiG-29 fighters were bought, and a deal worth up to $4 billion has been signed with Russia for more fighters. Iran is receiving shipments of large quantities of tanks, and it has bought three Kilo-class submarines from Russia. At the same time, Iran has been buying dual-technology equipment from Western sources. While Rafsanjani claims that Iran wants to normalize relations with the GCC countries, its military buildup casts doubts on his sincerity.

*Foreign Affairs.* During the 1980s Iran's foreign policy was dominated by its war with Iraq. Nevertheless, the Iranian leadership's intention to export its revolution to other states made Iran a primary security threat to Gulf nations. An Iranian-backed plot to overthrow the Bahraini government in 1981, Iran's support of Shi'ites who bombed Western embassies in Kuwait in 1983, and riots by Iranian pilgrims in Mecca for the holy pilgrimage in 1987, leaving 402 dead, were among the most troubling instances of Iranian subversion and agitation.

In response to Iran's threat to export revolution and its attacks on Gulf shipping, Jordan, Saudi Arabia, and Kuwait openly supported Iraq financially and militarily in its war with Iran. Among Middle Eastern and North African nations, only Syria, Libya, and the People's Democratic Republic of Yemen (South Yemen) supported Iran in the war. Since the end of the Iran-Iraq War, Iran has remained a regional outcast, even though it has moderated somewhat its position on the exportation of revolution.

In the Gulf War's aftermath, Iran sought to reassert itself as a regional power. Its negative reaction to the proposed Damascus Declaration of March 1991, whereby future Gulf security would be provided by GCC countries plus Egypt and

Syria, to the exclusion of Iran, was in large part responsible for the reconsideration of the plan. Iranian attempts at improved relations with the GCC countries were thwarted by a dispute between Iran and the United Arab Emirates over the island of Abu Musa. The underlying causes of the GCC countries' suspicion of Iran include ongoing territorial disputes, Iran's arms buildup, future Gulf security, Iranian support for extraterritorial fundamentalist groups, and the long rivalry of the Gulf Arabs and Persians. Fearing future Iranian "racial or religious chauvinism" or "Iraqi adventurism," several Arab Gulf countries have signed defense treaties with Western nations, a development that Iran opposes and claims causes regional instability. During the conflict over Kuwait, Iran normalized its relations with Egypt, Tunisia, Jordan, and the Arab Gulf states. Diplomatic ties were reestablished with Saudi Arabia on March 26, 1991, and subsequently Iranian pilgrims were able to participate in the 1991 hajj. Domestically, these were controversial measures; radical members of the Majlis opposed normalization of relations with Egypt, Jordan, and Saudi Arabia. Tehran has focused especially on improving relations with Saudi Arabia, primarily because the Saudis have the greatest influence over OPEC policies. Iran favors using stricter OPEC oil-production quotas to elevate prices and needs Saudi cooperation to achieve this goal.

In September 1990 Iran and the United Kingdom resumed diplomatic relations after Iran assured the United Kingdom of its respect for international law and its commitment to seeking the release of all Western hostages held in Lebanon. The European Community revoked its ban on senior-level diplomatic contact with Iran in October 1990. The single greatest obstacle to improved relations with the West remained Iran's perceived complicity with pro-Iranian terrorist groups in the holding of Western hostages in Lebanon. All Western hostages finally were released in June 1992. Despite further acts to improve relations with the West, Tehran refuses to revoke the condemnation of Salman Rushdie.

The end of the Iran-Iraq War in 1988, the withdrawal of Soviet forces from Afghanistan in early 1989, and Khomeini's death later in the year helped pave the way toward improved Soviet-Iranian relations. President Mikhail Gorbachev warmly received Rafsanjani in Moscow in June 1989. Negotiations between the two countries resulted in Soviet offers of military aid to Iran and a $15 billion economic development deal under which the Iranians were to purchase Soviet equipment, technology, and expertise.

The dramatic dissolution of the Soviet Union after August 1991 opened up the possibility of a new sphere of Iranian influence in Central Asia. Iran, Saudi Arabia, and Turkey are all vying for influence in the newly independent Muslim republics. While well positioned geopolitically, Iran is at a disadvantage linguistically and also because Central Asians are predominately Sunni Muslims. Lacking the economic resources to pursue its ambitions, Iran is seeking to enhance its position through bilateral agreements and through the revival of the Economic Cooperation Organization comprised of the Central Asian republics, Iran, Turkey, and Pakistan. There has been little warming in the relationship between the United States and Iran. While the release of U.S. hostages and some progress at the U.S.-Iran Claims Tribunal in the Hague, Netherlands, has reduced some of the tension, relations did not improve with the entrance of the Clinton administration. Iran remains for the United States one of the world's premier outlaw states. United States foreign policy toward Iran has remained one of active containment. Washington accuses Iran of fomenting terrorism, threatening its neighbors, assassinating political opponents abroad, and developing nuclear weapons. The Clinton administration has routinely opposed Iranian attempts to obtain international loans, and the United States is persistently trying to persuade allied nations to limit their trade with Iran. Tehran bitterly complains that its efforts to moderate its policies have not led the United States to soften its anti-Iranian policies.

Iran has consistently opposed the U.S.-sponsored Middle East peace talks. The United States accuses Iran of working to subvert the peace process through its active support of the militant Palestinian group Hamas. Iran condemned the September 1993 accord between Israel and the Palestine Liberation Organization, calling it treason. A rapprochement between Israel and its Arab neighbors would deprive Iran of the main issue through which it exercises influence in the Arab world. Consequently, Iran has supported Islamic parties in the Israeli-occupied territories and Hizballah in Lebanon. Although Iran's foreign policy has not been as revolutionary in the 1990s as it was during the Khomeini regime, it has been opportunistic.

## Outlook

The main challenge to Rafsanjani's government will be maintaining the pace of economic change, while keeping public dissatisfaction to a controllable level. The government's economic and financial problems have peaked at the same time as political apathy and demand for social change. Over the next several years the currency devaluation and economic restructuring will cause prices and unemployment to rise, making life even more difficult for weary Iranians. Government statistics indicate that per capita income in 1991 had declined to 50 percent of its pre-revolution figure.

While there is widespread disillusionment with Rafsanjani's government and general discontent about living standards, there is a general perception that there is no alternative to the current regime. The dissatisfied elements in society—the professional and middle classes, merchants, and the working class—merely tolerate rather than support the government, which they view as ineffective and corrupt. Nevertheless, the February 1994 assassination attempt on Rafsanjani and recent rioting indicate that deep and widespread dissatisfaction among the population may be reaching a critical level. The youth are particularly frustrated by social and cultural restrictions. With more than half of the population born after the revolution or too young to remember the shah, the Islamic republic is not a fulfillment of their dreams. They have known nothing but war, economic privation, and restrictive social rules. While politically apathetic, these young Iranians could present a formidable force for social change to the conservative religious leaders.

Iran's difficulty in paying its external debt comes at a time when it is desperate to prove its creditworthiness to attract foreign investment. Iran's options in fending off its creditors are problematic. In accepting Western assistance, Iran's finances would come under a degree of International Monetary Fund supervision. A direct Western role in the economy is anathema to the conservatives and would create serious political problems for Rafsanjani. Iran is hoping that Germany, its largest trading partner, will do a bilateral deal outside the purview of the international agencies.

The fortunes of the Iranian economy are tied to the performance of the petroleum sector. Despite improving performance by nonoil exports, oil still accounts for more than 90 percent of Iran's foreign exchange earnings. Without diversification of the economy, Iran remains vulnerable to the fluctuations of oil prices and market demand. Financial help from abroad will only provide a short reprieve from a financial crisis unless oil prices rise dramatically and the government is able to manage painful cuts in imports.

Internationally, attitudes toward Iran remain hostile. Since 1983 the United States has been leading an international campaign to isolate Iran economically and politically. Meanwhile, the most extreme groups feed off the resentment and suffering of Iranians struggling with deprivation to advance their own conservative agenda. While Iran may receive some help rescheduling its debts from its European creditors, it will otherwise have to cope on its own during this difficult period of transition.

# IRAQ

For seven months in late 1990 and early 1991, Iraq was the center of international attention. Its invasion of Kuwait was perceived as a grave threat to the international oil supply and a brutal attack against a defenseless neighbor. The resulting war in which a multinational coalition expelled Iraq from Kuwait with military force devastated Iraq and left it as one of the most isolated nations in the world.

After the war the United Nations continued to maintain an economic embargo against Iraq, with enforcement by U.S. warships in the Persian Gulf. But there were signs in late 1994 that Iraq's ordeal could soon end. The international community was tiring of the embargo, which prevented Iraq from repaying its international debts or trading with its neighbors. Some nations, however, notably the United States, were insisting that Iraq first abandon its claims to Kuwait.

Despite much of the population's disillusionment with the war and with deprivation created by the embargo, Iraqi president Saddam Hussein has kept a tight hold on power. His mercurial ruthlessness, combined with his domestic terror tactics, his xenophobia, and his political acumen, have enabled him to thwart coup attempts and ethnic upheavals. He has succeeded in building up his own personality cult and presenting himself as the only leader capable of holding Iraq together. Just as he had defied predictions that Iraq's eight-year war of attrition with Iran during the 1980s would lead to his removal, he has withstood Iraq's humiliating defeat in the Persian Gulf War and the hardships that followed. As long as Saddam leads Iraq, it will remain an international pariah.

## Geography

Iraq is located at the northern end of the Persian Gulf. The country's only access to the high seas is a thirty-mile coastline with two major ports, Umm Qasr on the Gulf itself and Basra, which is inland on the confluence of the Tigris and Euphrates rivers. The confluence is called the *Shatt al-Arab,* or "the river of the Arabs." South of Basra the Shatt al-Arab forms the international border between Iraq and Iran. When a river forms an international boundary, it is common to use the center of the main channel, or thalweg line, as the dividing line between countries. In this case the line was drawn down the Iranian bank of the river, giving control of the Shatt al-Arab entirely to Iraq. Over the years the placement of the boundary has been a source of dispute between the two countries, eventually contributing to the outbreak of the Iran-Iraq War in 1980.

A vast alluvial plain lies between Basra, Baghdad (the capital), and the Tigris and Euphrates rivers. This area is interlaced with irrigation canals and small lakes, and much of the land is fertile. Most Iraqis live on these plains near the two cities. The area east and north of where the Shatt al-Arab begins is a large, six-thousand-square-mile marshland that extends into Iran. West of the Euphrates River lies the Syrian desert, which extends into Jordan and Saudi Arabia. The Iraqi highlands cover the region between the cities of

Mosul and Kirkuk north to the Turkish and Iranian borders. Beginning as undulating hills, the land continues to rise to mountains as high as twelve thousand feet. Rainfall in this area, unlike most of the country, is sufficient to support agriculture.

Iraq's most valuable national resource is oil. The largest and most productive fields are around Mosul and Kirkuk. A series of smaller fields are located around Basra in the south. When its oil facilities are fully operational, Iraq has the capacity to produce as much as 3.5 million barrels per day (bpd) for limited periods. In 1988 Iraq's petroleum export earnings were $11.8 billion, second among the members of the Organization of Petroleum Exporting Countries (OPEC) to Saudi Arabia's. The international embargo against Iraq, in place since August 1990, has prohibited the sale of Iraqi oil.

Before the Iran-Iraq War, most of Iraq's oil was moved through pipelines to two oil terminals, at Khor al-Amaya and Mina al-Bakr in the Persian Gulf, where it was loaded onto tankers. Iranian attacks against these offshore terminals and other Iraqi oil facilities early in the war, however, severely reduced Iraqi oil exports. In addition, Syria reached an agreement with the government of Iran in 1982 to shut down the Banias line, a pipeline running from Iraq through Syrian territory to the Mediterranean Sea, in support of Iran's war effort. This prompted Baghdad to launch an ambitious pipeline construction program to avoid Iranian attacks and circumvent the Syrian blockade. Iraq expanded the capacity of a pipeline that runs from the Kirkuk fields to Ceyhan, a Turkish port on the Mediterranean. Iraq also built a pipeline from its southern oil fields to the Trans-Arabian Pipeline that runs to the Red Sea. A third pipeline, capable of carrying 1.6 million bpd across Saudi Arabia to the Red Sea, was under construction in 1989. These pipelines have been shut down as a result of the international embargo. *(Oil pipeline map, Chapter 5, p. 161)*

Aside from oil, Iraq has few natural resources. They include natural gas, produced at the Kirkuk fields and used domestically for power stations; limestone, which gives Iraq the capacity to export limited quantities of cement; salt; and gypsum. Iraq's potential for agricultural production is greater than that of most nations in the Middle East, but this potential has yet to be developed fully. Stone, metallic ore, timber, and other resources must be imported.

## Demography

Iraq's cultural, ethnic, linguistic, and religious diversity stems in part from its history of foreign domination. Once known as *Mesopotamia* or "the land between rivers," Iraq served as a frontier province for the Persian, Greek, Roman, Arab, Mongol, and Turkish empires. It was the Arab invasion in the seventh century A.D. that brought Islam and the Arabic language to Iraq. *Iraq* means "to take root" in Arabic, but no invader ever succeeded in completely conquering the region, and as each empire fell it left a cultural residue that survived succeeding invasions.

One consequence of Iraq's heterogeneous population has been that some subnational groups have never been assimilated into the mainstream of Iraqi society. One-quarter of Iraq's population speaks a language other than Arabic or an Arabic dialect that is unintelligible to the rest of the population. Illiteracy, estimated to be nearly 45 percent in urban areas and as high as 75 percent in the countryside, compounds the problem.

Historically, the religious, communal, ethnic, and linguistic minorities in Iraq have a tendency to identify with their parochial communities rather than with the central governing authority. For example, the early Arab settlers successfully converted the Kurdish inhabitants of the mountainous regions to Islam, but the Kurds retained their own language and hence their ethnic identity.

Religious heresies and schisms added to the already-complex cultural makeup of the region. In the seventh century A.D. the Islamic faith split into the *Sunni* and *Shi'ite* branches. The Shi'ite movement actually began in Iraq and spread rapidly among new converts to Islam who felt excluded from the Arab-dominated faith. Shi'ites

## Key Facts on Iraq

**Area:** 168,754 square miles.
**Capital:** Baghdad.
**Population:** 19,889,666 (1994).
**Religion:** 97 percent Muslim (mostly Shi'ite), 3 percent Christian or others.
**Official Language:** Arabic; Kurdish minority speaks Kurdish.
**GNP:** $38.0 billion; $2,000 per capita (1993).

*Source:* Central Intelligence Agency, *CIA World Factbook 1994.*

can now be found all through the Middle East, and they represent a majority of the population in Iran. Many Shi'ite martyrs are buried in Iraq, and shrines built to their memory attract large numbers of worshippers on holy days.

During Ottoman rule, which lasted from the sixteenth century until World War I, separate religious communities, called *millets,* were granted representation before the provincial Ottoman councils and were self-governing in communal matters. Because of weak or intermittent government, these groups were never forced to adapt their customs to those of most of the population, and they survived as coherent, nearly autonomous entities, often in conflict with the central government and with each other.

Kurds, an estimated 20 percent of the population, predominate in the isolated mountains of the north and are found in large numbers around the oil fields near Kirkuk. Arab Sunni Muslims generally live in the center of the country. Shi'ite Muslims, who make up about 60 percent of Iraq's population, are concentrated in the south around the oil fields near Basra.

## History

Foreign influences have shaped both the modern and ancient history of Iraq. British interests

wanted protection for trade routes from India and, after 1903, the Baghdad Railroad. In 1912, while Iraq was still under Ottoman domination, British, Dutch, and German entrepreneurs obtained a concession to explore for oil in the vicinity of Basra. Two years later the Ottoman Empire allied with Germany in World War I, and the British dispatched an expeditionary force to Iraq from India to maintain control. The British presence continued after the war. In 1920 the Treaty of Sevres placed Iraq and Palestine under a British mandate and Syria under the French. In 1921 the British created a constitutional monarchy in Iraq and placed at its head a Meccan prince, Faisal ibn Hussein (Faisal I), whose acceptance by the people derived from his being a descendant of the Prophet Muhammad. In 1932 Iraq became independent, but British influence over the ruling elite continued for another twenty-eight years.

The concept of nation was an alien one to most Iraqis, who identified more readily with ancient local orientations. Almost as soon as the constitutional monarchy was implanted on Iraqi soil, the process of fragmentation began. The Kurds revolted against the central government in Baghdad between 1922 and 1924. The death of King Faisal I in 1933 ended what political stability there was, and throughout the 1930s communal and tribal factions began to form around groups of European-educated intellectuals who advocated a wide variety of political solutions to Iraq's problems. The first of many coups came in 1936. It was led by anti-British army officers who advocated socialism. They, in turn, were deposed by pro-British and economically conservative officers who placed King Faisal's four-year-old grandson, Faisal II, on the throne in 1939. This last group managed to control Iraq until 1958.

During and after World War II, anti-imperialist sentiments began to grow. Opposition groups demanded the reduction of British influence in the country, the liberalization of politics, and land reform. On July 14, 1958, a group of officers led by Brig. Gen. Abdul Karim Kassim overthrew the Hashemite monarchy. King Faisal II, members of his family, and a number of persons who had assisted him in his rule were executed. The new regime reversed Iraq's international orientation and declared that Iraq was now part of the movement of nonaligned nations. Iraq's foreign policy became controlled by the drive to destroy Israel, which was regarded as the last vestige of imperialism in the Middle East.

The new Iraqi republic established relations with Communist nations and began purchasing military equipment from the Soviet Union. In March 1959 Iraq withdrew from the British-dominated Baghdad Pact, which had been formed four years before. The pact was a mutual defense treaty among Britain, Iran, Iraq, Pakistan, and Turkey. Its formation was promoted by U.S. president Dwight D. Eisenhower to counter potential Soviet aggression in the region. When Iraq withdrew, the organization moved its headquarters to Ankara, Turkey, and changed its name to the Central Treaty Organization (CENTO).

Iraq's domestic policies changed dramatically as well. The new Kassim government enacted land reform laws and greatly liberalized the political system. Previously suppressed segments within the society were granted access to the political process for the first time, and they began to press their parochial demands upon the central government. As a result, ancient local enmities increased as a factor in national politics. In March 1959 army officers from Mosul tried but failed to overthrow the Kassim regime because it was perceived as pro-Communist. In October supporters of Egypt's President Gamal Abdel Nasser unsuccessfully attempted to assassinate Kassim, because they wanted a union between Iraq and Egypt. In 1961 the Kurds launched an armed rebellion because they felt oppressed by the predominantly Arab government. Turks clashed with Kurds, Persians with Arabs, Shi'ite Muslims with Sunnis.

Out of this confusion emerged a group that eventually dominated Iraq's politics. A pan-Arab faction, opposed to the narrow nationalist policies of the Kassim government and in favor of union with Syria, formed the Arab Socialist Resurrection party, better known as the *Ba'ath* party. Aided by sympathetic members of Iraq's officer corps, the

Ba'ath party seized power in February 1963. It lost control nine months later as the result of a coup engineered by a pro-Nasser group of officers led by Col. Abdul Salem Arif. The Ba'athists were branded "deviationists" by the Arif regime, and many were forced to flee to Syria. In 1964 Arif created a joint presidency council that was intended to hasten the union of Egypt and Iraq, scheduled to take place in 1966. Later in 1964 Arif was killed in a plane crash and was succeeded by his brother, Abdul Rahman Arif.

Although it was obvious that union with Egypt was impractical, Abdul Rahman created an officially sponsored Iraqi Arab Socialist Union, patterned after the Egyptian model. It was intended to mobilize popular support for the regime's modernization schemes and to serve as the main channel of communication between the government and the people. It failed on both counts. By 1968 the Arif government had ruined the national economy and faced serious internal opposition.

A coup in July 1968 brought the Ba'athists back to power. Officers aligned with the Ba'ath party were led by Maj. Gen. Ahmed Hassan al-Bakr, a key figure in the 1958 and 1963 coups. He assumed the presidency and set a harsh authoritarian tone for his regime by directing that "all spies for the United States, Israel, imperialism, and Zionism" be arrested. A former president, two former prime ministers, numerous high-ranking officers, and prominent members of the Shi'ite Muslim and Kurdish communities were executed.

Many analysts have theorized that the driving force behind the new regime was al-Bakr's second in command and distant cousin, Saddam Hussein. Saddam's organization of a secret police force had been an important factor in the relatively easy Ba'ath seizure of power. Saddam began to enhance his personal position through contacts outside the party. His ties to the military resulted in his amassing supreme military rank and honors and even obtaining advanced degrees in military science. Saddam was able to gain the loyalty of key officers, in part by sponsoring a military build-up unparalleled in the Arab world.

Authoritarianism soon became the norm inside Iraq. Party and nonparty purges were routine. Saddam had experience in these matters; he allegedly had served as a Ba'ath party executioner in his early days and reportedly killed his brother-in-law because of his Communist party activities.

In 1979 Saddam eliminated all pretenses of power by placing al-Bakr under arrest and assuming the presidency himself. Saddam then embarked on a campaign to establish his own cult. Young Iraqis were taught Ba'ath party doctrine, and Saddam was extolled in literature, music, and film. Thirty-foot portraits of Saddam were erected in every city. His media image was carefully orchestrated to display him in various ethnic garbs and in every station of life. These careful efforts helped establish Saddam as the unchallenged leader of Iraq.

## Ba'athism

Ba'athism is first and foremost a pan-Arab movement with broad appeal to the diverse sectarian interests in Iraq. The party regards existing national borders as West-imposed artificial barriers that must one day be eliminated if Arab unity is to be achieved. During the 1970s this viewpoint

led to poor relations with some conservative Arab states, whose leaders were reluctant to relinquish their national identity for unity in an all-Arab federation presumably led by either Egypt or Iraq.

The philosophy of the Ba'ath party is central to Iraq's political organization and policies. Ba'ath socialism emerged during the 1940s when European policies toward Middle Eastern nations were particularly oppressive and when Jewish immigration to Palestine was a major Arab concern. The party's founders were three Paris-educated, middle-class Syrians—one a Sunni Muslim, one a Greek Orthodox Christian, and one a member of an extremist Shi'ite sect. Its basic tenets were pan-Arab, secular, and Socialist. They rejected communism as contrary to pan-Arabism and lacking in the spiritual qualities essential to the Arab way of life. Their national Socialist approach was meant to include all Arabs as a single indivisible political unit; that is, the Arab nation.

The Ba'ath party maintains that ethnic and linguistic modes of identity should be suppressed. Socialism is upheld as the only way to destroy the traditional Arab aristocracy and extend economic benefits to the lower classes. Private ownership of homes, businesses, and agricultural plots is permitted, but the renting of buildings and tenant farming is not.

A major factor in the Iraqi Ba'ath party's survival has been its capacity to control all the important functions of organized society. At each echelon of the state structure, beginning with local governments, there is a functionally parallel party organization that oversees the performance of the bureaucracy, sometimes even performing the bureaucratic service itself. Party links to the national level provide a line of vertical communication parallel to but distinct from that of the state. The heads of important bureaucracies are frequently high-ranking party members. At lower levels, the second in charge of an office often is a high-ranking party member who reports on his superior's performance and loyalty. Even Iraqi embassies have Ba'ath party cells, and Iraq's ambassador may not be the highest-ranking party member on the embassy's staff.

Party membership is selective and usually requires a long period of apprenticeship. There are only an estimated twenty-five thousand full party members, less than 0.2 percent of the population. If a member's behavior is judged by party leaders to be disloyal, scandalous, or imprudent, that member can be expelled from the party, imprisoned, or even executed.

During the early 1960s the Syrian and Iraqi Ba'ath parties were united, but in 1966 they split over differences concerning international issues and party leadership. Decision making in Iraq is centralized in the Ba'ath party's Revolutionary Command Council chaired by Saddam Hussein. Saddam, as president, commander in chief of the armed forces, head of the Ba'ath party, and prime minister—a position he assumed in May 1994—exerts nearly total control over Iraq's political system.

## Iran-Iraq War

The war with Iran overshadowed all other issues in Iraq from September 22, 1980, when Iraq attacked Iran, until Iran agreed to a cease-fire on July 18, 1988. Saddam Hussein's objective was to regain total control over the Shatt al-Arab. In addition, he hoped that an Iranian military defeat would cause the fall of the Ayatollah Khomeini.

At the time of the Iraqi attack the Iranian government appeared to be vulnerable. Eighteen months after the revolution in Iran, individuals and groups were still struggling for influence within the government, and the military was in total disarray following the purges of officers who had supported the shah.

A year after the war began, however, it became obvious that the Iraqi government had miscalculated. Initial success quickly turned to failure as a combination of poor strategy and equally bad tactical execution brought the invasion to a halt. By June 1982 Iran had driven the Iraqi army back to its own borders. Saddam announced a unilateral cease-fire and expressed a willingness to negotiate through the Saudi Arabian government and other potential mediators. Iran ignored the proposals and in July 1982 launched an attack across the border

*Saddam Hussein*

toward Basra. The Iranian offensive was stopped by the Iraqi army and the war degenerated into a bloody stalemate on Iraqi territory.

In the first years of the war, Iraq had few international supporters. The Ba'ath party's repressive treatment of the Communists in 1977 and the greater geopolitical importance the Soviet Union placed on Iran led Moscow to suspend the delivery of military weapons to Iraq. Soon after the war began, Syria, Libya, and North Korea began supplying Iran with Soviet military equipment, apparently with Moscow's blessings. The Soviet Union did not resume arms shipments to Iraq until late 1983. The conservative Arab nations on the Persian Gulf initially hedged their support for Iraq out of concern that Iran might retaliate against them. At first the only Western nation that supported Iraq's war effort was France.

As the war dragged on, however, and as Iran's foreign policy became more aggressive, the Arab states and some nations in the West backed Iraq in the conflict. Although hesitant initially, Jordan, Kuwait, and Saudi Arabia expedited the transport of consumer goods through their ports to compensate for Iraq's closing of its port facilities. Moreover, Saudi Arabia, Kuwait, and other Gulf states had extended Iraq tens of billions of dollars in aid and interest-free loans. To compensate for Iraq's loss of oil revenues, Saudi Arabia and Kuwait agreed to sell three hundred thousand barrels a day of their own oil to Iraq's customers, with the understanding that Iraq would pay it back at some future time.

Fearing the consequences of an Iranian victory, Western and most Arab nations continued supporting Iraq, despite internal repression by Saddam's regime, Iraq's attacks on neutral ships doing business with Iran, and Iraq's use of brutal tactics, including air strikes against Iranian cities and poison gas attacks against Iranian troops. In part because of the war, Iraq and the United States restored diplomatic relations on November 26, 1984. Iraq had severed ties in June 1967 because of U.S. support for Israel in the Six-Day War. In 1986 the renewed U.S.-Iraqi relationship was hurt by the disclosure that the administration of President Ronald Reagan had sold arms to Iran in an effort to build contacts among Iranian moderates and win the release of American hostages held in Lebanon. Iraq also accused the United States of providing it with false intelligence information. In May 1987 an Iraqi jet mistakenly fired a missile at the USS *Stark,* killing thirty-seven crew members. The United States accepted Iraq's explanation that the attack was an accident. The relationship improved that summer when the United States began naval patrols in the Persian Gulf to halt Iranian attacks on Kuwaiti ships. But another setback came in 1988 when the Reagan administration vigorously condemned Iraq for using chemical weapons against Kurdish rebels and civilians.

After several Iranian offensives in 1986 and 1987 failed to capture Basra, Iraqi forces pushed the exhausted Iranians back across the border in the spring and summer of 1988, causing Iran finally to accept a cease-fire. Although the war ended with Iraqi victories that allowed Saddam to claim success, the eight-year Iraqi war had left hundreds of thousands of Iraqis dead, while achieving none of Saddam's goals. Moreover, the Iran-Iraq War seriously damaged Iraq's economy by reducing oil exports and forcing huge expenditures on defense. To pay for the war Iraq went into debt and liberally injected new currency into its economy. The resulting inflation reduced the value of the Iraqi dinar and squeezed most workers who had to be content with prewar salaries. A period of economic recovery during which Iraq could pump and sell oil reserves at capacity was needed to rebuild the country.

## Invasion of Kuwait

The outcome of the war with Iran had both strengthened and weakened Saddam's position. Iraqi society was exhausted by the war, and its debts totaled a staggering $80 billion. Yet as the leader of the nation that had turned back the Iranian threat, Saddam's prestige among other Arab leaders was enhanced. The war also had resulted in a larger, battle-hardened Iraqi military, and Saddam took advantage of the end of the war to crush domestic opposition. Given these advantages and Saddam's perceptions that Iraq was owed a debt of gratitude by the rest of the Arab world, he was not content to preside over a quiet period of rebuilding.

During the first half of 1990 Saddam and his lieutenants bitterly denounced what he perceived as cheating on oil production quotas by Kuwait and the United Arab Emirates. In Saddam's view the high oil production rates of these countries was keeping prices low and reducing Iraqi oil revenues. Saddam's agenda was soon revealed to be broader than raising oil prices.

On August 2, 1990, Iraqi forces drove into Kuwait and occupied the country after facing minimal resistance. Saddam declared Kuwait to be Iraq's "nineteenth province" and announced Iraq's intention to annex it permanently. Saddam, however, did not anticipate the strong international response to his invasion. Led by the United States, the world community viewed Iraq's invasion as brutal aggression that gave Baghdad control over a large portion of the world's oil supply. The United States and its allies, including Saudi Arabia and the Persian Gulf states, moved to contain the Iraqi threat. Within a few weeks tens of thousands of foreign troops were deployed to defend Saudi Arabia and its oil fields from another Iraqi military thrust. By the end of the year, more than half a million troops had reached the Gulf region and were preparing to expel Iraq from Kuwait.

American policy toward Iraq focused on persuading Iraq—and Saddam Hussein in particular—that the United States and its allies were serious about waging war and that, if war came, Iraq would lose. American policy makers thought that Saddam's instinct for survival would lead him to withdraw from Kuwait if he believed he and his army were threatened. If he refused to pull his army out, they reasoned, it was only because he grossly overestimated his army's capabilities or believed that the United States was bluffing.

Evidence suggests that Saddam was not convinced the United States would go to war against him, especially if the war was likely to be a long one. According to the Iraqi transcript of the July 25, 1990, meeting in Baghdad between Saddam and U.S. ambassador April Glaspie, he remarked, "Yours is a society which cannot accept 10,000 dead in one battle." Arab, European, and American diplomats who had dealt with him in the past had reported that U.S. behavior during the Vietnam War had greatly influenced his opinions about the United States. Saddam's strategy seemed to be to present the United States with the prospect of a very bloody war by heavily fortifying Kuwait. If U.S. leaders perceived that coalition casualties would be high, they would be unlikely to order an attack.

If the coalition did attack, Saddam hoped that by inflicting heavy casualties Iraqi forces might cause American public backing for the war to erode, as it had during the Vietnam War. Such an erosion of support could force the Bush administration to seek a negotiated peace on terms favorable to Iraq. Iraq's experience in the Iran-Iraq War, during which well-fortified Iraqi defenders had inflicted appalling casualties on Iranian attackers, may have colored Saddam's judgment about how the battle would proceed.

It is possible, however, that Saddam accepted the impending war with the U.S.-led coalition even though he understood that by not leaving Kuwait he was subjecting his forces to an attack, probably with devastating results. In adopting this suicidal strategy, Saddam would have been seeking an outcome to war like those achieved by President Gamal Abdel Nasser, ruler of Egypt from 1954 to 1970. Nasser, an early hero of Saddam Hussein, had manufactured political victories out of two military defeats: the 1956 Suez crisis and the 1967 Six-Day War with Israel. During the Suez crisis British, French, and Israeli forces occupied the Sinai Peninsula and captured the Suez Canal; they later withdrew under pressure from President Eisenhower. During the Six-Day War, Israel easily crushed Egyptian forces and again captured the Sinai. Yet in both cases Nasser's regime survived and his reputation was strengthened. By taking on Israel and presenting himself as the leader of pan-Arabists, Nasser's prestige remained unmatched in the Arab world.

Saddam's confrontation of a coalition made up of the United States, former European colonial powers, wealthy Gulf Arab states, and others already had made him the most popular leader in many areas of the Arab world. If his forces could give the coalition a good fight and strike a few blows against Israel, Saddam would become a legend among dispossessed Arabs frustrated by Arab military weakness and passivity. Through military defeat, Saddam, like Nasser, could solidify his reputation as the only Arab leader willing to go to war to defend Arab rights and interests. In the process, he could weaken pro-Western Arab regimes that had sided with the coalition.

The theory that Saddam Hussein invited war is supported by his half-hearted efforts to avoid it. During the crisis Arab and Western officials put forward numerous diplomatic plans that were designed to allow the Iraqis to save face. None of them were seized with sufficient vigor or flexibility by Saddam and his diplomats to achieve a negotiated settlement. Saddam even rebuffed two last-minute diplomatic initiatives by the French and by UN Secretary General Javier Pérez de Cuéllar, when a positive response could have yielded substantial propaganda benefits.

## Gulf War

The short Gulf War that began on January 17, 1991, proved to be a disaster for Iraq. Before invading Iraq and Kuwait with ground forces, coalition aircraft carried out a thirty-seven-day bombing campaign that severely damaged Iraqi military industries and civilian infrastructure. Iraq was virtually helpless against the high-tech assault of Western aircraft. Rather than see its air force destroyed, Iraq sent more than one hundred warplanes to former-enemy Iran, which impounded them.

When the ground attack came on February 24, Saddam's vaunted army collapsed. Tens of thousands of Iraqi troops gave up without firing a shot, and whole Iraqi tank units were obliterated by the coalition blitzkrieg. In addition, despite several Iraqi conventional missile attacks against Israel, the Arab nations that had joined the U.S.-led effort remained firmly in the coalition. Saddam was celebrated in the occupied territories and in Palestinian refugee camps, but the magnitude of his army's defeat limited his heroic appeal in most of the Arab world.

One hundred hours after the ground attack began, U.S. president George Bush ordered a cease-fire. Iraq signed agreements committing it to abide by a series of tough UN Security Council resolutions establishing its postwar conduct. The international embargo that had been imposed shortly after the Iraqi invasion of Kuwait remained in force. Yet despite the military disaster Saddam survived in power.

## Ethnic Rebellion

The Iraqi defeat caused the Kurdish minority in northern Iraq and the Shi'ites in the south to rebel against Saddam. Early in the fighting during March 1991 it appeared that these rebellions might pose a danger to Saddam Hussein's regime. Despite the vast amount of military equipment lost during the Gulf War, however, Saddam still had enough military muscle in reserve to put down the rebellions.

The two rebel movements were grounded in their histories of discrimination and deprivation. Sunni control of the leadership structure has long been resented and opposed by the Shi'ite Muslims and the Kurds. Of these two groups the Shi'ites pose the most complex political problems for Saddam's regime. They form an impoverished and politically excluded majority of the Iraqi population. Historically, they were herders organized in tribal systems far from the settled areas. As a result, their representation in the bureaucracy and in the military has been low compared with their proportion of the whole population. Centuries of rule by the Sunni Muslim Ottoman Turks, and until 1958 by a Sunni Muslim Arab monarchy, reinforced their exclusion from the inner circles of power. The wretched living conditions in most Shi'ite villages prompted a massive urbanization of the poorest and least educated of their number and have given rise to sprawling urban slums. By the mid-1980s more than 60 percent of Iraq's population lived in urban areas, and most new arrivals in major cities came from the poorest Shi'ite districts in the south.

The Iranian revolution of 1979 radicalized existing Shi'ite political movements. After the outbreak of war, Iran's Arabic language broadcasts referred to Iraq's most distinguished and popular Shi'ite legist, Sayyid Muhammad Bakr al-Sadr, as the "Khomeini of Iraq." In 1980 Saddam executed him along with seven other Shi'ite leaders, six of them Iranian, who were suspected of involvement with antigovernment Shi'ite terrorist organizations.

Kurds live not only in Iraq but also in Iran and Turkey, and in smaller numbers in Syria and the Soviet Union. Kurds are Sunni Muslims but their Kurdish identity is salient. Their society was once tribal in organization, but insecurity resulting from conflict with the Iraqi, Turkish, and Iranian governments led to urbanization. Power has shifted away from the traditional feudal upper class to a growing urban intelligentsia. The emergence of this Kurdish intelligentsia has increased Kurdish national pride, which keeps hope alive for an autonomous Kurdish state.

Between 1961 and 1970 five major conflicts erupted between Kurdish tribes and Iraqi armed forces. After nearly a decade of intermittent guerrilla warfare a stalemate resulted, with the Kurds occupying the highlands and the Iraqi army holding the valleys.

By 1974 Kurdish forces had become better equipped and more numerous—an estimated hundred thousand strong. They occupied favorable terrain and had proved themselves to be excellent mountain fighters. Because of these factors they saw no reason to be accommodating. War broke out again in 1975, but this time a reequipped and retrained Iraqi army soon gained the upper hand, driving Kurdish forces to the Iranian border. The shah of Iran supplied military equipment to the Iraqi Kurds, but he was unwilling to use his armed forces against Iraq in their behalf.

In March 1975 the shah and Saddam Hussein, who was then vice president, met in Algiers and reached an agreement: the shah pledged to end his support for the Kurds while Iraq granted Iran navigational rights in the Shatt al-Arab. As a result of the agreement, the Kurds were forced to capitulate. Many were imprisoned, and more than two hundred of their leaders were executed. Thousands fled to Iran to escape further suppression by Baghdad.

When Khomeini deposed the shah in 1979, relations between Baghdad and Tehran deteriorated. The Algiers agreement collapsed and the Kurdish movement surfaced again. The war between Iran and Iraq that began in 1980 prevented Saddam's regime from focusing its armed might against the Kurds. Soon after a cease-fire was concluded in the summer of 1988, however, Baghdad initiated a military campaign to break Kurdish resistance. This campaign drew international condemnation, in part because of strong evidence that the Iraqi army used poison gas against Kurdish villages and camps in northern Iraq. Thousands of Kurds fled into Turkey to escape the Iraqi army.

The 1991 rebellions had divergent goals. The Iraqi Kurdistan Front, a coalition of the two largest Kurdish parties, wanted to establish an independent Kurdish state in northern Iraq. The Shi'ites, who comprise a majority of Iraq's population (Saddam Hussein is a Sunni Muslim), hoped to overthrow Saddam and establish a Shi'ite government in Baghdad. They were less organized than the Kurds, but they were receiving support from Iran's Shi'ite government.

Saddam's success at crushing the Kurdish and Shi'ite rebellions led Washington to take steps to protect these minorities. No-fly zones patrolled by American warplanes were established into which Iraqi aircraft could not fly. The Kurds received substantial U.S. humanitarian aid totaling more than a half billion dollars. The Shi'ites received more modest humanitarian aid.

The United States has been reluctant, however, to provide full backing for a Kurdish state or a Shi'ite rebellion. Washington policy makers fear that the success of such movements could splinter Iraq and open the way for Iranian dominance of the Gulf region. Nevertheless, the U.S. support for the no-fly zones has been portrayed by Baghdad as evidence of an international conspiracy to dismember Iraq. Many Iraqis do not want to see this happen and regard Saddam's regime as the only alternative to civil war.

## International Containment

Although Iraq did not repudiate the UN Security Council resolutions it had agreed to abide by after the Gulf War, it resisted implementation of them. In particular, Iraq resisted intrusive inspections by international investigators aimed at preventing a resumption of Iraq's programs to develop nuclear, chemical, and biological weapons. This attitude of defiance has caused the UN Security Council to continue the international embargo against Iraq.

Saddam's resistance also prompted President Bush and President Bill Clinton to take military action against Iraq. On January 13, 1993, a week before Bush left office, more than a hundred U.S. and allied warplanes attacked Iraq in retaliation for Iraqi incursions into Kuwait and Baghdad's refusal to cooperate with the international arms inspection efforts. On June 26, 1993, Clinton ordered a coordinated cruise missile strike against the Iraqi Intelligence Service headquarters in Baghdad. That attack was ordered after evidence showed that Iraq was behind a foiled assassination plot against former president Bush when he visited Kuwait earlier in the year. These attacks came as a psychological blow to those Iraqis who had hoped that the international embargo might be lifted against Iraq during 1993.

The pressure of the embargo led Saddam's regime on November 26, 1993, to formally announce that it would cooperate fully with international arms inspectors charged with verifying that Iran was not holding or building weapons of mass destruction.

In September 1994 an elaborate monitoring system was about to be activated. The system included cameras and high-tech monitoring equipment installed at as many as two hundred industrial and military installations throughout Iraq, unannounced searches by teams of inspectors, U.S. spy plane overflights, and patrolling helicopters equipped with radiation and chemical detection gear. Despite the unprecedented scope and intrusiveness of the monitoring effort, inspectors admitted that no system of verification would be foolproof.

Iraq's agreement to these procedures satisfied the most important condition for lifting the international embargo. This development led to a sharp dispute in the UN Security Council over how to proceed with Iraq. By early 1995 the inspection system would have gone through a trial period, and sentiment among several key nations was strongly in favor of lifting the embargo at that time. Turkey, in particular, voiced its opposition to sanctions, which were harming its own economy. Russia, China, and France also indicated their desire to see the sanctions lifted. The United States and Great Britain argued that such a move would be premature. They

insisted that the embargo stay in place until Iraq renounces its claims to Kuwait and recognizes the Iraqi-Kuwaiti border.

In early October 1994 Iraq gambled that it could bring about an end to international sanctions through calculated military pressure. Saddam redeployed at least two divisions of his well-trained Republican Guard troops to positions close to the Kuwaiti border. The Iraqi regime appeared to have hoped that the United States and other members of the coalition would not want to undertake an open-ended counter deployment in Kuwait. If they did not, Saddam would have considerable leverage in demanding that the sanctions be lifted, despite the weakness of his army relative to what it had been in 1990.

Saddam's gamble backfired. President Clinton ordered thirty-six thousand U.S. troops to Kuwait and Saudi Arabia, as well as aircraft carriers and additional air force squadrons. Within days, Iraqi forces backed away from their positions near the Kuwait border. Instead of eroding support for the sanctions, Iraq's aggressive move reinforced perceptions that Saddam's regime could not be trusted, and it strengthened the arguments of the United States and Great Britain to keep the sanctions in place. The Clinton administration declared that it intended to expand permanent U.S. military capabilities in the region to counter any further Iraqi threat.

## Economy

Evidence from inside Iraq suggested that the international embargo was devastating Iraq's economy. Iraq's inability to sell oil in the international marketplace left it without a source of revenue to buy food and consumer goods. Even though food and medicine were exempt from the embargo, the Iraqi government could not afford them in quantities to take care of its population. In addition, Saddam continued his practice of taking care of the needs of the army first.

In the months after the Gulf War, despite shortages of consumer goods and other sacrifices, Western observers in Baghdad noted that Iraqi daily life had not been overly disrupted. Through a decade of war, with only a brief interruption, the Iraqi people had become accustomed to deprivation.

Inflation was soaring by 1994, however, and shortages of consumer goods had become severe. Some basic items were doubling in price in a week's time during the summer. In the four years following the Iraqi invasion of Kuwait, consumer prices had risen approximately 1,500 percent. Because of the rapid inflation, a system of rationing had been established and a thriving black market had developed. Saddam attempted to deal with the black market through draconian punishments, including amputations of hands, but the desperate situation of many people perpetuated economic crimes. Because Saddam was unable to pay government officials their full salaries, his regime has tolerated corruption among bureaucrats and police as an alternative means of compensation.

The hard economic times led better-educated Iraqis to seek exit permits to leave the country. This trend has drained Iraq of many of its most productive citizens. The task of rebuilding will be complicated by the flight of talent and the already low level of education in Iraqi society.

The Iraqi government has been courting foreign companies to establish operations in Iraq as soon as the embargo is lifted. European and Japanese investors have traveled to Baghdad in large numbers to evaluate future business opportunities. But while foreign investment is essential, it was unlikely that it would constitute a panacea for Iraq's economic problems. Most investors will seek a role in rebuilding Iraq's infrastructure or involvement in Iraq's one profitable industry—oil. Other industries devastated by the war and the embargo could remain moribund.

## Outlook

Iraqi society impatiently awaits the end of the international embargo. Given the attitude of the United States government, it could continue for a number of years. It is also possible some arrangement will be concluded under which a partial lifting of the embargo is implemented to relieve the economic burden of nations bordering Iraq and those that are owed money by Iraq.

Once it is lifted a flurry of economic activity will occur. Iraq will pump all the oil it can to provide a quick infusion of cash to speed the rebuilding process. This will have implications for the international price of oil, which could fall as a result of a major oil producer's coming back into the market. Ironically, such a development would lower the per-barrel revenue coming into Iraq. Yet Saddam will not be in a position to limit production.

Iraq's huge oil reserves provide hope for its people that when the embargo is lifted the recovery may come quickly. Iraq also has more agricultural potential than any country in the Middle East. Yet the departure of many well-educated Iraqis during the embargo period will cause the Iraqi economy to depend even more heavily on oil revenues for basic sustenance.

Although Saddam will not have the resources to pursue an aggressive agenda for some years, his implacable hostility toward the West will make him a threat as long as he is in power. Despite the presence of international arms inspectors who will complicate Iraqi weapons development programs, few analysts expect Saddam to give up his goal of obtaining nuclear weapons.

Throughout his reign, Saddam Hussein has demonstrated his adeptness at clinging to power amidst numerous threats. The end of the international embargo will not end the threats to his regime. Kurds in the north and Shi'ites concentrated in the south will continue to clamor for autonomy and power. But the gravest threat to Saddam Hussein's regime may be the military itself. Saddam has attempted to maintain the predominance of the civilian wing of the Ba'ath party by placing trusted allies and members of his family in key command and intelligence positions within the military establishment. Nevertheless, he must constantly guard against coup attempts by the military, such as the one reported to have occurred in December 1988 that led to several executions. Since the Gulf War there have been many rumors of internal opposition to Saddam brought on by Iraq's deteriorating conditions.

As long as Saddam's regime stays in power, it will continue to dominate the political system through repression and stringent organizational control. Should Hussein be removed for any reason, the pervasiveness of the Ba'ath party in Iraqi society offers the possibility for a smooth transfer of political power to his successor. An orderly transition is contingent, however, upon general agreement within the party concerning who the successor should be. If that agreement is absent, it is likely that the religious, communal, ethnic, and linguistic rivalries that have caused so much violence for centuries will dominate Iraq's political scene.

# ISRAEL

During the entire existence of Israel, hostile relations with Arab neighbors have been the central feature of the country's political, economic, and social condition. The Jewish state has never known a time of complete peace. It has fought five wars against the Arabs—in 1948, 1956, 1967, 1973, and 1982—as well as innumerable skirmishes and a continuous war against Palestinian nationalism and its political manifestation—the Palestine Liberation Organization (PLO).

This situation led Israel early on to develop its military into the most potent fighting force in the region. It also developed an unacknowledged nuclear weapons capability and the means to deliver nuclear weapons efficiently. Throughout the 1970s and 1980s, Israel positioned itself as a staunchly pro-American power, keeping its borders secure through a strategy of deterrence based on its military strength. All of its defensive might, however, could not insulate Israel from the more subtle, yet explosive, threat from within.

Ruling more than a million Palestinians in the occupied territories seized by Israel during the Six-Day War in 1967 has proven to be a bloody and costly task, particularly since 1987 when the sustained Palestinian uprising known as the *intifada* began. The economic and human costs of occupation made Israelis increasingly eager for peace.

After the elections of 1992 brought Yitzhak Rabin and his Labor party back to power, Israel began a more concerted diplomatic effort to construct a compromise with the Palestinians and neighboring Arab states. In the early 1990s the collapse of the Soviet Union, the chief financial patron and arms supplier of the Arabs, and the decisive defeat of Iraq during the Persian Gulf War had strengthened Israel's negotiating position. With encouragement from Washington, a peace process ensued with the PLO and subsequently Jordan that has produced agreements ending their state of war with Israel and initiating a transfer of autonomy to the Palestinians in the occupied territories. Chances that the ongoing peace process could eventually bring tranquility to the region have brightened prospects not only for Israel's national security but also for its economy.

Today, Israel is enmeshed in negotiations with the PLO over the creation, character, and consequences of an autonomous Palestinian state in the West Bank and Gaza Strip. Considered an impossibility at the beginning of the decade, meetings between Israeli leaders and PLO representatives have been convened to iron out the details of Palestinian self-rule in Gaza and designated areas of the West Bank. These issues include the nature of a Palestinian police force, the status of Jewish settlers, border crossing arrangements, water rights, timing of the transfer of autonomy, and financing of the Palestinian administration of services.

Even if these and other contentious issues can be resolved as the negotiation of transferring autonomy moves forward, the peace process is threatened by violent rejectionists on both the Arab and Israeli sides who are not in favor of compromise. While the initial agreements have brought Israelis an increased sense of national security, fear and

# Key Facts on Israel

**Area:** 8,019 square miles.

**Capital:** Jerusalem; Tel Aviv is the diplomatic capital recognized by the United States.

**Population:** 5,050,850 (1994).

**Religion:** Predominantly Judaism (82 percent); Arab minority is largely Muslim (14 percent, mostly Sunni), 2 percent Christian, 2 percent Druze and others.

**Official Language:** Hebrew; Arabic is used by 15 percent of the population; English is widely spoken.

**GDP:** $65.7 billion; $13,350 per capita (1993).

*Source:* Central Intelligence Agency, *CIA World Factbook 1994.*

bloodshed have not abated. Suicide car bombings and other acts of terrorism by extremists have rocked Israel and Jewish targets overseas.

The immediate challenge for Israeli leaders will be to keep Arab and Jewish extremists from disrupting a process that even in the most stable environments is fraught with hurdles. The success of the peace process will depend on the Palestinian authorities' demonstrating that they can administer their territories without having the security of Israel or its people unreasonably threatened. Even if the autonomy experiment succeeds, there will be difficult issues to resolve before a Palestinian state can be created. The status of Jerusalem, cherished by both sides as a holy place, poses a particular challenge.

## Geography

A small country about the size of New Jersey, Israel is sandwiched between the Mediterranean Sea and a crescent of Arab nations: Lebanon to the north, Syria to the northeast, Jordan and the West Bank to the east, and Egypt to the southwest. Despite its size, Israel contains three disparate geographical regions: the coastal plain where most of the population resides, running from Haifa south to Tel Aviv; the Galilee region in the north, hilly and lush, and dominated by the Sea of Galilee; and the Negev Desert in the south, lacking material and natural resources.

Most of the country enjoys a temperate climate, except for the Negev, which is hot and dry throughout the year. Water is an important commodity in Israel because of the small amount of rainfall: twenty-eight inches annually in the north, nineteen to twenty-one inches in the central regions, and only one to eight inches in the Negev. Large investments have been made on desalinization, irrigation, and water conservation projects and water has featured prominently in Israel's disputes with Syria, Jordan, and Palestinians on the West Bank.

Almost totally devoid of natural resources of commercial value, Israel in its early years concentrated on agricultural production. Chemical manufacturing, diamond cutting and polishing, and developing high-technology products with commercial and military applications have surpassed agriculture as the most important areas of Israel's modern economy. One out of four Israeli workers today is employed directly or indirectly by the arms industry. Even the *kibbutz,* the Socialist agricultural cooperatives that were the most prominent and literal expression of the Jews' "Return to the Land," now earn more of their income through manufacturing than agricultural production.

## Demography

What Israel lacks in natural resources, it makes up for in the human talent of a culturally diverse population. Israel is a nation of immigrants. Israelis originate from more than a hundred countries. Among Israel's Jewish population, 57 percent are native born, 24 percent hail from Europe and the Western Hemisphere, and 19 percent were born in Asia and Africa. Those of Western origin—the original Zionist "pioneers" and ideologues—are called *Ashkenazim.* Jews from Eastern lands, including Spain, Turkey, Greece, Iraq, and Morocco, are called *Sephardim*. Sephardim and their native offspring now make up 60 percent of the Jewish population. Israel's Arab population is approximately 15 percent of the total.

The creation of the state of Israel in 1948 brought about significant demographic changes. During the course of hostilities, more than a half-million Palestinian Arabs living in what was to become the Jewish state fled or were expelled, ensuring an overwhelming Jewish majority of approximately 85 percent in the new nation.

Both the aftermath of the Holocaust and the formation of the Jewish state created conditions for a large-scale "ingathering" of Jews in Israel. In 1948 one hundred thousand Jews languishing in European "displaced persons'" camps emigrated to Israel. The next year saw a massive influx of Jewish immigrants, including two hundred fifty thousand from Turkey, Libya, Poland, and Romania, and almost fifty thousand from Yemen alone. From May 1950 to December 1951, Israel organized the emigration of one hundred thirteen thousand Iraqi Jews.

As a result of this influx, by 1951 Israel's 1948 Jewish population of six hundred fifty thousand had more than doubled to 1.4 million. Not surprisingly, the population boom strained the resources of the young country. Many new immigrants, especially the largely poor, illiterate masses of Sephardim, were forced to live in shantytowns far from the established Jewish settlements along the coastal plain, breeding a resentment that contributed to Labor's ouster in 1977. By 1992 the Sephardim, disillusioned with the Likud party, helped bring the Labor party back to power.

Much has been made of the antagonisms that exist within the Jewish community between Ashkenazim and Sephardim. These differences are as much the product of the economic gulf dividing the two communities as any cultural dissimilarities. The Ashkenazis are Israel's founders. Political Zionism is a European creed; the institutions of the state—the Knesset (parliament), the kibbutz economy, and most significantly the army—are Ashkenazi creations, to which the Sephardic majority has come late and the Arab minority hardly at all.

Israel's leadership welcomed the waves of Sephardic immigration in the 1950s, but the key to their integration into Israeli life was predicated on their adoption of the dominant Ashkenazi culture. Israeli society was European and reflected the traditions of Ashkenazi Jews, who viewed their coreligionists from Yemen and Iraq with disdain and not a little chauvinism. This kind of assimilation proved impossible for Sephardim, who possessed a varied and vibrant heritage of their own. In addition, their comparatively large families, lack of education, and meager financial resources put them at additional disadvantage.

The disparities dividing the two Jewish communities remain. In educational and economic achievement and political representation, the Sephardic majority still has not overcome structural barriers established in previous generations. Particularly when there is a recession, the poor Jewish residents of the inner city and development towns, along with Israeli Arabs, feel the brunt of retrenchment and cutbacks in state services.

Israel's Arab minority are ostensibly full members of Israel's political culture. They vote, and Arab politicians are present in the Knesset. As a community, however, they suffer as non-Jews in a Jewish state. This prejudiced condition is apparent in economic development and government assistance, education, employment, and housing—all sectors where state-supported discrimination exists and is supported by law.

The most recent wave of immigration has been composed of Jews from the former Soviet Union, particularly Russians. A much smaller number have recently emigrated from Ethiopia. Highly educated and ambitious, new Russian immigrants to Israel numbered more than half a million in 1993—approximately 10 percent of Israel's population—and their numbers are still increasing. They have swelled the percentage of Israelis born outside the state to more than 41 percent. Because many scientists and engineers have emigrated to Israel, the Jewish state now boasts the highest proportion of those professions per capita in the world.

Immigrant absorption is a monumental task. For each hundred thousand arrivals, there is a need for at least twenty thousand new jobs, thirty thousand housing units, and a proportional increase in other essential services, such as health care and education. Fully franchised, the new Russian immigrants have already had a significant impact on the political, economic, and cultural landscape of Israel. For example, by some estimates Russian voters helped the Labor party secure four parliamentary seats in the 1992 elections, contributing to a historic victory over Likud, whose policies many Russians felt were inadequately addressing their social and economic needs.

## Government and Religion

Israel has a parliamentary form of government: the prime minister is the head of government and the president is the head of state. The powers of the president are very limited; it is the prime minister who is responsible for maintaining a ruling coalition and for running the government. The Knesset, Israel's unicameral parliament, has 120 members. To form a government, a party must win a 61-seat majority (a feat that has yet to be accomplished) or form a coalition with one or more minority parties.

Unlike members of the U.S. Congress or British Parliament, Israel's legislators do not stand for election as representatives from a geographic district. Consequently, the primary allegiance of members is to their party, and party discipline is exacting. Candidates selected by the party apparatus run on a single slate. Voters therefore do not cast their vote for a particular candidate but for a single party. Each party can present a complete list of 120 candidates, although in practice only the two major parties make such an effort. The first name on each party list is that party's choice for prime minister.

The number of seats allocated to each party is determined by the percentage of votes it receives. To qualify for a Knesset seat a party must gain at least 1 percent of the votes cast. The total number of votes for all eligible parties is then divided by 120 to determine the minimum number of votes required for each seat. Each party is given the largest number of seats possible. Any seats not distributed in this fashion are awarded to those parties with the largest number of remaining votes. If any seats still remain unassigned, they are given to the parties with the largest number of seats.

This method of proportional representation has all but guaranteed a faction-ridden parliament and created a situation where never in Israel's short history has a single party commanded a Knesset majority, forcing the creation of a succession of coalition governments.

When no single party controls a majority of seats, it must join with smaller parties to gain control of the Knesset in a coalition government. After the election the president, in his most important role, consults with the leaders of all parties to determine which has the greatest likelihood of forming a government. He then asks the leader of that party to form a government within a specified period, which under certain circumstances can be extended.

Since before their nation was created, Israelis have debated the proper role of religion in the Jewish state. Although similar to secular democracies in its parliamentary form of government, Israel is unique in its foundation as a specifically constituted religious state in which Jews anywhere are automatically entitled to Israeli citizenship and privileged treatment by the government. This privileged position for Jews is the raison d'etre of the state, and its ramifications are a source of never-ending debate in Israel.

All issues of religious identification, marriage, birth certification, and divorce are the province of religious authorities, who, while supported by the state, exercise their authority relatively independently. There is, for example, no institution for secular marriage or divorce, which continues to be the province of Muslim, Christian, or Jewish religious authorities. For Jews in such cases, only the Orthodox Jewish establishment (as opposed to reform or conservative trends) is recognized as legitimate.

Political parties with religious roots and agendas have always been an active and dynamic force on the Israeli political landscape. By forming political parties, these organizations join coalitions and wield power disproportionate to their size. They are able to legislate and expand the role of orthodox religious principles in various aspects of public and private life, from divorce law to the playing of soccer on the Sabbath.

## Economy

Israel's economic development has been shaped by its isolation from the markets of neighboring countries, its lack of natural resources, and the requirements of maintaining extraordinary expenditures on defense.

During its first twenty years of existence, Israel had an annual average inflation rate of 7 percent. The tremendous costs of financing the October 1973 war, however, pushed inflation to nearly 40 percent by 1976. By the end of the decade annual rates were running at 130 percent. But the disruptive effects of such a spiral were almost completely offset by a complex scheme of indexation that ensured that the purchasing power of wage earners did not suffer.

The economic stimulation program implemented by a Likud government in the early part of the 1980s, combined with the expenditures required by the invasion of Lebanon, pushed Israel's inflation rate to almost 400 percent by 1984. A new currency, the third in less than a decade, was created. Unemployment, traditionally a rarity in Israel's full-employment economy, rose to 5.9 percent. Even so, Israel's economy has proved remarkably resilient. Its per capita gross domestic product is almost $9,750, by far the highest in the region (and higher than that of Spain and Ireland), and its standard of living approaches that of many countries in Western Europe.

Israel receives an annual grant of $3 billion from the United States and approximately $500 million in grants from the world Jewish community. It spends more than a fifth of its gross national product on defense. Since the prestate era, Israel has invested a large segment of its national wealth in creating an arms industry, primarily to ensure a reliable source of supply. Since the 1970s, however, the maintenance and expansion of a defense industry producing top-of-the-line weapons systems for the Israeli Defense Force (IDF) required Israel to join the international competition for foreign arms sales. Israel is today one of the world's leading arms exporters. Israel's military-industrial complex—which includes the kibbutz sector—and diamond cutting now dominate industrial production and export sales, a significant change from the era when citrus and agricultural products were the country's most significant earners of foreign currency and its most popular international symbols.

Complementing, and sometimes borne of, Israel's defense industry is its high-tech computer industry. The Israeli software industry recorded $600 million in sales in 1992, a 20 percent increase over 1990. Because of its exceptionally high standards of quality control and low costs of labor (30 to 50 percent of U.S. or European costs), Israel has succeeded in attracting major computer corporations interested in diversifying their holdings in software production.

The Palestinian uprising begun in late 1987 weakened the Israeli economy. It placed an additional burden on the system through increased expenditures by the defense, justice, and police ministries; an increase in reserve days of military service that Israeli Jewish men are required to serve; depressed exports to the territories; decreased tourism; and an erratic labor supply from the occupied territories.

Since 1992, however, Labor has accelerated deregulation and the privatization of state-run industries. In 1992 inflation fell by half to 9.4 percent and Israel's economy grew by 6.4 percent. Much of this growth was fueled by Israel's expanding domestic market caused by the large influx of Russian immigrants and the country's improved trade relations with China, India, and former Soviet bloc countries. With a vibrant export focus, corporate earnings in Israel grew by nearly 20 percent in 1993, according to Israeli investment research experts' estimates.

# History

Since the Roman destruction of Jerusalem's Second Temple in A.D. 70, the suppression of the Bar Kochba revolt sixty-five years later, and subsequent expulsion of Jews, the return to Zion has been a leitmotif of the Jewish people. The Old Testament proclaims the great religious significance of the Jews' return to Jerusalem: "If I forget thee, O Jerusalem, let my right hand forget her cunning. If I do not remember thee, let my tongue cleave to the roof of my mouth: if I prefer not Jerusalem above my chief joy."

Not until the mid-nineteenth century did the confluence of political emancipation, racially based theories of nationalism, and state-sponsored anti-Semitism throughout Europe create the conditions for an organized effort to reestablish Jewish sovereignty in Palestine. Early Zionist thinkers such as Moshe Hess, an associate of Karl Marx and author of *Rome and Jerusalem,* the first Zionist tract, Leo Pinsker, who in 1882 at the outset of the Russian pogroms wrote *Autoemancipation,* and Theodor Herzl, author of the seminal *Jewish State,* argued that the immutability of anti-Semitism and the "otherness" of Jews in nations created as expressions of non-Jewish cultural and racial purity required that Jews too create their own nation.

## Creating a Jewish State

From 1882 to 1914 more than 2.5 million Jews emigrated from Eastern Europe, the heart of Ashkenazi Jewry. The overwhelming majority, however, emigrated to countries in the West. Only small numbers of ideologically committed Zionists emigrated to Palestine, where they established a variety of communal and capitalistic agricultural settlements. To gain popular support for his idea of a Jewish state, the indefatigable Herzl convened the First Zionist Congress in Basel, Switzerland, in 1897. The World Zionist Organization was established at this conference as part of a program that stated, "The aim of Zionism is to create for the Jewish people a home in Palestine secured by public law. . . ."

While Herzl and his successors tried to win diplomatic recognition of Zionist enterprise from the European and Ottoman powers, from 1910 onward the exponents of "practical Zionism," notably Chaim Weizmann, worked to create a new reality in Palestine by fostering Jewish settlement that would be difficult to uproot.

The exigencies of World War I prompted Britain to issue the Balfour Declaration on November 2, 1917, which promised British support for "the establishment in Palestine of a national home for the Jewish people." The statement was designed to gain Jewish support for the British war effort and ensure British control over Palestine if the shaky Ottoman Empire collapsed. British support for a Jewish national home was, however, to be conditioned upon an understanding that "nothing shall be done which may prejudice the civil and religious rights of existing non-Jewish communities in Palestine." This policy established the contradictory impulses that were to affect British actions toward Palestine until Jewish independence.

Upon the defeat of the Ottoman Empire in World War I, Britain and France collaborated to divide its Middle Eastern holdings. Palestine was placed under a new form of colonial supervision—British mandatory authority. The British mandate in Palestine was legitimized in 1920 by the League of Nations.

While the growing Jewish community in Palestine, known as the *Yishuv,* viewed the British mandate as an opportunity to expand Jewish control there, Palestinian Arabs saw British rule as a threat to Arab sovereignty and an obstacle to independence such as that granted or promised to Egypt, Iraq, Syria, and Lebanon. The Yishuv therefore adopted a strategy of cooperation with the British authorities and under their protection constructed the administrative, economic, and military building blocks of Jewish sovereignty. Arab efforts, organized around clan-based political parties, were far less successful in achieving the Arab aim of an end to British control and the creation of an Arab state in Palestine.

In 1947 an exhausted and overextended Britain announced that it would terminate its mandate over Palestine and withdraw on May 15, 1948. The fledgling United Nations was entrusted with the problem of determining the successor to the mandate. On November 29, 1947, the UN General Assembly proposed the partition of Palestine into separate Arab and Jewish states and the internationalization of Jerusalem. The Zionist leadership supported the UN decision and prepared for statehood. Leaders of the Palestinian Arabs and the Arab League, a federation of seven Arab states formed in 1944, rejected partition.

In the succeeding months scattered warfare between Palestinian and Jewish irregulars occurred throughout Palestine. On May 14, 1948, David Ben-Gurion, the head of the Zionist Executive, the leadership body of the Yishuv, declared the establishment of the state of Israel and became the country's first prime minister and defense minister. From May until January 1949, when separate armistice agreements were initialed, armies from Egypt, Iraq, Syria, Jordan, and Lebanon fought unsuccessfully to abort Jewish statehood and, in Egypt's case, to prevent the expansion of Transjordan into most of the region earmarked for Palestinian Arab independence. Armistice agreements signed between the warring parties confirmed the viability of Jewish statehood, but they failed to fix permanent boundaries or to establish contractual peace between the new state and its neighbors.

### Arab-Israeli Wars

The issues left unresolved after the first Arab-Israeli War in 1948-49 have been a source of constant confrontation in succeeding decades. On four subsequent occasions—1956, 1967, 1973, and 1982—this endemic conflict erupted into full-scale military hostilities. *(For a detailed description of the five Arab-Israeli wars, see Chapter 2.)*

In October 1956 Israel, in coordination with France and Great Britain, launched an invasion into the Sinai aimed at toppling Egyptian leader Gamal Abdel Nasser, opening the port of Eilat to maritime commerce and neutralizing Palestinian *fedayeen* (guerrilla) attacks mounted from the Gaza Strip. The invasion did succeed in opening the port of Eilat to international commerce, but it boosted rather than deflated Nasser's prestige, and it brought unprecedented American pressure upon Israel to withdraw to the preinvasion boundaries. From this episode Israel learned the importance of gaining U.S. support for its military ventures. It would never again begin a major military operation without first receiving what it considered to be a "green light" from Washington.

In June 1967 Israel launched a successful preemptive attack against the Egyptian and Syrian air forces. In the following days the Israeli Defense Force gained control of Syria's Golan Heights, the Jordanian West Bank (including East Jerusalem), the Egyptian-administered Gaza Strip, and Egypt's Sinai Peninsula bordering the strategic Suez Canal. Israel thus gained control of the entire post-1921 mandatory Palestine. Israeli analysts contended that the addition of territory on three vulnerable fronts gave Israel the "strategic depth" necessary to defend its borders that pre-1967 Israel lacked.

Egypt and Syria, however, were determined to avenge their defeat. In the absence of any diplomatic progress, the two countries launched a coordinated, surprise offensive on October 6, 1973. Both Syria and Egypt had limited territorial objectives, aimed at recovering territories lost in June 1967. Jordan sat out the ensuing war.

The initial Syrian and Egyptian offensives took Israel by surprise. In the Sinai, Israel's vaunted Bar-Lev Line was breached, while in the Golan civilians were hurriedly evacuated from Jewish settlements constructed after 1967 as the Syrians advanced early in the fighting. These outposts proved to be an obstacle to, rather than a vehicle for, Israel's defense of the Golan.

Within days Israel, aided by timely U.S. resupply, had turned back the Arab assault and gained the military advantage. In negotiations following a cease-fire, Israel and Syria reached a detailed disengagement agreement that has been scrupulously maintained. Egyptian-Israeli talks resulted in an interim agreement on the Sinai, which opened the way to a complete Israeli withdrawal from occupied Egyptian territory and the Egyptian-Israeli peace treaty of 1979. *(Text of peace treaty, Appendix, p. 396)*

In June 1982 Israel launched an invasion of Lebanon. The Israelis hoped to decimate the political as well as the military power of the PLO, which had successfully frustrated Israeli efforts to win Palestinian acquiescence to permanent Israeli rule in the occupied West Bank and Gaza Strip. Israel also wanted to establish a new political order in Lebanon based on the rule of the Christian Phalange party led by its military leader, Bashir Gemayel. Finally, the Israelis aimed to humiliate Syria and remove it from its historical position of influence over Lebanese affairs. Although the Israeli military dominated the battlefield and destroyed Syrian air defenses in Lebanon, the war failed to achieve its objectives. It contributed to an ignominious end in 1983 to the tenure of Menachem Begin, Israel's longest-serving prime minister. The controversial nature of Israel's "war

of choice" created divisions among the Israeli people that have yet to heal.

## Politics and National Security

The victory of Menachem Begin's Likud party in 1977 was a political earthquake. For the first time since the establishment of the state, the political embodiment of Israel's pioneering and state-building generation, the Labor party, had been forced from power. The Likud was unambiguous in its view that the West Bank—*Judea and Samaria* in Likud's vocabulary—was an inseparable part of the "Land of Israel," promised by God to the Jewish people. It replaced the Labor alignment's security rationale for remaining permanently in the occupied territories with one based upon divine right.

Unfettered by Labor's desire to maintain a negotiating posture that did not rule out some degree of withdrawal from the territories as part of a peace settlement, the Likud embarked upon an ambitious settlement drive throughout the West Bank and Gaza, expanding the areas Labor had marked for eventual annexation. The Likud settlement program attempted to create a new reality of more than one hundred Jewish settlements and hundreds of thousands of Jewish settlers in the territories. Likud leaders believed such a settlement program would subvert any attempt to trade territory for peace as outlined in UN Security Council resolutions 242 and 338 adopted after the 1967 war. *(Texts of resolutions, Appendix, p. 395)*

The philosophy of the Herut (freedom) party, the dominant element of the Likud bloc, is rooted in the thinking of Vladimir Jabotinsky, a prestate Zionist leader who broke with Labor and Liberal Zionists over the means necessary to achieve Jewish sovereignty. Jabotinsky advocated a plan of militant resistance against both the British and the Arabs, best expressed in his theory that the Jewish community should erect an "Iron Wall" of Jewish sovereignty throughout the Land of Israel, against which the Arab world would eventually become reconciled. He and his followers, among them

Menachem Begin and Yitzhak Shamir, rejected any partition of the biblical Land of Israel and called for Jewish settlement on both sides of the Jordan River.

Israel's worsening economic condition, highlighted by a November 1980 announcement of an annual inflation rate of 200 percent, set the stage for the 1981 election contest.

Labor fielded a team headed by Shimon Peres, the party leader since 1977, and Yitzhak Rabin, the former prime minister and perennial challenger to Peres's leadership. Peres prevailed once again over Rabin in preelection party wrangling. Indeed, its election platform regarding the occupied territories was described by party elder Israel Galili as aimed at "refut[ing] the Likud's false assertions that if the Alignment comes to power it will guide the ship of state weak kneed back to the June 4, 1967, lines."

Begin, however, made Labor's ostensible "softness" on the issue of the territories the centerpiece of his electoral campaign. Begin labeled Peres a "Husseinist" for his advocacy of territorial compromise. The economy, too, enjoyed a temporary upsurge. A new finance minister manipulated fiscal and tax regulations to put more cash in the hands of Israeli voters. The destruction of Iraq's nuclear reactor by a daring Israeli air attack only weeks before the election also increased the popularity of Begin and his party. Peres, on the other hand, was pelted with tomatoes and prevented from addressing the annual festival of Moroccan Jews in Jerusalem. Sephardic antipathy toward Labor, the product of a generation of discrimination and neglect by Labor's Ashkenazi leadership, had yet to subside.

Labor and the Likud each won forty-eight seats in the Knesset balloting. The preference of the religious parties for the Likud led to a coalition government headed by Begin and marked Labor's second consecutive defeat.

The 1984 elections occurred against a background of military stagnation in Lebanon and growing economic problems. Begin, stunned by the death of his wife and traumatized by Israel's troubles in Lebanon and failure to end the PLO's political challenge to Israeli hegemony in the occupied territories, resigned the premiership in August 1983. His successor, Yitzhak Shamir, a veteran of the Jewish underground and the Mossad, Israel's CIA, was initially viewed as a caretaker whose tenure would not disrupt the ambitions of the Likud's second generation: Moshe Arens, David Levy, and Ariel Sharon. In the months following his appointment, Shamir wrestled with exploding inflation and dwindling foreign currency reserves, a crisis in Israel's Lebanon policy that portended a controversial, indefinite occupation of parts of that country, and incipient challenges to his leadership by the Likud's young guard.

The results of the July 1984 elections resulted in a national unity coalition government unique in Israeli history. The willingness of Israel's two major political blocs to rule together suggested that the issues separating them were more apparent than real. There had been one unity government previously, formed in the months before the June 1967 war under Labor's leadership. The 1984 coalition agreement, however, called for an unprecedented rotation of the premiership between Shamir and Labor party leader Peres. Each man would serve as prime minister for two years while the other was foreign minister, and both major parties would be awarded an equal number of cabinet portfolios.

It was widely anticipated that such a "two-headed" government was a prescription for disaster. The government confounded these expectations, however. Inflation was tamed without a significant increase in unemployment or decreases in purchasing power, postponing if not solving the country's economic problems. A compromise withdrawal of the IDF from Lebanon was effected, reestablishing the security zone run by the surrogate South Lebanese Army with IDF logistical and military support.

Colonization efforts in the occupied territories continued uninterrupted, albeit at a slower pace, during the stewardship of both Peres and Shamir.

"All the forces operative on the ground since Begin assumed power in 1977," wrote Israeli analyst Meron Benvenisti in 1986, "have continued to operate with tremendous drive under Peres. In the last two years the government has spent $300 million in order to advance Israeli interests in the territories. In comparison to cuts in other development budgets, the relative proportion of investments in the West Bank has even risen." Yet, even as investment remained steady, the number of Jewish settlers dwindled. In 1985, for example, only forty-eight hundred Jews moved to the West Bank, down from fifteen thousand in 1983.

Policy in the occupied territories was managed during the government's entire four-year tenure by Labor's Yitzhak Rabin. It was during this period that a new chapter in the "Iron Fist," a series of tough, repressive measures against a restive Palestinian population, emboldened by economic hardship, was put into effect. Deportation and administrative detention of Palestinian suspects, two measures that had fallen into relative disuse during the Begin era, were resurrected by Rabin as he attempted to quell the growing number of violent confrontations.

## Intifada

What has become known as the Palestinian uprising or intifada was sparked by a series of incidents in the Gaza Strip in the second week of December 1987. Violent confrontation between Palestinians of all ages and the IDF and Jewish settlers became a constant feature of life in the territories. Almost five hundred Palestinians and approximately twenty-five Israeli Jews were killed within two years, undermining the assumption that Israel could indefinitely maintain a peaceful and safe occupation. By 1993 the Israeli Information Center for Human Rights in the Occupied Territories reported that since the intifada began in December 1987, 97 civilians were killed by Palestinians, 67 Palestinians were killed by Israeli civilians, 54 Israeli soldiers were killed by Palestinians, and 1,067 Palestinians were killed by Israeli soldiers.

Israel's response to massive Palestinian protests involving the sustained participation of all sectors of the Palestinian community was grounded in its longstanding determination to crush any opposition to Israeli rule. "A political solution," Prime Minister Shamir explained, "is not always what puts an end to the opposition of one's enemy to one's existence. First of all, one must repel the dangers and then think about peace, if that is possible." Palestinian political demands, aimed at undermining the policies of de facto annexation and generating negotiations, were ignored.

Instead, Defense Minister Rabin described Israeli policy on January 21, 1988, as one of "force, might, and blows." By the end of February, eighty Palestinians had been killed and six hundred fifty wounded in almost five thousand recorded violent confrontations. A U.S. organization, Physicians for Human Rights, issued a report after a delegation visited the occupied territories. It charged the Israeli government with implementing "an essentially uncontrolled epidemic of violence by soldiers and police in the West Bank and Gaza Strip, on a scale and degree of severity that poses the most serious medical, ethical, and legal problems."

In January 1989 Amnesty International charged that the methods Israel employed in its unsuccessful effort to end the revolt "show that the Israeli Government is apparently not willing to enforce international human rights standards."

The political program of the uprising has always linked the allegiance of Palestinians in the occupied territories to the leadership of the PLO. The decision of the Palestine National Council to recognize Israel and endorse UN resolutions 242 and 338 in November 1988 was seen as a victory for Palestinians under occupation, who have long urged the PLO to adopt a realistic diplomatic posture toward Israel.

The intifada was seen as a vital complement to the PLO's diplomatic strategy aimed at winning an Israeli withdrawal from the occupied territories and the realization of Palestinian sovereignty.

The national unity government established after the 1984 elections served a full four-year term, which in itself was an achievement. The 1988 elections were in large measure a public referendum on the record of this unique form of political accommodation. The election, conducted against the background of the intifada and a poor economy, continued the drift of the Israeli electorate toward the religious, chauvinist right and confirmed continuing popular support for hard-line policies against the Palestinian uprising. Labor, led by Shimon Peres, won 39 seats in the 120-member Knesset. Shamir's Likud also won 39 seats.

The 1988 election underscored several important political trends. Israel's Arab voters emerged as the most significant electoral obstacle to the creation of a decisive right-wing majority. Small right-wing parties, and particularly anti-Zionist religious parties, emerged as key players in subsequent coalition negotiations. Labor, in contrast, was preoccupied with recriminations, directed primarily at Peres, who had failed to lead Labor to an electoral victory in four straight elections.

The U.S. decision to begin a "substantive dialogue" with the PLO in December 1988 contributed to the decision of Labor and Likud to reestablish the national unity government, if only to present Washington with a wall-to-wall coalition opposed to including the PLO in the diplomatic process. This new unity government, unlike its predecessor, would function under the unchallenged leadership of the Likud. The terms of this power-sharing agreement placed Yitzhak Shamir as prime minister for the life of the government. Labor's Yitzhak Rabin remained in the pivotal post of defense minister, the second most powerful position in Israel. Shimon Peres accepted the finance portfolio, a measure of Labor's preeminent concern to safeguard the future of its ailing kibbutz and industrial establishments, and also of Peres's eclipse as a political force.

## Persian Gulf Crisis

In the summer of 1990 a crisis unfolded in the Persian Gulf region that was to have dramatic repercussions for Israel and its relationship with the United States and the PLO. On the eve of August 2, Saddam Hussein ordered Iraqi troops to invade Kuwait and began an occupation that would unite most of the international community, including much of the Arab world, against him. *(Persian Gulf crisis, Chapter 4, p. 108)*

"Zionist plots" have been a feature of the rhetoric of Iraqi leader Saddam Hussein. Throughout the occupation and armed conflict, Saddam reiterated this theme. He accused the Kuwaiti royal family of having connections with "Zionist interests" and used this as a justification for invading Kuwait and establishing there a puppet government loyal to Baghdad. Saddam linked the Arab-Israeli dispute to Iraq's invasion, offering a mutual withdrawal whereby Iraqi forces would withdraw from Kuwait when Israeli forces withdrew from the West Bank and Gaza.

While nearly the entire international community rejected this "two wrongs make a right" logic, it resonated with the Palestinians of the occupied territories. Many, including the leadership of the PLO, initially saw Saddam Hussein as a hero. He appeared as a great Arab leader, able to defy the United States, Israel, and the Gulf Arabs, whom many considered to be in league with the West and far too parsimonious with their oil wealth.

After the U.S.-led coalition launched its massive air assault on Iraq on January 17, 1991, Saddam targeted Israel in an effort to transform his local territorial aggression into a pan-Arab issue. He ordered the launching of Scud missiles armed with conventional explosives at Israel. Iraq fired thirty-nine Scud missiles at Israel between January 17 and February 24, 1991. Forty-four percent of the Scuds were successfully intercepted by Patriot missiles, supplied and operated by the U.S. Army. While the Scuds killed few Israelis, more than two hundred injuries were reported, and hundreds of homes and apartments were damaged from falling debris.

Israel had the capability to retaliate and, in fact, threatened to do so after every missile landed. However, recognizing that they would be playing into Saddam's hands if they retaliated, Israeli leaders refrained from attacking Iraq. This decision allowed the United States to hold together Arab countries in the coalition, some of whom may have balked at fighting against an Arab country on the side of Israel. For this restraint, the United

*Yitzhak Rabin*

tion would not come through a military victory over Israel from an outside force.

For Israelis, many of whom were forced to spend nights in basements and air raid shelters with gas masks, the attacks underscored their vulnerability to missiles, which in the future might carry chemical, biological, or even nuclear warheads. Possession of the West Bank and Golan Heights no longer could guarantee Israeli security. With long-range missiles becoming more prevalent, the strategic value of the territories was becoming obsolete, while the political liability of the occupation remained.

## Path to Peace

Israel held elections in June 1992, in the aftermath of the Gulf crisis and amidst the sporadic, albeit unsettling, violence of the intifada. The central issues of the election were the economy, social problems, and the peace process. Although Likud was presiding over low inflation during the first half of 1992, billions of dollars were devoted to building Israeli settlements on the West Bank, an increasingly controversial priority. By diverting funds to the settlements from investment in the creation of new jobs, Likud's economic policy caused unemployment to soar to 12 percent, with newly arrived immigrants, military veterans, and residents in developing towns—traditionally Likud supporters—most likely to be without work. Additionally, the state comptroller's office cited widespread corruption in the construction programs in the territories administered by Israel's housing minister, Ariel Sharon.

The West Bank settlements also had a profound impact on U.S.-Israeli relations. The administration of President George Bush objected to the policy and refused to approve $10 billion in loan guarantees earmarked to help settle new immigrants until construction in the territories came to a halt. The dispute over the loan guarantees soured U.S.-Israeli relations, worrying Israelis on both the left and right. Shamir further alienated the electorate by vetoing an electoral-reform measure that had acquired strong public support.

States generously rewarded Israel after the Gulf War ended. It gave Israel in 1991, besides the regular foreign aid totaling $3 billion in military and economic support packages, additional emergency assistance of $3 billion for expenses incurred during the war. Once the danger of breaking the coalition was over, four Israeli jets flew over Iraqi airspace in October 1991. Claiming that the UN inspection of Iraqi nuclear weapons was insufficient, Israel seized this opportunity to demonstrate its air superiority by flying over Iraqi airspace with impunity.

The psychological impact of the Iraqi missile attacks on Israel was profound. Palestinians danced and cheered from rooftops as the missiles rained down—often close to, if not in, their own neighborhoods. Yet the quick and humiliating defeat of Saddam's army in February drove home to most Palestinians that their deliverance and libera-

## 1992 Elections

For Labor, Yitzhak Rabin's campaign emphasized his party's fresh leadership intent on focusing on education, infrastructure, industrial investment, and cleaning up the slums of Israel's towns and coastal cities. These priorities, he argued, along with military superiority, would make Israel strong, secure, and ready for peace.

As expected, both parties asserted they wanted peace. But Rabin while campaigning differentiated between settlements built for political purposes and those necessary for security and conceded the construction of the former should be stopped. Likud's Yitzhak Shamir continued to pledge that "not one inch" of Eretz Yisrael would be ceded to the Palestinians, a policy that secured ultra orthodox voters. For a great many Israelis, however, Shamir's intransigence had not advanced the cause of peace, and in the face of the intifada many swing voters were willing to try something new.

With the support of Soviet immigrants and Sephardim, who were also disenchanted with Likud because of its neglect of social issues, Labor won five additional seats while Likud lost eight. The smaller parties made the most impressive gains. To secure a majority and form a ruling government, Labor joined with Leftist parties, including two Arab parties. For the first time in Israeli history, the ruling party was in the unusual, and vulnerable, position of relying on Arab seats to form a government.

By ousting Shamir, Israeli voters sent a strong message to the PLO leadership. Chairman Yasir Arafat observed that "it was the results of the Israeli election that made a deal first seem possible. This was a very important signal that the Israelis were willing to achieve peace."

## Palestinian-Israeli Peace Accords

Seeds for the Palestinian-Israeli peace initiative can be traced back to December 1988, when the U.S. administration of President Ronald Reagan opened a dialog with the PLO after Arafat acknowledged Israel's right to exist on the basis of UN Resolution 242 and renounced terrorism. The same year, Rabin stated publicly before Labor party activists that "... you can't rule by force over 1.5 million Palestinians." Five years later Rabin was in a position to act on Israeli frustration with the moral and economic costs of the endless occupation.

Capitalizing on unparalleled U.S. influence in the region after the Gulf crisis in 1991, President Bush sent Secretary of State James A. Baker III to the Middle East eight times in an eight-month period to discuss the peace process with regional leaders. Bush and Soviet leader Mikhail Gorbachev sent invitations to Arab, Israeli, and Palestinian leaders to meet in Madrid in October to discuss avenues for peace. The early stages of the Madrid talks were widely acknowledged as fruitless, at best. Israel attended to appease the Bush administration but, under Shamir's leadership, had no intentions of changing the status quo. Shamir seemed intent on outlasting Bush and wearing down the opposition until events refocused domestic and international attention away from the Palestinian-Israeli question.

When Rabin came to power in mid-1992, the Labor coalition approved a partial housing construction freeze in the occupied territories. In doing so, Labor freed up loan guarantees from the United States, which were operable only under that condition, and sent a strong signal to the PLO that Israel was serious about making concessions for peace.

During the tenth round of Palestinian-Israeli peace negotiations, Israel and the PLO opened secret talks in Norway in February 1993. Outside the spotlight of the international media, Israeli foreign minister Shimon Peres met with senior PLO officials to propose a Palestinian self-rule agreement. During the course of fourteen rounds of talks, the parties agreed that Israel would withdraw from the Gaza Strip and the West Bank city of Jericho and transfer selected administrative responsibilities to Palestinians. The final status of the territories, Jerusalem, Jewish settlements, and other issues would be determined during the next five years. With its passage through the Knesset in August 1993, this agreement became the cornerstone upon which letters of mutual Israel-PLO recognition were signed.

With the White House as a dramatic backdrop, Rabin and Arafat exchanged letters of mutual recognition on September 13, 1993, and shook hands in a gesture of peace. The United States pledged $500 million over five years in aid to the Palestinian political entity that will emerge from the agreement. To sweeten the deal for Israel, President Bill Clinton assured Rabin that the United States would continue aid to Israel at the existing level of $3 billion a year, support the "Arrow" missile development, and provide twenty F-15E aircraft for Israeli defense. The peace accord calls for a transitional period of no more than five years, during which final status arrangements for a lasting and comprehensive peace settlement will be negotiated. In signing the accords, Israel essentially recognized that at the end of the road (in 1998, when the fate of the occupied territories is to be decided), a Palestinian state would be born.

### Jordan-Israeli Agreement

In July 1994 Israel followed up its agreement with the Palestinians by signing the Washington Declaration, a pact with Jordan to end the forty-six-year state of war with that country. Israel and Jordan had not actually engaged in significant fighting since the Six-Day War in 1967. Israeli leaders had long considered King Hussein of Jordan to be a negotiating partner who was preferable to Yasir Arafat or Syria's President Hafez al-Assad. But King Hussein could not be perceived as getting out in front of the Palestinians in negotiations with Israel, especially given Jordan's large and potentially destabilizing Palestinian population.

The PLO's agreement with Israel, however, opened the way for King Hussein to seek peace with Israel. The Washington Declaration led to intense negotiations that produced a formal Israeli-Jordanian peace treaty. It was signed on October 26, at a remote outpost on the border between the two countries. It established broad economic cooperation between Israel and Jordan and provided for a formal exchange of ambassadors. Especially important to Israel was Jordan's pledge not to allow a third party to use its territory as a staging area for attacks on Israel.

Although Yasir Arafat denounced the Israeli-Jordanian treaty, especially Israel's recognition of King Hussein's role as a guardian of Jerusalem's Islamic shrines, the agreement placed pressure on the PLO to move forward with the peace process.

## Current Issues

The signing of the accords between the PLO and Israel met with massive demonstrations in Israel and the territories, many in support of the act, some against. Four separate pro-peace demonstrations drew several thousand Palestinians on the West Bank and Gaza, while tens of thousands of Israelis also rallied in Tel Aviv.

The peace process has thrown Israel's Likud party into disarray, as it tries to keep pace with events and position itself as an opposition party. A significant portion of the electorate still supports the Likud party, for which this peace accord is a bombshell that clearly threatens the sanctity of Greater Israel. Although the accords have been accompanied by bloodshed and uncertainty, the Likud party, led by Binyamin Netanyahu, has been unable to react and solidify its leadership as the opposition party. In addition, political infighting has threatened to split the party between Netanyahu and his adversary, former foreign minister David Levy. Finally, Rabin has been actively courting smaller parties in the Likud coalition for his own coalition to help him sell the peace plan to the public—further splintering the Israeli right.

While Israel has benefited from its new relationship with the PLO by increased and improved ties with the international community, it has also suffered at the hands of extremists, both Jewish and Arab. Since the Palestinian-Israeli peace accord was signed in September 1993, deadly clashes have continued. Much of the violence has occurred in the territories involving Jewish settlers, the Israeli army, and Palestinians.

Causing the bloodiest day in the occupied territories since the War of 1967, on February 25, 1994, Baruch Goldstein, an American-born doctor who moved to a Jewish settlement on the West Bank, entered the Mosque at the Tomb of the Patriarchs in Hebron, the site where Abraham and Sarah are believed to be buried, and fired an automatic weapon at Muslim worshippers. Thirty Palestinians were killed. The incident ignited violence throughout the occupied territories and on the Temple Mount, where thirty more Palestinians died in clashes with the Israeli army in the month following the massacre.

The incident fueled the PLO's demand to disarm Jewish settlers and asked the UN to condemn the massacre and to approve an "international presence" in the occupied territories. Settlers are permitted to keep weapons at home while on reserve duty, which extends for decades for Israeli men. According to army rules, these weapons may be used only when lives are in danger. Several settlers have been arrested, however, for using the weapons to shoot Palestinians without justification. Most Palestinians in the territories are forbidden to carry guns.

Many Israelis seemed convinced that the fundamentalist Islamic Resistance Movement, or Hamas, which still rejects Israel's right to exist, has been growing more influential in the West Bank and may already have more influence in the Gaza Strip than the PLO leadership. In spite of deportations, Hamas has managed to execute deadly and embarrassing strikes against the Israeli army and civilians within Israel's borders. Propelled by economic hardship and disenchantment with the prospects for an independent homeland, young Palestinians began flocking to Hamas at the outset of the intifada in late 1987. Israeli army officials admit that Hamas has solid public backing and little need for organizational infrastructure or funding, since its operations involve groups of two or three men working within a decentralized framework.

Hamas claimed responsibility for a suicide car bomb attack that killed eight in the small town of Afula, Israel, in April 1994. The attack was the first of five acts of revenge for February's Hebron massacre. Both PLO and Israeli officials condemned the attack and vowed not to let terrorists alter the peace process or influence its agenda.

Israel's foreign policy had been defined by its conflict with its Arab neighbors and its de facto alliance with the United States, which has guaranteed Israel's military superiority over its enemies. Despite their differences, Israel's major parties have defined a national consensus supporting permanent Israeli hegemony in the area between the Mediterranean Sea and the Jordan River, the annexation of the Golan Heights won from Syria in the 1967 war, and the central importance of maintaining close military and political ties with the United States.

Israel and the United States have maintained good ties since Israel's creation in 1948, when the United States was the first country to grant Israel de facto recognition. Israel is the largest single recipient of U.S. foreign aid, currently amounting to $3 billion annually ($1.8 billion for military aid, $1.2 billion for economic aid) in outright grant assistance. Israel also has had the support of the Democratic and Republican parties, as well as the AFL-CIO. Israel has been the staunchest U.S. ally in the United Nations, voting with the United States more than any other country.

While no issue has challenged the essential comity of interests upon which U.S.-Israeli relations are based, there have been occasions when the two nations have clashed over goals, actions, and priorities. Israeli collaboration with the joint French-British invasion of Egypt in 1956 is the most notable instance of such conflict. More recent examples include the arrest of Jonathan Pollard, who passed U.S. secrets to Israel, Israel's opposition to the 1982 Reagan peace plan and Secretary of State George P. Shultz's "territory for peace" suggestions formulated in the wake of the intifada, and the inauguration of a U.S. dialogue with the PLO.

While both Labor and Likud share the commitment to maintaining U.S. support and assistance, the Likud has historically been less committed than Labor to maintaining the atmospherics of amity. Nevertheless, Washington's perceptions of its interests in the Middle East, Israel's enduring pro-American stance, and the strong support of American Jews for Israel ensure that Israel and the United States will remain close, regardless of who is in power in either nation.

As tensions between Israel and the PLO have eased, Israel's standing in the international community also has improved. Early in 1994 the Vatican established full diplomatic relations with Israel, ushering in an era of unprecedented goodwill between the church and Judaism. In April the Holy See staged a concert commemorating the victims of the Holocaust, which Pope John Paul II attended. One hundred survivors of Auschwitz, Buchenwald, Dachau, and the Warsaw Ghetto uprising were invited as special guests and met with the pope. Prominent Jews perceived these developments as profoundly important, conveying the message that "a sovereign Jewish state in the Middle East is a normal state of affairs," as Israel's ambassador to the Vatican, Itamar Rabinovich, observed.

The thaw between Israelis and Palestinians at the official levels also has increased U.S. and international pressure on the Arab League to consider dismantling, or easing, its boycott against Israel and against companies that do business with Israel. The league has stated that it will not consider dismantling its "primary boycott" against direct trade with the Jewish state so long as Israel still occupies Arab territories. The Arab countries see the boycott as one of the few bargaining chips they have left with Israel and do not want to give it up prematurely. In addition, several Levantine states fear domination by the aggressive and sophisticated Israeli economy and want to have some measure of control over economic agreements with Israel to prevent loss of domestic markets and industries.

Several major holes have already been poked in the boycott. Morocco has opened economic links with Israel. Kuwait and Saudi Arabia, thankful for the protection the United States provided against

Iraq, unofficially ignore the ban against third-country businesses having trade ties to Israel, known as the "secondary boycott." According to the president of Koor Industries, Israel's largest conglomerate, clandestine trade between Israelis and Arabs is estimated to total $500 million annually. However, an official end to the boycott would provide Rabin with a significant economic and diplomatic lift, well timed to quell strident opposition of the Israeli far right to the peace accords.

The agreements between Israel and the PLO and Jordan have left Syria as the one major frontline Arab power that has not agreed to make peace with Israel. American diplomatic efforts have focused on promoting negotiations between President Assad and the Israeli government. Prime Minister Rabin has offered a plan to dismantle Israeli settlements in the Golan Heights in exchange for a comprehensive peace with Syria. Although Rabin came under significant domestic criticism for the plan, Assad did respond with a detailed, comprehensive reply, indicating that there is some willingness to enter into negotiations. Though it may be in Assad's long-term interest to conclude a compromise with Israel, he is unchallenged domestically and can maneuver at his leisure for the best deal possible.

In addition to the status of the Golan Heights, Lebanon is an issue in Syrian-Israeli talks. Lebanon, as a nation, has never posed a military danger to Israel, but its destruction has resulted in the use of its sovereign territory by irregular forces hostile to Israel. In military terms Israel considers Lebanon an extension of its hostile border with Syria and, as the 1982 invasion demonstrated, an arena of potential Israeli-Syrian military confrontation. In recent years the vacuum of central authority has enabled both Israel and Syria to employ Lebanon as an arena for creating buffer zones and competing spheres of influence. Israel has established a "security zone" in Lebanese territory administered by the IDF-supported South Lebanese Army. Syria dominates the Lebanese government in Beirut and has extensive influence with Hizballah leaders in South Lebanon.

## Outlook

The sharp contrast between the atmosphere of reconciliation at the official meetings between PLO and Israeli representatives and the blood of the streets shows that elements in both communities have not accepted the basic premises of the peace accords. Random and bloody acts of terror on Israeli soil, if frequent enough, could erode the support of Israel's moderates, which is vital to the success of the peace accords.

If the experiment with Palestinian autonomy in Gaza and Jericho is successful, however, Israel could flourish economically alongside a developing Palestinian entity. Many Israelis are hoping that with peace accords in place with its neighbors, Israel will benefit from a "peace dividend" and divert some of the approximately $7 billion defense budget to other needs. A further lifting of the Arab economic embargo would boost the Israeli economy. If Israel can maintain a good-faith effort in the peace process, it will benefit from increased trade and investment as the international financial community looks to the region for high-growth markets. Access to and use of fresh-water resources will continue to take a high priority in discussions with neighboring states. The peace with Jordan is especially encouraging to many Israelis because it was achieved in an atmosphere of friendship. Unlike the peace treaty with Egypt in 1979, which in practice resulted in a "cold peace" of minimal cooperation during the 1980s, the treaty with Jordan is expected to generate broad economic dividends. It has the potential to demonstrate to other Arabs the economic advantages of making peace with Israel. Securing the long border with its neighbor to the east also may ease the Israelis' sense of encirclement.

Despite the impasse in Syrian-Israeli talks, most analysts do expect those two nations to eventually reach an agreement. The status of the Golan Heights, captured by Israel in 1967, is the main issue to be resolved. President Assad has stated that he will accept only a complete return of the territory. Israel has been seeking a compromise that would return part of the Golan, or perhaps most of it under conditions that would guarantee Israeli security.

The road to a complete Palestinian-Israeli peace must eventually address the issues of establishing an independent Palestinian state and deciding the fate of Jerusalem. No point will surpass Jerusalem and its future status as an obstacle to a final peace between Israel and its neighbors. It evokes such powerful passions among Israelis and Palestinians that it is difficult to conceive how its future could be successfully negotiated. Prime Minister Rabin has spent much energy declaring that despite his willingness to compromise on just about every other issue, the status of Jerusalem is not negotiable. Like Israeli leaders before him he has stated that Jerusalem must remain an undivided city under the control of Israel. As a holy city for Muslims, Jews, and Christians, Jerusalem will undoubtedly be a flash point for violence and political unrest between Arabs and Israelis.

# JORDAN

Since its origins in the aftermath of World War I, Jordan has been challenged by its stronger and wealthier neighbors. Its Hashemite kings in the early years were the targets of innumerable assassination attempts. The current king, Hussein ibn Talal, was present when his grandfather was killed on the steps of the Al-Aqsa Mosque in Jerusalem in 1951 by a young Palestinian. Sixteen-year-old Hussein survived that day only because a medal on his tunic deflected the bullet intended for him. The challenges to the rule of the Hashemites continue today.

Jordan is a poor nation surrounded by regionally powerful states. Most of the attention and aid Jordan has received since 1948 from the great powers and from other Arab states have been given because of Jordan's pivotal position in the Arab-Israeli conflict. King Hussein, who until 1988 claimed to represent the West Bank and had extensive ties to the Palestinian population there, was viewed by many nations since he became king in 1953 as one of the most important players in the Arab-Israeli conflict. With his own kingdom having a population that is about 60 percent Palestinian, Hussein has struggled to preserve its integrity and his leadership and to achieve a resolution to Arab-Israeli and inter-Arab conflicts that would be conducive to a peaceful, prosperous Jordan.

This shrewd tactician and master of cautious flexibility weathered many Arab-Israeli and inter-Arab conflicts for thirty-five years before removing himself, in effect, from the heart of the Arab-Israeli dispute by giving up all claims and legal connections to the Israeli-occupied West Bank in

July 1988. This important decision freed him from his previous rivalry with the Palestine Liberation Organization (PLO) and others for leadership of the Palestinians. The move also allowed Hussein to devote greater attention to the demanding internal problems of Jordan. It came none too soon, for in April 1989 rioting broke out in several Jordanian towns over dissatisfaction toward government economic policies. Hussein responded politically by permitting general elections to choose an eighty-seat parliament for the first time since the 1967 war with Israel. This move toward democracy, together with his renunciation of claims to the West Bank, had the result of enhancing his popularity as king, even though the November 1989 elections brought a significant number of opposition deputies into the reestablished parliament.

This enhanced popularity proved vital in helping Hussein to weather the next crisis faced by the kingdom: the dilemma posed by Iraq's August 1990 invasion and occupation of Kuwait. Jordan had close economic ties to Iraq. Although the king repeatedly voiced his opposition to Iraq's annexation of Kuwait, he also resisted supporting the U.S.-led international coalition that marshaled forces to oust the Iraqi army from Kuwait. This stance isolated Jordan and led to much economic pain as the international community withdrew aid to and restricted trade with Jordan. But the king's position greatly reinforced his popularity domestically.

Movement in the Arab-Israeli peace process during the early 1990s, however, repaired Jordan's status in the West, as the king was seen as an indispensable participant in the negotiations. The agreement between the PLO and Israel, reached in September 1993, opened the way for a Jordanian-Israeli pact. On July 25, 1994, King Hussein signed the Washington Declaration with Prime Minister Yitzhak Rabin of Israel. The agreement ended the state of war between Jordan and Israel and was followed by a formal peace treaty signed on October 26, 1994.

The challenge before King Hussein and his government is how to translate the kingdom's enhanced political stability and the regional peace process into long-term economic development. Failure to improve the economy may undermine the hard-won political gains made during the early 1990s.

## Geography

Jordan is bounded on the north by Syria, the east by Iraq and Saudi Arabia, the south by Saudi Arabia, and the west by Israel and the Israeli-occupied West Bank. Jordan's only port is located on the Gulf of Aqaba in a narrow crescent of coastline between Israel and Saudi Arabia.

About the size of Indiana, Jordan covers a territory of 34,445 square miles. Only a small percentage of the land (under 10 percent) is arable. Virtually all the rest is steppe or desert primarily suitable for nomadic grazing and periodic pasturage. A small forested region in the northwest near Ajlun covers about 1 percent of Jordan's territory.

The Jordan River Valley and the Wadi al-Araba (officially the Wadi al-Jayb) are an extension of the great rift that begins in East Africa and continues up the Red Sea into Jordan. The Jordan River, which rises in Lebanon and Syria, descends from an elevation of 9,842 feet to Earth's deepest land-surface depression at the Dead Sea, some fourteen hundred feet below sea level. The East Bank of the Jordan River rises precipitously to form a sharp escarpment cut by numerous valleys and gorges. From the top of the plateau, the extremely arid land (receiving less than twelve inches of rain a year) extends to the east as part of the Great Syrian Desert. The land near the East Bank tributaries of the Jordan River is the only area to receive sufficient rainfall for intensive cultivation.

Jordan's main crops are fruits and vegetables. Although various other crops are grown, the country must import foodstuffs to meet its needs. Jordan has developed several light industries and prosperous phosphate mining operations located at the Dead Sea. With the demise of many banks and commercial enterprises in Beirut caused by Lebanon's civil war, Amman, the capital of Jordan, attracted a number of these concerns because of the country's economic stability and active governmental support.

During the early 1980s as many as four hundred thousand Jordanians—many of them Palestinians with Jordanian passports—lived and worked outside the country. Many of them remitted a portion of their income to family members in Jordan. Remittances were estimated to be running at $1.3 billion a year in the mid-1980s, but they fell sharply later in the decade. Nearly all remittances were lost after the 1990-91 Persian Gulf crisis, when as many as three hundred thousand of the expatriate workers were forced to return to Jordan. Their return meant not only a loss of funds from outside Jordan, but also added domestic unemployment and strains on the resources of the state.

## Demography

In 1994 Jordan's population was close to 4 million. Ethnically, 98 percent of the population is Arab with Arabic the official language, although English is widely spoken and understood. About 92 percent of the population are Muslims, nearly all of whom are Sunnis; most of the remaining Jordanians are Christians. Jordanian authorities proudly claim that more than 70 percent of the population is literate, which indicates the government's emphasis on education and the degree to which education is viewed as a key to social mobility.

Hashemite leadership in Jordan is built upon the political support of the numerically small Bed-

## Key Facts on Jordan

**Area:** 34,445 square miles.

**Capital:** Amman.

**Population:** 3,961,194 (1994).

**Religion:** 92 percent Sunni Muslim, 8 percent Christian.

**Official Language:** Arabic; English is widely spoken by upper and middle classes.

**GDP:** $11.5 billion; $3,000 per capita (1993).

*Source:* Central Intelligence Agency, *CIA World Factbook 1994.*

ouin tribes—only 6 to 8 percent of the population. Abdullah ibn Hussein, who became emir of Transjordan in 1921, developed a special relationship with these groups during the early 1920s. This relationship has been strengthened and institutionalized by his grandson King Hussein. The Bedouins constitute the core of Jordan's army, which is the power source of the existing monarchy. Hussein, like his grandfather, has an intense personal interest in the welfare of these tribesmen and continues to spend considerable time visiting and socializing with them. Originally a martial, desert people, the Bedouins of today are more sedentary and their political influence has diminished somewhat. Bedouins, however, still occupy key positions in the military, and they remain committed to Hussein and the Hashemite regime.

An estimated 60 percent of Jordan's population is ethnic Palestinian. Many of the Palestinians who arrived in Jordan during the late 1940s and the early 1950s were better educated than the native population, and they tended to prosper economically. Palestinians who settled in Jordan during the 1960s, however, brought with them considerably fewer skills and resources. Many of them simply moved from refugee settlements on the West Bank to similar ones on the East Bank.

The ingestion of a large Palestinian population into Jordan has resulted in serious dislocation. The problem of absorbing hundreds of thousands of displaced persons, coupled with the more traditional and conservative orientation of the East Bank social and political elites, has led to mutual suspicion and distrust between Jordanians and Palestinians. Palestinian support for military action against Israel has resulted in numerous confrontations with Jordan's leadership. The most serious and potentially catastrophic of these conflicts occurred in September 1970 when the PLO challenged Hussein's political leadership throughout the country. In a series of bloody skirmishes, the Jordanian military was able to defeat the PLO forces and preserve Hashemite rule. Since that time Hussein has made a concerted effort to integrate more Palestinians into the mainstream of Jordanian society, thereby enhancing his kingdom's political stability.

## History

The Old Testament recounts the settlement of present-day Jordan by Gilead, Ammon, Moab, Edom, and Joshua. Others such as the Nabataeans, Greeks, Romans, Arabs, and European crusaders held sway at various times until the Ottoman Empire extended its domination over much of the Arabian Peninsula and Jordan in the early 1500s.

The British and their Arab allies in 1918 ousted the Ottomans from Palestine and Transjordan (which would later be named Jordan), and the area was briefly ruled by Prince Faisal as part of the Hashemite Kingdom of Syria. Faisal's ejection by the French in 1920 placed Transjordan under the loose administration of Britain. The territory comprising Palestine, Transjordan, and Iraq was awarded to Britain under the League of Nations mandate and the provisions of secret agreements concluded during World War I.

Hussein ibn Ali, the king of Hijaz, and his sons, Faisal and Abdullah, opposed the creation of the mandates, arguing that independence had been promised to the Arabs if they sided with the Allies against the Ottomans during the war. Although the Allies balked at granting independence, Faisal and Abdullah were allowed to set up partially autonomous kingdoms for themselves in Iraq and Transjordan, respectively. In May 1923 Britain recognized the independence of Transjordan within informal parameters established by the British.

Abdullah sought to meld the disparate Bedouin tribes into a cohesive group capable of maintaining Arab rule in the face of increasing Western encroachment. To maintain his rule, Abdullah accepted financial assistance from Britain and agreed to accept advice on financial and foreign affairs. It was during this period that the fabled Arab Legion—British officered but staffed with Bedouin troops—was established as the cornerstone of the regime. The British mandate over Transjordan ended May 22, 1946. Three days later Abdullah was proclaimed king of the newly independent state of Transjordan.

The British abdicated their Palestinian mandate on May 14, 1948, and Jewish leaders proclaimed the state of Israel the next day. Transjordan joined its Arab neighbors in attacking the new Jewish state. When the fighting ended in 1949, Transjordan controlled central Palestine (the West Bank) and East Jerusalem. In April of that year the regime in Amman announced that Transjordan would henceforth be known as Jordan. Nearly a half million Palestinian Arabs who had fled the fighting found that they could not return to their homes and were forced to remain refugees in Jordan.

Abdullah, seeking to use his occupation of the West Bank as a stepping-stone to the creation of a Hashemite-led Greater Syria, annexed the West Bank in 1950. He conducted a number of discussions with the Israelis in an attempt to resolve some of the Arab grievances against Israel. On July 20, 1951, a Palestinian assassinated King Abdullah for his hostility to Palestinian nationalist aspirations.

Abdullah's eldest son, Talal, was proclaimed his successor on September 5, 1951, but mental illness led to his forced abdication in favor of a regency for Talal's eldest son, Hussein. The new king, Hussein, away at the Sandhurst Military Academy

in Britain, returned to be crowned king on his eighteenth birthday, May 2, 1953.

The next two decades were difficult times for the young monarch. In 1955 and 1956 anti-Western, pro-Egyptian sentiments made Jordan's ties to Britain a serious political liability. To calm the political turmoil, Hussein relieved the British commander of the Arab Legion, Gen. John Glubb (popularly known during his twenty years of service in Jordan as Glubb Pasha), of his post and severed Jordan's mutual defense pact with Britain. Hussein also refused to join the pro-Western Baghdad Pact, even though he had been involved in its creation. Hashemite rule in Jordan under Hussein barely survived a military plot uncovered in 1957 and a number of assassination attempts—including one effort by the Egyptian air force to shoot down Hussein's plane. Hussein was able to stay in power because the army continued to back him in his efforts to curb domestic unrest and foreign meddling.

To withstand the forces arrayed against him, Hussein sought to form a union with his uncle, King Faisal of Iraq. The Iraqi revolution and the killing of Faisal in July 1958, however, destroyed that avenue of assistance. The revolution emboldened anti-Hashemite elements in Jordan to defy the king and his government. Hussein, fearing a concerted anti-Hashemite campaign directed by Egypt's president, Gamal Abdel Nasser, requested British and American assistance. In response, the British stationed troops in Jordan from July 17 to November 2, 1958, and the United States greatly increased its economic assistance to the kingdom.

In the years immediately following this successful defense of his crown, Hussein kept a low profile in inter-Arab politics while trying to ameliorate domestic tensions within his country. The more-or-less tolerable state of peace between Jordan and Israel was broken on June 5, 1967, by Israel's surprise attack against Arab states. Israeli warplanes destroyed almost the entire air forces of Egypt, Syria, and Jordan during the first few hours of the Six-Day War, leaving Jordan's forces vulnerable to air attack and with almost no chance to stop the Israeli advance. After a spirited defense of East Jerusalem, Jordanian units were forced to withdraw from the entire length of the West Bank with sizable casualties and loss of equipment.

## Jordanian Civil War

After the war, guerrilla commandos of the Palestinian resistance movement—better known as the *feyadeen*—expanded their organizational and recruitment activities in Jordan, Syria, and Egypt and used these countries as bases for their assaults. Their attacks against Israeli targets captured the imagination of the Arab world. In particular, Palestinian expatriates saw in these fighters hope for regaining their homeland from Israeli control. Hashemite claims to the West Bank had never been supported by most Palestinians or the other Arab states, and the military debacle of the Arab governments in the 1967 Arab-Israeli War destroyed any lingering Palestinian support for the Jordanian position.

In the immediate aftermath of the 1967 war, Hussein permitted the PLO to organize and strike at Israel from Jordanian territory in the hope that he would be able to have some degree of influence over their operations. By 1970 these hopes had been dashed as the PLO sought to establish its political dominance within the Palestinian refugee community and ultimately in all of Jordan.

By September 1970 the rising tensions had escalated into a full-scale civil war in Jordan. Ostensibly, the Popular Front for the Liberation of Palestine triggered the war by hijacking three commercial airplanes belonging to American, British, and Swiss airlines. The hijackers held four hundred passengers hostage on a deserted airstrip in Jordan. Hussein viewed the hijacking and standoff in the desert as the beginning of a power struggle for control of Jordan. He decided to hurl his army against the Palestinian resistance movement in an effort to save his throne.

Intense fighting erupted between the Jordanian army and the PLO in Amman and in a string of villages and towns near the Syrian border. Syrian armored units, camouflaged to look like Palestine Liberation Organization units, charged across the Jordanian border on September 20, 1970. After consultations with the Americans to see how they might support him, Hussein decided to throw his small air force against the invading Syrian armor. Syrian air force commander Hafez al-Assad, noting Israel's mobilization along the Jordanian and Syrian border, decided not to support the Syrian tanks with air cover, thereby allowing Jordanian air power to pummel the nearly defenseless tanks as they retreated back into Syria. The lightly armed PLO guerrilla forces were no match for the artillery, tanks, and aircraft of the Jordanian army and lost ground everywhere.

Foreign ministers of surrounding Arab states met in Cairo on September 22, 1970, to try to resolve the conflict. King Hussein and PLO leader Yasir Arafat signed an agreement calling for substantial concessions by the fedayeen. Nevertheless, tensions continued. In July 1971 the Jordanian army crushed the last PLO positions in the pine forest above the northwestern Jordanian village of Ajlun. The fighting was reported to have been so bitter that many PLO fighters sought to swim the

Jordan River and surrender to the Israelis rather than face the Jordanian army.

Although Hashemite rule was preserved in Jordan, the regime was forced to bear an onerous political burden. Jordan had come to be viewed as the enemy of the Palestinian movement, and the PLO swore revenge. The first of many casualties of this shadowy war was Jordan's prime minister, Wasfi al-Tal, who was assassinated in Cairo in November 1971.

## Regional Politics

In October 1974 at the Rabat Arab summit conference, the PLO was declared the officially recognized representative of the Palestinian people, the objections of King Hussein notwithstanding. Hussein argued that the PLO would never be able to wrest Palestine from the Israelis militarily or to effect a political settlement. Grudgingly, he acquiesced to the Rabat decision. At the same time, however, cautious Hussein maintained his options by strengthening his contacts with the Palestinian community on the West Bank, cooperating more with Syrian authorities, and intimating that he remained open to discussions with Israel on a wide range of issues.

Jordan's performance during the 1973 October war did not increase its political standing with other Arab countries. Hussein did not opt to enter the war until it was well into its final stages and then only by sending armored units to fight in the Syrian Golan Heights. The border between Israel and Jordan remained quiet during the entire war.

The civil war in Lebanon that began in 1975 gave Jordan an opportunity to decrease its political isolation. Hussein watched the Arab consensus that had formed after the October war and the Rabat summit come unglued, thereby increasing his maneuvering room. Beginning in 1977 an uneasy reconciliation took place between Hussein and PLO chairman Arafat.

Egyptian president Anwar Sadat's 1977 visit to Jerusalem was followed in 1979 by the Camp David peace treaty between Egypt and Israel. The agreement visualized a role for Jordan in a future settlement of the Palestinian issue, raising considerable skepticism in Amman. To Hussein, Sadat seemed to be opting out of the struggle for Palestinian national rights and bypassing the truly difficult issues—the political nature of the Palestinian entity on the West Bank, the level of Israel's official presence there, and the future of Jerusalem. Hussein believed that if Egypt, with all of the support of the United States behind it at Camp David, could not coax a viable compromise out of the Israelis, then he had little chance of doing so. The role envisaged for Jordan in the Camp David accords was nothing but a recipe for disaster, he feared.

Without the outline of a settlement in sight that at least addressed most of the issues critical to the Palestinians, Hussein resolved not to move too far ahead of the Arab consensus. Influential members of the Likud party in Israel emphatically suggested that Jordan really was the Palestinian state. Such assertions angered King Hussein.

From late 1982, after the PLO was pushed out of Lebanon by the Israeli army, until early 1986, King Hussein sought to co-opt and to subordinate PLO leader Arafat by negotiating with him on the formation of a joint Palestinian-Jordanian position and, possibly, negotiating team. Arafat, politically weakened in the wake of his defeat in Lebanon, agreed in February 1985 to an accord for political coordination with Hussein, although the details were unclear. Hussein continued to try to obtain Arafat's agreement on PLO acceptance of United Nations Security Council Resolution 242, but Arafat, whose leadership of the PLO had been rendered tenuous by more radical elements within the organization, refused. In February 1986 King Hussein broke off the dialogue with the PLO, and his relations with the organization returned to their normal coolness. (Text of UN Resolution 242, Appendix, p. 395)

Unsuccessful in his negotiations with Arafat and stung by the refusal of the U.S. Congress in 1985 to sell Jordan mobile I-Hawk air defense missiles, F-16 aircraft, and Stinger missiles, Hussein focused his attention on relations with other Arab states. The Iran-Iraq War and the attacks on shipping in the Persian Gulf by both combatants had pushed the Palestinian issue lower on the agenda of the Arab nations and the international community. King Hussein worked hard to achieve reconciliation among the Arab states, especially to gain acceptance of Egypt's return to the Arab fold. Although his main attention was now on the Arab world, he quietly made several gestures aimed at cultivating a moderate, non-PLO leadership on the West Bank, including announcement of an ambitious $1.3 billion West Bank development plan in mid-1986.

In April 1987 King Hussein secretly met with Israeli Labor party leader Shimon Peres in London and reached an agreement to work for a five-power international peace conference. This attempt at advancing negotiations foundered when Peres failed to secure the support of the Israeli cabinet for the initiative.

Jordan's relations with Iraq, Egypt, and Saudi Arabia were good, and its relations with Syria—very hostile because of Jordanian support of Iraq and Syria's support of Iran during the Iran-Iraq War—had begun to improve slightly in late 1985. Hussein tried to bring Syria together with Iraq. Saudi Arabia and the conservative Arab states of the Gulf also put pressure on Syria, especially after the Iranian threat to the Arab states of the Gulf was manifested in the Mecca riots by Iranian pilgrims in August 1987.

The high point of Hussein's diplomatic efforts in the Arab world came in November 1987 when he hosted an Arab League summit in Amman. Through relentless diplomacy, Hussein secured unanimous agreement among Arab states on two contentious issues. First, Iran's ally, Syria, agreed to join a resolution condemning Iran for holding Iraqi territory and for failing to accept a UN-sponsored cease-fire. Second, although Syria still did not agree that Egypt could rejoin the Arab League, Syrian president Hafez al-Assad agreed to a resolution explicitly permitting Arab League states to restore diplomatic relations with Egypt. Most important for King Hussein, Arafat and the PLO received little attention at the summit. The Palestinian issue—so often the main topic of Arab

summits—was clearly secondary to the Iran-Iraq War.

The popular Palestinian uprising on the West Bank and Gaza known as the *intifada* that began in December 1987 transformed Jordan's diplomatic position and had serious consequences for its domestic situation. Unlike the other Arab countries abutting Israel, Jordan faced more than a foreign policy matter in the Palestinian problem. Hussein feared that the uprising could spill over and affect the Palestinians of the East Bank, who had become more or less integrated into the Jordanian polity since the Jordanian-Palestinian war of 1970. Moreover, the intifada threatened to diminish his role in the Middle East peace process relative to the PLO, which, although it had not started and did not control the uprising, still commanded the allegiance of most West Bank and Gaza Palestinians. Hussein pinned his hopes on international efforts to restart the peace process; the United States and moderate factions in Israel remained firmly committed to a key role for Jordan in the process and outcome of any Arab-Israeli negotiations. Although Hussein could not agree to the proposals of U.S. secretary of state George P. Shultz in March 1988 because they went too far in front of Arab consensus on the conflict, he was cordial to U.S. attempts to restart negotiations, knowing that he would be a key player in any American effort.

Arafat, meanwhile, took advantage of the uprising to strengthen his leadership role. The PLO leader succeeded in assembling an extraordinary conference of the Arab League in June 1988. There the Arab heads of state (minus Egypt, which had still not been permitted to rejoin) gave their full attention to the Palestinian issue. The Jordanian king could not prevent the summit from adopting Arafat's proposal to give the PLO full financial control over support to the Palestinians in the occupied territories. In an even more threatening proposal, Arafat suggested that, as leader of the PLO, he should be the sole legal representative of all Palestinians everywhere. The summit did not adopt this stand, but it was affirmed by the Palestine National Council in November 1988. This

*Hussein ibn Talal*

proposal was an insult and a threat to the king of Jordan, whose population is 60 percent Palestinian.

## Renunciation of West Bank Claims

In response to these events, and perhaps hoping to insulate his kingdom from the continuing violence in the occupied territories, King Hussein formally severed his connections to the West Bank on July 31, 1988. This bold move renounced Jordanian claims to the area that had existed since 1950, and it called on the PLO to take responsibility for the Palestinians in the occupied territories that it had long claimed. Hussein quickly implemented this decision by severing all legal and administrative ties to the area: he dissolved the Jordanian parliament (half of whose members represented the West Bank); he ordered the Jordanian passports held by West Bank Palestinians to be changed into two-year travel documents; and he

cut off salaries to West Bank residents who were being paid by Jordan to administer the West Bank but who had not been able to perform their jobs since 1967 because of the Israeli occupation.

This surprising change in Jordanian policy profoundly altered the situation in the Middle East. Pressure grew on the PLO to act like a proclaimed state-in-exile, and by the end of 1988 the PLO had proclaimed the independence of Palestine (which King Hussein recognized immediately), accepted UN Security Council Resolution 242, recognized the existence of Israel in a formula acceptable to the United States, and moved into formal dialogue with the latter.

The United States and moderate Israeli leaders were unhappy with the king's announcement, having hoped for a long time to avoid the establishment of a Palestinian state by some arrangement with the kingdom of Jordan. Both the United States and Israel had viewed Hussein as the Arab leader around whom a solution to the Arab-Israeli conflict could be most likely constructed, but neither had given him much help in his efforts to maintain his leadership of the West Bank. The United States had provided Jordan with considerable economic assistance over the years, but recent U.S. administrations had found Congress mistrustful of Jordan and unwilling to sell King Hussein the weapons he regarded as essential.

## Trend Toward Democracy?

An important result of the king's renunciation of claims to the West Bank was to decrease Jordan's influence regionally. But the decision freed him to devote more attention to Jordan's pressing domestic problems. In April 1989 Hussein announced the establishment of a new National Assembly to be chosen democratically from citizens of the kingdom solely on the East Bank to which the frontiers of Jordan were now clearly limited. The elections which took place in November were the first that had been held in Jordan since 1967 war with Israel.

A notable feature of the new eighty-person National Assembly was the election of Islamic fundamentalist candidates to about 40 percent of the parliamentary seats. Campaigning under the slogan, "Islam is the solution," the Islamists, whose principal goal was the revival of Islamic law in Jordan, emerged as the largest bloc in the National Assembly, but they did not control it. Reacting pragmatically rather than ideologically to their new-found political strength, they tended to support the king's policies, despite disagreement with some, including his policy of disengagement from the West Bank.

The king's commitment toward increased democratization also was apparent in the diminishing role of the security services that formerly had played an important role in securing the stability of his regime. In November 1989 Hussein announced his intention to appoint a royal commission for the purpose of drafting a national charter that would legalize political parties—banned since 1957—and regulate political life in Jordan. In April 1990 he appointed a sixty-member commission for this purpose and accepted the draft of its work in January 1991. In June of that year the charter was formally ratified and implemented.

Perhaps the chief highlight of the national charter, which may be thought of as a constitutional basis for future governments of Jordan, was its assertion of a social contract between the monarchy and its politically active subjects. Where political opposition in Jordan historically had expressed itself by questioning the legitimacy of the monarchy, the charter provided for the expression of all political views in return for the stated allegiance of any recognized political party to the institution of the monarchy. In short, the charter sought to channel political opposition away from the king and increase the potential for political participation in Jordan, yet enable the king to continue to play the decisive role in Jordanian politics.

## The Agony of the Gulf Crisis

These dramatic domestic developments proceeded during the midst of the Gulf crisis provoked by Iraqi president Saddam Hussein's inva-

sion and occupation of Kuwait in August 1990. The Gulf crisis posed a difficult dilemma for King Hussein. Jordan and Iraq had developed a particularly close relationship, especially during the 1980s when Iraq was fighting for its existence during the prolonged war with Iran. Iraq had become highly dependent on Jordan as a transhipment route for war materials and other goods reaching Iraq via the Jordanian port of Aqaba. Jordan, too, had become highly dependent on Iraq, which supplied it with more than 90 percent of its petroleum requirements and nearly 50 percent of its international trade. Many Jordanian businessmen had profited from and were dependent on the brisk trade in goods and services between Iraq and the outside world. King Hussein favored a strong Iraq as an ultimate guarantor of Jordanian national security in the event of a serious conflict with Israel, or even with Syria.

Yet the traditionally pro-Western Jordanian monarchy also had close ties with Egypt, Saudi Arabia, the smaller Arab Gulf states, and the principal Western powers—the United States and other countries that coalesced to oppose the Iraqi invasion of Kuwait. King Hussein was quick to condemn the Iraqi aggression and worked to diplomatically reverse it. But at the same time, he opposed the U.S.-led coalition's commitment to resolve the crisis by force, if necessary.

The economic embargo imposed on Iraq hurt Jordan perhaps more than the more self-sufficient Iraq. Caught between "Iraq and a hard place," as many pundits noted, Jordan pursued a policy of effective neutrality. In the king's view this stance was principled. But in the eyes of most members of the anti-Iraq coalition, it was tantamount to supporting the Iraqi dictator. Fortunately for King Hussein, despite the economic hardships that flowed from general adherence to the economic embargo, the loss of aid from members of the anti-Iraq coalition, and a large influx of refugees from Iraq and Kuwait, his policy was popular among most sectors of the Jordanian population. Indeed, some analysts even suggested that any other policy might have toppled the Hashemite monarchy.

Jordan suffered serious consequences as a result of the Gulf crisis. It quickly experienced severe shortages and had to impose rationing on basic commodities, such as rice, sugar, and powdered milk. A rapid decline in international trade threw the country almost immediately into an economic recession from which it was difficult to emerge after the end of the crisis. A sudden influx of nearly three hundred thousand refugees from Iraq and Kuwait increased the size of Jordan's resident population by nearly 8 percent in the space of just a few weeks. This added population compounded the unemployment problem and represented a loss in worker remittances from the Gulf, which had amounted to $623 million in 1989.

Lost too was the economic aid that Jordan previously had received from Saudi Arabia and the other small, oil-rich Arab Gulf states. Some estimates of Jordan's economic losses resulting from the Gulf crisis ranged as high as $2 billion (higher if the loss were projected over a number of future years). In addition, the crisis brought the economic burden of a flood of refugees to Jordan who had fled hardship and potential war in Kuwait and Iraq.

Jordan experienced near-complete international isolation during the Gulf crisis. Jordan's official adherence to the sanctions imposed on Iraq cut it off from effective relations with that country. Meanwhile Jordan's neutrality brought the hostile reactions of Saudi Arabia and the Gulf states as well as most of the major Western powers, including the United States. The Saudi government, with which King Hussein had always had close ties, was especially vindictive over Jordan's stand during the crisis. In September 1990 Riyadh suspended deliveries of oil to Jordan and expelled twenty Jordanian diplomats in retaliation for King Hussein's position.

Domestically, however, King Hussein's popularity in Jordan soared to new heights. Jordanian support for his policy toward Iraq and his ongoing initiatives at promoting democratic trends in Jordan combined to strengthen the legitimacy of his throne.

## Jordan and the Peace Process

Although improvement in relations between Jordan and the Arab Gulf states was very slow following the Gulf crisis, relations with the United States and other Western countries improved rapidly. The vital role required of Jordan in the American- and Soviet-sponsored Arab-Israeli peace initiative that followed soon after the end of the Gulf crisis meant that Jordan would escape some of the isolation that had affected the country during the crisis. By July 1991 the United States had restored $35 million in economic aid to Jordan that had been frozen during the Gulf crisis, and following Jordan's participation in the first round of the Arab-Israeli peace talks held in Madrid in October 1991, a further $22 million in military aid from the United States was extended.

Following Syria's agreement to participate in the Madrid summit, Jordan indicated its acceptance as well. The participation of Jordan made it possible for a Palestinian delegation to participate within the framework of a joint Jordanian-Palestinian delegation. Otherwise, Israel indicated that it would refuse to join the negotiating process. Once talks began, however, Jordanian members of the delegation assiduously avoided addressing questions related to the occupied territories, referring them to the Palestinian members of the contingent who spoke for themselves rather than as an element of a joint delegation. It soon became clear that the Palestinian delegation was negotiating separately from the Jordanian contingent and was coordinating its positions with PLO headquarters in Tunisia. The PLO therefore was present in a de facto sense, despite historic Israeli commitments never to negotiate with the PLO.

Such developments were possible because of general agreement that a Jordanian-Palestinian confederation and not an independent Palestinian state would be the farthest-reaching outcome that could result from the peace process. In June 1992, however, the Labor party replaced the Likud party as the government of Israel. Soon the new Israeli government led by Prime Minister Yitzhak Rabin opened a secret direct dialogue with the PLO, a dialogue that culminated in mutual recognition and the formal signing of a Declaration of Principles in Washington on September 13, 1993. *(Text of declaration, Appendix, p. 404)*

Like other parties involved in the peace process, Jordan was caught by surprise by the Israel-PLO agreement. But King Hussein quickly endorsed it and authorized the signing and publication of the Jordan-Israeli agenda for an eventual settlement that had been worked out in the bilateral negotiations between their two delegations. Others in Jordan, particularly the Islamist members of the parliament and some leftists, denounced the Israel-PLO agreement and also opposed the Israel-Jordan agenda. The question of what status the Palestinian majority in Jordan would have following a comprehensive Arab-Israeli settlement quickly became an issue of concern that the king sought to ameliorate by assurances that all Jordanians, whatever their origins, had a place in his kingdom.

## Peace with Israel

The issues separating Jordan and Israel had less to do with bilateral disputes than with regional tensions. With the PLO heavily engaged with Israel in a peace process, Jordan had plenty of political cover to pursue its own agreement with Israel. Jordanian-Israeli enmities were far less extreme than those that existed between Israel and the PLO and Israel and Syria. Since the 1967 Six-Day War, Jordan and Israel had not engaged in significant combat. Moreover, the Israeli leadership and King Hussein had already established a working relationship. Hussein had long been the Israeli government's preferred negotiating partner.

In the wake of Israel's withdrawal from the Gaza Strip and Jericho in the late spring of 1994, Israel and Jordan moved quickly toward ending the state of war between them. On July 18, for the first time, Israeli and Jordanian peace negotiators met on their own territory. They held sessions in a large tent that straddled the Israeli-Jordanian border a few miles north of the Gulf of Aqaba. Israeli

foreign minister Shimon Peres visited Jordan two days later.

On July 25 King Hussein and Prime Minister Rabin arrived in Washington for the ceremonial signing of an agreement between the two countries. The "Washington Declaration" was not a full peace treaty; rather, it was an agreement ending the forty-six-year state of war that existed between the two countries and providing for further negotiations on a range of issues leading toward a comprehensive agreement. Such a treaty was signed by Israel and Jordan on October 26. It provided for an exchange of ambassadors and broad cooperation in trade, tourism, water allocation, transportation, communications, environmental protection, and border arrangements. Both nations pledged not to allow third parties to use their territory for an attack against the other and Israel recognized Jordan's role as a guardian of Islamic holy places in Jerusalem. Both leaders hoped their improved relationship would translate into trade and other economic benefits that would build a strong constituency for peace among the people of both countries.

## Current Issues

Jordan historically has been forced to balance a number of powerful, conflicting pressures. Neighboring countries—Iraq, Syria, Saudi Arabia, and even the PLO—have at various times competed with the Jordanian regimes for the loyalties of certain segments of the population. During the 1950s and 1960s it was primarily the Nasserist-inspired theme of Arab nationalism and unity that posed a constant challenge to the stability of the Jordanian monarchy. Following the 1967 war with Israel, itself a severe humiliation for the king, it was primarily the rapidly emerging PLO that competed with King Hussein for the loyalty of the large number of Jordanian citizens of Palestinian origin. After the September 1970 Jordanian civil war between the regime and the PLO, the king was able to exert a strong hand over the affairs of his country.

Large infusions of foreign aid during the oil boom years of the 1970s and early 1980s greatly aided the king in consolidating the strength of the monarchy over an otherwise resource-poor state. But growing dependence on foreign aid weakened his ability to be fully independent of foreign influences and demands. Diminishing oil revenues in the late 1980s threatened to reverse the situation and ultimately led the king, under pressure from the Palestinian intifada, to undertake the political reforms of the late 1980s. These measures served to maintain the stability of the regime but did nothing to reverse the deterioration of the Jordanian economy, which received its most serious shock during the Gulf War.

Economic issues, far more than political issues, therefore, were the key challenge facing the Jordanian government during the 1990s. Jordan had a foreign debt of more than $7 billion at the end of 1993 and a negative current accounts balance of about $600 million. It suffered from high unemployment, and its refusal to support the anti-Iraq coalition had cut it off from most financial assistance from the Gulf states. Unlikely to be relieved of these pressures in the near term (Saudi King Fahd was reported to have said he would never speak to King Hussein again during his lifetime), Jordan's best hope seemed to reside in an effective resolution of the Arab-Israeli conflict that would open borders throughout the region to enlarged trade and new sources of development capital.

Yet a resolution of the Arab-Israeli conflict held several economic uncertainties for Jordan. An agreement between the PLO and Israel might direct significant aid to the new Palestinian self-governing authority, while leaving Jordan largely forgotten. The prospect that the new Palestinian entity would be more closely linked economically by treaty with Israel than Jordan was also worrisome. In addition, the very real likelihood that many Palestinians unhappy with the Israel-PLO settlement (such as the Islamic militants of Gaza) might eventually find their way to Jordan could aggravate unemployment and budget shortfalls. Finally, the possibility that long-time Palestinian residents of Jordan might begin to invest their capital in the new Palestinian political entity rather than Jordan implied that the country's economic crisis might be worsened rather than resolved as a result of peace.

In the face of these possibilities, an expansion of economic ties to Israel and the emerging Palestinian state is imperative for Jordan. The peace between Israel and Jordan has already begun to stimulate commerce between them. In addition, in response to Jordan's step toward peace, the United States has forgiven $220 million of Jordan's $700 million debt to the United States. Forgiveness of the rest of the amount has been promised by the Clinton administration.

## Outlook

King Hussein has never been able to sit easily on his throne. Although the reasons have differed through the years, and today he is riding at the crest of his popularity, he will continue to face difficult dilemmas through the last decade of the twentieth century. He has ruled his country for more than forty years and is now one of the world's longest-serving heads of state. Yet he will observe only his sixtieth birthday in 1995 and could have many more years to rule. A successful operation for cancer in 1992 raised consciousness concerning his mortality but also demonstrated his popularity when thousands poured into the streets to welcome his return following the operation. His brother and designated successor, Crown Prince Hassan, is also popular and respected in the country and may favor Jordan's democratic experiment more than Hussein himself. A smooth succession in the event of the king's untimely death seems likely, especially in the new political environment created by the national charter, which seeks to permanently legitimize the monarchy as a Jordanian political institution.

Hussein's commitment to the democratization process was again demonstrated by the holding of new parliamentary elections in November 1993. That he still dominated the political process was apparent in the method he chose before the elections to decree a new electoral law opposed by the parliament as a means of weakening the strength of Islamist and other opposition deputies elected to the 1993 parliament.

The future inclusion of some Palestinian inhabitants of the West Bank under Jordanian rule could alter the demographic character of Hussein's kingdom, making Palestinians and Jordanians of Palestinian origin the overwhelming majority of Jordan's population. If this demographic change were to come about as a result of the peace process, it could bring a negative backlash on the part of the king's native Jordanian population, which historically has been the backbone of his support. In addition, Hussein's regime would be more vulnerable to the factionalism associated with Palestinian politics, including the split between those who have come to terms with the need to reach accommodation with Israel and those who have not.

Hussein, unlike some of the authoritarian rulers in the region, has never seemed comfortable with repressive methods of governing. There are limits, however, to how far he will extend political liberalization. He could clamp down, perhaps more severely than ever before, if he believes that Palestinian agitation, whether from the West Bank or from Palestinians in Jordan, threatens his kingdom or his power.

Economically, Jordan is emerging from the losses caused by the Gulf crisis. A European Community economic assistance package of $380 million in 1993 helped to provide some relief, and the U.S. cancellation of a part of Jordan's $7 billion external debt has been a basis of some optimism. Moreover, an April 1994 agreement to modify the mechanism for enforcing the economic embargo against Iraq by inspecting maritime cargoes on shore at the Port of Aqaba rather than at sea in the Gulf of Aqaba promised to lift some of the restraints that previously had seriously depressed Jordanian trade.

With Jordan's signing of a peace treaty with Israel, King Hussein appears to be betting that Jordan's economic future lies with Israel and the West. Signing the agreement has completely repaired Jordan's relations with the United States, which were damaged by King Hussein's sympathetic posture toward Iraq during the Persian Gulf War. It is imperative that the treaty with Israel yield quick economic benefits. If it does, King Hussein should be able to blunt internal criticism of the accord and other Arab leaders will come under increasing pressure to follow Jordan's lead.

# KUWAIT

Kuwait is recovering from a nightmare: invasion, occupation, systematic destruction, and the exile of the ruling family and more than half of the population. The Iraqi invasion in August 1990 shattered Kuwait's belief that no neighboring country would ever invade it. During a seven-month occupation, the Iraqi forces inflicted horrendous suffering on the Kuwaiti population, destroyed the country's infrastructure, stole or pillaged public and private property, and ignited 723 oil wells. The fires burned away a portion of the country's precious natural resource and left Kuwait shrouded in black smoke for eight months.

The complete rebuilding of the ruined infrastructure is largely on course. A more difficult problem for the government is the uncertain state of the country's finances and the unpopular policies it must implement to manage the debt and revive the economy. The ruling family also must contend with the continuing debate over political participation, the question of citizenship rights for naturalized citizens, and the status of women, including their right to vote.

For a time in late 1994 Kuwait was shaken by events disturbingly similar to those that preceded the onset of the 1990 nightmare. Iraqi president Saddam Hussein again massed troops near the Kuwait border as if preparing to invade. But this time Kuwait and its allies moved quickly to call Saddam's bluff and halt an invasion before it could begin. American president Bill Clinton dispatched a sizable force to the area and warned Saddam in a televised address October 10 that his action "requires a strong response from the United States and the international community." Saddam, he said, "has shown the world ... he cannot be trusted."

Iraq's saber rattling was seen as somehow related to its desperate efforts to have the United Nations lift the economic sanctions imposed against Iraq after the 1990 invasion. The embargo was causing serious shortages of food and medicine, gaining Iraq some sympathy and support in the UN for removing the sanctions. But the United States was resisting any easing of the embargo until Iraq renounced its claims to Kuwait and abandoned its hope of developing nuclear weapons. *(Iraq profile, p. 228)*

## Geography and People

*Kuwait*—meaning "little fortress"—lies at the head of the Persian Gulf, bordering Iraq and Saudi Arabia and facing Iran across the Gulf. Roughly the size of New Jersey, the country covers 6,880 square miles. It possesses ten offshore islands, the main ones being Bubiyan, Warba, and Failaka.

Kuwait's terrain is mainly flat desert with a few oases. Blazing summer temperatures often reach well into the hundreds with frequent dust and sand storms. Winters are mild with occasional frost at night. With little rainfall, drinking water is largely supplied by piped distilled sea water from the Shatt al-Arab waterway, which runs into the Persian Gulf. The oil that Iraq released into the Gulf during the war caused considerable damage to the desalination facilities and to the fishing industry.

# Key Facts on Kuwait

**Area:** 6,880 square miles.
**Capital:** Kuwait City.
**Population:** 1,819,322 (1994).
**Religion:** 85 percent Muslim, 15 percent Christian, Hindu, Parsi, and other.
**Official Language:** Arabic; English is widely spoken.
**GDP:** $25.7 billion; $15,100 per capita (1993).

*Source:* Central Intelligence Agency, *CIA World Factbook 1994.*

Agriculture is extremely limited; only 0.4 percent of the land is arable. As a result, most of the country's food is imported.

Indigenous Kuwaitis are primarily descendants of Arabian tribes. The first tribal settlers, the Anaiza from the Nejd (central Arabia), were led by the al-Sabah family. Another tribal group, the Kenaat, arrived from the Basra region of Iraq. A few notable families are of southwestern Persian (Iranian) origin. Comprising the group that are considered second-class citizens are former Palestinians and stateless Arab nomads from Syria, Jordan, and Iraq called the *bedoon* (meaning "without"). Kuwait is 85 percent Muslim, mostly Sunni, including the ruling al-Sabah family, with the rest Shi'ite. Nearly two-thirds of Kuwait's inhabitants live in Kuwait City, the capital city and principal harbor. The oil towns of Ahmadi, Jahra, Hawalli, and Farwaniya are the other principal cities.

Before the 1991 Gulf War, only 40 percent of the population was indigenous to Kuwait. Kuwait relies heavily on foreign labor for its work force, and it was one of the few Gulf countries to allow families to migrate together. Many expatriate Arabs were drawn to Kuwait by employment opportunities in the oil industry.

In 1987, however, the Kuwaiti government issued a five-year plan aimed at reducing the number of Arab and Iranian expatriates working in Kuwait. Fears of internal unrest and terrorism related to Islamic fundamentalism and the Palestinian quest for a homeland had prompted the Kuwaiti government to quietly work toward changing the work force from one dominated by Arabs and Iranians to one that relied more on workers from India, Pakistan, and other parts of Asia.

The aftermath of the 1991 Gulf War created conditions under which the government could take its most assertive steps toward reducing expatriates. Many of the Palestinians still in Kuwait were deported on the grounds that they had collaborated with the Iraqi occupiers. Kuwait also induced large numbers of non-Palestinian Arab expatriates to leave. In mid-1990 the total Kuwaiti population was estimated at 2.14 million. By mid-1992 it had decreased to just 1.30 million, mainly as a result of the departure of non-Kuwaiti residents. By 1994 it had climbed to 1.82 million.

Oil wealth transformed Kuwait by the 1960s into the ultimate cradle-to-grave welfare state. Despite not paying income tax, throughout the 1980s Kuwaitis enjoyed unparalleled access to subsidized social services, including free education, free medical care, and virtually free housing. Cash gifts also could be obtained to defray the costs of weddings and funerals. Electricity and water charges were negligible, and petroleum products were provided at deep discounts. Even domestic telephone calls were free. Until the mid-1980s Kuwaitis enjoyed per capita incomes ranking among the top five in the world.

While Kuwaiti citizens were entitled to a wide range of free services, immigrant workers' benefits were limited. This situation led to hostility between the minority native Kuwaiti population and the majority immigrant population. Kuwaiti citizenship is highly restricted even for families that have lived in Kuwait for generations.

Beginning in 1985, however, government benefits to citizens were substantially cut back because of budgetary and political constraints. A series of austerity budgets raised domestic energy prices and imposed user fees on other goods and services that previously had been free. After liberation from the Iraqi occupation, the non-Kuwaiti resident population was largely ineligible for government services and compensatory benefits. The expiration in May 1992 of existing residence permits led to a mass exodus of resident aliens of "hostile" nationalities, particularly Palestinians, Jordanians, Yemenis, and Sudanese. Foreign workers allowed into the country are, for the most part, not permitted to bring dependents with them.

## History

Kuwait's modern history dates from the founding of Kuwait City by members of the Anaiza tribe at the beginning of the eighteenth century. The ruling al-Sabah dynasty dates from 1756, when the Kuwaiti settlers decided to appoint a sheik to administer their affairs, provide for their security, and represent them in dealings with the Ottoman Empire.

During the latter half of the nineteenth century, Kuwait looked to Britain as a counterbalance to Ottoman dominance in the region and for protection from the raiding Wahhabi tribes of central Arabia. In return Kuwait recognized British trading rights in the Persian Gulf. In 1899 Mubarak al-Sabah "The Great" signed an agreement with the United Kingdom effectively establishing Kuwait as a British protectorate.

This arrangement, under which Britain controlled Kuwait's foreign affairs and security, lasted until 1961. The British intervened in Kuwait's behalf at three critical junctures. In 1899 it prevented an Ottoman invasion. In 1920 Britain repelled attacks from Wahhabi tribesmen, but Kuwait nevertheless lost some 40 percent of its territory to the expanding Saudi kingdom. The 1922 Treaty of Uqair settled this conflict and established a neutral zone south of Kuwait.

In 1961, shortly after Kuwaiti independence, Iraq claimed sovereignty over Kuwait based on old Ottoman records. When Baghdad threatened to invade, Kuwait asked for and received British military assistance, effectively deterring an Iraqi occupation. An Arab League peacekeeping force representing Saudi Arabia, Jordan, the United Arab

Republic, and Sudan arrived in September 1961 to replace the British. In 1963 Kuwait was admitted to the the Arab League and the United Nations. The new Iraqi government also recognized Kuwait's independence in 1963.

### Government and Domestic Politics

Kuwait is a hereditary constitutional monarchy ruled by an emir. The current emir, Sheikh Jaber Al-Ahmad al-Sabah, succeeded his uncle to the throne December 31, 1977. Descendants from Sheikh Mubarak's two sons, Jaber and Salim, are appointed alternately to succeed as emir. The second most powerful post of crown prince and prime minister goes to the alternate side. The current crown prince and prime minister is Sheikh Sa'ad Abdallah al-Salim al-Sabah. The Council of Ministers is appointed by the emir and headed by the prime minister. The major cabinet positions are held by the al-Sabah family members, including the key portfolios of foreign affairs, defense, and interior.

In 1961 an election was held to choose twenty members to the Constituent Assembly; the other members being ministers. This assembly drafted a new constitution in 1962 vesting legislative authority in a fifty-member National Assembly. Kuwait is the only Gulf country with a National Assembly entirely elected by popular vote. Suffrage, however, is restricted to first-class male Kuwaiti citizens—those who can prove that their ancestry dates before 1920, which is only 5 percent of the population. Women, immigrants, illiterates, and all under age twenty-one are excluded from the franchise. The press has enjoyed greater freedom after the Gulf War but still practices self-censorship. Political parties are banned, though informal caucuses (diwaniyya) comprising tribal constituencies, Arab nationalists, and Islamists have existed since the early 1980s.

Domestic politics are focused on four points of conflict: internal competition among the ruling family along dynastic lines; the relationship between the old established merchant families and the ruling family; the regime and those advocating a change in the political order—nationalists, Islamists, and secular politicians; and first-class male Kuwaiti citizens pitted against the nonenfranchised population.

The assembly was suspended from 1976 to 1981 because the emir feared its increasingly vocal criticism of the monarchy could contribute to instability. The emir suspended the assembly again in July 1986 citing security concerns, excessive division, and the need for unity in the face of the Iran-Iraq War. Assembly members had become increasingly vocal in their attacks on official corruption and government economic policy.

In late 1989 former parliamentarians demanded the revitalization of the 1962 constitution, the restoration of parliament, and the retention of the election law dividing the country into twenty-five electoral zones. Prodemocracy street demonstrations were suppressed by the government. In a conciliatory move the emir announced the formation of a provisional assembly to deliberate on a new constitution.

International pressure on the ruling family dur-

ing and after the 1991 Gulf War forced the emir to hold new elections for the National Assembly in October 1992. Although Kuwaiti women and naturalized Kuwaitis were not permitted to vote in that election, the ruling family has agreed in principle to extend voting rights to them.

## International Politics

Kuwait's regional foreign policy during the 1960s, 1970s, and early 1980s was predicated on its commitment to Arab causes and nonalignment in inter-Arab disputes. It supported mainstream Arab goals—such as Palestinian rights, Yemeni unity, and Lebanon's integrity—with political support and generous financial aid. Because of its small size and vulnerable location, Kuwaiti leaders did not believe security could be achieved through a strong Kuwaiti defense. Consequently, Kuwait sought to ensure its security by maintaining an accommodating posture toward its neighbors.

Despite its small size, Kuwait became an influential player in the Arab world through its financial resources. Using the Kuwait Development Fund, the government distributed millions to Third World countries. This checkbook diplomacy was a means of co-opting critics and rewarding friends and allies.

Kuwait took a neutral stance in the inter-Arab conflicts of the 1960s and tried to mediate in the Yemen and South Arabian conflict. During the 1967 Arab-Israeli War, Kuwait declared its support for the Arab countries and contributed heavily to the reconstruction of Egypt, Jordan, and Syria.

Kuwaiti forces stationed along the Suez Canal during the October 1973 Arab-Israeli War took part in the fighting and Kuwait contributed substantial financial aid to other involved Arab states. Kuwait also played a major role in convening a meeting of the Organization of Arab Petroleum Exporting Countries (OAPEC) to develop an Arab policy for use of oil as a weapon to pressure Western countries, particularly the United States, to force an Israeli withdrawal from occupied Arab lands. Kuwait joined other Gulf countries in a 70 percent increase in the posted price of crude petroleum, and it participated in the total embargo on petroleum shipments to the United States in 1973. At the Baghdad Arab summit in November 1978, Kuwait pressed for unanimity in condemning the Egyptian-Israeli peace agreement and supported sanctions against Egypt.

Along with Saudi Arabia, the United Arab Emirates, Qatar, Oman, and Bahrain, Kuwait was a founder of the Gulf Cooperation Council (GCC) in 1981. In the hostile climate created by the Iran-Iraq War, the oil-producing Gulf countries hoped that economic integration and political coordination would increase their security.

## The Iran-Iraq War

Fearing a spill-over of Iranian fundamentalism, Kuwait backed Iraq financially throughout the eight-year Iran-Iraq War. Kuwait also allowed Iraq access to Kuwaiti ports, enabling Iraqi petroleum exports to continue. However, Kuwait refused Iraqi requests for access to the strategic islands of Bubiyan and Warba. In retaliation for Kuwait's support of Iraq, Iran targeted Kuwaiti territory and shipping. It bombed Kuwaiti oil installations near the Iraqi border in September 1981. Terrorist attacks at the end of 1983 and in early 1984 increased concern for Kuwait's security. Six bombs exploded in Kuwait City in December 1983, killing five people and wounding sixty-one. Al-Jihad Al-Islamiya (Islamic Holy War), militant Shi'ite Muslims with acknowledged connections to Iran, claimed responsibility.

The threat of domestic unrest from the country's own fundamentalist Shi'ites led to the deportation of more than six hundred Iranian workers and increased restrictions on their free passage through Kuwait. The bombings in May 1984 of two Kuwaiti oil tankers in the Gulf were perceived as warnings to Kuwait to reduce its support for Iraq in the war with Iran. In December 1984 tensions heightened when a Kuwaiti airliner was hijacked and forced to land in Tehran. The hijackers demanded the release of the seventeen Shi'ites imprisoned for the 1983 bomb attacks. The terrorists were overwhelmed after killing two Americans.

In May 1985 an Iraqi member of the banned Al-Dawa Al-Islamiya (Voice of Islam) organization attempted to assassinate Emir Jaber Al-Ahmad by driving a car bomb into a royal procession. During 1985 and 1986 other terrorist incidents followed, including explosions at Kuwait's main export refinery and deadly bombings in Kuwait City. Security became an obsession. Almost twenty-seven thousand expatriates, many of them Iranians, were deported, and the National Assembly unanimously approved the death penalty for terrorist acts that result in loss of life.

To punish Kuwait for loading petroleum in Iraq's behalf, Iranian forces began attacking merchant ships and seizing cargoes sailing to or from Kuwait. In an attempt to deter attacks, Kuwait sought protection in December 1986 for its oil tankers from both the United States and the Soviet Union. After the Soviets offered protection, the United States agreed to Kuwait's request. The American decision was designed to block growing Soviet influence in the Gulf. In May 1987 eleven Kuwaiti tankers were re-registered under the protection of U.S. naval forces. Kuwaiti oil tankers also sailed under the flags of Liberia, the Soviet Union, and the United Kingdom. Within days, a reflagged tanker hit a mine. The United States and Saudi Arabia helped in clearing mines, and in August, after initially refusing, France and Great Britain sent minesweeping vessels to the Gulf, as did the Netherlands, Belgium, and Italy in September.

In April 1988 a Kuwait Airways Boeing 747 was hijacked by a group believed to be affiliated with a pro-Iranian Shi'ite organization in Lebanon. After landing in Iran the group demanded the release of the seventeen Shi'ite Muslims imprisoned in Kuwait for terrorism. The fifteen-day hijacking ordeal, in which two Kuwaitis were killed, eventually ended in Algeria where the plane had been forced to land. The Algerian government negotiated the release of the hostages in exchange for safe passage out of the country for the hijackers.

*Jaber Al-Ahmad al-Sabah*

## Prelude to 1991 Gulf War

The 1988 UN-sponsored cease-fire between Iran and Iraq raised the confidence of the region and held the promise of stability for an exhausted region. After years of war and recession, Kuwait's economy began to improve. In its drive for market share to increase oil revenues, beginning in 1987 Kuwait consistently ignored OPEC production quotas. Iraq's economy, on the other hand, was exhausted by its war effort and on the verge of a financial crisis. Kuwait expected repayment for the equivalent of $16 billion in cash and oil sales that it had provided Iraq. Meanwhile, Iraq considered the massive debts that it had accumulated during the war the minimum contribution that Iraq's sacrifices merited in defense of the Arab world. Iraq also believed that the primary purpose of Kuwaiti overproduction was to weaken the Iraqi economy.

In July 1990 President Saddam Hussein of Iraq accused unspecified countries of petroleum overproduction in violation of quotas, which had been fixed at a May 1990 OPEC meeting. He accused Kuwait of stealing $2.4 billion worth of oil reserves from a well in an area where the borderline was undemarcated. Saddam also demanded border modifications and the leasing of Bubiyan Island. In severe economic straits after its war with Iran, Iraq sought redress through the Arab League. Iraqi foreign minister Tariq Aziz demanded that Kuwait cancel Iraq's war debt, compensate it for lost revenue incurred during its war with Iran and as a result of Kuwait's overproduction, and provide $10 billion in emergency aid. In addition, Iraq accused Kuwait of violating its borders by establishing military posts and drilling wells on Iraqi territory.

Iraqi threats against Kuwait raised tension in the region. Iraqi and Kuwaiti representatives met in Saudi Arabia on August 1 in an attempt to resolve the conflict. Kuwait refused to cede territory but was willing to pay half of the amount demanded by Iraq. Consequently, the talks collapsed. Despite assurances by Saddam Hussein to President Hosni Mubarak of Egypt and King Hussein of Jordan that Iraq would not use military force against Kuwait, and further attempts by King Fahd of Saudi Arabia to mediate a solution, Iraq prepared to attack.

On August 2, 1990, Iraq invaded Kuwait with a force of one hundred thousand troops. Kuwait's total military strength numbered twenty thousand. Emir Jaber and the royal family fled to Saudi Arabia along with some three hundred thousand Kuwaiti citizens. Many others were already abroad on holiday. Only one in four Kuwaitis remained in the country, together with the bedoon and Palestinian populations who had few options for resettlement.

The invasion had caught Kuwait by surprise. In the days leading up to the attack, Kuwaiti military officials had pressed the government to allow them to call a partial or complete military alert. The Kuwaiti regime, however, believed that such a move could give Iraq a pretext for an invasion. Consequently, when the assault did occur, as many as three-quarters of the Kuwaiti armed forces personnel were on leave or away from their military posts. Kuwaiti military leaders have asserted that had they been able to prepare their forces they could have slowed the Iraqi invasion force for several days.

## Iraqi Occupation

Saddam Hussein formally annexed Kuwait on August 8 and declared it the nineteenth province of Iraq on August 28. Kuwaiti rejection of Iraqi rule was broad and deeply rooted. Even opposition leaders, who criticized the al-Sabahs' rule, declared their support for Emir Jaber as head of state.

From the first day of occupation, Iraqi troops plundered, burned, and ransacked the country. They also kidnapped, tortured, raped, and assassinated Kuwaiti citizens and foreigners. What they could not steal they destroyed in a seemingly deliberate effort to efface all traces of the Kuwaiti culture. Resistance to Iraqi occupation took two forms: sabotage by Kuwaiti soldiers and policemen who infiltrated Kuwait from Saudi Arabia, and attacks on Iraqi troops and equipment by organized groups of resistance fighters within occupied Kuwait. With little outside coordination, the resistance activists, composed largely of the lower classes, who could not afford to flee, succeeded in building up their groups within Kuwait. The resistance inflicted persistent if minor damage on the occupying forces.

The Kuwaiti government in exile was headquartered in Taif, Saudi Arabia. The Kuwait Investment Office in London was used as a national treasury to pay living expenses of Kuwaiti citizens stranded abroad. On October 13 the al-Sabahs held a national convention attended by a thousand delegates. This convention was designed to present a united front against Iraq, counter Iraq's popular appeal with the Arab and Muslim masses, demonstrate the legitimacy of al-Sabah rule, and accommodate U.S. and Arab wishes to see a more democratic Kuwait worthy of the international efforts being made for its liberation. The opposition mem-

bers of the dissolved National Assembly used the event to extract concessions for democratic reforms. Determined to present a strong national front, the al-Sabahs relented and agreed to "consolidate democracy under the 1962 constitution" after liberation and to nullify the June 1990 elections and hold new elections according to the provisions of the constitution.

The al-Sabahs acted to solidify the support of regional powers. The Kuwaitis gave $2.5 billion to anti-Iraq coalition members Egypt and Turkey and forgave Egypt's huge debt. In contrast, all aid was cut off to Jordan, the Palestine Liberation Organization (PLO), and Yemen for their support of Iraq. Kuwait moved to reestablish ties with Iran and expressed satisfaction that Iran condemned the occupation of Kuwait. In exile and under occupation, the Kuwaitis could do little but wait for the anti-Iraqi coalition to liberate them.

## The Gulf War and Aftermath

On January 17, 1991, the UN-backed, U.S.-led multinational force launched its military campaign to liberate Kuwait. After an intense aerial bombardment of Iraq, ground forces entered Kuwait on February 24. Within three days, Iraqi troops had been driven from the country and Saddam Hussein agreed to accept all UN Security Council resolutions governing disposition of the crisis.

The ruling family returned in early March to a Kuwait under martial law. Most of Kuwait's government buildings, desalination plants, and harbor facilities were destroyed or damaged. Enormous structural and environmental war damage had left the country in a state of unrest. Human rights groups alleged that Palestinians suspected of collaboration were being tortured by security forces. Middle East Watch, a human rights monitoring group, claimed several weeks after liberation that Kuwaiti security forces and freelance gangs had detained and tortured approximately two thousand Palestinian residents of Kuwait who were suspected of collaborating with Iraqi troops. Many Palestinians complained of abuse and said that Kuwaiti authorities were not providing as much food and water to Palestinians as other residents of Kuwait received.

Repatriation of the national population was one of the government's highest priorities. The regime initiated a program to register all non-Kuwaiti nationals resident in the country, and it prohibited the return of non-Kuwaitis until labor requirements were calculated. The government exploited the Iraqi invasion's displacement of expatriates by announcing a restriction on the number of non-Kuwaiti residents to less than 50 percent of the precrisis total. The Palestinian population declined from a precrisis high of four hundred thousand to no more than forty thousand after the occupation.

The Kuwaiti public was discontented over the government's failure to restore supplies of electricity, food, and water in a timely manner. The regime announced that elections would take place within a year, following the return of Kuwaiti exiles and the compilation of a new electoral roll.

Before the invasion, many Kuwaitis were unhappy with the form and substance of the al-Sabahs' rule. The ruling family had occasionally loosened its grip on power and allowed its citizens to dabble with various constitutional and parliamentarian reforms, but these reforms have never endured. Many Kuwaitis who survived Iraqi atrocities felt empowered to demand change. With the royal family in exile, the invasion provided fertile ground for the Kuwaiti resistance movement to organize and gain strength and purpose. A new willingness to challenge the old order was manifest by the claims of some Kuwaitis that the resistance movement did not receive from the Kuwaiti government-in-exile the material and financial assistance it needed to be effective, because the royal family did not want the resistance to pose a threat after liberation. There also was sentiment among some Kuwaitis that the emir could have prevented the Iraqi invasion with more astute foreign and economic policies.

While many Kuwaitis were clamoring for more democratic freedoms and stronger voice in the country's decision making, there were many others who believed the al-Sabahs needed to unify the country under their rule. After the trauma of the Iraqi invasion, many Kuwaitis did not want divisive domestic political debates to invite subversion or foreign aggression. These supporters of the royal family and the royal family itself may be intolerant of any challenge to the old order from below. Days after the country was liberated, a well-known former member of the Kuwaiti parliament and critic of the royal family was shot, sending a clear signal to other dissidents that democratic change would not come easily.

## Oil and the Economy

Before the development of the oil industry, the Kuwaiti economy was based on fishing, trading, and pearling. Oil was discovered in 1938 by the Anglo-Persian Oil Company (now British Petroleum) and the Gulf Oil Corporation. The wells were capped at the onset of World War II, and further development was delayed until 1948. But by 1956 Kuwait was the largest oil producer in the Middle East. Kuwait bought out British Petroleum and Gulf Oil in March 1975, thereby becoming the first Arab petroleum-producing nation to achieve complete control of its own output. The Kuwait Petroleum Corporation is the twelfth largest such company in the world.

Kuwait has channeled its income from petroleum sales into five areas: industrial diversification, the development of substantial social services, the creation of the Reserve Fund for Future Generations, overseas investment through the Kuwait Investment Office, and aid to poorer countries—Arab, African, and Asian—through the Kuwait Fund for Arab Economic Development.

Despite government efforts to diversify the economy and to provide alternative sources of employment, oil and gas production dominates the economy, accounting for approximately 50 percent of gross domestic product and 90 percent of export earnings.

Kuwait's considerable overseas investments have allowed it to withstand periods of economic uncertainty. In 1986, for the first time, income from its overseas investments yielded higher revenues than petroleum exports. Nevertheless, the onset of the oil glut of the 1980s inflicted on Kuwait serious financial difficulties that have been compounded by the Persian Gulf War.

In the early 1980s, due to lower oil prices that accompanied the Iran-Iraq War, Kuwait suffered its first budget deficits. The economy slid in 1982 into a recession that lasted until the end of the decade. The breakdown of Kuwait's unofficial stock market, Souk Al-Manakh, in September 1982 lead to a prolonged financial crisis. The collapse impoverished many businessmen and Kuwaiti banks were burdened with huge nonperforming loans. Subsequently, Kuwait's position as the Gulf's major business center was lost to Abu Dhabi.

From the Iraqi invasion in August 1990 until July 1991, Kuwait was solely dependent on its income from its international financial investments and profits from Kuwait Petroleum International, which operates Kuwaiti petroleum companies in Europe and Asia. Kuwait's investments were drained from $100 billion to $40 billion to fund the government's efforts during the 1990-91 crisis.

The occupying Iraqi forces severely damaged Kuwait's oil-producing facilities. An estimated eight hundred of the country's nine hundred fifty oil wells had been sabotaged, with 723 set aflame by the retreating troops. The cost of repairing the wells and extinguishing the fires, combined with losses of oil revenues, was estimated at more than $40 billion. Rehabilitation of the petroleum sector became the highest economic priority for the government.

The cost of the Gulf War and disruption of petroleum production exacerbated the budget deficit. Between 1990 and 1993 the Kuwaiti national debt was run up to more than $60 billion. Kuwait committed approximately $100 billion to the cost of the war—$16 billion in direct military expenditure, $19 billion in aid and other indirect costs, and $60 billion in reconstruction costs and lost oil revenues. Kuwait is claiming $64 billion in reparations from Iraq for damages, theft, and lost revenues from oil production as well as unpaid Iraqi debts.

The government's 1992 buyout of personal and corporate debts dating back to the Souk Al-Manakh crisis accounts for a third of the cumulative debt. Many of the major debtors are members of the royal family, and until the problem of equitable repayment is resolved private sector initiatives will remain stalled, delaying economic recovery. The new assembly passed a public funds protection law in January 1993 imposing greater transparency and accountability on state-owned investment companies' dealings.

The growth in the economy stimulated by postwar reconstruction has slowed down. Oil production capacity reached 2.5 million barrels a day in November 1993 but Kuwait's OPEC's quota remains at about 2.0 million barrels a day. Kuwait believes it has the right to maximize its output to recoup revenues lost during and after the Iraqi invasion. With oil prices down and forecast to remain low, they could fall further if OPEC countries do not respect their quotas and Kuwait could suffer the loss of OPEC's goodwill.

A November 1993 World Bank report on Kuwait recommends wide-scale privatization, economic liberalization, reduction of welfare subsidies, and cutting the bloated bureaucracy. The state employs an estimated 95 percent of the national work force. The private sector enjoys protected markets, subsidies, and bailouts in the event of financial losses.

## Foreign Policy

The 1991 Gulf War shattered Kuwait's assumption that no regional power would ever challenge its existence and security. After the war, Kuwait was confronted with a profound security challenge. Its former ally, Iraq, was a weakened but still looming threat on its border. Iran remained as dangerous as before, especially given that Iraq could no longer be considered a counterweight to Iranian adventurism in the Gulf region.

Immediately after the war, Kuwait participated in the development of the so-called Damascus Declaration of March 1991. This was a defense agreement between the Gulf Cooperation Council nations, including Kuwait, and Syria and Egypt. The agreement, however, drew the strident opposition of Iran, which objected to the presence of non-Gulf Arabs in the Gulf region. In addition, disputes between Egypt and Kuwait regarding compensation for Egyptian workers expelled from Kuwait and payment for Egyptian military support caused the Gulf states to reconsider the Damascus Declaration.

Recognizing its inability to defend itself and the declining chances that a purely Arab security arrangement could be effective, Kuwait sought bilateral defense agreements with its Western allies. The Kuwaiti defense minister signed a ten-year defense pact with the United States in September 1991.

Kuwait also moved ahead with plans to increase the size and efficiency of its armed forces. Two-year military service became compulsory for male Kuwaiti nationals. The financial burden of reconstruction and the limited capabilities of its small population, however, ensure that Kuwait will not be able to provide for its own defense. Nevertheless, Kuwait plans a $350 million upgrading of its Ali Al-Salem and Ahmed Al-Jabar bases.

A number of nations that had been beneficiaries of Kuwaiti largess—the PLO, Yemen, and Jordan—were sympathetic to Iraq during the Persian Gulf War. In addition, Sudan, Tunisia, and Mauritania did not condemn the invasion. Kuwait's sense of betrayal by these countries runs deep. Financial aid to them was discontinued. Foreign aid is now directed to the Arab countries that provided military support in the anti-Iraq coalition, especially Egypt, Syria, and Morocco.

Despite its break with the Jordanian and PLO leaderships, Kuwait welcomed the historic agreement between Israel and the PLO in September of 1993. Kuwait became the first country after Egypt to relax its boycott of Israel.

## U.S. Relations

Since the Persian Gulf War, Kuwait has regarded the United States as its ultimate strategic defender. Despite its criticism of U.S. policy toward Israel, Kuwait believes that the United States can be counted on to come to its aid. At the same time, Kuwait is under U.S. pressure to continue democratic reforms. Given the continuing threat to Kuwaiti security from Iraq and Iran, the United States has some leverage it can apply on the al-Sabah regime.

The American reflagging of Kuwaiti tankers during the Iran-Iraq War put the U.S.-Kuwait relationship on firm ground after it had been shaken in the mid-1980s by Washington's refusal to sell Stinger antiaircraft missiles to Kuwait and by the revelation of U.S. weapons sales to Iran. After the Iran-Iraq War, Kuwait sought to downplay its relationship with the United States to avoid charges of being too close to an outside power. Kuwait also wanted to diversify its arms purchases and improve relations with the Soviet Union and other European and Arab states. Even as Iraq became increasingly aggressive in 1989, Kuwait did not want to align itself with the West against an Arab country, and so it made no moves to foster a defense treaty with the United States.

The liberation of Kuwait by the U.S.-led coalition resulted in a dramatic shift in policy from neutrality toward overt dependence on the United States (as well as Great Britain and France) for military protection. Despite continuing cynicism about U.S. intentions in the region, the ten-year defense treaty signed by Kuwait and the United States in the aftermath of the Gulf War provides for the stockpiling of U.S. military equipment in Kuwait, U.S. access to Kuwaiti ports and airports, and joint training exercises and equipment purchases. Kuwaiti air defenses were bolstered by the purchase of Patriot and Hawk missiles, and Kuwait received the first of forty F-18 aircraft from the United States in 1992. Kuwait signed similar defense arrangements with the United Kingdom and France, and a more limited agreement with Russia in 1993.

With large amounts of capital invested in the United States and other Western nations, Kuwait has a vested interest in the continued health of these economies. This is a powerful incentive for Kuwait to ensure a continual supply of oil to fuel Western industries. The U.S. interest in the Gulf is essentially oil. The GCC countries are an integral part of the United States' strategic, political, and economic agenda in the Middle East.

## Outlook

After a harrowing opening to the 1990s, Kuwait is in a period of transition. Having resisted the brutal Iraqi occupation without the leadership of their government, many Kuwaitis had expected that the end of occupation would bring long promised democratic reforms, and that the al-Sabahs would rule with greater accountability. Reforms have been modest. But with new confidence in their own abilities, Kuwaitis are asserting their right to play a broader political role in liberated Kuwait.

The 1991 Gulf War forced to the surface large issues that the regime had previously sought to avoid, including the potential appeal of Islamic fundamentalism, pressure for democratic reforms, the difficulty of achieving national security, and challenges to the management of the country's resources. The regime is likely to make concessions on reform, while trying to reinforce its control over Kuwaiti society.

Kuwait must remain on guard against future aggression by its dominate neighbors. The Iraqi threat remains alive and, despite improved relations, Iran's major rearmament program and its undecipherable foreign policy provoke unease. Ironically, Kuwaiti will to provide for a greater share of its own defense has grown, while Kuwaiti ability to pay for large investments in defense has decreased. Kuwait has embarked upon a defense buildup, but purchases will be constrained by reduced oil revenues. Moreover, exorbitant expenditure on defense equipment and facilities is not likely to reduce Kuwait's reliance on the United States and other Western allies to ensure its security. The Kuwaiti regime must contend with potential opposition to the relationship with the United States from Islamists and Arab nationalists. Reli-

ance on the United States also opens Kuwait to pressure from Washington to achieve meaningful democratic reform.

The country's reconstruction program has been swift and successful. The economy, however, has not been so easy to fix. Although Kuwait has increased its oil production, demand for oil has been flat, holding down prices.

Balancing the budget has become a top priority for the government. The International Monetary Fund and World Bank, in a report critical of the economy's inefficiency and low productivity, warned Kuwait to curtail its postwar spending spree. It recommended cutting welfare programs and trimming subsidies. The regime must weigh the political risks of ending payments that Kuwaitis have come to expect against the risks of economic problems caused by high budget deficits. Despite a reduction in the number of non-Kuwaitis receiving social services, the government is likely to increase user fees and reduce the subsidy element of government services.

It is clear, however, that the solution to the deficit will come with a price. While the fundamental problems of the state-dominated economy are longstanding and officially acknowledged by the ruling family, there is little consensus about how to resolve them. In this budgetary environment, Kuwait will continue to pump oil near its capacity.

Kuwaiti citizens traumatized by the brutal Iraqi occupation are no longer placatable solely by public services. Their heightened political consciousness has focused greater attention on Kuwait's investments abroad and the country's security and defense. After a six-year absence, the new National Assembly is self-confident and confrontational in exposing corruption and demanding greater accountability from the government. Despite pressure from the assembly and Islamists, the ruling al-Sabah family continues to be resistant to change, considering the old way as the best way.

# LEBANON

After fifteen years of sectarian conflict and factional violence following its devastating civil war of 1975-76, Lebanon has recovered a modicum of domestic political tranquillity. The groundwork for the improved security situation was laid by the Ta'if Agreement, an Arab League-sponsored accord among Lebanese parliamentarians signed in October 1989. Stability was achieved after the forcible ouster from Lebanese politics in October 1990 of Gen. Michel Aoun, former commander of the Lebanese army, who had remained the principal opponent of Syrian hegemony in Lebanon.

Aoun's ouster was accomplished during the buildup in Saudi Arabia by Western coalition forces responding to Iraq's invasion of Kuwait. Syrian armed forces attacked Aoun's strongpoints in Beirut, forcing him to find refuge first in the French embassy and ultimately in France. With Aoun out of the picture, Syria finally solidified its position as the dominant outside player in internal Lebanese affairs, a circumstance that was consolidated by the signing of a treaty of "fraternity, cooperation and coordination" between Syria and Lebanon in May 1991.

Syria's hegemony over Lebanon constituted a clear infringement of Lebanese national sovereignty and independence. However, it did have the impact of clarifying issues of leadership and power in Lebanon. As a result, Lebanon, albeit under Syrian tutelage, has been able to renew the process of rebuilding its institutions and planning for future development.

Parliamentary elections in the summer of 1992, the first held since 1972, marked an important stage in the revival of established Lebanese political institutions. The elections were boycotted by certain sectors of the Lebanese public, primarily by elements of the Christian Maronite community, who sought to cast doubt on the legitimacy of the electoral process. But deputies in due course were chosen from each electoral district, and the boycott failed to achieve its intended objective.

Progress toward the redevelopment of Lebanon has been slow. Despite the compromises of the Ta'if Agreement, no fundamental resolution of the issues that divided the various Lebanese factions had been achieved. Therefore, although most Lebanese have found new grounds for hope in their collective future, many also express fears that the era of "dialogue by the gun" may not be over. Secondly, Lebanon, once a haven for foreign refugees and expatriates of many nationalities, has ceased to be a country where persons of foreign origin, especially Westerners, can feel secure. The hostage-taking of the mid-1980s succeeded in eliminating most of the foreign presence in Lebanon, and continuing anti-Western sentiment deters the return of foreign investment.

Finally, one key area of Lebanon—the south—remained beyond the authority of the central Lebanese government. Here, the Israeli-supported South Lebanon army (SLA) and the Iranian-financed Shi'ite Muslim militia Hizballah continued to vie for control of an anarchic no-man's land. Lebanon and its Syrian overlord continued to have concerns that the anarchy of southern Lebanon might spread north once again, enveloping Lebanon as it had in the past. The continuing involvement of both Syria and Lebanon in the Arab-Israeli peace talks inaugurated in Madrid in October 1991 gave hope, however, that an overall settlement of Arab-Israeli issues, including the problem of south Lebanon, might be achieved.

## Geography: Vulnerable Location

Lebanon is a small country of 4,015 square miles (smaller than the state of Connecticut) located on the eastern edge of the Mediterranean Sea. From north to south it has a maximum length of 135 miles, and its average width from west to east is less than 35 miles. It shares a two-hundred-mile internationally recognized border with Syria to the north and east. To the south its 45-mile border with Israel marks the United Nations-sponsored cease-fire line agreed upon by Lebanon and Israel in 1949. During the 1967 Arab-Israeli War, however, Israel abrogated this agreement. Then, in the Israel-Lebanon agreement of May 17, 1983, it was accepted again as the permanent boundary. Less than a year later, in March 1984, the government of Lebanon, at Syria's urging, abrogated the agreement. Lebanon's southern border with Israel therefore remained unsettled and legally undefined in terms of international law.

Lebanon's geographical position jeopardizes its security. Its only two neighbors, Syria and Israel, have a long history of mutual hostility, and each has attempted to exploit the underlying diversity and disunity of Lebanon to pursue its own strategic advantage. Both countries are far stronger than even a politically unified Lebanon could be, and both have vested security interests in the foreign and domestic policies of Lebanon. Over the years, Lebanese governments have had to walk a fine line between competing pressures related to the Arab-Israeli conflict. Recent moves toward peace between Israel and its Arab neighbors have raised hopes of an escape from the security dilemma imposed on Lebanon by its geography.

Within its compact land area, Lebanon is divided into four distinct, parallel geographical regions: (1) a narrow coastal plain that runs the full length of the 135-mile Mediterranean coast, where the major port cities of Tripoli, Beirut, Sidon, and Tyre are located; (2) a coastal mountain range (known as Mount Lebanon), where the country's principal non-Sunni Muslim religious communities (Maronite Christians, Druze, and Shi'ite Muslims) have their roots; (3) the fertile, grain-producing Bekaa Valley, which varies from five to eight miles in width; and (4) a lower, interior mountain range (called the anti-Lebanon), through which runs the border with Syria. Each of these regions has a different climate, soil, water supply, density of settlement, life style, and history.

Within the main Mount Lebanon range, deep valleys stretch back several miles from the coast and divide the mountains into a number of distinct districts that give the Jbaylis, Kisrawanis, Metnis, Shufis, and other Lebanese living in them a strong sense of local identity. Most Lebanese define themselves according to their town, city, district, or region, as well as to their clan and religious community. The local, tribal, and religious identifications of the people, however, compete with a broader sense of national identity.

The climate of the country's coastal plain, where more than half the population lives, is typically Mediterranean—hot and humid with little rain during the long nine-month summer, and quite rainy but with almost no snow during the short three-month winter. The climate of coastal Lebanon contrasts sharply with the climate of the mountains, where heavy snows fall in the winter, the summers remain cool and invigorating, and the four seasons are distinct.

## Economy: Severe Deterioration

Aside from its largely self-subsistent agricultural base, Lebanon is poor in natural resources. As a result, its modern economic structure developed around trade, banking, and tourism. Before the 1975-76 civil war, two-thirds of the country's gross national product (GNP) was based on these service industries. The routing of most Middle Eastern trade with the West through the port of Beirut gradually transformed that city into the major com-

## Key Facts on Lebanon

**Area:** 4,015 square miles.
**Capital:** Beirut.
**Population:** 3,620,395 (1994).
**Religion:** 70 percent Muslim, 30 percent Christian.
**Official Language:** Arabic; French and English are widely spoken.
**GDP:** $6.1 billion; $1,720 per capita (1993).

*Source:* Central Intelligence Agency, *CIA World Factbook 1994.*

mercial and financial entrepôt of the region. Sidon and Tripoli, the sites of two major oil pipeline terminals and refining facilities, also profited.

Lebanon's economic growth, boosted by enterprise and a laissez-faire approach to government interference, was spectacular but uneven. Although Beirut became a glittering center of international trade, some parts of Lebanon, such as the Shi'ite-inhabited southern regions and the northern Bekaa, remained primitive and undeveloped. The attraction of Beirut led to the haphazard development of housing that quickly deteriorated into massive slums, particularly in the southern suburbs. There large numbers of rural poor, especially Shi'ite Muslims and Palestinian refugees, settled to seek work in the city.

As a result of the civil war, which was mainly an urban conflict fought in Beirut, the entire structure of the Lebanese economy changed. The commercial center of the city—where most of Lebanon's banks, hotels, and international businesses were located—was almost totally destroyed and remains in shambles. Nevertheless, some Lebanese entrepreneurs, businessmen, and traders continued to function through a number of militia-controlled "illegal" ports that sprang up along the Lebanese coast. Israel's 1982 invasion of Lebanon and the chaos that followed further deepened economic deterioration.

## Demography: A Nation of Minorities

Historically, Lebanon has been a haven for religious, ethnic, and political minorities. Canaanite (Phoenician) in biblical times and largely Christianized prior to the rise of Islam, Lebanon later became a country where Christian and non-Sunni Muslim minorities could maintain a relatively autonomous communal existence. This was particularly true in the Mount Lebanon region. Its northern end was occupied by Maronite Christians, its central portion by the Druze, and its southern end by Shi'ite Muslims. These three sects are the principal religious communities of Mount Lebanon, around which the unique historical development of the country has turned. Fiercely independent, they have alternately banded together to resist external control and battled one another to keep any one group from becoming dominant.

The major cities along the coast—Tripoli, Beirut, and Sidon—existed apart from Mount Lebanon for centuries and became populated by Sunni Muslims. The few Christians who lived in these towns were usually Greek Orthodox. Only in the mid-nineteenth century did large numbers of Maronites, Druze, and Shi'ites begin to settle in the coastal towns, and then primarily in Beirut. Tyre, the main coastal city in southern Lebanon, has long been inhabited principally by Shi'ite Muslims.

The Bekaa Valley and its neighboring anti-Lebanon mountains did not share the special heritage of Mount Lebanon as a political or ideological refuge. These regions historically served as arenas of contest between the prevailing powers in Mount Lebanon and the Syrian interior. Nevertheless, the Bekaa is characterized by sectarian diversity: in the north, Shi'ite Muslims; in the central valley, Sunni Muslims, Greek Orthodox, and Greek Catholics (Greek Orthodox who adhered to Rome in the late eighteenth century); and in the south, Druze.

In 1920 France created Grand Liban, or "greater Lebanon," the current Lebanese state. To make the new state more economically and demographically viable, it expanded the boundaries of traditional Mount Lebanon, and in so doing joined disparate groups under a single political authority. In creating Lebanon, France was acting in behalf of the Maronite Christian community, which in the nineteenth century had become a virtual French client. Expansion of Lebanon's demographic base enabled Maronite political leaders to gain power. They cultivated the allegiance of more politically passive groups, especially the Sunni Muslim community of coastal Lebanon, as a means of dominating the Druze and Shi'ite Muslims, who fiercely resented Maronite control of the new Lebanese state.

Lebanon was granted its independence from the French in 1941, and three years later it reinstituted constitutional procedures based on sectarian politics. A national census in 1932 had determined that the ratio of Christians to Muslims was six to five. This gave rise to the formula for apportioning parliamentary representation. The census defined the Maronite and the Sunni Muslim communities as the two largest sectarian groups (30 percent and 20 percent of the population, respectively), and on this basis agreement was reached that the president of Lebanon would be a Maronite and the prime minister a Sunni Muslim. The agreement was called the National Covenant of 1943, and it remained the formula, however obsolete, upon which the weak and ineffective Lebanese government was structured in the 1980s.

In fact, the formula was fragile from the beginning because it represented an agreement between the political leaders of only two of Lebanon's many sectarian communities. It also reinforced the notion that sectarian affiliation was politically significant, thereby hindering the development of national unity. The chief weakness of the National Covenant, however, was its rigidity and inability to anticipate socioeconomic and demographic changes. Its implicit assumption of Maronite-Sunni Muslim collaboration in governing Lebanon was flawed. Despite this fundamental weakness, the formula worked with a reasonable degree of effectiveness for more than thirty years, in part because the Lebanese feared the consequences of its failure.

By 1975, however, many questioned the validity of the National Covenant. Lower birthrates and higher rates of emigration among the more prosperous Christian communities—combined with higher birthrates and less emigration among the more disadvantaged Muslim and Druze communities—greatly changed the country's demographic makeup. Tens of thousands of deaths during the civil war and massive emigration in response to new flareups of violence have further distorted the country's demographic picture. Some analysts believe the Christian-Muslim ratio in Lebanon has reversed, although this is difficult to verify because no official census has been taken since 1932.

Lebanon has a population of about 3.6 million, roughly 93 percent of which is Arab. Hundreds of thousands of Palestinian refugees flocked to Lebanon following the 1948 Arab-Israeli War and Jordan's civil war in 1970. Although there were one hundred eighty-two thousand Palestinians officially registered in Lebanon in December 1971, estimates of their numbers during the 1980s were as high as three hundred fifty thousand.

## The Ottoman Period, 1516-1918

Mount Lebanon became incorporated into the vast Ottoman Empire as a result of Istanbul's conquest of Syria in 1516. Nevertheless, for most of the Ottoman period it remained an autonomous political entity under the rule of an indigenous emir who recognized the sovereignty of the Ottoman sultan. These emirs (the Maan dynasty followed in 1697 by the Chehab dynasty) were Druze, but they governed on behalf of all the inhabitants of the mountain, providing them with a sense of unique political identity within the empire. The Lebanese emirate began to weaken, however, during the first half of the nineteenth century.

In 1826, in an effort to revive its rapidly declining power, the Ottoman central government embarked on a program of reform, known as the Tanzimat. One aim of the program was to break down centers of local authority and impose a centralized system of administration throughout the empire. Another factor that weakened the emirate was the steady growth of the Maronite Christian population in northern Lebanon. Maronites expanded gradually into the Druze-inhabited area of central Lebanon, provoking Druze hostility while making the Maronites the principal champions of Lebanese autonomy. As noted earlier, France forged close commercial, religious, and cultural ties with the Maronite community. Faced with the centralization policies of the Ottoman government, the Maronites viewed French protection as the best guarantee of political autonomy.

### Establishment of the Mutasarrifiyah

In 1860—after nearly thirty years of mounting unrest, Druze massacres of Maronite Christians in central Lebanon, and the spread of sectarian conflict to Damascus—an international commission headquartered in Beirut was established to resolve the crisis. Its members represented the five principal European powers (Great Britain, France, Austria, Prussia, and Russia) plus the Ottoman government.

The regime imposed on Lebanon by the commission did not resolve conflicting sectarian interests, but it did restore general order and security. The six-power international treaty of June 9, 1861, served as a kind of constitution for Mount Lebanon for the next fifty years, until its abrogation by Turkey during World War I. Ottoman ambitions to administer the country were satisfied by making the governor or mutasarrif of Lebanon an Ottoman appointee. French and Maronite concerns were met by a provision that the governor be a non-Lebanese Ottoman Christian acceptable to the European powers.

The treaty created a twelve-member central administrative council with representatives from the principal religious communities in the country: two Maronites, two Druze, two Greek Orthodox, two Greek Catholics, two Shi'ite Muslims, and two Sunni Muslims. The council had the authority to assess taxes, manage the budget, and give advice on questions submitted to it by the governor. This system of confessional representation (political participation based on quotas allotted to different religious sects) later characterized the independent Lebanese government.

### Growth and Development

As time passed, the Ottoman-appointed governor became more of a figurehead, and the authority of the central administrative council increased. The period of the mutasarrifiyyah (1860-1914) proved to be a time of great social and economic development. Roads and railroads opened up not only Lebanon but also the whole Syrian interior to international commerce. Beirut began to flourish as a commercial center and to attract many immigrants from the countryside, gradually transforming the traditional, largely Sunni Muslim town into a thriving multisectarian and cosmopolitan city. This was also the time of the so-called Arab renaissance in learning and culture. The Syrian Protestant College, later renamed the American University of Beirut, was established by American missionaries in Beirut in 1866, and French Jesuits established the Université de St. Joseph in Beirut in 1875.

By the end of the nineteenth century Lebanon had emerged as one of the most tranquil, prosperous, and highly developed regions of the Ottoman Empire. Many former Maronite and Druze peasants acquired real estate and became prosperous landowners. In the larger mountain towns, artisans and tradesmen prospered, and in the coastal cities of Tripoli, Beirut, and Sidon, trading families rose to positions of great wealth.

The political impact of these developments was the emergence of a strong sense of Lebanese identity among the people of Mount Lebanon, especially among the Maronites, who tended to perceive themselves as the vanguard of progress in the country, partly because of their closer links with the West, particularly France. Even more important was Lebanese leadership of the Arab nationalist movement against Turkish rule. The despotic policies of Sultan Abdul Hamid (1876-1909), and of the Young Turk regime (1908-18) that deposed him several months after it took power, led Christians and Muslims throughout Syria, Lebanon, and Palestine to organize into clandestine political opposition groups. The end of Turkish rule, however, was less the result of Arab nationalist activity than of the Allied armies' victory over the Turks in World War I. The Allied powers, France and Britain in particular, had agendas of their own for that region of the world that did not include the immediate independence of any new state.

## French Mandate, 1918-43

Following World War I, France was granted a League of Nations mandate to oversee the political development of Syria and Lebanon, and its first action on September 1, 1920, expanded the frontiers of the traditional Ottoman Mount Lebanon mutasarrifiyyah to include the major coastal towns, part of the Akkar plain to the north of Mount Lebanon, the Bekaa and portions of the anti-Lebanon range, and the largely Shi'ite Muslim-inhabited Jabal Amil, the extension of the Mount Lebanon range south of the Litani River.

On May 26, 1926, an elected Lebanese representative council, the direct descendant of the Ottoman central administrative council, adopted a constitution that transformed the expanded Lebanon into the Lebanese Republic. Although amended many times by successive governments, this constitution has remained the fundamental document outlining the organization of the Lebanese government and defining its powers.

The constitution provided for equitable representation of the various sectarian communities in Lebanon, but it did not establish a fixed ratio for such proportional representation, nor did it reserve specific government positions for members of different communities. These matters were left to be resolved by representatives of the various groups.

Constitutional amendments in 1927 and 1929 transformed the originally bicameral legislature into a unicameral body and extended the renewable three-year term of the president to a nonrenewable six-year term. Both these reforms became permanent features of Lebanon's government. Although members of parliament were popularly elected from established electoral districts, the president was elected by parliament rather than by popular vote—a provision that provided a degree of stability in turbulent times. Because of the civil war of 1975-76 and subsequent turmoil in the country, the parliament elected in 1972 for a normal four-year term did not stand for reelection until 1992. Presidential elections, however, were conducted in 1976, 1982, and again in 1989.

The first president of Lebanon, elected in 1926, was not a Maronite Christian, as later became customary, but a prominent Greek Orthodox lawyer and journalist. In 1932 a prominent Sunni Muslim jurist ran for president, but when it appeared that he would win the French high commissioner temporarily suspended the constitution. France's interests in both Syria and Lebanon and its ties with the Maronite Christian community precluded the election of a Sunni Muslim as president.

The most significant problem of the French

mandate era was conflict between Maronite Christians, who generally supported the concept of an independent Lebanon, and Sunni Muslims, who opposed the creation of greater Lebanon and favored the reincorporation, with Syria, of those regions that France had annexed to Mount Lebanon in 1920. The conflict continued until an alliance was formed between an increasingly powerful Maronite party, led by Bishara al-Khoury, who favored Lebanese independence on the basis of cooperation with the Sunni Muslim community, and a Sunni Muslim bloc, led by Riyad al-Solh, who favored an independent Lebanon and cooperation with the Maronites as a means to end the French mandate.

The principal catalyst in cementing this alliance was British, and later American, support for Lebanese and Syrian independence following the Allied reoccupation of Lebanon and the deposition of the Vichy-appointed high commissioner in 1941. Although Free French officials continued to administer Lebanese affairs for two years following the 1941 proclamation of independence, British support enabled the Khoury-Solh coalition to lead the movement for Lebanese sovereignty. With the restoration of the constitution in 1943, Bishara al-Khoury was elected the first president of the newly independent state, and he immediately named Riyad al-Solh as his first prime minister. Even so, the Maronite-Sunni coalition was fragile from the beginning and had many opponents who opposed Lebanese independence.

## Lebanese Politics, 1943-75

After Lebanon gained independence in 1943, a strong presidency proved to be the principal stabilizing element in an otherwise chaotic political environment. Not surprisingly, the most profound political crises occurred at the time of presidential elections in 1952, 1958, 1976, 1982, and 1989, although there have been countless subplots in the drama of Lebanese politics. In general, however, a consensus prevailed that no one party or power should predominate and thus destabilize the delicate political status quo established in 1943. In 1975 this consensus was breached, and more than

fifteen years passed before a degree of order could be reestablished in the country.

Lebanese politics from 1943 to 1975 were based almost exclusively on family networks and patron-client relationships between the country's dominant political figures and less central actors. All of Lebanon's major sectarian communities had leading families who dominated the country's politics: the Khourys, Eddes, Chamouns, Chehabs, Franjiehs, and Gemayels among the Maronites; the Solhs, Salams, Yafis, and Karamis among the Sunnis; the Jumblatts and Arslans among the Druze; and the Assads and Hamadahs among the Shi'ites. Below this tier were other families, closely associated with the premier families, who were counted among the Lebanese "aristocracy" but had not yet attained a position of dominance. Through a combination of wealth and political influence these families were able to build powerful patron-client relationships in the mountain districts or urban quarters that served as the principal base of their national political influence. The political parties that did exist tended to be the creations of the leading families, who thus controlled voting blocs in parliament. Political status generally passed from father to son, and with certain exceptions members of the families who dominated Lebanon at the time of independence remained key political figures into the 1980s.

The dynamics of the Lebanese political system flowed from the National Covenant of 1943. That agreement stipulated that Lebanon's president should be a Maronite Christian, while its prime minister should be a Sunni Muslim. This arrangement spurred competition among leading Maronite political figures. Candidates allied with other leading sectarian politicians to form parliamentary blocs strong enough to capture a majority vote. Sunni Muslims also vied with one another to become prime minister.

### Khoury and Chamoun

Lebanon's first president, Bishara al-Khoury (1943-52), governed effectively during the first four years of his six-year term. In 1947, however, he was charged with influencing elections to secure a parliament that would amend the constitution and thus enable him to extend his term in office. When parliament did extend his term, his protégé Camille Chamoun turned against him. Chamoun, Kataeb party leader Pierre Gemayel, Druze leader Kamal Jumblatt, and others formed an alliance known as the Socialist Front, which called for an end to sectarianism and the corruption and favoritism they accused the regime of fostering. The death of Prime Minister Riyad al-Solh in 1951 increased the president's political vulnerability. In the summer of 1952 the Socialist Front successfully organized a countrywide general strike to force al-Khoury to resign. Following his capitulation, the Lebanese parliament on September 23 elected Chamoun president.

Like his predecessor, Chamoun governed with reasonable effectiveness during the first years of his term (1952-58). Unlike al-Khoury, however, who had based his power on a strong alliance with his Sunni Muslim prime minister, Chamoun sought to dominate the Muslim community by changing prime ministers regularly and by playing Sunni politicians off against each other. To weaken the political strength of his Maronite rivals and to improve his own popularity, Chamoun presented himself as a populist leader of all Lebanese citizens. Charges of election fraud, however, eroded his support.

Chamoun, like al-Khoury in 1947, was accused of fraudulently influencing parliamentary elections in 1957 and of seeking a constitutional amendment that would enable him to be reelected. Unable to resist effectively through constitutional procedures, his opponents turned to violence and terrorism following the parliamentary elections. Unlike the 1952 crisis, the absence of a rival Maronite candidate for president made the conflict appear as a distinctly sectarian clash, although Chamoun had many Muslim supporters and Maronite detractors.

Regional developments again played an important role in aggravating the domestic crisis. During the mid-1950s Egyptian president Gamal Abdel Nasser had emerged as a charismatic champion of Arab nationalism. At a time when Chamoun was perceived as undermining the Muslim role in Lebanese politics, Nasser's appeal was strong. Chamoun believed the growth of pan-Arab sentiment in Lebanon, inflamed and supported by Egyptian influence, threatened Lebanon's independence, and he looked to the West for support. In March 1957, in spite of strong Muslim opposition, the Lebanese government accepted the so-called Eisenhower Doctrine—a resolution the U.S. Congress passed in January 1957 declaring that "if the President determines the necessity . . . [the United States] is prepared to use armed forces to assist . . . any nation or groups of nations requesting assistance against armed aggression from any country controlled by international communism."

## Rise of Chehabism

Dramatic regional developments in the spring and summer of 1958 fueled the Lebanese domestic crisis. The formation of the United Arab Republic (UAR) in February by a union of Egypt and Syria was viewed enthusiastically by many Lebanese Muslims, who demonstrated in favor of Lebanon's joining the UAR. In May an anti-Chamoun journalist was assassinated. This transformed the general tension into open violence that quickly spread to all non-Maronite districts. The armed capability of the rebels was seen as evidence that men, arms, and ammunition were being infiltrated into Lebanon by pan-Arab forces in Syria. President Chamoun ordered Gen. Fuad Chehab, the commander of the Lebanese army, to crush the revolt, but Chehab refused, arguing that the army's role was to deter external aggression, not to resolve domestic political disputes.

Finally, the outbreak of a bloody pro-Egypt military coup d'état in Iraq on July 14 raised general expectations throughout the Arab world that the long-awaited day of Arab political unity, inspired by Nasser, was at hand. Fearful not only for the independence of Lebanon but also for his life, and having already presented to the United Nations Security Council a formal complaint accusing the UAR of interference in domestic Lebanese politics, President Chamoun invoked the Ei-senhower Doctrine and called upon the United States to send troops to Lebanon.

By the evening of July 15, 1958, the first of approximately fifteen thousand U.S. Marines had landed without armed opposition in Lebanon. The American action deterred any other foreign inter-vention and provided a security umbrella for a U.S. negotiator, Under Secretary of State Robert Murphy, to mediate among the country's compet-ing politicians. President Chamoun assured his ri-vals that he planned to leave office on the last day of his term, September 22, 1958. Sunni Muslim leaders made it known that they considered Gen-eral Chehab, who had gained their favor by refus-ing to deploy the army against them, the only acceptable Maronite to replace Chamoun as presi-dent. Duly elected by the parliament on July 31, Chehab did not take office until September 23, the day after Chamoun stepped down. With the transition of power accomplished, the U.S. Ma-rines withdrew from Lebanon between October 4 and 25.

Fuad Chehab, a descendant of Lebanon's for-mer ruling Druze family, which had converted to Maronite Christianity in the nineteenth century, was the quintessence of Lebanese aristocracy. He had served as commander of the Lebanese army since 1945. Not a professional politician, Chehab sought to cultivate the image of a statesman who was above the hurly-burly of daily politics. Using the formula "no victor, no vanquished" as his slogan for resolving the 1958 crisis, he reestab-lished political stability by drawing pro- and anti-Chamoun politicians into his government. The old political system based on powerful regional lead-ers, which Chamoun had tried to suppress, re-emerged under Chehab's seemingly aloof and yet dominating rule. Like Bishara al-Khoury, Chehab cultivated a close Maronite-Sunni relationship by sharing power primarily with a single prime minis-ter, Rashid Karami, the dominant Sunni politician of Tripoli. Karami continued to serve under Chehab's successor, Charles Helou (1964-70).

Chehab pursued a deliberately neutralist for-eign policy that sought to be inoffensive to neigh-boring Arab regimes, especially Egypt, yet accept-able to the West. According to his political philosophy, later called Chehabism, the govern-ment should serve Christians and Muslims equally. He relied on the army's Deuxième Bureau (mili-tary intelligence) to monitor and report on domes-tic political developments, a policy that made his presidency akin to a military regime.

In addition, Chehab concentrated on infrastruc-ture development throughout the country, includ-ing the areas outside of Mount Lebanon that had been largely neglected by al-Khoury and Chamoun. Chehab brought considerable stability to Lebanon. Elitist rather than populist (like Chamoun), or more traditionally patrimonial (like Khoury), Chehab gained many adherents, and Chehabism continued to have partisans for a num-ber of years.

## Chehab Successor

As his predecessors had done, Chehab consid-ered seeking a second term, but when opposition emerged he gave his support to Charles Helou, who was elected president in 1964, rather than risk destabilizing the country. A former banker, jour-nalist, and diplomat, Helou was an able and ac-complished individual. Because Helou had no per-sonal base of power except for the Chehabist-controlled government and parliament, Chehab appointees continued to run Lebanon during his term of office. Helou lacked the political authority either to control his own government or to deal effectively with the country's other powerful politi-cians.

Under these circumstances, following the 1967 Arab-Israeli War, Lebanese politics became in-creasingly polarized over regional issues. Although Lebanon had avoided becoming a combatant in the war, it could not avoid involvement in the ongoing Arab-Israeli conflict after the war. The gradual emergence of the Palestine Liberation Organization (PLO) as an autonomous political and military force in the late 1960s strongly af-fected Jordan and Lebanon because of their large concentrations of Palestinian refugees (in Lebanon's case, about 10 percent of the resident population). The PLO and its cause became a divisive political issue that ultimately provoked Lebanon's civil war.

Maronite politicians looked for a way that would enable Lebanon to support the Palestinian cause yet oppose the armed activities of the PLO in Lebanon. Muslim politicians, however, also seeking to reflect the will of their constituencies, generally supported the PLO. President Helou was unable to act decisively because of powerful political pressures from both sides. His use of the Deuxième Bureau to monitor developments and to try to control them provoked serious resentment.

## The Civil War

Although it was sparked by a specific event—the April 13, 1975, attack by unknown gunmen on Maronite worshipers at a Sunday church service in the Beirut suburb of Ayn Rummaneh—the Lebanese civil war had deeper causes that were years in the making. The polarization of the Lebanese public over government policy toward the PLO could be seen as early as December 1968, when an Israeli commando raid on Beirut International Airport destroyed thirteen Lebanese civilian aircraft. Undertaken in retaliation for airplane hijackings and commando raids by the PLO, this Israeli raid paralyzed the Lebanese government and rapidly radicalized public opinion.

Further Israeli attacks in southern Lebanon in response to PLO guerrilla operations led to the collapse of the Lebanese government in May 1969; Prime Minister Karami resigned rather than sanction Lebanese military actions against the PLO. Unable to form a new cabinet with another Sunni prime minister, President Helou resolved the crisis by acceding to the Egyptian-sponsored Cairo agreement in November 1969. This agreement confined the PLO armed presence to certain localities in southern Lebanon.

The Syrian Socialist Nationalist party (SSNP), the Lebanese Communist party (LCP), the Lebanese branch of the Syrian Ba'ath party, and other new ideological parties, often closely affiliated with the PLO, attracted more and more adherents during the late 1960s. Many of these parties were disillusioned with established Muslim politicians who used their influence to protect the PLO but failed to actively support it. The result was the formation of the multiparty Lebanese National Movement (LNM) in 1969. Its leader was Kamal Jumblatt, the powerful head of Lebanon's Druze community, who since 1949 had organized his own political followers into the Progressive Socialist party (PSP).

### Franjieh's Victory

In the August 1970 presidential election, Suleiman Franjieh, a Maronite politician from Zghorta in northern Mount Lebanon, defeated his Chehabist rival, Elias Sarkis, just before King Hussein's war against the PLO in Jordan. Franjieh's election was generally perceived as a victory for those who sought to crush the PLO's growing strength in Lebanon. The parliamentary vote electing him, however, had been only 50-49, and the decisive vote had been cast by LNM leader Jumblatt, who in siding with Franjieh was really voting against continued Chehabist control of the government.

Owing his election at least partly to the LNM, Franjieh began his presidency as a radical reformer, seeking to co-opt the LNM's opposition by trying to implement needed changes in government administration. Entrenched political interests, however, stymied the reforms, and he soon abandoned the effort. After 1972 Franjieh's rule was increasingly based on personal control of the government bureaucracy and defense of the established political system. The LNM, angered by this reversal of policy, tried to mobilize public opinion against the government. One significant reform Franjieh had been able to make, however, was the liquidation of the Chehabist-controlled Deuxième Bureau. This deprived the government of an effective intelligence service at a time of increasing disorder and tension in the country.

Following the defeat of the PLO in Jordan in

1970-71, Lebanon became the last center of armed Palestinian resistance against Israel. Israeli retaliatory raids against Palestinian guerrilla bases located in Lebanese border villages produced a steady exodus of Shi'ite Muslims from southern Lebanon to Beirut. Shantytowns sprang up, usually in and around the long-established Palestinian refugee camps that ringed Beirut. Disillusioned with their political leaders, who had failed to protect their homes and land from either the PLO or Israel, these restless and impoverished Shi'ite Muslims provided ready recruits to the militias of the LNM. At this time a populist Shi'ite organization called Amal (meaning "hope") was established. It sought a larger role for the Shi'ite community in the Lebanese political system. Rampant inflation during the early 1970s, partly due to the growing flow of Arab oil money into Lebanon's thriving banking sector and to the absence of controls over the country's freewheeling economy, accentuated the gap between rich and poor and increasingly associated the political conflict in Lebanon with class distinctions.

During the 1972 parliamentary elections, the LNM pressed hard to elect antiestablishment candidates, but the outcome demonstrated the traditional leaders' powerful hold over the electoral process. To those who sought radical transformation in Lebanon, revolutionary violence seemed the only available route. Nevertheless, the election of a few radical deputies—especially the overwhelming victory of a pro-Nasserist candidate over an established conservative rival in Beirut—sent tremors through the conservative political establishment.

In April 1973 Israeli commandos raided the heart of Beirut, killing three top PLO leaders. The LNM organized mass demonstrations against the government to protest its passivity toward Israeli aggression. President Franjieh and other Maronite leaders, however, decided the government could not delay longer in moving against the PLO. Heavy fighting on May 2 between the army and PLO fighters in the Burj al-Barajina refugee camp quickly spread to other parts of the country. But the government policy provoked powerful opposi-

tion and Maronite leaders, as yet unprepared to carry on alone the fight against the PLO, had to back down. The May 18, 1973, settlement at Melkart basically reaffirmed the provisions of the Cairo agreement of 1969, but it did not resolve the fundamental issue that had provoked the fighting. Further showdowns were inevitable. In the months that followed, the Maronite leaders, the parties of the LNM, and the PLO intensified recruitment efforts and searched worldwide for the arms and funds necessary to meet the challenge that awaited them.

## War Among Militias

The Lebanese civil war that finally erupted in April 1975 was not so much a conflict between Christians and Muslims, as widely reported in the Western press, as it was a battle between the militias of the dominant Maronite leaders of the established political order and the various militias of the LNM, whose leaders sought to overthrow the traditional political system. Indeed, the vast majority of Lebanese were victims rather than active participants in the conflict. The fighting could continue only because of the army's political incapacity to intervene. The established Muslim politicians refused to countenance army intervention so long as the conflict remained a fundamentally domestic one. But the army did intervene when the PLO, which at first had held back from the fighting, entered the fray in late 1975 to shore up the sagging fortunes of the LNM militiamen in Beirut's hotel district.

The army became an enemy of the joint PLO-LNM forces and a tacit ally of the Maronite militias. Sensing impending victory, the Maronites undertook a massive destruction and depopulation campaign against Palestinian and Shi'ite Muslim refugee camps on the east side of Beirut. This action brought the PLO fully into the conflict and prompted retaliatory attacks against strategically located Maronite towns in areas otherwise controlled by the joint PLO-LNM forces. As these campaigns continued during January 1976, morale within Lebanon's multiconfessional army could not be sustained. By early February the army had totally collapsed, and many of its soldiers took sides with one or another of the fighting militias. Lebanon plunged into full-scale civil war.

## Syrian Intervention

Unlike 1958, when U.S. intervention played a role in stabilizing Lebanon, in 1975 Lebanon's president had no relatively disinterested external party to turn to for help in stemming the political chaos. To Lebanese nationalists, particularly Maronites, independence primarily meant independence from Syria. Yet in 1975-76 only Syria had the vital interest in the outcome of the Lebanese crisis to expend the political, military, and financial resources necessary to bring it under control. It was strategically important that Lebanon not become either a base or a corridor for an Israeli invasion of Syria.

### Assad's Fear of Radical Regime

Prior to 1975 Syria had strongly supported the PLO and the LNM in Lebanon. By late March 1976 a PLO-LNM victory seemed imminent. Syrian president Hafez al-Assad became convinced that such a victory would lead to Israeli intervention—an action that he wanted to preempt. At the same time, Lebanon's Maronite leaders and their Muslim political colleagues also feared the possible results of a PLO-LNM victory. Consequently, Assad began to seek—and the Maronite leaders began to accept—the principle of a primary role for neighboring Syria in resolving the Lebanese conflict.

Syrian forces dispatched to Lebanon defended the presidential palace in Baabda in March 1976, provided security for the presidential elections held in May, and in June forcibly restored the pre-April 1975 political status quo. But fighting, primarily between Syrian and PLO-LNM forces, continued throughout the summer. The better-trained Syrian units gradually managed to achieve strategic superiority. In October representatives of the various warring parties concluded a generally

accepted cease-fire agreement in Riyadh, Saudi Arabia.

A summit of the Arab League, which then included all the Arab states, ratified the Riyadh agreement in Cairo on October 25. A key provision was the establishment of the Arab Deterrent Force (ADF), which was to provide security throughout the country while a process of national reconciliation was undertaken. Placed technically under the authority of the newly elected Lebanese president, Elias Sarkis (the Chehabist rival of President Franjieh, who was favored by Syria in the May elections), the ADF was to be composed of units from several Arab countries. It was tacitly understood, however, that Syrian elements would form the main body of the force. By this means, Syria's role in Lebanon gained legitimacy. As various units from other Arab countries were recalled in the months that followed, the ADF became a completely Syrian force, albeit supported and at least partially financed by the multinational Arab League.

Syrian intervention in Lebanon's civil war temporarily restored order to most of the country, but, because the intervention did not resolve the fundamental problems, the peace was short-lived. Conflict and violence, often in the form of terrorist bombings and attacks, soon dominated Lebanese political life once again.

Although Syria had intervened in behalf of Lebanon's Maronite leaders against the PLO and LNM, it had not put an end to PLO activity in Lebanon. Indeed, the Riyadh agreement specifically affirmed the 1969 Cairo agreement. The terms of the Cairo agreement, however, had never been accepted by the non-Chehabist Maronite leadership. Thus, the honeymoon between Syria and these leaders—grouped together as the Lebanese Front—was brief. In May 1977, only days after Menachem Begin was elected prime minister of Israel, the front issued a statement declaring that the Cairo agreement was null and void and that the Maronite militias would remain armed as long as the PLO did.

Even during the civil war, the Maronite leaders had entered into covert arms deals with Israel's

Labor government. With the coming to power of Menachem Begin, who openly supported the Lebanese Front, the Maronite leaders dared to challenge Syria directly with assurances of Israeli support, making confrontation between Syria and the Maronite militias inevitable.

Under the terms of the Riyadh agreement, PLO fighters returned to southern Lebanon in spite of warnings by Israel that it would not tolerate a resumption of commando activity in the region. As the PLO returned, Israel responded by arming and helping to organize a local, predominately Christian militia commanded by Maj. Saad Haddad, a renegade Lebanese officer who sought to counter and contain PLO and LNM expansion into the border area.

Israel's higher profile in Lebanon following the civil war was closely linked to Syria's presence there. After Syrian forces entered Lebanon in 1976, Israel announced the existence of an undefined "red line" somewhere in southern Lebanon, beyond which it would not tolerate Syrian troops.

The line was generally considered to be in the vicinity of the Litani River. Syria never seriously challenged this Israeli condition, and southern Lebanon, historically one of Lebanon's most neglected and underdeveloped areas, became a virtual no man's land where neither Lebanese, Syrian, nor even Israeli authority extended. Bloody conflict among the supporters of Saad Haddad, the PLO, the LNM militias, and the predominately Shi'ite population that lived in the area poisoned the political atmosphere elsewhere in Lebanon, where every group in the south had its supporters.

### Divide-and-Rule Strategy

Syria's conservatism in dealing with security problems also escalated tensions. Syria sought to mediate agreements among Lebanon's various militias and political parties, but it did not seriously try to disarm them even though it was authorized to do so by the Riyadh agreement. As a result, the militias remained armed, and Lebanon continued to live on the edge of violence and renewed civil war. Syria's policy for containing conflict was to move in with sufficient strength to crush violence when it erupted. Such a policy, although it produced respect, also produced resentment, and it did little to halt the growing number of terrorist acts used by the various militias. As a result of its divide-and-rule strategy—tolerating every group but really supporting none—Syria was increasingly perceived by most Lebanese as serving no particular interest except its own.

Disenchantment with the PLO also grew during the late 1970s, especially among Lebanon's southern Shi'ites, who previously had perceived themselves as sharing a common plight with the Palestinians. Three events in 1978 and early 1979 helped to rally support for the populist Amal organization: Israel's invasion of southern Lebanon in March, the unexplained disappearance of Amal leader Musa Sadr while on a visit to Libya in September, and the successful example of a Shi'ite revolution in Iran. The escalating conflict in the south between the Shi'ite Muslim population and the PLO laid the basis for the Shi'ites' popular reception of Israeli armed forces during their summer 1982 invasion of Lebanon. The sectarian solidarity of the community, however, also laid the basis for the ultimate failure of Israeli policy in Lebanon.

## Israeli Invasions of 1978, 1982

Israel's invasions of southern Lebanon in March 1978 and June 1982, although allegedly provoked by Palestinian terrorist incidents, were aimed at achieving broader policy goals. The principal result of the 1978 invasion was the clearing of an area several kilometers wide along Israel's northern frontier to serve as a security zone under the control of Maj. Saad Haddad's Free Lebanon Militia (FLM). The inability of the FLM to achieve this mission was the chief factor necessitating Israel's military intervention.

In spite of the operation's success, PLO groups continued to find ways to cross the frontier and to conduct terrorist operations in northern Israel. The presence in southern Lebanon of some six thousand soldiers of the United Nations Interim Force in Lebanon (UNIFIL) undoubtedly ameliorated the problem, but UNIFIL failed to deploy in the security zone because of Israeli opposition and its own inability to control all Palestinian movements in southern Lebanon. Moreover, various PLO groups acquired long-range artillery and multiple-rocket launchers capable of firing over the heads of both UNIFIL and the FLM. This created a new danger that led Begin's government to devise strategies for dealing with the threat to northern Israel.

Other developments in Lebanon in 1980-81 had a significant impact on how the 1982 invasion was eventually carried out. The Maronite militias (except for that of former president Franjieh) joined together under the leadership of Bashir Gemayel, son of Maronite Kataeb party leader Pierre Gemayel. This made Bashir the principal Maronite wielding military power and thus a viable presidential candidate in the 1982 elections. For him to be elected, however, Syrian opposition to his candidacy had to be neutralized. Militantly opposed to the PLO and Syrian presence in Lebanon, Bashir favored decisive action to end the vicious cycle of violence that had killed so many. Like the Israelis, Amal followers, and a growing number of ordinary Lebanese citizens, Bashir Gemayel largely attributed violence to the PLO's continuing presence in Lebanon. Increasingly isolated, the PLO found it advantageous on July 24, 1981, to enter into a cease-fire agreement with Israel that had been negotiated by U.S. special envoy Philip C. Habib. The isolation of the PLO also cleared the way for Israel to launch a full-scale invasion of Lebanon in June 1982 targeted at the PLO. *(Arab-Israeli conflict, Chapter 2, p. 45)*

As a result of that invasion, the PLO was formally expelled from Beirut and southern Lebanon in August. Lebanon's Maronite leaders understandably interpreted this as a victory for their cause and particularly for Bashir Gemayel, who was duly elected president. Although Bashir was assassinated before he could take office, his brother Amin was quickly elected to take his place.

The victory claimed by the Maronites over the PLO, however, was illusory. It had been achieved by Israeli military strength, not the Maronite militias. The continuing occupation of Lebanon by both Israeli and Syrian forces transformed the domestic conflict into a regional one in which Lebanon remained the principal arena of death and destruction.

## U.S. Involvement, 1982-84

In September 1982 the United States, France, Italy, and the United Kingdom dispatched a five-thousand-man multinational peacekeeping force (MNF) to Beirut to bolster the confidence of the new Lebanese government. At the same time, U.S. diplomats sought to broker agreements that would lead to the full withdrawal of Syrian, PLO, and Israeli forces, provide for the security of Israel's northern border, and strengthen the Lebanese government's authority. Unresolved conflict between Syria and Israel in other areas, especially regarding the status of the Golan Heights, which Israel had effectively annexed in December 1981, made even indirect negotiations between these two countries impossible.

After receiving assurances from Syria that it would leave Lebanon if Israel unconditionally withdrew, the United States sought to mediate a withdrawal agreement between Israel and Lebanon. On May 17, 1983, representatives of Israel, Lebanon, and the United States initialed such an agreement. It contained guarantees that Israel would withdraw its forces completely from Lebanon in return for Lebanese political, economic, and military concessions that Israel considered necessary for the security of its northern frontier. After the initialing of the document, however, Israel tied full implementation to a similar commitment by Syria to withdraw its forces from Lebanon.

Syria immediately asserted that its forces would not withdraw unless the agreement was abrogated. Damascus objected to the agreement's establishment of special security zones in southern Lebanon and a joint Lebanese-Israeli committee that would hold ultimate authority over matters of security within these zones. These and other provisions were perceived by Syria as placing unacceptable restrictions on Lebanese sovereignty, in effect partitioning the country into zones of Israeli and Syrian influence and increasing the Israeli threat to Syria.

The agreement was rejected by most Lebanese political factions, which had leagued together as the National Salvation Front to resist it. Moreover, Syrian forces, from their strategically dominant position in the hills overlooking Beirut, supported Lebanese groups opposing the agreement and intimidated the Maronite community with shellfire and threats. Meanwhile, the high cost of sustaining the Israeli occupation, the increasingly heavy Israeli casualties from Lebanese resistance, and the September 1982 massacres at the Sabra and Shatila refugee camps, in which hundreds of Palestinians were killed by Maronite militiamen under the nose of the Israeli army, had begun to erode support at home for Israel's involvement in Lebanon.

Militia groups virtually crushed by Israel's invasion in 1982 regrouped with Syrian support during the summer of 1983. Events climaxed in September 1983 when Israel undertook a partial, unilateral withdrawal from its forward positions along the Beirut-Damascus highway to more defensible positions below the Awali River short of Sidon. Fighting erupted throughout the Shuf region in central Lebanon between Druze militias, supported by PLO and Shi'ite elements on the one hand, and the Lebanese armed forces and Maronite militia forces on the other. Druze forces prevailed, causing a mass flight of Maronite Christians from their villages in the region and enabling Walid Jumblatt (who had become Druze leader after pro-Syrian forces assassinated his father, Kamal, in March 1977) to consolidate his authority throughout the Shuf, although the Lebanese army succeeded in maintaining control over militias in West Beirut.

On October 23, 1983, a terrorist bombing of the American Marine barracks in Beirut killed 241 servicemen. This attack and the earlier April 18, 1983, bombing of the U.S. embassy in Beirut, which had killed 63 persons, diminished U.S. public support for a military role in Lebanon.

Following the collapse of Lebanese government authority in West Beirut in early February 1984, the United States announced its decision to withdraw its MNF contingent. The last U.S. Marines were evacuated in March. Italy, Britain, and France also withdrew their forces during early 1984.

# Revived Syrian Hegemony

With the departure of Western troops, Syria reemerged as the dominant external power influencing affairs in Lebanon. Lebanese president Amin Gemayel moved quickly to restore relations with Damascus, and on March 5, 1984, the Lebanese government announced its abrogation of the May 17, 1983, Lebanon-Israel agreement. Following further discussions between Syrian representatives and Lebanese political leaders, a government of "national unity" was formed in April, and a security plan aimed at restoring government authority throughout the country was agreed upon.

Implementation of the plan proved impossible, however, because of sectarian conflict, particularly over the continuing Israeli occupation of southern Lebanon. Shi'ite, Druze, and other militia groups there refused to disarm while Israeli troops still occupied the region. Attacks against Israeli forces escalated, even as Israel's new government elected in 1984 adopted an "iron fist" policy.

## Turmoil in Southern Lebanon

With the disintegration of its previous policy objectives in Lebanon, Israel in the spring of 1985 began a graduated, unilateral withdrawal from Lebanon. As it did so, however, it left in place an expanded security zone under the control of a surrogate militia, the South Lebanon Army, now commanded by retired Lebanese general Antoine Lahad. Although the zone was designed to promote the security of Israel's northern border and was controlled ultimately by Israel—which had armed, funded, and advised the SLA—the zone's presence provoked continuing resistance on the part of the mainly Shi'ite inhabitants of southern Lebanon. The Shi'ite resistance to the SLA was split into two rival factions. The first, more closely linked with Syria, was the Amal organization, which sought to demonstrate to Israel its capability and determination to control the PLO in Lebanon and thus remove any pretext for Israel to maintain the security zone. In May 1985 Amal's efforts to control PLO activities by maintaining a siege around Palestinian camps in Beirut and southern Lebanon erupted into open warfare. The Shi'ite-Palestinian "camp wars" continued until January 1988, when Amal leader Nabih Berri lifted the siege of the camps following the outbreak of the Palestinian *intifada* in the Israeli-occupied West Bank and Gaza.

The rival Shi'ite faction to Amal was the Hizballah (party of God) movement, which received inspiration and support from Iran. Unlike Amal, which sought a stronger Shi'ite role in Lebanon's multisectarian political system, the partisans of Hizballah favored the establishment of Lebanon as a fully Islamic state. Imbued with fanatical determination, the Hizballahis competed with Amal for Shi'ite attention and loyalty by conducting spectacular suicidal attacks against SLA and Israeli patrols in southern Lebanon. In addition, they preferred to collaborate with Palestinian guerrillas in their struggle against Israel and opposed Amal's efforts to contain Palestinian military activity. These different approaches occasionally provoked intra-Shi'ite conflict and violence.

Another tactic (in most cases associated with Hizballah) was the taking of Western hostages. Beginning in early 1984, soon after the withdrawal of the U.S. Marines from Lebanon, isolated kidnappings of Americans and later French, British, West German, Saudi, and even South Korean nationals began to occur. Among other motives, the kidnappers sought to win the release of Shi'ite prisoners in Kuwaiti, Israeli, or Western jails and to enhance their influence in local Lebanese and regional affairs. The kidnappings greatly reduced the Western presence in Lebanon and consequently the ability of Western nations to exert influence in that country or to react forcibly because of the potential danger to the hostages.

Israel's efforts to contain Shi'ite and Palestinian guerrilla activity in southern Lebanon through commando raids, air strikes, artillery shelling, and the capture of guerrilla leaders intensified the region's turmoil and provoked retaliation. An example was the hijacking of TWA Flight 847 in June 1985 by three Lebanese Shi'ites who killed one American serviceman and held thirty-nine people hostage in an effort to force Israel to release some seven hundred Lebanese Shi'ites imprisoned in Israel. The eventual arrest and trial of one of these hijackers, Muhammad Ali Hamadai, in West Germany provoked yet another round of kidnappings of West German citizens in Lebanon by a group, probably centered around relatives of Hamadai, called the Organization of the Oppressed of the Earth.

## Tripartite Agreement

Efforts by the Gemayel government to reconcile with Syria in 1984 prompted elements of the militant Maronite Christian Lebanese Forces militia in northern Lebanon to revolt in early 1985 against central government authority. The Lebanese Forces regarded Gemayel's accommodation toward Syria as evidence that the government was caving in to Syrian efforts to establish hegemony.

Syria in December 1985, working with Sunni prime minister Rashid Karami but not with President Gemayel, managed to forge a "tripartite agreement" among Elie Hubayka, representing a counterfaction of the Lebanese Forces; Druze leader Walid Jumblatt; and Amal leader Nabih Berri. The agreement was aimed at reaching a compromise settlement of the Lebanese conflict, centered around the principal militias rather than the traditional politicians. To be implemented, it required Hubayka and Berri to assert control over the more radical factions of their respective communities. Despite increased Syrian support, neither proved able to do so, and fierce intra-Maronite and intra-Shi'ite conflict occurred during the spring and summer of 1986.

Continued deterioration of the security situation throughout the country finally led Syria in August 1986 to reintroduce about seven hundred troops into Beirut. In February 1987 President Assad increased his commitment by sending into Lebanon an additional seven thousand troops supported by tanks and heavy artillery. With the reimposition of Syrian military control in West Beirut and central Lebanon, Damascus began slow but deliberate efforts to strengthen Amal at the expense of Hizballah and PLO elements remaining in Beirut and southern Lebanon. Syrian leaders, however, were careful to avoid jeopardizing relations with Iran, whose alliance with Syria against Iraq took priority over any heavy-handed effort to crush the Hizballah movement entirely. Anti-Syrian resistance was growing, symbolized by the emergence during 1987 of a new terrorist group, the Lebanese Liberation Front, which assassinated Syrian officials and soldiers in Syrian-controlled areas of Lebanon. Nevertheless, the Syrian influence in Lebanon by the summer of 1988 was sufficiently strong to have a decisive bearing on Lebanese presidential elections, which were mandated by the constitution to occur before September 23.

## Syrian-Maronite Conflict

To help counter Syrian efforts to dictate the outcome of the election, the Lebanese Forces found a willing ally in Iraqi president Saddam Hussein, who, having achieved a cease-fire in his war with Iran in August, looked for ways to retaliate against Syria for supporting Iran. Iraqi arms began reaching Lebanon in October, and the Lebanese Forces led a movement to block the election of presidential candidates favored by Syria. As a result, no presidential election could take place. Just before his term of office expired, President Gemayel appointed Lebanese armed forces commander Michel Aoun as acting Maronite prime minister to preside over an interim military government until elections could be held. When the government of Sunni Muslim prime minister Selim al-Hoss refused to step down and recognize the new

government of General Aoun, Lebanon found itself with two acting governments, one recognized as legitimate by Syria and its Muslim allies and the other by the Lebanese Forces and most of the Maronite community.

Efforts by the Arab League in late January 1989 to mediate the impasse led Aoun in mid-February to assert the authority of his government and armed forces over the various independent militias in Lebanon. Beginning with the Lebanese Forces, which at first resisted his offensive against them in a series of bloody clashes, Aoun ordered the army to take over militia headquarters and barracks in the greater Beirut area and to bring all illegal militia-controlled ports under the control of the army. As this operation succeeded, he extended the order in early March to include illegal ports controlled by the Druze and Muslim militias and attempted to impose a naval blockade on them. Druze and Muslim militias countered Aoun by shelling Maronite areas. Aoun considered these attacks to be inspired by Syria. Consequently, he responded to Druze and Muslim shelling by targeting Syrian military positions, although many of these were located in heavily populated residential areas of Beirut. At the same time, he sought to appeal to increasingly widespread anti-Syrian sentiment in all sectors of the Lebanese population by calling for a general uprising against the Syrian occupation and a liberation of Lebanon from Syrian control.

Iraqi support of Aoun (and reportedly support from Israel as well) virtually guaranteed that Syria would determinedly resist Aoun's efforts to weaken its position in Lebanon. Aoun could not expect to dislodge the Syrian occupation by force alone, and he hoped for international intervention and mediation on behalf of continued Lebanese sovereignty and independence. Arab League efforts in late April did result in a cease-fire agreement, and Aoun lifted his blockade of Druze and Muslim ports. Continued efforts by Aoun and the Lebanese Forces, however, to receive military supplies through ports along the Maronite portion of the Lebanese coast prompted Syria to shell the ports and to blockade ships serving them. Continued retaliatory shelling by Aoun's army and the Lebanese Forces against Syrian military positions made the cease-fire agreement a dead letter and the summer of 1989 one of the bloodiest and most violent seasons in Lebanon's fourteen-year conflict. Ironically the bitter summer of 1989 proved to be the catalyst for at least a partial settlement of the conflict in Lebanon.

*The Ta'if Agreement*

General Aoun failed to understand that with the rapid deterioration of communism in Eastern Europe and the former Soviet Union, a corresponding decline of the West's interest in Lebanon was taking place. The Lebanese conflict could no longer be cast as a Cold War move by a pro-Soviet Syria to consolidate its influence in Lebanon at the West's expense. Indeed, both the United States and the Soviet Union, desirous of remaining out of the Lebanese quagmire, lent support to a Saudi-sponsored Arab League effort to mediate the conflict of 1989.

On September 30, 1989, the Saudi government convened a summit of the Lebanese parliament in Ta'if, Saudi Arabia. Sixty-two of the seventy-one living members of the original ninety-nine-member parliament that had been elected in 1972 were present for the opening session. For more than three weeks the deputies contentiously debated the text of a national reconciliation charter that had been drafted by a committee of the Arab League and coordinated with Syria. Finally, mindful that the continued legitimacy of the Lebanese government was in their hands, fifty-eight of the assembled deputies on October 22 signed an amended charter that soon became known as the Ta'if Agreement.

By no means a revolutionary document, the Ta'if Agreement made only minor alterations to the traditional, confessional Lebanese political system. The composition of the parliament, which had been fixed at a ratio of six Christians to five Muslim deputies, was restructured on a 50-50 ratio. To ensure that no sect would lose seats because of this change, the size of the chamber was in-

creased from ninety-nine to one hundred eight deputies. In addition, the deputies agreed that the whole confessional system would be reviewed with the aim of abolishing it some time in the future. The powers of the Sunni Muslim prime minister and his cabinet were significantly enhanced at the expense of the Maronite president. Most significantly, however, the agreement, every provision of which had been cleared by Damascus, tasked "Syrian forces" with assisting "the forces of the legitimate Lebanese government to extend the authority of the Lebanese state within a period not exceeding two years...." Following the two-year period, the Lebanese government, newly reestablished under Syrian supervision, would negotiate with Syria the terms for the withdrawal of the latter's armed forces.

The terms of the Ta'if Agreement, therefore, more fully legitimized the Syrian presence in Lebanon. This outcome was quite the opposite from what General Aoun had desired, and he vowed to resist implementation of the agreement. Syria moved quickly, however, convening the Lebanese parliament on November 4 to elect René Muawwad as the new president of Lebanon. Quick international recognition of the Muawwad government, including recognition by the United States, should have communicated to Aoun his isolation. But buoyed by significant popular support, he continued his resistance and refused to vacate the presidential palace at Baabda where he was headquartered. Syria demonstrated its control of the situation when, after the car bomb assassination of Muawwad eighteen days after his election, it supervised yet another election on November 24 in which Elias Harawi was chosen to replace Muawwad.

## Second Lebanese Republic

Despite a number of threats, Syria and the Harawi government failed to move forcibly against Aoun, concentrating instead on institutionalizing the reforms adopted in the Ta'if Agreement. Meanwhile intense conflict erupted in early 1990 between Aoun and Samir Jaja, head of the Maro-

*Elias Harawi*

nite Lebanese Forces, who had decided to accept the Ta'if Agreement and collaborate with the Harawi government.

While Aoun continued to hold on, the Lebanese parliament in August 1990 passed amendments to the constitution that formally incorporated the compromises reached at Ta'if. Aoun violently rejected these constitutional changes and called for the overthrow of Harawi. Despite Aoun's threat, Harawi formally approved the constitutional amendments, making them law on September 21. By thus limiting his own powers, Harawi also proclaimed the establishment of the Second Lebanese Republic.

The coup de grace for Aoun came two weeks later, on October 13, when a combined force of Syrian and Lebanese armed forces moved against him. This attack was facilitated by the Persian Gulf crisis provoked by Iraq's invasion of Kuwait in August. Syria's decision to join that United States-led coalition against Iraq had resulted in

much improved U.S.-Syrian relations. That Syria had a green light to move against Aoun without fear of provoking a serious Western reaction was apparent when Israeli aircraft failed to come up to challenge Syrian planes bombing Aoun's positions. By the end of the day, Aoun had taken refuge in the French embassy after ordering his men to follow the orders of Gen. Emile Lahoud, the legitimate armed forces commander of the Harawi government.

## Consolidation of State Authority

With the collapse of the resistance posed by General Aoun, relative calm settled over much of Lebanon, as the Lebanese reconciled themselves to the inevitability of the new order mandated by the Ta'if Agreement and enforced by Syria. Most Lebanese were weary of fighting and recognized the dominant position of Syria. They also regarded the Ta'if Agreement as having addressed at least some of the root causes of the Lebanese conflict, namely the perceived inequity of the old political system.

The new government of Elias Harawi negotiated agreements with the various Lebanese militias to remove themselves from Beirut, to place their weapons in storage, and to return to civilian occupations. Increasingly, in early 1991, Lebanese armed forces took over former militia checkpoints and sought to extend the state's authority beyond the outskirts of Beirut. In early February, taking advantage of renewed conflict in south Lebanon between the PLO, Israel, and the Israeli-supported South Lebanon Army, elements of the Lebanese army began deploying toward the south. Despite the army's success in confining the PLO within the Palestinian refugee camps, Israel remained skeptical of Lebanon's ability to guarantee the security of its border with Israel and refused to withdraw support from the SLA or to allow the Lebanese army to deploy into the Israeli-defined south Lebanon security zone.

By April all militias except for Hizballah in southern Lebanon had agreed to disarm; Lebanese troops had deployed throughout most of the country; militia checkpoints had disappeared; citizens increasingly felt free to move about; new construction and reconstruction was getting under way; and commercial life was beginning to regain momentum.

At this stage Syria and Lebanon took steps to approve a new Treaty of Brotherhood, Cooperation and Coordination, which was officially signed by President Harawi of Lebanon and President Hafez al-Assad of Syria in Damascus on May 22, 1991. Requiring total cooperation and coordination between the two governments, including defense and foreign affairs, the treaty formally affirmed Syria's recognition of Lebanese sovereignty and independence. As the dominant partner in the alliance, however, Syria clearly expected Lebanese decision making to be coordinated with Damascus.

In early June the Lebanese president, prime minister, and Speaker of parliament collectively appointed forty new deputies to the parliament. These included thirty-one to fill seats that had become vacant since the last election in 1972, and nine others to fill seats created by the Ta'if Agreement. The decision to appoint rather than elect these deputies proved controversial, as most of the deputies chosen were pro-Syrian. The term of office of the new chamber was to be for four years, but in 1992 the government reversed its position and held general parliamentary elections.

The growing consolidation of government authority, backed by Syria, was apparent by the fall of 1991 with the gradual release of all foreign hostages held in Lebanon (although a full accounting of several missing Israelis in Lebanon was never achieved). The spread of army and police personnel throughout the country made eventual detection of hostage locations likely, leading the kidnapping groups to compromise on their terms for release. Nevertheless, for each hostage liberated, some quid pro quo was obtained, usually the release of several Lebanese prisoners held by Israel. Iranian intervention and influence also played a role in achieving the release of the hostages.

Yet another manifestation of increasing Lebanese government authority was the agreement by Yasir Arafat's PLO to close down its military operations in Lebanon and to ship its heavy weapons out of the country. Although anti-Arafat Palestinian groups remained intact, their activities were sharply circumscribed in Lebanon, as they were in Syria.

## Lebanon and the Peace Process

The virtual shutdown of PLO military activities in Lebanon coincided with the surprise July 1991 announcement by Syrian president Hafez al-Assad of his agreement to accept a joint U.S.-Soviet invitation to enter negotiations with Israel. Lebanon followed the Syrian lead, and it too had a delegation at the Madrid summit, which opened on October 30. The Lebanese played a peripheral role in the series of multilateral negotiations in Washington that followed the initial summit, as the agendas of Syria, Israel, Jordan, and the Palestinians all took precedence.

The Lebanese perspective was different, as the Lebanese delegate at Madrid said when he noted that the Lebanese concern in the negotiations was UN Security Council Resolution 425, more than 242. The former resolution, adopted at the time of Israel's first invasion of Lebanon in 1978, called for Israel to withdraw its forces completely from Lebanon. Nevertheless, UN Resolution 242 proved to be the dominant issue in the negotiations, leaving the Lebanese delegation frustrated, despite Syrian assurances that no settlement would be reached that did not take into account both UN resolutions.

## Continuing Problem in South Lebanon

Fighting in south Lebanon flared up dramatically in 1991, following the Lebanese government's increasingly successful consolidation of authority throughout most of the rest of the country. Israel's skepticism concerning Lebanese capability to provide security along its northern border led it to maintain its self-declared security zone and support for the SLA which governed the zone. The Lebanese government, unable to deploy into the security zone, did not press the Hizballah Shi'ite militia to disarm like other militias. As a result,

Hizballah continued to conduct attacks against SLA positions and Israeli troops in southern Lebanon, inviting Israeli retaliatory operations. In response to the Israeli operations, Hizballah forces occasionally were able to fire Katyusha rockets or conduct military operations across the border into Israel itself. These actions invited even more massive Israeli retaliation. In February 1992 and July 1993 Israel conducted heavy bombing and shelling of Shi'ite positions and villages in southern Lebanon.

Despite the intensity and bitterness of the conflict, Israel proved unable to stop Hizballah operations. Hizballah activities reinforced the view of Israeli policy makers that they had no alternative to maintaining the security zone as a buffer protecting Israel's northern border.

Notably, instability in the south did not spread to the rest of Lebanon as it had in the past. Indeed, in July 1993, Lebanon even sent small contingents of Lebanese soldiers into the UNIFIL area, up to the border of the security zone. Exhibiting an unexpected degree of initiative, the new Lebanese government sought to communicate that if Israeli power could not maintain order in the security zone, Lebanon was ready and willing to prove that it could do better.

### Parliamentary Elections at Last

Perhaps the most dramatic development in post-civil war Lebanon was the parliamentary elections of August-September 1992. The last elections had been held in 1972, and the deputies elected at that time had maintained some limited power. During the presidential crisis of 1988-89, the parliament remained the only source of legitimacy for the Lebanese government. But with about one-third of its members dead and many more advancing in years, the parliament could not claim to be a current reflection of the Lebanese electorate. The appointment of forty deputies in the summer of 1991 to fill empty seats could not restore this fading legitimacy. Thus the electoral process organized in 1992 was a major step toward reinvigorating the Lebanese government.

Even so, the elections proved to be controversial and were boycotted by many in the Maronite community who sought to cast doubt on the legitimacy of what they perceived as a Syrian-rigged electoral process. Nevertheless, popular turnout was high in other parts of the country, and the process appeared to be conducted with reasonable fairness, within the limitations that came with Syrian hegemony. Finally, even Maronite-inhabited Kisrawan province returned deputies in a late special election held in October. The election placed many new faces in the parliament along with some of the old ones. Many of the militias, including Hizballah, which had fought for recognition during Lebanon's long era of anarchy and violence, now found themselves represented by deputies in parliament. This circumstance created hope that Lebanese politics may have moved away from the battlefield and into the parliament.

## Outlook

The changing circumstances of the international and regional environments—the end of the Cold War, the restructuring of inter-Arab relations associated with the Gulf crisis, and the subsequent efforts to settle the Arab-Israeli conflict—seem to bode well for Lebanon. Government authority has been at least partially restored, significant reconstruction and redevelopment has been set in motion, and except for the south most of the conflict and violence that the Lebanese had known for a decade and a half has disappeared. Occasional terrorist bombings, such as that at the American University of Beirut in November 1991 and at Phalange party headquarters in East Beirut in December 1993, have occurred, but these no longer seem to lead to a general breakdown of law and order in the larger society.

The circumstances of the new Second Lebanese Republic are different from those of the first, however. Previously, Lebanon had looked to the West—France in the first instance, and later Britain and the United States—as the principal guarantors of its security and independence. Today, Syria, and in a larger sense the collective Arab world, which formally recognized the idea of an independent Lebanese state in the Ta'if Agreement of October 1989, now play this role. To many Lebanese who have deep-rooted fears of the old Arab nationalist idea that Lebanon should be subsumed in a larger, unified Arab state, this is an uncomfortable position. Fears exist that the current dominant Syrian role in Lebanese politics may only be a prelude to further assertions of Syrian governmental authority in Lebanon. Others fear the consequences for Lebanon of a disintegration of political stability in Syria following a change of regime in Damascus.

For the moment, the Lebanese have little alternative but to accept and adjust to the new political situation. It has brought a relative degree of peace and tranquillity to the country, which the war-weary Lebanese desire to maintain. Furthermore, there is little hope that any Western nation will arise to play a protective role for Lebanon. The Western nations have supported the Ta'if process and shown clear disinclination to embroil themselves further in the intricacies and brutalities of Lebanese politics. In addition, the legacy of the hostage crisis and continuing fears that Lebanon may remain too dangerous a country for various categories of foreigners acts to deter Western nations from becoming involved in Lebanon in any capacity.

Lebanon's near-term destiny, therefore, is intimately tied to developments in the larger region of which it is a part. Movement toward resolution of the Arab-Israeli conflict and increased stability in the region will benefit Lebanon. Revived regional instability, due either to renewed interstate conflict or to heightened levels of ideological conflict, such as between Islamic fundamentalists and existing secular regimes, would likely produce similar reverberations in always-volatile Lebanon.

# L I B Y A

The September 1969 coup d'etat that replaced King Idris I with a Revolutionary Command Council (RCC) headed by Muammar al-Qaddafi ushered in a dramatic social and political transformation of Libya. The nation was transformed from a loose collection of relatively conservative Arab societies into a sometimes bizarre blend of dictatorship, pan-Arabism, militarism, Islamic extremism, socialism, and foreign militancy. The common thread running through Libyan society was Qaddafi, who functioned not only as the top political leader, but also as chief ideologist.

Qaddafi's radicalism appears linked to his conscious desire to follow the early policies of his hero, Gamal Abdel Nasser of Egypt. Qaddafi was profoundly influenced by the broadcasts of Radio Cairo to which he listened while growing up during the height of Nasser's influence. Like several other military takeovers in the Arab world, the 1969 coup in Libya was a clear emulation of Nasser's 1952 revolution. As chairman of Libya's Revolutionary Command Council, Qaddafi seems to have wanted to go beyond Nasser in his devotion to Arab unity, his hostility toward Israel, and his leadership of Arab and African nations.

As long as Qaddafi could use Libya's huge oil profits to improve the country's standard of living, the small Libyan population tolerated his foreign adventures and unorthodox ideas and he enjoyed considerable popularity. Falling oil prices during the 1980s, however, severely weakened the Libyan economy. Qaddafi's domestic repression and the disorder resulting from his erratic political and economic policies eroded the Libyan leader's sup-

port among his people. Qaddafi enjoys little popularity and controls Libya largely by virtue of his command of the military and security forces.

Meanwhile, Libya's foreign activities have made it a pariah state under significant (though far from total) international economic sanctions. The West, especially the United States, watched with alarm Qaddafi's transformation of Libya and the radicalization of its foreign policy. By the 1980s many Westerners regarded Qaddafi as a madman because of his radical foreign policy; his pursuit of weapons of mass destruction; and his support of terrorists, subversive groups, and assassins abroad. To the Reagan administration in particular he was seen as a diabolical nemesis of the West.

Libya's profound international isolation has further complicated the lot of the Libyan people and Qaddafi's rule. In September 1993 elements of the Libyan military rebelled against Qaddafi. He was able to overcome this challenge by calling on loyal air force units to bomb the barracks of the coup participants. This was not the first challenge to Qaddafi, however, and his rule is likely to remain precarious.

## Geography

Libya is located in the center of the North African coast of the Mediterranean Sea. It is bounded by Egypt on the east, Sudan on the southeast, Tunisia and Algeria on the west, and Niger and Chad on the south. Except for those bordering Tunisia and Egypt, the areas of Libya adjacent to its neighbors are inhabited very sparsely, if at all.

With an area of 679,359 square miles (about two-and-a-half times the size of Texas), Libya is the fourth-largest country in Africa. Most of the country is desert, and more than 90 percent of its people live in less than 10 percent of the country, primarily in the fertile areas along the 1,100-mile Mediterranean coast. The coastal strip has a Mediterranean climate of warm summers, mild winters, and scant rainfall, but most of Libya has arid, desert weather with no rainfall and no permanent rivers. There are two small areas of hills and mountains in the northeast and northwest regions and another zone of hills and mountains in the Sahara in the south and southwest.

Libya is made up of three distinct regions that, until independence in 1951, were relatively unrelated to one another. Tripolitania—about 16 percent of the nation's land area—extends from the center of the Libyan coast westward to Tunisia and has been linked with the Maghreb, a term used historically to denote Tunisia, Algeria, and Morocco. Directly to the south of Tripolitania is the region called Fezzan—33 percent of the nation and mostly desert. The entire eastern part of Libya, from the Mediterranean to the border with Chad, is Cyrenaica, which comprises 51 percent of Libya's land area. This region has been more closely associated with the Arab states of the East than with the Maghreb.

## Demography

The Libyan population is still quite small, estimated in 1994 at about 5 million people. Because of the country's underpopulation, the government has encouraged a high birth rate. The population growth rate is a strong 3 percent. In addition, Libya has imported many foreign workers to fill essential jobs in the economy. As many as half a million foreigners work in Libya, most of them in the major cities of Tripoli and Benghazi.

Well over 90 percent of the Libyan people are Arabic-speaking Sunni Muslims who are ethnically a mixture of Arab and Berber stock. The rest are mainly pure Berbers, Tuareg tribespeople (Muslim nomads of the central and western Sahara), black Africans, or members of various foreign communities of longstanding residence (especially Greek and Maltese). The Arabic dialect of the western parts of Libya in Tripolitania and Fezzan is similar to those of the other Maghreb nations to the west, while the Arab dialect prevalent in Cyrenaica is closer to that of Egypt. Although Libya is steadily becoming more urbanized, there are still nomadic and seminomadic Bedouin tribes in the desert and adjacent areas. Qaddafi himself is from one such tribe.

## Oil and the Libyan Economy

Petroleum production dominates Libyan economic life. In addition to oil, Libya's mineral resources include large iron deposits, salt beds, and construction materials (gypsum, limestone, cement rock, and building stone). Other than some cement and gypsum, these nonpetroleum mineral resources have only begun to be exploited.

After oil was discovered in Algeria in the early 1950s, exploration began in Libya under the rule of King Idris I. The first oil was found in 1957 in western Fezzan and the first major strike occurred in 1959 in Cyrenaica. By 1961 oil was being exported by Esso. Although there are dozens of major and minor oil fields (including some offshore), the major strikes of the late 1950s and early 1960s were in Sirtica, an arid zone in the center of Libya's coastal area, and this remained the source of most of Libya's oil exports. Unlike other Middle Eastern oil-producing states that granted rights to develop their oil to a single company, Libya gave oil concessions to many petroleum companies in the United States, Great Britain, West Germany, and other nations.

Several factors have made Libyan oil particularly marketable. First, Libyan light crude has a low sulphur content, which makes it more attractive for engine use because it burns more cleanly, thereby producing less air pollution. Second, because of its proximity to the coastline, most Libyan oil can be piped directly from the well to the

## Key Facts on Libya

**Area:** 679,359 square miles.
**Capital:** Tripoli.
**Population:** 5,057,392 (1994).
**Religion:** 97 percent Sunni Muslim.
**Official Language:** Arabic; Italian and English are widely spoken in major cities.
**GDP:** $32.0 billion; $6,600 per capita (1993).

*Source:* Central Intelligence Agency, *CIA World Factbook 1994.*

tanker. A third factor is the proximity of Libya to major European oil-importing nations. Libyan tankers need not go through the Suez Canal or around Africa to reach European ports, as is the case with almost all Persian Gulf oil. Finally, Libya's late start in the petroleum export business proved to be beneficial. The expertise already acquired in other Middle Eastern and North African oil fields made Libyan oil operations more efficient.

The overthrow of King Idris I in 1969 brought changes in Libyan oil policy. Although Libya had joined the Organization of Petroleum Exporting Countries (OPEC) in 1962, it encouraged foreign competition for oil exploration and provided concessionary terms for foreign companies. After Qaddafi came to power, however, oil policy became increasingly attuned to political objectives. Soon efforts were under way to "Libyanize" employment, increase posted oil prices, establish Libyan government control over the rate of oil production, and increase government ownership of the oil companies. The government demanded that foreign oil companies agree to Libyan participation or be nationalized. In September 1973 Libya nationalized 51 percent of the assets of all foreign oil companies, and six months later the government completely nationalized the Libyan holdings of three American corporations: Texaco, California-Asiatic (a subsidiary of Standard Oil of Califor-

nia), and Libyan-American (a subsidiary of Atlantic-Richfield). After nationalizing foreign oil interests, Libya began a policy of joint production instead of simply granting concessions to foreign concerns.

Libya's domestic energy needs are still quite limited, and very little oil is refined in Libya. Although Libyan petroleum reserves (including both oil and natural gas) are substantial, experts have estimated that they will last no more than about forty years, depending on the rate of production.

In 1992 Libya was the thirteenth largest oil producer in the world, producing at a rate of about 1.5 million barrels per day. Oil accounts for one-third of Libya's gross domestic product and virtually all of its export earnings.

## History

The term "Libya" was used historically—especially by the Greeks—to denote most of North Africa, and the modern nation-state of Libya is not equivalent to the area denoted by the ancient name. In fact, unlike Egypt, for example, Libya has no history as an identifiable nation before independence in 1951. Its history is that of several regions, groups, and tribes out of which the modern state of Libya was formed.

The Libyans' identification with a region—either Cyrenaica, Tripolitania, or Fezzan—persisted well after independence united the three zones. In ancient times the people of Tripolitania came in contact with Phoenician civilizations farther west along the coast and the inhabitants of Cyrenaica had ties with the Greeks. In modern times the two regions of Libya—separated by the desert of the Sirtica Basin—have tended to be oriented to the adjacent areas of North Africa. Fezzan has maintained contacts with the coastal areas but also has ties to the African nations in the Sahel to its south: Chad, Niger, and to a lesser extent Mali.

The coastal zone appears to have been inhabited since neolithic times. Although the origin of the indigenous Berber people is still unknown, some scholars conjecture that they migrated from southwestern Asia beginning around 3000 B.C. The coast of what is now Libya was once the site of Phoenician, Greek, and Roman settlements.

Undoubtedly the most important single phenomenon of Libya's history was the advent of Islam in the middle of the seventh century. Only a little more than a decade after the death of the Prophet Muhammad in 632, Arab Muslim armies took control of Cyrenaica and overcame fierce resistance from Berbers in Tripolitania. By 663 they controlled Fezzan, and by 715 Andalusia in present-day Spain also had come under Arab Muslim rule. North Africa, like most of the great Arab empire, was ruled by caliphs (successors to the Prophet Muhammad), governing first from Damascus and later from Baghdad and then Cairo. Tripolitania lay within the realm of the semiautonomous Maghrebi dynasties that ruled most of Morocco and Algeria, while Cyrenaica was controlled by the rulers of Cairo. After a brief period of Spanish rule in Tripolitania, Ottoman authority was established, at least nominally, and by the end of the sixteenth century even Fezzan had been brought under Ottoman authority.

Early in the eighteenth century a local Turkish officer began a dynasty in Tripolitania that extended into parts of Cyrenaica. The piracy supported by the rulers in Tripoli was feared by European merchants, and in 1799 the United States, like many European states, paid tribute to Tripoli to prevent attacks against its vessels. When the United States did not quickly meet Tripoli's demand for an increase in its payment in 1801, the American consulate was attacked and the consul expelled from Tripoli. Only after a small-scale naval war with the United States was peace restored. Political turmoil and economic problems in Tripolitania prompted reimposition of direct Ottoman rule in 1835.

In 1879 Cyrenaica was separated administratively from the rest of the country. The Ottomans exercised limited control over the more inaccessible parts of Cyrenaica and Fezzan, and in the coastal areas where the Ottomans retained control their rule was repressive, corrupt, and unpopular.

Also during the nineteenth century an Islamic

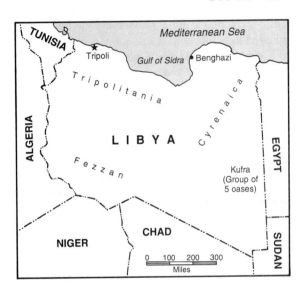

religious sect began to change the lives of the people of Cyrenaica. Muhammad bin Ali al Sanusi, a native of what is now Algeria, settled in Cyrenaica in the 1840s and attracted Bedouins and town dwellers to a new approach to Islam, one that combined the mysticism of Sufi Muslims and the rationalism of orthodox Sunnis. He was soon venerated by tribal adherents, although such sainthood is abhorrent to orthodox Islam. His descendants increased the following of what became known as the Sanusi order, and by the beginning of the twentieth century it had the allegiance of virtually all Cyrenaican Bedouins as well as followers in Egypt, the Sudan, and even Arabia.

Italy was a latecomer in the European colonial rivalry in the Middle East and Africa, but by 1912 it had wrested what is now Libya from the weakened Ottoman Empire. The Italian government, however, had great difficulty subduing its new domain. Members of the Sanusi order inflicted heavy losses on Italian troops in Libya's hinterland. Nevertheless, Italy maintained control of much of Libya.

By 1916 leadership of the Sanusis was in the hands of young Muhammad Idris al Sanusi (who would become King Idris of Libya). Although the United Kingdom and Italy recognized Idris as emir (prince) of the Cyrenaican hinterland and granted him substantial autonomy over his realm, the victorious allies of World War I recognized Italy's sovereignty over Libya as a whole. The nationalists of Tripolitania, who wanted independence from Italy, were badly divided by personalities and tribal affiliations. They apparently realized that agreement on one of their own number was impossible and that a united front against the Italians was needed. Consequently, they offered Idris in 1922 the title of emir of Tripolitania and thus the leadership of their region. Idris did not aspire to authority in Tripolitania, where he had few followers, but he accepted the role within a few months. This resulted in a split with the Italians, who by then were convinced that Idris threatened their control. In late 1922 Idris fled to Egypt, where he continued to guide his followers from exile.

Following Prime Minister Benito Mussolini's accession to power in 1922, Italy again attempted to subjugate its Libyan possessions. By 1931, through a brutal campaign, it finally succeeded despite strong resistance from Libyan nationalists. The Italian government exploited Libya's resources and encouraged colonization of its North African holdings aimed at relieving unemployment and overpopulation at home. More than a hundred thousand Italian colonists settled in Libya during the 1930s. In 1939 Libya was formally annexed to Italy. Although Italian colonial rule brought some economic progress, the life of the indigenous population was little improved in the cities and became worse in the countryside, where grazing land was confiscated for distribution to Italian settlers. The leaders of the Sanusi sect remained for the most part outside of the country.

World War II provided Libyan nationalists with the opportunity to oust the Italians by cooperating with the British, in the hope that Britain would support Libyan independence when the war was won. Despite serious disagreements between the nationalists from Cyrenaica and Tripolitania, the two regions agreed to accept the leadership of Idris, the leader of the Sanusi sect, and to provide volunteers to the British forces. The Libyan Arab Force fought alongside the Allies under British command until the Axis forces were driven out of Libya in February 1943.

Cyrenaica and Tripolitania were administered by the British, and Fezzan by the French, from 1943 until 1951. Although the Libyan people enthusiastically welcomed Idris back into Libya, and the British allowed him to form an independent Sanusi emirate in Cyrenaica, the European powers did not believe Libya was ready for independence. Various transitional plans were devised during the late 1940s, but the Europeans were slow to reach a consensus on how to administer the former Italian colonies.

In some ways, Libya was not ready for independence, although a majority of its inhabitants apparently favored it. United as a single entity only since 1939, social and political divisions between Cyrenaica and Tripolitania persisted. Tripolitanians demanded a republic, and Cyrenaicans called for a Sanusi monarchy, fearing domination by the larger and more sophisticated Tripolitanian population. Fezzan, a tribal society like Cyrenaica, had its own leading family. The economic situation was profoundly unpromising: Libya had no known natural resources and depended heavily on external aid.

Finally, a United Nations resolution was agreed upon that called for establishment of an independent, unified Libyan state by the beginning of 1952. An international council (including Libyans from each of the three regions) was set up to assist in establishing a government. A National Constituent Assembly began deliberations in late 1950 and, despite some dissent, decided upon a federal system with Idris as the monarch. On December 24, 1951, King Idris I formally declared Libya an independent state.

Although there was a legislature, the king held most of the political power. His rule was conservative and pro-Western. Occasionally the regions challenged the central government's power, and political parties were banned when they showed signs of dissent, but Idris's eighteen-year reign was generally stable. He established close ties with the British and with the Americans, who were granted military base rights in exchange for economic assistance. Idris changed the constitution in 1963 in an effort to bring greater centralization to the federal form of government established in 1951. He hoped that the change would help to unify Libya and erode the regionalism that was pervasive throughout Libya's history.

Under the conservative monarchy of King Idris, Libya enjoyed particularly good relations with other conservative Arab and African nations such as Saudi Arabia and Ethiopia. Libya remained somewhat removed from the Arab-Israeli conflict.

The low literacy rate and rising prosperity because of oil revenues might have enabled Idris to insulate his country from external conflicts and upheavals if it had not been for two related factors. First, the growing influence of Egypt's President Nasser permeated Libya as Egyptian broadcasts carried his speeches throughout the Arab world. Second, the June 1967 Arab-Israeli War, and the attendant humiliation of the Arab nations, galvanized Libyans as it did Arabs everywhere. Young people and workers began to rally to the call of Arab nationalism.

Idris did not succeed in creating a Libyan nation united around the institution of the monarchy. After nearly two decades as ruler, he was still mistrusted by Tripolitanians. Support for the monarchy eroded as many Libyans in urban areas became disillusioned with the failure of the king to spread the benefits of oil income to all segments of the population. Although Idris supported subsidies to the "front line" Arab states of Egypt and Jordan, he generally continued to pursue policies that favored the West at a time when anti-Western sentiments were becoming more pronounced throughout the Arab world. In September 1969 King Idris was overthrown by a coup launched by army units in Benghazi.

## Qaddafi's Regime

Although the names of the twelve members of the Revolutionary Command Council that seized power on September 1, 1969, were not released until the following year, a week after the coup one

*Muammar al-Qaddafi*

of the RCC members, Capt. Muammar al-Qaddafi, was promoted to colonel and named commander in chief. He was just twenty-seven years old. Since then Qaddafi has been the predominant political and ideological force in Libyan politics.

Qaddafi's Bedouin background, his education in Muslim schools, and his adolescence during the height of anti-imperialism and Nasserism all influenced his thinking. Scholars have traced his puritanical personal life, his aversion to both capitalism and communism, and his inclination to egalitarianism to his early life and upbringing.

The new government quickly championed Arab unity, the Palestinian cause, and an Arab-Islamic style of socialism. From the beginning, Qaddafi and the Free Officers' movement, a group of young reformist military men who had carried out the coup, looked to Nasser's Egypt as the model for their new government. The slogans about socialism and Arab unity, the titles (the Free Officers' movement, the Revolutionary Command

Council), and the organizations (the Arab Socialist Union as the political party) all were an expression of Qaddafi's hero worship of Nasser. Nasser himself had learned, by 1969, to temper his political objectives according to prevailing political realities, but Qaddafi was ready immediately to pursue all the goals that his new government espoused. A few weeks after the coup, Qaddafi's deputy, Abdel Sallem Jalloud, traveled to Egypt and the Sudan to propose unification of the three nations. Qaddafi repeatedly demonstrated an obsession with achieving Arab unity through schemes to unify profoundly different political systems.

After the coup the new regime sought to mollify foreign friends of the deposed king by declaring that Libya would adhere to its treaty obligations. Despite such assurances, the United States and the United Kingdom—each with ties to Idris—were soon disillusioned. The new regime prosecuted (mostly in absentia) former officials and expelled many Jews and Italians. Libya's relations with the West deteriorated. Even before Qaddafi seized power, the United States had agreed to leave Wheelus Air Force Base in Libya. A national holiday was declared on the day the U.S. evacuation was completed in June 1970.

In the mid-1970s Qaddafi began to move closer to the Soviet Union and its allies, principally through arms transfer agreements. Nevertheless, Qaddafi never reneged on his denunciation of communism as a form of atheism and never permitted the establishment of a Communist (or indeed any other nongovernment) party in Libya.

Observers of Libyan internal politics have been puzzled by Qaddafi's disappearance from public view in 1972 and again in 1974. In both instances, Qaddafi left his administrative duties in the hands of his trusted second-in-command, Jalloud, who was appointed prime minister in 1972. On both occasions Qaddafi retained the post of commander in chief of the armed forces. Qaddafi's brief withdrawals from politics in 1972 and 1974 are now viewed by analysts as periods in which he devoted himself to political reflection and the formulation of his ideology. These "retreats" do not appear to have resulted in a diminution of Qaddafi's power.

Qaddafi's political philosophy has developed through several stages. In 1973 he introduced a "cultural revolution" reminiscent of China's in the mid-1960s. Castigating the Libyan people for their lack of revolutionary fervor, Qaddafi ordered the annulment of all pre-1969 laws and the repression not only of communism but also of capitalism, the Muslim Brotherhood (a militant Sunni group), and any manifestation of atheism. He rejected all "non-Islamic thinking" and established "people's committees" throughout the country and at every level of the government. He declared that this program marked the beginning of a return to the true Islamic heritage of decision making by consultation.

The next stage in Qaddafi's political thinking resulted from his 1974 retreat. The following year he reorganized the party he had created after the coup—the Arab Socialist Union—into people's congresses. People's congresses are large gatherings of Libyans that operate, in Qaddafi's view, as manifestations of direct democracy. At a people's congress, individuals are technically free to express their views openly. In practice, these meetings often tend to be little more than rallies to back government policy. Despite Qaddafi's condemnation of representation, congresses at lower levels do send people to the General People's Congress. This apparent contradiction has never been explained by the government.

In 1977 the General People's Congress became the main organ of government in Libya, and the country's name was changed to the Socialist People's Libyan Arab Jamahiriya (an invented word meaning roughly "state of the masses").

During Qaddafi's 1974 retreat he assembled his political philosophy into a book. His "Green Book, Part I," which is entitled "The Solution of the Problem of Democracy," was published in 1976. This was followed in 1978 by "The Green Book, Part II: The Solution of the Economic Problem—Socialism." In Part I he declared that representation is an inherently undemocratic concept. He explicitly rejected not only representational democracy but also parliaments, referendums, majoritarian electoral systems, and multiparty and single-party systems. In Part II of the "Green Book" Qaddafi proclaimed his belief that every man has the right to a house, an income, and a vehicle. While mandating rights to private ownership of one house (and no more), Qaddafi urged the abolition of business, and in 1978 he encouraged the takeover by people's committees of many business establishments, especially retailing operations. Qaddafi's fundamental theory, what he calls the "Third International Theory," rejects capitalism and communism and claims to establish in Libya true, direct democracy.

The implementation of Qaddafi's eccentric ideas has wrought havoc with daily life in Libya. One such plan in the late 1980s called for moving the capital and transferring the government ministries to scattered locations around the nation. A more expensive endeavor has been the building of the "great man-made river"—an extraordinarily costly water pipeline linking aquifers deep in the desert to the coastal areas. This twenty-five-year project, begun in 1983, is projected to cost $25 billion. Because few Libyan lands can be converted to agriculture, even with irrigation, the project is of dubious value and could create unintended environmental problems.

Other actions have damaged the economy severely in the interest of Qaddafi's utopian notions of equality, such as the abolition of retail trade, the seizure of bank accounts and businesses, the destruction of land tenure records, and a proposal for the abolition of money.

## Domestic Issues

As long as Qaddafi kept the standard of living of the population high and had the money for projects, such as water wells, schools, and housing, that directly benefited the Libyan people, there was a general tolerance for his rule. The world oil glut of the early 1980s dramatically lowered Libya's oil earnings from about $22 billion in 1980 to less than half that amount in 1985. A year later they were almost halved again. Foreign exchange reserves dropped by 80 percent in the same period.

Although oil earnings recovered somewhat, they are still far below 1980 levels.

Unlike many developing nations, Libya has not taken out significant loans from foreign countries and banks. Nevertheless it owes billions of dollars in unpaid bills to foreign businesses for purchases of industrial equipment and other items and services. It owes Russia about $4 billion from purchases of Soviet military equipment.

Libya experiences shortages of food and consumer goods, due to bureaucratic inefficiency and unpaid bills abroad. Inflation is only partially disguised by price controls. Almost three-quarters of the labor force is employed by the government, and sudden salary cuts and dismissals of personnel without university educations have created insecurity among workers. Travel restrictions have been imposed both by the Libyan government and by Western governments. Opportunities for Libyans to study abroad have been curtailed as well.

In addition to these troubling economic conditions, Libyans must contend with a politically repressive regime. Reports indicate that hundreds of Libyans have been executed over the two-and-a-half decades of Qaddafi's rule and thousands of political prisoners are in his jails. There is no mechanism for political activity other than that sanctioned—and controlled—by the government. All political parties are banned.

Qaddafi remains in power by balancing the agents of his repression. Like most military dictators, he fears the army most of all. He has relied on three principal groups to stay in power—and has played them off against one another to prevent any of the three from gaining ascendancy: his old colleagues from the RCC (especially his second-in-command, Jalloud); relatives from his own Qadadfa tribe; and his "Revolutionary Guards"— small detachments of young men established all over the country, even in the military itself. The latter were involved in the assassination of Libyan dissidents abroad; they "kept order" in the capital after a major dissident attack in May 1984; and they maintain a watchful and sometimes violent vigilance over the population at large.

## Foreign Policy Issues

Three aspects of Qaddafi's foreign policy have remained more or less unchanged since the 1969 coup: his ardent desire for Arab unity through mergers with other Arab nations, his staunch opposition to outside powers—especially Western—seeking to affect the course of events in the Middle East, and his hostility to Israel, which he viewed as a manifestation of Western imperialism in the region.

During the early 1970s U.S. policy toward the new Libyan leader was somewhat ambivalent because anticommunism was an early hallmark of Qaddafi's regime. During the 1970s, however, as Qaddafi and Egyptian president Anwar Sadat became increasingly estranged because of Egypt's U.S.-sponsored reconciliation with Israel, the American perception of Qaddafi as a threat to U.S. interests grew. As Sadat moved toward an agreement with Israel after the October 1973 Arab-Israeli War, Qaddafi moved into the forefront of the hard-line Arab nations that repudiated Sadat's policies. The closer American interests became identified with Sadat and his policies toward Israel, the closer Qaddafi edged toward the Soviet Union.

Like Nasser, Qaddafi has not been content simply to rule; he has tried to formulate a philosophy of government to be implemented in his own nation and exported abroad. He has been a leader in the Arab rejectionist movement—those nations that refused to participate in any peace process with Israel and that cut ties with Egypt for doing so. But while many other rejectionist nations (and the Palestine Liberation Organization) have renewed formal ties with Egypt and occasionally taken a conciliatory stand toward Israel, Qaddafi has remained steadfastly hostile to both countries.

During the l980s Libyan support (mostly financial, sometimes logistical) of international terrorists who attacked American citizens and interests intensified the already-hostile relationship between the United States and Libya. The Reagan administration responded first with economic sanctions, and then with military confrontation. On April 14,

1986, President Ronald Reagan ordered a coordinated air strike against Libya in response to evidence that Qaddafi had supported terrorist activities. The U.S. raid destroyed several military targets and killed dozens of Libyan military personnel and civilians, including Qaddafi's daughter.

The attention focused on Qaddafi's support of Iran in the Iran-Iraq War, of radical factions of the PLO (especially the extremist Abu Nidal organization that has concentrated its attacks on American targets), and of subversive groups outside the Middle East (including the Irish Republican Army) accentuated an image of Libyan power in the region. Yet the Libyan military has generally performed poorly. Although Qaddafi purchased an impressive arsenal of Soviet weapons, he has not made major attempts to use the Libyan military except in Chad, where he intervened in 1973, 1980, 1983, and 1987. Twice in 1987 Chadian forces, equipped and supported by the French and Americans, routed invading Libyan troops, who reportedly lost three thousand (out of ten thousand) men and $1 billion of equipment. This embarrassing defeat of Qaddafi's costly military machine in its only substantial conflict was not reported by the official Libyan news media, but it became known widely in the country nonetheless. Libyan forces also were beaten in several clashes with the United States (most notably the 1986 American bombing raid of Libya).

Indeed, many discussions of Libyan radicalism and subversion abroad neglect to mention that Libya's tiny population and its weak economy, based on depleting oil resources, make this large desert nation an unlikely candidate for regional leadership.

Qaddafi's principal foreign policy problem is his isolation. None of the governments of Libya's neighboring states likes or trusts him, for good reasons. Each of them has been the target of verbal abuse and, in several cases, subversion or attack. Their relations with Tripoli change according to several factors: Qaddafi's own interest in reaching accommodation with them, their own need for funds or aid from Libya, the degree of polarization in the Arab world, and their desire to see diminished Libyan aid to their own dissident groups or external enemies. Attempts at unity with Egypt, Sudan, and Syria (beginning in 1970), with Tunisia (1974), with Syria (1980), and with Morroco (beginning in 1984) ended in acrimony. Yet the nations of the Middle East and North Africa do not consider Qaddafi to be the madman he is often portrayed as in the Western press, and they generally have backed him pro forma in his military confrontations with the United States.

Libya's isolation in the Arab world was accentuated by political developments in the late 1980s and early 1990s. The end of the Iran-Iraq War (in which Libya had backed non-Arab Iran), Egypt's reentry into the Arab fold, and the PLO's moderated stance and dialogue with the United States all undermined Qaddafi's ambition to play a leading role in a radicalized, rejectionist Arab world.

The Soviet Union's economic crisis and eventual disintegration in 1991 was a heavy blow to Libya. Successor state Russia, troubled by its own economic and political difficulties, has neither the resources nor the inclination to support an unpredictable dictator of a country clearly outside its area of vital interest. Even during the Cold War, Moscow had maintained more distance from the unpredictable Qaddafi than some of its client states. With Russia clearly concentrating on domestic affairs, Libya was left without a patron.

In 1993 Libya was one of the few countries to voice outright opposition to the Israeli-PLO peace accord, placing it at odds with other more prominent Arab states. The accord and the ongoing peace process have devalued Libya's rejectionist strategy within the Arab League. On February 27, 1994, the Libyan government announced that it was withdrawing from the Arab League.

Libya is the subject of significant, though not total, international economic sanctions stemming from its role in the bombing of Pan Am Flight 103 on December 21, 1988. The crash killed 259 people on board and 11 people on the ground in Lockerbie, Scotland. After an extensive investigation, the United States and Scotland indicted two Libyan nationals, Abd al-Baset Ali al-Megrahi and Al-Amin Khalifah Fhimah. The men were identified as Libyan intelligence agents. French authorities announced that they also were suspects in the bombing of a French jet over Niger in 1989 that killed 171 people.

Libya's refusal to turn over the men for trial in Scotland has led the United Nations Security Council to adopt three resolutions calling for the extradition of the suspects and placing sanctions on Libya until it complies. The sanctions include a limited freeze on Libyan assets abroad and a ban on sales of oil equipment to Libya.

Although the sanctions are not devastating, they have expanded Libya's isolation. At times during the 1980s many nations believed that U.S. efforts to oppose Libya went too far. But Libya's refusal to extradite the bombing suspects created an issue upon which a UN consensus could be constructed.

Libya's relations with the United States remain extremely bad. There is no official contact between the two nations, and broad American economic sanctions, first imposed in 1981, remain in effect. The possibility of continued small military confrontations between American naval forces and Libya in the Mediterranean remains, although such clashes have became less likely since President Reagan, who seemed to have a personal obsession with the Libyan leader, left office.

Although the West Europeans did enact sanctions against Libya in 1986, and Great Britain severed its relations with Libya in 1988 following a terrorist incident at the Libyan embassy in London, the Europeans retain economic ties with Libya. Several thousand West Europeans live in Libya, and Libya has outstanding debts to businesses in Italy and Germany. France, Germany, Great Britain, and Spain also still have investments in Libya.

## Outlook

Qaddafi is unlikely to change many of his extreme foreign policy positions—on Israel, on the United States, on peacemaking—because such changes would force him to deny his own ideology and back down from frequently stated policy goals.

If Qaddafi's maneuverability abroad is circumscribed, he may devote more of his attention to domestic affairs. One possibility might be a move toward a closer embrace by the government of Islamic principles in an effort to solidify the support of Islamist segments of the population. On February 18, 1994, the Libyan government announced that it would begin the implementation of *shari'a,* Islamic Law based on the Koran.

Even if Qaddafi increased his attention to domestic politics he might not be able to prevent his eventual downfall. There were coup conspiracies and other challenges to Qaddafi's rule by dissident forces during the 1980s and 1990s. A few opposition groups exist, most notably the Libyan National Salvation Front, which reportedly has received assistance from the United States.

Yet, a major uprising seemed unlikely, despite the unpopularity of the regime, but forces such as Islamic fundamentalism could provide a rallying point of opposition against Qaddafi. He retained firm control of the clergy, but some of his policies, such as putting women in the military, making divorce easier for women to obtain, and dis-

couraging polygamy, alienated many devout Muslims. Although Qaddafi himself claims to be a devout Muslim, and leads a rather ascetic life, his religious views and policies are quite unorthodox.

Libya's economy is not likely to improve, given its isolation and the handicap of Qaddafi's dictates. Yet its still-significant oil reserves probably ensure that it will not sink into poverty any time soon. European nations depend on Libyan oil, which is easily transported across the Mediterranean. They are likely to resist any move by the United States to impose tougher sanctions on Libya. Because of the $4 billion Libya owes it, Russia also will oppose further weakening the Libya economy.

Qaddafi has demonstrated over the last twenty years that he has the political skill necessary to remain in power. Nevertheless, a military coup, whether by Islamic fundamentalist or pragmatic officers, remains a real possibility. In a closed society such as Libya there is often little sign of a dramatic change until the moment it occurs. If Qaddafi is removed from power, the event is likely to be as much of an immediate surprise as was Qaddafi's own coup d'etat in 1969.

# PERSIAN GULF STATES

Not long ago, the desert sheikdoms on the Persian Gulf were remote and generally unassuming, mostly peopled by nomadic camel herders and pearl harvesters. The world was barely conscious of Bahrain, Abu Dhabi, Dubai, Oman, and Qatar.

But that was before the dramatic increase in demand for oil, coupled with price hikes by the Organization of Petroleum Exporting Countries (OPEC). Since 1973-74, when oil prices increased sharply, the Persian Gulf states have become significant forces in the world economy, with Abu Dhabi and Qatar enjoying per capita incomes exceeding those of many Western industrialized nations. Oil revenues produced substantial funds for domestic development projects and investments overseas.

The oil glut of the mid-1980s, however, sent oil prices plummeting and cut the oil revenues of the Persian Gulf states. Their leaders were forced to reduce spending for social services, construction, economic development, and defense. While oil is still their main source of income and oil prices recovered somewhat in the late 1980s, the Gulf states are trying to diversify their economies as a hedge against falling oil prices and in preparation for future times when oil reserves have been depleted. The Gulf countries also are attempting to reduce the central role that public expenditures play in their economies. To this end, governments throughout the Gulf are reducing red tape, establishing free trade zones, and setting up stock exchanges to encourage private investment and expand trade.

The Gulf states are dependent to varying degrees on Saudi Arabia for policy guidance and the United States for security, yet all are determined to maintain as much independence as possible. In response to the threats posed by the Iran-Iraq War, the states of Bahrain, Kuwait, Qatar, the United Arab Emirates (UAE), Oman, and Saudi Arabia joined to create the Gulf Cooperation Council (GCC) in 1981. The organization's purpose is to enhance regional security and prosperity through greater military, economic, and political coordination. However, recent geopolitical developments in the region have challenged the efficacy of the GCC. The council was powerless to stop Iraq's invasion of Kuwait and it has not played a significant role in the Palestinian-Israeli peace process.

## BAHRAIN

**Area:** 239 square miles.
**Capital:** Manama.
**Population:** 585,683 (1994).
**Religion:** 70 percent Shi'ite Muslim, 30 percent Sunni Muslim.
**Official language:** Arabic; Farsi, Urdu, and English are widely spoken.
**GDP:** $6.8 billion; $12,000 per capita (1993).

Bahrain, the smallest of the Persian Gulf states, was the first to export oil in the 1930s. It established the foundations for a modern, industrialized economy earlier than its neighbors, enabling it to become a regional banking and service center during the oil boom of the 1970s.

During the 1980s Bahrain faced a number of challenges to its political and economic stability. Soon after the Ayatollah Khomeini seized power in Iran, Tehran tried to incite Bahrain's Shi'ite population to begin a fundamentalist revolution in the Gulf. The depression of the oil market in the mid-1980s further aggravated social tensions and complicated the government's development plans. With rapidly diminishing oil resources, Bahrain became more dependent on its Gulf neighbors.

Although the threat of Islamic revolution diminished greatly with the death of Khomeini in 1989, the Bahraini regime continues to face the twin challenges of having a politically disenfranchised Shi'ite majority and a domestic economy that will soon become the first in the Gulf to enter the postpetroleum era.

## Geography

*Bahrain,* meaning "two seas," is an archipelago of about thirty-five islands, six of which are inhabited. Al-Bahrain, the largest island and the location of the capital, Manama, is also the country's namesake. Situated in the Persian Gulf, Bahrain lies between the Saudi Arabian coast and the Qatari Peninsula. Its total land mass is one-fifth the size of Rhode Island.

Al-Muharraq, connected to Manama by a causeway, is the second principal island and the location of Bahrain's international airport. Bahrain's climate is hot and humid most of the year with daytime temperatures often exceeding 100 degrees Fahrenheit. Oil and gas are the country's only significant natural resources. Pearling, a traditional industry, has virtually ceased.

## Demography

The vast majority of the approximately five hundred eighty-six thousand Bahrainis are Muslims. Bahrain has a higher proportion of native citizens to resident aliens than many Gulf countries. The immigrant residents, nearly one-third of the inhabitants, are mostly non-Arab Asians from India, Iran, and Pakistan. Bahrain is also the only Gulf country besides Iran and Iraq where Shi'ite Muslims outnumber Sunnis. Seventy percent of Bahrain's population is Shi'ite, although the ruling al-Khalifa family is Sunni. Shi'ites do not hold wealth and power in proportion to their numbers. Arabic is the official language, but Persian is often spoken among the Iranian-descended Bahrainis. By Gulf standards, Bahrain has a sophisticated population, noted for its intellectual tradition and articulate labor force.

## History

Bahrain was the site of the ancient civilization of Dilmun, which flourished as a trading center from 2000 to 1800 B.C. Portuguese sailors captured the strategically important islands from local Arab tribes in 1521 and ruled until 1602. The islands were then alternately controlled by Arab and Persian forces until the Arabian Utub tribe expelled the Persians in 1783. The members of the al-Khalifa family established themselves as sheiks in 1782 and have ruled ever since.

British interests in the Persian Gulf developed in the early nineteenth century as London sought safe passage for its ships to India, Iraq, and Iran. By 1820 the British established hegemony over the islands, taking over the responsibility of defense and foreign affairs. The al-Khalifa family claimed suzerainty over neighboring Qatar until 1868, when at the request of Qatari notables the British opposed Bahraini claims.

Bahrain's special relationship with Great Britain continued until 1971. British interference in Bahraini domestic affairs was minimal and both countries enjoyed the support of the other. After World War II, Great Britain moved its regional ambassador from Iran to Bahrain.

In 1968 the United Kingdom announced its intention to end its treaty obligations to the Persian Gulf sheikdoms by 1971. Bahrain then joined Qatar and the Trucial States (now called the United Arab Emirates) in negotiations aimed at forming a confederation. Plans for a union failed, and in 1971 Bahrain became an independent state.

## Current Issues

Bahrain is officially a constitutional monarchy under the dynastic rule of the al-Khalifa family. A thirty-seat national assembly elected in 1973 was dissolved in August 1975 after alleged subversive activity by some assembly members. Emir Isa bin Sulman al-Khalifa, who ascended to the throne on November 2, 1961, at the age of twenty-eight, now rules through an appointed cabinet. All major ministerial posts are held by members of the al-Khalifa family. Political parties are prohibited by law. The traditional administrative system of *majlis,* whereby residents directly present petitions to the emir, remains.

Bahrain's modest petroleum reserves provided steadily decreasing revenues in the 1980s. By the early 1990s oil experts agreed that the end of Bahrain's oil reserves was imminent, and that Bahrain would soon become a net oil importer. These forecasts compelled Bahrain to intensify its efforts to diversify its economy. To this end, Bahrain expanded its petroleum refining and aluminum smelting industries and developed a ship repair center. Much of Bahrain's export earnings come from processed petroleum products. Bahraini leaders, however, put most of their effort toward developing their emirate into an international financial center, replacing the void created by Beirut's destruction during Lebanon's protracted civil war.

Bahrain established a relatively stable environment for offshore banking services largely by exempting financial institutions from regulation or taxation. As a result, more than a hundred international banks have opened offices in Bahrain. At the height of the oil boom, Bahrain succeeded in becoming the region's financial and banking capital, surpassing Hong Kong in total assets. A number of factors, however, have since stymied Bahrain's progress in this arena: the collapse of world oil prices in the mid-1980s; continued defaulting of loans to lesser developed countries; and Iraq's invasion of Kuwait, which scared away some investors. The resulting decline in revenues severely depressed Bahrain's economy and forced cuts in government spending.

Tensions created by the economic slowdown raised the threat of discontent from the politically disenfranchised in Bahrain. Of principal concern to the al-Khalifa regime has been the potential for domestic unrest among its majority Shi'ite population. Shortly after the Ayatollah Khomeini seized power in Iran in 1979, unrest increased among Bahrain's Shi'ites. In 1981 security officials uncovered an attempted coup that was thought to be directed by Imam Hadi al-Mudarasi, an Iranian Shi'ite formerly in exile in Bahrain. The government believed that all seventy-three convicted conspirators, representing the Islamic Front for the Liberation of Bahrain, received guerrilla training in Iran. In February 1984 an arms cache discovered in Bahrain's Shi'ite section was attributed to Iran. Another plot to overthrow the government was discovered in 1985, and a plan to sabotage Bahrain's major petroleum refinery was disclosed in December 1987.

The al-Khalifa regime has made considerable efforts to conciliate the Shi'ite community. While strengthening its internal security forces, the government has shown leniency to Shi'ite dissidents. It chose to waive the death penalty for the perpetrators of the aborted 1981 coup. The regime also has increased Shi'ite representation in the bureaucracy and has shown greater respect for Shi'ite religious rituals and traditions.

Since the mid-1980s the level of support among Bahraini Shi'ites for the Iranian government has diminished, as most became disenchanted with the direction of Iran's revolution and the Iran-Iraq War. Still, disaffection among the Shi'ite citizenry will likely remain a problem for the regime as long as they are less well off than Sunni citizens and feel inadequately represented in the government.

Furthermore, the example of Kuwait's democracy movement after its liberation from Iraq did not go unnoticed. In an attempt to preempt calls for more open and participatory political processes, the royal family expressed its support for more democracy in Bahrain. In December 1992 Skeik al-Khalifa announced plans to form a thirty-member "consultative council." Composed of appointed members, the council's role would be solely advisory, without any real power to enact legislation or challenge decisions made by the royal family. While hardly a true democratic innovation, this was nevertheless the first move toward broadening political participation since 1973, when a parliamentary body was elected, only to be dissolved two years later. Unfortunately, announcing the creation of the council backfired, and the three major dissident political organizations—the Islamic Front for the Liberation of Bahrain, the Bahrain National Liberation Movement, and the Popular Front—issued a joint statement rejecting the proposed council on grounds that it did not respond to popular sentiment.

Of equal concern to the Bahraini regime are issues of regional security. Because of Bahrain's small size and important strategic position, it is particularly vulnerable to instability in the Gulf and depends heavily on collective defense arrangements. In 1981 Bahrain signed a bilateral defense pact with Saudi Arabia and joined four other Gulf states in forming the Gulf Cooperation Council. In 1984 Bahrain received funds from the GCC for improvement of its defenses and participated with Qatar and other Gulf states in the GCC's "peninsula shield" military exercises. By the end of the Persian Gulf War, Bahrain also bought four F-16s from the United States and began constructing an air base. Bahrain already has an onshore facility for American forces, and there is a large U.S. Navy presence in the country.

Bahrain and Qatar have disputed their border with regard to the Hawar Islands and the Fasht al-Dibal and Jaradah shoals, located between the two countries. Although uninhabited, these lands have potential for oil and gas exploration and therefore are of extreme importance to both countries, each of which faces dwindling reserves.

## Outlook

Although Bahrain managed to escape the Iran-Iraq War and the invasion of Kuwait relatively unscathed, it still remains vulnerable to the geopolitical aspirations of its powerful neighbors. As its oil reserves dwindle, Bahrain will become in-creasingly dependent on its income from peripheral industries servicing the better-endowed Gulf countries. Joint industrial projects undertaken by the GCC will become more important to Bahrain's prosperity, as will construction of the King Fahd Causeway, a twenty-five-kilometer link between Bahrain and Saudi Arabia.

If stable oil prices and political conditions are maintained, Bahrain's future as a trade and economic service center in the region is bright. Although the Bahraini banking industry was scaled down in the mid-1980s because of declining oil revenues and competition from Kuwaiti and Saudi banks, Bahrain is still a preferred location for business in the region, because of its first-rate communications, permissive banking laws, tolerance of Western social customs, and time zone, which allows dealers to trade with Tokyo and Singapore in the morning and London and New York in the afternoon. Bahrain recently became the first country in the Gulf to allow 100 percent foreign-owned businesses into the country without local sponsorship.

Bahrain will still remain highly vulnerable to the uncertainties in the oil market and instability in the region. Future downturns in oil prices would jeopardize Bahrain's extensive industrial projects and expanding financial markets. The resumption of hostilities in the Gulf could threaten the Bahraini economy by destroying international business confidence and placing the country's own security at risk.

Shi'ites are in the majority, unlike in most Arab Gulf states. Bahrain must keep close watch over political and religious developments in Iran. Tehran still maintains an eighteenth-century territorial claim to Bahrain and has been persistent in its desire to gain control of the island. As a majority with fewer rights and riches than the minority Sunnis in power, the Shi'ites continue to be an unpredictable force in Bahraini politics. The traditionally vocal Shi'ite community is likely to demand greater political and economic equality, using its ethnic and religious identities as a rallying point. Another potential source of domestic unrest arises from Bahrain's young educated class. They may press for white-collar jobs, personal freedom, and political participation if the al-Khalifa regime does not move forward with political reforms.

# OMAN

**Area:** 82,030 square miles.
**Capital:** Muscat.
**Population:** 1,701,470 (1994).
**Religion:** Muslim, 75 percent from the Ibadhi sect.
**Official language:** Arabic; English, Baluchi, Urdu, and Indian dialects are also spoken.
**GDP:** $16.4 billion; $10,000 per capita (1993).

During the past quarter century, the sultanate of Oman has experienced perhaps the most dramatic social and economic progress of any Middle East nation. Formerly known as the sultanate of Muscat and Oman, the country changed its name in 1970 after the current sultan, Qaboos bin Said, gained power. Before then, Oman was notable as perhaps the most isolated nation in the Middle East. Surrounded by sea and desert, its rulers rejected virtually all outside influences. The palace coup that brought Sultan Qaboos to power ushered in an era of development in which Oman used its oil revenues to increase living standards, build a modern infrastructure, and establish social services for the populace. In 1970 Oman had just three schools, one hospital, and ten kilometers of paved roads. By 1991 Oman had seven hundred twenty-one schools, fifty hospitals, and more than four thousand kilometers of paved roads.

Oman has followed an independent foreign policy line based on strong cooperation with the West, especially the United States. Considered by most U.S. statesmen as America's most reliable ally in the Persian Gulf, Oman was the only Gulf nation that endorsed the Camp David accords and refused to sever relations with Egypt because it made peace with Israel. Since 1980, when Oman signed a defense agreement with the United States, it has become increasingly involved in U.S. strategic plans for projecting force in the Middle East. Oman was a valuable ally during the Persian Gulf crisis and war.

## Geography

Oman stretches for a thousand miles from the mouth of the Persian Gulf around the southeast coast of the Arabian Peninsula and borders on the west with Yemen. Most of Oman's territory is empty flat desert. The country has four distinct regions: the Musandam Peninsula, a small noncontiguous province that juts into the Persian Gulf at the strategic Strait of Hormuz; the Batinah, a fertile and prosperous coastal plain that lies northwest of Muscat, the capital; the expansive Inner Oman, which is located between the Jabal al-Akhdar (Green Mountains), where heights reach 9,900 feet, and the Rub al-Khali (Empty Quarter) desert; and the Dhofar region that stretches along the southern coast to Yemen.

During most of the year Oman's desert climate is hot and exceptionally humid. The coastal area of Dhofar, however, is more tropical with less extreme temperatures. The southern coastal tip of Oman receives monsoon summer rains that support a small tropical fruit industry and cattle farming.

## Demography

Although no official census has ever been conducted in Oman, the population is estimated to be slightly more than 1.7 million people. Nearly half of all Omanis live in the central hill region of Inner Oman; the most densely populated area is the Batinah Plain where about one-third of Oman's people live. The Dhofar province has approximately sixty thousand inhabitants. The al-Shahouh tribes dwell in the Musandam Peninsula and number about fifteen thousand.

About three-fourths of Omanis, including the royal family, are Ibadhi Muslims, a small Islamic sect that believes in a nonhereditary caliphate, or temporal ruler. About 20 percent of the population are Sunni. Expatriate labor in Oman is rapidly increasing, numbering at least two hundred thousand workers. Most come from India, Pakistan, Bangladesh, and Sri Lanka.

## History

Oman's early history is obscure. Converted to Islam in the seventh century A.D., native Omanis embraced Ibadhism, which traces its roots to the Kharijite movement, an early Islamic offshoot. European influence began in 1507 when Portugal seized much of the Omani coastline. Seventeenth-century Portuguese fortifications on the Omani coast still stand in and around Muscat.

The Portuguese were ousted in 1650 as an Omani renaissance began. Elected Ibadhi imams of the central hill region and hereditary sultans situated in Muscat became the political leaders of the region. Divisions between the coast and interior of the country were exacerbated in 1786 when the capital moved from Rostaq to coastal Muscat. The Muscat rulers were responsible for extending Oman's control to Zanzibar (near Tanzania), a large part of the Arabian Peninsula, and the Makran coast (Pakistan). By the early nineteenth century, Omani power was unchallenged in southern Arabia and East Africa.

Oman has remained independent since 1650, except for a brief period of Persian rule from 1741 to 1744. Ahmad ibn Said defeated the Persians and shortly thereafter founded the al-Bu Said dynasty, which is still in power today.

Oman's regional power began to decline during the latter half of the nineteenth century when it was forced to relinquish control of its East African colonies. In 1958 Oman sold its last colonial possession, Gwadur, to Pakistan for three million pounds.

Ibadhi Muslims in the interior pressed for greater independence from Muscat around the beginning of the twentieth century. Two rebellions flared up in 1950 when the people of Inner Oman, under their own elected imam, resisted the efforts of Sultan Said bin Taimur to extend his control into the interior. With the aid of the British, the insurgents were defeated in 1959. Later the sultan invalidated the office of the elected imam.

The government of Sultan Said was regarded as one of the most traditional and conservative in the Arab world in its day. Slavery was still common, and social and economic development was completely ignored, despite growing oil revenues. In 1964 a major tribal revolt occurred in the southern province of Dhofar. The rebels operated from bases in neighboring South Yemen, conducting a war of attrition against Sultan Said and his successor for more than ten years.

In a palace coup Sultan Qaboos overthrew his father's stifling rule in 1970 and embarked on a program of modernization. Although Oman's economic progress partially stemmed the insurgents' rebellion, fighting nevertheless continued. In 1974 rebel forces formed the People's Front for the Liberation of Oman (PFLO). In December 1975, after a rebel offensive was crushed, Sultan Qaboos declared complete victory.

The rebellion flared up again in June 1978 when exiles from South Yemen reported renewed support of the PFLO by Cuba. This development caused the Omani government to close its border with South Yemen in June 1981 and put its defense forces on full alert. Tensions then receded, and in October 1982 Oman and South Yemen reestablished diplomatic relations and signed an agreement ending the conflict. According to official Omani sources, the PFLO is now defunct.

## Current Issues

Oman is an absolute monarchy dominated by the sultan. No constitution or parliament exists because the sultan legislates by decree. He acts as the premier, foreign minister, defense minister, and finance minister. In 1981, however, the sultan established the State Consultative Council (*Majlis Al Shura*). The council's fifty-five members are appointed from a list of freely elected candidates made up mostly of government officials, selected merchants and business leaders, and tribal leaders from various regions. Chaired by the sultan himself, the council has no legislative powers. Nevertheless, it performs a valuable advisory function for the sultan, and it has been seen as a vehicle through which Omanis might begin to participate in government.

Sultan Qaboos is noted for his strong leanings toward the West. About twenty of his closest advisers are said to be either Britons, Americans, or Arabs who have encouraged Oman's Western orientation. A 1980 defense agreement with Oman grants the United States access to Omani military installations, emergency landing rights, and the authority to pre-position military hardware at Omani storage facilities. After the Iraqi invasion of Kuwait, the first American soldiers sent to Saudi Arabia used military equipment that had been pre-positioned in Oman.

The Musandam Peninsula facility, an Omani military base near the Strait of Hormuz to which the United States has access, is a valuable listening post for monitoring activity in Iran and became a strategic focal point from which the United States coordinated logistical operations in support of Operation Desert Storm. Oman also sent combat troops to fight Iraq under Saudi command in Desert Storm.

Despite its close ties to the West, Oman has pursued an independent foreign policy. The sultan has been known to go to great lengths to demonstrate a neutrality in inter-Arab and regional disputes. For example, in 1988 Oman and Syria agreed to establish formal relations at a time when Syria's involvement in Lebanon was a source of frustration for Washington and its Arab allies. Oman maintained relations with Iraq throughout the Iran-Iraq War, again breaking ranks with most other Arab states. In 1987 the Omanis upgraded diplomatic relations with the Soviet Union to the ambassadorial level, following the example of Kuwait and the United Arab Emirates. Establishing diplomatic relations with the Soviet Union helped pave the way for improved relations with South Yemen, a Soviet ally and long-time regional rival.

A founding member of the Gulf Cooperation Council, Oman has been an advocate of an integrated GCC defense force. As its close ties with the United States indicate, however, Oman has recognized that the GCC cannot ensure the security of its members from attacks by the region's larger states without Western assistance.

Throughout its recent history, Oman's economy has been largely dependent on the oil industry, which provides the government with most of its revenues. In 1993, 77 percent of Oman's revenues of $4.3 billion came from the petroleum industry. Compared with those of other Gulf states, Oman's oil reserves are of moderate size, slightly in excess of 4.3 billion barrels. They are expected to last only another twenty years.

Oman is not a member of the Organization of Petroleum Exporting Countries (OPEC) or the Organization of Arab Petroleum Exporting Countries (OAPEC) and hence does not abide by their quota system. This has enabled Muscat to weather the world oil glut by adjusting its output to partially compensate for low petroleum prices.

Yet even Oman's freedom from OPEC could not insulate its economy from the volatile oil prices of the late 1980s. The country's capacity to pump is restricted by its relatively small and inaccessible fields. As a result, falling prices led to falling government revenues and budget slashing. Numerous development projects and military purchases were delayed or discontinued and the Omani riyal was devalued. By 1990 the Central Bank of Oman was forced to introduce a bond program to finance the country's budget deficit.

The sultan has made a concerted effort especially since 1989 to diversify Oman's economy. Fortunately, Oman's picturesque mountains and coastline can be exploited for tourism. The government is easing restrictions on visas for tourists and businesses to encourage foreigners to come to Oman. This sector will take some time to develop, given Oman's complete isolation from outsiders prior to 1970 and its focus on the petroleum industry since then.

The possibilities for developing fishing, agriculture, and mining are better than in the rest of the region. Gold and chromite resources were recently identified, and Oman has turned to the private sector to develop them. To encourage investment, the Muscat stock exchange opened in 1990, and trade volumes initially exceeded expectations. Nevertheless, Oman has not lodged its hopes in becoming a center of international commerce like Bahrain. Omani leaders have sought to develop long-term investment projects.

The most significant economic developments for Oman have been in the industrial sector. Oman is setting up joint ventures and providing technical assistance for petroleum refining projects in some of the newly independent states and other parts of Asia. The Oman Oil Company is involved with several projects in Kazakhstan, Thailand, and Russia. In addition, Oman has taken a lead in strengthening its economic ties with India. Both countries are investigating major joint ventures, including the construction of new refineries and of a natural gas pipeline linking the two nations. Of the Western countries, Great Britain is the most heavily involved in the Omani economy.

## Outlook

Sultan Qaboos enjoys broad support and the public generally approves of his foreign and domestic policies. Throughout Oman, no significant political opposition or abuse of human rights exists. As Oman's development continues, however, the sultan will have to meet the growing expectations of his increasingly well-educated population. If Oman's long-term growth or the state's paternal distribution of wealth is ever disturbed, perhaps the sultan's staunch commitment to the principle of monarchal rule, with no popular representation, will become less tolerable to Omanis.

Oman's major concern for the future must focus on how to best diversify its economy beyond the petroleum sector. Thus far, Oman's efforts to diversify have proven successful, in part because its reliance on oil was never so dramatic and absolute as that of its neighbors. Oman's gross domestic product (GDP) registered an impressive growth rate of 10.4 percent in 1992—the bulk of which reflected increased exports from the nonoil sector. However, with an educated middle class growing rapidly, meeting rising expectations with an expanding economy will be the principal domestic challenge for the sultan.

Without an heir, Sultan Qaboos (unmarried

and fifty-five years old in 1994) has left open for speculation the question of the form of Oman's future government.

## QATAR

**Area:** 4,247 square miles.
**Capital:** Doha.
**Population:** 512,779.
**Religion:** Muslim, mostly Sunni from the Wahhabi sect.
**Official language:** Arabic; English is widely spoken.
**GDP:** $8.8 billion; $17,500 per capita.

Qatar has gone through a profound period of social transformation since oil production began in 1947. Before then Qatar (KAH-tar) was one of the poorest and least developed countries of eastern Arabia. The economy depended heavily on fishing and pearling. Petroleum production and export rapidly converted a nomadic population into a mostly urban and settled people, with one of the highest per capita incomes in the world.

The ruling al-Thani family is one of the largest ruling families in the region, numbering in the thousands. Its members dominate all important government functions and all major ministries—interior, defense, and foreign affairs. Qatari society is staunchly religious and conservative, with strong ties to Saudi Wahhabism.

Qatar like all Gulf states felt the economic recession and regional instability that rocked the Gulf in the 1980s. Although its shipping was endangered during the Iran-Iraq War, Qatar was not seriously challenged during that decade by foreign intrigue or domestic unrest.

During the 1990s Qatar has pursued an independent foreign policy that emphasizes accommodation with its three large neighbors: Saudi Arabia, Iraq, and Iran. Qatari leaders have attracted controversy for speaking out against the economic embargo of Iraq, making overtures to Israel, and signing a defense cooperation agreement with the United States.

## Geography

Qatar occupies a thumb-shaped desert peninsula, about the size of Connecticut, that stretches north into the Persian Gulf. In the south it borders the United Arab Emirates and Saudi Arabia. The peninsula is a low, flat, barren plain, consisting mostly of sand-covered limestone. The climate is hot and humid. One-half of Qatar's water supply is provided by sea-water desalination.

On the west coast is a chain of hills, the Dikhan Anticline, beneath which lie oil reserves that contain an estimated 3.7 billion barrels of crude oil. Off the northeast Qatari coast lies one of the world's largest concentrations of natural gas not associated with oil. Qatar has known reserves of 162 trillion cubic feet of high-quality natural gas, more than 4 percent of worldwide reserves.

## Demography

Indigenous Qataris share their country with Arabs from neighboring states, and large numbers of Iranian, Pakistani, and Indian immigrants. Qatari society constituted one of the most ethnically homogeneous communities among all Gulf states until petroleum production began in the late 1940s. Today foreign workers—principally from Iran, Pakistan, and India—constitute the overwhelming majority of Qatar's work force. Detailed rules closely govern their entrance into the country and their political rights. Although laws restrict the industrial and commercial activities of non-Qataris, foreign workers are usually content to forgo civil and political rights in exchange for high wages.

Most Qataris adhere to the Wahhabi school of Sunni Islam. Approximately 16 percent of the population, composed primarily of expatriates, is Shi'ite. More than 80 percent of all Qatar's inhabitants reside near the capital city of Doha.

The ruling family is divided into three main branches, each quite independent of the other: Bani Hamad, Bani Ali, and Bani Khalid. The current emir, Sheik Khalifa bin Hamad al-Thani, comes from the Bani Hamad branch.

## History

Qatar was formerly dominated by Bahrain's ruling al-Khalifa family, which regarded Qatar as an errant province. Rising to prominence in the nineteenth century, the al-Thani family established its own dynasty in Qatar, gaining independence and legitimacy through successive agreements with Great Britain. At the request of leading Qatari families, the British in 1868 opposed the Bahraini claim in exchange for a larger British role in Qatar's affairs.

The British-Qatari relationship was interrupted in 1872 when the Ottoman Turks occupied Qatar. After the Ottomans evacuated the peninsula in the beginning of World War I, however, the al-Thani dynasty entered into treaty obligations with Great Britain and became a formal British protectorate in 1916. A 1934 treaty gave Britain a more extensive role in Qatari affairs. Oil was discovered in 1940, but exploitation was delayed by World War II. During the 1950s and 1960s, gradually increasing oil revenues brought prosperity, rapid immigration, and social progress.

From 1947 to 1960 Qatar was led by Emir Ali, who was forced from his throne by his son Ahmad with the help of a British gunboat in Doha harbor. Ahmad's profligate and venal rule, however, was ended by a 1972 bloodless coup by his cousin Khalifa bin Hamad al-Thani, the current emir.

Qatar declared its independence on September 1, 1971, after attempts to form a union with neighboring Gulf emirates (Bahrain and the Trucial States) failed. Later that year British forces concluded their withdrawal from the region.

## Current Issues

Emir Khalifa holds absolute authority to enact all laws, appoint members to the advisory council (a consultative assembly), and amend the provisional 1970 constitution. Qatar's constitution or "basic law" is officially designated as a provisional document to be replaced by a final constitution following a transitional period. However, there is no indication that a new constitution is forthcoming. Currently, no popularly elected governmental body exists.

Emir Khalifa rules under the guidance of strict Islamic law. On major decisions he seeks a family consensus. The Qatari throne is hereditary within the al-Thani family, but it is not automatically passed from father to son. Instead, the ruler is designated by the consensus of leading family members. The emir's son, Sheik Hamad bin Khalifa al-Thani, is the crown prince and likely successor to the throne.

The emir's rule is constrained by rival families and by the conservative religious establishment. The al-'Atiyyah family continuously vies with the al-Thanis for predominance within Qatar's economy and armed forces. Other family clans also have challenged the al-Thanis, but to date no challenge has been successful. In May of 1992, for example, fifty-four prominent Qataris presented Emir Khalifa with a petition demanding parliamentary elections, a written constitution, and greater personal and political freedoms. Some of the signatories were called in for questioning or had their passports confiscated. The petition did not inspire any changes, as a ruling in July 1993 barring television satellite dishes indicates. In a move to counter what the emir saw as a corrupting influence of some foreign television stations, as well as an effort to boost the government's own cable service, the government requires any resident wishing to view foreign broadcasts to subscribe to Qatari state cable service, strictly regulated by the government's Office of Telecommunication.

Yet Qatar is generally less puritanical than its neighbor, Saudi Arabia. It allows movie theaters and women drivers, but it prohibits the importation, manufacturing, and consumption of alcohol. Qatar provides free education and medical services to all its citizens.

The successful integration of Qatar's growing population has traditionally depended upon revenues generated by the emirate's principal export, petroleum. Oil accounts for about 90 percent of Qatar's national income. As a result, Qatar's economy suffered when oil prices fell in the latter half of the 1980s. By the end of the 1980s, government revenues were half of the level they were in the mid-1980s, and Qatar's GDP was approximately $15,000 per capita, less than half of what it was in 1981 ($36,000).

The focus of the government's economic diversification effort has been the development of its North Field project, designed to exploit Qatar's large offshore natural gas resources. In 1987 the government began construction of offshore production facilities linked to the shore by submerged pipelines. With proven natural gas reserves estimated at 150 trillion cubic feet, the North Field is expected to produce 700 million cubic feet per day, becoming a valuable source of energy for cement, steel, and petrochemical industries as well as income for Qatar for the next hundred years. Qatar also recently signed agreements with French and Japanese companies to research, build, and operate a liquefied natural gas facility with transportation and marketing services.

Qatar joined the Gulf Cooperation Council in 1981 and supported Iraq throughout the Iran-Iraq War. In 1982 Qatar signed a bilateral defense agreement with Saudi Arabia and generally follows its lead in policy matters. However, border disputes in 1992 between the two countries have complicated otherwise good relations. The border dispute resulted from Qatari accusations that Saudi troops were attacking border posts at al-Khaffoss in an attempt to redefine the border. With a rift opening in Gulf regional security, Egypt's President Hosni Mubarak mediated a compromise by calling a joint committee to set the boundary.

Qatar also is engaged in long-running border disputes with its other neighbor, Bahrain. In April 1986 Qatar raided the island of Fasht ad-Dibal, which had been reclaimed from an underlying coral reef by the Bahraini government. The Qatari forces seized twenty-nine foreign workers who were building a Bahraini coast guard station on the island. The dispute was finally resolved when Bahrain and Qatar agreed to destroy the island and to submit future disputes to international arbitration. In addition to Fasht ad-Dibal, Qatar and Bahrain have each claimed the town of Zubara on the mainland of Qatar and Hawar Islands off the coast of Qatar.

While Qatar remained strongly pro-Western, its relationship with the United States was strained in March 1988 when Washington learned that Qatar had secretly acquired thirteen American-made Stinger antiaircraft missiles. After Qatar refused to disclose where it got the missiles, the U.S. Senate voted to prohibit weapons sales to Qatar. Later in 1988 Qatar became the fourth Gulf state to establish diplomatic relations with the People's Republic of China and the Soviet Union.

As with most of its neighbors, Qatar strengthened its ties to the United States in the wake of Iraq's invasion of Kuwait. Qatari troops played a major role in the first land battle of the Persian Gulf War near the town of Khafji, where a large Iraqi unit penetrated into Saudi territory before being repelled by coalition forces. In March 1991 Qatar joined the other Gulf states in endorsing a security plan with the United States to ensure the security of the region through a multinational peacekeeping force, U.S. naval deployments, and frequent joint maneuvers. In June 1993 Qatar signed a bilateral defense cooperation agreement with the United States.

Nevertheless, Qatar has pursued good relations with Iran and Iraq since the Gulf War. Qatar signed a major trade pact with Iran in 1993, and it sent an ambassador back to Baghdad shortly after the war. Qatar's foreign minister, Hamad bin Jassim bin Jabir, stated in early 1994 that if Iraq recognizes Kuwait, international economic sanctions against Iraq should be lifted.

## Outlook

Like many of the Gulf sheikdoms, Qatar faces a combination of challenges any one of which could dramatically change the political or economic landscape. With a world oil glut, prices have fallen, dragging down the government's main source of revenue. As a result, Qatar will have to continue to diversify its economy to maintain its high standard of living and contented population. Qatar's huge natural gas reserves will provide a cushion against low oil revenues.

While calls for radical changes or greater par-

ticipation in the government are a relatively recent phenomenon, they are no doubt tied to frustrations of an educated population. Despite the rapid pace of development, Qatari society has been unable to adequately absorb the more than two thousand secondary school and college graduates that enter the work force each year. At the same time few Qataris are able or willing to fill the technical and laboring jobs that are critical to the economy. Such inconsistencies in the labor market are likely to cause increasing frustration among Qatar's native population, while making it more difficult for the government to reduce the number of foreign workers in the country. Foreign workers seem content to reap the benefits of Qatar's oil economy despite the constraints placed upon them. If the ruling family can maintain national revenues and foreign workers remain quiescent, then the threat to the political status quo is minimal.

Despite the recession of the 1980s, Qatar's economic future remains promising. In the short term, the country's oil reserves are expected to support its conservative economic path, and the development of the North Field natural gas project promises continued prosperity in the postoil era. Still, as a small state, Qatar has interests that are tied closely to the fortunes of OPEC and the regional security provided by the GCC. One potential threat to Qatar's future economic prospects is an Iranian claim to a substantial portion of the North Field gas reservoir. While Tehran's claim does not affect the first stage of Qatar's development program, the dispute could evolve into a major political confrontation.

# UNITED ARAB EMIRATES

**Area:** 29,182 square miles.
**Capital:** Abu Dhabi.
**Population:** 2,791,141.
**Religion:** 96 percent Muslim, 4 percent Christian, Hindu, and others.
**Official language:** Arabic; Persian, English, Hindi, and Urdu are also spoken.
**GDP:** $63.8 billion; $24,000 per capita.

The United Arab Emirates (UAE), formerly known as the Trucial States, is the only federation of states in the Middle East. By 1972 seven disparate emirates ruled by individual tribal sheiks had merged to create a federal framework within which they could preserve their local autonomy and avoid being dominated by their two large neighbors, Saudi Arabia and Iran.

Commercial development of petroleum resources, which began in the late 1950s, stimulated population growth and development in the emirates. The combined population of the emirates increased from one hundred eighty thousand in 1968 to more than 1 million by 1980, largely because of immigration. Development among the emirates proceeded unevenly, however, and the smaller emirates that lacked oil were left almost untouched by petroleum riches.

Inequalities persist in size, population, development, and wealth. Abu Dhabi and Dubai stand out among the other emirates for their vast oil revenues, large populations, and expansive territory. More than 1.5 million of the 2.8 million people in the UAE live in Abu Dhabi, Dubai, or Sharjah, a latecomer to oil production. Ajman, with a hundred square miles and only sixty thousand inhabitants, is the smallest emirate.

All the states fiercely compete with each other for development funds and projects, often at the expense of national unity and economic planning. Because of the absence of a strong centralized government, duplication of many facilities, such as international airports and harbors, has occurred throughout the country.

## The Seven Emirates

Abu Dhabi, the largest, most populous, and influential of the seven emirates, is the federal capital. With the advent of petroleum production, Abu Dhabi became a classic example of a traditional society transformed almost overnight by tremendous oil wealth. The UAE's largest oil producer, Abu Dhabi has proven reserves of 31 billion barrels and accounts for more than 60 percent of the federation's gross national product.

Dubai, second only to Abu Dhabi in oil riches, has a long tradition of entrepôt trading. Dubai boasts one of the Gulf's most important deepwater ports, Jebel Ali. Recently, this port has become a major reexporting center and free trade zone for foreign goods destined for Iran.

After Sharjah began oil production in 1974, it joined Abu Dhabi and Dubai to form an elite group of oil producers within the federation. Ras al-Khaimah entered the federation in February 1972 after its fruitless efforts to recapture the two Tunb islands and the islet of Abu Musa, which Iran overran on March 30, 1971. Comparatively large and fertile, Ras al-Khaimah contains only minor offshore oil reserves, which were discovered in 1983. Fujairah, Ajman, and Umm al-Qaiwan are subordinate to the wealthier emirates and rely on their largess for development programs and to overcome economic and social disparities.

## Geography

The UAE extends for 746 miles along the southern rim of the Persian Gulf, where six of the emirates are located. Fujairah faces the Gulf of Oman, a part of the Arabian Sea. Sharjah also has additional, noncontiguous territory along the coast with Fujairah.

About the size of South Carolina, the UAE has approximately twenty-nine thousand square miles of mostly barren flat land. Temperatures sometimes soar to 140 degrees Fahrenheit. Its undefined southern border with Saudi Arabia merges into the great, virtually uninhabited wasteland of the *Rub al-Khali* (Empty Quarter). In the east along the Omani border lie the Western Hajar Mountains.

The UAE's major natural resources are oil and natural gas. The UAE is OPEC's third largest producer after Saudi Arabia and Iran. Its proven published reserves in 1992 were estimated at 98 billion barrels of petroleum, the bulk of which is located in Abu Dhabi. Abu Dhabi also possesses most of the UAE's 199 trillion cubic feet of natural gas reserves.

## Demography

Indigenous inhabitants of the seven emirates account for less than 20 percent of the federation's nearly 3 million people. Most of the immigrant residents are Indian, Pakistani, and Iranian. Among the expatriate Arab population are Omanis, Palestinians, Jordanians, Egyptians, and Yemenis. Nearly 91 percent of the labor force is foreign.

The country is overwhelmingly Sunni, with about 16 percent following the Shi'ite branch of Islam. Hindus and Christians reside in the foreign communities; few are granted citizenship rights. Bedouin nomads, making up 5 to 10 percent of the population, live around oases and are slowly settling towns or migrating to urban areas.

## History

During the early nineteenth century the Qawasim tribe was the dominant Arab power in the lower Gulf coast. After Wahhabi warriors from the Arabian Peninsula overran their territory in 1805, the tribe turned from sea trading to piracy. These armed outlaws made the sea perilous for British maritime traders. To secure the lower Gulf for safe trading, Britain negotiated a peace treaty in 1820 with what was then known as the Pirate Coast and thereafter as the Trucial Coast. The local sheiks signed with Great Britain a perpetual maritime truce in 1853 and an exclusive agreement in 1892 that gave Britain control over the Trucial States' foreign policy.

Britain supported Abu Dhabi in a 1955 dispute with Saudi Arabia over the Buraimi Oasis and other territories in the south. The oasis is now shared by Abu Dhabi and Oman. The border between the UAE and Saudi Arabia remains undemarcated. Minor boundary differences still persist with Oman. After Britain announced in 1968 its intention to withdraw from the Gulf by the end of 1971, Qatar, Bahrain, and the Trucial States initiated plans to form a confederation. Qatar and Bahrain, however, decided in favor of independent sovereign status.

On December 2, 1971, the UAE proclaimed its independence and immediately entered into a treaty of friendship with Britain. Originally only six emirates signed the act of confederation, but after two months Ras al-Khaimah accepted membership.

Since then Sheik Zayed ibn Sultan al-Nahayan of Abu Dhabi has ruled as president of the UAE. He heads the highest body in the country, the Supreme Council of the Union (SCU), which is composed of the rulers of the federation's seven member states. The SCU is responsible for the election of the president and vice president, for general federal policy, for the ratification of federal laws, and for appointing the legislative body. Abu Dhabi and Dubai have veto power over all federal matters. The forty-member Federal National Council functions primarily as a consultative assembly and forum for debate. Members are chosen by each emir.

The government of the UAE is based on a provisional constitution promulgated in 1971, which has been renewed at five-year intervals. The establishment of a permanent constitution has been delayed by the reluctance of individual emirates to relinquish their autonomy—particularly in the areas of natural resources and defense. Contributions to the federal budget have also been a source of dispute, as Abu Dhabi has become increasingly reluctant to continue contributing more than 80 percent of the total budget.

Family rivalries also have influenced interemirate politics. In June 1987 Abdul Aziz, the older brother of Sheik Sultan of Sharjah, tried to replace his younger brother as ruler of the emirate. Abu Dhabi favored Abdul in the power struggle, while Dubai supported Sheik Sultan. Finally, after days of uncertainty, the other members of the GCC stepped in to help negotiate a compromise in which Sheik Sultan regained power while Abdul Aziz was made crown prince.

## Current Issues

The economy of the UAE has historically been sensitive to the world oil market. Because of the oil glut in 1982, the government began running budget deficits for the first time in its history; a number of development projects were postponed, canceled, or scaled down. When oil prices collapsed in 1986, oil revenues fell 40 percent below those of 1984, leading to a dramatic decline in gross national product. To maintain a surplus in their balance of payments, the emirates now place greater emphasis on economic diversification through the development of industry and trade. In 1993 the UAE began constructing a multimillion-dollar facility to produce steel for domestic and export markets. In addition, the UAE has aggressively pursued developing its natural gas fields with Japanese partners.

The emirates were thrust into the international spotlight in 1991 over the collapse of the Bank of Credit and Commerce International (BCCI). Seventy-seven percent owned by Abu Dhabi's leader, Sheik Zayed, the bank was shut down after auditors in England and other countries disclosed fraud, improper loans, and deceptive accounting and accused the bank of catering to drug dealers, arms merchants, and Third World dictators. Although the government of Abu Dhabi agreed to pay $2.2 billion to creditors in exchange for an agreement not to sue the bank or Abu Dhabi for losses stemming from the bank's collapse, victims have accused Abu Dhabi of foot dragging in criminal investigations. However, Abu Dhabi contends it was a major victim also, losing nearly $6 billion of the $10 billion in worldwide losses from the bank's closure. BCCI reportedly stole between $1.5–$2.0 billion from Sheik Zayed himself to cover up enormous losses from fraudulent loans. Finally, two years after the bank collapsed, the UAE indicted thirteen BCCI officers on criminal and forgery charges.

In foreign policy, the federation has tried to pursue a strategy of balance. In October 1984 it opened diplomatic relations with China. In November 1985 it became the third Gulf state to establish ties to the Soviet Union. Regional stability is also of prime importance to the UAE. The federation attempted to steer a neutral course during the Iran-Iraq War. While joining with the other Arab Gulf states to form the GCC in 1981 and entering into a bilateral defense agreement with Saudi Arabia in 1982, the UAE maintained stable relations with Iran, permitting Sheik Zayed to play a mediating role as the Iran-Iraq War escalated in the mid-1980s.

In spite of the UAE's relatively good rapport with Iran, the two countries have one unresolved dispute over the islands of Abu Musa, Greater and Lesser Tunbs, and part of Ras al-Khaimah. In 1971 the shah of Iran sent a small force to claim the islands, but he agreed with the UAE to cede administrative control and split offshore oil revenues. In September 1992 Iran claimed full sovereignty, causing the UAE to seek Egypt's involvement in a peaceful resolution. Negotiations are currently at a standstill.

## Outlook

While Yemen, Kuwait, Bahrain, and even Saudi Arabia have been forced to confront domestic calls to broaden political participation, no such pressure appears to affect the UAE. For the foreseeable future, the ruling families' generous, albeit paternalistic, political tradition will continue to satisfy the UAE's forty thousand citizens. The UAE's principal political concern is its heavy reliance on foreign labor. Although the federal government has stepped up efforts to "nationalize" employment, the small size of the country's native labor force and its strong commitment to industrial development have given the federation no option but to retain a large number of foreign workers. Although the expatriates have remained relatively quiescent, the large foreign majority may threaten the emirates' conservative culture and political system.

The issue of political succession also will need to be resolved. Sheik Zayed, who was elected for his fourth term in 1986, is in his seventies; and Sheik Rashid, the UAE's prime minister and emir of Dubai, has been incapacitated by serious illness since 1981. While both leaders have designated their eldest sons as heirs, their offspring lack their experience and commitment to the federation.

A stable oil market in the 1990s will greatly

benefit the UAE, buying time and revenues to complete its diversification and petroleum modernization programs. The UAE has earmarked $500 million to boost oil production capacity by six hundred thousand barrels a day to about 3 million barrels a day by 1995. It also expects to spend more than $1 billion over an undisclosed time to expand gas and refining sectors. Abu Dhabi, which produces 75 percent of the UAE's petroleum exports, will likely retain its preeminent position within the UAE. Dubai will most likely increase its reliance on its transportation and export trade.

In foreign affairs, the UAE is likely to continue to maintain close ties with the conservative, pro-Western group of GCC states, while seeking to develop a balanced relationship with both Iran and Iraq. The UAE is in the unfortunate position of being the trip-wire against Iran's foreign policy posture. It must engage Iran diplomatically and economically to strike a balance of strength and friendship to protect its territory and natural resources. In the coming years, the UAE may be forced to accept Iranian "settlements" regarding the disputed islands to avoid larger confrontation.

In the meantime, the UAE will continue to exploit its market position through Jebel Ali, the UAE free trade zone where companies can operate without paying taxes yet have access to cheap oil and other economic incentives. Situated close to Iran, Jebel Ali stands to cash in on Iran's reentry to the international economy and become the center of nonpetroleum industry for the UAE.

# SAUDI ARABIA

The 1990s began disastrously for the Kingdom of Saudi Arabia. Iraq's invasion of Kuwait in August 1990 posed the most serious threat to the security of the kingdom in its modern history. In the war's aftermath, Saudi Arabia faces daunting challenges to its safety, economic stability, and monarchical rule.

The Iraqi invasion shattered Saudi Arabia's foreign policy assumptions. Despite the kingdom's careful cultivation of inter-Arab alliances through consensus diplomacy and the disbursal of billions in aid, longtime allies became archenemies overnight. After years of discreet relations with Washington, Fahd ibn Abdul Aziz, king of Saudi Arabia, requested that American forces be deployed to defend his country. With its very existence threatened, a more decisive Saudi Arabia put its European and Asian allies on warning that all future contracts were dependent on their active participation against Iraqi aggression. As a new regional order was emerging, security remained Saudi Arabia's first priority. The kingdom embarked on an upgrade of its defense capabilities, and it is renewing relations with old enemies.

Saudi Arabia is under increasing pressure to control its spending. The enormous cost of the 1991 Persian Gulf War has been compounded by low world oil prices and flat demand for petroleum. Nevertheless, Saudi Arabia is committed to spending on domestic modernization and social projects, as well as new orders of U.S. and British weapons. With reduced revenues, the Saudi government will have difficulty supporting the high standards of living to which its citizens have be-

come accustomed, especially given the significant diminution of Saudi financial reserves.

The unprecedented number of foreigners in the kingdom during the Gulf War electrified the traditional society. Many Saudis seized on the crisis as an opportunity to push for change, including a call by the middle class and intellectuals for greater political participation. The monarchy responded by establishing the Consultative Council, but because its role is purely advisory, its formation has done little to satisfy desires for more political participation.

Like many of its neighbors, Saudi Arabia has not been immune from the pressure of politically activist Islamic movements. Conservative religious leaders who see Islam undermined by the waywardness of the ruling family and Westernization have demanded reform. Though they have not captured the imagination of the majority of Saudis, they have a significant following.

## Geography and People

The Kingdom of Saudi Arabia extends over four-fifths of the Arabian Peninsula. The country—approximately eight hundred thousand square miles or about one-third the size of the continental United States—stretches from the Gulf of Aqaba and the Red Sea in the west to the Persian Gulf in the east. It borders Jordan, Iraq, Kuwait, Bahrain, Qatar, the United Arab Emirates (UAE), Oman, and the Republic of Yemen. Many of the Saudi boundaries with the UAE and with Yemen remain undefined. Saudi Arabia faces

Iran across the Persian Gulf and, across the Red Sea, Egypt, the Sudan, and Ethiopia.

Geographically, the country can be divided into regions characterized by distinctive terrain: coasts, sand deserts, plateaus, escarpments, and mountains. Along the eastern shore of the Red Sea, a narrow plain running the length of the coastline called the Tihama rises gradually from the sea to mountain ranges of four thousand to seven thousand feet. Adjoining the Red Sea is the Hijaz region, which contains the Islamic holy cities of Mecca and Medina. South of the Hijaz, the rugged coastal highland of the Asir region has peaks rising above nine thousand feet. East of the mountainous coast is the central rocky plateau region or Najd, the birthplace of Saudi Arabia, and the location of the capital Riyadh. The Syrian desert in the north extends southward into the twenty-two thousand square miles of the reddish Al-Nufud desert. A narrow strip of desert known as Al-Dahna separates the Najd from eastern Arabia and arcs downward toward one of the largest sand deserts in the world, the Rub Al-Khali (empty quarter). With more than two hundred fifty thousand square miles, it is about the size of Texas. The Eastern Province, sloping toward the sandy coast along the Persian Gulf, contains Saudi Arabia's rich oil fields and Al-Hasa, the world's largest oasis.

With no permanent rivers or bodies of water, Saudi Arabia is the driest land on earth. Rainfall is erratic and averages about two to four inches a year, except in the mountainous Asir region, which often receives torrential downpours and flash floods and averages twenty inches of annual rainfall. The Rub Al-Khali may receive no rain for up to ten years. Rainfall, ground water, desalinated sea water, and very scarce surface water supply the country's growing needs. At current rates of depletion, the known nonrenewable water resources will last only about twenty years. Saudi Arabia plans to invest billions of dollars in additional desalination projects. During the 1991 Persian Gulf War, Iraq engineered an intentional oil spill that fouled much of Arabia's Persian Gulf shoreline with serious consequences for the ecosystem, desalination plants, and the fishing industry.

Heat is intense during the summer months, frequently exceeding 120 degrees Fahrenheit in some areas, and coastal humidity is excessive. Snow and ice are rare in winter, although temperatures sometimes drop below freezing in the central and northern regions. Strong winds called the shamal frequently whip up dust and sandstorms along the eastern coast.

Almost all Saudis can trace their lineage from the indigenous Arabian tribes. The remaining minorities—mostly Turks, Iranians, Indonesians, Indians, and Africans—are the descendants of pilgrims to Mecca who settled in the Hijaz region.

The population of Saudi Arabia is about 18.2 million according to the 1994 estimates. Almost 5.0 million of that number are resident foreigners. The annual population growth rate is approximately 3.3 percent. Half of the population is under the age of eighteen. Much of the population is concentrated in the commercial city of Jiddah on the Red Sea; the holy cities of Mecca and Medina; the resort town of Ta'if; the capital Riyadh; and the major industrial and petrochemical centers on the Persian Gulf, including the Dammam-Hofuf complex.

About 95 percent of all Saudis are Sunni Muslims adhering to the strict Wahhabi interpretation of Islam; the remainder are Shi'ites. Many Shi'ites, indigenous to the oil-rich Eastern Province, consider themselves oppressed and are viewed with apprehension by the government because of their suspected sympathy to predominately Shi'ite Iran.

Because of Saudi Arabia's limited labor supply, the government has recruited foreign workers. Many upper-level managerial and executive positions have been filled by Westerners, while the balance of workers are mainly Egyptians, Yemenis, Jordanians, Bahrainis, Pakistanis, Indians, and Filipinos. Saudis comprise only 10 percent of the private sector work force. The presence of foreigners has long been viewed as a threat to the country's traditional Islamic society. The government frequently has declared its intention to curtail the influx of workers, but several factors have hampered its ability to do so. Despite the increasing number of female university graduates, social con-

## Key Facts on Saudi Arabia

**Area:** 756,981 square miles; some borders undefined.

**Capital:** Riyadh; diplomatic capital located at Jiddah.

**Population:** 18,196,783 (1994).

**Religion:** 95 percent Sunni Muslim, 5 percent Shi'ite Muslim.

**Official Language:** Arabic.

**GDP:** $194 billion; $11,000 per capita (1993).

*Source:* Central Intelligence Agency, *CIA World Factbook 1994.*

straints limit their employment to more traditional fields. Although numerous training programs are available to Saudi nationals to increase their competitiveness, they often are less qualified than foreign nationals for business positions. Foreign labor fills the supply of low-skilled, low-pay occupations that Saudis will not accept.

Reducing the kingdom's dependence on foreign labor was a key feature of the government's five-year development plan for 1985-90. Plans also were made to double enrollments in the country's vocational training programs and to increase the number of women in the educational system. The fifth development plan (1990-95) again calls for a reduction in the number of foreign workers and their replacement with indigenous workers.

## History

Arabian history, while traceable to earliest civilizations, is generally the account of small urban settlements subsisting mainly on trade, living in the midst of nomadic tribes that survived by raising livestock and raiding. Arabia remained largely unsettled until the peninsula came under the suzerainty of the Ottoman sultans of Istanbul in the early sixteenth century. At the same time, European merchant adventurers began exploring the

Persian Gulf. The Portuguese arrived first, followed by the British, Dutch, and French. But by the nineteenth century Great Britain had become the dominant European power in the Gulf.

Meanwhile, the Najd or central Arabia was the scene of a religious upheaval. The puritanical and reforming Wahhabi movement launched by Muhammad Ibn Abd Al-Wahhab called for a return to the concept of the absolute oneness of God. His unitarian message was unwelcome among the Arabian tribes, and he was driven to seek refuge among the Al-Sauds, the ruling family in the Najd settlement of Diriya, who were willing to support him. In 1744 the Al-Wahhab and Al-Saud families sealed a pact dedicated to the preservation and propagation of pure Islam.

This union provided the Al-Saud with a clearly defined religious message that became the basis of their political authority. Bent on destroying the hold of Ottoman occupiers, the Wahhabi movement had spread by 1800 to Ottoman territories, including Mecca and Medina in the Hijaz. The Ottoman sultan called upon his viceroy Muhammad Ali of Egypt in 1816 to drive out the Wahhabis. His son Ibrahim Pasha finally completed the task, laying waste to Diriya in 1818 and driving the Al-Saud into exile. During the Egyptian occupation, the power of the Rashid family grew at the expense of its rival, the Saud family. The Rashids ruled much of Arabia during the late 1800s, while the Najdi city of Riyadh became the new base of Saudi rule.

In 1902 Abd Al-Aziz, a member of the deposed Saud family and known also as Ibn Saud, returned to the Najd from exile in Kuwait to regain the family's former domain. In a legendary battle, Abd Al-Aziz captured Riyadh, expelled the Rashidi dynasty, and proclaimed himself ruler of the Najd. Ibn Saud's loyal Wahhabi Bedouin forces, known as the *Ikhwan* (brethren), abandoned their nomadic lifestyle for agricultural settlements in remote desert areas in order to spread Wahhabi doctrine.

By 1913 Ibn Saud's armies had driven the Ottomans from the Hasa coast of the Persian Gulf (now the Eastern Province), a move that led to closer contact with the British. During World War I Ibn Saud was able to expand his domain to encompass the northern regions then held by the Rashidi tribes loyal to the Turks. In 1915 Ibn Saud signed a treaty with the British recognizing him as the independent ruler of the Najd and its dependencies under a British protectorate.

The final step in Ibn Saud's goal of unifying the Arabian Peninsula under his leadership was realized in 1926 when he ousted his chief rival, Hashemite leader Sherif Hussein (King Hussein of Jordan's great-grandfather), from the Hijaz. Ibn Saud, a traditional Arab clan leader, now had to consider the varied constituencies that his expanding realm encompassed, from the cosmopolitan Hijazis to his fervent Ikhwan Bedouin followers.

As the only truly independent Arab leader after World War I, Ibn Saud played a wider role in Arab politics. His adoption of Western technologies and an increasing presence of non-Muslim foreigners in the country were not acceptable to the Ikhwan. Defying the authority of Ibn Saud, the Ikhwan launched attacks against Saudi tribes in 1929 and pushed beyond borders set up after World War I into Iraq. The border violation was intolerable to the British, and Ibn Saud was obliged to take on the Ikhwan militarily. With British support, he put down the rebellion. The short civil war ended in 1930, when British forces captured the rebel leaders in Kuwait and delivered them to Ibn Saud.

On September 24, 1932, Ibn Saud unified the kingdoms of the Hijaz, the Najd, and their dependencies under the name the Kingdom of Saudi Arabia. It is the only nation in the world named after the ruling family.

During World War II Abd Al-Aziz retained a neutral stance, but his preference for the Allied cause was apparent. Recognizing the importance of the country's oil and strategic geographic location, Franklin D. Roosevelt declared in 1943 that the defense of Saudi Arabia was of vital interest to the United States and dispatched the first U.S. military mission to the kingdom. Roosevelt and Ibn Saud sealed this alliance in 1945 when they met aboard the cruiser USS *Quincy* in the Suez

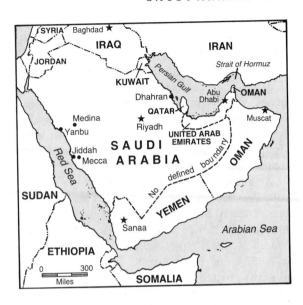

Canal. Ibn Saud nominally declared war on Germany in 1945, a move that ensured Saudi Arabia's charter membership in the United Nations and made it eligible for American lend-lease aid. The same year, Abd Al-Aziz was instrumental in the formation of the Arab League.

## Postwar Developments

Ibn Saud died in November 1953 at the age of seventy-one and was succeeded by the oldest of his thirty-four surviving sons, Crown Prince Saud. Faisal, another son, became the crown prince and prime minister. King Saud's incompetent leadership and profligate spending to the detriment of the country's development led to growing dissatisfaction by more liberal princes and the foreign-educated sons of the rising middle class.

Relationships with its Arab neighbors, as well as domestic politics, tested the growing nation. Hostility between Saudi leaders and Egyptian president Gamal Abdel Nasser dominated Saudi-Egyptian relations during Nasser's tenure from 1954 to 1970. Nasser encouraged revolutionary attitudes in Arab countries and criticized royal regimes. The Saudis were shocked by the merger of Syria and Egypt in 1958 into the United Arab

Republic. Tensions flared in 1962 when Egypt and Saudi Arabia backed opposing sides in the Yemeni civil war. In 1961 Saudi Arabia responded to newly independent Kuwait's request for assistance in deterring Iraqi expansionist threats by sending troops. Brig. Gen. Abdul Karim Kassim had recently overthrown the Hashemite monarchy in Iraq and now sought territorial rights over Kuwait. (Iraq first claimed Kuwait in the 1930s.) Saudi troops remained in Kuwait until 1972.

An alleged conspiracy by King Saud to assassinate President Nasser of Egypt led senior members of the Al-Saud family to pressure King Saud to relinquish power to Crown Prince Faisal. On March 24, 1958, Faisal assumed executive powers of foreign and internal affairs. By means of an austerity program, Faisal balanced the budget and improved the country's fiscal health, but his cuts in royal subsidies incensed Saud and drove him to reassume the post of prime minister. After almost a decade of external and internal pressure to depose Saud, the *ulama,* or religious scholars, supported by the royal family, issued a *fatwa* (religious decree) on November 2, 1964, deposing Saud and declaring Faisal king.

King Faisal designated his half-brother Khalid crown prince, and Sultan, another half-brother, minister of defense and aviation. Faisal reorganized the Central Planning Organization to develop priorities for economic development and invested oil revenues to stimulate growth. Education was emphasized as crucial to development. The annual expenditures for education increased to about 10 percent of the budget.

The United States became an important ally to Saudi Arabia during the Cold War. Both King Saud and King Faisal warned against Communist influence in Arab and Muslim countries. Between 1952 and 1962 the United States maintained an air base at Dhahran on the Persian Gulf. The arrangement was not renewed in 1961, due partly to Saudi Arabia's opposition to U.S. support of Israel.

Saudi Arabia supported the Arab cause in the Six-Day War against Israel in 1967. At the Khartoum Conference in August 1967, Saudi Arabia agreed to contribute $140 million to rebuild the economies of those countries involved in the June 1967 war.

Political and economic developments during the 1970s catapulted Saudi Arabia to the forefront of world politics. Despite good relations with the United States, heightened regional pressures for a resolution to the Arab-Israeli conflict caused King Faisal to use oil as a political weapon against Israel and the United States. When the Arab-Israeli War of October 1973 erupted, and the United States continued its support of Israel despite repeated warnings of an embargo, Saudi Arabia led a movement by the Arab oil-producing countries to exert pressure on the United States by reducing oil exports. The kingdom joined with ten other oil-producing Arab nations in cutting by 5 percent each month the amount of oil sold to the United States and other Western countries. On October 18 Saudi Arabia independently cut oil production by 10 percent to bring direct pressure on the United States. Two days later, after President Richard Nixon unveiled plans for additional U.S. aid to Israel, Riyadh announced a total halt in oil exports to the United States. Members of the Organization of Arab Petroleum Exporting Countries (OAPEC) joined the embargo.

The embargo triggered serious discussions in the United States about using military force to keep the oil flowing, but force was not used to resolve the crisis. At a meeting in Vienna on March 18, 1974, Saudi Arabia lifted the five-month-old embargo against the United States. The action was joined by Algeria, Egypt, Kuwait, Abu Dhabi, Bahrain, and Qatar; only OAPEC members Libya and Iraq dissented. The tripling of oil prices after 1973 vastly increased the revenues available to the Saudi government for domestic programs.

## Discovery of Oil

Oil discoveries around the Persian Gulf in the 1920s suggested that the peninsula might also contain petroleum deposits. In 1933 Standard Oil of California (now Chevron) was granted an exclusive sixty-six-year concession to explore for, produce, and eventually export Saudi Arabia's oil under the operating name Arabian-American Oil Company (Aramco). The liberal terms of the grant reflected Ibn Saud's need for funds, his low estimate of oil's potential, and his weak bargaining position. The terms of the original agreement were modified in 1938, with substantially higher payments to the Saudi government, after oil was discovered in Saudi Arabia. Other U.S. oil companies acquired shares in Aramco. By 1948 Standard Oil of California, Standard Oil of New Jersey (later Exxon), and Texaco each owned 30 percent of the company and Mobil Oil owned 10 percent.

Saudi Arabia marked 1950 with two momentous events: the completion of a 753-mile oil pipeline by the Aramco subsidiary, Trans-Arabian Pipeline Company (Tapline), across Jordan, Syria, and Lebanon to the Mediterranean Sea, and the signing of a 50-50 profit-sharing agreement with Aramco, thereby greatly increasing the government's revenues. Other oil-rich Middle East nations would later negotiate similar terms.

In 1962 Saudi Arabia created the General Petroleum and Mineral Organization (Petromin) to increase state participation in the petroleum and gas industries. The 1960s and 1970s saw spectacular expansion of petroleum output in response to rising world demand. Production increased from 1.3 million barrels per day (bpd) in 1960 to 8.5 million bpd in 1984. Increased output was accompanied by rising prices. Petroleum revenues rose from $1.2 billion in 1970 to $22.6 billion in 1974.

Convinced that the strength or weakness of Western economies had a major effect on its own fortunes, Saudi Arabia emerged after the events of 1973-74 as a pro-Western influence in OPEC, using its high potential output to hold down petroleum prices. The shortfall in petroleum output in early 1979 caused by the revolution in Iran was filled by Saudi Arabia's increased output from below 8.5 million bpd to 10 million bpd. Nevertheless, prices increased sharply in response to the West's fear of shortages. Saudi production was raised again in 1980 to compensate for lost output due to the Iran-Iraq War.

In 1980 the Saudi government made final payments to Aramco's parent companies for total ownership of Aramco, a purchase process begun in 1973. In 1988 Aramco was renamed Saudi Arabian Oil Company (Saudi Aramco), a totally Saudi-owned company with responsibility for all domestic exploration and development. A 1990 acquisition of a South Korean oil refining company established Saudi Aramco as the world's largest petroleum-producing company. Through 1995 the government's priorities for the oil industry include restructuring, upgrading and improving existing facilities to raise sustainable development to 10 billion bpd, and developing the downstream network.

## Pricing Policy and OPEC

The kingdom's oil pricing policy is guided by three factors: maintaining moderate oil prices to ensure the long-term use of crude oil as a major energy source; developing sufficient excess capacity to stabilize oil markets and maintain the kingdom's importance to the West; and generating adequate oil revenues to further economic development and prevent fundamental changes to its political system. Saudi policy has conflicted often with other members of the Organization of Petroleum Exporting Countries (OPEC) since its founding in 1960. Nevertheless, as the OPEC nation with the largest oil reserves, Saudi Arabia has positioned itself to influence the organization's pricing and production policies. In the aftermath of the Gulf War, Saudi Arabia emerged as the unchallenged leader within OPEC. *(Oil politics and pricing, Chapter 5, p. 142)*

During much of the late 1970s the Saudis held their prices down and their production levels high, which forced other countries to hold the line on prices. This kept the world oil market relatively stable. Saudi light crude in 1981, at $32 a barrel, was the cheapest in OPEC. Other organization members' prices ranged as high as $41 a barrel.

During the 1970s and early 1980s the Saudi position was that excessive price hikes would reduce world oil consumption and encourage investment in alternative sources of energy—two developments that would lower OPEC's long-term income. To force other OPEC members to reduce their prices, the Saudis pumped 10 million bpd in the spring of 1981 and vowed to continue until other countries lowered prices. Despite Saudi efforts, prices remained high, causing an oil glut.

Oil production in the non-Communist world outside OPEC jumped 25 percent from 1979 to 1984. At the same time, world demand for oil dropped 15 percent because of energy conservation and permanent shifts to natural gas and coal.

To avoid a collapse of prices, OPEC countries slowed production. In 1982 the Saudis alone cut production by about 7 million bpd. Together the thirteen OPEC members produced about 16 million bpd in 1984, down from 31.6 million bpd in 1979 and 23.5 million in 1981. Prices had fallen to a benchmark price in 1985 of $28 a barrel for Saudi light crude.

Saudi Arabia bore the brunt of the production cuts to prevent poorer OPEC countries—those that relied almost exclusively on oil income—from bearing the burden. Some of those same countries, however, offered secret discounts to Western suppliers to keep the oil dollars flowing, a factor that undercut OPEC's—and Saudi Arabia's—price and production scheme.

In October 1984 Saudi Arabia agreed to become OPEC's "swing producer," cutting its own production to keep prices and production levels as high as possible for other OPEC nations. At the time, the Saudis could afford this sacrifice because of a cash surplus of more than $100 billion.

By mid-1985, however, the kingdom's economic situation had deteriorated. Saudi production dropped off sharply and the country's oil revenues rapidly declined. Under significant domestic pressure, King Fahd finally decided to abandon Saudi Arabia's role as swing producer and to substantially increase production. The government's intention was to force the price of oil to decline in an effort to discipline OPEC members and coerce non-OPEC countries into limiting their production, thereby enabling Saudi Arabia to regain what it considered its "fair share of the market."

The strategy resulted in the collapse of oil prices during the first half of 1986. As Saudi Arabia increased its production to 5.7 million bpd, other OPEC members refused to rein in their production to accommodate the extra Saudi output. The corresponding oil glut led prices to tumble below $10 a barrel (about one-third the level of the early 1980s). The Saudi oil industry was therefore generating only a fraction of the previous year's revenue. In desperation, the kingdom abandoned its "fair-share" policy in October, and it dismissed longtime oil minister Ahmed Zaki Yamani, who had designed the plan.

In December 1986 OPEC agreed to a new Saudi proposal that established a target price of $18 a barrel, supported by strictly enforced restrictions on output. Under the agreement, Saudi Arabia was allotted a nominal quota, again effectively making it a swing producer.

Saudi Arabia sought to sustain the $18 target in 1987 through a series of threats of price cutting and hints of production concessions to encourage the rest of OPEC to curb its output. When Kuwait and the United Arab Emirates failed to oblige, the Saudis resorted to full quota production and price cutting.

Overproduction, however, only caused oil prices to decline further, falling to below $12 in September 1988. In response, the Saudis again independently boosted oil production, a violation of the quota agreement intended to jolt OPEC members into respecting their own output targets. This time the tactic proved effective. In late November 1988 OPEC reached a new quota agreement for the first time since 1983, and oil prices began to recover by the end of the year.

Oil prices remained well short of OPEC's target price of $18 per barrel throughout 1989, mainly because of the constant overproduction by the UAE and Kuwait. At the July 1990 OPEC meeting, Iraq threatened UAE and Kuwait with military action if they did not respect the quota agreement.

Iraq invaded Kuwait in August 1990. Panic buying of crude petroleum drove prices up to $28 a barrel, and OPEC production—with the absence of Iraqi and Kuwaiti supplies—was 4 million bpd below the agreed upon July ceiling. Saudi Arabia announced that it would increase its output by 2 million barrels unless OPEC agreed to hold an emergency meeting. Despite the members' agreement to suspend quotas and increase production during an August emergency meeting, fear of hostilities in the Gulf caused prices to rise above $40 a barrel for the first time in nearly a decade. Saudi Arabia increased its output in 1991 to 8.2 million bpd, taking in $43.5 billion in revenues. Throughout 1992 oil production was market driven. The continued recession in consuming countries decreased total demand for oil. Overall, OPEC countries were able to maintain the ceiling on production agreed upon at the May 1992 meeting. Kuwait was allowed a higher production quota to compensate for its losses during the Iraqi occupation.

At the September 1993 OPEC meeting, in response to falling oil prices, Saudi Arabia signaled its willingness to temper its drive for market share in the interest of price stability.

*Fahd ibn Abdul Aziz*

## Government and Politics

Saudi Arabia is ruled as an absolute monarchy, headed by the king and a crown prince chosen as the heir apparent. The Koran, the holy book of Islam and the basis of *shari'a* or Islamic law, serves as the constitution. Major decisions are usually made by consensus with senior princes of the Al-Saud clan, in close consultation with the ulama. Since 1953 the Council of Ministers, appointed by the king, has advised Saudi rulers on policy and on administration of the growing bureaucracy. Not all of Saudi Arabia's estimated four thousand princes play a major role in the government, but at least a few hundred do. The Saud family always has been careful to cultivate its bonds with the two other influential families in the country, the Sudeiris and the Al-Shaykh, who backed the Al-Sauds' 1750 to 1926 campaign for control of most of the Arabian Peninsula.

In 1982 at the age of sixty Fahd ascended the throne after the death of his half-brother King Khalid, aged sixty-nine. Abdullah, a half-brother of Fahd and commander of the National Guard since 1962, became crown prince and first deputy prime minister. Sultan, second deputy prime minister and minister of defense and aviation since 1962, became second in line of succession.

Fahd served in top government posts for nearly three decades before taking the throne. He was appointed the first minister of education in 1953, and during King Faisal's reign (1964-75) he served as minister of the interior. As crown prince under the ailing King Khalid, Fahd was the chief spokesman for the kingdom and a major architect of Saudi economic and foreign policies. Fahd has played an important mediating role in inter-Arab conflicts. His visit to Egypt in March 1989 marked the end of Egypt's isolation. Together with Algeria and Morocco, King Fahd convened the Lebanese National Assembly in Ta'if in 1989 to develop a peace initiative for Lebanon.

Fahd's leadership abilities are hampered by his poor health and his tendency toward extravagance.

He is afflicted with diabetes, heart problems, and obesity. He has built a number of palaces for himself, both in Saudi Arabia and abroad, and he has a personal Boeing 747 passenger jet. He is insulated from daily Saudi life and his subjects.

The close association with the ulama has provided the Al-Saud family with its primary source of religious legitimacy. In exchange for the recognition of their political influence, the ulama provides tacit or public approval, when requested, on potentially controversial policies. During the Gulf War, for example, the ulama supported King Fahd's decision to permit non-Muslims to be stationed in the kingdom to protect the territory.

In February and May 1991, King Fahd was urged by two petitions from a group of conservative clerics to bring the kingdom's policies into closer accord with the shari'a. The growing assertiveness of Islamic conservatives in the debate on the future of the country was in contrast to the position of liberal intellectuals and businessmen. In April 1991 they too petitioned the king, but they urged the institution of national and municipal councils and the curbing of the *mutaween* (religious police). The mutaween patrol Saudi towns and cities apprehending blasphemers, persons consuming alcohol, or others breaking Islamic law.

In response to domestic unrest following the 1991 Gulf War and pressure for democratization from Saudi Arabia's Western allies, King Fahd published three decrees on March 1, 1992. In them the king established a Basic Law defining the Saudi system of government, promised to appoint within six months a Majlis Al-Shura or Consultative Council, and issued new regulations covering municipal administration. These decrees represented key elements of reforms promised but unimplemented for thirty years.

The Basic Law is as near as Saudi Arabia has come to having a formal constitution. In accordance with the shari'a, it codifies for the first time economic and judicial principles, social welfare and education programs, and the process of succession. In August 1993 King Fahd named the sixty members of the Consultative Council plus an appointed chairman, deputy chairman, and secretary-general. The council is to play an advisory role to the Council of Ministers and the king, but it will not have actual legislative powers. In September 1993 the membership of new councils for provincial administration in the kingdom's thirteen regions were also announced.

Legislation in Saudi Arabia is enacted by royal decree and must follow the tenets of the Koran and the *hadith-sunnah,* the chronicled sayings and traditions of the Prophet Muhammad. Judges appointed by the ulama head a system of religious courts. The king serves as the highest court of appeal and has the right to issue pardons. Alcohol is forbidden, women are segregated, and shari'a penalties of flogging, dismemberment, and beheadings are applied for criminal acts. Political parties, labor unions, professional associations, and non-Islamic religious ceremonies are banned. The media exercises self-censorship.

For more than sixty years the Saudi citizenry has accepted the rule of the royal family with little resistance. The monarchy has sought to preserve wide popular support by relying on its Islamic legitimacy and by dramatically increasing government services. The Saudi government provides free education, medicine, and health care services to all Saudi citizens, and pensions to widows, orphans, the elderly, and the permanently disabled. Electricity and gasoline are heavily subsidized. Social aid helps victims of natural disasters and persons who are temporarily disabled. In the past, the government also supplied interest-free loans for home mortgages, small businesses, and construction and agricultural development projects. All this is provided without taxes.

## Islamic Unrest

In November 1979 an extremist group laid siege to the Mosque in Mecca, raising the specter of militant Islamic revolt. The armed insurgents were mostly Saudis with some Yemenis, Sudanese, Kuwaitis, and students recruited from Medina University. While many in the Muslim world supported in principle the group's attacks on Saudi corruption, they were outraged by the violation of Islam's sanctuary by guns and bloodshed. For two weeks the rebels held the mosque until army, national guard, and police units received the approval of the nation's top religious leaders to storm the site. One hundred three insurgents and 127 Saudi troops were killed. Afterward, enforcement of shari'a penalties increased.

The Iranian Revolution initially sparked unrest among the Shi'ite of the Gulf. Successive attempts to disrupt the *hajj* (the annual pilgrimage of Muslims to Mecca) and turn it into a political demonstration against Saudi Arabia were thwarted by authorities until July 1987 when Iranian pilgrims clashed with Saudi security forces. With more than one hundred fifty thousand Iranians present, a demonstration by Iranian pilgrims around the Ka'bah, Islam's holiest shrine, sparked violent riots, resulting in the deaths of 402 people, 275 of whom were Iranian. In the following days, mass demonstrations took place in Tehran. The Saudi embassy was sacked, and Iranian leaders vowed to avenge the pilgrims' deaths by overthrowing the Saudi ruling family. Shortly afterward, two powerful explosions were reported at Saudi oil installations in the Eastern Province. The explosions were widely believed to be acts of sabotage by Shi'ite workers with connections to Iran.

The pattern of disturbances during the hajj increased tensions between Saudi Arabia and Iran. Saudi Arabia responded by creating national quotas for hajj pilgrims based on a formula of one pilgrim per one thousand people. Iran announced that it was boycotting the 1988 pilgrimage. In July 1989, on the anniversary of the 1987 riots, two bombs exploded in Mecca, killing one person and injuring sixteen others. The worst tragedy of any pilgrimage occurred, however, in a July 1990 accident, when 1,426 pilgrims suffocated or were trampled to death in a tunnel near the pilgrimage sites, giving the Iranian government another opportunity to declare that the Saudi rulers were not fit to administer Islam's holy cities.

The Saudi regime responded to these threats to its Islamic legitimacy by expanding the influence of the religious authorities in affairs of state, and calling more often upon the religious leaders to sanction government actions. In 1986, to further deemphasize his monarchical status and to enhance his Islamic legitimacy, King Fahd dropped the honorific "His Majesty" and adopted the title "Custodian of the Two Holy Mosques" (Mecca and Medina).

To stem the tide of unrest by the Shi'ite Muslims community in the oil-rich Eastern Province, the Saudi government bolstered its security forces and accelerated government-funded development in these relatively deprived areas. The regime also broadened the social and religious rights of the Shi'ites.

The combination of money and repression, however, has not eliminated the appeal of Muslim fundamentalists in Saudi Arabia. Islam has become the main vehicle to express discontent. Fundamentalism is growing in popularity among young Shi'ites and Sunnis alike. Opposition clerics and other fundamentalists have distributed audio tapes and literature that harshly criticize the Saudi regime for its close relationship to the West, its extravagance, its failure to provide for the defenses of the country, and its failure to implement an even more rigorous standard of Islamic law. While many Saudis do not identify with them, the fundamentalists have become the focus of opposition by including mainstream concerns about security, finances, and political participation in their attacks on the regime.

## The Economy

The production of crude petroleum and petroleum products dominates the Saudi economy. Saudi Arabia has the capacity to pump more than 10 million bpd, although the oil glut that developed in the mid-1980s prompted significant production cuts. Saudi Arabia controls about one-quarter of the world's oil. With reserves estimated at about 260 billion barrels, Saudi Arabia can expect to have more than eighty years of production at 1993 levels.

In 1962 Crown Prince Faisal announced his program for using the ever-increasing oil revenues to modernize the country's agricultural, industrial, and infrastructural base. Since 1970 the development of the Saudi economy has been moved forward by a series of five-year plans. The first plan (1970-75) committed a modest $80 million to developing basic infrastructure and improving government social services. The dramatic rise in petroleum revenues from $1.2 billion in 1970 to $22.6 billion in 1974 allowed the government to underwrite a massive program of industrialization and modernization under the second plan (1975-80). In an action described by Saudi minister of planning Hisham Nazer as an "experiment in social transformation," the government allocated $149 billion in the second plan for investment, primarily in defense, followed by education, urban development, and industrial and mineral production. Central to the plan to increase industrial output was the creation of two new industrial cities: Jubail on the Gulf coast and Yanbu on the Red Sea.

During the 1970s oil revenues accumulated faster than the country's capacity to spend them. Surpluses generated high levels of foreign currency reserves, largely invested in Europe, Japan, and the United States. Saudi Arabian foreign assets grew from $4.3 billion in 1973 to more than $120.0 billion in 1982.

But oil production tumbled after 1981. As world demand for oil declined, Saudi production fell from a high of 10.0 million bpd in 1980 to an estimated 2.5 million bpd by 1985. The slowdown was felt by all sectors of the economy. Early in 1985 the government stopped work on two refineries, even though orders were already taken and engineering work was nearly complete.

The Saudis tried to balance their budget by cutting back government spending. The regime reduced expenditures by 20 percent in 1984. The Saudis were able to weather the drop in oil revenues by drawing upon their enormous financial reserves.

The success of these plans in constructing the basic transportation and communications facilities of a modern industrial state permitted the government to shift the emphasis from infrastructure to the productive sectors in the third five-year plan

(1980-85). The plan stressed agriculture and the goal of achieving food security by reducing dependence on imports, worker training to reduce reliance on foreign labor, and encouraging Saudi private investors to play a more prominent role in the economy. The planned investment figure of $235 billion did not include the amount for defense spending.

The results of the third plan were mixed. The non-oil sector showed steady growth and accounted for 24.2 percent of government revenue in 1983. There was also a sharp increase in production of cement, chemical fertilizers, and many agricultural crops, particularly wheat, which Saudi Arabia now exports. Wheat production, however, is not efficient because it requires large quantities of scarce water for irrigation.

The government's intensive industrialization program dramatically improved Saudi Arabia's petroleum refining capacities. The country produces its own fuel oil, kerosene, and other petroleum products. Since 1981 the Saudis also have tapped the country's natural gas resources to fuel industrial complexes and generate electric power.

The fourth plan (1985-90) focused on improving the efficiency of existing resources, enhancing non-oil revenue-generating activities (particularly in manufacturing, agriculture, and financial services), promoting private-sector initiatives, and developing a better-trained work force to reduce dependence on foreign labor.

The plan contained the Saudi government's sobering recognition that its expansion period had come to a close: "The expansive environment of the last decade has ended, and now the Saudi Arabian private sector faces normal world conditions where business success will depend on tight financial controls, high standards of product quality and service, and efficient and well planned marketing strategies."

Declining oil prices further reduced revenues in 1986, but by 1988 the fourth development plan appeared to be leading the Saudi economy toward a modest recovery. According to the Saudi Ministry of Finance, the country achieved a real growth rate of 3.2 percent in 1988, compared with 0.8

percent in 1987 and 2.3 percent in 1985. The industrial sector was reported to have risen by 4.7 percent, compared with only 1.9 percent in 1987. Industrial growth was led by the petrochemical and refining industries, which nearly doubled their profits in the first half of 1988. The agricultural sector grew an unprecedented 10.8 percent.

The Saudi economy received an additional boost from the rise in crude oil prices that followed the achievement of a new quota agreement among the members of OPEC in December 1988. Yet as oil prices and production remained far below levels set during the boom years in the late 1970s, the country registered significant budget deficits. Saudi Arabia's vast foreign reserves adequately covered these deficits. But as reserves declined from $114 billion in 1985 to an estimated $75 billion in 1989, the government become more reluctant to draw upon them, for fear of diminishing future investment income.

Owing to the crisis in the Gulf, the fifth development plan (1990-95) allocated about 34 percent of total expenditure to defense. Much of the increased Saudi defense expenditure has gone for a major upgrade of its weapons systems. Promotion of Saudi industry was to be reinforced by the "30 percent rule," whereby at least 30 percent of government contracts would be awarded to Saudi Arabian companies.

The conflict with Iraq is estimated to have cost Saudi Arabia between $42 billion and $65 billion. Funds to pay for the war came directly from Saudi financial reserves. Not only did Saudi Arabia finance a major portion of the cost of the war, it also provided assistance to other countries affected by the crisis. Saudi Arabia also spent billions to increase oil production to fill the gap left by the disruption of Iraqi and Kuwaiti output.

Despite its incredible oil wealth, which generates about $40 billion in annual income, the Saudi government is running a budget deficit of about $10 billion a year. This situation has led foreign analysts to conclude that Saudi Arabia faces a financial crisis in the near future unless it cuts spending, institutes income taxes, or finds some other means to raise revenue. Several Saudi banks, including the large National Commercial Bank of Saudi Arabia, are saddled with bad debts. A loss of investor confidence could send the Saudi stock market tumbling, threatening the entire financial system.

Foreign analysts have prescribed fiscal reforms, but the monarchy has not shown an inclination to adopt major spending cuts. Such cuts would have to come in defense, social services, or the personal allowances of the Saudi elite. Each would increase the Saudi monarchy's vulnerability—from foreign invasion, internal discontent, or elitist machinations.

## Saudi National Security

Saudi Arabia's vast oil wealth makes it an inviting prize for a potential aggressor. Until the Gulf War it had avoided a security alliance with the United States because of the fear of Western influences, differences over the Arab-Israeli conflict, and the discontent such an alliance could create among conservative Muslims.

The Saudis therefore sought to ensure their security through high-technology arms purchases and through regional security arrangements, even as they maintained a close, but "over the horizon," relationship with the United States. The Saudis were the driving force behind the creation of the Gulf Cooperation Council (GCC) in 1981. The six GCC members are Saudi Arabia, Kuwait, Bahrain, the United Arab Emirates, Qatar, and Oman. The GCC was created to promote economic cooperation and collective security. The instability in the Gulf caused by the rise of Ayatollah Khomeini and the Iranian Islamic revolution in 1979, as well as the outbreak of the Iran-Iraq War in 1980, provided Saudi Arabia and the smaller Persian Gulf countries the impetus to form the military alliance. The GCC, however, was not up to the task of ensuring its members' security.

Perhaps the most pressing problem confronting the Saudis during the 1980s was the Iran-Iraq War. Although the Saudis were highly suspicious of the Iraqis, the potential threat from Iran was sufficient to induce them to support Iraq throughout the eight-year war, providing $25.7 billion, according to Saudi officials. *(Iran-Iraq War, Chapter 4, p. 105)*

As the tanker war escalated during 1984, the kingdom appeared to be on the verge of becoming directly involved. On June 4 Iranian F-4 fighter planes flew over Saudi territorial waters, presumably seeking naval targets. They were intercepted by Saudi F-15s and shot down. Despite the threatened disruption of tanker traffic in the Gulf during the latter half of the war, the Saudis resisted U.S. intervention to safeguard the region. Concerned about Arab reaction abroad and anti-American sentiment at home, Saudi Arabia refused to give the United States access to military facilities on its territory. Yet the Saudis did countenance the U.S. decision to escort reflagged Kuwaiti tankers in the Gulf in June 1987, when they provided essential cooperation in clearing mines and extending surveillance operations to the area.

Fearing a widening of the conflict, Saudi Arabia and its GCC allies supported diplomatic efforts to bring sanctions against Iran if it refused to halt the war. In November 1987 Saudi Arabia joined the other members of the Arab League in unanimously condemning Iran for prolonging the war, deploring its occupation of Iraqi territory, and urging it to accept without preconditions UN Security Council Resolution 598, which called for an end to the hostilities. *(Text of Resolution 598, Appendix, p. 398)*

Saudi Arabia came close to a confrontation with Iran again in 1987, following the July 31 clashes between Iranian pilgrims and Saudi security forces in Mecca. As the level of hostility rose between Riyadh and Tehran, Iranian leaders threatened armed retaliation for the deaths of the pilgrims. Eventually the tense situation culminated in Saudi Arabia's April 1988 decision to sever diplomatic relations with Iran.

Tehran's moves toward normalization of relations with Western countries, its neutrality during the Gulf War, and Riyadh's concerns about postwar Iraq led to a reestablishment of diplomatic relations with Iran in 1991.

The dramatic breakup of the Soviet Union, its withdrawal from Afghanistan, and its support during the Gulf War facilitated a change in attitude by Saudi policy makers. Formal relations were restored with Russia in 1990 (and also with China) after a hiatus of about fifty years. Saudi Arabia has extended some financial assistance to the six predominately Muslim Central Asian republics of the former Soviet Union.

## Relations with the United States

Since the 1940s Saudi Arabia has shared a close strategic alliance with the United States, despite U.S. support for Israel. The commitment of Harry S. Truman to Ibn Saud to support the territorial integrity and political independence of Saudi Arabia became the basis for the 1951 mutual defense assistance agreement, under which the United States provided military equipment and training for the Saudi armed forces. The U.S.-Saudi security relationship was an outgrowth of Saudi Arabia's preoccupation with regime and regional security. The United States' interest in Saudi Arabia was to ensure its own access to oil resources and preserve the kingdom as a bulwark against the encroachment of communism.

Since the fall of the shah of Iran in 1979, the United States has increasingly relied on Saudi Arabia as its major strategic ally in the Persian Gulf. During the early 1980s Saudi cooperation was considered critical to the Reagan administration's "strategic consensus" policy that sought to mobilize the anti-Communist states of the Middle East to counter threats of Soviet encroachment in the region. Maintaining that the Soviet Union, and not the Arab-Israeli conflict, was the main threat to regional security and oil supplies to the West, the White House supported the sale of sophisticated military equipment to the Saudis, often over Israel's objections. Saudi suspicions of Soviet intentions in the Middle East were intensified by the Soviet invasion of Afghanistan in 1979. Throughout the nine-year occupation, Saudi Arabia financed the rebels fighting the Soviets.

Washington also sought Saudi assistance in

dealing with the Middle East peace question. In 1983, when President Ronald Reagan called for a partial Israeli withdrawal from the occupied territories and self-rule for West Bank Palestinians, he asked the Saudis to pressure the Palestine Liberation Organization (PLO) to allow Jordan's King Hussein to speak for the Palestinians.

In the mid-1980s a common interest in containing the spread of Iranian revolutionary activity and securing free shipping in the Gulf provided additional areas for cooperation between Saudi Arabia and the United States. In 1986 Washington finally delivered sophisticated AWACS surveillance planes that the Saudis had purchased in 1981, and Riyadh provided essential aid to the U.S. naval convoys that began escorting reflagged Kuwaiti tankers through the Gulf in June 1987. Nevertheless, Riyadh refused to allow U.S. access to its military facilities there.

Differences over the Arab-Israeli conflict, however, continued to strain relations between Washington and Riyadh. American support for Israel led to restrictions on U.S. military sales to Saudi Arabia and reduced the willingness of Saudi leaders to support U.S. policies in the region. The kingdom's reluctance to pressure its Arab neighbors toward a peace settlement has frustrated some American leaders.

In early 1987 congressional opposition to supplying sophisticated weapons to an Arab country forced the Reagan administration to withdraw its proposal to sell the Saudis Stinger missiles, F-15 planes, and Maverick antitank missiles. In frustration, the Saudis vastly increased their purchase of weapons from the United Kingdom, ultimately leading the British to displace the United States as the Saudis' main supplier of arms.

In March 1988 the disclosure that Riyadh had secretly purchased an unspecified number of CSS-2 medium-range missiles from China led to a diplomatic confrontation between Washington and Riyadh. The missiles had a range of 2,600 kilometers and were capable of carrying nuclear weapons. Washington was stunned that the Saudis had acquired the missiles and had kept the deal hidden for more than two years.

## The Gulf War and Aftermath

The Iraqi invasion of Kuwait on August 2, 1990, took Saudi Arabia and the world by surprise. Fearful that Saddam Hussein planned to seize the Eastern Province's oil fields and installations, King Fahd abandoned the illusion of Arab solidarity and discreet diplomacy. He requested the deployment of U.S troops on Saudi soil to defend its territory, in contravention to longstanding policy to keep U.S. forces "over the horizon" on naval platforms in the Arabian sea. Saudi fears regarding U.S. commitment to the security relationship were dissolved by the United States' dispatch of more than four hundred thousand troops to defend the kingdom against aggression during the 1991 Gulf War. After years of maintaining discreet ties with Washington, King Fahd openly declared himself a friend of the United States.

From mid-August to the outbreak of hostilities on January 16, 1991, Arab states attempted to mediate a solution, but the United States and increasingly King Fahd would settle for nothing less than Iraq's full compliance with UN Security Council Resolution 660 calling for Iraq's complete and unconditional withdrawal from Kuwait.

When war came, Saudi Arabia operated as a full participant and host of the anti-Iraqi alliance. But the Gulf War success has not contributed to a long-term sense of pride in Saudi Arabia.

The invasion of Kuwait demonstrated the vulnerability of Saudi Arabia despite the billions it invested in arms purchases. The obvious need to resort to foreign forces to defend the kingdom sparked widespread domestic criticism of the government's failure to construct a viable military deterrent to regional threats. King Fahd promised a major expansion of the armed forces, despite the implications for regime security, including a doubling of the army's size and the creation of a reserve system.

Traditionally, Saudi Arabia has pursued two primary foreign policy objectives: regional security and Islamic solidarity. Fearing aggression and externally supported subversion as threats to its security, Saudi Arabia has worked to maintain stability in the entire Middle East area surrounding the Arabian Peninsula. Iraq and Iran, its more populous and powerful neighbors, have been particular security concerns.

Oil revenues have provided the means for a generous and extensive aid program throughout the Islamic world, yet this aid failed to ensure the loyalty in the Gulf crisis of several principal beneficiaries—Iraq, Jordan, Yemen, and the PLO. The Gulf War effectively split the Arab world in two: those countries that supported the U.S.-led coalition and those who were neutral or opposed to it. Saudi retribution against Arab nations that supported Iraq was swift and severe. Oil supplies and the $400 million in annual aid to Jordan ceased. Funding to the PLO, $6 million monthly since 1989, also stopped. Thousands of Palestinians were expelled from the kingdom. Yemen's neutral stand, as well as its continuing claims on Saudi territory, led to a suspension of its annual $400 million subsidy and to the expulsion of more than eight hundred thousand Yemenis from Saudi Arabia.

Meanwhile, Saudi Arabia expanded aid programs to its allies in the Gulf crisis. Syria received between $1.5 billion and $2.5 billion for its participation in the multinational force. Egypt was extended massive debt relief and promises of future financial aid and labor contracts.

As the U.S. military downsizes, officials in the Clinton administration regard arms sales to the Saudis as crucial for maintaining jobs for American arms makers. To ensure that the Saudis will be able to afford the pending purchases of $30 billion in weapons and $6 billion in commercial airliners, the Saudis will be able to buy on credit what they once bought with cash. Saudi Arabia is, however, unwilling to institutionalize defense relations with the United States because of criticism from Arab countries. Riyadh therefore reversed its acceptance of the "Memorandum of Understanding on Gulf Security," which outlined the U.S. role in the security of the Gulf.

The historic signing by Israel and the PLO of the "agreement on guidelines" in September 1993, as well as the Jordanian-Israeli peace concluded in

July 1994, hold the promise of a new era for the Middle East. The United States is expecting Saudi Arabia to be a major contributor toward the development of Jericho in the West Bank and Gaza once the Palestinians assume control.

## Outlook

In the late 1990s and beyond, domestic challenges will demand more of the Saudi government's attention. Earlier, during the 1970s and 1980s, the Saudi royal family maintained broad support with the help of prominent clerics and an unstated social bargain: the monarchy would use Saudi Arabia's immense oil wealth to provide Saudi citizens with a good living in return for the people's tolerance of absolute rule by the monarchy. But flat world demand for crude oil, the expensive war with Iraq, and the royal family's unwillingness to cut back on extravagant expenditures have placed in doubt the Saudi leadership's ability to continue this bargain.

Many analysts believe the kingdom's current economic and fiscal path is unsustainable. There is increasing pressure on the government to cut spending. To finance its budget deficit, the government has relied primarily on its financial reserves and its own ailing domestic commercial banks. In the future, however, if the deficits continue, the country will have to turn to foreign borrowings.

To maintain domestic tranquility, the monarchy has relied on subsidies and patronage to tribal, religious, and military leaders. By doing so, the Saudi government has given important groups a financial stake in maintaining the status quo. But the financial crisis may lead to domestic spending cuts that could heighten domestic unrest. The flush years of the oil boom have created high economic expectations among the Saudi people that will be hard to meet. Austerity measures could create severe domestic discontent. But failure to do anything to meet the nation's financial problems until a crisis forces action is the most dangerous course for the regime.

While Saudi Arabia considers a resolution to the Israeli-Palestinian conflict positive—not least because it may reduce radical elements in the Gulf—the United States' expectations for significant financial support for development of the West Bank and Gaza are still a sensitive issue because of the PLO's alliance with Iraq. Saudi aid to Islamic countries in general will be scaled back and will not be filtered through their respective governments.

Saudi Arabia has emerged from the Gulf conflict as the undisputed leader of OPEC, which no doubt will allow it greater influence in oil pricing policy. But with the Iraqi economy in ruins, the Iranian economy struggling, and Kuwait rebuilding, other major Gulf producers will want to pump as much oil as possible. Unresolved border disputes between Saudi Arabia and its neighbors remain another possible area of conflict, especially as oil exploration and the granting of concessions continue.

Security will remain the top priority for the kingdom. Although billions were spent on weapons in the past, the Gulf War demonstrated that Saudi Arabia's military was not up to the task of defending against a concerted attack by a regional power. The kingdom is acting to enhance its national and regional security by a comprehensive upgrade of its defense systems with the ultimate goal of becoming self-reliant in the twenty-first century. Saudi officials assert that they will not cut back on some $30 billion worth of U.S. arms orders—although they have requested payment rescheduling. Despite this program, it is highly unlikely that the Saudi military capacity will improve dramatically. The weaknesses of the military have much more to do with its small size, its questionable morale, and its internal rivalries than with its equipment. Moreover, so long as the government and the military believe that Western nations will come to their rescue in an emergency, the Saudi military is unlikely to feel an urgency to achieve self-sufficiency.

The promised establishment of new institutions in which ordinary citizens can participate has not been fulfilled. King Fahd opened the inaugural meeting of the Consultative Council on December 29, 1993, but most people believe that it will wield very limited power. The monarchy retains substantial support. But without political and economic reforms, Saudi citizens will increasingly turn to Islamic fundamentalists critical of the regime who offer an alternative course.

# SYRIA

Syria has had stable rule for more than two decades under President Hafez al-Assad. This period of relative calm followed more than two decades of intensive political tumult. Syria experienced more than a dozen coups and attempted coups between 1946, when the departure of French soldiers left Syria independent, and 1970, when Assad seized power. Under his rule Syria not only achieved domestic stability but it also gained a leading role in regional politics.

After a period of sharp economic decline and growing international isolation in the 1980s, in part due to Syria's support for Iran in the Iran-Iraq War, Syria began to rebound during the early 1990s. Assad consolidated and extended close relations with Egypt and Saudi Arabia and other Persian Gulf states during the crisis provoked by Iraq's August 1990 invasion and occupation of Kuwait. He also adjusted to the collapse of the Soviet Union, Syria's principal patron during the Cold War years, by joining the U.S.-sponsored coalition of armies that forced Iraq from Kuwait in February 1991. In Operation Desert Storm, Syria amazingly fought as an ally of the United States in circumstances that saw arch-rival Israel marginalized as a strategic asset of the United States. Because of the perceived fragility of the anti-Iraq coalition, Israel could only watch from the sidelines, while Syria associated itself with Egypt and Saudi Arabia as principal Middle Eastern allies of U.S. policy in the Gulf crisis. Finally, Assad was able to take advantage of the changing regional strategic situation by moving in October 1990, during the buildup of the Gulf crisis, to

consolidate Syrian control in Lebanon. This he achieved with scarcely a murmur of dissent from the West, which in earlier years undoubtedly would have interpreted the development as an advance for Soviet influence.

The early 1990s also saw a significant rebounding of the Syrian economy. Economic reforms, modest but important oil discoveries, a reduction in the size of the military, and a resolution to the fighting in Lebanon contributed to gross domestic product (GDP) growth rates of between 5 and 8 percent in the early 1990s, among the highest in the world.

Syria was approaching the end of the twentieth century with a newly found sense of confidence that enabled the government in 1991 to respond positively to joint U.S.-Russian overtures inviting it to enter negotiations with Israel over issues related to the Arab-Israeli conflict. President Assad's agreement to join the summit convened in Madrid in October 1991 and the subsequent rounds of negotiations that followed was a surprise to many who grounded their understanding of Syria on its long history of rejectionist behavior with regard to the Arab-Israeli conflict.

Assad apparently perceived a new regional strategic situation, largely a result of the Gulf crisis of 1990-91, in which he could hope to negotiate more evenly with Israel. One key regional rival, Iraq, had been effectively marginalized, and with the support of others, especially Egypt and Saudi Arabia, Syria could negotiate with Israel from a stronger diplomatic position than at any time since the 1967 Arab-Israeli War. Therefore Assad was prepared to abandon more than forty years of rejectionist intransigence and to enter the diplomatic process with Israel. The Jewish state's peace agreements with the Palestine Liberation Organization (PLO) and Jordan have fueled speculation that a peace agreement between Israel and Syria will soon follow.

A dark cloud that continues to hang over Syria's future, however, is the nature of the Assad regime itself. Despite recent modest political liberalizations and the release of many political prisoners, it remained a highly centralized authoritarian regime buttressed by extensive domestic security forces. The regime's long history of human rights abuses toward its opponents had not been abandoned.

Assad remained firmly in control of the country's near-term destiny, having won a December 1991 national referendum that gave him a fourth seven-year term as president. The victim of a heart attack in 1984, however, and rumored to have a number of other physical ailments, such as diabetes, Assad (born in 1930) may not have the vigor of his earlier years. A number of personnel shifts in the government in early 1993 gave rise to speculation that Assad was preparing for his succession, possibly in behalf of Basil, his eldest son. But Basil was killed in an automobile accident, leaving the future of Syria after Assad an open question. The country was characterized by a high degree of political instability before Assad, leading some analysts to speculate that it will revert to the same pattern after him.

## Geography

Syria is located at the eastern end of the Mediterranean Sea and shares borders with Turkey to the north, Iraq to the east, Jordan to the south, Israel to the southwest, and Lebanon to the west. It has a land area of 71,498 square miles (including the 500 square miles of the Golan Heights, which is currently occupied by Israel).

Syria is geographically divided into an inland plateau in the east and a much smaller coastal zone in which two mountain ranges enclose a fer-

tile lowland. A chain of low mountains crosses the inland plateau diagonally, extending from the mountainous Jebel Druze area in the southwest corner of Syria to the Euphrates River that flows from the mountains of Turkey diagonally across Syria to Iraq. South of these mountains, along the eastern portion of the Syrian-Jordanian border and the southern portion of the Syrian-Iraqi border, is the Hamad desert region. The largest fertile area of Syria, where modest amounts of oil have been discovered, is known as the Jazirah "island," which is northeast of the Euphrates.

About 50 percent of Syria's land is arable, but only about 31 percent is under cultivation. Syria is one of the few nations of the Middle East that still have unexploited arable land. Most of Syria's water is supplied by its rivers (80 percent from the Euphrates alone) and underground reservoirs.

Syria's largest cities are located in fertile areas: Latakia (a major port) is on the coastal plain, and Damascus, Aleppo, Hamah, and Homs are in fertile river plains. All of these cities except Latakia are inland of the coastal mountain ranges and have been traditional centers of trade.

The climate of Syria is varied. The coastal zone receives fairly plentiful rainfall as the mountain ranges catch precipitation blown from the Mediterranean. The barren desert regions of the southeast receive little rain. The 75 percent of the country that lies between these two regions has a semiarid climate; the rivers there supply most of the water.

Arable land is Syria's most important resource, although relatively small oil and gas deposits have added to the economy in recent years. Otherwise Syria's only natural resources are low-grade phosphate deposits and small amounts of natural asphalt, rock salt, and construction materials (sand, stone, gravel, and gypsum). Syria's oil and gas deposits are quite small by regional standards and were late in being exploited. Oil was first discovered in 1956 but production did not begin until 1968. Still larger fields were found in 1984. Oil and gas production has provided the Syrian economy with a small but important boost since the 1970s. Syria also profits from two petroleum pipe-

## Key Facts on Syria

**Area:** 71,498 square miles, including about 500 square miles occupied by Israel.

**Capital:** Damascus.

**Population:** 14,886,672 (1994).

**Religion:** 74 percent Sunni Muslim; 16 percent Alawite, Druze, and other Muslim sects; 10 percent Christian.

**Official Language:** Arabic; Kurdish, Armenian, and French are also spoken.

**GDP:** $81.7 billion; $5,700 per capita (1993).

*Source:* Central Intelligence Agency, *CIA World Factbook 1994.*

---

lines that cross its territory transporting petroleum products to the Mediterranean Sea from the oil-producing states bordering the Persian Gulf. The pipeline from Iraq has been closed since 1982, however.

## Demography

In Syria, like neighboring Lebanon, demography has had a powerful effect on the country's political situation. The people are mostly Arab (about 90 percent) and Sunni Muslim (at least 70 percent). Ethnic minorities include Kurds (about 5 to 7 percent), Armenians (about 3 percent), and much smaller numbers of Turkomans, Circassians, Assyrians, and Jews. Major religious minorities include several small Islamic sects (the two most important being the Alawis and the Druze), as well as Greek Orthodox Christians and various other Christian sects.

Religious and ethnic identification in Syria is usually accompanied by certain regional, social, and economic characteristics. Although Alawis make up less than 15 percent of the population as a whole, they represent a majority in the coastal province of Latakia and are mostly poor farmers. Druze, who make up perhaps 3 percent of the population, are located primarily in the Jebel Druze in the southwest corner of Syria, the Golan Heights, and Damascus. Traditionally denied political influence by the Sunni majority and lacking means of advancement other than free military training, the Alawis and Druze flocked to the military and to the secular Ba'ath party. With the advent to power of the Ba'ath party, these two minority groups gained political influence disproportionately greater than their numbers or economic clout. Because President Assad is a member of the Alawi minority and supports secular rule, Muslim fundamentalists—especially the Sunni Muslim Brotherhood—have often opposed his leadership.

The Alawi and Druze sects are offshoots of Shi'ite Islam, the religion of Iran, rather than the orthodox Sunni sect. The theologies of Alawis and Druze diverge sharply from orthodox Sunni Islam, and even from Shi'ite Islam. They are considered heretical by most Sunnis and Shi'ites. This compounds Assad's difficulties, not only in dealing with Sunni fundamentalism at home, but also with his support of Shi'ite Iran and Shi'ite elements in Lebanon.

## Early History

The modern nation of Syria did not come into existence until the twentieth century. The name *Syria,* used first by the Greeks, historically denoted the region at the eastern end of the Mediterranean lying between Egypt and Asia Minor. This larger region—generally called Greater Syria to distinguish it from the nation-state that bears the name today—has a rich history. Containing some fertile farmland and located at the crossroads of three continents, Greater Syria was the invasion route of armies, the battleground of adjacent empires, and an arena of conflict for centuries. The waves of migration and invasion in ancient times and the ever-changing religious and political leaders left Greater Syria a mosaic of ethnic and religious groups.

Because no single indigenous power has ever been able to control all of Greater Syria, people in the area have closely identified with their city or region. This has left its mark on the modern nation of Syria, where religious and ethnic differences are often reinforced by differences of region. Geography has been a fragmenting influence; the two distinctive zones separated by mountains (the coastal plain and the interior plateau) and the lack of navigable rivers have reinforced Syrians' historical identification with their own region and group.

Damascus, one of the oldest continuously inhabited cities in the world, may have been settled as early as 2500 B.C. It was dominated by various civilizations over the centuries: Aramean, Assyrian, Babylonian, Persian, Greek, Roman, Nabatean, and Byzantine. In A.D. 636 Damascus came under Muslim rule. The city rose to its peak of power as the capital of the Umayyad Empire, which stretched from India to Spain and lasted from 661 to 750.

After the downfall of the Umayyads, Greater Syria became the prey of powerful neighboring states and empires in Mesopotamia, Anatolia, and Egypt. Religious conflict is an integral part of the history of this area. The Fatimid rulers of Egypt did much to spread Islam in Greater Syria, often by force. When the Christian crusaders came to the area to fight the Muslims, some local Christian groups provided aid, thereby creating bonds between Levantine and European Christians and encouraging hostility between Muslim and Christian inhabitants of Greater Syria. Damascus was a provincial capital of the Mameluke Empire from 1260 until 1516 when the rule of the Ottoman Turks began.

The four hundred years of Ottoman rule strongly influenced what would one day become the nation-state of Syria. The Ottoman Empire was extraordinarily heterogeneous, including most of the lands of the eastern and southern Mediterranean coast. The Ottoman system provided substantial autonomy not only to provincial governors but also to different religious groups, as long as taxes were paid to the Ottoman government. The system allowed each recognized religious community, or *millet,* to run its own system of personal law and perform certain civil functions. This accentuated

the localism and communal separatism that resulted from the presence of so many different groups. The people continued to identify with their own city or region rather than with a larger political entity.

By the nineteenth century the Ottoman Empire had weakened and European nations had begun to develop direct ties with minority groups in Greater Syria: the French with the Catholics, especially the Maronites of Mount Lebanon (the mountains near the coast of what is now Lebanon); the Russians with the Orthodox; the British with the Protestants and the Druze.

Shortly after the turn of the twentieth century, Ottoman authorities, fearing the growth of Arab nationalism, clamped down on Greater Syria. Ottoman repression, however, did not succeed in quelling the Arab independence movement. Many Syrians supported Sherif Hussein, the leader of Mecca in the Arabian Peninsula, in his efforts to break away from Ottoman control. Sherif Hussein and Arab nationalists throughout the area believed that the British would support the establishment of independent Arab states in the eastern Mediterranean after the end of World War I. In 1918 Prince Faisal, son of Sherif Hussein, gained control of Damascus. By the time the Ottoman Empire collapsed at the end of the war, there was already an

Arab administration in Damascus and in the interior areas of what is now Syria. The British controlled Palestine and the French controlled the Syrian coastal areas.

The victorious Europeans made conflicting promises, however, concerning the future of the region. In 1915 Britain assured Sherif Hussein that independent Arab entities would be established in parts of the former Ottoman Empire. The 1916 Sykes-Picot Agreement between Britain and France (kept secret until 1917 when it was disclosed by the revolutionary government of Russia) divided Greater Syria between the British and French, and the 1917 Balfour Declaration promised British support for the establishment of a Jewish homeland in Palestine.

Although Syrian nationalists called for an independent nation with Faisal as king in 1919, the 1920 San Remo Conference of the victorious allies placed the area that is now Syria and Lebanon under French control. French troops entered Damascus, and in 1922 the League of Nations formally recognized France's mandate over the area.

French rule was oppressive and divisive. The French split the mandated area into regions that roughly corresponded to religious and ethnic groupings, undoubtedly to discourage unified opposition to French rule. Mount Lebanon was the major location of the Maronite Christians, a group with strong historic ties to France, and this district was enlarged by adding the coastal cities and the Bekaa Valley to the east. This had the effect of increasing the area dominated by Maronites but at the same time diluting Maronite strength in the region as Druze from the mountains and Muslims from the adjacent areas were added. Other areas of the mandate were also administered by the local dominant groups: Latakia (Alawis), Alexandretta (Turks), Jebel Druze (Druze), and Aleppo and Damascus (Sunni Muslims).

French control was not imposed easily. European nations and inhabitants of the French mandate pressured France to discuss the future independence of the area, and negotiations between the French and local Arab nationalists were held throughout the late 1920s. A major point of disagreement concerned the links between Mount Lebanon, Jebel Druze, Alexandretta, and the rest of the region. Arab nationalists insisted that the entire area under French control become independent as one nation, while the French were intent on protecting the autonomy of certain minority groups, especially the Maronites of Mount Lebanon. Local nationalists were further alienated from France when it granted the area around Alexandretta (Iskenderun, known also as the Hatay province) to Turkey in 1939.

Not until World War II did Syria achieve independence. When the Free French took over Syria from the Vichy government representatives in 1941, they promised independence to gain local support. Formal de jure independence was granted in late 1941, and an elected government under President Shukri al-Kuwatly took power in 1943, the same year that neighboring Lebanon achieved independence. The last French soldiers were not withdrawn until 1946, however, and even then the French were reluctant to leave.

## Syrian Independence

The first twenty-five years of Syrian independence were characterized by political instability. Syria developed a reputation as the Arab state that was most prone to military coups. The civilian government of Shukri al-Kuwatly was overthrown in March 1949 in a bloodless coup by the army chief of staff, Col. Husni al-Zayim. Syria's poor military showing in the first Arab-Israeli War in 1948, bickering among the members of the civilian government, and a weak economy prompted the insurrection.

This first military coup was the beginning of more than twenty years of instability and military involvement in political affairs. The phenomenon not only has given minority groups that are disproportionately represented in the army greater power than the majority Sunnis but also has politicized the Syrian army, with harmful effects on its combat capability.

The first military regime was toppled only four

and a half months later by another military group, which was itself overthrown in December 1949. The new regime, led by Lt. Col. Adib al-Shishakli, seemed relatively liberal in its first two years in power: a constitution was enacted in 1950 and a parliament was elected that permitted free speech within limits. Rising opposition, however, triggered repressive measures beginning in late 1951, and these steps resulted in Shishakli's overthrow in February 1954.

The next four years of democratic government saw frequent cabinet changes and the rapid growth of political parties with strong ideological bases, most importantly the Arab Socialist Resurrection party (the Ba'ath party). The Ba'ath party was the result of a merger in 1953 of two political groups with two distinctive ideological objectives. From one group the Ba'athists inherited a Socialist orientation, although they explicitly rejected Marxism. From the other they received an emphasis on Arab unity. Although the party recognizes the connection between Arabism and Islam, it is not based on Islamic solidarity. Ba'athism has broad appeal in other Arab countries and ultimately came to be the ruling ideology in Iraq as well, although a factional split between Ba'athists in Syria and Iraq has been a divisive factor in Syrian-Iraqi relations for many years.

The Syrian Ba'athists worked assiduously to build party support within the army. The secular ideology of the party attracted many young officers of minority religious groups. Two other parties with strong ideological orientations, the Syrian Communist party and the Syrian National party, also actively sought to increase their power during the 1954-58 period. The Ba'athists were represented in the cabinet for the first time in 1956 and soon began to accrue power disproportionate to their numbers.

By late 1957 the Ba'athists feared that the Communist party was overtaking them in their efforts to control policy in Damascus. The appeal of the political left in Syria grew not only because of the ineptitude of the democratic governments but also because of the wave of anti-Western feeling that had swept the Arab countries in the late 1940s and the 1950s. The creation of Israel in 1948 and the 1956 Suez crisis accelerated opposition to the West. Egyptian president Gamal Abdel Nasser's appeals for Arab nationalism gave the Ba'athists the opportunity to salvage their threatened domestic situation by asking the Egyptian leader to form a union with Syria. Nasser had cracked down severely on Communists in Egypt and could be expected to do the same in Syria if a union were established. Although the Ba'athists knew that their own party would be restricted as well, they favored a union because they believed it would eliminate the threat from the far left. Although Nasser was reluctant initially, the United Arab Republic was announced in February 1958.

The three and one-half years of Syrian union with Egypt were not pleasant for Syrian politicians. Nasser insisted that he would accept only a complete merger, not a federation, and the much smaller Syrian nation was submerged in the union. Although the religious leaders, landowners, and wealthy business people who made up the traditional political elite in Syria most strongly opposed the union, the Ba'athists as well soon regretted their plea for union with Egypt. In 1961 Nasser began to emphasize socialism, and Syria suffered a drought and an economic downturn. These may have been the last straws for disaffected Syrians, and the coup of September 1961 brought to power in Damascus traditional political figures who immediately brought about Syria's secession from the union.

The coup of September 1961 ushered in another period of confusion and instability in Syrian politics. Government succeeded government, and popular discontent grew as the traditional Sunni politicians, both inside and outside the military, proved incapable of providing stable leadership.

In March 1963 the Ba'ath party assumed power following another coup, and since then elements of the party have ruled Syria. The party itself became the arena of political conflict, and until Hafez Assad took power in 1970 the leftists and the centrists of the Ba'ath party leadership contested for power.

*Hafez al-Assad*

# Syria Under Assad

In July 1963 an attempted coup by pro-Nasser officers was violently suppressed by the Ba'ath regime. This marked a change in the relatively peaceful pattern of coups in Syria up to that point. Lt. Gen. Amin al-Hafez became president and ruled for the next two and one-half years. In February 1966 a coup by Alawi officers ushered in a period of civilian Ba'athist rule, although Gen. Salah Jadid was clearly the final arbiter of Syrian politics. Between 1966 and 1970 tension grew between the more radical civilian wing of the Ba'ath party and the more pragmatic military wing. The civilian leaders of the country were ardent supporters of pan-Arabism and the PLO, while the military group led by air force lieutenant general Hafez al-Assad, a forty-year-old Alawi, represented greater support of Syrian national objectives. In November 1970 a coup brought Assad to power.

During the first five years of his rule, Assad consolidated power domestically and strengthened ties abroad. Gradually Syria began to emerge from the isolation imposed by years of domestic instability. Although Assad was careful to place loyal Alawi officers in key positions, especially in intelligence, he broadened the base of his regime by bringing various leftist elements into the government. As early as 1973 Sunnis demonstrated against the regime, but objections to the political domination of the Sunni majority by an Alawi minority did not become politically significant until the latter part of the 1970s, perhaps because most Syrians were relieved at the stability the new regime offered and the relatively liberalized political atmosphere established by Assad in his early years in power.

The foreign policy of Assad's first five years achieved friendly relations with most of the Arab states, improved relations with the Soviet Union after some strain in late 1970, and even renewed diplomatic relations with several Western nations (Great Britain in 1973, the United States and West Germany in 1974).

Assad's cooperation with other Arab states reached its peak in the close coordination with Egypt that led to the October 1973 Arab-Israeli War. Despite Syria's failure to retake the Golan Heights from Israel, the war was regarded by many Syrians as a success because their troops performed well during the fighting.

By the mid-1970s, however, serious domestic and foreign problems began to plague Assad's regime. Political dissent, especially from disaffected Sunnis, became more violent, and the civil war in Lebanon put Assad in the difficult position of reconciling his support of Arab nationalism and the Palestinians with Syrian national interests.

## Involvement in Lebanon

The involvement of Syrian troops after 1976 in the Lebanese civil war complicated every aspect of Syria's foreign policy. Syrian troops supported virtually every faction in the Lebanese war at one time or another, and Syrian activities in Lebanon were impossible to understand without a clear grasp both of the conflicting goals of Syrian foreign policy and of specific Syrian objectives in Lebanon.

Since the beginning of Ba'athist domination of Syria in 1963, there has been a contradiction between the concepts of Syrian nationalism and Arab nationalism. Ba'athist ideology focuses enormous attention on Arab nationalism. Although Assad's 1970 coup represented the victory of the less radical, more pragmatic wing of the party, Syria remained committed to the concept of an Arab nation. At the heart of Arab nationalism lies the Palestinian conflict with Israel, and so the Syrian commitment to Arab nationalism implied strong support of the PLO. On the other hand, Syrian national interests have often been in conflict with general Arab objectives. Syria's intervention in Lebanon highlighted the contradiction between these two threads of Syrian foreign policy and vastly complicated Assad's desire to maintain good relations with his fellow Arab leaders and to play a leading role in the Arab world.

Syrian objectives in Lebanon are rooted in the history of Syria and Lebanon before their independence. In 1920 the French added areas with Muslim majorities to the predominantly Maronite Christian Mount Lebanon region and ruled this area separately from the rest of its mandate. Syrian nationalists viewed French policy as an unjustified division of one national entity, and Syrian governments never openly accepted the legitimacy of a separate Lebanon. Despite the close ties between the two states, Syria has never had diplomatic relations with Lebanon.

Migration, trade, and other forms of contact with Lebanon have continued throughout Syria's history. Some of the minority groups that make up the fractured Lebanese polity are also found in Syria.

Given these close connections and the fragility of the Lebanese government, Syria had always sought to influence events in Lebanon. Some Syrians even advocated annexing Lebanon to Syria outright, but Assad never aspired to do so. He appears to favor a compliant Lebanese government in which Syrian influence plays a strong hand. Annexation of Lebanon, with its quarreling factions and bitter religious-political differences, might destabilize Syria itself. In addition, for many years the Druze of Syria competed with the Alawis for influence in the Ba'ath party, and Assad is unlikely to want to add some two hundred thousand Lebanese Druze (with an armed and combat-ready militia) to his own country.

Assad's objective in Lebanon appears to be the creation of a peaceful, prosperous climate with a weak, politically moderate central government dependent upon Syria for its survival, a goal he substantially achieved by 1990. This goal helps to explain the shifts in Syrian support for the various Lebanese factions over the years.

After the 1970 Jordanian-Palestinian war, most PLO troops had been displaced to Lebanon, the one Arab state adjacent to Israel where they could operate without being threatened by a strong government. The arrival of PLO troops upset the fragile balance of the Lebanese political system and in April 1975 triggered civil war. At first Syria played a constructive role, receiving praise from other Arab states, as well as the United States and France, for its attempts to reconcile warring factions.

By mid-1976, however, it appeared that an alliance of the PLO and the Lebanese left was about to triumph over the conservative Christian Maronites and their allies. The prospect of a radical government in Beirut and a PLO unresponsive to Syrian control prompted Assad to send his troops into Lebanon in June 1976 to prevent the collapse of the Maronite coalition. With the aid of Syrian forces, the Maronites were able to avoid defeat.

The Arab states were appalled at the sight of Syrian troops attacking the PLO and participating in the Maronite assault on Palestinian refugee camps. In response some Arab states broke their ties with Syria. By the end of 1976 a temporary halt in the fighting had been achieved. Saudi Arabia helped to mediate a compromise: an Arab peacekeeping force would patrol Lebanon to prevent violence, and the Syrian forces already present would make up the majority of these peacekeepers. Saudi Arabia and other Arab oil producers agreed to pay most of the expenses incurred by the presence of Syrian troops in Lebanon.

This compromise allowed Syrian rapprochement with some of its Arab critics. The surprise 1977 visit of Egyptian president Anwar Sadat to Israel caused Arab governments angry with Egypt to reaffirm close relations with Syria. Relations between Syria and the Lebanese Maronites cooled as Assad cultivated improved relations with the PLO, the Lebanese left, and other anti-Israeli and therefore anti-Sadat forces in the Arab world. Although Assad had agreed to a U.S.-sponsored disengagement agreement with Israel in May 1974, he had opposed Sadat's growing rapprochement with the United States. He condemned Sadat's November 1977 trip to Jerusalem and became a leader of the Arab states that rejected the 1979 Camp David peace treaty and any other compromises with Israel.

Fearful of the new direction in Syrian policy, the Maronites by 1978 had begun to turn to Israel for external aid, a circumstance Assad found threatening. Arab strength was further weakened by Iraqi president Saddam Hussein's 1980 decision to declare war on Iran, which Assad interpreted as the withdrawal of yet another important Arab state from the common struggle against Israel. As a result, Assad stressed Syrian national interests and became even more determined to control affairs in Lebanon.

When Israel invaded Lebanon in June 1982, Syrian forces in Lebanon's Bekaa Valley suffered serious losses. Although the Soviet Union quickly replaced weapons and military equipment lost during the fighting, the damage to Syrian military prestige was substantial and underlined Syria's inability to use military means to reverse Israel's annexation of the Golan Heights. Assad's foreign policy problems were compounded by political dissent at home, which he violently suppressed.

As usual, however, Assad rebounded from the lackluster performance of his troops in Lebanon in 1982. Taking the lead of the diverse and mutually suspicious factions that shared only an opposition

to Israel, for three years Assad worked to push the Israelis out of Lebanon and reassert his influence over that country. By 1985 a May 1983 U.S.-brokered agreement between Israel and Lebanon, which Assad opposed, had been abandoned by the powerless government of Amin Gemayel; the American marine force had been withdrawn in disarray following the 1983 bombing of its barracks; and in June 1985 Israel withdrew the bulk of its forces, leaving a few units to aid the pro-Israeli South Lebanon Army militia in southern Lebanon.

This resurgence of Syrian power in Lebanon, however, was soon challenged. Israeli influence had been removed except from the areas adjacent to the border, but soon Assad was again in conflict with the PLO and even with pro-Iranian segments of the Shi'ite community. In early 1987 Syria increased its military contingent in Lebanon and attempted once again to control Beirut. Although Syria controlled one of the small factions within the PLO, it failed in its efforts to exercise decisive influence over Arafat and the organization as a whole. In early 1988 Syria tried to get the PLO out of Beirut by pushing Amal, the Shi'ite militia allied with Syria, to lay siege to the Palestinian refugee camps where the PLO held sway. After weeks of fighting, Amal lifted the siege and the PLO moved to the predominantly Sunni town of Sidon on the southern coast of Lebanon. Bitterness remained between the PLO and Assad and between pro-Iranian and pro-Syrian factions within the Shi'ite community.

Syrian conflict with the most important Maronite militia, the Lebanese Forces, was more straightforward. For Assad, the Lebanese Forces were reactionary, pro-Israeli diehards who stood in the way of his domination of Lebanon. The Lebanese Forces regarded Assad as a relentless enemy who wanted to take over Lebanon and destroy the Maronite community, politically if not physically. The Syrian attempt failed in the fall of 1988 to force the rump Lebanese parliament to select as president pro-Syrian Maronite and former president Suleiman Franjieh. Assad was also unsuccessful in having another pro-Syrian Maronite, Michel

Daher, elected in September. The deadlock ended with President Amin Gemayel stepping down at the end of his term and naming the Christian commander of the armed forces, Gen. Michel Aoun, as head of government. Syria and those factions allied with it refused to accept this and viewed Gemayel's last prime minister, Selim Hoss, as the head of government. In early 1989 Aoun, after attempting to unify the Christian militias, challenged the Syrians directly by calling for the evacuation of all foreign forces from Lebanon. In response, the Syrians bombarded Christian sections of Beirut and areas outside the capital.

Aoun, now strengthened by material assistance from Iraqi president Saddam Hussein, resisted fiercely, and together Aoun and Assad made the spring and summer of 1989 the worst year in Lebanon's long fifteen-year period of civil war and violence. Although he knew he could not defeat the Syrians, Aoun had hoped he could provoke international outrage over Syrian brutality and prompt foreign intervention that would lead to a withdrawal of Syrian forces from Lebanon. He had miscalculated, however, and failed to grasp that, with the decline of the Soviet Union, Western nations no longer viewed a consolidation of Syrian control in Lebanon as an advance for Soviet influence. Indeed the Soviet Union and the United States, both desirous of avoiding involvement in the conflict, together blessed a Saudi-sponsored Arab League initiative during 1989 to resolve the conflict at the regional level. Convening a sufficient number of deputies from the Lebanese parliament in Ta'if, Saudi Arabia, during October 1989, the Saudi government took a leading role in trying to mediate a settlement of the Lebanese crisis.

The Ta'if Agreement of October 22, 1989, which was closely coordinated with Syria, recognized the existence of a special relationship between Syria and Lebanon. It prescribed that a reformed Lebanese government reconstituted under Syrian tutelege should negotiate the final withdrawal of Syrian forces from Lebanon. Cornered, Aoun continued to resist the Syrian presence and the Ta'if Agreement, which authorized Syria to oversee new presidential elections as a prelude to undertaking further reforms agreed upon at Ta'if. Assad quickly demonstrated his ability to reconstitute central authority in Lebanon. He oversaw the election of René Muawwad as Lebanese president in November 1989 and then Elias Harawi three weeks later after the car-bomb assassination of the former. The success of Syrian efforts resulted in the marginalization of Aoun, who finally succumbed to a combined force of Syrian and Lebanese soldiers in October 1990.

Assad's final move against Aoun coincided with the buildup of U.S.-led Western forces in Saudi Arabia to dislodge Iraqi forces from Kuwait. Courted by the United States, which wanted the broadest possible coalition against Iraqi president Saddam Hussein, Assad offered forces to be part of the effort, cemented relations with other members of the coalition (especially Saudi Arabia), and achieved tacit acquiescence for a forcible resolution of affairs in Lebanon. This international acquiescence was apparent when Syrian aircraft launched raids on Aoun's positions on the morning of October 13, 1990, and Israeli aircraft did not come up to meet them. By the end of the day, Aoun had fled to the French embassy in Beirut, and further resistance to Syrian hegemony in Lebanon collapsed.

## Syrian Economy in the 1990s

The success of Assad's Lebanon policy was accompanied by a significant turn-around in the Syrian economy. In part, this change arose from reforms Assad adopted beginning in the mid-1980s. Influenced by the decline and final collapse of fellow Socialist regimes in Eastern Europe, Assad had inaugurated a gradual economic liberalization program aimed at reversing some of the Socialist policies that had prevailed since the coming to power of the Ba'ath party in 1963. The deadening effect of a large bureaucracy had contributed to Syria's deep economic and foreign exchange crisis. Centralized economic planning suppressed both agricultural production and industrial development.

In response Assad had reduced consumer subsidies, devaluated the national currency, relaxed central control of agriculture, and granted greater freedom for individuals and private companies to participate in international trade. By 1989 Syria had achieved a balance-of-trade surplus of $1.2 billion, the first such trade surplus in more than thirty years.

Undoubtedly, some of this trade surplus derived from earnings on a commodity relatively new to Syria—oil. By the late 1980s Syria was beginning to benefit from the new light, high-quality crude oil discovered in the northeastern part of the country in 1984. Although Syria's oil deposits were only a fraction of the size of those of the oil-rich Arab states, the discovery freed Syria from having to expend valuable foreign exchange earnings on oil imports. By 1993 production of more than five hundred thousand barrels a day, about half of which was now being exported, were projected to earn Syria more than $2 billion for the year.

Many observers of economic change in Syria have focused on "Law Number Ten," promulgated in May 1991. This law was aimed at encouraging private investment. By late 1992 more than 735 private ventures valued at nearly $2 billion had been established.

Assad's strategic shift in late 1990, when he sided with the Western alliance against Iraq, also had a positive economic dimension. Following the conflict, the Gulf states collectively pledged $10 billion in development funds for those Arab countries that had supported the victorious alliance. Although this figure was subsequently reduced, Syria reportedly had received $1.5 billion by 1993 for investment in its economic infrastructure.

As a result of these developments, Syria experienced significant economic growth in the early 1990s. As is often the case in developing countries, growth in the private sector increased income differentials in Syria. Although shops were now filled with goods that previously had been unavailable, only a small fraction of the Syrian population could afford these newly available products. As many as 65 percent of the people were estimated to have fallen below the poverty line. Many in this

category were government employees, public sector workers, and landless peasants—historically important bases of support for the ruling Ba'ath party.

The poverty problem was compounded by rapid population growth of 3.4 percent a year. At that rate the population of 15 million in 1994 was expected to exceed 20 million by the year 2000. Moreover, nearly 60 percent of Syrians were under the age of twenty, making the population nonproductive economically and placing heavy demands on the state for education, health care, and future employment.

Syria also must contend with a huge foreign debt left over from the 1980s. It owes the former Soviet Union approximately $15 billion and the rest of the world another $10 billion. Nevertheless, if it can sustain favorable economic conditions and good relations with the wealthy Persian Gulf countries, Syria will have a better capability than many debtor nations to handle its debt.

## Subtle Political Change

Assad's effort to encourage a more liberal economic policy was not matched by a parallel effort to advance political liberalization. His regime remained a highly centralized, authoritarian structure based on an extensive deployment of security forces throughout the country.

Nevertheless, Assad tried to adapt to changing circumstances with a subtle shift in political strategy. Gradually, he moved from a reliance on his traditional base of political support—the rural and urban working classes—to a closer relationship with the emerging mercantile class that has been the principal beneficiary of the new liberal economic policies.

This change was apparent in the electoral process that returned Assad to office as president of Syria in December 1991. In the run-up to this election, which Assad won by 99.98 percent of the votes, the ruling Ba'ath party played virtually no role. Instead, Assad presented himself as a populist candidate representing all the people of the country, rather than as the heroic leader of an ideological vanguard party representing the interests of the oppressed in society. Emphasis was placed on mass demonstrations by people both from within and outside the party and also on the testimony of well-known independent personalities and the support of professional associations.

In parliamentary elections that preceded those for the presidency, Assad also had diminished the stature of the Ba'ath party by declining to convene it prior to the election and by reserving eighty seats of the two hundred fifty-member Peoples' Assembly for nonparty independents. Although the electoral process was structured so that the party controlled by Assad would maintain control of the chamber, the fairly open competition for the eighty nonparty seats provided a new democratic dimension to Syrian political life. The elections brought into prominence a number of new faces who were grateful to Assad for giving them a voice in politics. The new deputies constituted a bloc that not only benefited from Assad's changed economic policies but also constituted a potential lobby for further changes. The minority status of these elements in Syrian politics, however, guaranteed that in the short run their influence would be limited.

## Joining the Peace Process

In July 1991 Assad surprised the international community by responding positively to a joint U.S.-Soviet invitation requesting Israel and its Arab neighbors to convene negotiations aimed at resolving the Arab-Israeli conflict. Syria's participation in the coalition that had defeated Iraq in the 1991 Persian Gulf War and its agreement to negotiate with Israel marked a significant departure from previous Syrian foreign policy.

Syrian goals in the Arab-Israeli conflict had long been twofold: to lend support to the "Palestinian cause" and, since 1967, to recover the Golan Heights from Israel, which had seized them by force in the June 1967 war. In pursuit of these goals, Assad since 1973 had held steadfastly to three key policy positions: that any Arab-Israeli negotiation should take place under UN sponsorship, where Soviet and Third World support could buttress the Arab negotiating position; that only a joint-Arab delegation representing a common Arab position should negotiate directly with Israel; and that Israel should withdraw from territories occupied in 1967, as demanded in UN Security Council resolutions 242 and 338, as a precondition for the start of negotiations.

Meanwhile, conscious that these conditions were unacceptable to Israel, Assad pursued a policy of achieving "strategic parity" with the Jewish state in an effort to develop a position of relative strength from which to negotiate. During the 1970s and 1980s, Syria had cultivated its relationship with the Soviet Union, which supplied Syria with its arms.

But as Syria worked to improve its military strength, its diplomatic position weakened. Syria's ambivalent policies toward both the PLO and Lebanon, its support of Iran in the Iran-Iraq War, and its deepening reliance on the Soviet Union undercut its position in the Arab world.

By 1990, however, the efficacy of the military track had sharply declined due to the coming collapse of the Soviet Union. Meanwhile, Iraq's invasion of Kuwait in August brought an opportunity for Syria to revive the diplomatic dimension. Syria's participation in the anti-Iraq coalition led to a renewed alliance with Egypt and Saudi Arabia, and to much improved relations with the United States and other Western countries. Assad could now consider achieving by diplomatic means those same objectives for which previously he had been totally reliant on the military option.

Buoyed by the new spirit of economic growth and political optimism that seemed to be emerging in Syria in the early 1990s, Assad was able to take risks he previously would have avoided. In July 1991, therefore, he found himself able to respond positively to the joint U.S.-Soviet invitation to participate in the United States-sponsored peace conference that opened in Madrid, Spain, in October. Doing so also forced Israel's hand and led a recalcitrant government of Yitzhak Shamir to respond favorably as well in August, despite serious misgivings about the terms of reference for the negotiations.

In agreeing to enter the peace talks, however, Assad compromised significantly on a number of issues—namely that the talks be held under UN auspices and that Israel first withdraw from the Golan Heights as a precondition for negotiations. The position that the Arabs should negotiate together as one delegation was finessed by an inter-Arab agreement of the various Arab parties to the talks—Syria, Lebanon, Jordan, and the PLO (Israel did not yet recognize a role for the PLO)—to coordinate their positions between each round of the Arab-Israeli talks. On key issues—that the Palestinians should achieve their "legitimate national rights" and that Israel should withdraw entirely from the Golan Heights by the end of the negotiating process—Assad remained adamant.

By the late summer of 1993, following the initial "symbolic session" of the Madrid peace talks in October 1991, eleven sessions of negotiations had been held in Washington. Little progress on any of the substantive issues had been made. Nevertheless, some observers were predicting an imminent breakthrough between Israel and Syria. Israel, now led by Prime Minister Yitzhak Rabin, had indicated that compromise on the Golan was possible, and Assad had made it known that a "liberated" Golan could remain demilitarized.

At this point, in late August, it was announced that secret PLO-Israeli talks had culminated in an agreement formally signed in Washington on September 13. This "Gaza and Jericho first" agreement could not be and was not condemned outright by Syria. The Syrian president, however, did criticize the PLO for failure to coordinate its moves with other members of the Arab negotiating group and also expressed skepticism concerning the wisdom of an agreement that would divert attention away from the Golan Heights issue. Indeed, from the Syrian perspective the agreement had the impact of derailing the joint-Arab negotiating process in which Syria was the key player. It weakened Assad's ability to obtain through negotiation a return of the Golan Heights on his terms. Syrian spokesmen continued to announce, however, the country's commitment to an eventual comprehensive settlement of the Arab-Israeli conflict.

During 1994 Syria and Israel engaged in sporadic but serious negotiations through the shuttle diplomacy of U.S. secretary of state Warren Christopher. The conclusion in July of an agreement ending the state of war between Jordan and Israel left Syria as the last major frontline Arab nation to remain in a state of war against Israel. Both Assad and Rabin recognize that it is in their interest to eventually conclude an agreement, and both have offered genuine proposals on resolving the Golan Heights issue. Israel has already agreed in principle to a phased withdrawal from the Heights in conjunction with an internationally guaranteed demilitarization of the Golan. But Assad is proceeding cautiously, seeking the best deal he can obtain on the Golan, as well as on many issues related to Lebanon. He also wants to ensure that any agreement with Israel will bring with it a new U.S.-Syrian relationship that includes economic assistance and contacts.

## Outlook

Syria of the mid-1990s had a more positive and stable outlook than it had had for many years. Though it was still deeply involved in Lebanon, it was no longer bogged down there. Economically, it was beginning to enjoy a modest prosperity based on a somewhat liberalized economic order. Regionally, it had escaped its isolation of the 1980s and was closely allied with Egypt and Saudi Arabia, the two principal Arab countries dominating regional politics following the 1991 Persian Gulf War. President Assad's participation in the Gulf War had enabled him to diminish the legacy of his earlier close relationship with the former Soviet Union and to establish improved relations with the United States. These relations were augmented by the positive response Assad gave Washington regarding Syria's willingness to enter direct negotiations with Israel. Whether an eventual settlement with Israel will ever be reached remains an open question. Remaining committed to do so, however, gives Syria a more positive international image than it had for decades.

Whether Syria will stay the course that Assad had adopted during the early 1990s depends on a variety of factors, not the least of which is the fate of the Syrian president himself. The current stability and strength of Syria is closely associated with the pragmatic and adaptive policies Assad has pursued through the years. But this stability and strength has been purchased at a considerable price—the relative absence of political liberty in Syria.

Numerous challenges face Syria as it approaches the end of the twentieth century. One of these is the type of regime that will govern the country after Assad. Still another is the pressure of demographic growth that will place increasingly strong demands on the resources of the state. Yet another is developing suitable water-sharing arrangements with Turkey and Iraq over the flow of the Euphrates River, which is a source of disagreement among the three riparian states.

To address each of these challenges, including the maintenance of continued economic development, Syria would benefit from a reasonable settlement of the Arab-Israeli conflict. Assad, however, cannot compromise too extensively on what Syrians see as the key issues—the Golan Heights and the legitimate rights of the Palestinians—without jeopardizing the legitimacy of his own rule, which has been built partly on championship of these causes. In the end, a final settlement of the Arab-Israeli conflict may not be the most vital objective from Assad's point of view.

Other factors that could greatly affect Syria's position within the region would include a significant regime change in either Saudi Arabia or Egypt, possibly due to the influence of Islamic fundamentalist forces, or a return to power of the less compromising Likud party in Israel. The failure of Syria's current policy of cultivating closer relations with the West to gain concessions from Israel could lead Assad to consider its revision. In sum, the Syrian regime is not fully master of its own destiny in the context of the larger, turbulent region in which it sits. Syria's influence and role in the Middle East historically has ebbed and flowed in reactions to events and developments in the region. There is little reason to doubt that the future will be any different.

# YEMEN

In mid-1994 the Republic of Yemen was emerging from a short but bloody civil war that pitted the country's formerly separate halves against each other. Northern military units occupied the primary southern city of Aden on July 7, bringing the civil war to a close, although guerrilla war remained a possibility.

Divided since the early 1700s, North Yemen and South Yemen recently had tried to achieve the daunting task of unifying two disparate economic and political systems into one country. Prior to unification in 1990, relations between the North and South were fractious and cool at best. In February 1979 tension between them led to a border war that had international ramifications. Throughout the 1980s, North and South Yemen exploited each other's tribal rivalries to foment internal dissension.

Although the two Yemens had publicly committed themselves to the principle of unification for several years, it was not until the late 1980s, with the demise of the Soviet Union and the end of Cold War geopolitics, that this goal was seen to be realistic. With their sagging economies and regional instablility in the wake of the Iran-Iraq War, the Yemens took a risk to combine resources and position themselves for a regional leadership role in the next decade.

But the civil war revealed the deep differences between the political elites of the North and South. With many southern secessionist leaders at large in other countries and the leadership of the North willing to use military force to maintain control of the South, the future of Yemen's unification experiment was in grave doubt.

## Geography

With a total area of 203,849 square miles, Yemen is roughly twice the size of the state of Wyoming. Yemen occupies the southwestern corner of the Arabian Peninsula, bordered by the Red Sea on the west, the Arabian Sea on the south, Oman on the east, and Saudi Arabia on the north and northeast. It also controls the small, strategic island of Perim in the Bab al-Mandab Strait and the much larger island of Socotra in the Gulf of Aden.

The country is divided roughly into three ecosystems: a semidesert coastal plain, called the Tihama, that stretches along the Red Sea and Arabian Sea coasts and extends about forty miles inland; a chain of highlands and mountains in the interior; and a vast, sandy desert, known for being one of the most inhospitable places on Earth, the Empty Quarter *(Rub al-Khali)*.

Yemen's poorly defined borders have led to armed conflict with its neighbors and between North and South Yemen. Control over remote desert outposts took on great economic significance after the discovery of oil on the peninsula. The 1934 Saudi-Yemeni treaty of friendship settled one clash, but border disputes with Saudi Arabia still flare. The mix of heat and humidity makes the coast uncomfortable, and in the interior summer temperatures soar to about 130 degrees Fahrenheit. Although only 6 percent of the country's land is considered arable, abundant rainfall makes the interior highlands of the North one of the most important agricultural areas on the Arabian Peninsula. In the southern region, only scant and irregular rains fall from the tail end of the Indian monsoons, severely limiting agriculture. Southern Yemeni culture depended heavily on fishing and nomadic herding.

Sanaa, the capital city of former North Yemen, is Yemen's largest city and now capital of the unified country. Aden, once one of the busiest and most significant ports in the world, was the capital of former South Yemen and has been designated as the new country's economic and commercial capital.

## Demography

Yemen's population of more than 11 million is the second largest on the Arabian Peninsula after Saudi Arabia. According to most estimates, Yemen's population is growing rapidly at a rate of almost 3.4 percent annually. In religion the country is Muslim, divided between Sunnis and Sh'ites, with a heavy concentration of Sunnis in the South. Arabic is spoken nearly everywhere, although a few people in the extreme eastern part of the country continue to speak a pre-Arabic dialect.

Life expectancy is about forty-five years and the illiteracy rate is approximately 60 percent. Education and health services, confined to Yemen's urban centers, are woefully inadequate. Malnutrition and poverty are rampant in the hinterlands of the South, where the lack of basic services and facilities, small dispersed communities, and rugged terrain have hindered development. Yemen suffers from one of the highest infant mortality rates in the world.

Yemen's human resources are greatly underdeveloped. More than half of the work force is engaged in agriculture. Most of the remaining workers provide unskilled labor to the labor-poor, capital-rich countries of the Arabian Peninsula, such as Saudi Arabia and the United Arab Emirates. Throughout the 1970s and the 1980s, the wages paid to these workers provided a steady capital inflow that, along with foreign aid, has been vital to the country's economic stability.

Ethnically, Yemenis in the South pride themselves on being primarily Qahtani or southern Arabs, those with the most ancient roots, as opposed to Adnani or northern Arabs. Northern Yemenis fall into two principal Islamic groups of almost equal size: the *Zaydis*, belonging to a Shi'ite sect, and the *Shafi'is*, who are Sunnis. The Zaydi-Shafi'i division has plagued northern Yemen throughout its history and continues to be a major obstacle to the country's political development. The tension between the two sects has been sustained primarily by the political and military dominance of the Zaydis.

## History

Yemeni territory, known to the ancient Arabs as *Al-Yaman*, was divided into kingdoms and enclaves of various sizes. Strategically poised at the junction of major trading routes between Africa and India and endowed with an abundance of fertile land, Yemen's ancient kingdoms grew prosperous and powerful. Among Yemen's centers of civilization was the fabled Kingdom of Saba ruled by the Queen of Sheba of biblical fame.

In about 1000 B.C. the Kingdom of Saba was a great trading state with a major agricultural base supported by a sophisticated system of irrigation, at the heart of which was the Marib dam, a regional wonder. In the north of Yemen, the Kingdom of the Mineans arose, coexisting with Saba and maintaining trading colonies as far away as Syria. During the first century B.C., the Kingdom of Himyar was established, reaching its greatest extent and power in the fifth century A.D. Christian and Jewish kings were among its leaders.

Developments in the Roman Empire were largely responsible for the decline of pre-Islamic civilization in Yemen. New trade routes bypassed the old caravan trails, and Christian Romans did not need the frankincense used in pagan funeral rituals. By the sixth century A.D. the Marib dam had collapsed, symbolizing a process of political disintegration in southern Arabia that helped pave the way for Islam.

When followers of the Islamic Shi'ite sect split off from the mainstream Sunni religion in what is today Iran and Iraq, many persecuted Shi'ites fled

## Key Facts on Yemen

**Area:** 203,849 square miles.
**Capital:** Sanaa.
**Population:** 11,105,202 (1994).
**Religion:** Muslim.
**Official Language:** Arabic.
**GDP:** $9 billion; $800 per capita (1993).

*Source:* Central Intelligence Agency, *CIA World Factbook 1994.*

during the eighth and ninth centuries to the highlands of northern Yemen. Claiming descent from the Prophet Muhammad, one of their leaders proclaimed himself *imam* and established the Rassid dynasty, which espoused a sect of Shi'ite Islam called *Zaydism.*

Zaydism dominated the tribes of the northern and eastern mountains, but the Sunni doctrine prevailed in the coastal plain and in other parts of Yemen. The religious division was to dominate Yemeni politics for generations.

In the sixteenth century the Ottoman Turks captured the Yemeni plains and the port of Aden, but a young Zaydi imam led a successful resistance, forcing the Ottomans to conclude a truce and eventually leave Yemen in 1636. One of his successors unified the mountains and plains into a single state extending to Aden, with the northern city of Sanaa as its capital. But war and chaos soon returned to Yemen. In 1728 the sultan of the southern province broke away from the Zaydi regime and forced the division between North and South that prevailed until 1990.

The Ottoman sultan in Istanbul continued to claim suzerainty over Yemen, but his control was tenuous. In the meantime, the British, jointly with the Dutch at first, had established a trading post in Yemen's coffee-rich area of Mocha and by 1770 had become major coffee traders. After Napoleon's seizure of Egypt in 1798, Britain took control of Aden to protect its routes to India via the Suez.

A small Turkish military presence in Yemen came to an end after Turkey's defeat in World War I. The Zaydi imam Yahya was left in control of the area evacuated by the Turks. He subsequently tried to consolidate his control over Yemen, but his efforts were opposed by the British and their local protégés in the South and by the Saudis in the North. War ensued, ending in a humiliating defeat for Yahya in 1934, although he remained in control of part of Yemen.

After the building of the Suez Canal and the development of large steamships in the nineteenth century, the port of Aden gradually became a major international fueling and bunkering station between Europe, South Asia, and the Far East. In 1937 the British made Aden a crown colony and divided the hinterland sultanates in the South into the Western and Eastern Aden Protectorates.

The British further developed the port facilities in Aden in the 1950s and built an oil refinery. Consequently, Aden became the dominant economic center in southern Arabia—a densely populated urban area with a rapidly growing working class.

Yahya, whose isolationism and despotism had alienated a large number of Yemenis, was assassinated in an attempted coup in 1948. His son, Ahmad, succeeded him. Growing nationalism among the Arab countries after World War II, exemplified by the rise of Egypt's Gamal Abdel Nasser as a pan-Arab leader, as well as improving communications and the emergence of Arab oil wealth, forced Ahmad to abandon the isolationist policies of his father. He joined Egypt and Syria in the ill-fated United Arab Republic in 1958 and sought aid from Communist and capitalist nations alike.

## The Yemeni Republics

Ahmad's repressive domestic policies touched off a coup on September 26, 1962, that established the Yemen Arab Republic, with Sanaa as its capital. This coup put an end to the Rassid dynasty, one of the oldest and most enduring in history. Established in about A.D. 897, the Rassid dynasty claimed descent from the Prophet Muhammad and produced 111 imams (kings and religious leaders) before it was uprooted by the 1962 revolution.

To the south, where the other Yemen still was under British colonial rule, the coup was a great inspiration to underground groups agitating for political freedom. This nationalism combined with severe urban problems in congested Aden to create an unstable situation in southern Yemen. The British, hoping to withdraw gracefully from the area while protecting their interests, persuaded the sultans in the Western and Eastern Protectorates to join Aden in 1963 in forming the Federation of South Arabia, which was to be the nucleus of a future independent state.

Arab opponents of the British plan mounted a campaign of sabotage, bombings, and armed resistance. Britain, failing to persuade the various opposing factions to agree on a constitutional design for a new independent state, announced early in 1966 that it would withdraw its military forces from Aden and southern Arabia by the end of 1968. (Britain had signed a treaty in 1959 guaranteeing full independence to the region by 1968.)

London's announcement turned the anti-British campaign of terror into one of interfactional competition. The National Front for the Liberation of South Yemen (or National Liberation Front, NLF), backed by the British-trained South Arabian army, emerged as the victor among the various factions, and on November 30, 1967, Aden and southern Arabia became an independent state under the name of the People's Republic of Southern Yemen (later changed to the People's Democratic Republic of Yemen). The NLF leader, Qahtan al-Sha'bi, became the republic's first president.

## North Yemen

Civil war raged in North Yemen for eight years after the establishment of the Yemen Arab Republic. When the last monarch, Iman Muhammad al-Badr, fled Sanaa after the 1962 coup, he mustered loyal tribal warriors and waged war against the republican government. Aid from Saudi Ara-

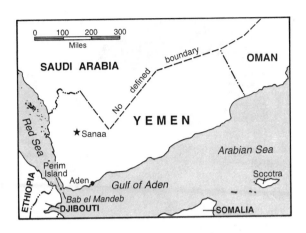

bia and Jordan helped to sustain his resistance movement. In response, the new president, Col. Abdullah al-Sallal, turned to Nasser, who sent a military force to support the new republic.

Hostilities continued on and off until 1967 when Arab-Israeli tensions made it imperative for Egypt to withdraw its forces from North Yemen. In the meantime, fighting broke out among the republican leaders themselves, and President al-Sallal was removed from office. Moderate republicans, led by Gen. Hasan al-Amri, seized power and managed to push back a serious monarchist offensive against Sanaa. After the withdrawal of Egyptian forces, Saudi Arabia began to reduce its commitment to al-Badr's followers, and in 1970 it recognized the Yemeni republic after the monarchists agreed to drop their claims and cooperate with the republican regime.

During the early 1970s the formation of a three-person republican council headed by Judge Abd al-Rahman al-Iryani seemed to have produced stability. During that period, Saudi Arabia became a major provider of foreign aid, perhaps to forestall greater Communist aid to Sanaa and to counter the growing Marxist orientation of South Yemen. Relations between the two Yemens deteriorated and flared into border fighting, pushing North Yemen closer to Saudi Arabia.

In 1976 Col. Ibrahim al-Hamdi ousted the civilian government of al-Iryani and embarked on a major program of healing old factional and reli-

*Ali Abdullah Salih*

gious wounds. Though a popular leader, al-Hamdi was assassinated in 1977. His successor, Ahmad al-Ghashmi, was assassinated in 1978. Lt. Col. Ali Abdullah Salih then took over and has remained in power ever since.

Under Salih's rule North Yemen continued to be beset by turmoil, much of it resulting from tensions between the two Yemens that erupted in the 1979 border war. Salih actively sought arms from the Soviet Union, and in mid-1979 Sanaa concluded a new arms agreement with Moscow. The agreement was partly spurred by the Saudis' anger over the March 1979 announcement of merger plans between North and South Yemen and by the Saudis' subsequent decision to scale down military aid to North Yemen.

Early in 1979, during the border war between the two Yemens, Saudi Arabia had considered direct military intervention in support of North Yemen and had been willing to underwrite U.S. arms sales to Sanaa. But in late 1979 and early 1980 Saudi Arabia suspended military and economic aid to its neighbor, and the U.S. arms program that was to sell $390 million worth of modern arms to North Yemen was terminated. Salih's government sought to reassure Saudi Arabia that it was not abandoning North Yemen's traditional policy of nonalignment, and that its proposed merger with South Yemen did not mean the emergence of a Soviet-oriented alliance.

In the 1980s the major threat to the Salih government came from the National Democratic Front (NDF), a coalition of opponents engaged in political and military action against the government backed by South Yemen. By the fall of 1981 the NDF occupied much of the southern part of North Yemen and seemed on the point of winning a war of attrition. Over the next few months, however, Salih turned the menacing situation around through vigorous military action and an astute political compromise with South Yemen leader Ali Nasser Muhammad reached in May 1982. Muhammad agreed to halt support for the NDF if amnesty for and political incorporation of NDF elements were forthcoming. This agreement led to a gradual normalization of the situation in North Yemen and strengthened Muhammad against his hard-line opponents in Aden, who wanted to support NDF military operations vigorously.

With his southern opponents neutralized, Salih turned his attention to rebellious northerners, who were more loyal to local clan leaders than to the central authorities. Thanks to the discovery of oil, Salih was able to finance the building of schools, hospitals, and better roads, as well as to dispense other jobs and services that increased government presence and co-opted local inhabitants in tribal areas. In 1985 Yemeni citizens (farmers, merchants, businessmen, and some women) were encouraged to vote for the newly created Local Council for Cooperative Development, which became responsible for the administration of village development projects. This extension of the state bureaucracy to remote areas was somewhat successful in diminishing the entrenched power of the local tribal leaders.

In 1988 Salih permitted elections to establish the long-promised Consultative Assembly. In the voting, 1.2 million Yemenis chose twelve hundred delegates to the assembly, which is not authorized to initiate legislation but is permitted to amend or critique it. One of its first official acts was to name Salih as head of state de jure. His landslide victory illustrated the public's general approval of (and resignation to) Salih's political ambitions.

## South Yemen

Since its independence in 1967 as the People's Republic of Southern Yemen, South Yemen had a strong Socialist orientation. The ruling party, the National Front for the Liberation of South Yemen, preached "scientific socialism" with a Marxist flavor. President Qahtan al-Sha'bi sought closer ties with the Soviet Union and China as well as with the more radical Arab regimes.

Al-Sha'bi's orientation, however, was not radical enough for some elements of the NLF. In 1969 he was overthrown by a group of militants led by Salim Rubayyi' Ali, and in 1970 the country was renamed the People's Democratic Republic of Yemen. The new regime took extreme steps, including repression and exile, to break traditional patterns of tribalism and religion and eliminate the vestiges of the bourgeoisie and familial elites.

Externally, relations between Aden and Sanaa were soured by political and ideological differences—despite mutual advocacy of Yemeni reunification. Saudi Arabia joined with North Yemen in actively opposing South Yemen's Marxist regime and backing opposition efforts in the South.

Salim Rubayyi' Ali had a powerful rival in the person of Abd al-Fattah Isma'il, secretary general of the NLF (renamed the National Front). Ali was considered a Maoist with pro-China sympathies, while Isma'il was thought of as a pragmatic Marxist loyal to Moscow. In June 1978 Isma'il seized power and executed Ali. He reorganized the National Front into the Yemeni Socialist party (YSP), became chairman of the Presidium of the People's Supreme Assembly, and named Ali Nasser Muhammad as prime minister. In October 1979 Isma'il signed a friendship and cooperation treaty with the Soviet Union.

Isma'il, however, was unable to hold on to power. In April 1980 he relinquished his posts as Presidium chairman and YSP secretary general. The party indicated that he had resigned because of poor health, but it appeared that Isma'il had lost a power struggle, in part because of his foreign policy positions. The YSP Central Committee named Ali Nasser Muhammad to take his place. Isma'il had intended to further cement ties with the Soviet Union and Eastern Europe, and on this point there was agreement between him and Muhammad. The latter, however, also wanted to improve relations with Saudi Arabia and other Gulf countries to end South Yemen's isolation in the Arab world, secure new sources of foreign aid, and facilitate union between the two Yemens.

Muhammad began his tenure with visits to the Soviet Union, Saudi Arabia, North Yemen, and other neighboring countries. He signed agreements on economic and technical cooperation with the Soviets, and in late 1980 he agreed to a friendship and cooperation treaty with East Germany. The Soviet military presence in South Yemen increased significantly. The number of East German and Cuban military personnel in Aden also increased in 1980.

Overall, Muhammad's regime attempted to pursue a more moderate path, cultivating economic ties with the West, achieving political reconciliation with North Yemen and Oman, and moderating between as many tribal rivalries as possible. But in the fall of 1985 Isma'il, Muhammad's predecessor, precipitated a power struggle by returning from his self-imposed exile in the Soviet Union.

In January 1986 a bloody coup attempt by supporters of Isma'il escalated to civil war. Pitched tank battles and anarchy broke out in Aden as Muhammad was driven from power and forced to flee the country. Some ten thousand people died during twelve days of fighting and thousands more fled the country.

Ironically, Isma'il himself disappeared during

the fighting and was presumed dead. Haider Abu Bakr al-Attas, the prime minister in Muhammad's government who happened to be out of the country during the conflict, returned to Aden January 25 and was named provisional president. In October 1986 he was elected president for a full term. His government also followed a local brand of "pragmatic Marxism," pursued a close relationship with the Soviet Union, discussed unification with North Yemen, and supported mainstream Arab causes. South Yemen restored diplomatic relations with Egypt in 1988 and considered reestablishing ties with the United States.

## Unification of the Yemens

North and South Yemen pursued their independent destinies in a climate of mutual suspicion throughout much of the 1980s. In the latter stages of the decade, however, fundamental changes in the global and regional geopolitical map set the stage for Yemeni unification.

Most observers trace the beginning of the unification process back to the spring of 1988, when presidents from both countries met to reduce tensions at the common border, create an economic buffer zone for joint investment, and revive discussions regarding unification. The meeting reduced tensions between the countries. In 1989 North Yemen initiated a series of talks with the South aimed at unification.

The crumbling of the Soviet Union and its inability to provide economic and military aid led Aden to the decision that unification with the North was in its best interest. South Yemen's economy sagged under socialist principles. After the country became independent, industrial production declined, the once-famous port of Aden lay in disrepair, and workers' remittances provided half of the government's annual budget. Due in part to substandard Soviet technology, South Yemen's oil sector, which had the potential to give the country an economic lift, was in shambles.

North Yemen's leadership had equally compelling arguments for considering unification. Salih saw merger as a means to increase the power and influence of his country. By incorporating South Yemen, Salih would have control over more land and loyalties unfettered by tribal allegiances. Finally, it is said that Salih himself was eager to broker unification to secure for himself a prominent position in the history of Yemen, whose people had long dreamed of unification.

In the final agreement, the two countries divided the ministerial positions, although local bureaucracies in the North and South remained intact. Salih retained his position as head of state. The two economies were generally left to function as they had previously, and the militaries exchanged senior staffs but left most rank-and-file personnel unintegrated.

Soon after its union in May 1990, Yemen fell under a plague of internal political violence and tribal warfare. High-level officials from nearly every political persuasion were the objects of assassination attempts or harassment. Conspiracy enthusiasts accused everyone from the House of Saud to Iranian hit squads.

This internal instablility was compounded by Iraq's invasion of Kuwait on August 2, 1990. Yemen showed sympathy for Iraq and condemned the involvement of Western forces in what it considered an Arab problem. By doing so it offended its wealthy Gulf neighbors. Saudi Arabia expelled hundreds of thousands of Yemeni workers whose remittances were crucial to Yemen's economy. Unemployment and poverty statistics jumped in 1991. Popular frustration and disillusionment with the new government, more bloated and inefficient under unification than before, mounted.

In 1992 Yemen was buffeted by riots brought on by the postponement of elections and severe economic problems. Yemen's riyal was devalued nearly 50 percent to encourage foreign investment, causing thousands of the nation's public sector workers to strike in protest. In December 1992 the country convulsed again in protest over the rising cost of living. Several military mutinies occurred and taxi and bus drivers attacked public buildings. Thousands of protesters marched to the parliament building in Sanaa demanding action.

On April 27, 1993, Yemen finally held its first

free, multiparty elections. Some five thousand candidates competed for 301 seats in parliament. Before election day the ruling coalition, headed by President Salih, and the Yemeni Socialist party, the party of power in former South Yemen, traded accusations over buying votes, inflating the electoral register, and unfair use of the media. The government deployed more than thirty-five thousand troops on the streets of Sanaa to keep order on election day.

With a large and peaceful turnout, Salih's People's Congress party won a plurality of the parliamentary seats. International observers declared the vote fair and several opposition parties won. They now occupy seats in the legislature—a step toward multiparty democracy virtually unprecedented in the Gulf region. Salih promised to form a coalition government that included Socialists from the South and fundamentalists, essentially continuing the process of co-opting his opponents that began in the 1970s with tribal clan leaders. However, he formed a coalition with the Yemeni Alliance for Reform, a party with strong Islamic influences. Ali Salem Beidh, leader of the Yemeni Socialist party, became vice president in the union, but his party was in a weak position. In August 1993 Beidh boycotted the five-person Presidential Council and returned to Aden, accusing Salih of refusing to integrate the military and hiding oil revenues. Beidh subsequently charged Salih and his followers with being responsible for the assassination of key Yemeni Socialist party officials and supporters.

## Civil War

Yemen's unification had been popular with most ordinary Yemenis, despite persistent ethnic, tribal, and religious divisions. But the army units, police forces, and bureaucracies from the two Yemens had not been fully integrated. Rivalries within the government based on the former division were strong. During late 1993 and early 1994 frequent skirmishes broke out between northern and southern units of the military.

On May 5, when Salih fired Ali Salem Beidh as vice president, armed conflict erupted. Beidh declared a separate government on May 21 and led the southern rebellion against Salih. He established a presidential council and a rump parliament to lead the "Democratic Republic of Yemen."

The larger northern army invaded the South and drove toward Aden and the oil port of Mukalla three hundred miles to the east. An eight-thousand-troop northern unit that had been stationed in the South managed to avoid capture and participated in the assault. Thousands of foreigners fled Aden and the surrounding region. The United States government advised all Americans in Yemen, numbering approximately five thousand, to leave. The UN Security Council adopted two resolutions calling for a cease-fire, without results. The United Nations, Arab League, and Russia all became involved in unsuccessful mediation efforts.

Southern forces used their superiority in combat aircraft to slow the northern advance, but the numerically superior forces from the North could not be stopped. As northern troops approached Aden in early July, fierce artillery duels seemed to forecast a bloody fight for the city. But before northern forces entered Aden and Mukalla, southern fighters abandoned the city or melted into the populace. The capture of Aden and Mukalla on July 7 effectively ended the fighting.

## Economy

The civil war was the latest economic blow to Yemen, which has never been an economic powerhouse in the region. Prior to unification, North and South Yemen relied on a combination of workers' remittances, coffee exports, a thriving fishing industry, and foreign assistance to supplement revenue from oil and gas exports.

During the oil booms of the 1970s and 1980s, many Yemenis found service-sector jobs in other Gulf countries. Their remittances were the largest and most reliable sources of foreign exchange for both North and South Yemen. However, their spending power created income disparities and sparked a strong demand for consumer goods that was hard to meet after the downturn in oil prices in the early 1980s. Moreover, the exodus of workers made it difficult for Yemen to develop its own agricultural and industrial bases. As Yemeni demonstrators took to the streets of Sanaa in support of Iraq's invasion of Kuwait, hundreds of thousands of workers were expelled from Saudi Arabia and repatriated.

The port of the city of Aden was traditionally the center of economic activity in South Yemen. In the past, the port serviced thousands of oil tankers and its refineries competed favorably with those of other Gulf oil states. But as political instability and extremism wracked South Yemen and oil tankers increased their range and depended less on refueling stops, Aden's port activity waned. This decline enhanced the importance of agriculture and fishing, but these sectors have not been able to generate sufficient income for the fast-growing population.

Both North and South Yemen depended on foreign aid to a large extent since the 1970s. Assistance came from Communist countries, particularly the Soviet Union, China, and East Germany, and from Western nations, including the United States. North Yemen managed to solicit other major sources, including Saudi Arabia, Kuwait, and the World Bank. As with remittances, this external aid often brought undesired consequences. North Yemen's economy was vulnerable to the capriciousness of the world economy and foreign governments. During the early and mid-1980s North Yemen's economy suffered because previous funding from Arab donors was diverted to sustain Iraq's war effort, and a global recession diminished other external sources of finance. The Republic of Yemen agreed to assume the international obligations of the two former countries, bequeathing the unified nation a combined official debt of approximately $7 billion.

Yemen's economy has been hampered by the widespread social habit of *qat* chewing. The mildly narcotic leaves of the qat shrub are chewed daily by men and women of all social classes. Qat chewing encourages lethargy, and North Yemenis tend to spend inordinate portions of their meager incomes on the leaves. A portion of Yemen's indigenous wealth and labor productivity is literally chewed away.

Qat has also affected North Yemen's agricultural industry. Most experts agree that for a farmer a qat bush is easy to grow, tolerates frequent cropping, and provides instant cash returns. Many fields that previously grew edible and exportable crops have been converted into qat fields. Some analysts argue that qat growing has saved the rural economy by returning money to the villages from the urban consumers. After centuries of food self-sufficiency, however, North Yemen has been transformed into an import-dependent country whose agricultural base has been slow to recover from the impact of prolonged droughts, civil strife, and qat growing.

Government efforts to discourage qat production have largely foundered. Recently the government appears to have accepted qat's prevalence and importance in Yemeni culture. Instead of attempting to limit its production, the authorities have tried to tax it.

With a low level of domestic industrial and agricultural output, Yemen today is dependent on revenues from its oil sector for virtually all of its essential needs. Estimates of Yemen's total oil reserves are about 4 billion barrels, and the likelihood for discovering more is high, especially in the South. In addition, Yemen has bountiful natural gas reserves in the North.

The discovery of oil in the eastern part of what was then North Yemen occurred in the early 1980s. By late 1988 North Yemen's oil production was targeted at two hundred thousand barrels a day. In 1987 South Yemen began producing oil, and by 1989 it began to export oil in significant quantities. Yemen's total oil production in 1994 stood at about three hundred twenty thousand barrels a day.

Kidnappings and hijackings are common in Yemen, particularly among oil company personnel working in remote areas where tribal leaders still operate their own fiefdoms with impunity. In February 1993 Yemen's oil minister warned that he could not guarantee the safety of foreign nationals working in Yemen. The government declared in September 1993 that it would establish a special force to protect foreign oil companies. The civil war threatened the substantial Western investment in Yemeni oil facilities and called into question further investment.

## Outlook

The civil war has soured most southern Yemenis' attitudes toward unification, although few were willing to back an all-out war of secession. Western correspondents reported that when Aden fell most residents greeted the end of the fighting with relief. Many analysts, however, have predicted that elements of the southern military will carry out a protracted guerrilla war against the government. Given the many remote areas in Yemen that could sustain guerrilla tactics and the presence of weapons throughout the country, such a war could be hard to put down.

About nine thousand southerners returned to Yemen under a general amnesty that ended on August 15, 1994. Some southern leaders have engaged the Sanaa government in discussions about how to put the country back together, but others remain abroad vowing to carry on a guerrilla war. Beidh, who fled to Oman, is said to have retired from political life. His vice president in the secessionist southern government, Abd al Rahman Jifri, has been one of the strongest advocates of continued struggle.

Continuing instability in Yemen would affect Saudi Arabia because tribal loyalties and connections cross the Saudi-Yemeni border. Guerrilla warfare in Yemen could create a refugee crisis or invite Iran or the Sudan to infiltrate the Islamic elements of the Sanaa government. Saudi Arabia and the Gulf states have been sympathetic toward Beidh and the South in this dispute, despite their Marxist past. The Saudi royal family remains angry at Sanaa's support for Iraqi president Saddam Hussein during the Persian Gulf War.

Most analysts are pessimistic that Yemen can be peacefully united in the near future, especially if foreign powers back opposite factions in the struggle. The civil war has rekindled old rivalries and suspicions. In addition, the recent confirmation of oil deposits in the South has caused southern leaders to believe that they would be better off economically on their own. The oil discoveries give Sanaa a more powerful incentive to hold onto the South by force.

Significantly, however, hope for eventual peace and unification remains because the civil war was not brought on by animosity between the citizens of the North and the South. The public does not see the political, economic, and social problems faced by their country as stemming from unification.

The civil war was a tragedy for the advancement of democracy on the Arabian Peninsula. By conducting relatively free and fair national elections, Yemen had proven itself an innovator among the countries of the Gulf. It had set a positive example of moving toward a free and democratic society, much faster than Kuwait and Saudi Arabia, whose populations have been clamoring for a similar commitment to pluralism and democracy from its leadership. Although the Yemeni civil war was not directly caused by the elections, it may make other Gulf leaders even more reticent to take steps toward democracy.

The ongoing crisis also increases the likelihood that President Salih will retain political control over the Yemeni People's Congress for the foreseeable future. No military officer or tribal leader appears to have sufficient charisma, influence, and ethnic ties to mount a credible challenge to his rule through normal political processes.

# APPENDIX

SKETCHES OF LEADERS

MAJOR EVENTS, 1990-94

DOCUMENTS

BIBLIOGRAPHY

# SKETCHES OF
# MIDDLE EAST LEADERS

---

Following are biographical sketches of some leading twentieth-century political figures in the Middle East.

*Abd-ul-Ilah (1913-58).* Regent of Iraq (1939-53); crown prince (1953-58). Educated at Victoria College, Alexandria. Became regent when his cousin King Faisal II succeeded to the throne at age three. Known for his loyalty to the boy king, his opposition to violent nationalism, and his cooperation with the West. Relinquished power to Faisal II when he reached majority in 1953. Assassinated with the king in Baghdad uprising July 14, 1958.

*Abdullah ibn Hussein (1882-1951).* Emir of Transjordan (1921-46); Hashemite king of Jordan (1946-51). Born in Mecca, second son of Hussein ibn Ali (later king of Hijaz). Played major role in Arab revolt against Turkey during World War I. In 1920 boldly occupied Transjordan; recognized as emir by the British, who held a mandate over the region. Established Transjordan as an entity separate from Palestine, extracting a pledge from British that Jews would not settle in his emirate.

In World War II sent his army, the Arab Legion, to assist British troops in Iraq and Syria. In 1946 rewarded with independence by Britain, renamed country Jordan, and became king. After the partition of Palestine in the 1948 Arab-Israeli War, Abdullah's army captured Old Jerusalem and held central Palestine for Arabs. When Jordan annexed these territories, Abdullah angered Egypt, Saudi Arabia, and Syria, which supported an independent Arab Palestine. Accused of betraying the Palestinian cause by negotiating with Israel and trying to settle Palestinian refugees in Jordan. Assassinated in Aqsa Mosque, Jerusalem, July 20, 1951, by a young Palestinian Arab.

*Abdullah al-Salem al-Sabah (1895-1965).* Emir of Kuwait in 1961 when British withdrew protection over the emirate and recognized Kuwait's independence. When Iraq threatened to make Kuwait a province, Abdullah deterred Iraqi action by obtaining British aid. Modernized the country by using vast oil wealth; shared riches with people to give Kuwait one of the world's highest standards of living.

*Abdel-ul-Shafi, Haidar (born 1919).* Headed Palestinian delegation to the 1991 Madrid Peace Conference. An influential medical doctor, born in Gaza. Also head of the Palestinian Red Crescent Society and founding member of the Palestine National Council. Participated in negotiations leading to Declaration of Principles in 1993 but openly criticized the 1994 Gaza-Jericho Accord, decrying Palestine Liberation Organization (PLO) concessions as capitulation to Israeli demands.

*Abu-Jaber, Kamal (born 1932).* Head of the Jordanian-Palestinian joint delegation to the Madrid Conference. A U.S.-educated professor of political science and foreign minister of Jordan.

*Aflaq, Michel (1910-89).* Syrian political thinker, born in Damascus. Co-founded the Ba'ath party with Salah al-Bitar. Promoted pan-Arabism, greatly influencing the postwar history of many Arab countries.

*Aoun, Michel (born 1936).* Former commander of the Maronite Christian brigades of the Lebanese army. Head of the provisional military government appointed by outgoing president Amin Gemayel in December 1988.

Became prime minister of East Beirut Christian military government, but Lebanon's Muslim community did not accept his premiership. Led unsuccessful Christian opposition to Syrian presence in Lebanon in 1989. Exiled in France since August 1991.

*Arafat, Yasir (born 1929).*   Head of the Palestine Liberation Organization since 1968. Trained as a guerrilla fighter, founded Al Fatah, a militantly nationalist Palestine organization, in 1957. Condemned the separate peace treaty between Egypt and Israel that was signed March 26, 1979. Evicted from Beirut September 1982 following the Israeli bombardment and set up new headquarters in Tunis.

In November 1988 became president of the newly formed Palestinian government in exile. Gained U.S. recognition of the PLO in December 1988 after explicitly renouncing terrorism and accepting UN resolutions 242 and 338. Stridently supported Iraq during the Persian Gulf War. Signed the Declaration of Principles with Israel in 1993. Took further steps toward Palestinian autonomy with the 1994 signing of the Gaza-Jericho Accord. Winner, along with Israeli leaders Yitzhak Rabin and Shimon Peres, of 1994 Nobel Peace Prize.

*Arens, Moshe (born 1925).*   Israeli defense minister (1990-92). Born in Lithuania; emigrated to the United States in 1939, then to Israel in 1948. Elected to the Israeli Knesset in 1977. Ambassador to Washington (1982-83) until appointed minister of defense when Ariel Sharon resigned in 1983.

Became minister without portfolio in the national unity government in 1984. Placed in charge of Arab affairs in 1986. Served as foreign minister in the 1988 national unity government.

*Arif, Abdul Rahman (born 1916).*   Ba'ath party leader, president of Iraq (1966-68). Became president when his brother, President Abdul Salem Arif, was killed in a helicopter crash April 13, 1966. Tried to end Kurdish revolt in northeast Iraq. During the 1967 Arab-Israeli War, sent troops to the Sinai and Jordan; cut off oil supplies to the West; severed diplomatic relations with the United States, Britain, and West Germany. The Arab defeat, Kurdish troubles, and economic problems led to his overthrow in a bloodless coup July 17, 1968; living in exile.

*Arif, Abdul Salem (1921-66).*   Headed the Ba'athist army coup that overthrew Iraqi dictator Abdul Karim Kassim, making Arif the Iraqi president in 1963. Improved relations with oil companies; dropped Iraqi claims to Kuwait. Killed in a helicopter crash near Basra April 13, 1966.

*al-Assad, Hafez (born 1930).*   President of Syria since 1971. Became defense minister in 1965; headed Nationalist faction of Ba'ath party. After an unsuccessful February 1969 coup, led a successful coup in November 1970, deposing President Nureddin al-Atasi. Assumed the presidency March 1971. Improved rela-

tions with Saudi Arabia and other conservative Arab states as well as with Egypt. Launched war against Israel on the Golan Heights in October 1973 but agreed to troop disengagement with the Jewish state in 1974. U.S.-Syrian relations, broken off in 1967, were resumed in 1974. Accepted massive Soviet military aid and Soviet advisers in Syria during the 1970s and 1980s. Took Syria into the Lebanese conflict in mid-1976. Supported Iran in the Iran-Iraq War and sent troops to fight in the anti-Iraq coalition during the 1991 Gulf War. Reelected president in 1991 for a fourth seven-year term. Demonstrated increased inclination to negotiate with Israel for peace, although progress was impeded by the Golan Heights issue and others.

*al-Atasi, Louai (born 1926).*   Syrian army officer and statesman. In March 1963 led the pro-Nasser military faction that seized control of the Syrian government. Commander in chief of Syria's armed forces and president of the Revolutionary Council (March-July 1963). Helped establish Ba'ath party predominance, ending its twenty-year clandestine existence. Resigned in 1963; in exile in Egypt since 1969.

*al-Atasi, Nureddin (born 1929).*   Syrian medical doctor and government official. Led Progressive faction of the Ba'ath party, favoring strong ties to the Soviet Union and a Marxist economy. Became president in 1966; deposed by Hafez al-Assad in a November 1970 bloodless coup and subsequently imprisoned. Reportedly released in the 1980s but prohibited from engaging in politics.

*Aziz, Tariq (born 1936).*   Iraqi Christian politician. Minister of information (1974-77). Deputy prime minister under Saddam Hussein (1979-83). Foreign minister (1983-91). In 1991 became deputy prime minister again, and a member of the Revolutionary Council Command. Acted as Iraq's chief negotiator throughout the Gulf crisis. In January 1991 met with U.S. secretary of state James A. Baker III in a failed attempt to avoid war. Appeared before the United Nations Security Council in May 1994, pleading on Saddam's behalf for a termination of sanctions against Iraq.

*Bakhtiar, Shahpur (1914-91).*   Iranian prime minister and opposition leader. Appointed by the shah in January 1979 to form a new civilian government just before the monarch left the country; expelled from membership in the National Front opposition coalition upon assuming the premiership. Resigned on February 12, 1979, when forces loyal to Muslim leader Ayatollah Khomeini took over the government. Fled to France, where he founded the National Resistance Movement. Assassinated in Paris in 1991.

*al-Bakr, Ahmed Hassan (1912-82).* President of Iraq (1968-79). Seized power in a bloodless coup on July 17, 1968, and assumed the presidency and premiership. Under his regime Iraq sought to end the Kurdish revolt by granting Kurds a measure of autonomy; but after Iraq settled differences with Iran, which had armed the Kurds, al-Bakr ordered the military to crush the revolt in March 1975. In April 1972 signed a fifteen-year friendship treaty with the Soviet Union; in June 1972 nationalized the Petroleum Co. Resigned for health reasons July 1979.

*Bani-Sadr, Abolhassan (born 1932).* Opponent of the shah of Iran, exiled to France where he became a leader of students abroad opposed to the shah. In direct contact with the exiled Ayatollah Khomeini after 1972. Following the shah's downfall, elected in January 1980 as first president of the Islamic Republic. In a victory for Iranian extremists, dismissed by Khomeini as president in June 1981. Fled to France in July 1981. In 1991 wrote *My Turn to Speak,* an account of his political career.

*al-Barzani, Mustafa (1904-79).* General and leader of the Kurdish revolt against Iraq. Declared war on the Baghdad government in 1974 after turning down an offer of limited autonomy. Iraqi armed forces crushed the revolt in March 1975. Fled into exile in Iran. Died a refugee in the United States.

*Begin, Menachem (1913-92).* Prime minister of Israel (1977-83). Commander of Irgun Jewish underground organization (1943-48), which launched a series of attacks against the British mandate authorities. In 1948 founded Herut opposition party. Became prime minister of Israel in June 1977 as leader of the conservative Likud bloc. His surprise election victory cast doubt over Israel's willingness to compromise on the Palestinian question and on the West Bank and Gaza Strip territories. Winner, along with Egypt's Anwar Sadat, of 1978 Nobel Peace Prize. Signed Camp David peace treaty with Egypt on March 26, 1979, at the White House in Washington, D.C. Reelected in June 1981. Resigned August 1983 and retired from public life.

*Ben-Gurion, David (1886-1973).* Zionist leader and Israel's first prime minister. Born in Poland; went to Palestine in 1906 as a laborer. Founded the Labor party. During World War I was expelled from Palestine by the Turks; went to New York where he formed the Zionist Labor party. Joined the Jewish Legion, part of British forces in Palestine. From 1918, lived in Tel Aviv and headed the Labor party.

Founded the underground Haganah organization in 1920 as a fighting force to defend the Jewish community in Palestine. At Tel Aviv May 14, 1948, read the public declaration of Israel's independence. Became prime minister and defense minister of the new state, holding both posts until 1963 except for one interlude. Sent troops into the Suez Canal conflict of 1956. Resigned as premier in June 1963 but remained in the Knesset until 1970.

*Ben-Zvi, Isaac (1884-1963).* Second president of Israel (1952-63). Went to Palestine in 1907 and helped found the Hashomer, a Jewish self-defense organization. After his exile by the Turks in 1915, went to New York and, with David Ben-Gurion, established the Hechalutz (Pioneer) movement and the Jewish Legion. Founder and chairman of the Vaad Leumi (National Council of Palestine Jews). Signed the Israeli declaration of independence. Elected to the Knesset in 1949 and the presidency on December 8, 1952, after Chaim Weizmann's death.

*Berri, Nabih (born 1938).* Leader of the Amal Shi'ite movement in Lebanon. Joined the Shi'ite movement known as the Movement of the Dispossessed shortly after it was founded by Imam Musa Sadr. In 1975, when Amal was created as the military wing of Imam Sadr's movement, became a member of its politburo. Elected to head Amal in 1980; reelected in 1986. Considered a moderate in Shi'ite politics and an ally of the Syrians; has had difficulty controlling radical factions within Amal and rival Shi'ite movement Hizballah. Became a minister under Amin Gemayel but remained for the most part an opponent of the government. Became minister of justice in national unity government formed in 1984; reappointed to the position by Lebanese Muslim government created in 1988. Became Speaker of parliament in 1992.

*al-Bitar, Salah (1912-80).* Syrian prime minister. Helped create the Socialist Ba'ath party, which became Syria's ruling party, and the short-lived United Arab Republic, a union between Syria and Egypt. Led a pro-Nasser coup in Syria that on March 8, 1963, resulted in Bitar's becoming premier. Held that post intermittently until 1966. Killed in Paris in 1980 by assassins allegedly under Syrian orders.

*Chamoun, Camille (1900-87).* President of Lebanon (1952-58) and prominent Maronite politician. In 1958 his pro-Western policies led to open Muslim revolt. At his request President Dwight D. Eisenhower sent U.S. Marines into Lebanon in July 1958 to help restore order. In July 1975 became defense and foreign minister in "rescue cabinet" formed to end bloody Muslim-Christian clashes over Palestinian refugee issue in Lebanon. Headed the National Liberal party

(1958-86). From 1984 until his death, served as Lebanese finance minister.

*Chehab, Fuad (1903-73).* President of Lebanon (1958-64). Served as commander in chief of the Lebanese army, prime minister, interior minister, and defense minister. As president, pursued a neutralist policy acceptable to Arabs and the West. Put down an attempt to overthrow his government by the Syrian Popular party, which sought Lebanese union with Syria.

*Dayan, Moshe (1915-81).* Israeli military commander and political leader. Member of Jewish police force (1936-39). Chief of staff for all Israeli forces (1953-58); prepared plans for the invasion of the Sinai Peninsula during the 1956 Suez crisis. Elected to the Knesset in 1959 on the Labor party ticket. Appointed defense minister in 1966 and became a hero of the 1967 Six-Day War. Quit the cabinet in 1974 after criticism over the army's lack of preparedness during the 1973 Arab-Israeli War. In 1977 defected from the Labor party to become foreign minister in Menachem Begin's government. Resigned as foreign minister in October 1979 in protest of Israel's hard-line settlements policy.

*Eban, Abba (born 1915).* Israeli diplomat and member of the Knesset. Deputy prime minister of Israel (1963-66); foreign minister (1966-74). Worked to maintain strong U.S.-Israeli ties; architect of several Middle East peace plans. Appointed chairman of Knesset Foreign Affairs and Security Committee in 1984. Excluded in 1988 from list of candidates to the Knesset.

*Eshkol, Levi (1895-1969).* Finance minister of Israel when David Ben-Gurion resigned the premiership in 1963; succeeded him as prime minister (1963-69). Under his leadership, Israel defeated the Arab states in the Six-Day War of 1967.

*Fadlallah, Muhammad Hussein (born 1939).* Spiritual leader of Lebanon's Shi'ite Hizballah organization, a radical fundamentalist group with ties to Iran. Thought to maintain some influence over Islamic Jihad and other radical fundamentalist groups in Lebanon.

*Fahd ibn Abdul Aziz (born 1922).* Succeeded Khalid as king of Saudi Arabia in June 1982. As crown prince after King Faisal's death in 1975 and later as king, Fahd has been regarded as the most important figure in shaping Saudi foreign policy. Wrote the first Middle East peace initiative sponsored by Saudi Arabia in 1981. The Iraqi invasion of Kuwait compelled Fahd to break traditional Saudi policy and allow deployment of multinational armed forces to the kingdom. After the Gulf War, Fahd established consulta-

tive councils and implemented some minor political changes.

*Faisal ibn Abdul Aziz al-Saud (1906-75).* King of Saudi Arabia (1964-75). Became crown prince when his brother, King Saud, ascended to the throne in 1953. Served as prime minister, foreign minister, defense minister, and finance minister. Became king in March 1964 when Saud was legally deposed. Supported pan-Arab and pan-Islam solidarity. Pressed for economic and educational advances.

A Muslim ascetic and anti-Communist, Faisal called for Israel to evacuate Islamic holy places in Jerusalem and all occupied Arab territory. Fostered ties with United States and supported conservative Arab regimes. During 1973 Arab-Israeli War, enforced the Arab oil embargo and price hike against the United States, Western Europe, and Japan. Assassinated by a nephew March 25, 1975, in Riyadh.

*Faisal I (Faisal ibn Hussein) (1885-1933).* King of Iraq (1921-33). Horrified by Turkish anti-Arab actions, led an Arab revolt, assisted by T. E. Lawrence (Lawrence of Arabia) and the British, against the Ottomans in World War I. To consolidate an Arab state in Syria, served briefly as king of Syria in 1920 until expelled by the French, who held a mandate for Syria. With British help, elected in 1921 to a second throne in Baghdad.

*Faisal II (1936-58).* King of Iraq (1939-58). Inherited the throne at age three upon the accidental death of King Ghazi. Crowned May 2, 1953. During his five-year reign, Iraq pursued an anti-Communist course, culminating in the 1955 Baghdad Pact in which Britain, Iran, Iraq, Pakistan, and Turkey pledged to thwart possible Soviet intrusion into the Middle East. Assassinated July 14, 1958, with most members of the royal family in Baghdad revolution, which resulted in Iraq's being declared a republic.

*Farouk I (1920-65).* King of Egypt (1936-52). Reign marked by his quarrel with the dominant Wafd party and with the British over the Sudan. The disastrous campaign against Israel in 1948 and charges of corruption connected with arms purchases damaged his public standing. Forced to abdicate after a military coup in July 1952. Died in exile in Italy.

*Franjieh, Suleiman (born 1910).* President of Lebanon (1970-76). Maronite Christian and strong supporter of Syria. During the crisis of 1975 between rightist Christians and leftist Muslims, could not develop a formula for a government placating all sides. Refused to leave the presidency, even after a petition from parliament and a military assault on his residence, until his term of office expired in September 1976. His staunch support of Syria alienated leaders of Maronite Lebanese Forces.

*Fuad I (1868-1936).* King of Egypt (1922-36). Proclaimed king when Britain relinquished its protectorate over Egypt in 1922. Fuad's reign was marked by a struggle between the Wafd party and palace parties centering around the king. Established the first Western-style Egyptian university, the Fuad I (now Cairo) University, in 1925.

*Gemayel, Amin (born 1942).* President of Lebanon (1982-88). Son of Pierre Gemayel. Elected September 1982 to succeed his slain brother, Bashir. Although Amin was a Phalangist deputy, Phalange extremist groups refused to recognize him as their leader. His pro-American policies also antagonized other sects. Retained only nominal control of the country amidst continued civil unrest. His six-year term ended without the election of a successor. Appointed Michel Aoun as the head of an interim military government in the last minutes of his presidency. Retired from politics in 1988.

*Gemayel, Bashir (1947-82).* Son of Pierre Gemayel and brother of Amin Gemayel. Commander of Phalange militia. Elected August 1982 as president of Lebanon with Israeli support and pressure. Once elected, Gemayel tried to adopt a more neutral stance. Killed by a bomb while speaking at Phalange party headquarters in East Beirut September 1982.

*Gemayel, Pierre (1905-84).* Leader of the Phalange party in Lebanon. Became member of parliament in 1960 and held office in most Lebanese governments. Ran for the presidency in 1970 but withdrew in favor of neutral candidate Suleiman Franjieh.

*Habash, George (born 1925).* Palestinian leader of "rejection front" that refuses to consider coexistence with Israel. In 1970 his Popular Front for the Liberation of Palestine (PFLP) became known for its hijacking of foreign planes. The PFLP was held responsible for triggering the Jordanian civil war in 1970 and for helping spark the Lebanese civil war in 1975. Opposes Arafat's peace with Israel.

*Harawi, Elias (born 1930).* Lebanese president and Maronite Christian. In 1989, after assassination of the newly elected René Muawwad, Harawi was elected president for a six-year term. His policies are guided by Syria in accordance with a 1991 Lebanese-Syrian treaty. Under Syrian direction, he has increased the Lebanese territory his regime controls and has dissolved many opposing militias.

*Hassan ibn Talal (born 1947).* Crown Prince of Jordan. Brother of King Hussein and heir to the throne. Appointed crown prince in 1965. Ombudsman for National Development since 1971; founder of the Royal Scientific Society in Jordan.

*Helou, Charles (born 1911).* President of Lebanon (1964-70). Former banker, journalist, and diplomat who was a compromise choice for president in 1964. Steered a neutralist course between the West and neighboring Arab countries. Retired from politics after his presidential term expired in 1970.

*Herzog, Chaim (born 1918).* President of Israel (1983-93). Previously a member of the Knesset and Israel's ambassador to the United Nations (1975). Military governor of the West Bank (1967) and Israel's first chief of military intelligence.

*Hussein ibn Ali (Sherif Hussein, 1854-1931).* Emir of Mecca (1908-16); king of Hijaz (now part of Saudi Arabia, 1916-24). During World War I his negotiations with the British led to Arab revolt against Turkey. Opposed mandatory regimes imposed on Syria, Palestine, and Iraq by the Versailles Treaty. Hijaz kingdom attacked by Ibn Saud of the Wahhabi sect; Hussein forced to abdicate in 1924 and exiled to Cyprus. Hussein's son Ali was king of Hijaz briefly; another son, Abdullah, became king of Jordan; a third son became King Faisal I of Iraq.

*Hussein, Saddam (born 1937).* President of Iraq since July 1979. Succeeded Ahmed Hassam al-Bakr, who resigned for health reasons. Former vice chairman of the Revolutionary Command Council. Helped bring about détente with Iran in 1975, but as president launched an invasion of that country September 1980 that developed into a costly eight-year war. Moved away from alliance with the Soviet Union and toward a closer relationship with moderate Arab states during the war. Restored diplomatic relations with the United States 1984. Concluded a cease-fire with Iran August 20, 1988. Ordered the use of chemical weapons against Kurdish population in northern Iraq in the late 1980s.

In August 1990 invaded Kuwait. Gained favor and support in some Arab countries by promoting his aggression as a holy war. Refused to withdraw from Kuwait until decisively defeated by U.S.-led coalition in early 1991. Despite Gulf War destruction, an international embargo, and Kurdish and Shi-ite independence movements, has maintained power in Iraq. Moved troops close to Kuwait border again in October 1994 but pulled back under U.S. pressure.

*Hussein ibn Talal (born 1935).* King of Jordan

since 1953. Educated at Royal Military Academy, Sandhurst, England. Crowned May 2, 1953, after his father, King Talal, was declared mentally ill. In 1956 abrogated Jordan's treaty with Britain. Accepted U.S. economic aid.

Supported Nasser in Egypt's 1967 war against Israel. After losing half his kingdom (West Bank of the Jordan River), tried to deal indirectly with Israel to recover lost lands. Crushed Palestinian guerrilla enclaves during 1970 civil war between his army and Palestinians. At Rabat summit conference of the Arab League in 1974, the right to negotiate for return of the West Bank was taken from Hussein and given to the Palestine Liberation Organization. Hussein denounced the Egyptian-Israeli peace treaty signed in March 1979 and broke off relations with Egypt. Restored diplomatic ties with Egypt September 1984. Surrendered Jordan's claim to the West Bank in favor of the PLO and announced the breaking of all legal and administrative ties to the Israeli-occupied territory in August 1988. Faced sharp international criticism for his pro-Iraqi stance in the Gulf War but remained popular with his subjects. In July 1994 signed the Washington Declaration, ending a forty-six-year state of war with Israel and taking first steps toward a comprehensive peace.

*Ibn Saud (1880-1953).*  First king of Saudi Arabia (1932-53). Made war on King Hussein of Hijaz, forcing him to abdicate and leading to the merger of the Hijaz and Najd kingdoms into Saudi Arabia in 1932. Worked to consolidate his realm and improve relations with his enemies in other Arab states.

In 1933 granted a sixty-year oil concession to a U.S. oil company that became ARAMCO. Oil royalties greatly enriched his treasury. In 1945 helped form the Arab League.

*Idris I (1890-1983).*  King of Libya (1951-69). As emir of Cyrenaica, fought Italian occupation of Libya. Was declared constitutional monarch when Libya was made an independent state in 1951. Deposed September 1, 1969, by a coup led by Col. Muammar al-Qaddafi, who declared Libya a Socialist republic. Lived in exile in Egypt until his death in May 1983.

*Isa bin Sulman al-Khalifa (born 1933).*  Emir of Bahrain. Declared Bahrain's independence after Britain quit the Persian Gulf in 1971. Rejected a proposed federation of Bahrain with neighboring Qatar and United Arab Emirates.

*Isma'il, Abd al-Fattah (1939-86).*  President of South Yemen (1978-80). Pro-Soviet politician, served as secretary general of the National Liberation Front (1971-78). Following coup against Rubayi Ali in 1978 became general secretary of the reorganized Yemen Socialist party and was elected head of state. Resigned from both positions and moved to Moscow in 1980, presumably because of an internal power struggle. Returned to South Yemen in 1985 and was elected to the politburo. His return precipitated January 1986 coup and subsequent civil war. Wounded during the fighting and presumed dead.

*Jumblatt, Kamal (1917-77).*  Father of Walid Jumblatt. Leader of leftist forces in Lebanese civil war. Strong supporter of the Palestinian cause and of secular reforms that would change the practice in Lebanon of distributing public offices among the country's religious factions. Assassinated in March 1977.

*Jumblatt, Walid (born 1949).*  In 1977 succeeded his father, Kamal, as leader of Lebanon's Druze-dominated Progressive Socialist party, which maintains a close political-military relationship with Syria. A leader of the revolt against Amin Gemayel in 1983. Druze military victories established him as an influential politician. Subsequently joined the cabinet but remained one of Gemayel's most vociferous opponents. Minister of public works, transport, and tourism in the Muslim government created in 1988. Retired from public affairs in 1990.

*Karami, Rashid (1921-87).*  Four-time prime minister of Lebanon and influential Sunni politician. Born in Tripoli; educated in Cairo. Served as prime minister under Camille Chamoun (1955-56) but resigned after a dispute with Chamoun. Served as prime minister again under Fuad Chehab and Charles Helou (1958-69) until resigning in 1969 to protest the violent suppression of a pro-Palestinian demonstration. Reappointed prime minister by Suleiman Franjieh during the civil war (1975-76). Held the office for a fourth time beginning in 1984 under Amin Gemayel, with whom he had a strained relationship. Made numerous unsuccessful attempts to promote national reconciliation. Resigned May 1984, but his resignation was not accepted. Assassinated in June 1987.

*Kassim, Abdul Karim (1914-63).*  Iraqi dictator (1958-63). As an army general, led July 14, 1958, military revolution that killed young King Faisal II and most of the royal family. After the revolution a republic was proclaimed and Kassim was named prime minister. Withdrew Iraq from the Baghdad Pact and improved relations with the Soviet Union and China. Escaped an attempted assassination in October 1959.

Crushed a Kurdish revolt in 1962. Laid claim to Kuwait after its independence in 1961, but British sent troops to Kuwait's aid, deterring any Iraqi action. Executed after a coup by "free officers" of Ba'ath party in 1963.

*Khalaf, Salah (1933-91).* PLO security chief. Born in Jaffa. Educated at University of Cairo, where he joined Yasir Arafat in the Palestinian Student's Union. In 1970 took part in Black September Palestinian fighting in Jordan. Member of the Palestine Central Council since 1973. A leader of al-Fatah and close ally of Arafat. Assassinated in 1991 in Tunis reportedly by associates of Abu Nidal.

*Khalid ibn Abdul Aziz (1913-82).* King of Saudi Arabia (1975-82). Became vice president of the Council of Ministers, 1962; elevated to crown prince, 1965; succeeded to throne when King Faisal was assassinated in March 1975. Died of a heart attack in June 1982.

*Khalifa bin Hamad al-Thani (born 1937).* Emir of Qatar. Assumed power after deposing his cousin, Emir Ahmad bin Ali bin Abdullah al-Thani, in a bloodless coup February 22, 1972. Headed a program of social and economic improvements made possible by oil revenues. Joined in the Arab oil embargo against the West in 1973.

*Khamenei, Ayatollah Ali (born 1939).* Iranian spiritual leader. A disciple of Ayatollah Ruhollah Khomeini in Qom, Khamenei was one of the most active Shi'ite clerics in the Iranian revolution. Imprisoned twice for opposition to the shah. Cofounded the Islamic Republic party in 1978. Elected as third president of the Islamic Republic in October 1981. Reelected to a second presidential term 1985. Appointed spiritual leader of Iran upon Khomeini's death in June 1989.

*Khomeini, Ayatollah Ruhollah (1902-89).* Shi'ite Muslim leader of Iran (1979-89) who established the Islamic Republic. Educated in the theological center in Qom. Led political protests against the shah's social reforms (1962-63), resulting in his exile to Turkey in 1963, then Iraq a year later. During his fifteen-year exile, Khomeini issued statements guiding the antishah protests of clerics in Iran. Expelled from Iraq in 1978 for conducting political agitation. Lived in France until the overthrow of the shah, returning to Iran on February 1, 1979.

Khomeini forces formed Council of the Islamic Revolution to replace the shah-appointed Bakhtiar government. In March 1981 he ordered a national referendum to seek support for the new Islamic Republic. Decided to accept a cease-fire of the eight-year Iran-Iraq War July 1988, reversing his unflinching commitment to overthrow Iraq's President Saddam Hussein. Died in Tehran June 3, 1989.

*al-Khoury, Bishara (1895-1964).* Elected president of Lebanon in 1943 while the Free French controlled the country. After the French arrested Khoury and other government officials, an insurrection led to restoration of the Lebanese government. In 1946 France relinquished its Lebanese mandate and Lebanon became independent. During Khoury's presidency, Beirut became a trade and financial center. Khoury's abuses of power angered the public and he was deposed by a popular movement in 1952.

*Kuwatly, Shukri (1891-1967).* Twice Syrian president. During 1920s and 1930s emerged as a nationalist leader opposed to the French mandate. Elected president in 1943 while the Free French controlled Syria; secured the withdrawal of the French and attainment of Syrian independence in 1946. Overthrown by a 1949 coup. Returned from exile in 1954 and advocated a broad Arab union led by Egypt. Elected president again in 1955, serving until 1958, when United Arab Republic of Egypt and Syria was inaugurated.

*Meir, Golda (1898-1978).* Israeli prime minister (1969-74). Also served as ambassador to the Soviet Union, minister of labor, and minister of foreign affairs. A native of Kiev, Russia, Meir was brought to the United States in 1906; she emigrated to Palestine in 1921. Active in labor movement, World Zionist Organization, and Haganah movement to establish a Jewish state.

While prime minister maintained an inflexible policy vis-à-vis Arab states. Her government received criticism for lack of preparedness for the 1973 Arab-Israeli War. Unable to form a new government after several tries, she relinquished premiership in 1974.

*Montazeri, Ayatollah Hussein Ali (born 1922).* Iranian religious leader. Studied theology in Isfahan, then went to Qom where he met Ayatollah Khomeini. Entered politics in the early sixties, assuming leadership of a sit-in protest against the shah. After the Islamic revolution, elected to the Council of Experts, later becoming its Speaker. Khomeini designated him as his successor in November 1985. Lost favor with Khomeini and resigned under pressure in March 1989 amidst turmoil within Iran's political leadership.

*Mossadeq, Muhammad (1880-1967).* Iranian prime minister. Largely responsible for nationalizing the Anglo-Iranian Oil Company in 1951. His efforts to obtain more political power led to strained relations with the shah. Overthrown by the military in April 1953; later sentenced to a three-year prison term for treason.

*Mousavi, Mir Hossein (born 1941).* Iranian prime

minister (1981-89). Founded the Islamic Society of Students in Iran. Arrested in 1973 for opposing the monarchy. Elected prime minister in November 1981; reelected in 1985 and 1988. Involved mainly in domestic issues. Believed to be an advocate of strong government control of industry and trade. Lost post in July 1989 when office of prime minister was abolished by a constitutional referendum.

*Mubarak, Hosni (born 1928).*   President of Egypt. Appointed air force chief of staff 1969; became its commander in 1972; credited with air force's successful performance in the early days of the October 1973 war with Israel. Appointed vice president in 1975. Presided over cabinet meetings and attended most international discussions on Middle East policy. Elected president of Egypt following the assassination of Anwar al-Sadat on October 6, 1981. Reelected for a third six-year term in 1993. During Gulf War, took unyielding stance against the Iraqi invasion, leading Arab opposition to it.

*Naguib, Muhammad (1901-84).*   President of Egypt when it was declared a republic in 1953. Leader of the Free Officer junta that opposed King Farouk. Ousted after a power struggle with Nasser in 1954.

*Nasser, Gamal Abdel (1918-70).*   Egyptian president (1954-70). As head of the Revolutionary Command Council, Nasser led a revolt that deposed King Farouk and established a republic on June 18, 1953. Became president after a power struggle with President Naguib. Negotiated the withdrawal of British troops from the Suez Canal zone in 1954 and nationalized the canal in 1956, prompting Anglo-French-Israeli military intervention. After the United States forced allies to withdraw, Nasser's prestige grew in the Arab world. Created the United Arab Republic, a union between Egypt and Syria, in 1958 and served as its president until Syria seceded in 1961.

Israel's defeat of Egypt in 1967 led to détente between Nasser and conservative Arab states that had distrusted his revolutionary goals. Received revenues from Saudi Arabia and Kuwait and arms from the Soviet Union. At home, pursued a course of social justice, redistribution of land, improved medical care, and education. Construction of the Aswan Dam symbolized his achievements. Died of a heart attack following the September 1970 conference in Cairo that ended the Jordanian civil war.

*Pahlavi, Muhammad Reza (1919-80).*   Shah of Iran (1941-79). Became shah upon the abdication of his father, Reza Shah Pahlavi. Established a close alliance with the United States. Staged a counter-coup in 1953 to regain control of the government from prime minister

Mossadeq. Launched a land and social reform program known as the White Revolution in the 1960s. The shah's thirty-seven-year reign as monarch ended January 16, 1979, when he left Iran for an "extended vacation," a few weeks before Muslim leader Ayatollah Khomeini returned from exile to set up the new Islamic Republic. In 1980 Iranians demanded return of the shah for trial as a condition for release of American hostages. Died in Cairo of cancer, July 27, 1980.

*Pahlavi, Reza Shah (1878-1944).*   Shah of Iran (1925-41). Gained the throne after a coup deposed Ahmad Shah. Autocratic ruler who ignored constitutional safeguards. Built Trans-Iranian Railway; developed road system. Sought machinery and technicians from Germany, which led to the World War II occupation of Iran by British and Soviet troops. Forced to abdicate by the British and the Soviets in 1941 in favor of his son, Muhammad Reza Pahlavi.

*Peres, Shimon (born 1923).*   Israeli Labor party politician. Became acting prime minister in April 1977 when Yitzhak Rabin resigned because of a scandal. Designated as Labor's choice for prime minister in 1977 and 1981, but was defeated by Menachem Begin's conservative Likud party. Prime minister of Israel for twenty-five months (1984-86). Was instrumental in bringing about the withdrawal of the Israeli army from Lebanon. Rotated out of the premiership in accordance with a coalition agreement between the Labor and Likud parties. Served as foreign minister for the remainder (1986-88) of the coalition's fifty-one-month term. Became finance minister under the coalition government formed in December 1988. Became minister of foreign affairs again in 1992. Winner, along with Prime Minister Yitzhak Rabin and PLO Chairman Yasir Arafat, of 1994 Nobel Peace Prize.

*Qaboos bin Said (born 1942).*   Sultan and absolute ruler of Oman since 1970 when he overthrew his father, Sultan Said bin Taimur, one of century's most tyrannical despots. Educated in Britain, Qaboos embarked on an ambitious program of social and economic development after assuming power. Defeated Dhofari rebels after a military offensive in 1975. Also improved relations with his Arab neighbors, particularly members of the Gulf Cooperation Council. Established relations with the Soviet Union in 1985, while maintaining close ties with the United States.

*al-Qaddafi, Muammar (born 1942).*   Chairman of the Revolutionary Command Council of Libya since 1969 when he led a coup that overthrew King Idris. Educated at the University of Libya and the Libyan Military Academy. Evicted the United States and Britain from Libyan military bases and nationalized Libya's oil industry. Tried unsuccessfully to extend his influence and achieve Arab unity through merger schemes with Egypt and Tunisia.

Known for his implacable enmity toward Israel and the United States. Strong supporter of Palestinian "rejectionist front" and other radical Arab movements. The United States bombed Libyan targets in 1986 in retaliation for Qaddafi's support of terrorism. Built modern army from Soviet-supplied weapons but suffered military defeats in Chad after Libya invaded that country in 1987. Suspected of link to terrorist bombing of Pan Am Flight 103 over Lockerbie, Scotland, on December 21, 1988.

*Rabin, Yitzhak (born 1922).* Prime minister of Israel (1974-77; 1992- ). Chief of staff of the Israeli army; credited with planning Israel's overwhelming victory in the 1967 war. Served as ambassador to Washington (1982-83). Became prime minister when Golda Meir retired in 1974. After a scandal involving an illegal bank account held in Washington by his wife, Rabin resigned as prime minister in April 1977. Became defense minister in 1984 and retained the post in 1988 coalition government.

Elected prime minister in 1992. Implementing a progressive strategy of compromise, Rabin took the first steps toward a comprehensive peace for Israel, first signing the Declaration of Principles with the PLO in September 1993 and then the Washington Declaration with Jordan in July 1994. Rabin also has demonstrated a commitment to finding a peace with Syria as discussions of Israeli withdrawal from Golan have commenced. Winner, along with Foreign Minister Shimon Peres and PLO Chairman Yasir Arafat, of 1994 Nobel Peace Prize.

*Rafsanjani, Ali Akbar Hashemi (born 1934).* President of Iran since 1989. Studied under Khomeini in Qom, organized opposition movements in Iran leading to the 1979 revolution. In 1980 elected to Majlis (parliament) as a member from Tehran and elected Speaker later the same year. Was Khomeini's representative on the Supreme Defense Council. In June 1988 appointed acting commander in chief of Iranian armed forces. Elected president in July 1989 following Khomeini's death. Reelected president in 1993 for a second four-year term. Since 1989 has tried to lead Iran in a more pragmatic direction. Was target of an assassination attempt in January 1994.

*al-Rifai, Zaid Samir (born 1936).* Jordanian prime minister (1985-89). In 1972 became a political adviser to King Hussein and was later appointed minister of defense and minister of foreign affairs (1974-76). Ac-

cused by the Black September organization in Jordan of playing a leading role in the Jordanian effort to liquidate the Palestinian resistance during the 1970-71 struggles. Became prime minister upon the resignation of Ahmad Ubeidat April 1985. Resigned April 1989 amidst public protests against government price hikes and accusations of corruption.

*al-Sabah, Jaber Al-Ahmed (born 1920).* Emir of Kuwait. Ruled Kuwait since the 1977 death of Sabah al-Salem al-Sabah. In 1980 revived the National Assembly, which had been suspended since 1976. Suspended assembly again in July 1986 amid acrimonious debates on foreign affairs and internal matters.

Escaped to Saudi Arabia and established a government in exile following the Iraqi invasion of August 1990. Returned to the emirate after liberation in February 1991. Responded to calls for reform by announcing formation of a new Council of Ministers and 1992 elections for the National Assembly. Retained full control, however, over the vital matters of defense, foreign affairs, and the interior.

*al-Sadat, Anwar (1918-81).* President of Egypt (1970-81). Educated at Military College, Cairo. Deputy to President Nasser in organizing the secret revolutionary brotherhood that overthrew the monarchy. Speaker of the National Assembly and twice vice president. Became president when Nasser died in 1970.

In 1972 ordered twenty thousand Soviet military advisers out of Egypt. Became Arab hero in the 1973 war with Israel when Egypt won initial victories. Agreed to troop disengagement accords in the Sinai in 1975. Moved his country away from the radical socialism of Nasser to attract Western capital.

In June 1975 reopened the Suez Canal after an eight-year closure. Participated in the Camp David peace talks that won him and Israel's Menachem Begin the 1978 Nobel Peace Prize. In March 1979 signed the Egyptian-Israeli peace treaty with Israel, incurring the wrath of Egypt's Arab neighbors. Assassinated October 6, 1981, by Muslim extremists.

*Said, Nuri (1888-1958).* Iraqi officer and influential politician. Prime minister eight times between 1930 and 1958, often also serving as foreign or defense minister. Instrumental in developing the institutions of the Iraqi state and obtaining its independence. Assassinated in a 1958 coup.

*Salih, Ali Abdullah (born 1942).* President of North Yemen since 1978 and president of the Republic of Yemen since its unification in 1990. Elected North Yemen president in July 1978 following the assassination of Ahmed ibn Hussein al-Ghashmi. Attempts by southern leaders to secede and Salih's military response led the Republic of Yemen into a civil war with an uncertain future.

*Sarkis, Elias (1924-86).* President of Lebanon (1976-82). Assumed office September 1976 during civil war, succeeding Suleiman Franjieh. Supported by Syrians over Raymond Edde. Died in exile in Paris June 1986.

*Saud ibn Faisal (born 1941).* Foreign minister of Saudi Arabia since 1975. Saudi prince; fourth of the eight sons of the late King Faisal. Educated at Princeton University. Possible future king.

*Saud IV (1902-69).* King of Saudi Arabia (1953-64). Succeeded his father, Ibn Saud. Expanded his father's modernization program. Continued friendship with the United States and all Arab nations. Suspicious of communism and firmly opposed to Israel. Abdicated in 1964 after the royal family effectively transferred power to his brother, who became King Faisal.

*Shah of Iran.* See *Muhammad Reza Pahlavi.*

*Shamir, Yitzhak (born 1915).* Prime minister of Israel in the national coalition government formed in December 1988. Born in Poland, emigrated to Palestine in 1935 and studied law in Jerusalem. Member of Irgun underground resistance organization (1937-40). Later joined the Stern Gang, a more radical underground organization, becoming its leader in 1942. Israeli intelligence operative abroad 1948-65.
Elected to the Knesset in 1973 on the Herut party list, serving as parliamentary Speaker 1977-80. Foreign minister (1980-83); then appointed prime minister after Begin's resignation in 1983. In 1984 Shamir's Likud party concluded a coalition agreement with the Labor party that provided for a rotating premiership. Shamir served as foreign minister (1984-86), then as prime minister (1986-88). After the 1988 elections another coalition government was formed, in which Shamir continued as prime minister until 1992.

*Sharon, Ariel (born 1928).* Defense minister during Israel's invasion of Lebanon. Served as military officer in 1967 and 1973 wars. Elected to the Knesset in 1973 on the Likud party ticket; resigned in 1974. Appointed minister of defense in second Begin government in 1981. Planned January 1982 invasion of Lebanon. Personally involved in all stages of the Lebanese war; frequently charged with concealing his moves from the prime minister. Forced to resign as defense minister after the massacres at the Sabra and Shatilla refugee camps, but remained in the cabinet as minister without portfolio.

Appointed minister of industry and trade in 1984 and reappointed by the coalition government of 1988. Served as minister of housing 1990-92. Sharply criticized Israeli-PLO accord. Remains active in Likud politics.

*al-Solh, Rashid (born 1926).* Lebanese premier (1973-75). Resigned amid criticism of his handling of the bloody Christian-Muslim riots that put Lebanon on the brink of civil war. Deputy in parliament during the 1980s. Briefly served again as prime minister in May-October 1992.

*al-Tal, Wasfi (1920-71).* Prime minister of Jordan five times between 1962 and 1971. Assassinated in Cairo November 1971 by Black September, a Palestinian terrorist organization, in reprisal for the Jordanian government's crushing of Palestinian strongholds in Jordan.

*Talal (1909-72).* King of Jordan (1951-52). Deposed in 1952 after being declared mentally ill by the Jordanian parliament. Spent rest of his life in a mental institution in Turkey. Succeeded by his son, King Hussein.

*Wazir, Khalil (1933-88).* Former military chief of the Palestine Liberation Organization. Also known as Abu Jihad. After June 1967 Six-Day War, became responsible for Palestinian military operations launched against Israel from Jordan, Syria, and Lebanon. Served as commander in chief of PLO in Yasir Arafat's absence. Became a close associate of Arafat and enjoyed wide prestige within the PLO. Assassinated April 1988 at his home in Tunis by a commando unit suspected to have been dispatched from Israel.

*Weizman, Ezer (born 1924).* President of Israel. Commander of Israeli air force (1958-66), army deputy chief of staff (1966-69), and businessman until appointed defense minister in 1977. Played major role in negotiating Egypt-Israel peace treaty. Resigned May 1980 to protest government's settlement policy in occupied territories. Returned to politics in 1984. Served as minister of science and development 1988-90. Elected president in 1993.

*Weizmann, Chaim (1874-1952).* First president of Israel (1948-52). Born in Russia; educated in Germany. Headed British Admiralty Laboratories that created synthetic acetene for explosives in World War I. Rewarded with Balfour Declaration, a British white paper that called for creation of a homeland for Jews in Palestine. President of the World Zionist Organization (1920-31). In 1947 headed the Jewish Agency delegation to the United Nations.

*Yamani, Ahmed Zaki (born 1930).* Saudi Arabia's minister of petroleum and mineral resources (1962-86). A commoner descended from desert tribesmen; educated at the University of Cairo, New York University, and Harvard. Leader in formulating participation agreements with oil companies in Arab states, in devising 1973-74 oil embargo against the West, and in setting Organization of Petroleum Exporting Countries (OPEC) oil prices. Dismissed in 1986 because of disagreements with the Saudi leadership over future oil policies.

*Zayed ibn Sultan al-Nahayan (born circa 1916).* Emir of Abu Dhabi, president of the federation of the United Arab Emirates since its formation in December 1971. Used vast oil wealth to modernize his sheikdom and provide social programs for its people.

# MAJOR EVENTS, 1900-94

*Following is a chronological listing of major events in Middle Eastern history from the beginning of the twentieth century through October 1994.*

*1900.* Russia lends Persia funds to secure Russian commercial and political influence throughout the region.

*1901.* Fifth Zionist Congress begins collections for the Jewish National Fund to purchase land in Palestine. May, Iran grants William D'Arcy a concession to search for oil.

*1902.* First Aswan Dam opens, greatly expanding irrigation and food production in Egypt. Ibn Saud makes successful raid on Riyadh against Ottoman forces.

*1903.* August 22, Zionist Congress opens at Basel, Switzerland.

*1904.* April, Anglo-French Entente Cordiale ends contest for control of Egypt.

*1905.* Death of Muhammad Abduh, leader of Egyptian Islamic modernist movement opposed to foreigners and imperialist occupation. December, prominent Iranian business and religious leaders protest shah's corruption and demand "House of Justice" for safe expression of views opposing the government.

*1906.* May 13, Sinai Peninsula officially becomes part of Egypt after the British force the Ottomans to withdraw from Taba. December, Iranian revolution erupts in response to British and Russian intervention and local corruption; shah is forced to grant constitution.

*1907.* January 4, Muzaffar Ali Shah, Persian monarch, dies. August 31, Anglo-Russian agreement divides Iranian territory into separate spheres of influence.

*1908.* May 26, first major oil strike in Iran is made at Masjed Soleyman. July, Muhammad Ali Shah is forced to abdicate in Iran. July 21, after uniting under Committee of Union and Progress, Young Turk movements demand the sultan's immediate restoration of Ottoman constitution.

*1909.* Anglo-Persian Oil Company is formed to exploit the D'Arcy concession in Iran. April, Ottoman counterrevolt quashes the Ottoman Third Army and deposes Abdulhamid II.

*1910.* February 10, Premier Butros Ghali of Egypt is assassinated.

*1911.* The Italian army invades Libya and defeats the Ottoman forces. Lord Herbert Kitchener takes power in Egypt.

*1912.* Ottomans cede Libya to Italy. Ibn Saud establishes his army of Ikhwan (brothers) from Wahhabi soldiery.

*1913.* January, Committee of Union and Progress takes direct control of Ottoman government. June, Arab Congress convenes in Paris supporting an Ottoman government in which every nation under its rule would have equal rights and obligations.

*1914.* August, Ottomans enter World War I on the side of Germany. November, British declare war on the Ottomans, annex Cyprus, and land troops in lower Iraq. December 18, British declare protectorate over Egypt.

*1915.* February, Ottoman forces attack the Suez Canal. April 25, allied troops mount an amphibious operation at Gallipoli designed to knock the Ottoman Empire out of the war by seizing Istanbul, the imperial capital; the British fail to capture the Dardanelles. November 16, Sir Henry MacMahon promises Hussein ibn Ali, the emir of Mecca, that Britain will support Arab independence if the Hashemites rebel against Ottoman rule.

*1916.* Arab revolt against Turks begins; British appoint T. E. Lawrence as political and liaison officer to Faisal's (Hussein's son's) army. May, Britain, France, and Russia conclude the Sykes-Picot Agreement outlining the future division of Ottoman lands. July 19, second Ottoman campaign against the Suez begins. December 15, British recognize Hussein as king only of Hijaz.

*1917.* November 2, Britain issues Balfour Declaration calling for "support of the establishment in Palestine of a national home for the Jewish people." December 9, Turks surrender Jerusalem to Gen. Edmund Allenby.

*1918.* June, Emir Faisal ibn Hussein and Zionist

leader Chaim Weizmann meet in Transjordan to discuss future cooperation between the Arab and Jewish national movements. October, British and Arabs capture Damascus, then Aleppo.

*1919.* March, Egyptians rebel against British after the deportation of nationalist leader Saad Zaghlul. June, King-Crane commission, appointed by Paris peace conference, arrives in Syria to determine wishes of the population concerning the future of Palestine and Syria. August, proposed Anglo-Persian treaty stirs national opposition in Iran and is never ratified by Persian Majlis (parliament).

*1920.* March, Syrian National Congress proclaims Faisal king of Syria and Palestine. April 24, through League of Nations' San Remo Agreement, Britain is awarded mandates over Iraq and Palestine, and France over Syria and Lebanon. July, French forces evict Faisal from the throne in Damascus and Faisal's brother Abdullah is offered the throne in Baghdad, causing large-scale riots in Palestine and Iraq. August, French high commissioner creates Greater (modern) Lebanon in an attempt to utilize religious differences, particularly between Christians and Muslims, to ease the task of French administration.

*1921.* February, Reza Khan seizes power in Iran. March, organized by the British under Winston Churchill, the Cairo Conference names Faisal ibn Hussein king of Iraq and Abdullah ibn Hussein emir of Transjordan (which was carved out of Palestine).

*1922.* February 28, Britain unilaterally terminates its rule over Egypt while retaining control over communications vital to the empire, foreign interests, the Sudan, and minority rights in a policy known as the Four Reserved Points. March, Fuad takes title of king of Egypt. July 22, Council of the League of Nations confirms mandate allocations made to Britain and France two years earlier. October 10, Anglo-Iraqi Treaty signed. November, Mustafa Kemal abolishes the Ottoman sultanate.

*1923.* April, Egypt drafts constitution and holds elections. May 15, Britain recognizes Transjordan as a self-governing state. October, Kemal officially proclaims Turkish republic and begins his fifteen years as president.

*1924.* Ibn Saud takes Hijaz from Hashemites. March, Kemal abolishes the caliphate. November, Sir Lee Stack, governor-general of Sudan, is murdered in Egypt.

*1925.* April, Hebrew University in Jerusalem opens. December 12, Iranian Majlis approves Reza Khan's establishment of Pahlavi dynasty; he becomes Reza Shah Pahlavi.

*1926.* January 8, Ibn Saud is proclaimed king of the Hijaz. May 26, Lebanese constitution adopted.

*1927.* May, British recognize Ibn Saud as king of the Najd and Hijaz.

*1928.* April, Turkey is declared a secular state and adopts the Latin alphabet.

*1929.* August, prolonged Arab-Jewish riots spring from conflict over claims that the Jews were seeking control of the Temple Mount; the riots eventually lead to a pro-Arab turn in British policies.

*1930.* October 20, Britain issues Passfield White Paper, limiting Jewish immigration to "economic absorptive capacity" and restricting land sales to Jews.

*1931.* February, Responding to Jewish criticism of Passfield White Paper, Prime Minister Ramsay MacDonald sends letter assuring Chaim Weizmann that Britain will promote a national Jewish home in Palestine in accordance with its mandate.

*1932.* June 1, oil is discovered in Bahrain. September 24, Ibn Saud issues royal decree unifying the kingdoms of Hijaz and Najd into Saudi Arabia. October 3, Britain grants Iraq independence but retains military bases and oil interests.

*1933.* August, Assyrian uprising in Iraq suppressed. September 8, King Faisal of Iraq dies.

*1934.* Kuwait grants first oil concession, for seventy-four years, to the Kuwait Oil Company.

*1935.* March, Iran becomes the official name for Persia. October, Italians invade Ethiopia.

*1936.* April-October, Arab general strike is mounted in Palestine. July, Montreux Convention gives Turkey control of Straits of Dardanelles.

*1937.* Sa'dabad Treaty is concluded among Afghanistan, Iran, Iraq, and Turkey, implicitly designed to block Soviet expansion. July, Peel commission calls for partition of Palestine.

*1938.* Oil discovered at al Burqan just south of Kuwait City. Saudi Arabian oil exports begin. November, Woodhead commission declares partition plan for Palestine unworkable.

*1939.* February, Anglo-Arab Conference on Palestine held in London. May 17, British publish white paper limiting Jewish immigration into Palestine. September, most independent Middle East countries declare their neutrality as World War II begins.

*1940.* September 12, Italian forces in Libya invade Egypt. November 25, French freighter *Patria,* holding eighteen hundred illegal Jewish immigrants who were prevented from entering Palestine by British authorities, explodes and sinks in Haifa harbor. December 27, British announce no quota for Jewish immigration to Palestine will be set for October 1930 to March 1941.

*1941.* June, a nationalist coup d'état in Iraq, led by military commanders sympathetic to Germany, prompts Britain to invade Baghdad and Basra areas, then occupy Syria and Lebanon. August 26, British and Soviet forces invade Iran. September 16, Reza Shah is forced to abdicate in favor of his son, Muhammad Reza Pahlavi.

*1942.* January, Britain and the Soviet Union sign

treaty guaranteeing Iranian independence and securing vital communications between Soviet and Allied forces in the Middle East. February, British force King Farouk to appoint pro-Allied cabinet. May, Zionists issue Biltmore Program. July, Allies halt German advance in Egypt. October 23, Allied forces begin decisive assault against German lines at El Alamein in Egypt.

*1943.* November, Lebanon declares its independence; its Christians and Muslims adopt their "National Pact." December, Syrian state absorbs Jebel Druze.

*1944.* February 3, the Arabian-American Oil Company (ARAMCO) announces plans to build a refinery in Saudi Arabia. October 8, Syria, Transjordan, Iraq, Lebanon, and Egypt sign a protocol providing for establishment of the Arab League. November 6, Jewish "Stern Gang" assassinates Lord Moyne, the British resident minister in the Middle East.

*1945.* March 22, the Arab League is founded by Egypt, Iraq, Lebanon, Syria, Saudi Arabia, and Transjordan. November 13, the United States and Great Britain create the Anglo-American Committee of Inquiry to examine the problems of European Jews and Palestine.

*1946.* March 5, the United States protests Soviet retention of troops in Iran. March 22, the British mandate in Transjordan ends. May 6, Soviet troops leave Iran. April 30, the Anglo-American Committee of Inquiry recommends the admission of a hundred thousand Jews into Palestine and continuation of the British mandate in Palestine until a United Nations trusteeship is established. October 4, President Harry S. Truman expresses support for a "viable Jewish state."

*1947.* February 14, the London Conference on Palestine closes without an agreement between Arab and Jewish delegates. August 31, the UN Special Committee on Palestine recommends that Palestine be split into separate Arab and Jewish states by September 1, 1949. October 11, the United States endorses the UN committee's report. December 8, the Arab League pledges to help Palestinian Arabs resist any move to partition Palestine.

*1948.* April 1, the UN Security Council adopts a U.S. resolution calling for a truce in Palestine and a reexamination of the partition issue. May 13, the Arab League declares war against Palestinian Jews. May 14, the British mandate for Palestine ends and the state of Israel is proclaimed. May 15, President Truman recognizes Israel at 12:11 a.m., eleven minutes after its independence, and Arab armies invade the new state. May 17, the Soviet Union recognizes Israel. June 11, a four-week Arab-Israeli truce goes into effect. September 17, UN mediator Count Folke Bernadotte is assassinated, allegedly by Jewish terrorists. September 20, the Arab League announces establishment of an Arab government for Palestine. October 22, Israel and Egypt agree to halt renewed fighting, but the truce does not hold.

*1949.* January 6, Egypt and Israel agree to a final cease-fire on all fronts. January 10, Israel withdraws its troops from Egyptian territory. January 25, the Labor party is victorious in the first Israeli election. March 11, Israel and Transjordan sign a cease-fire agreement. April 26, Transjordan announces that the correct name of the country is Jordan. April 28, the Israeli government refuses to allow Arab refugees to return to their homes inside Israel. May 11, Israel is admitted to the United Nations. July 20, Syria and Israel sign an armistice. December 16, Israeli prime minister David Ben-Gurion announces that Jerusalem will become Israel's capital on January 1, 1950.

*1950.* April 13, Israel rejects Arab League terms for peace negotiations. April 24, Jordan formally annexes eastern Palestine, including the Old City of Jerusalem. November 21, Great Britain refuses to abide by Egypt's request that it withdraw its troops from the Suez Canal.

*1951.* March 7, Iranian premier Gen. Ali Razmara is assassinated. April 28, Iran nationalizes the British-owned Anglo-Iranian Oil Company. July 20, Jordan's King Abdullah is assassinated. September 6, Abdullah's son Talal is crowned king of Jordan. September, Iran expels the remaining British oil workers. October 27, Egypt nullifies its 1936 Treaty of Alliance with Great Britain. December 24, the Federation of Libya gains its independence.

*1952.* January 18, British troops battle with Egyptian guerrillas. May 3, Britain offers a conditional withdrawal of its troops from the Suez Canal. July 23, a military coup deposes Egypt's King Farouk. August 11, the Jordanian parliament declares King Talal mentally unfit to rule and declares Crown Prince Hussein the new king. September 18, Lebanese president Bishara al-Khoury resigns in the face of general strikes. September 23, Camille Chamoun is elected president of Lebanon. October 22, Iran breaks diplomatic ties with Great Britain.

*1953.* February 12, Great Britain and Egypt sign a pact establishing self-government in the Sudan. May 2, King Faisal II of Iraq is crowned. August 16, the shah of Iran seeks sanctuary in Iraq after his unsuccessful attempt to dismiss Premier Muhammad Mossadeq. August 19, a loyalist revolt ousts Premier Mossadeq. November 29, the Sudan's first general election yields a victory for forces seeking a union with Egypt.

*1954.* April 18, Gamal Abdel Nasser replaces Muhammad Naguib as premier of Egypt; Naguib remains president. July 27, Egypt and Great Britain sign an agreement ending their dispute over the Suez Canal. November 14, Egypt's ruling military junta deposes President Naguib.

*1955.* February 24, Iraq and Turkey sign the Baghdad Pact, a mutual defense treaty; Great Britain, Iran, and Pakistan join the alliance later in the year. October

20, Egypt and Syria sign a mutual defense treaty. November 22, the five Baghdad Pact members announce a permanent political, military, and economic alliance.

*1956.* January 30, Israel appeals to the United States for arms. April 18, the United States becomes a member of the Economic Committee of the Baghdad Pact. May 9, the United States declines to sell arms to Israel. June 13, Great Britain ends its occupation of the Suez Canal. June 24, Nasser becomes president of Egypt. July 20, the United States refuses to lend Egypt funds for the Aswan High Dam project. July 27, Nasser nationalizes the Suez Canal. October 29, Israel attacks Egypt to provide Great Britain and France with a justification to seize the Suez Canal. October 31, British and French aircraft attack Egypt. November 5, British and French troops enter the fight against Egypt. November 6, under U.S. pressure, Great Britain and France accept a cease-fire. November 7, the UN General Assembly calls for withdrawal of British, French, and Israeli troops from Egypt. November 21, the withdrawal of British, French, and Israeli troops from the Sinai begins.

*1957.* January 5, President Dwight D. Eisenhower calls for American action to counter Communist expansion in the Middle East. March 1, Israel withdraws its troops from the Gaza Strip. May 5, King Hussein announces that his government has defeated leftist elements in Jordan. September 5, the United States announces arms shipments to Jordan, Lebanon, Turkey, and Iraq.

*1958.* February 1, Egypt and Syria merge into the United Arab Republic (UAR). March 24, King Saud of Saudi Arabia transfers some of his power to his brother, Crown Prince Faisal. July 14, revolutionaries overthrow the Iraqi government, kill King Faisal, and proclaim a republic. July 15, the United States sends five thousand troops to Lebanon to protect that country's independence. July 17, Great Britain sends troops to Jordan at the request of King Hussein. July 19, the UAR and the new Iraqi regime sign a mutual defense treaty. July 31, Gen. Fuad Chehab is elected president of Lebanon. September 22, Lebanon's pro-Western cabinet resigns. September 24, Rashid Karami becomes premier of Lebanon.

*1959.* January 17, Egypt and Great Britain sign the British-Egyptian Suez Pact. March 5, Iran and the United States sign a mutual defense treaty. March 24, Iraq withdraws from the Baghdad Pact. August 18, the Baghdad Pact is renamed the Central Treaty Organization (CENTO).

*1960.* January 18, Egypt announces that the Soviet Union will finance the second stage of the Aswan Dam. September 15, the Organization of Petroleum Exporting Countries (OPEC) is established. December 21, Prince Faisal resigns as premier of Saudi Arabia.

*1961.* June 19, Great Britain grants independence to Kuwait. July 20, Kuwait joins the Arab League. September 19, Arab League troops replace British soldiers guarding Kuwait against Iraq's claims of sovereignty. September 28, dissident Syrian army units overthrow the government and dissolve the union with Egypt the next day.

*1962.* August 29, Saudi Arabia and Jordan agree on a plan to merge their militaries and economic policies. September 26, Yemen's Imam Badr is driven from power by a military revolt led by Col. Abdallah al-Sallal, who is backed by Egypt. November 6, Saudi Arabia breaks ties with Egypt, charging that Egyptian planes bombed Saudi villages near the Yemen border.

*1963.* February 8, the Iraqi air force overthrows the government of Premier Abdul Karim Kassim. March 8, a pro-Nasser coup ousts the Syrian government. May 21, Nasser announces that Egyptian troops in Yemen will not leave until royalist factions have been put down. July 22, Nasser renounces an agreement to unite Egypt, Syria, and Iraq. August 25, Israeli and Jordanian forces clash in Jerusalem. November 18, Iraq's President Abdul Salem Arif announces that his forces have overthrown the civilian Ba'athist government.

*1964.* March 28, Saudi Arabi's King Saud turns over his powers to his half-brother Crown Prince Faisal. August 22, the Libyan government announces that the United States and Great Britain will give up their military bases in Libya. November 2, the Saudi Arabian cabinet and consultative counsel proclaim Crown Prince Faisal the king of Saudi Arabia, thus dethroning King Saud.

*1965.* January 12, thirteen Arab nations issue a communiqué saying they will take joint action against nations that recognize Israel or aid its "aggressive military efforts." March 16, Egyptian president Nasser is elected to another six-year term. August 24, Saudi Arabia and Egypt sign an agreement aimed at halting the fighting in Yemen. November 24, Sabah al-Salem al-Sabah is crowned emir of Kuwait after the death of his brother.

*1966.* April 13, Iraqi president Abdul Salem Arif dies in a helicopter crash; he is succeeded as president by his brother, Abdul Rahman Arif. May 19, the United States reports the sale of tactical bombers to Israel. December 7, Syrian leader Nureddin al-Atasi calls on Jordanians and Palestinians to overthrow King Hussein of Jordan and offers arms to dissident groups.

*1967.* April 20, skirmishes erupt between Iraqi and Kuwaiti troops on their border. May 15, Egypt puts its military forces on alert. May 20, at the request of Egypt, the UN Emergency Force in the Middle East ends its patrols in the Gaza Strip and at Sharm el Sheikh at the mouth of the Gulf of Aqaba. May 22, Egypt closes the Strait of Tiran to Israeli shipping. May 30, Jordan and Egypt sign a mutual defense pact. June 5, the Six-Day

War begins when Israeli warplanes attack airfields in Egypt, Syria, and Jordan. June 7, Israel captures the Old City of Jerusalem. June 8, the USS *Liberty* is attacked by Israeli planes. June 9, the Egyptian National Assembly rejects Nasser's resignation. June 10, Israel captures the Golan Heights. June 12, Israel refuses to withdraw its forces from the territory it has occupied. President Lyndon B. Johnson offers a five-point Middle East peace proposal. June 28, Israel proclaims the unification of Jerusalem. September 24, Israel announces that it will move Jewish settlers into occupied territories. November 22, the UN Security Council unanimously adopts Resolution 242. November 28, Great Britain declares the independence of South Yemen.

*1968.* February 15, fighting between Jordanian and Israeli forces erupts on their border. July 17, Ahmed Hassan al-Bakr comes to power in a coup in Iraq. December 5, King Hussein sends a message to other Arab nations urging unified action to liberate Arab lands from Israel. December 28, in retaliation for an earlier attack on an occupied Israeli airliner, Israeli forces destroy thirteen unoccupied Arab airliners at Beirut International Airport.

*1969.* February 26, Israeli prime minister Levi Eshkol dies of a heart attack. March 7, Foreign Minister Golda Meir becomes prime minister of Israel. April 22, UN Secretary General U Thant says Egypt and Israel are engaged in "a virtual state of war" in the Suez Canal sector. August 3, Israel announces that it intends to keep the Golan Heights, the Gaza Strip, and part of the Sinai Peninsula as buffer zones. August 21, a fire damages the Al Aqsa Mosque in Jerusalem, leading to Arab protests. September 1, Libya's King Idris is overthrown; Col. Muammar al-Qaddafi emerges as leader of the new regime. October 28, the new Libyan regime orders the United States to vacate its airbase near Tripoli.

*1970.* February 2, heavy fighting breaks out between Israel and Syria on the Golan Heights. April 14, Yemeni civil war ends with Saudi Arabia's agreement to stop supplying royalist rebels. June 24, U.S. intelligence reports indicate that Soviet troops have taken over Egypt's air defenses and Soviet pilots are flying missions over Egypt. August 7, a ninety-day Egyptian-Israeli cease-fire begins. September 6, the Popular Front for the Liberation of Palestine hijacks three airliners. September 16, King Hussein declares martial law. September 19, Syrian units enter Jordan to support Palestinian guerrillas against the Jordanian army. September 27, Jordanian civil war ends with the signing of an agreement in Cairo by Arab heads of state. September 28, President Nasser dies of a heart attack. October 17, Anwar Sadat is sworn in as president of Egypt. November 13, Syrian president Nureddin al-Atasi is arrested in a coup.

*1971.* March 13, Hafez al-Assad is proclaimed president of Syria. May 27, Egypt and the Soviet Union sign a fifteen-year treaty of friendship and cooperation. November 28, Jordanian premier Wasfi al-Tal is assassinated while visiting Cairo. December 2, the United Arab Emirates declares its independence.

*1972.* March 15, King Hussein unveils a plan to make Jordan a federated state comprising two autonomous regions, one on the East Bank of the Jordan River and the other on the West Bank. May 9, Israeli commandos rescue ninety passengers on a hijacked airliner at Lod Airport in Tel Aviv. May 30, three Japanese terrorists recruited by the Popular Front for the Liberation of Palestine stage an attack at Lod Airport, killing twenty-six people. July 18, President Sadat expels Soviet military advisers from Egypt. September 5, eleven Israeli athletes participating in the Munich Olympics are killed by Arab terrorists of the Black September group. November 27, King Hussein confirms reports of an aborted coup to overthrow him.

*1973.* February 21, Israeli forces shoot down a Libyan airliner that had strayed over Israeli occupied territory and had failed to heed warnings; 106 passengers and crew are killed. August 29, Egypt and Libya announce a gradual approach toward unifying the two countries. October 6, the 1973 Arab-Israeli War begins with Egyptian forces crossing the Suez Canal and attacking Israeli units; Syrian forces attack in the Golan Heights. October 7, Israeli forces counterattack. October 12, Israeli forces advance to within eighteen miles of Damascus. October 15, the United States announces that it is resupplying Israel with military equipment; an Israeli detachment establishes a bridgehead on the west side of the Suez Canal. October 20, Saudi Arabia halts all oil shipments to the United States. October 21, other Arab oil-producing states cut off shipments to the United States. October 22, the UN Security Council adopts Resolution 338 calling for a cease-fire in the Middle East. October 23, Israeli forces cut off the Egptian III Corps. October 25, President Richard Nixon puts U.S. forces on worldwide military alert in response to indications that the Soviet Union might intervene in the Middle East. October 27, Egypt and Israel agree to negotiate on implementing a cease-fire. October 29, Syria accepts a cease-fire with Israel. November 11, Israel and Egypt sign a cease-fire accord. December 21, the first Arab-Israeli peace conference opens in Geneva.

*1974.* January 18, Israel and Egypt sign a Suez disengagement accord. January 25, Israel begins withdrawing from its positions on the Suez. February 28, the United States and Egypt restore full diplomatic ties after a seven-year break. March 4, Israel completes its Suez withdrawal. March 18, the Arab oil embargo against the United States is lifted by all Arab oil producers but Libya and Syria. April 10, Golda Meir resigns as Israeli prime minister. May 31, Syria and Israel sign disengagement accords. June 14, during a visit to the Middle East President Nixon signs a friendship accord with President Sadat of Egypt. June 16, Syria and the United States restore full diplomatic ties, broken since the 1967 war. October 28, twenty Arab League heads of state at a summit in Rabat, Morocco, recognize the Palestine Liberation Organization (PLO) as the "sole legitimate representative of the Palestinian people on any liberated Palestinian territory." November 13, PLO head Yasir Arafat addresses the UN General Assembly.

*1975.* March 5, Iran and Iraq sign an agreement resolving border and other disputes. March 22, the Kurdish resistance in Iraq collapses under attacks from Iraqi troops. March 25, Saudi King Faisal is shot to death by his nephew, Prince Faisal ibn Musaed; Crown Prince Khalid becomes king. June 5, the Suez Canal opens after an eight-year closure to commercial shipping. July 1, Lebanese premier Rashid Karami forms a "rescue cabinet" to try to end the Lebanese civil war. September 1, Egypt and Israel sign a new Sinai pact providing for further Israeli withdrawal. November 10, the UN General Assembly adopts a resolution defining Zionism as "a form of racism or racial discrimination." December 4, Israeli planes attack Palestinian refugee camps in Lebanon, killing seventy-four persons.

*1976.* January 28, in an address to the U.S. Congress, Israeli prime minister Yitzhak Rabin rules out any talks with the PLO. May 8, Elias Sarkis is elected president of Lebanon. May 31, Syrian troops advance into Lebanon. June 16, two U.S. diplomats are shot to death in Beirut. June 27, a jetliner in Athens carrying numerous Jewish passengers is hijacked to Uganda. July 4, Israeli commandos stage a raid that frees the hostages in Uganda. July 16, amidst increasing violence, the U.S. embassy in Beirut closes and urges all Americans to leave the country. September 17, President Sadat is elected to a second term in Egypt. October 25, all members of the Arab League but Iraq and Libya approve a Lebanese peace plan at a summit in Riyadh. November 15, Syrian peacekeeping troops take up positions in Beirut.

*1977.* January 19, President Sadat repeals proposed price increases after violent demonstrations in Cairo. March 9, King Hussein and Yasir Arafat meet for the first time since Jordan's "Black September" rout of Palestinian guerrillas in 1970. March 15, an Israeli newspaper discloses that Prime Minister Rabin's wife has an illegal bank account. April 7, amid scandal, Rabin withdraws from the Labor party ticket. May 17, Israel's Likud party unexpectedly wins a plurality in the Israeli election. June 21, Menachem Begin becomes prime minister of Israel. August 25, the PLO denounces

U.S. peace efforts in the Middle East. September 26, a U.S.-arranged cease-fire in southern Lebanon goes into effect, but it lasts only ten days. October 26, Egypt suspends payment of its military debt to the Soviet Union. November 19, Sadat arrives in Israel. November 6, Yasir Arafat says Palestinian forces will not pull out of southern Lebanon. November 15, Prime Minister Begin formally invites President Sadat to address the Israeli Knesset. November 17, Sadat accepts Begin's invitation. November 20, Sadat addresses the Knesset. December 5, Egypt breaks ties with Syria, Iraq, Libya, Algeria, and Lebanon. December 25, Begin and Sadat hold a summit in Ismailia, Egypt.

*1978.* January 18, Sadat denounces Israel's negotiating posture at talks in Jerusalem and recalls the Egyptian delegation. February 14, the Carter administration announces a $4.8 billion arms package for Egypt, Israel, and Saudi Arabia. March 14, Israel launches an all-out attack on Palestinian bases in Lebanon in retaliation for a Palestinian raid that killed thirty Israelis; Israeli forces occupy a six-mile security belt in southern Lebanon. July 1, Syrian troops attack Christian militia in Beirut, resulting in pitched battles that kill hundreds. September 5, talks between Begin, Sadat, and President Jimmy Carter begin at Camp David, Maryland. September 8, hundreds of Iranian antigovernment demonstrators are killed by troops in Tehran. September 17, Begin, Sadat, and Carter sign two historic agreements mapping the normalization of relations between Egypt and Israel. October 12, negotiations on an Egyptian-Israeli draft peace treaty begin in Washington. November 6, the Iranian government declares martial law in response to an oil worker strike. December 15, the Israeli cabinet rejects the latest Egyptian-Israeli draft treaty proposal by the United States.

*1979.* January 6, in response to widespread riots, the shah of Iran installs a new civilian government under Shahpur Bakhtiar. January 16, the shah leaves Iran for a "vacation" that becomes permanent exile. February 1, Ayatollah Khomeini returns to Iran after fifteen years in exile. February 11, armed revolutionaries overthrow the Bakhtiar government in Iran; a provisional government formed by Ayatollah Khomeini takes power. February 14, the U.S. embassy in Tehran is occupied by leftist guerrillas, but Khomeini supporters later free the personnel. March 13, at the end of a diplomatic mission to the Middle East, Carter announces at the Cairo airport that Sadat has approved a proposed peace treaty. March 26, Begin and Sadat sign the Egyptian-Israeli peace treaty at a White House ceremony. March 31, the foreign ministers of eighteen Arab League countries vote to impose an economic boycott on Egypt. April 1, Ayatollah Khomeini proclaims an Islamic republic in Iran. May 25, Israel begins withdrawing from the Sinai Peninsula. July 16, President Ahmed al-Bakr of Iraq resigns, naming Gen. Saddam Hussein as his successor. November 4, Iranian students seize the U.S. embassy in Tehran and take U.S. diplomats hostage. November 14, President Carter freezes Iranian assets in the United States. December 15, the shah leaves the United States for Panama after receiving cancer treatments. December 24, the Soviets launch an invasion of Afghanistan.

*1980.* January 23, President Carter outlines the "Carter Doctrine" pertaining to the security of the Persian Gulf. April 7, Iraq expels seven thousand Iranians, and both nations put their armies on alert. April 8, Ayatollah Khomeini calls for the ouster of Iraqi president Saddam Hussein. April 25, a U.S. commando mission to rescue the hostages in Tehran is aborted because of equipment failure. June 22, the Israeli government announces the transfer of the cabinet room from West Jerusalem to East Jerusalem. July 27, the shah of Iran dies of cancer in Cairo. July 30, the Israeli Knesset adopts a law affirming Israel's claim to all of Jerusalem. September 17, Saddam Hussein declares the 1975 Iran-Iraq border agreement void. September 22, border clashes escalate to full-scale war between Iran and Iraq. October 7, Syria declares its support for Iran in its war with Iraq. December 28, the United States announces a proposal to trade the release of frozen Iranian assets for the return of U.S. hostages in Tehran.

*1981.* January 20, minutes after Ronald Reagan is sworn in as president, Iran frees the U.S. hostages. April 2, Lebanese Christian militia engage in fierce battles with Syrian troops in Beirut. April 21, the Reagan administration announces a massive arms sale package for Saudi Arabia, including five AWACS radar defense planes. April 28, for the first time, Israeli forces intervene on the side of Lebanese Christian troops fighting Syrian forces. April 29, Syria moves surface-to-air missiles into the Bekaa Valley. May 25, the Gulf Cooperation Council (GCC) is established. June 7, Israeli warplanes destroy Iraq's Osirak nuclear reactor near Baghdad. June 22, Ayatollah Khomeini dismisses President Abolhassan Bani-Sadr. June 30, the Likud party wins a narrow plurality of Knesset seats in the Israeli elections. July 17, Israeli jets attack PLO headquarters in downtown Beirut, killing three hundred people. July 20, the United States suspends delivery of six F-16s to Israel. July 24, Israel and the PLO endorse separate cease-fire agreements. August 7, Saudi prince Fahd offers an eight-point peace plan that recognizes Israel's right to exist. October 6, Egyptian president Sadat is assassinated. October 13, Vice President Mubarak is elected president of Egypt. October 28, the U.S. Senate approves the AWACS sale to Saudi Arabia. November 30, the United States and Israel sign a memorandum of understanding on strategic cooperation. December 14, the Israeli Knesset passes a bill annexing the Golan Heights. December 18, the United States suspends the memorandum of understanding in response to Israel's annexation of the Golan Heights.

*1982.* February 2, an uprising by Muslim fundamentalist rebels in the Syrian city of Hama leads to heavy fighting that kills thousands. March 22, Iran launches a spring offensive that forces Iraqi troops to retreat. April 11, an Israeli soldier kills two Arabs and wounds many in a shooting spree at the Dome of the Rock mosque in Jerusalem. April 25, Israel returns the final portions of the Sinai Peninsula to Egypt. June 3, Shlomo Argov, the Israeli ambassador to Great Britain, is wounded in London; Israel blames the PLO and launches air strikes in retaliation. June 6, Israel invades Lebanon. June 9, Israeli planes destroy Syrian air defenses in the Bekaa Valley. June 13, King Khalid of Saudi Arabia dies of a heart attack and is succeeded by Crown Prince Fahd. June 24, the United States closes its embassy in Beirut. August 4, Israeli forces enter West Beirut. August 19, Israel accepts a U.S. plan providing for the withdrawal of PLO forces from Lebanon. August 21, the PLO departure from Lebanon begins. August 23, Bashir Gemayel is elected president of Lebanon. September 1, President Reagan offers a Middle East peace plan in a major address. September 14, president-elect Bashir Gemayel is assassinated. September 15, Israeli troops reenter West Beirut. September 18, hundreds of Palestinian civilians are massacred in the Sabra and Shatila refugee camps outside Beirut by Lebanese Christian militia. September 20, Amin Gemayal is elected president of Lebanon. September 22, Israeli defense minister Ariel Sharon acknowledges that Israel allowed militia into the PLO camps to conduct an antiterrorist operation. December 14, Jordan and the PLO agree to coordinate their diplomacy.

*1983.* February 8, the Israeli commission investigating the Beirut refugee camp massacres recommends dismissing Ariel Sharon and several Israeli officers. February 11, Sharon resigns but stays in the government as a minister without portfolio. April 18, a car bomb partially destroys the U.S. embassy in Beirut, killing sixty-three persons. June 1, more than twenty members of Yasir Arafat's Al Fatah wing of the PLO announce their support for an internal PLO rebellion against Arafat. June 24, Syria expels Arafat after he accuses Syria of aiding PLO rebels against him. July 24, heavy fighting breaks out in Lebanon between PLO rebels and Arafat loyalists. August 29, Israeli prime minister Begin announces that he will resign. September 16, U.S. naval guns begin firing at targets in Syrian-controlled territory in Lebanon. October 23, a truck bomb destroys the barracks of U.S. peacekeeping forces in Beirut, killing 241 servicemen. November 16, Yasir Arafat sets up headquarters in Tripoli, Lebanon, after PLO rebels capture the Beddawi refugee camp, an Arafat stronghold. December 20, Arafat and four thousand PLO troops are evacuated from Tripoli under an agreement brokered by the UN.

*1984.* February 7, President Reagan orders U.S. peacekeepers to withdraw from Lebanon. February 27, Iraq blockades Iranian oil facilities at Kharg Island. March 12, President Gemayal opens national reconciliation talks in Switzerland with leaders of Lebanese Muslim factions. March 30, U.S. ships leave the waters off Lebanon. April 29, Israel says it uncovered a plot by Jewish terrorists to blow up Arab buses in Israel. June 23, the Lebanese cabinet approves a plan to restructure the army to provide for more equal representation. July 4, a reconstituted Lebanese army assumes control of Beirut and begins destroying the Green Line wall dividing Muslim and Christian sectors. September 13, the Labor and Likud parties agree to form a coalition government in Israel. September 25, Jordan announces it will restore relations with Egypt. November 22-29, the PLO National Council meets in Amman and reaffirms support for Yasir Arafat. November 26, the United States and Iraq restore diplomatic ties after a seventeen-year split. December 4, Arabs hijack a Kuwaiti passenger jet and divert it to Tehran. December 9, Iranian police storm the hijacked aircraft and free the passengers, but Tehran refuses to extradite the hijackers.

*1985.* February 22, Jordan releases the text of a PLO-Jordanian agreement on the Middle East peace process. April 17, after heavy fighting between rival Muslim factions in Beirut, the one-year-old Lebanese unity cabinet resigns. May 19, heavy fighting breaks out between PLO fighters and Amal Shi'ite militia near Beirut. May 25, Kuwaiti emir Sheikh Jaber al-Ahmed al-Sabah narrowly survives a suicide bomb attempt. June 10, the Israeli army completes its withdrawal from Lebanon. June 14, TWA Flight 847 carrying 153 passengers, including 104 Americans, is hijacked by members of the Islamic Jihad group and forced to land in Beirut. June 30, a two-week hostage drama ends with the release of 39 American hostages from Flight 847. September 14, U.S. hostage Benjamin Weir is released in Beirut. October 1, Israeli warplanes bomb PLO headquarters in Tunis. October 7, Palestinian gunmen hijack the *Achille Lauro,* an Italian cruise ship. October 9, the *Achille Lauro* hijackers surrender in Egypt after gaining assurances of safe passage. October 10, U.S. warplanes intercept an Egyptian plane carrying the hijackers and force it to land in Sicily, where the hijackers are charged with murder. October 21, Israeli prime minister Shimon Peres tells the UN General Assembly he would be willing to participate in an "international forum" on Middle East peace. November 21, Jonathan Pollard is arrested outside the Israeli embassy in Washington and charged with conducting espionage for Israel against the United States. November 23, an Egyptian airliner lands in Malta after being hijacked by followers of Palestinian

terrorist Abu Nidal. November 24, fifty-nine passengers aboard the Egyptian airliner are killed when Egyptian special forces storm the plane. December 1, Prime Minister Peres apologizes to the United States for the Pollard spy scandal. December 27, Palestinian gunmen attack travelers at El Al Israeli Airlines check-in counters in Rome and Vienna.

*1986.* January 7, in response to alleged Libyan sponsorship of terrorism, President Reagan ends all economic activity between the United States and Libya. January 13, South Yemen President Ali Nasser Muhammad's attempt to assassinate rival Politburo members leads to a bloody coup and short civil war in which he is deposed. February 11, Iranian forces capture the strategic Iraqi oil port of Fao. February 19, King Hussein announces he is ending a year-long joint effort with the PLO to revitalize the Arab-Israeli peace process. April 5, a terrorist bomb in a West Berlin night club kills two and injures more than two hundred. April 14, American bombers carry out a raid against targets in Libya; President Reagan says the attack is in response to evidence that Libya was behind the West Berlin bombing. May 25, U.S. national security adviser Robert C. McFarlane leads a secret diplomatic mission to Tehran aimed at freeing American hostages in Lebanon. June 4, Jonathan Pollard pleads guilty to espionage. June 25, Avraham Shalom, head of Israel's security agency, resigns amid allegations that he ordered and then covered up the killings of two Palestinian bus hijackers in 1984. July 22, Prime Minister Shimon Peres meets with King Hassan II of Morocco in Ifrane, Morocco. August 18, Soviet and Israeli officials meet in Helsinki in the first diplomatic contacts between the two countries in nineteen years. October 20, Prime Minister Peres trades jobs with Foreign Minister Yitzhak Shamir in accordance with a power-sharing agreement resulting from the 1984 Israeli election. November 3, a pro-Syrian Beirut weekly magazine discloses Robert McFarlane's secret trip to Tehran in May. November 13, President Reagan admits his administration sent arms to Iran. November 25, Attorney General Edwin Meese III discloses that members of the administration helped divert millions of dollars from the Iranian arms sales to the Nicaraguan contra rebels.

*1987.* January 12, Iraq accuses the United States of supplying it with false intelligence information. January 20, Anglican church emissary Terry Waite disappears in Lebanon. January 24, three Americans and one Indian are kidnapped from the Beirut University campus. February 22, thousands of Syrian troops enter West Beirut in response to calls for Syrian intervention to halt bloody fighting between Lebanese Muslim groups. March 23, the United States offers to protect Kuwaiti oil tankers sailing in the Persian Gulf. May 17, an Iraqi warplane launches a missile that seriously damages the frigate

USS *Stark*. May 19, the United States announces an agreement with Kuwait to reflag eleven Kuwaiti tankers that will receive U.S. naval protection while in the Gulf. June 1, Lebanese prime minister Rashid Karami is killed when a bomb explodes in his helicopter. July 20, the UN Security Council unanimously adopts Resolution 598 calling for a cease-fire between Iran and Iraq. July 22, the U.S. Navy begins escorting Kuwaiti tankers. July 31, protests by thousands of Iranian pilgrims near the Grand Mosque in Mecca lead to a riot in which more than four hundred people are killed. September 21, U.S. helicopters disable an Iranian ship reportedly laying mines in the Persian Gulf. November 8-11, at an emergency Arab League summit in Amman, Arab leaders focus on the Iran-Iraq War while largely ignoring the Arab-Israeli conflict. December 9, a general uprising in the occupied territories begins when Palestinians in the Gaza Strip confront Israeli soldiers with rocks and molotov cocktails. December 21, Palestinians in Israel hold a general strike in support of the uprising in the occupied territories.

*1988.* January 19, Israeli defense minister Yitzhak Rabin says Israel will combat the Palestinian uprising with "force, might, and beatings," to reduce the number of Palestinians being killed. February 15, Israeli news sources confirm that the army arrested two soldiers for allegedly burying four Palestinian protesters alive. February 17, U.S. Marine Lt. Col. William R. Higgins, a UN observer, is taken captive near Tyre, Lebanon. March 28, the Israeli army announces that it will seal off the occupied territories. April 16, Khalil Wazir, the PLO's military chief, is killed in his home in Tunisia by a commando team presumed to be Israeli. April 18, Iraq recaptures the Fao Peninsula from Iran. May 25, Libya announces that it will end its armed conflict with Chad and recognize the government of President Hissene Habra. July 3, the American cruiser USS *Vincennes* shoots down an Iranian passenger airliner after mistaking it for an attacking aircraft. July 18, Iranian president Ali Khamenei accepts UN Security Council Resolution 598, which calls for a cease-fire between Iran and Iraq. July 30, Iraq opens an offensive to crush Kurdish resistance in northern Iraq. July 31, King Hussein renounces Jordan's claim to the West Bank in favor of the PLO. August 20, a cease-fire between Iran and Iraq goes into effect. September 22, President Gemayal appoints Gen. Michel Aoun as acting premier of a provisional Lebanese government after the Lebanese parliament fails to elect Gemayal's successor. November 15, the Palestine National Council proclaims an independent Palestinian state in Gaza and the West Bank. December 14, Yasir Arafat explicitly renounces terrorism and recognizes Israel's right to exist at a press conference in Geneva, leading the United States to open a dialogue with the PLO. December 21, a bomb blows a Pan Am airliner

out of the sky over Scotland, killing 259 people aboard and 11 on the ground.

*1989.* January 4, two U.S. Navy warplanes down two Libyan fighters over waters near Libya. February 14, Ayatollah Khomeini calls on Muslims everywhere to kill Indian-born British author Salman Rushdie for writing *The Satanic Verses*. March 14, Maronite Christian leader Michel Aoun declares "a campaign of liberation against the Syrian presence in this country." March 28, Ayatollah Hussein Ali Montazeri, the heir of Iranian spiritual leader Ayatollah Khomeini, announces his resignation after Khomeini asks him to step down. April 18, riots break out in Jordan over an increase in food prices. May 22, Egypt rejoins the Arab League. June 3, Ayatollah Khomeini dies in a Tehran hospital. July 5, Prime Minister Shamir accepts right-wing conditions on his election plan for the occupied territories, ending Arab consideration of the plan. July 12, Israel announces that it will gradually reopen schools in the West Bank. July 28, in southern Lebanon, Israeli commandos abduct Sheik Abdul Karim Obeid, a spiritual leader of the pro-Iranian Shi'ite Hizballah group. July 31, a videotape is released by hostage takers in Lebanon reportedly showing the hanging of Lt. Col. William Higgins. August 13, Syrian troops in Lebanon launch an offensive against Christian forces. August 17, Iranian president Ali Akbar Hashemi Rafsanjani takes the oath of office in Tehran. November 6, the United States returns $567 million in Iranian assets that had been frozen since 1979. November 22, newly elected Lebanese president René Muawwad is assassinated by a bomb in Beirut. November 24, the Lebanese parliament elects Elias Harawi president. December 27, Syria and Egypt restore diplomatic relations, broken since 1979.

*1990.* February 4, terrorists attack a tour bus in Egypt, killing nine Israeli tourists. March 15, Prime Minister Shamir loses a no-confidence vote in the Israeli Knesset. April 2, Saddam Hussein threatens to use chemical weapons against Israel if Israel attacks Iraq. April 22, American hostage Robert Pohill is freed by his Lebanese kidnappers after three years in captivity. April 30, American hostage Frank Reed is freed in Beirut. May 22, North and South Yemen announce their merger into a unified state. May 30, Israeli forces capture two heavily armed speedboats piloted by Palestinians on their way to attack Israeli beaches. June 8, Yitzhak Shamir announces the formation of a governing coalition comprised of the Likud party and several small right-wing parties. June 20, President George Bush suspends the U.S. dialogue with the PLO over the PLO's failure to denounce recent terrorist activities. June 21, an earthquake in northern Iran kills more than thirty-five thousand people. July 17, Saddam Hussein accuses unnamed Gulf leaders of plotting to keep oil prices low. July 25, the American ambassador to Iraq, April

Glaspie, meets with Saddam Hussein in Baghdad. August 1, talks between Iraq and Kuwait in Jiddah, Saudi Arabia, break down. August 2, Iraq invades and occupies Kuwait, touching off the Persian Gulf War. August 6, the UN Security Council imposes mandatory economic sanctions on Iraq. August 7, U.S. forces begin deploying in Saudi Arabia. August 10, twelve Arab League members vote for a resolution backing Arab troop deployments to Saudi Arabia. August 16, U.S. ships begin enforcing a naval blockade of Iraq. August 17, Iraq announces that it will place Western hostages at strategic defense sites. August 18, Iraq begins withdrawing its troops from Iran under the terms of a hastily concluded peace agreement. August 28, Iraq releases women and children hostages. September 11, President Bush explains U.S. goals in the Persian Gulf in an address to Congress. October 8, a clash between Israeli police and Palestinian protesters in Jerusalem leaves as many as twenty-one Palestinians dead. October 13, Lebanon's General Aoun abandons his fight against Syrian forces and takes refuge in the French embassy. November 8, Bush announces a dramatic increase in U.S. forces deployed in Saudi Arabia. November 29, the UN Security Council adopts Resolution 678 authorizing the use of "all necessary means" to expel Iraq from Kuwait. December 6, Saddam announces that all hostages in Iraq and Kuwait will be freed. December 13, the last flight carrying hostages leaves Iraq.

*1991.* January 4, Iraq accepts Bush's offer of talks in Geneva. January 9, a meeting between U.S. secretary of state James A. Baker III and Iraqi foreign minister Tariq Aziz in Geneva fails to resolve the Gulf crisis. January 12, the U.S. Congress authorizes the use of force against Iraq. January 17, at 12:50 a.m. Saudi time, coalition forces begin a massive air campaign against targets in Iraq and Kuwait. January 18, Iraq hits Israel with Scud missiles carrying conventional warheads. January 25, the United States accuses Iraq of deliberately leaking oil into the Persian Gulf. January 26, Iraqi pilots begin flying warplanes to Iranian airfields rather than have them destroyed. February 13, four hundred Iraqi civilians are killed in a coalition bombing raid on what was believed to be a military communications center. February 22, Bush sets a deadline for complete Iraqi compliance with coalition terms. February 24, at 4:00 a.m. Saudi time, coalition ground forces attack Iraqi positions. February 26, Iraqi forces abandon Kuwait City. February 27, U.S. forces engage in a tank duel with Republican Guard units that destroys more than two hundred Iraqi tanks. February 28, at 8:00 a.m. Saudi time, a cease-fire goes into effect. March 3, Iraqi leaders accept all allied terms for formally ending the Gulf War at a meeting with Gen. Norman Schwarzkopf near the Iraqi town of Safwan. March 4, Iraq begins freeing its prisoners of war. March 6, Kurdish leaders

announce they have begun a large-scale offensive against Iraqi forces in northern Iraq. March 31, the Kurdish insurgency collapses. April 5, the United States announces an air drop of supplies to Kurdish refugees in northern Iraq. April 17, U.S., British, and French forces secure a "safe zone" in northern Iraq and begin to build refugee camps for the Kurds. May 13, the United States transfers control of Kurdish refugee camps to the UN. June 23-28, Iraq obstructs UN inspectors from obtaining full access to its weapons facilities. July 18, Syria accepts a joint U.S.-Soviet invitation to a Middle East peace conference to be held in Madrid. September 6, the Shamir government requests $10 billion in loan guarantees from the United States to help settle Russian Jewish immigrants. September 24-26, Iraq temporarily detains UN arms inspectors. October 30, the Middle East peace conference opens in Madrid. November 6, the last of the more than seven hundred Kuwait oil wells set on fire by Iraqi forces is capped. December 1-3, the last three American hostages in Lebanon are freed. December 10, Arab-Israeli peace talks begin in Washington after several days' delay by the Israeli delegation. December 16, the UN General Assembly votes 111-25 to overturn a 1975 resolution that equates Zionism with racism.

*1992.* February 16, Hizballah leader Sheikh Abbas al-Musawi is killed when Israeli aircraft attack his motorcade in southern Lebanon. February 19, the Israeli Labor party names Yitzhak Rabin as its leader, replacing Shimon Peres. March 17, a bomb destroys the Israeli embassy in Buenos Aries; the Islamic Jihad claims responsibility. March 20, Iraq agrees to UN demands for arms inspections after a month of defiance. April 8, Yasir Arafat survives a plane crash in Libya. May 19, Kurds hold free elections to choose a legislature in their zone in northern Iraq. June 23, the Labor party wins a convincing victory in Israeli parliamentary elections. July 13, the Israeli Knesset approves the formation of Rabin's Labor-led coalition government. July 26, after three weeks of refusing to let UN inspectors examine a building in Baghdad, Iraqi authorities relent. August 11, the United States and Israel agree on terms for provision of $10 billion in U.S. loan guarantees to Israel. August 23, Lebanon begins its first parliamentary elections in twenty years. August 26, the United States, Great Britain, and France establish a "no-fly zone" in southern Iraq for Iraqi aircraft. September 11, President Bush approves the sale of seventy-two F-15s to Saudi Arabia. October 5, parliamentary elections are held in Kuwait. October 22, Lebanese president Harawi appoints Rafik al-Hariri as premier. December 17, Israel deports to its security zone in southern Lebanon four hundred Palestinians allegedly linked to militant Arab groups. December 18, Lebanon refuses to admit the deportees.

*1993.* January 12, the Arab League urges the United Nations to impose sanctions on Israel for not allowing the Palestinian deportees to return. January 13, U.S. warplanes strike Iraqi targets in response to Iraqi incursions into Kuwait and Baghdad's refusal to cooperate with international weapons inspectors. January 19, Israel repeals a law prohibiting contacts with PLO members. March 10, Palestinian leaders reject a U.S.-Russian proposal to resume peace negotiations with Israel. March 25, Benyamin Netanyahu is elected to replace Yitzhak Shamir as leader of Israel's Likud party. March 30, Prime Minister Rabin says that in response to a surge of violence, Israel is sealing off the occupied territories. April 14-16, former president Bush visits Kuwait. April 21, Arab negotiators announce that they will resume peace talks with Israel. June 11, Iranian president Rafsanjani is elected to a second four-year term. June 26, in response to evidence that Iraq sponsored an assassination plot against former president Bush when he visited Kuwait, the United States launches a cruise missile attack against the Iraqi intelligence service headquarters in Baghdad. July 25, Israel carries out intense air and artillery assaults into southern Lebanon in retaliation to rocket attacks by Hizballah guerrillas. July 31, a U.S. mediated cease-fire agreement in southern Lebanon is concluded. August 15, Israel announces a two-phased repatriation of Palestinians deported the previous December. August 30, Foreign Minister Shimon Peres discloses a draft statement of principles on Palestinian self-rule negotiated at secret Israeli-PLO talks in Norway and Tunisia. September 10, Yasir Arafat and Yitzhak Rabin exchange letters of mutual recognition. September 13, at a White House ceremony Shimon Peres and PLO negotiator Mahmoud Abbas sign a declaration of principles for interim Palestinian self-rule. October 1, a conference of forty-three nations meeting in Washington pledges $2 billion in aid for the new Palestinian entity. October 19, Israel begins releasing about six hundred Palestinian prisoners in Israeli jails. November 11, the UN Security Council tightens economic sanctions on Libya in reaction to its refusal to extradite terrorists implicated in the 1988 bombing of a PanAm jet. November 26, Iraq agrees to abide by UN Security Council Resolution 715, requiring full inspections to prevent its development of weapons of mass destruction. December 13, the target date for the beginning of a transfer of power to a Palestinian authority in the Gaza Strip and Jericho, passes without an agreement on details.

*1994.* January 16, President Assad voices Syria's willingness to negotiate a peace treaty with Israel. February 9, Israeli and PLO representatives sign the Cairo Document, which details security procedures related to the transfer of power to a Palestinian authority. February 25, an Israeli settler kills twenty-nine Arab worshippers in a crowded mosque in Hebron on the West Bank; Arab delegations break off talks with Israel. February 28, Yasir Arafat calls for an international presence in the occupied territories. March 18, U.S. secretary of state Warren Christopher announces that Syria, Jordan, and Lebanon have agreed to resume talks with Israel. March 31, the PLO agrees to reopen talks with Israel. April 12, in Cairo, Israeli and PLO negotiators agree on terms for Israel's release of five thousand Palestinian prisoners and the PLO's establishment of a police authority in Palestinian-administered areas. April 14, U.S. warplanes mistakenly shoot down two U.S. helicopters on a UN mission over northern Iraq. April 21, Prime Minister Rabin says Israel would be willing to tear down settlements in the Golan Heights as part of a peace agreement with Syria. May 4, Yasir Arafat and Yitzhak Rabin sign an agreement implementing Palestinian self-rule in the Gaza Strip and Jericho. May 13, the first Palestinian police enter Jericho. June 26, an Israeli commission says the Israeli army bears no blame in the Hebron massacre. July 1, Yasir Arafat returns to the Gaza Strip after twenty-seven years in exile. July 5, Arafat visits Jericho where he takes an oath of office as president of the Palestinian National Authority. July 7, northern Yemeni forces capture the southern city of Aden, ending a two-month civil war. July 18, Jordanian and Israeli peace negotiators meet in a tent straddling their border. July 25, King Hussein and Prime Minister Rabin sign the Jordan-Israel Washington Declaration at a White House ceremony. August 29, Israel and the PLO sign an accord granting the Palestinian National Authority administrative power over some functions throughout the West Bank. September 5, Cairo hosts the UN Conference on Population and Development. October 5, two Iraqi Republican Guard divisions are observed moving into southern Iraq near Kuwait. October 8, President Bill Clinton orders a U.S. military buildup in Saudi Arabia and the Persian Gulf in response to the Iraqi deployments. October 11, Iraqi forces begin pulling back from the Kuwaiti border. October 14, Yasir Arafat, Yitzak Rabin, and Shimon Peres are named recipients of the Nobel Peace Prize. October 14, a kidnapped Israeli soldier, three Palestinian kidnappers, and an Israeli commando are killed when Israeli forces storm the kidnappers' safe house in the West Bank. October 17, Israel and Jordan initial the first peace treaty between Israel and an Arab state since the Egyptian-Israeli Treaty of Peace in 1979. October 19, a member of Hamas blows up an Israeli bus in Tel Aviv, killing himself and twenty-one passengers. October 26, with President Clinton in attendance, Prime Minister Rabin and Prime Minister Abdul-Salam al-Majali of Jordan sign a formal peace treaty on the Jordanian-Israeli border.

# DOCUMENTS

*Following are texts of selected documents, resolutions, and speeches that have played a prominent role in Middle East affairs since 1967. The texts are arranged in chronological order.*

## UN Security Council Resolution 242

*Following the Six-Day War, the UN Security Council on November 22, 1967, unanimously approved Resolution 242 aimed at bringing peace to the Middle East.*

November 22, 1967

*The Security Council,*
  *Expressing* its continued concern with the grave situation in the Middle East,
  *Emphasizing* the inadmissibility of the acquisition of territory by war and the need to work for a just and lasting peace in which every State in the area can live in security,
  *Emphasizing further* that all Member States in their acceptance of the Charter of the United Nations have undertaken a commitment to act in accordance with Article 2 of the Charter

1. *Affirms* that the fulfilment of Charter principles requires the establishment of a just and lasting peace in the Middle East which should include the application of both the following principles:
   (i) Withdrawal of Israel armed forces from territories occupied in the recent conflict;
   (ii) Termination of all claims or states of belligerency and respect for the acknowledgement of the sovereignty, territorial integrity and political independence of every State in the area and their right to live in peace within secure and recognized boundaries free from threats or acts of force.
2. *Affirms further* the necessity

(a) For guaranteeing freedom of navigation through international waterways in the area;
(b) For achieving a just settlement of the refugee problem;
(c) For guaranteeing the territorial inviolability and political independence of every State in the area, through measures including the establishment of demilitarized zones.

3. *Requests* the Secretary-General to designate a Special Representative to proceed to the Middle East to establish and maintain contacts with the States concerned in order to promote agreement and assist efforts to achieve a peaceful and accepted settlement in accordance with the provisions and principles in this resolution.
4. *Requests* the Secretary-General to report to the Security Council on the progress of the efforts of the Special Representative as soon as possible.

## UN Security Council Resolution 338

*Between 1967 and 1973 the UN Security Council reaffirmed Resolution 242. Attempting to end the October war of 1973, the Security Council passed Resolution 338.*

October 22, 1973

*The Security Council,*

1. *Calls upon* all parties to the present fighting to cease all firing and terminate all military activity immediately, not later than 12 hours after the moment of the adoption of the decision, in the positions they now occupy;
2. *Calls upon* the parties concerned to start immediately after the ceasefire the implementation of Security Council Resolution 242 (1967) in all of its parts;
3. *Decides that,* immediately and concurrently with the

ceasefire negotiations start between the parties concerned under appropriate auspices aimed at establishing a just and durable peace in the Middle East.

# Resolution of Arab Heads of State

*In Rabat, Morocco, on October 28, 1974, Arab heads of state declared the Palestine Liberation Organization the sole representative of the Palestinian people, removing this title from King Hussein of Jordan.*

Rabat, October 28, 1974

The Conference of the Arab Heads of State:

1. *Affirms* the right of the Palestinian people to return to their homeland and to self-determination.
2. *Affirms* the right of the Palestinian people to establish an independent national authority, under the leadership of the PLO in its capacity as the sole legitimate representative of the Palestine people, over all liberated territory. The Arab States are pledged to uphold this authority, when it is established, in all spheres and at all levels.
3. *Supports* the PLO in the exercise of its national and international responsibilities, within the context of the principle of Arab solidarity.
4. *Invites* the kingdoms of Jordan, Syria and Egypt to formalize their relations in the light of these decisions and in order that they be implemented.
5. *Affirms* the obligation of all Arab States to preserve Palestinian unity and not to interfere in Palestinian internal affairs.

# Egyptian-Israeli Treaty of Peace

*Following is the text of the Treaty of Peace between the Arab Republic of Egypt and Israel, signed in Washington March 26, 1979, by President Anwar Sadat of Egypt and Prime Minister Menachem Begin of Israel and witnessed by U.S. president Jimmy Carter.*

The Government of the Arab Republic of Egypt and the Government of the State of Israel;

## Preamble

Convinced of the urgent necessity of the establishment of a just, comprehensive and lasting peace in the Middle East in accordance with Security Council Resolutions 242 and 338;

Reaffirming their adherence to the "Framework for Peace in the Middle East Agreed at Camp David," dated September 17, 1978;

Noting that the aforementioned Framework as appropriate is intended to constitute a basis for peace not only between Egypt and Israel but also between Israel and each of the other Arab neighbors which is prepared to negotiate peace with it on this basis;

Desiring to bring to an end the state of war between them and to establish a peace in which every state in the area can live in security;

Convinced that the conclusion of a Treaty of Peace between Egypt and Israel is an important step in the search for comprehensive peace in the area and for the attainment of the settlement of the Arab-Israeli conflict in all its aspects;

Inviting the other Arab parties to this dispute to join the peace process with Israel guided by and based on the principles of the aforementioned Framework;

Desiring as well to develop friendly relations and cooperation between themselves in accordance with the United Nations Charter and the principles of international law governing international relations in times of peace;

Agree to the following provisions in the free exercise of their sovereignty, in order to implement the "Framework for the Conclusion of a Peace Treaty between Egypt and Israel":

## Article I

1. The state of war between the Parties will be terminated and peace will be established between them upon the exchange of instruments of ratification of this Treaty.
2. Israel will withdraw all its armed forces and civilians from the Sinai behind the international boundary between Egypt and mandated Palestine, as provided in the annexed protocol (Annex I), and Egypt will resume the exercise of its full sovereignty over the Sinai.
3. Upon completion of the interim withdrawal provided for in Annex I, the Parties will establish normal and friendly relations, in accordance with Article III (3).

## Article II

The permanent boundary between Egypt and Israel is the recognized international boundary between Egypt and the former mandated territory of Palestine as shown on the map at Annex II, without prejudice to the issue of the status of the Gaza Strip. The Parties recognize this boundary as inviolable. Each will respect the territorial integrity of the other, including their territorial waters and airspace.

## Article III

1. The Parties will apply between them the provisions of the Charter of the United Nations and the principles of international law governing relations among states in times of peace. In particular:
   a. They recognize and will respect each other's sovereignty, territorial integrity and political independence;
   b. They recognize and will respect each other's right to live in peace within their secure and recognized boundaries;
   c. They will refrain from the threat or use of force, directly or indirectly, against each other and will settle all disputes between them by peaceful means;
2. Each Party undertakes to ensure that acts or threats of belligerency, hostility or violence do not originate from and are not committed from within its territory, or by any forces subject to its control or by any other forces stationed on its territory, against the population, citizens or property of the other Party. Each Party also undertakes to refrain from organizing, instigating, inciting, assisting or participating in acts or threats of belligerency, hostility, subversion or violence against the other Party, anywhere, and undertakes to insure that perpetrators of such acts are brought to justice.
3. The Parties agree that the normal relationship established between them will include full recognition, diplomatic, economic and cultural relations, termination of economic boycotts and discriminatory barriers to the free movement of people and goods, and will guarantee the mutual enjoyment by citizens of the due process of law. The process by which they undertake to achieve such a relationship parallel to the implementation of other provisions of this Treaty is set out in the annexed protocol (Annex III).

## Article IV

1. In order to provide maximum security for both Parties on the basis of reciprocity, agreed security arrangements will be established including limited force zones in Egyptian and Israeli territory, and United Nations forces and observers, described in detail as to nature and timing in Annex I, and other security arrangements the Parties may agree upon.
2. The Parties agree to the stationing of United Nations personnel in areas described in Annex I. The Parties agree not to request withdrawal of the United Nations personnel and that these personnel will not be removed unless such removal is approved by the Security Council of the United Nations, with the affirmative vote of the five Permanent Members, unless the Parties otherwise agree.
3. A Joint Commission will be established to facilitate the implementation of the Treaty, as provided for in Annex I.
4. The security arrangements provided for in paragraphs 1 and 2 of this Article may at the request of either party be reviewed and amended by mutual agreement of the Parties.

## Article V

1. Ships of Israel, and cargoes destined for or coming from Israel, shall enjoy the right of free passage through the Suez Canal and its approaches through the Gulf of Suez and the Mediterranean Sea on the basis of the Constantinople Convention of 1888, applying to all nations. Israeli nationals, vessels and cargoes, as well as persons, vessels and cargoes destined for or coming from Israel, shall be accorded non-discriminatory treatment in all matters connected with usage of the canal.
2. The Parties consider the Strait of Tiran and the Gulf of Aqaba to be international waterways open to all nations for unimpeded and non-suspendable freedom of navigation and overflight. The Parties will respect each other's right to navigation and overflight for access to either country through the Strait of Tiran and the Gulf of Aqaba.

## Article VI

1. This Treaty does not affect and shall not be interpreted as affecting in any way the rights and obligations of the Parties under the Charter of the United Nations.
2. The Parties undertake to fulfill in good faith their obligations under this Treaty, without regard to action or inaction of any other party and independently of any instrument external to this Treaty.
3. They further undertake to take all the necessary measures for the application in their relations of the provisions of the multilateral conventions to which they are parties, including the submission of appropriate notification to the Secretary General of the United Nations and other depositories of such conventions.
4. The parties undertake not to enter into any obligation in conflict with this Treaty.
5. Subject to Article 103 of the United Nations Charter, in the event of a conflict between the obligations of the Parties under the present Treaty and any of their other obligations, the obligations under this Treaty will be binding and implemented.

## Article VII

1. Disputes arising out of the application or interpretation of this Treaty shall be resolved by negotiations.
2. Any such disputes which cannot be settled by negotiations shall be resolved by conciliation or submitted to arbitration.

## Article VIII

The Parties agree to establish a claims commission for the mutual settlement of all financial claims.

## Article IX

1. This Treaty shall enter into force upon exchange of instruments of ratification.
2. This Treaty supersedes the agreement between Egypt and Israel of September, 1975.
3. All protocols, annexes and maps attached to this Treaty shall be regarded as an integral part hereof.
4. The Treaty shall be communicated to the Secretary General of the United Nations for registration in accordance with the provisions of Article 102 of the Charter of the United Nations.

Done at Washington, D.C. this 26th day of March, 1979, in triplicate in the English, Arabic, and Hebrew languages, each text being equally authentic. In case of any divergence of interpretation, the English text shall prevail.

For the Government of the
Arab Republic of Egypt:                  A. Sadat
For the Government of Israel:             M. Begin
Witnessed by:                 Jimmy Carter, President of
                              the United States of America

# UN Security Council Resolution 598

*The UN Security Council on July 20, 1987, unanimously approved Resolution 598, which called for an end to the war between Iran and Iraq.*

*The Security Council,*

*Reaffirming* its resolution 582 (1986),

*Deeply concerned* that, despite its calls for a cease-fire, the conflict between Iran and Iraq continues unabated, with further heavy loss of human life and material destruction,

*Deploring* the initiation and continuation of the conflict,

*Deploring also* the bombing of purely civilian population centres, attacks on neutral shipping or civilian aircraft, the violation of international humanitarian law and other laws of armed conflict, and, in particular, the use of chemical weapons contrary to obligations under the 1925 Geneva Protocol,

*Deeply concerned* that further escalation and widening of the conflict may take place,

*Determined* to bring to an end all military actions between Iran and Iraq,

*Convinced* that a comprehensive, just, honourable and durable settlement should be achieved between Iran and Iraq,

*Recalling* the provisions of the Charter of the United Nations, and in particular the obligation of all Member States to settle their international disputes by peaceful means in such a manner that international peace and security and justice are not endangered,

*Determining* that there exists a breach of the peace as regards the conflict between Iran and Iraq,

*Acting* under Articles 39 and 40 of the Charter of the United Nations,

1. *Demands* that, as a first step towards a negotiated settlement, Iran and Iraq observe an immediate cease-fire, discontinue all military actions on land, at sea and in the air, and withdraw all forces to the internationally recognized boundaries without delay;
2. *Requests* the Secretary-General to dispatch a team of United Nations Observers to verify, confirm and supervise the cease-fire and withdrawal and further requests the Secretary-General to make the necessary arrangements in consultation with the Parties and to submit a report thereon to the Security Council;
3. *Urges* that prisoners-of-war be released and repatriated without delay after the cessation of active hostilities in accordance with the Third Geneva Convention of 12 August 1949;
4. *Calls upon* Iran and Iraq to co-operate with the Secretary-General in implementing this resolution and in mediation efforts to achieve a comprehensive, just and honourable settlement, acceptable to both sides, of all outstanding issues, in accordance with the principles contained in the Charter of the United Nations;
5. *Calls upon* all other States to exercise the utmost restraint and to refrain from any act which may lead to further escalation and widening of the conflict, and thus to facilitate the implementation of the present resolution;
6. *Requests* the Secretary-General to explore, in consultation with Iran and Iraq, the question of entrusting an impartial body with inquiring into responsibility for the conflict and to report to the Security Council as soon as possible;
7. *Recognizes* the magnitude of the damage inflicted during the conflict and the need for reconstruction

efforts, with appropriate international assistance, once the conflict is ended and, in this regard, requests the Secretary-General to assign a team of experts to study the question of reconstruction and to report to the Security Council;

8. *Further requests* the Secretary-General to examine, in consultation with Iran and Iraq and with other States of the region, measures to enhance the security and stability of the region;

9. *Requests* the Secretary-General to keep the Security Council informed on the implementation of this resolution;

10. *Decides* to meet again as necessary to consider further steps to ensure compliance with this resolution.

# Iran's Acceptance of Resolution 598

*President Ali Khamenei accepted UN Resolution 598 on behalf of Iran in a July 18, 1988, letter to UN Secretary General Javier Pérez de Cuéllar. The letter was the first step in establishing a truce in the Iran-Iraq war.*

In the name of God, the Compassionate, the Merciful.

Excellency,

Please accept my warm greetings with best wishes for Your Excellency's success in efforts to establish peace and justice.

As you are well aware, the fire of the war which was started by the Iraqi regime on 22 September 1980 through an aggression against the territorial integrity of the Islamic Republic of Iran has now gained unprecedented dimensions, bringing other countries into the war and even engulfing innocent civilians.

The killing of 290 innocent human beings, caused by the shooting down of an Airbus aircraft of the Islamic Republic of Iran by one of America's warships in the Persian Gulf is a clear manifestation of this contention.

Under these circumstances, Your Excellency's effort for the implementation of Resolution 598 is of particular importance. The Islamic Republic of Iran has always provided you with its assistance and support to achieve this objective. In this context, we have decided to officially declare that the Islamic Republic of Iran—because of the importance it attaches to saving the lives of human beings and the establishment of justice and regional and international peace and security—accepts Security Council Resolution 598.

We hope that the official declaration of this position by the Islamic Republic of Iran would assist you in continuing your efforts, which has always received our support and appreciation.

# Hussein's Renunciation of Claim to West Bank

*In a July 31, 1988, speech King Hussein of Jordan renounced his nation's claims to the West Bank and severed all legal and administrative links with it.*

*In the name of God, the compassionate, the merciful and peace be upon his faithful Arab messenger*

Brother citizens.... [W]e have initiated, after seeking God's assistance, and in light of a thorough and extensive study, a series of measures with the aim of enhancing the Palestinian national orientation, and highlighting the Palestinian identity. Our objective is the benefit of the Palestinian cause and the Arab Palestinian people.

Our decision, as you know, comes after thirty-eight years of the unity of the two banks, and fourteen years after the Rabat Summit Resolution, designating the Palestine Liberation Organization (PLO) as the sole legitimate representative of the Palestinian people. It also comes six years after the Fez [Morocco] Summit Resolution of an independent Palestinian state in the occupied West Bank and the Gaza Strip....

The considerations leading to the search to identify the relationship between the West Bank and the Hashemite Kingdom of Jordan, against the background of the PLO's call for the establishment of an independent Palestinian state, are twofold:

I. The principle of Arab unity, this being a national objective to which all the Arab peoples aspire, and which they all seek to realize.

II. The political reality of the scope of benefit to the Palestinian struggle that accrues from maintaining the legal relationship between the two banks of the kingdom....

... We respect the wish of the PLO, the sole legitimate representative of the Palestinian people, to secede from us in an independent Palestinian state. We say this in all understanding. Nevertheless, Jordan will remain the proud bearer of the message of the great Arab revolt; faithful to its principles; believing in the common Arab destiny; and committed to joint Arab action.

Regarding the political factor, it has been our belief, since the Israeli aggression of June 1967, that our first priority should be to liberate the land and holy places from Israeli occupation.

Accordingly, as is well known, we have concentrated all our efforts during the twenty-one years since the occupation towards this goal. We had never imagined that the preservation of the legal and administrative links between the two banks could constitute an obstacle to the liberation of the occupied Palestinian land. . . .

Lately, it has transpired that there is a general Palestinian and Arab orientation towards highlighting the Palestinian identity in a complete manner. . . . It is also viewed that these [Jordanian-West Bank] links hamper the Palestinian struggle to gain international support for the Palestinian cause, as the national cause of a people struggling against foreign occupation. . . .

. . . [T]here is a general conviction that the struggle to liberate the occupied Palestinian land could be enhanced by dismantling the legal and administrative links between the two banks, we have to fulfill our duty, and do what is required of us. At the Rabat Summit of 1974 we responded to the Arab leaders' appeal to us to continue our interaction with the occupied West Bank through the Jordanian institutions, to support the steadfastness of our brothers there. Today we respond to the wish of the Palestine Liberation Organization, the sole legitimate representative of the Palestinian people, and to the Arab orientation to affirm the Palestinian identity in all its aspects. . . .

Brother citizens. . . . We cannot continue in this state of suspension, which can neither serve Jordan nor the Palestinian cause. We had to leave the labyrinth of fears and doubts, towards clearer horizons where mutual trust, understanding, and cooperation can prevail, to the benefit of the Palestinian cause and Arab unity. This unity will remain a goal which all the Arab peoples cherish and seek to realize.

At the same time, it has to be understood in all clarity, and without any ambiguity or equivocation, that our measures regarding the West Bank, concern only the occupied Palestinian land and its people. They naturally do not relate in any way to the Jordanian citizens of Palestinian origin in the Hashemite Kingdom of Jordan. They all have the full rights of citizenship and all its obligations, the same as any other citizen irrespective of his origin. They are an integral part of the Jordanian state. They belong to it, they live on its land, and they participate in its life and all its activities. Jordan is not Palestine; and the independent Palestinian state will be established on the occupied Palestinian land after its liberation, God willing. There the Palestinian identity will be embodied, and there the Palestinian struggle shall come to fruition, as confirmed by the glorious uprising of the Palestinian people under occupation.

National unity is precious in any country; but in Jordan it is more than that. It is the basis of our stability, and the springboard of our development and prosperity. It is the foundation of our national security and the source of our faith in the future. It is the living embodiment of the principles of the great Arab revolt, which we inherited, and whose banner we proudly bear. It is a living example of constructive plurality, and a sound nucleus for wider Arab unity.

Based on that, safeguarding national unity is a sacred duty that will not be compromised. Any attempt to undermine it, under any pretext, would only help the enemy carry out his policy of expansion at the expense of Palestine and Jordan alike. Consequently, true nationalism lies in bolstering and fortifying national unity. Moreover, the responsibility to safeguard it falls on every one of you, leaving no place in our midst for sedition or treachery. With God's help, we shall be as always, a united cohesive family, whose members are joined by bonds of brotherhood, affection, awareness, and common national objectives. . . .

The constructive plurality which Jordan has lived since its foundation, and through which it has witnessed progress and prosperity in all aspects of life, emanates not only from our faith in the sanctity of national unity, but also in the importance of Jordan's Pan-Arab role. Jordan presents itself as the living example of the merger of various Arab groups on its soil, within the framework of good citizenship, and one Jordanian people. This paradigm that we live on our soil gives us faith in the inevitability of attaining Arab unity, God willing. . . .

Citizens, Palestinian brothers in the occupied Palestinian lands, to dispel any doubts that may arise out of our measures, we assure you that these measures do not mean the abandonment of our national duty, either towards the Arab-Israeli conflict, or towards the Palestinian cause. . . . Jordan will continue its support for the steadfastness of the Palestinian people, and their courageous uprising in the occupied Palestinian land, within its capabilities. I have to mention, that when we decided to cancel the Jordanian Development Plan in the occupied territories, we contacted, at the same time, various friendly governments and international institutions, which had expressed their wish to contribute to the plan, urging them to continue financing development projects in the occupied Palestinian lands, through the relevant Palestinian quarters.

. . . No one outside Palestine has had, nor can have, an attachment to Palestine, or its cause, firmer than that of Jordan or of my family. Moreover, Jordan is a confrontation state, whose borders with Israel are longer than those of any other Arab state, longer even than the combined borders of the West Bank and Gaza with Israel.

In addition, Jordan will not give up its commitment to take part in the peace process. We have contributed to the peace process until it reached the stage of a consensus to convene an international peace conference on the Middle East. The purpose of the conference would be to achieve a just and comprehensive peace settlement to the Arab-Israeli conflict, and the settlement of the Palestinian problem in all its aspects. . . .

Jordan, dear brothers, is a principal party to the Arab-

Israeli conflict, and to the peace process. It shoulders its national responsibilities on that basis.

I thank you and salute you, and reiterate my heartfelt wishes to you, praying God the almighty to grant us assistance and guidance, and to grant our Palestinian brothers victory and success.

May God's peace, mercy, and blessings be upon you.

## Arafat Statement on Israel, Terrorism

*At a December 14, 1988, press conference in Geneva, Palestine Liberation Organization leader Yasir Arafat explicitly recognized Israel's right to exist, renounced terrorism, and accepted UN Security Council resolutions 242 and 338. Arafat's statement prompted the United States to open a dialogue with the PLO. Following is the text of Arafat's statement.*

Let me highlight my views before you. Our desire for peace is a strategy and not an interim tactic. We are bent on peace come what may, come what may.

Our statehood provides salvation to the Palestinians and peace to both Palestinians and Israelis.

Self-determination means survival for the Palestinians and our survival does not destroy the survival of the Israelis as their rulers claim.

Yesterday in my speech I made reference to United Nations Resolution 181 as the basis for Palestinian independence. I also made reference to our acceptance of Resolution 242 and 338 as the basis for negotiations with Israel within the framework of the international conference. These three resolutions were endorsed by our Palestine National Council session in Algiers.

In my speech also yesterday, it was clear that we mean our people's rights to freedom and national independence, according to Resolution 181, and the right of all parties concerned in the Middle East conflict to exist in peace and security, and, as I have mentioned, including the state of Palestine, Israel and other neighbors, according to Resolution 242 and 338.

As for terrorism, I renounced it yesterday in no uncertain terms, and yet, I repeat for the record. I repeat for the record that we totally and absolutely renounce all forms of terrorism, including individual, group and state terrorism.

Between Geneva and Algiers, we have made our position crystal clear. Any more talk such as "The Palestinians should give more"—you remember this slogan?—or "It is not enough" or "The Palestinians are engaging in propaganda games, and public-relations exercises" will be damaging and counterproductive.

Enough is enough. Enough is enough. Enough is enough. All remaining matters should be discussed around the table and within the international conference.

Let it be absolutely clear that neither Arafat, nor any for that matter, can stop the intifada, the uprising. The intifada will come to an end only when practical and tangible steps have been taken towards the achievement of our national aims and establishment of our independent Palestinian state.

In this context, I expect the E.E.C. to play a more effective role in promoting peace in our region. They have a political responsibility, they have a moral responsibility, and they can deal with it.

Finally, I declare before you and I ask you to kindly quote me on that: We want peace. We want peace. We are committed to peace. We are committed to peace. We want to live in our Palestinian state, and let live. Thank you.

## Bush Announcement of Troop Deployments

*On August 8, 1990, President Bush delivered a televised address from the Oval Office on his decision to send U.S. military forces to Saudi Arabia to help it defend itself against possible aggressive actions by Iraq.*

In the life of a nation, we're called upon to define who we are and what we believe. Sometimes, these choices are not easy. But today, as president, I ask for your support in a decision I've made to stand up for what's right and condemn what's wrong, all in the cause of peace.

At my direction, elements of the 82nd Airborne Division, as well as key units of the United States Air Force, are arriving today to take up defensive positions in Saudi Arabia. I took this action to assist the Saudi Arabian government in the defense of its homeland. No one commits American armed forces to a dangerous mission lightly, but after perhaps unparalleled international consultation and exhausting every alternative, it became necessary to take this action.

Let me tell you why. Less than a week ago in the early morning hours of August 2, Iraqi armed forces, without provocation or warning, invaded a peaceful Kuwait. Facing negligible resistance from its much smaller neighbor, Iraq's tanks stormed in blitzkrieg fashion through Kuwait in a few short hours. With more than 100,000 troops, along with tanks, artillery, and surface-to-surface missiles, Iraq now occupies Kuwait.

This aggression came just hours after [Iraqi President] Saddam Hussein specifically assured numerous countries in the area that there would be no invasion. There is no justification whatsoever for this outrageous and brutal act of aggression.

A puppet regime, imposed from the outside, is unacceptable. The acquisition of territory by force is unacceptable.

No one, friend or foe, should doubt our desire for peace, and no one should underestimate our determination to confront aggression.

Four simple principles guide our policy.

First, we seek the immediate, unconditional, and complete withdrawal of all Iraqi forces from Kuwait.

Second, Kuwait's legitimate government must be restored to replace the puppet regime.

And third, my administration, as has been the case with every president from President [Franklin D.] Roosevelt to President [Ronald] Reagan, is committed to the security and stability of the Persian Gulf.

And fourth, I am determined to protect the lives of American citizens abroad.

Immediately after the Iraqi invasion, I ordered an embargo of all trade with Iraq, and, together with many other nations, announced sanctions that both froze all Iraqi assets in this country and protected Kuwait's assets.

The stakes are high. Iraq is already a rich and powerful country that possesses the world's second-largest reserves of oil and over a million men under arms. It's the fourth largest military in the world.

Our country now imports nearly half the oil it consumes and could face a major threat to its economic independence. Much of the world is even more dependent on imported oil and is even more vulnerable to Iraqi threats.

We succeeded in the struggle for freedom in Europe because we and our allies remain stalwart. Keeping the peace in the Middle East will require no less.

We're beginning a new era. This new era can be full of promise, an age of freedom, a time of peace for all peoples. But if history teaches us anything, it is that we must resist aggression, or it will destroy our freedoms.

Appeasement does not work. As was the case in the 1930s, we see in Saddam Hussein an aggressive dictator threatening his neighbors. Only fourteen days ago, Saddam Hussein promised his friends he would not invade Kuwait. And four days ago, he promised the world he would withdraw. And twice we have seen what his promises mean. His promises mean nothing.

In the last few days I've spoken with political leaders from the Middle East, Europe, Asia, the Americas, and I've met with [British] Prime Minister [Margaret] Thatcher, [Canadian] Prime Minister [Brian] Mulroney, and NATO Secretary General [Manfred] Wöerner. And all agree that Iraq cannot be allowed to benefit from its invasion of Kuwait.

We agree that this is not an American problem or a European problem or a Middle East problem. It is the world's problem, and that's why soon after the Iraqi invasion, the United Nations Security Council, without dissent, condemned Iraq, calling for the immediate and unconditional withdrawal of its troops from Kuwait.

The Arab world, through both the Arab League and the Gulf Cooperation Council, courageously announced its opposition to Iraqi aggression. Japan, the United Kingdom, and France, and other governments around the world have imposed severe sanctions.

The Soviet Union and China ended all arms sales to Iraq, and this past Monday, the United Nations Security Council approved for the first time in twenty-three years mandatory sanctions under Chapter VII of the United Nations Charter.

These sanctions, now enshrined in international law, have the potential to deny Iraq the fruits of aggression, while sharply limiting its ability to either import or export anything of value, especially oil.

I pledge here today that the United States will do its part to see that these sanctions are effective and to induce Iraq to withdraw without delay from Kuwait. But we must recognize that Iraq may not stop using force to advance its ambitions.

Iraq has massed an enormous war machine on the Saudi border, capable of initiating hostilities with little or no additional preparation. Given the Iraqi government's history of aggression against its own citizens as well as its neighbors, to assume Iraq will not attack again would be unwise and unrealistic. And therefore, after consulting with [Saudi] King Fahd, I sent Secretary of Defense Dick Cheney to discuss cooperative measures we could take.

Following those meetings, the Saudi government requested our help and I responded to that request by ordering U.S. air and ground forces to deploy to the kingdom of Saudi Arabia.

Let me be clear: The sovereign independence of Saudi Arabia is of vital interest to the United States. This decision, which I shared with the congressional leadership, grows out of the longstanding friendship and security relationship between the United States and Saudi Arabia. U.S. forces will work together with those of Saudi Arabia and other nations to preserve the integrity of Saudi Arabia and to deter further Iraqi aggression.

Through the presence, as well as through their training and exercises, these multinational forces will enhance the overall capability of Saudi armed forces to defend the kingdom.

I want to be clear about what we are doing and why. America does not seek conflict, nor do we seek to chart the destiny of other nations. But America will stand by her friends. The mission of our troops is wholly defensive. Hopefully, they will not be needed long.

They will not initiate hostilities, but they will defend themselves, the kingdom of Saudi Arabia, and other friends in the Persian Gulf.

We are working around the clock to deter Iraqi aggression and to enforce UN sanctions. I'm continuing my conversations with world leaders. Secretary of Defense Cheney has just returned from valuable consultations with President [Hosni] Mubarak of Egypt and King Hassan of Morocco. Secretary of State [James A.] Baker [III] has consulted with his counterparts in many nations, including the Soviet Union. And today he heads for Europe to consult with President [Turgut] Ozal of Turkey, a staunch friend of the United States. And he'll then consult with the NATO foreign ministers.

I will ask oil-producing nations to do what they can to increase production in order to minimize any impact that oil-flow reductions will have on the world economy. And I will explore whether we and our allies should draw down our strategic petroleum reserves.

Conservation measures can also help. Americans everywhere must do their part.

And one more thing: I'm asking the oil companies to do their fair share. They should show restraint and not abuse today's uncertainties to raise prices. Standing up for our principles will not come easy. It may take time and possibly cost a great deal, but we are asking no more of anyone than of the brave young men and women of our armed forces and their families, and I ask that—and the churches around the country—prayers be said for those who are committed to protect and defend America's interests.

Standing up for our principles is an American tradition. As it has so many times before, it may take time and tremendous effort, but most of all, it will take unity of purpose. As I've witnessed throughout my life in both war and peace, America has never wavered when her purpose is driven by principle, and on this August day, at home and abroad, I know she will do no less.

Thank you, and God bless the United States of America.

# UN Security Council Resolution 678

*On November 29, 1990, the UN Security Council passed Resolution 678. It authorized member nations to use "all necessary means" after January 15, 1991, to force Iraq to withdraw from Kuwait and comply with all UN Security Council resolutions related to its aggression. The vote was 12-2 with 1 abstention.*

*The Security Council,*

*Recalling and reaffirming* its resolutions 660 (1990), 661 (1990), 662 (1990), 664 (1990), 665 (1990), 666 (1990), 667 (1990), 669 (1990), 670 (1990) and 674 (1990),

*Noting that,* despite all efforts by the United Nations,

Iraq refuses to comply with its obligation to implement resolution 660 (1990) and the above subsequent relevant resolutions, in flagrant contempt of the Council,

*Mindful* of its duties and responsibilities under the Charter of the United Nations for the maintenance and preservation of international peace and security,

*Determined* to secure full compliance with its decisions,

*Acting* under Chapter VII of the Charter of the United Nations,

1. *Demands* that Iraq comply fully with resolution 660 (1990) and all subsequent relevant resolutions and decides, while maintaining all its decisions, to allow Iraq one final opportunity, as a pause of goodwill, to do so;

2. *Authorizes* Member States cooperating with the Government of Kuwait, unless Iraq on or before 15 January 1991 fully implements, as set forth in paragraph 1 above, the foregoing resolutions, to use all necessary means to uphold and implement Security Council resolution 660 (1990) and all subsequent relevant resolutions and to restore international peace and security in the area;

3. *Requests* all States to provide appropriate support for the actions undertaken in pursuance of paragraph 2 of this resolution;

4. *Requests* the States concerned to keep the Council regularly informed on the progress of actions undertaken pursuant to paragraph 2 and 3 of this resolution;

5. *Decides* to remain seized of the matter.

# Bush Announcement of Cease-Fire

*On February 27, 1991, President George Bush delivered a televised speech from the White House in which he announced the liberation of Kuwait and a cease-fire in the Persian Gulf War.*

Kuwait is liberated. Iraq's army is defeated. Our military objectives are met. Kuwait is once more in the hands of Kuwaitis, in control of their own destiny. We share in their joy, a joy tempered only by our compassion for their ordeal.

Tonight, the Kuwaiti flag once again flies above the capital of a free and sovereign nation, and the American flag flies above our embassy.

Seven months ago, America and the world drew a line in the sand. We declared that the aggression against Kuwait would not stand, and tonight America and the world have kept their word.

This is not a time of euphoria, certainly not a time to gloat. But it is a time of pride: pride in our troops, pride in the friends who stood with us in the crisis, pride in our nation and the people whose strength and resolve made victory quick, decisive, and just. And soon, we will open wide our arms to welcome back home to America our magnificent fighting forces.

No one country can claim this victory as its own. It was not only a victory for Kuwait, but a victory for all the coalition partners.

This is a victory for the United Nations, for all mankind, for the rule of law, and for what is right.

After consulting with Secretary of Defense [Dick] Cheney, the chairman of the Joint Chiefs of Staff [Gen. Colin L.] Powell [Jr.], and our coalition partners, I am pleased to announce that at midnight tonight, Eastern Standard Time, exactly one hundred hours since ground operations commenced, and six weeks since the start of Operation Desert Storm, all United States and coalition forces will suspend offensive combat operations.

It is up to Iraq whether this suspension on the part of the coalition becomes a permanent cease-fire. Coalition political and military terms for a formal cease-fire include the following requirements:

Iraq must release immediately all coalition prisoners of war, third-country nationals, and the remains of all who have fallen.

Iraq must release all Kuwaiti detainees. Iraq also must inform Kuwaiti authorities of the location and nature of all land and sea mines.

Iraq must comply fully with all relevant United Nations Security Council resolutions. This includes a rescinding of Iraq's August decision to annex Kuwait and acceptance in principle of Iraq's responsibility to pay compensation for the loss, damage, and injury its aggression has caused.

The coalition calls upon the Iraqi government to designate military commanders to meet within forty-eight hours with their coalition counterparts, at a place in the theater of operations to be specified, to arrange for military aspects of the cease-fire.

Further, I have asked Secretary of State [James A.] Baker [III] to request that the United Nations Security Council meet to formulate the necessary arrangements for this war to be ended.

This suspension of offensive combat operations is contingent upon Iraq's not firing upon any coalition forces, and not launching Scud missiles against any other country. If Iraq violates these terms, coalition forces will be free to resume military operations.

At every opportunity, I have said to the people of Iraq that our quarrel was not with them, but instead with their leadership, and above all with Saddam Hussein. This remains the case. You, the people of Iraq, are not our enemy. We do not seek your destruction. We have treated your POWs with kindness. Coalition forces fought this war only as a last resort, and looked forward to the day when Iraq is led by people prepared to live in peace with their neighbors.

We must now begin to look beyond victory and war. We must meet the challenge of securing the peace. In the future, as before, we will consult with our coalition partners. We've already done a good deal of thinking and planning for the postwar period.

And Secretary Baker has already begun to consult with our coalition partners on the region's challenges. There can be and will be no solely American answer to all these challenges, but we can assist and support the countries of the region and be a catalyst for peace.

In this spirit, Secretary Baker will go to the region next week to begin a new round of consultations.

This war is now behind us. Ahead of us is the difficult task of securing a potentially historic peace. Tonight, though, let us be proud of what we have accomplished. Let us give thanks to those who risked their lives.

Let us never forget those who gave their lives.

May God bless our valiant military forces and their families, and let us all remember them in our prayers. Good night, and may God bless the United States of America.

# Israeli-Palestinian Declaration of Principles

*Following is the text of "Declaration of Principles on Interim Self-Government and Arrangements" signed by Israeli foreign minister Shimon Peres and PLO foreign affairs spokesperson Mahmoud Abbas, in Washington, D.C., on September 13, 1993.*

The Government of the State of Israel and the P.L.O. team (in the Jordanian-Palestinian delegation to the Middle East Peace Conference) (the "Palestinian Delegation"), representing the Palestinian people, agree that it is time to put an end to decades of confrontation and conflict, recognize their mutual legitimate and political rights, and strive to live in peaceful coexistence and mutual dignity and security and achieve a just, lasting and comprehensive peace settlement and historic reconciliation through the agreed political process. Accordingly, the two sides agree to the following principles:

## Article I
### Aim of the Negotiations

The aim of the Israeli-Palestinian negotiations within the current Middle East peace process is, among other things, to establish a Palestinian Interim Self-Government Authority, the elected Council (the "Council"), for the Palestinian people in the West Bank and the Gaza Strip, for a transitional period not exceeding five years, leading to a permanent settlement based on Security Council Resolutions 242 and 338.

It is understood that the interim arrangements are an integral part of the whole peace process and that the negotiations on the permanent status will lead to the implementation of Security Council Resolutions 242 and 338.

## Article II
### Framework for the Interim Period

The agreed framework for the interim period is set forth in this Declaration of Principles.

## Article III
### Elections

1. In order that the Palestinian people in the West Bank and Gaza Strip may govern themselves according to democratic principles, direct, free and general political elections will be held for the Council under agreed supervision and international observation, while the Palestinian police will ensure public order.
2. An agreement will be concluded on the exact mode and conditions of the elections in accordance with the protocol attached as Annex I, with the goal of holding the elections not later than nine months after the entry into force of this Declaration of Principles.
3. These elections will constitute a significant interim preparatory step toward the realization of the legitimate rights of the Palestinian people and their just requirements.

## Article IV
### Jurisdiction

Jurisdiction of the Council will cover West Bank and Gaza Strip territory, except for issues that will be negotiated in the permanent status negotiations. The two sides view the West Bank and the Gaza Strip as a single territorial unit, whose integrity will be preserved during the interim period.

## Article V
### Transitional Period and Permanent Status Negotiations

1. The five-year transitional period will begin upon the withdrawal from the Gaza Strip and Jericho area.
2. Permanent status negotiations will commence as soon as possible, but not later than the beginning of the third year of the interim period, between the Government of Israel and the Palestinian people representatives.

3. It is understood that these negotiations shall cover remaining issues, including: Jerusalem, refugees, settlements, security arrangements, borders, relations and cooperation with other neighbors, and other issues of common interest.
4. The two parties agree that the outcome of the permanent status negotiations should not be prejudiced or preempted by agreements reached for the interim period.

## Article VI
### Preparatory Transfer of Powers and Responsibilities

1. Upon the entry into force of this Declaration of Principles and the withdrawal from the Gaza Strip and the Jericho area, a transfer of authority from the Israeli military government and its Civil Administration to the authorised Palestinians for this task, as detailed herein, will commence. This transfer of authority will be of a preparatory nature until the inauguration of the Council.
2. Immediately after the entry into force of this Declaration of Principles and the withdrawal from the Gaza Strip and Jericho area, with the view to promoting economic development in the West Bank and Gaza Strip, authority will be transferred to the Palestinians on the following spheres: education and culture, health, social welfare, direct taxation, and tourism. The Palestinian side will commence in building the Palestinian police force, as agreed upon. Pending the inauguration of the Council, the two parties may negotiate the transfer of additional powers and responsibilities, as agreed upon.

## Article VII
### Interim Agreement

1. The Israeli and Palestinian delegations will negotiate an agreement on the interim period (the "Interim Agreement").
2. The Interim Agreement shall specify, among other things, the structure of the Council, the number of its members, and the transfer of powers and responsibilities from the Israeli military government and its Civil Administration to the Council. The Interim Agreement shall also specify the Council's executive authority, legislative authority in accordance with Article IX below, and the independent Palestinian judicial organs.
3. The Interim Agreement shall include arrangements, to be implemented upon the inauguration of the Council, for the assumption by the Council of all of the powers and responsibilities transferred previously

in accordance with Article VI above.

4. In order to enable the Council to promote economic growth, upon its inauguration, the Council will establish, among other things, a Palestinian Electricity Authority, a Gaza Sea Port Authority, a Palestinian Development Bank, a Palestinian Export Promotion Board, a Palestinian Environmental Authority, a Palestinian Land Authority and a Palestinian Water Administration Authority, and any other Authorities agreed upon, in accordance with the Interim Agreement that will specify their powers and responsibilities.

5. After the inauguration of the Council, the Civil Administration will be dissolved, and the Israeli military government will be withdrawn.

## Article VIII
### Public Order and Security

In order to guarantee public order and internal security for the Palestinians of the West Bank and the Gaza Strip, the Council will establish a strong police force, while Israel will continue to carry the responsibility for defending against external threats, as well as the responsibility for overall security of Israelis for the purpose of safeguarding their internal security and public order.

## Article IX
### Laws and Military Orders

1. The Council will be empowered to legislate, in accordance with the Interim Agreement, within all authorities transferred to it.

2. Both parties will review jointly laws and military orders presently in force in remaining spheres.

## Article X
### Joint Israeli-Palestinian Liaison Committee

In order to provide for a smooth implementation of this Declaration of Principles and any subsequent agreements pertaining to the interim period, upon the entry into force of this Declaration of Principles, a Joint Israeli-Palestinian Liaison Committee will be established in order to deal with issues requiring coordination, other issues of common interest, and disputes.

## Article XI
### Israeli-Palestinian Cooperation in Economic Fields

Recognizing the mutual benefit of cooperation in promoting the development of the West Bank, the Gaza Strip and Israel, upon the entry into force of this Dec-

laration of Principles, an Israeli-Palestinian Economic Cooperation Committee will be established in order to develop and implement in a cooperative manner the programs identified in the protocols attached as Annex III and Annex IV.

## Article XII
### Liaison and Cooperation with Jordan and Egypt

The two parties will invite the Governments of Jordan and Egypt to participate in establishing further liaison and cooperation arrangements between the Government of Israel and the Palestinian representatives, on the one hand, and the Governments of Jordan and Egypt, on the other hand, to promote cooperation between them. These arrangements will include the constitution of a Continuing Committee that will decide by agreement on the modalities of admission of persons displaced from the West Bank and Gaza Strip in 1967, together with necessary measures to prevent disruption and disorder. Other matters of common concern will be dealt with by this Committee.

## Article XIII
### Redeployment of Israeli Forces

1. After the entry into force of this Declaration of Principles, and not later than the eve of elections for the Council, a redeployment of Israeli military forces in the West Bank and the Gaza Strip will take place, in addition to withdrawal of Israeli forces carried out in accordance with Article XIV.

2. In redeploying its military forces, Israel will be guided by the principle that its military forces should be redeployed outside populated areas.

3. Further redeployments to specified locations will be gradually implemented commensurate with the assumption of responsibility for public order and internal security by the Palestinian police force pursuant to Article VIII above.

## Article XIV
### Israeli Withdrawal from the Gaza Strip and Jericho Area

Israel will withdraw from the Gaza Strip and Jericho area, as detailed in the protocol attached as Annex II.

## Article XV
### Resolution of Disputes

1. Disputes arising out of the application or interpretation of this Declaration of Principles, or any subsequent agreements pertaining to the interim period,

shall be resolved by negotiations through the Joint Liaison Committee to be established pursuant to Article X above.

2. Disputes which cannot be settled by negotiations may be resolved by a mechanism of conciliation to be agreed upon by the parties.

3. The parties may agree to submit to arbitration disputes relating to the interim period, which cannot be settled through conciliation. To this end, upon the agreement of both parties, the parties will establish an Arbitration Committee.

## Article XVI
### Israeli-Palestinian Cooperation Concerning Regional Programs

Both parties view the multilateral working groups as an appropriate instrument for promoting a "Marshall Plan," the regional programs and other programs, including special programs for the West Bank and Gaza Strip, as indicated in the protocol attached as Annex IV.

## Article XVII
### Miscellaneous Provisions

1. This Declaration of Principles will enter into force one month after its signing.

2. All protocols annexed to this Declaration of Principles and Agreed Minutes pertaining thereto shall be regarded as an integral part hereof.

DONE at Washington, D.C., this thirteenth day of September, 1993.

## Annex I
### Protocol on the Mode and Conditions of Elections

1. Palestinians of Jerusalem who live there will have the right to participate in the election process, according to an agreement between the two sides.

2. In addition, the election agreement should cover, among other things, the following issues:
   a. the system of elections;
   b. the mode of the agreed supervision and international observation and their personal composition; and
   c. rules and regulations regarding election campaign, including agreed arrangements for the organizing of mass media, and the possibility of licensing a broadcasting and TV station.

3. The future status of displaced Palestinians who were registered on 4th June 1967 will not be prejudiced because they are unable to participate in the election process due to practical reasons.

## Annex II
### Protocol on Withdrawal of Israeli Forces from the Gaza Strip and Jericho Area

1. The two sides will conclude and sign within two months from the date of entry into force of this Declaration of Principles, an agreement on the withdrawal of Israeli military forces from the Gaza Strip and Jericho area. This agreement will include comprehensive arrangements to apply in the Gaza Strip and the Jericho area subsequent to the Israeli withdrawal.

2. Israel will implement an accelerated and scheduled withdrawal of Israeli military forces from the Gaza Strip and Jericho area, beginning immediately with the signing of the agreement on the Gaza Strip and Jericho area and to be completed within a period not exceeding four months after the signing of this agreement.

3. The above agreement will include, among other things:
   a. Arrangements for a smooth and peaceful transfer of authority from the Israeli military government and its Civil Administration to the Palestinian representatives.
   b. Structure, powers and responsibilities of the Palestinian authority in these areas, except: external security, settlements, Israelis, foreign relations, and other mutually agreed matters.
   c. Arrangements for the assumption of internal security and public order by the Palestinian police force consisting of police officers recruited locally and from abroad (holding Jordanian passports and Palestinian documents issued by Egypt). Those who will participate in the Palestinian police force coming from abroad should be trained as police and police officers.
   d. A temporary international or foreign presence, as agreed upon.
   e. Establishment of a joint Palestinian-Israeli Coordination and Cooperation Committee for mutual security purposes.
   f. An economic development and stabilization program, including the establishment of an Emergency Fund, to encourage foreign investment, and financial and economic support. Both sides will coordinate and cooperate jointly and unilaterally with regional and international parties to support these aims.
   g. Arrangements for a safe passage for persons and transportation between the Gaza Strip and Jericho area.

4. The above agreement will include arrangements for coordination between both parties regarding passages:

a. Gaza-Egypt; and
b. Jericho-Jordan.

5. The offices responsible for carrying out the powers and responsibilities of the Palestinian authority under this Annex II and Article VI of the Declaration of Principles will be located in the Gaza Strip and in the Jericho area pending the inauguration of the Council.

6. Other than these agreed arrangements, the status of the Gaza Strip and Jericho area will continue to be an integral part of the West Bank and Gaza Strip, and will not be changed in the interim period.

## *Annex III*
## Protocol on Israeli-Palestinian Cooperation in Economic and Development Programs

The two sides agree to establish an Israeli-Palestinian Continuing Committee for Economic Cooperation, focusing, among other things, on the following:

1. Cooperation in the field of water, including a Water Development Program prepared by experts from both sides, which will also specify the mode of cooperation in the management of water resources in the West Bank and Gaza Strip, and will include proposals for studies and plans on water rights of each party, as well as on the equitable utilization of joint water resources for implementation in and beyond the interim period.

2. Cooperation in the field of electricity, including an Electricity Development Program, which will specify the mode of cooperation for the production, maintenance, purchase and sale of electricity resources.

3. Cooperation in the field of energy, including an Energy Development Program, which will provide for the exploitation of oil and gas for industrial purposes, particularly in the Gaza Strip and in the Negev, and will encourage further joint exploitation of other energy resources. This Program may also provide for the construction of a Petrochemical industrial complex in the Gaza Strip and the construction of oil and gas pipelines.

4. Cooperation in the field of finance, including a Financial Development and Action Program for the encouragement of international investment in the West Bank and the Gaza Strip, and in Israel, as well as the establishment of a Palestinian Development Bank.

5. Cooperation in the field of transport and communications, including a Program, which will define guidelines for the establishment of a Gaza Sea Port Area, and will provide for the establishing of transport and communications lines to and from the West Bank and the Gaza Strip to Israel and to other

countries. In addition, this Program will provide for carrying out the necessary construction of roads, railways, communications lines, etc.

6. Cooperation in the field of trade, including studies, and Trade Promotion Programs, which will encourage local, regional and inter-regional trade, as well as a feasibility study of creating free trade zones in the Gaza Strip and in Israel, mutual access to these zones, and cooperation in other areas related to trade and commerce.

7. Cooperation in the field of industry, including Industrial Development Programs, which will provide for the establishment of joint Israeli-Palestinian Industrial Research and Development Centers, will promote Palestinian-Israeli joint ventures, and provide guidelines for cooperation in the textile, food, pharmaceutical, electronics, diamonds, computer and science-based industries.

8. A program for cooperation in, and regulation of, labor relations and cooperation in social welfare issues.

9. A Human Resources Development and Cooperation Plan, providing for joint Israeli-Palestinian workshops and seminars, and for the establishment of joint vocational training centers, research institutes and data banks.

10. An Environmental Protection Plan, providing for joint and/or coordinated measures in this sphere.

11. A program for developing coordination and cooperation in the field of communication and media.

12. Any other programs of mutual interest.

## *Annex IV*
## Protocol on Israeli-Palestinian Cooperation Concerning Regional Development Programs

1. The two sides will cooperate in the context of the multilateral peace efforts in promoting a Development Program for the region, including the West Bank and the Gaza Strip, to be initiated by the G-7. The parties will request the G-7 to seek the participation in this program of other interested states, such as members of the Organization for Economic Cooperation and Development, regional Arab states and institutions, as well as members of the private sector.

2. The Development Program will consist of two elements:
   a) an Economic Development Program for the West Bank and the Gaza Strip.
   b) a Regional Economic Development Program.
   A. The Economic Development Program for the West Bank and the Gaza Strip will consist of the following elements:
      (1) A Social Rehabilitation Program, including a

Housing and Construction Program.

(2) A Small and Medium Business Development Plan.

(3) An Infrastructure Development Program (water, electricity, transportation and communications, etc.).

(4) A Human Resources Plan.

(5) Other programs.

B. The Regional Economic Development Program may consist of the following elements:

(1) The establishment of a Middle East Development Fund, as a first step, and a Middle East Development Bank, as a second step.

(2) The development of a joint Israeli-Palestinian-Jordanian Plan for coordinated exploitation of the Dead Sea area.

(3) The Mediterranean Sea (Gaza)-Dead Sea Canal.

(4) Regional Desalinization and other water development projects.

(5) A regional plan for agricultural development, including a coordinated regional effort for the prevention of desertification.

(6) Interconnection of electricity grids.

(7) Regional cooperation for the transfer, distribution and industrial exploitation of gas, oil and other energy resources.

(8) A Regional Tourism, Transportation and Telecommunications Development Plan.

(9) Regional cooperation in other spheres.

3. The two sides will encourage the multilateral working groups, and will coordinate towards their success. The two parties will encourage intersessional activities, as well as pre-feasibility and feasibility studies, within the various multilateral working groups.

## Agreed Minutes to the Declaration of Principles on Interim Self-Government Arrangements

A. General Understandings and Agreements

Any powers and responsibilities transferred to the Palestinians pursuant to the Declaration of Principles prior to the inauguration of the Council will be subject to the same principles pertaining to Article IV, as set out in these Agreed Minutes below.

B. Specific Understandings and Agreements

### Article IV

It is understood that:

1. Jurisdiction of the Council will cover West Bank and Gaza Strip territory, except for issues that will be negotiated in the permanent status negotiations: Jerusalem, settlements, military locations, and Israelis.

2. The Council's jurisdiction will apply with regard to the agreed powers, responsibilities, spheres and authorities transferred to it.

### Article VI(2)

It is agreed that the transfer of authority will be as follows:

(1) The Palestinian side will inform the Israeli side of the names of the authorised Palestinians who will assume the powers, authorities and responsibilities that will be transferred to the Palestinians according to the Declaration of Principles in the following fields: education and culture, health, social welfare, direct taxation, tourism, and any other authorities agreed upon.

(2) It is understood that the rights and obligations of these offices will not be affected.

(3) Each of the spheres described above will continue to enjoy existing budgetary allocations in accordance with arrangements to be mutually agreed upon. These arrangements also will provide for the necessary adjustments required in order to take into account the taxes collected by the direct taxation office.

(4) Upon the execution of the Declaration of Principles, the Israeli and Palestinian delegations will immediately commence negotiations on a detailed plan for the transfer of authority on the above offices in accordance with the above understandings.

### Article VII(2)

The Interim Agreement will also include arrangements for coordination and cooperation.

### Article VII(5)

The withdrawal of the military government will not prevent Israel from exercising the powers and responsibilities not transferred to the Council.

### Article VIII

It is understood that the Interim Agreement will include arrangements for cooperation and coordination between the two parties in this regard. It is also agreed that the transfer of powers and responsibilities to the Palestinian police will be accomplished in a phased manner, as agreed in the Interim Agreement.

### Article X

It is agreed that, upon the entry into force of the Declaration of Principles, the Israeli and Palestinian delegations will exchange the names of the individuals designated by them as members of the Joint Israeli-Palestinian Liaison Committee. It is further agreed that each side will have an equal number of members in the Joint Committee. The Joint Committee will reach decisions by agreement. The Joint Committee may add other technicians and experts, as necessary. The Joint Committee will decide on the frequency and place or places of its meetings.

### Annex II

It is understood that, subsequent to the Israeli withdrawal, Israel will continue to be responsible for external security, and for internal security and public order of settlements and Israelis. Israeli military forces and civilians may continue to use roads freely within the Gaza Strip and the Jericho area.

Done at Washington, D.C., this thirteenth day of September, 1993.

## Israeli-Jordanian Washington Declaration

*Following is the "Washington Declaration," signed by Israel's Prime Minister Yitzhak Rabin and Jordan's King Hussein in Washington, D.C., on July 25, 1994.*

A. After generations of hostility, blood and tears and in the wake of years of pain and wars, His Majesty King Hussein and Prime Minister Yitzhak Rabin are determined to bring an end to bloodshed and sorrow. It is in this spirit that His Majesty King Hussein of the Hashemite Kingdom of Jordan and Prime Minister and Minister of Defense, Mr. Yitzhak Rabin of Israel, met in *Washington* today at the invitation of President William J. Clinton of the United States of America. This initiative of President William J. Clinton constitutes an historic landmark in the United States' untiring efforts in promoting peace and stability in the Middle East. The personal involvement of the president has made it possible to realize agreement on the content of this historic *declaration*. The signing of this *declaration* bears testimony to the president's vision and devotion to the cause of peace.

B. In their meeting, His Majesty King Hussein and Prime Minister Yitzhak Rabin have jointly reaffirmed the five underlying principles of their understanding on an agreed common agenda designed to reach the goal of a just, lasting and comprehensive peace between the Arab States and the Palestinians, with Israel.

1. Israel and Jordan aim at the achievement of just, lasting and comprehensive peace between Israel and its neighbors and at the conclusion of a treaty of peace between both countries.

2. The two countries will vigorously continue their negotiations to arrive at a state of peace, based on Security Council Resolutions 242 and 338 in all their aspects, and founded on freedom, equality and justice.

3. Israel respects the present special role of the Hashemite Kingdom of Jordan in Muslim holy shrines in Jerusalem. When negotiations on the permanent status will take place, Israel will give high priority to the Jordanian historic role in these shrines. In addition, the two sides have agreed to act together to promote interfaith relations among the three monotheistic religions.

4. The two countries recognize their right and obligation to live in peace with each other as well as with all states within secure and recognized boundaries. The two states affirmed their respect for and acknowledgment of the sovereignty, territorial integrity and political independence of every state in the area.

5. The two countries desire to develop good neighborly relations of cooperation between them to ensure lasting security and to avoid threats and the use of force between them.

C. The long conflict between the two states is now coming to an end. In this spirit the state of belligerency between Israel and Jordan has been terminated.

D. Following this *declaration* and in keeping with the agreed common agenda, both countries will refrain from actions or activities by either side that may adversely affect the security of the other or may prejudice the final outcome of negotiations. Neither side will threaten the other by use of force, weapons, or any other means, against each other and both sides will thwart threats to security resulting from all kinds of terrorism.

E. His Majesty King Hussein and Prime Minister Yitzhak Rabin took note of the progress made in the bilateral negotiations within the Israel-Jordan track last week on the steps decided to implement the sub-agendas on borders, territorial matters, security, water, energy, environment and the Jordan Rift Valley.

In this framework, mindful of items of the agreed common agenda — borders and territorial matters — they noted that the boundary sub-commission has reached agreement in July 1994 in fulfillment of part of the role entrusted to it in the sub-agenda. They also noted that the sub-commission for water, environment and energy agreed to mutually recognize, as the role of their negotiations, the rightful allocations of the two sides in Jordan River and Yarmouk River waters and to fully respect and comply with the negotiated rightful allocations, in accordance with agreed acceptable principles with mutually acceptable quality.

Similarly, His Majesty King Hussein and Prime Minister Yitzhak Rabin expressed their deep satisfaction and pride in the work of the trilateral commission in its meeting held in Jordan on Wednesday, July 20th, 1994, hosted by the Jordanian prime minister, Dr. Abdessalam al-Majalim and attended by Secretary of State Warren Christopher and Foreign Minister Shimon Peres. They voiced their pleasure at the association and commitment of the United States in this endeavor.

F. His Majesty King Hussein and Prime Minister Yitzhak Rabin believe that steps must be taken both to overcome psychological barriers and to break with the legacy of war. By working with optimism toward the dividends of peace for all the people in the region, Israel and Jordan are determined to shoulder their responsibilities towards the human dimension of peacemaking. They recognize imbalances and disparities are a root cause of extremism which thrives on poverty and unemployment and the degradation of human dignity. In this spirit, His Majesty King Hussein and Prime Minister Yitzhak Rabin have today approved a series of steps to symbolize the new era which is now at hand.
1. Direct telephone links will be opened between Israel and Jordan.
2. The electricity grids of Israel and Jordan will be linked as part of a regional concept.
3. Two new border crossings will be opened between Israel and Jordan — one at the southern tip of Aqaba-Eilat and the other at a mutually agreed point in the north.
4. In principle, free access will be given to third-country tourists traveling between Israel and Jordan.

5. Negotiations will be accelerated on opening an international air corridor between both countries.

The police forces of Israel and Jordan will co-operate in combating crime with emphasis on smuggling and particularly drug smuggling. The United States will be invited to participate in this joint endeavor.

6. Negotiations on economic matters will continue in order to prepare for future bilateral co-operation including the abolition of all economic boycotts.

All these steps are being implemented within the framework of regional infrastructural development plans and in conjunction with the Israel-Jordan bilaterals on boundaries, security, water and related issues and without prejudice to the final outcome of the negotiations on the items included in the Agreed Common Agenda between Israel and Jordan.

G. His Majesty King Hussein and Prime Minister Yitzhak Rabin have agreed to meet periodically or whenever they feel necessary to review the progress of the negotiations and express their firm intention to shepherd and direct the process in its entirety.

H. In conclusion, His Majesty King Hussein and Prime Minister Yitzhak Rabin wish to express once again their profound thanks and appreciation to President William J. Clinton and his administration for their untiring efforts in furthering the cause of peace, justice and prosperity for all the peoples of the region. They wish to thank the president personally for his warm welcome and hospitality. In recognition of their appreciation to the president, His Majesty King Hussein and Prime Minister Yitzhak Rabin have asked President William J. Clinton to sign this document as a witness and as a host to their meeting.

His Majesty King Hussein
Prime Minister Yitzhak Rabin
President William J. Clinton

# BIBLIOGRAPHY

## Books

Abir, Mordechai. *Saudi Arabia in the Oil Era: Regime and Elites, Conflict and Collaboration.* Boulder, Colo.: Westview Press, 1988.

Abrahamian, Evrand. *Iran Between Two Revolutions.* Princeton, N.J.: Princeton University Press, 1982.

Afkhami, Gholam R. *The Iranian Revolution: Thanatos on a National Scale.* Washington, D.C.: Middle East Institute, 1985.

Ajami, Fouad. *Arab Predicament: Arab Political Thought and Practice Since 1967.* New York: Cambridge University Press, 1981.

_____. *The Vanished Imam: Musa al Sadr and the Shia of Lebanon.* Ithaca, N.Y.: Cornell University Press, 1986.

Al-Khalil, Samir. *Republic of Fear: The Inside Story of Saddam's Iraq.* New York: Pantheon Books, 1990.

Altorki, Soraya, and Donald Cole. *Arabian Oasis City.* Austin: University of Texas Press, 1989.

Anderson, Irvine H. *Aramco, the United States, and Saudi Arabia: A Study of the Dynamics of Foreign Policy, 1933-1950.* Princeton, N.J.: Princeton University Press, 1981.

Ansari, Hameid. *Egypt, the Stalled Society.* Albany: State University of New York Press, 1986.

Avineri, Shlomo. *The Making of Modern Zionism: The Intellectual Origins of the Jewish State.* New York: Basic Books, 1981.

Bakhash, Shaul. *The Reign of the Ayatollahs: Iran and the Islamic Revolution.* New York: Basic Books, 1984.

Baker, Raymond William. *Sadat and After: Struggles for Egypt's Political Soul.* Cambridge: Harvard University Press, 1990.

Bar-Siman-Tov, Yaacov. *The Israeli-Egyptian War of Attrition, 1969-1970.* New York: Columbia University Press, 1980.

_____. *Israel, the Superpowers, and the War in the Middle East.* New York: Praeger, 1987.

Bhatia, Shyam. *Nuclear Rivals in the Middle East.* New York: Routledge, 1988.

Bidwell, Robin. *The Two Yemens.* Boulder, Colo.: Westview Press, 1983.

Bill, James A. *The Eagle and the Lion: The Tragedy of American-Iranian Relations.* New Haven: Yale University Press, 1988.

Braun, Aurel, ed. *The Middle East in Global Strategy.* Boulder, Colo.: Westview Press, 1987.

Bulloch, John. *The Persian Gulf Unveiled.* New York: Congdon and Weed, 1985.

Burgat, Francois. *The Islamic Movement in North Africa.* Bloomington: Indiana University Press, 1993.

Carter, Jimmy. *The Blood of Abraham: Insights into the Middle East.* Boston: Houghton Mifflin, 1985.

Cattan, Henry. *The Palestine Question.* New York: Croom Helm, 1988.

Cole, Juan R. I., and Nikki R. Keddie. *Shi'ism and Social Protest.* New Haven: Yale University Press, 1986.

Congressional Quarterly. *The Iran-Contra Puzzle.* Washington, D.C.: Congressional Quarterly, 1987.

Cordesman, Anthony H. *After the Storm: The Changing Military Balance in the Middle East.* Boulder, Colo.: Westview Press, 1993.

Cottam, Richard W. *Iran and the United States: A Cold War Case Study.* Pittsburgh: University of Pittsburgh Press, 1988.

Cottrell, Alvin J., and Michael L. Moodie. *The United States and the Persian Gulf, Past Mistakes and Present Needs.* New York: Strategy Information Center, 1984.

Dann, Uriel. *The Great Powers in the Middle East, 1919-1939.* New York: Holmes and Meier, 1988.

Dawisha, Adeed I. *Syria and the Lebanese Crisis.* New York: St. Martin's Press, 1980.

Dayan, Moshe. *Breakthrough: A Personal Account of the Egypt-Israel Peace Negotiations.* New York: Knopf, 1981.

Deeb, Marius. *The Lebanese Civil War.* New York: Praeger, 1980.

Drysdale, Alaisdair, and Raymond A. Hinnebusch. *Syria and the Middle East Peace Process.* New York: Council on Foreign Relations Press, 1991.

Elazar, Daniel J. *The Camp David Framework for Peace: A Shift Toward Shared Rule.* Washington, D.C.: American Enterprise Institute for Public Policy Research, 1979.

Esposito, John L. *The Islamic Threat: Myth or Reality.* New York: Oxford University Press, 1992.

Fernea, Elizabeth Warnock, and Mary Evelyn Hocking, eds. *The Struggle for Peace: Israelis and Palestinians.* Austin: University of Texas Press, 1992.

Fisher, Michael M. J. *Iran: From Religious Dispute to Revolution.* Cambridge: Harvard University Press, 1980.

Frankel, William. *Israel Observed.* New York: Thames Hudson, 1981.

Freedman, Lawrence, and Efraim Karsh. *The Gulf Conflict, 1990-1991: Diplomacy and War in the New World Order.* Princeton: Princeton University Press, 1993.

Freedman, Robert O. *Soviet Policy Toward the Middle East Since 1970.* 3d ed. New York: Praeger, 1982.

Freiberger, Steven Z. *Dawn Over Suez: The Rise of American Power in the Middle East, 1953-1957.* Chicago: I. R. Dee, 1992.

Friedman, Thomas L. *From Beirut to Jerusalem.* New York: Farrar, Straus, Giroux, 1989.

Fromkin, David. *A Peace to End All Peace.* New York: Avon Books, 1989.

Fuller, Graham E. *The "Center of the Universe": The Geopolitics of Iran.* Boulder, Colo.: Westview Press, 1991.

Gerner, Deborah, J. *One Land, Two Peoples: The Conflict Over Palestine.* Boulder: Westview Press, 1991.

Ghanem, Shukri M. *OPEC: The Rise and Fall of an Exclusive Club.* New York: Kegan Paul International, 1986.

Gold, Dore. *America, the Gulf, and Israel: CENTCOM and Emerging U.S. Regional Security Policies in the Middle East.* Boulder, Colo.: Westview Press, 1989.

Goldschmidt, Arthur, Jr. *A Concise History of the Middle East.* Boulder, Colo.: Westview Press, 1991.

Grossman, David. *Sleeping on a Wire: Conversations with Palestinians in Israel.* New York: Farrar, Straus & Giroux, 1994.

Harris, William W. *Taking Root: Israeli Settlement in the West Bank, the Golan, and Gaza-Sinai, 1967-1980.* New York: John Wiley and Sons, 1980.

Heikal, Mohammed. *Autumn of Fury: The Assassination of Sadat.* New York: Random House, 1983.

Heller, Mark A. *A Palestinian State: The Implications for Israel.* Cambridge: Harvard University Press, 1983.

Helms, Christine Moss. *Iraq: Eastern Flank of the Arab World.* Washington, D.C.: Brookings Institution, 1984.

Hiltermann, Joost. *Behind the Intifada.* Princeton: Princeton University Press, 1991.

Hinnebusch, Raymond A. *Peasant and Bureaucracy in Ba'thist Syria.* Boulder, Colo: Westview Press, 1989.

Hiro, Dilip. *Desert Shield to Desert Storm: The Second Gulf War.* New York: Routledge, 1992.

Hourani, Albert. *A History of the Arab Peoples.* Cambridge: Belknap Press, 1991.

Hudson, Michael. *Arab Politics: The Search for Legitimacy.* New Haven: Yale University Press, 1977.

Hunter, Shireen. *Iran After Khomieni.* Washington, D.C.: Center for Strategic and International Studies, 1992.

Ismael, Tareq Y., and Jacqueline S. Ismael, eds. *The Gulf War and the New World Order: International Relations of the Middle East.* Gainesville: University Press of Florida, 1994.

Issac, Rael J. *Party and Politics in Israel: Three Visions of a Jewish State.* New York: Longman, 1980.

Jabber, Paul, et al. *Great Power Interests in the Persian Gulf.* New York: Council on Foreign Relations, 1989.

Johns, Richard, and David Holden. *House of Saud.* New York: Holt, Rinehart, and Winston, 1981.

Kandiyoti, Deniz. *Women, Islam and the State.* Philadelphia: Temple University Press, 1991.

Katouzian, Homa. *The Political Economy of Modern Iran: Despotism and Pseudo-Modernism, 1926-1979.* New York: Columbia University Press, 1981.

Kauppi, Mark V., and R. Craig Nation. *The Soviet Union and the Middle East in the 1980s: Opportunities, Constraints, and Dilemmas.* Lexington, Mass.: Lexington Books, 1983.

Keddie, Nikki. *Roots of Revolution: An Interpretive History of Modern Iran.* New Haven: Yale University Press, 1981.

Kedourie, Elie. *Democracy and Arab Political Culture.* Washington, D.C.: Washington Institute for Near East Policy, 1992.

_____. *Politics in the Middle East.* Oxford; New York: Oxford University Press, 1992.

Kepel, Gilles. *Muslim Extremism in Egypt.* Berkeley: University of California Press, 1993.

Khadduri, Majid. *The Gulf War: The Origins and Implications of the Iraq-Iran Conflict.* New York: Oxford University Press, 1988.

Khalaf, Samir. *Lebanon's Predicament.* New York: Columbia University Press, 1987.

Khalidi, Rashid. *The Origins of Arab Nationalism.* New York: Columbia University Press, 1991.

Khalidi, Walid. *Conflict and Violence in Lebanon.* Cambridge: Harvard University Press, 1979.

Kipper, Judith, and Harold H. Saunders, eds. *The Middle East in Global Perspective*. Boulder, Colo.: Westview Press, 1991.

Korany, Bahgat, Paul Noble, and Rex Brynen. *The Many Faces of National Security in the Arab World*. New York: St. Martin's, 1993.

Lacey, Robert. *The Kingdom*. New York: Avon, 1983.

Lapidus, Ira M. *A History of Islamic Societies*. Cambridge: Cambridge University Press, 1988.

Laqueur, Walter, and Barry Rubin. *The Israel-Arab Reader: A Documentary History of the Middle East*. New York: Penguin, 1984.

Ledeen, Michael, and William Lewis. *Debacle: The American Failure in Iran*. New York: Random House, 1981.

Lenczowski, George. *American Presidents and the Middle East*. Durham, N.C.: Duke University Press, 1990.

Lesch, Ann Mosely. *Transition to Palestinian Self-Government*. Bloomington: Indiana University Press, 1992.

Lewis, Bernard. *The Jews of Islam*. Princeton: Princeton University Press, 1984.

_____. *The Political Language of Islam*. Chicago: University of Chicago Press, 1988.

Lewis, Norman N. *Nomads and Settlers in Syria and Jordan, 1800-1980*. New York: Cambridge University Press, 1987.

Licklider, Roy. *Political Power and the Arab Oil Weapon: The Experience of Five Industrial Nations*. Berkeley: University of California Press, 1988.

Lippmann, Thomas W. *Egypt After Nasser: Sadat, Peace, and the Mirage of Prosperity*. New York: Paragon House, 1988.

Lukacs, Yehuda, and Abdulla M. Battah, eds. *The Arab-Israeli Conflict: Two Decades of Change*. Boulder, Colo.: Westview Press, 1988.

Lytle, Mark H. *The Origins of the Iranian-American Alliance, 1941-1953*. New York: Holmes and Meier, 1987.

Mack, John E. *A Prince of Our Disorder: The Life of T. E. Lawrence*. Boston: Little, Brown, 1976.

Mansour, Camille. *The Palestinian-Israeli Peace Negotiations*. Washington, D.C.: Institute for Palestine Studies, 1993.

Martin, David C., and John Walcott. *Best Laid Plans: The Inside Story of America's War Against Terrorism*. New York: Harper and Row, 1988.

McDermott, Anthony. *Egypt from Nasser to Mubarak: A Flawed Revolution*. London: Croom Helm, 1988.

Mofid, Kamran. *The Economic Consequences of the Gulf War*. New York: Routledge, Chapman and Hall, 1991.

Morris, Benny. *The Birth of the Palestinian Refugee Problem 1947-1949*. New York: Cambridge University Press, 1988.

Munson, Henry. *Islam and Revolution in the Middle East*. New Haven: Yale University Press, 1988.

Muslih, Muhammad. *The Origins of Palestinian Nationalism*. New York: Cambridge University Press, 1988.

Norton, Augustus Richard. *Amal and the Shia: Struggle for the Soul of Lebanon*. Austin: University of Texas Press, 1987.

Owen, Roger. *The Middle East in the World Economy*. London: I.B. Tauris & Co., 1993.

Parker, Richard B. *The Politics of Miscalculation in the Middle East*. Bloomington: University of Indiana Press, 1993.

Peck, Malcolm C. *The United Arab Emirates: A Venture in Unity*. Boulder, Colo.: Westview Press, 1986.

Peretz, Don. *Government and Politics of Israel*. 2d ed. Boulder Colo.: Westview Press, 1984.

_____. *Intifada: The Palestinian Uprising*. Boulder, Colo.: Westview Press, 1989.

_____. *The Middle East Today*. 5th ed. New York: Praeger, 1988.

Peterson, J. E. *Yemen: The Search for a Modern State*. Baltimore: Johns Hopkins University Press, 1982.

Quandt, William, ed. *The Middle East: Ten Years After Camp David*. Washington, D.C.: Brookings Institution, 1988.

_____. *Peace Process: American Diplomacy and The Arab-Israeli Conflict Since 1967*. Washington, D.C.: Brookings Institution, 1993.

Rabinovich, Itamar. *The Road Not Taken: Early Arab-Israeli Negotiations*. New York: Oxford University Press, 1991.

_____. *The War for Lebanon, 1970-1983*. Ithaca, N.Y.: Cornell University Press, 1983.

Rafael, Gideon. *Destination Peace: Three Decades of Israeli Foreign Policy*. New York: Stein and Day, 1981.

Ramazani, R. K. *The United States and Iran: The Patterns of Influence*. New York: Praeger, 1982.

Richards, Alan, and John Waterbury. *A Political Economy of the Middle East*. Boulder, Colo.: Westview Press, 1989.

Rubin, Barry. *Paved with Good Intentions: The American Experience and Iran*. London: Oxford University Press, 1980.

Rubin, Jeffrey Z. *Dynamics of Third Party Intervention: Kissinger in the Middle East*. New York: Praeger, 1983.

Sachar, Howard M. *History of Israel*. New York: Knopf, 1976.

Sadowski, Yahya. *Scuds or Butter? The Political Economy of Arms Control in the Middle East.* Washington: Brookings Institution, 1992.

Said, Edward. *The Question of Palestine.* New York: Random House, 1992.

Salibi, Kemal S. *Crossroads to Civil War, Lebanon 1858-1976.* New York: Caravan Books, 1976.

Seale, Patrick. *The Struggle for Syria: A Study of Postwar Arab Politics, 1945-1958.* 2d. ed. New Haven: Yale University Press, 1987.

Segev, Tom. *Nineteen Forty-Nine, the First Israelis.* New York: Free Press, 1993.

Shaked, Haim, and Itamar Rabinovich, eds. *The Middle East and the United States.* New Brunswick, N.J.: Transaction Books, 1980.

Shawcross, William. *The Shah's Last Ride: Fate of an Ally.* New York: Simon and Schuster, 1988.

Shipler, David K. *Arab and Jew: Wounded Spirits in the Promised Land.* New York: Times Books, 1986.

Shlaim, Avi. *Collusion Across the Jordan: King Abdullah, the Zionist Movement, and the Partition of Palestine.* New York: Columbia University Press, 1988.

Sick, Gary. *All Fall Down: America's Tragic Encounter with Iran.* New York: Random House, 1985.

Sish, Timothy D. *Islam and Democracy.* Washington: U.S. Institute for Peace, 1992.

Sluglett, Marion-Farouk, and Peter Sluglett. *Iraq Since 1958: From Revolution to Dictatorship.* New York: Methuen, 1988.

Spiegel, Steven L. *The Other Arab-Israeli Conflict: Making America's Middle East Policy from Truman to Reagan.* Chicago: University of Chicago Press, 1985.

St. John, Ronald Bruce. *Qaddafi's World Design: Libyan Foreign Policy, 1969-1987.* London: Saqi Books, 1987.

Stowasser, Barbara Freyer. *The Islamic Impulse.* Washington, D.C.: Center for Contemporary Arab Studies, 1987.

Taylor, Alan R. *The Islamic Question in Middle East Politics.* Boulder, Colo.: Westview Press, 1988.

Tillman, Seth P. *The United States in the Middle East.* Bloomington: Indiana University Press, 1982.

Toubia, Nahid. *Women of the Arab World.* London: Zed Books, 1989.

Twinam, Joseph Wright. *The Gulf, Cooperation and the Council: An American Perspective.* Washington, D.C.: Middle East Policy Council, 1993.

Vance, Cyrus. *Hard Choices.* New York: Simon and Schuster, 1983.

Waterbury, John. *The Egypt of Nasser and Sadat.* Princeton, N.J.: Princeton University Press, 1983.

Watt, W. Montgomery. *Islamic Fundamentalism and the Modern World.* New York: Routledge, Chapman, and Hall, 1989.

Wenner, Manfred W. *Modern Yemen, 1918-1966.* Baltimore: Johns Hopkins University Press, 1967.

Wright, Robin. *Sacred Rage: The Wrath of Militant Islam.* New York: Simon and Schuster, 1984.

Yaniv, Avner. *Dilemmas of Security: Politics, Strategy, and the Israeli Experience in Lebanon.* New York: Oxford University Press, 1987.

Yergin, Daniel. *The Prize: The Epic Quest for Oil, Money, and Power.* New York: Simon and Schuster, 1990.

Yodfat, Aryeh. *The Soviet Union and the Arabian Peninsula: Soviet Policy Toward the Persian Gulf and Arabia.* New York: St. Martin's Press, 1983.

## Articles

Adelman, M. A. "Oil Fallacies." *Foreign Policy* (Spring 1991): 3-16.

Ajami, Fouad. "The Summer of Arab Discontent." *Foreign Affairs* (Winter 1990/91): 1-20.

Akins, James E. "The New Arabia." *Foreign Affairs* (Winter 1990/91): 36-49.

Alexander, Nathan. "The Foreign Policy of Libya: Inflexibility Amid Change." *Orbis* (Winter 1981): 819-846.

Ali, Sheikh R. "Holier Than Thou: The Iran-Iraq War." *Middle East Review* (Fall 1984): 50-57.

Anderson, Ewan W. "The Vulnerability of Arab Water Resources." *Arab Affairs* (Summer/Fall 1988): 73-81.

Atherton, Alfred Leroy, Jr. "The Shifting Sands of Middle East Peace." *Foreign Policy* (Spring 1992): 114-133.

"Bahrain: A MEED Special Report." *Middle East Economic Digest,* October 17-23, 1987, 20-45.

Bannerman, M. Graeme. "Arabs and Israelis: Slow Walk Towards Peace." *Foreign Affairs* (Winter 1992/93): 142-157.

Bar-on, Mordechai. "Trend in the Political Psychology of Israeli Jews." *Journal of Palestine Studies* (August 1987): 21-36.

Bassiouni, M. Chelif. "An Analysis of Egyptian Peace Policy Toward Israel: From Resolution 242 (1967) to the 1979 Peace Treaty." *New Outlook* (January 1981): 27-33.

Beinin, Joel. "The Communist Movement and Nationalist Political Discourse in Nasirist Egypt." *Middle East Journal* (Autumn 1987): 568-584.

Belfiglio, Valentin J. "Middle East Terrorism." *International Problems* (Summer 1987): 21-28.

Bill, James A. "The United States and Iran: Mutual Mythologies." *Middle East Policy* (No. 3, 1993): 98-106.

Bishara, Ghassan. "Israel's Power in the U.S. Senate." *Journal of Palestine Studies* (Autumn 1980): 58-79.

Brown, L. Carl. "The Middle East: Patterns of Change, 1947-1987." *Middle East Journal* (Winter 1987): 26-39.

Bulliet, Richard W. "The Future of The Islamic Movement." *Foreign Affairs* (November/December 1993): 38-44.

Carter, Jimmy. "The Middle East Consultation: A Look to the Future." *Middle East Journal* (Spring 1988): 187-192.

Chalabi, Ahmad. "Iraq: The Past as Prologue." *Foreign Policy* (Summer 1991): 20-29.

Chomsky, Noam. "The United States and the Middle East." *Journal of Palestine Studies* (Spring 1987): 25-42.

Christison, Kathleen M. "Myths About Palestinians." *Foreign Policy* (Spring 1987): 109-127.

Cohen, Benjamin. "Israel's Expansion Through Immigration." *Middle East Policy* (No. 2, 1992): 120-135.

Cooley, John K. "The Libyan Menace." *Foreign Policy* (Spring 1981): 74-83.

Cooper, Mary H. "Persian Gulf Oil." *Editorial Research Reports,* October 30, 1987, 566-575.

Cottam, Richard W. "Inside Revolutionary Iran." *Middle East Journal* (Spring 1989): 168-185.

Cottam, Richard W., et al. "The United States and Iran's Revolution." *Foreign Policy* (Spring 1979): 3-34.

Dawisha, Karen. "The USSR in the Middle East: Superpower in Eclipse." *Foreign Affairs* (Winter 1982/1983): 438-451.

Deeb, Mary-Jane. "Shia Movements in Lebanon: Their Formation, Ideology, Social Basis, and Links with Iran and Syria." *Third World Quarterly* (April 1988): 683-698.

Eban, Abba. "Camp David: The Unfinished Business." *Foreign Affairs* (Winter 1978/1979): 343-354.

Ebert, Barbara Gregory. "The Gulf War and Its Aftermath: An Assessment of Evolving Arab Responses." *Middle East Policy* (No. 4, 1992): 77-95.

Elon, Amos. "Letter from Israel." *New Yorker,* February 13, 1989, 74-80.

Esposito, John, and James Piscatori. "Democratization and Islam." *Middle East Journal* (Summer 1991): 427-440.

Fishelson, Gideon. "The Economics of Peace." *New Outlook* (September/October 1986): 16-18.

Fischer, Stanley. "Building Palestinian Prosperity." *Foreign Policy* (Winter 1993/94): 60-75.

Gigot, Paul A. "A Great American Screw-Up." *The National Interest* (Winter 1990/91): 3-10.

Gimlin, Hoyt. "Egypt's Strategic Mideast Role." *Editorial Research Reports,* February 24, 1989, 106-115.

Green, Jerrold D. "Ideology and Pragmatism in Iranian Foreign Policy." *Journal of South Asian and Middle Eastern Studies* (Fall 1993): 57-75.

Hadar, Leon T. "What Green Peril?" *Foreign Affairs* (Spring 1993): 27-42.

Haddad, Yvonne. "Islamists and the Problem of Israel." *Middle East Journal* (Spring 1992): 266-285.

Hamad, Jamil. "Learning from History: The Lessons of Arab-Israeli Errors." *International Relations* (November 1987): 176-186.

Hirsch, Seev. "Trade Regimes and the Middle East Peace Process." *World Economy,* March 1987, 61-74.

Hochstein, Joseph M. "Israel's Forty-Year Quandary." *Editorial Research Reports,* April 15, 1988, 186-199.

Hudson, Michael. "After the Gulf War: Prospects for Democratization in the Middle East." *Middle East Journal* (Summer 1991): 407-426.

Hunter, Robert E. "Seeking Middle East Peace." *Foreign Policy* (Winter 1988/1989): 3-21.

Hunter, Shireen T. "After the Ayatollah." *Foreign Policy* (Spring 1987): 77-97.

——. "Iran and the Spread of Revolutionary Islam." *Third World Quarterly* (April 1988): 730-749.

Ibrahim, Saad Eddin. "Crises, Elites and Democratization in the Arab World." *Middle East Journal* (Spring 1993): 292-305.

Indyk, Martin. "Watershed in the Middle East." *Foreign Affairs* (Winter 1992): 70-93.

Joffe', E. G .H. "Relations Between the Middle East and the West." *Middle East Journal* (Spring 1994): 250-267.

Kedourie, Elie. "Iraq: The Mystery of American Policy." *Commentary* (June 1991): 15-19.

Kepel, Gilles. "God Strikes Back: Re-Islamization Movement." *Contention* (Fall 1992): 159-178.

Khalidi, Rashid. "The Uprising and the Palestinian Question." *World Policy Journal* (Summer 1988): 497-517.

Knauerhase, Ramon. "Saudi Arabia Faces the Future." *Current History,* February 1986, 75-78.

Kuutab, Jonathan. "The Children's Revolt." *Journal of Palestine Studies* (Summer 1988): 26-35.

Lake, Anthony. "Confronting Backlash States." *Foreign Affairs* (March/April 1994): 45-55.

Laqueur, Walter. "Why the Shah Fell." *Commentary,* March 1979, 47-55.

Lebovic, James H., and Ashfaq Ishaq. "Military Burden, Security Needs, and Economic Growth in the Middle East." *Journal of Conflict Resolution* (March 1987): 106-138.

Lederman, Jim. "Dateline West Bank: Interpreting the Intifada." *Foreign Policy* (Fall 1988): 230-246.

Lesch, Ann Mosely. "Contrasting Reaction to the Persian Gulf War Crisis: Egypt, Syria, Jordan and the

Palestinians." *Middle East Journal* (Winter 1991): 30-50.

Lewis, Bernard. "Rethinking the Middle East." *Foreign Affairs* (Fall 1992): 99-119.

Long, David. "Prospects for Armed Conflict in the Gulf in the 1990s: The Impact of the Gulf War." *Middle East Policy* (No. 1, 1993): 113-125.

Lustick, Ian S. "Israel's Dangerous Fundamentalists." *Foreign Policy* (Fall 1987): 118-139.

——. "Reinventing Jerusalem." *Foreign Policy* (Winter 1993/94): 41-59.

Marcus, Jonathan. "The Politics of Israel's Security." *International Affairs* (London), September 1989, 233-246.

Mattar, Philip. "The PLO and the Gulf Crisis." *Middle East Journal* (Winter 1994): 31-46.

Maynes, Charles William. "Dateline Washington: A Necessary War?" *Foreign Policy* (Spring 1991): 159-177.

Miller, Judith. "The Challenge of Radical Islam." *Foreign Affairs* (Spring 1993): 43-56.

Moench, Richard U., ed. "The Impact of Fluctuating Oil Prices on State Autonomy in the Middle East." *Arab Studies Quarterly* (Spring 1988): 155-238.

Mylroie, Lori. "The Baghdad Alternative." *Orbis* (Summer 1988): 339-354.

Oren, Michael B. "Escalation to Suez: The Egyptian-Israeli Border War, 1949-1956." *Journal of Contemporary History* (April 1989): 347-374.

Parsons, Anthony. "Iran and Western Europe." *Middle East Journal* (Spring 1989): 218-229.

Peres, Shimon. "A Strategy for Peace in the Middle East." *Foreign Affairs* (Spring 1980): 887-901.

Peretz, Don. "Intifadeh: The Palestinian Uprising." *Foreign Affairs* (Summer 1988): 965-980.

Perthes, Volker. "Incremental Change in Syria." *Current History* (January 1993): 23-27.

Peterson, J. E. "The Political Status of Women in the Arab Gulf States." *Middle East Journal* (Winter 1989): 34-50.

Pipes, Daniel, and Patrick Clawson. "Ambitious Iran, Troubled Neighbors." *Foreign Affairs* (Winter 1993): 124-141.

Prince, James M. "A Kurdish State in Iraq?" *Current History* (January 1993): 17-22.

Quandt, William. "Camp David and Peacemaking in the Middle East." *Political Science Quarterly* (Spring 1986): 357-377.

——. "The Gulf War: Policy Options and Regional Implications." *American-Arab Affairs* (Summer 1984): 1-7.

Ramati, Yohanan. "A PLO State and Israel's Security." *Midstream* (April 1989): 3-6.

Ramazani, Nesta. "Women in Iran: The Revolutionary Ebb and Flow." *Middle East Journal* (Summer 1993): 409-428.

Reed, Stanley. "The Battle for Egypt." *Foreign Affairs* (September/October 1993): 94-107.

Richards, Alan. "Economic Imperatives and Political Systems." *Middle East Journal* (Spring 1993): 217-227.

Roumani, Maurice M. "The Sephardi Factor in Israeli Politics." *Middle East Journal* (Summer 1988): 423-435.

Sadowski, Yahya. "Economic Crisis in the Arab World: Catalyst for Conflict." *Overseas Development Council* (September 1991): 1-11.

——. "Revolution, Reform or Regression: Arab Options in the 1990 Gulf Crisis." *Brookings Review* (Winter 1990/91).

Said, Edward W. "Inside Islam." *Harper's,* January 1981, 25-32.

——. "Irangate: A Many-Sided Crisis." *Journal of Palestine Studies* (Summer 1987): 27-49.

Salame, Ghassan. "Islam and the West." *Foreign Policy* (Spring 1993): 22-37.

Sharabi, Hisham. "Modernity and Islamic Revival." *Contention* (Fall 1992): 127-138.

Sick, Gary. "Trial by Error: Reflections on the Iran-Iraq War." *Middle East Journal* (Spring 1989): 230-246.

"Squeezed." *The Economist,* May 12, 1990, 3-26.

Stanislaw, Joseph, and Daniel Yergin. "Oil: Reopening the Door." *Foreign Affairs* (September/October 1993): 81-93.

Starr, Joyce R. "Water Wars." *Foreign Policy* (Spring 1991): 17-36.

Tal, Lawrence. "Is Jordan Doomed?" *Foreign Affairs* (November/December 1993): 45-58.

Telhami, Shibley. "Israeli Foreign Policy After the Gulf War." *Middle East Policy* (No. 2, 1992): 85-95.

Tetreault, Mary Ann. "Kuwait: The Morning After." *Current History* (January 1992): 6-10.

Troxler, Nancy C. "The Gulf Cooperation Council: The Emergence of an Institution." *Millennium* (Spring 1987): 1-19.

Tuma, E. H. "Institutionalized Obstacles to Development: The Case of Egypt." *World Development,* October 1988, 1185-1198.

Vaziri, Haleb. "Iran's Involvement in Lebanon: Polarization and Radicalization of Militant Islamic Movements." *Journal of South Asian and Middle Eastern Studies* (Winter 1992): 1-16.

Weinbaum, Marvin. "The Israel Factor in Arab Consciousness and Domestic Politics." *Middle East Policy* (No. 1, 1993): 87-102.

Wizarat, Talat. "The Role of the Gulf Cooperation Council in Regional Security." *Strategic Studies* (Winter 1987): 69-78.

# INDEX

Page numbers in **boldface** refer to biographical sketches.